BUSINESS LAW

BUSINESS LAW

Second Edition

Michael P. Litka

Head, Department of Finance
College of Business Administration
The University of Akron

I.S.B.N. 0-88244-108-6
Library of Congress Catalog Card Number 76-2999

1 2 3 4 5 6 ▦ 1 0 9 8 7 6

Business Law, Second Edition, was edited by Kathy Williams, stylized by
Elaine Clatterbuck, production manager. Cover design by Marcie Clark. The
text was set in Times Roman by S M Data Center, Inc. Ashland, Ohio.

CONTENTS

PART II: CONTRACTS

PART III: THE AGENCY AND EMPLOYMENT RELATIONSHIP

PART IV: PARTNERSHIPS

PART V: CORPORATIONS

PART VI: INSURANCE AND SELLING

PART VII: COMMERCIAL PAPER

Case for Review
Case Problems
Endnote

Presentment for Payment
Presentment for Acceptance
Dishonor
Notice
Protest
Legal Principles
Case for Review
Case Problems

Personal Defenses
Real Defenses
Discharge
Payment or Satisfaction
Cancellation and Renunciation
Impairment of Recourse or Collateral
Reacquisition
Material Alteration
Certification of Checks
Acceptance Varying Drafts
Delay in Conditions Precedent
Legal Principles
Case for Review
Case Problems

PART VIII: PROPERTY

Freehold Estates
Nonfreehold Estates
Legal Principles
Case for Review
Case Problems

Joint Tenancy
Tenancy in Common
Tenancy by the Entireties
Community Property
Legal Principles
Case for Review
Case Problems

PART IX: FINANCIAL TRANSACTIONS

EDITOR'S PREFACE

The publication of the second edition of Mike Litka's *Business Law* is a milestone for the Grid Series in Law. The concept of the Series is to provide innovative teaching materials especially for undergraduate courses in law. Although subject matter coverage varies, instructors face common problems in determining the most effective teaching techniques for presenting legal material to students who have no previous legal study.

The Grid Series provides a variety of texts on undergraduate legal topics so that instructors (experimentors and traditionalists alike) will have a viable choice of teaching materials. It will no longer be necessary for instructors in some areas to face the Hobson's choice of using a law school text written for more advanced students, or of using library assignments and mimeographed materials as the sole "text" in the course.

Last year saw the publication of four books in the Series which covered a variety of subjects including mass media law, antitrust law and labor law. The publication this year of *Business Law* and several more texts designed for traditional courses in the field of business law/legal environment significantly expands the foundation of the Series. Plans are already underway for building on this base. Outstanding and able authors are under contract to produce additional texts encompassing both traditional business law subjects and more specialized courses in undergraduate education in law.

Already a popular and well regarded text, Litka's *Business Law* has been further strengthened by substantial revision and expansion. Ten new chapters have been added including those covering crimes and torts, the attorney, employment, the accountant, insurance, trusts, and bankruptcy. Many new case excerpts and case problems have been added and the well-received practice of chapter summaries has been continued. *Business Law* now matches or exceeds its competitors in its comprehensiveness and its concise, relevant treatment of subject matter. It should fill excellently the needs of students taking the basic first course in business law.

Thomas W. Dunfee
Wharton School
University of Pennsylvania

PREFACE

Business Law, Second Edition, does not purport to offer definitive answers to specific legal questions. What it does provide is a problem-solving, logical approach to commercial law to help the reader develop awareness of the law's relevance to business problems. With this awareness the student will gain some of the flexibility needed to adapt to our changing environment. By acquiring an understanding of the process of legal reasoning he can develop the logical framework necessary to make legally sound business decisions.

The content of the text reflects current thinking and recent changes in the law. *Business Law* is not offered as a Code or non-Code edition because the Uniform Commercial Code does not affect the bulk of the subject matter. However, the discussion of sales, commercial paper, and secured transactions are based on Code provisions. The text covers nine fundamental areas of business law: Contracts, Agency, Partnerships, Corporations, Sales, Commercial Paper, Secured Transactions, Real Property, and Personal Property and Bailments. The Second Edition also includes new chapters on The Accountant, Regulation of the Employer and Employee Relationship, Federal Securities Regulation, Federal Regulation of Corporation, Insurance, Trusts, Bankruptcy, and Bankruptcy Proceedings. An introductory section examines the interrelationship of law with society.

Each chapter begins with background or conceptual material relevant to the particular aspect of the commercial law to be covered. Each chapter in Parts II through IX contains a summary of the rules of law dealt with in that chapter. Since principles are more likely to be understood when their use is illustrated by actual situations, various cases turning on these points of law are included in the text. These cases have been carefully selected to reflect recent legal solutions and edited to delete material not pertinent to the legal principles under study. Case problems at the end of each chapter contrast in some instances with the cases and supplement them in others. They are designed to encourage the student to exercise his powers of reasoning in analyzing legal variables.

The object of *Business Law,* Second Edition is to enable the student to comprehend the legal significance of business decisions. Intended to be both readable and teachable, it is a concentrated study within a framework that seeks to avoid both oversimplification and needless complexity. It presents detailed material without slighting fundamental concepts.

No commercial law text represents the efforts of a single individual, and many scholars and teachers have contributed to the wealth of material that is presented here. Special mention, however, is due Professor Gola Waters of Southern Illinois University and Professor James E. Inman of The University of Akron. Finally, a great deal of credit for the successful completion of *Business Law,* Second Edition must go to my wife, Ellie, whose patience and understanding enabled me to accomplish the task.

Michael P. Litka, J.D.
Professor of Law

PART I
LAW AND SOCIETY

THE EVOLUTION OF LAW   1

Law is basically a device to regulate the economic and social orders of society. It is a formalized code of behavior to which all the members, both natural and legal, of a particular society are urged to conform. Law is created, interpreted, and enforced at the direction of a society's government. It is the government's responsibility to see that the law is pertinent to the needs of the people and their business entities, responsive to change, and justly enforced. These responsibilities imply the right to levy penalties on those who break the law.

The purpose of a legal system is to preserve the economic and social welfare of a society by introducing an element of control into the daily activities of its citizens and its business enterprises. If man lived in complete isolation, carrying on no economic activity and recognizing no superior authority, laws would not exist, nor would they be necessary. Citizens and business firms, however, which operate within a common society and share a common government, inevitably come in contact with one another. Social contacts and business operations give rise to controversies because each entity has different needs and desires. Some needs and desires are more urgent than others and some are more crucial to the welfare of the society. The legal regulatory device is a means of giving priority to the needs and desires of the individual or business firm in relation to the needs, desires, purposes, and responsibilities of the society as a whole. (Thus, when citizens or corporations pay taxes, their financial needs are balanced with respect to the financial needs of the society as a whole.)

A society cannot hope to be peaceful and prosperous unless each entity realizes that it must respect the needs and desires of other entities to have its own respected. By acting in accordance with this idea, natural and legal members contribute to the order and harmony of society. The family, churches, schools, and an individual's own desires for order and peace all exert influences upon the orderly interaction of people in daily activities. The same influences are felt by the human beings running the economic order within society. Practically speaking, however, these means of control are not forceful enough to induce the desired restraint and cooperation. It is the job of the legal system, therefore, to specify the rights of individuals, the duties of individuals to one another, their duties to society, and the rights of society and its duties to its citizens. In much the same manner it is the function of law to prescribe the conduct of business firms in the economic order of society. It imposes certain duties on the business firm and gives certain rights to the members of society. Having made these distinctions, it is then the responsibility of the system to see that they are upheld.

The use of law as a regulatory device is given different interpretations in different societies. We see examples of the law used simply as a means of subjugation. The person or group in power regulates the activities of those not in power by enforcing a code of behavior that allows the subjugated to carry on their activities only within narrowly defined limitations. In societies such as ours the law serves quite a different purpose. It does prescribe what the citizens can *not* do, but the law of a free society also informs the citizens of their rights and of their obligations as responsible citizens—what they *can* do and what they *must* do. For example, murder is prohibited, property ownership is permitted and payment of taxes is prescribed.

In addition to being a regulatory or controlling factor, the law of a free society guarantees individual freedoms, allows free enterprise, ensures against both their infringement and their abuse, and provides a means of bringing controversies to a peaceful solution.

THE ORIGINS OF MODERN LEGAL CONCEPTS

A society's legal system reflects its inherent characteristics. Laws tell us a great deal about the customs, habits, traditions, and moral standards of the people in a particular society. Moreover, because all human societies are intended to satisfy the needs of, and provide protection for, human life, they share fundamental similarities in the sense that there are certain situations every society finds it desirable to regulate. Legal systems, then, reflect social characteristics and reveal the methods different societies have devised or adopted to cope with fundamental human problems.

A society's laws are only as effective as they are relevant to the conditions of life among its people. Thus, as social, political, and economic changes occur governments must modify and append the laws of their societies to keep the legal regulatory device strong and meaningful. To study the evolution of law is to study the manner in which laws have been created, interpreted, enforced, and modified in relation to the progress of human civilization.

One of the most significant aspects of the legal evolutionary process is the fact that certain legal concepts have endured for long periods of time without significant alterations and despite a wide variety of sociological changes. Such laws have taken on something of a universal character because of their effectiveness in bringing order to many different types of societies. One might include in this category, for example, the principles of the Ten Commandments. The influence of these guidelines for civil, religious, and administrative activities is evident in one form or another in a number of legal systems throughout the world. They form an integral part of the American system, where their influence is greatly felt in municipal law.

The discussions that follow trace the origins of some of our most important legal concepts back to the societies of Babylon, Israel, Greece, Rome, and England.

BABYLONIAN LAW

The Babylonian legal system was the product of a society that engaged extensively in business and commercial dealings. Theirs was perhaps the earliest system in which commercial custom and law played an integral part.

The nature of the Babylonian laws indicates that the members of this society were entitled to a wide degree of individual initiative and freedom with respect to their domestic and business activities. The use of writing was widespread among the Babylonians and they kept records of all transactions. Tablets uncovered from the ruins of this ancient kingdom bear written evidence of the use of documents for a great many legal transactions—contracts for the purchase and sale of real estate, leases, mortgages, bailments, the charging of interest, agency, partnerships, marriage contracts, marine insurance, and the use of wills to establish inheritance. The tablets reveal that many legal procedures common today were employed in the Babylonian community. They show, for example, (1) the execution of contracts in duplicate; (2) the execution of contracts before witnesses or a public officer (similar to the modern notary public); (3) the practice of having parties to a contract place their signatures upon it; (4) the use of rent contracts that were generally for a length of one year and for which it was customary to pay part of the rent in advance; (5) the use of leasing contracts containing numerous conditions and covenants; (6) the use of mortgage contracts containing rights of redemption and foreclosure; and (7) the stipulation in land deeds of borders and boundaries. (One tablet was even found that recorded a suit for the recovery of real estate somewhat similar to the present practice of ejectment.)[1]

The importance of mentioning these specific features of Babylonian law is that whereas it is difficult to determine the exact origins of many of our modern laws because so many were unwritten long before they were formally set down, the Babylonians have provided us with tangible evidence of the existence of many fundamental legal principles and procedures, especially in regard to commercial transaction, as early as 2000 B.C.

Any discussion of Babylonian law and business must mention the Babylonian king Hammurabi, who ruled about 1900 B.C. It was he who promulgated the famous Code of Hammurabi, the oldest written code of laws and the only substantially complete pre-Hebrew code that has been discovered. It set forth basic concepts relating to public and private rights and liabilities. The legal principles embodied in this Code represent the first step in the evolutionary process that resulted in the Roman civil law, which prevails in many European countries today. The laws as set down by Hammurabi levied strict punishments for crimes. The most famous of these penalties derived from the concept of "an eye for an eye," which was applied to criminal law and illustrated the principle of equating the punishment with the crime. The Code was also one of the earliest attempts to distinguish negligence from accident. For example, according to the Code, "if a builder build a house for a man and do not make its construction firm . . . he shall rebuild the house which collapsed from his own property." On the other hand, "if a man hire an ox . . . and a lion kill it . . . it is the owner's affair."[2] The measures of control set forth in the Code indicate that whereas an individual was free to carry on his own affairs, the penalties for infringing on the rights of others or contributing to violence or fraud were intended to discourage such disruptive actions.

In addition to having civil significance, the Hammurabic Code recognized many ways of disposing of property—sale, lease, barter, gift, dedication, loan, pledge—all of which were matters of contract. In the handling of controversies between individuals, no claim was admitted unless substantiated by documents or oaths of witnesses; and in business matters the rule was that the buyer had to convince himself of the validity of the seller's title. The deeds employed contained many provisions that are used in present-day convey-ancing practice, such as the description of the premises, the names of the parties, the consideration given, and the kind of title conveyed. Records also reveal a distinction between the warranty deed and a quit claim deed.[3]

The Code of Hammurabi was studied for 1500 years after its first composi-tion. Its great distinction, and perhaps the key to its endurance, was the fact that its articles seemed to have been chosen with a view to universal applica-tion, not to the customs of any single city. It contained the concept that per-sonal property was the possession of the individual. Individual responsibility was beginning to become an integral part of the law. It also represented the rudimentary beginnings of criminal law. Babylonian law was the first civilized legal system that influenced the development of other legal systems. Its im-portance today is mainly historical: it provides us with much more certainty as to the law than we have regarding any other ancient system except the Roman.

MOSAIC LAW

Mosaic Law is said to have been issued to man "by Almighty God Himself." According to Hebrew tradition, the primary provisions of the Law, in the form of the Ten Commandments (also called the Decalogue), were received from God by Moses, the leader of the Israelites, on the Mount of Sinai. The complete body of the Law is to be found in the first five books of the Old Testament, called the Pentateuch.

The Ten Commandments are not to be regarded as strictly spiritual, or religious, in nature. In fact, only the first two of the ten may be so classified. The other eight deal almost entirely with the organization of human society and have come to form the basis of modern municipal law. The influence of Mosaic Law can be seen in the municipal-law prohibitions against killing, stealing, and adultery and in the observance of a periodic day of rest and religious worship. As an example of the extent to which these principles in-fluence our lives today, a recent case reached the United States Supreme Court upholding the Sunday Closing Laws of Maryland. The Court com-mented, "it is common knowledge that the first day of the week has come to have a special significance as a day of rest in this country." (McGowan v. Maryland, 366 U.S. 420 (1961).)

As seen in the context of the Pentateuch, the Ten Commandments formed the foundation for an extensive legal system that bound the twelve tribes of Israel together. Features of this legal system include the use of the oath, witnesses, and the prohibition against giving false testimony. The Com-mandments defined domestic relations and were the basis for the formulation of laws pertaining to property ownership and to the administration of justice along lines similar to modern jurisprudence. There are also numerous refer-ences in the Old Testament to proper conduct in commercial transactions. For example, a prohibition was placed on all forms of usury; the penalty for vio-lating the loan agreement was forfeiture of the interest on the loan with the remaining right to recover the principal. Today, each of the fifty states in this country has usury laws with much the same penalties. Again, the rule of inheritance under Mosaic Law was that all real estate should descend to male children in equal shares, with the eldest descendent, however, receiving a double share.

It is well to note, in comparing Mosaic Law to our present system, that just as this ancient code served to unify the twelve tribes of Israel, so our own laws serve to maintain the unity of the fifty states. Also, in the sense that laws reflect the characteristics of the society they protect, the Pentateuch is rich with references to the customs, traditions, and features of daily life among the pastoral people of Israel.

Finally, the Pentateuch contains numerous examples of the manner in which the principles of the Ten Commandments were applied to cases involving the conflict of individual rights. These accounts point up the fact that interpretation is a key function of any legal system. The simple commandment to "honor" one's father and mother can be taken quite literally, or allowances can be made in those cases where one's father or mother was a murderer, a thief, an adulterer, and so on.

Perhaps the primary contribution of Mosaic Law to our American system is its refinement of the principle that each individual is legally responsible for his own acts and the acts of those for whom he has voluntarily made himself responsible.

GREEK LAW

The Greek legal system was a product of the political disunity and the democratic institutions of the various Greek city-states. They did not have codes of law because the emphasis was not on the strict rule of law but on the general justice of the case. The Greek contribution was not codes, but rather concepts of law and justice. It was in Greece that the study of jurisprudence began.

Greek law was essentially based on democratic principles, with a general participation by the people. In fact, the term "democratic" derived from the Greek word "demos," meaning "the people." The Greeks believed that all citizens should have equal rights and that these rights should be exercised in open meetings. However, although the government appeared democratic it was actually a democracy of the ruling class, because there were a great number of non-citizens and slaves excluded from government.

The drafters of the Declaration of Independence and the United States Constitution were influenced by Greek jurisprudence, and many of the legal concepts incorporated in these documents were first expounded by the Greek philosophers. To Plato law existed by nature. Single laws, like natural phenomena, were thought to emanate from one universal and divine law, without which chaos would result. Aristotle saw both consistency and change in the law. Natural law had force everywhere; however, controversies subject to legal determination were resolved according to concepts of fairness, applied to the circumstances of the case.

The principles of Greek law are very similar to our own. There is a distinction between the written and the unwritten law because custom and habits were law long before anything was written. The difficulty with the Greek system was its failure to develop a competent tribunal to apply the law. It would seem that details of law were not regarded as worth the closest attention of those who busied themselves with such matters as the nature of wisdom, virtue, and the good life.

Perhaps the greatest contribution of the Greeks was in the realm of legal draftsmanship for commercial purposes. While not concerning themselves with details of law, the Greeks, like the Babylonians, adopted the practice of putting all commercial transactions in writing. In the matter of contractual relations, pledges, mortgages, and commercial ventures, the written contract precluded proof of any other contract made. For example, today when one buys a piece of real estate, he has the title searched or obtains an abstract of the title from the seller. This practice had its precedents in Greek law. They had an excellent system of land recording through which the title to land would be checked before it was bought. A record has been found at Tenos, dated 200 B.C., which contains some fifty entries of land transfers and appears in a standardized form intelligible to any modern title-searcher. Leases and forms of leases were equally well developed, though it must be realized that the Greek craftmanship relevant to these may have been derived from earlier civilizations.

ROMAN LAW

The Roman contributions in the field of law may well be the greatest contribution of this civilization to the modern world. Two vehicles that created the law were the Roman courts and a professional class of lawyers. In almost all the departments of law there was a procedural solution for legal controversies. That solution would not differ except in unusual cases from the solution that would be reached in our courts, while the main elements in our procedure can be traced directly back to the Roman law.

The famous civil law of Rome was developed from the Laws of the Twelve Tables by successive Praetorian Edicts. In 527 Justinian I became the ruler of the Roman Empire of the East. Justinian was able not only to partially restore the old Roman Empire, but to codify the Roman civil law (Corpus juris civilis). The Code of Justinian is a collection of all the enactments of the law of Rome existing and in effect at the time of the compilation. It is a remarkable work and is especially noted for its conciseness. Its method of classification according to subjects and its enumeration of the enactments were followed in the Revised Statutes of the United States, written in 1874.

The Code of Justinian was a compilation of early Roman laws and legal principles, illustrated by cases and combined with an explanation of new laws and future legislation to be put into effect. It was divided into four parts: the *Institutes,* the *Digest,* the *Code,* and the *Novels.* This development and evolution of the legal process not only contributed to future legal systems, but it also served the needs and pressures of a far-flung but closely unified empire by providing a uniform system to hold the empire together.[4]

The *Institutes* were a general classification of the principles of the Roman law and served as a general book of instruction for law students, similar to Blackstone's Commentaries. The *Digest,* which contained the bulk of the law, consisted of extracts from writers on the law. A collection of the laws promulgated by different emperors was compiled in the form of the *Code*. Finally, a series of laws was promulgated to supplement the *Code* and the *Digest*. These new laws were called the *Novels* (or new laws) and put into statutory form every long-established custom. They included a law of descent and distribution that served as a model for our present law.

Business life in Rome was complex, resembling in many ways a modern business society. Consequently, much of our business law can be traced to Roman influence. For example, the Romans upheld the sanctity of the contract. A contract was held to be binding because of the intention of the parties and not because of any written agreement. In addition to the binding promise of the contract, a religious ritual was involved in finalizing the agreement. However, Roman contracts did not contain what we know as "consideration," nor did the Romans have bilateral or unilateral contracts. (In lieu of the latter was an arrangement called a penalty contract that produced the same result.)

The Romans knew the intricacies of deposit, bailment, pledge, and mortgage. They employed all legal implements of credit and banking and for the transfer of funds in their business ventures. There were very few concepts of recovery of money or property of which the Romans were unaware. Interest on loans was eventually legalized at 12 percent, although Justinian reduced it to 8 percent on business loans and eventually to a 6 percent general rate, which is close to the amount allowed today in a number of American states.

Although U.S. laws concerning leases of lands are derived most directly from the feudal system, few essential differences exist between these principles and those of the Romans in these matters. One difference, however, was that the Romans felt that whatever personal property a tenant brought onto the land should be recognized as security for payment of rent.

Even though there were no "corporations" in Rome as we know them today, there were forms of corporate bodies such as the unions or craft guilds. Banking was practiced to satisfy the needs of big business and money was borrowed on mortgages or other security. Sometimes no security was needed, as the general credit of the borrower sufficed. Syndicates of bankers existed to finance commercial ventures, comparable to modern syndicates.

The Roman world was more restricted in commercial law and the forms of transaction than in any other area. This limitation is reflected in the fact that the Romans had "bills and notes" but no "negotiable instruments." That is, they knew and used promissory notes, written promises to pay, but knew nothing about notes passed by indorsement or by delivery from person to person free of any defenses that the original maker might have had against the original payee. Other restrictions in business were a lack of bankruptcy laws and only rudimentary insurance provisions. Laws respecting transfers of property came into use as needed by the parties. The Romans also mastered the concept of possession and understood the rights relevant to property-holders.

The use of wills in Rome was almost universal because of the feeling that arbitrary rules of descent violated sentiment. It was, in fact, to ensure the succession of property to close relatives that wills were most often used.[5]

In sum, the modern world is indebted to Rome for its formal codification, classification, general theory, and method of applying law. The Roman civil law provides the basis of much of the law in the modern world. The nations of continental Europe adopted national legal codes based on principles similar to those of the Code of Justinian. This civil-law system was spread through colonization to Central and South America, the state of Louisiana in the United States, and to portions of Canada. The majority of the world's peoples today live under a legal system that is formally codified along Roman lines.

ENGLISH LAW

The development and evolution of the English common law has affected the American system of lawmaking more than any other single factor. The history of common law can be traced from the early invasions and settlement of the English sphere, through the reigns of all the English monarchs up to the present.

The influence of the common law was strongest in those countries where the English settled or governed. The United Kingdom and its colonies, the United States, Canada, Australia, New Zealand, Ghana, Nigeria, and India are all common-law countries in a sense. Though their individual systems may differ, they all bear characteristics of common law: the institution of the jury, the right to speedy trial, the tradition of the powerful and independent judiciary. By comparison, there are civil-law countries such as Italy, France, and Germany whose legal systems derive primarily from Roman law. Perhaps the most obvious point of contrast between common-law and civil-law systems is that in those countries where civil law prevails, legal regulations are embodied in legislative codes, while under common-law systems the judge, instead of being guided by a code, relies on decisions made by judges in previous cases. The common law thus operates on the idea of precedent, which might be understood as a built-in evolutionary process. The concept of precedent lends to the legal process measures of flexibility and adaptability that have made possible the endurance and success of the common law over the centuries.

In the earliest days of the common-law courts, when the law was evolving, there would have been no need to resort to any other source for an equitable decision. The law itself was capable of modification to meet the needs of justice. However, by the end of the fifteenth century the common law had ceased to accommodate itself to changing conditions. The process of granting new writs to meet new demands for all practical purposes had ceased. This forced litigants to appeal to the king, who, under the law, was the source of all justice, for the relief they thought was being denied to them by the courts. Due to the volume of these appeals the king began to refer them to his chancellor, whose duty it was to assist him in the discharge of the obligations of his coronation oath. Though at the outset this was probably a temporary measure, reference to the chancellor of problems of failure or inadequacy of legal remedy became a common practice. Although there was opposition from time to time from the established courts, the result was the creation of a separate series of courts alongside the common-law courts.

The early chancellors did not consider themselves bound by any fixed rules. Conscience was asserted to be the foundation of the chancellors' discretionary power. Petitions referred to them asked for "what ought to be done," "what justice demands," "according to law and reason," or "what reason and conscience required." The chancellors did, however, set certain guidelines to aid themselves in handling matters that came before them. The principle was early established that the Chancellor would not grant relief unless it could be shown that the petitioner had no legal remedy, having exhausted all available legal remedies, or that if a remedy at law existed, it was inadequate. (The common-law remedy in a contract action was an award of money damages.) At the chancellor's discretion contracts for the sale of real property were enforced. Specific performance is granted today under similar circumstances. The chancellor also granted relief for fraud and error in contract actions. The principle was also established that equity courts acted "in personam" (upon the person). The courts could issue orders commanding a person to do or refrain from doing a certain thing. If the person failed to comply with the decree, he was in contempt of court and might be fined or sent to jail, or both. The use of the injunction is an example of this principle that is still part of our legal system.

LAW AND CHANGE

The law in modern society is an ever-changing, dynamic process. The body of laws that governs a society must constantly be expanded to deal with new situations created by sociological or technological change. For example, the now common usage of the airplane has placed restrictions on the legal principle that "to whomever the soil belongs, he also owns the sky and to the depths." The Supreme Court, in keeping with what it called "the traditional policy of the courts to adapt the law to the economic and social needs of the time," refused in 1932 to enjoin the defendent Curtiss Airports Corporation from flying aircraft above the plaintiff's land.[6] In this situation, precedence was of no value in resolving the controversy because there were no previous formulas for giving priority to human desires with respect to the issues at hand. New law had to be established. It was determined that the owner of the land was entitled to a reasonable use of the airspace; likewise, the airline companies had to be reasonable in their use of the sky.

QUESTIONS FOR DISCUSSION

1. Is a legal system a necessary element of an organized society?
2. Can any society be classified as a "free" society?
3. Is there an element that is common to the legal system of every organized society?
4. What does a study of a society's legal system tell us about that particular society?
5. Why is it necessary for one society to borrow from another society's legal system?

ENDNOTES

1. Hon. M.F. Morris, *The History of the Development of Law* (Washington, D.C.: Byrne, 1909), pp. 52-58.
2. William A. Robson, *Civilization and the Growth of Law* (New York: Macmillan, 1935), p. 10.
3. Rene A. Wormser, *The Story of the Law* (New York: Simon and Schuster, 1962), p. 6.
4. Wormser, *op. cit.,* pp. 44-83.
5. *Ibid.,* pp. 126-149.
6. Swetland v. Curtiss Airports Corp., 55 F.2d 201, 203 (1932).

THE AMERICAN LEGAL SYSTEM

2

The Pilgrim fathers brought to America ideas about law and the organization of society that had been evolving in England for generations. A synthesis of these inherited concepts provided the New World with its first legal document, the Mayflower Compact. This "strongly English" pact, signed November 11, 1620, by forty-one of the Pilgrim fathers, was their agreement to "combine . . . together into a civil Body Politick" that would formulate the laws to which the people of the Pilgrim settlement in Plymouth, Massachusetts, would be expected to give "due Submission and Obedience."[1]

As additional colonists came from Europe and settled in different locations along the Eastern seaboard, numerous new bodies of law were created. Prominent individuals among the early settlers are generally credited with the promulgation of the laws of the various colonies. Among these were many religious men: John Calvin, Nathaniel Ward, Cotton Mather, Thomas Hooker, and John Wise, to mention a few. Despite superficial differences, the new bodies of law being promulgated were built around two basic legal concepts: the protection of the people of the community and the freedom of every individual to do as he pleased as long as his actions did not endanger the interests of the community. To quote John Wise:

> The end of all good government is to cultivate humanity, and promote the happiness of all, and the good of everyman in his rights, his life, liberty, estate, honor, etc., without any injury or abuse to any.[2]

Because of their strong religious beliefs and the hardships with which they were faced, the laws adopted by the early settlers were primarily restrictive. The Ten Commandments were made the basis of the criminal law, and many of the punishable crimes were those that ran contrary to the teachings of the different religious sects. The magistrates administered a type of justice dependent on their interpretation of the divine law, based largely on their discretion in cases not expressly covered by enacted law. Local freedom to interpret the law was carried to its most abusive extremes when the enforcement of the law was directed at the cruel punishment of those persons believed to be witches.

THE BEGINNINGS OF A BUSINESS FRAMEWORK

Technically, the colonies were under England's jurisdiction. However, the mother country did little more than acknowledge their existence. Given a free rein, the first colonists went about developing their own business framework. Laws were administered simply and without technicality; decisions were based on local statutes and the discretion of the courts rather than on the common law.

As the American economy grew, and as people in England began to recognize the economic potential of the New World, pressure was put on Parliament for tighter control of the business enterprises of the colonies and the laws of the commerce became more confining. The Americans, chafing under the new restrictions inhibiting trade, soon grew impatient. Moreover, aware of the abundance of land and resources of the New World, the colonists had become vitally concerned with developing this wealth, enlarging their share of international trade, and reaping profits free from British interference. For these reasons and many more, they demanded and fought for independence.

THE EFFECTS OF INDEPENDENCE

The immediate effect of independence in the United States was a decrease in commerce because of the loss of the British market. Ships therefore set sail to China and the Orient, where they established a very substantial trade, in competition with Britain. This trade soon expanded to include Hawaii and the Pacific Coast of North America. Although these feats were highly regarded, the effort needed to establish the new trade was far out of proportion to the monetary benefits derived. The reason was that the Articles of Confederation, adopted by the thirteen original states in 1781 to serve as the first official constitution, placed a considerable hindrance on business. Drawn up by men fearful of giving too much power to a central government, the Articles left the matter of regulating trade largely up to the individual states. Each state retained the right to make its own tariff laws and to adopt its own retaliatory measures in case of foreign discrimination against commerce. The complications and hardships that resulted from this lack of legislative and judicial control by the federal government soon made it clear that a different system of government was necessary.

The Constitution that emerged from the Convention of 1787 in Philadelphia was far superior to the Articles in meeting "the exigencies of the Union." It reflected many centuries of legal and political thought and had been drafted by men familiar with the operations of the common law as well as the civil law system and with such documents as the Magna Carta and the Bill of Rights. These men could likewise draw on their experience in drafting the state constitutions and running state governments. Much then was borrowed; yet there was some definite innovation. The notion of "the people" giving powers to a federal government and retaining those powers not granted was unknown in the history of law. Likewise, the separation of the central government into executive, legislative and judicial branches, with a system of constitutional "checks and balances" to permit some blending of the separate powers, contributed a new concept to legal history.

The Constitution gave Congress control over interstate and international commerce, abolished interstate tariffs, and put almost unlimited treaty-making powers in the hands of the President and Senate. These provisions helped protect the power of Congress to levy and collect import duties. Although a tariff for protection was not specifically mentioned, the manufacturer was certain that his special welfare was in the interest of the "general welfare of the United States."

Because of the tremendous market that developed for goods, everyone seemed to take an interest in invention. The Constitution specifically empowered Congress "to promote the progress of science and useful arts by securing for limited times to authors and inventors the exclusive right to their respective writings and discoveries" (Article I, Sec. 8). Pursuant to this, in 1790, Congress enacted the country's first patent law, whereby inventors had the sole right "to make, use, and vend" their inventions in this country for a period of seventeen years. This law was revised in 1793, and again in 1836, and still serves as the framework for the patent system. To prevent an inundation of applications for patents, the later revision provided that patents would be issued only after it had been determined that the inventions were new and were "sufficiently useful and important." Aside from the regulation of patents, the federal government made no attempt to regulate business.

Some of the most significant pieces of land legislation came out of the early years of the Republic. In fact, the principles of our modern property law were drawn up during this period. Congress, by the Ordinance of May 20, 1785, adopted what is known as the rectangular system of land surveys, which is still in use.

The Ordinance of 1787 established an important precedent in property law by its provision that new states created from the public domain "shall never interfere with the primary disposal of the soil by the United States nor with any regulations that the United States may find necessary for securing the title in such soil to the bonafide purchasers." The individual title derived from the federal government was to encompass the entire transfer of ownership of the soil, without any interference by any of the various state governments. It provided that what each man got, he got in fee simple, with a deed to a specific tract. Ownership was purely allodial,[3] with all the rights we associate with ownership. This represented a departure from the concept that ownership was in the sovereign.

This legislation provided the basis for our present laws of descent and distribution. It stated that estates of landowners dying intestate (i.e., without a will) should "descend to, and be distributed among their children, and the descendants of a deceased child, in equal parts," subject to the dower rights of the widow. Ownership would not revert to the sovereign.

In the years following 1790 a factory system developed in the United States. In order to produce the greatest amount of goods as cheaply as possible, factory owners resorted to child labor, long hours, and the most meager of working conditions. Manufacturing was dominated by the constant appeal of greater profits. In colonial days, a distrust of royal charters and the privileges that went with them prevented the rise of the corporation as a form of business organization. However, after independence was achieved, many corporations were formed, receiving their charters from the states in which they were located. In 1789 Massachusetts incorporated the Beverly Cotton Manufactory under its general incorporation statute. A wave of general incorporation acts by states in 1837 was prompted by the Dartmouth College case, which protected the corporate charter from legislative interference.[4] By 1860 nearly all the states had adopted such statutes, which paved the way for the large scale business organizations that developed after the Civil War.

THE INDUSTRIAL REVOLUTION

After the Civil War, liberty of contract and free enterprise, sustained by a laissez faire philosophy of government, brought about unrestricted competition that led to the construction of thousands of miles of railroads, the exploitation of natural resources, and the expansion of the West. Vast fortunes were amassed, and large corporations, trusts, and monopolies developed. At this point in the evolution of American business the courts and Congress found it necessary to make inquiries into the legality of certain procedures followed by the various companies.

Transportation was the focal point of these investigations because of its necessity in the distribution of goods. The cheaper the cost of transportation, the more profit an industry could make. Rate discrimination became a source of controversy during the period from 1870 to 1917. It took two forms: discrimination against specific shippers producing the same product and discrimination between different localities. In the early days agitation for regulation came principally from farmers. The main charge against the railroads was that lower rates were being extended to a few favored shippers as part of a concerted effort to eliminate competition and build trusts. Rebates of rates and special rates were sometimes induced by competition between railroads for a large shipper's business, but more often they appeared to be part of the movement toward monopoly.

In the 1870's and 1880's many complaints were voiced by small businessmen to the effect that they were being treated unfairly. The Granger movement was founded in 1867 to protect farmers of the Middle West, South, and Southwest from the excessive rates being charged by middleman operations. Intensive competition soon led to reductions in rates, but the evils of discrimination in rates and the threat to the public interest in railway agreements remained unabated. It is not surprising, therefore, that the first national regulatory act was aimed at ensuring a fair level of rates, eliminating discrimination, and preventing existing methods of combination.

REGULATION OF BUSINESS

A basic feature of our American system is that all law has a constitutional origin or sanction. Since federal authority is limited to the enumerated powers, many economic measures were enacted based on the constitutional provisions covering currency, patents and copyrights, and bankruptcy. However, legislation affecting business had rested largely on the commerce clause and the welfare clause.

Until almost the beginning of the twentieth century, the direct regulation of economic affairs in the United States was left almost wholly to the states. The Supreme Court gave repeated expression to the doctrine that competition was an unregulated and unrestricted process conducted without public rules or penalties. From 1801 to 1835, the Supreme Court, under Chief Justice John Marshall, established a broad interpretation of national power within which the nation's economy could develop. State laws that threatened national economic expansion were ruled unconstitutional as "impairing the obligation of contracts."

Chief Justice Taney, who led the Court from 1836 to 1864, followed primarily the pattern set by the Marshall Court. However, in the years following the Civil War, the Supreme Court began to support the states in their efforts to curb some of the more flagrant abuses of the growing industrial complex. The states found much encouragement in the Court's view of the "police power," their broad authority to protect the public health, public safety, public morals, and public welfare.

The first comprehensive federal regulation of business was the Interstate Commerce Act of 1887. It was followed by the Sherman Anti-Trust Act of 1890. The former, with its various amendments, was an attempt to regulate interstate railroad rates and practices, the latter struck at trusts and monopolies.

The Interstate Commerce Act applied to rail transportation, or joint rail-water transportation under the same management or control. It contained provisions on rates, pooling, and methods of administration. With regard to rates: (1) it set the general standard that all rates should be just and reasonable, (2) it prohibited various forms of discrimination, and (3) it prescribed publication of rates.

To administer the Act, the Interstate Commerce Commission was created. Its function was to hear complaints, initiate investigations, require production of papers and testimony of witnesses, make findings and reports, and issue orders. It could appeal to the circuit courts if carriers failed to comply with its directives or requirements.

The Sherman Act declared any combination in restraint of trade to be illegal and any person monopolizing, attempting to monopolize, or conspiring to monopolize trade or commerce to be guilty of a misdemeanor. Though seemingly specific in its words and phrases, this Act generated much legal controversy. Some judges wanted the provisions of the Act taken in their strictest and most limited meaning, while others wanted a broader interpretation favoring business. This problem of interpretation is reflected in the diverse judicial decisions handed down in the business disputes that followed passage of the Act.

The constitutional provision most often referred to in attempting to determine the extent of the grant of power given to Congress to regulate the nation's economy is the commerce clause (Article I. Sec. 8[3]): "The Congress shall have power . . . to regulate commerce with foreign nations, and among the several States, and with the Indian tribes." This is all the Constitution has to say on the subject of regulation. The constitutional questions, the questions about what the Congress can do, are in the last analysis left for the courts to decide. (See Chapter 3).

The decade which included our entry into World War I and Woodrow Wilson's administration (1913-21) is referred to by historians as a "trust busting" era. The Antitrust Division was established in the Department of Justice in 1903, with an Assistant Attorney General in charge of its operation. This same year, President Theodore Roosevelt set up the Bureau of Corporations for "diligent investigation into the business of any corporation or corporate combination." A part of the newly organized Department of Commerce and Labor, it was authorized to suggest corrective action for industrial problems. Woodrow Wilson was elected on a platform that stressed antitrust action. During his administration, the Federal Trade Commission Act (1914) and the Clayton Act (1915) were passed.

These acts were both designed principally to eliminate unfair competition. Section 5 of the Federal Trade Commission Act provides "that unfair methods of competition in commerce are hereby declared unlawful," and Section 2 of the Clayton Act states that it is unlawful for any person in commerce to discriminate in prices "where the effect of such discrimination may be to substantially lessen competition or to tend to create a monopoly in any line of commerce." To add to this description, the FTC Act "was intended primarily to prevent abuses rather than to punish for infractions of the law," and the Clayton Act "forbade discrimination in prices between different customers, the holding of stock by [one] corporation in others if the result was to diminish competition, and interlocking directorates between companies serving the same market."

The so-called "trust busting" efforts were largely terminated with an adverse decision in the United States Steel case in 1920. In that case, by a 4-3 vote, the Supreme Court held that the United States Steel Corporation, the largest industrial holding company of its kind, was legal. This seemed to sanction any merger short of monopoly. The Court reasoned that though the main objective of such a combination was the elimination of competition, though its power was great, though it engaged with competitors in collusive price tactics, still it was not illegal if the collusive tactics had been discontinued, if coercive tactics were not used against outsiders, and if monopoly was not achieved. Also, evil intent in formation was not sufficient; unexerted power was not evil; and a holding company as a method of organization was itself not illegal. This reasoning declares the company to be free of predatory practices at the time it is prosecuted.

The period following the steel case, 1920 to 1937, was a time of both great prosperity and great depression. There was little government interference with business activity in the prosperous twenties and an almost complete halt to antitrust activity with the passage of the National Industrial Recovery Act of 1933.

In 1936, the Robinson-Patman Act, passed as an amendment strengthening Section 2 of the Clayton Act (the section referring to price discrimination), and the Miller-Tydings Act, passed in 1937, exempted retail price fixing agreements under the states' "fair trade" laws from the antitrust laws.

Since 1937, the Supreme Court has voided only three acts of Congress, none of them relating to economic regulation of business activity. A survey of recent Court decisions also reveals a liberal reinterpretation of both the commerce and general welfare clauses of the Constitution. Thus, it would seem that the power to regulate has been established and that the Court has adopted the view that Congress is entitled to exercise fully its powers to meet the needs of the growing complexities of a modern business society.

BUSINESS AND THE LAW

Business is regulated or controlled, at least in part, by the workings of the free-market economy. Society does, however, impose some regulations and restrictions. Society must, for example, create, maintain and enforce the standards of weight, exchange and measurement that are vital to the development of uniform facilities for commercial transactions in the economy. Private ownership of property is a fundamental concept of our economic system made possible through legal sanctions. It is through law that the corporation is available as a means for combining the funds of many investors into a large firm or firms. Commercial law offers the enforceable contract, the concept of agency, commercial paper, the secured transaction and other instruments vital to the conduct of the business operation. The government also manages the economy by setting rules, such as the antitrust laws, and providing agencies to enforce these rules. In the last analysis, business administration is making business decisions within a legal framework. It is in the best interests of everyone to be aware of what actions society as represented by government will take, why they are taken, and how they will affect business.

UNIFORM COMMERCIAL LAWS THROUGHOUT THE FIFTY STATES

Toward the end of the nineteenth century it had become apparent to the business community that the laws governing business had become somewhat cumbersome and showed very little uniformity among the various states. Contributing to this were the rapid geographical expansion of the nation, the development of modern transportation facilities, and a significant increase in the volume of interstate commercial transactions.

In 1891 the quest for uniformity resulted in the formation of the National Conference of Commissioners on Uniform State Laws, with representatives appointed by the governors of the States. The first uniform statute promulgated by this body was the Negotiable Instruments Act. Covering the subjects of checks, promissory notes, and bills of exchange, it was proposed in 1896, and by 1924 it was adopted in all jurisdictions.

The first uniform act was followed by the Uniform Sales Act and the Uniform Warehouse Receipts Act in 1906. In 1909 the Uniform Bills of Lading Act and the Uniform Stock Transfer Act were adopted. The Commissioners approved the Uniform Partnership Act in 1914, and the Uniform Limited Partnership Act in 1916. The Uniform Conditional Sales Act was promulgated in 1918, the Uniform Business Corporation Act in 1928, and the Uniform Trust Receipts Act in 1933.

Although a number of states enacted these uniform laws, the rules of law governing commercial transactions in the various jurisdictions showed very little actual uniformity until recently. This variation existed primarily because judicial decisions interpreting the statutes varied from state to state both in those states adopting uniform laws and in those geographic areas not covered by the uniform statutes. Also, many states changed provisions of the uniform laws prior to their adoption.

In order to eliminate these variations in judicial interpretation and to secure some degree of uniformity, the National Conference of Commissioners on Uniform State Laws and the American Law Institute, with the aid of countless others, prepared the Uniform Commerical Code in the early 1950's. Their work was the first attempt to promulgate a comprehensive act covering the entire realm of commercial transactions.

PURPOSES OF THE UNIFORM COMMERCIAL CODE

The purposes of the Uniform Commerical Code, hereafter referred to as the Code, are to simplify commercial transactions; to permit continued expansion of commercial practices through custom, usage, and agreement of the parties; and to make the law uniform among the various jurisdictions. Although uniformity is the expressed purpose, numerous sections of the Code are prefaced by the words "unless otherwise agreed," emphasizing the agreement between the parties. In giving effect to the agreement; however, the Code does specify certain conditions as being contrary to public policy.

The basic principles of commercial law are not rewritten or significantly changed by the Code. However, they are expanded, and significant changes are made in the manner in which these basic principles are applied. For example, the Code represents a departure from legal tradition in that it is oriented toward the particular transaction and the intention of the parties themselves rather than concerned primarily with the application of a rule of law to a transaction.

SCOPE

The Uniform Commercial Code is limited in its scope to transactions involving various aspects of sales, financing, and security interests in personal property. Contracts, agency, partnerships, real property, and bailments remain essentially common law subjects. Specifically the Code regulates three areas: sales of goods, commercial paper, and secured transactions in personal property. It also covers particular aspects of banking, letters of credit, warehouse receipts, bills of lading, and investment securities. It contains nine articles, eight of which deal in detail with specific aspects of commercial transactions. The remaining article contains general provisions applicable to the whole body of Code law. The Uniform Commercial Code has been adopted by every state except Louisiana and by the District of Columbia and the Virgin Islands.

QUESTIONS FOR DISCUSSION

1. What principles formed the basis of early American legal systems?
2. What "new" political and legal principles were written into the United States Constitution?
3. What is the allodial concept of land ownership?
4. What is the "police power" of the several states?
5. What factor limits congressional regulation of the economy?

ENDNOTES

1. Rene A. Wormser, *The Story of the Law* (New York: Simon and Schuster, 1962), p. 305.
2. *Ibid.,* p. 316.
3. *Allodial:* absolute ownership or land; free from rent or service; as opposed to *feudal.*
4. *Dartmouth College* v. *Woodward,* 4 Wheat 518 (1819).

THE CONSTITUTION   3

The primary document of the legal system in our society is the United States Constitution. The framers of this document, considering historical precedent, emphasized the importance of distributing governmental power among the legislative, executive, and judicial branches of government. In order to prevent an undue concentration of power in the federal government, they not only separated governmental powers, they gave to the federal government only a portion of the power at their disposal. Powers not vested in the federal government were reserved to the states and to the people. In addition, certain basic and "unalienable" rights of property and personal liberty were guaranteed to individuals and placed beyond the control of any government. These guarantees cannot be changed except by the people themselves through the amending process.

The concept of separation of power was supplemented by a series of checks that each branch may exercise against the others. The President has a right to veto legislation, which checks or limits the exercise of legislative power by Congress. Certain appointments made by the President must be confirmed by the Senate, which limits executive power. Additionally, there are some areas of overlap among the powers of the three branches. For example, in connection with the passing of legislation, Congress may make investigations, thus exercising judicial power. In recent years, there has been a further tendency to modify the separation concept by delegation to administrative agencies of executive, legislative and judicial powers.

Legislative and executive power was further restricted by the practice of judicial review. In 1803, in the case of *Marbury* v. *Madison,* the Supreme Court decided that a portion of the Judiciary Act was contrary to the Constitution.[1] With this decision the Court established a precedent for the enforcement only of those statutes which it considers to be in accordance with the Constitution. Challenges to the constitutionality of a statute may be raised during any step of the legal process; however, any definitive interpretation of the United States Constitution must be made by the United States Supreme Court.

If a portion of a statute is held by the Court to be unconstitutional the entire statute will fall when it is clear that the legislature would not have passed that portion by itself. Where the entire statute is determined to be unconstitutional such declaration does not usually affect the result of earlier cases.

There are certain checks which may be exercised by the President and Congress to curtail the power of the Supreme Court. For example, the President has the power to fill vacancies that may occur on the court, subject to the approval (advise and consent) of the Senate. The size of the Court is a matter of legislative determination, subject to the requirement that sitting incumbents shall not be thrown out of office. Another check rests on the fact that most of the Supreme Court's jurisdiction is the result of congressional action. Where there is a wide diversity of opinion over a given case, therefore, the Court's jurisdiction could be limited or even eliminated without going through the tedious process of a constitutional amendment.

BASIC GUARANTEES

In criminal law certain actions are defined as being so contrary to accepted social behavior that commission of such an act may lead to the imposition of a fine or a deprivation of one's physical liberty. It is necessary, however, to ensure that society's desire to punish the perpetrator of the act does not result in a departure from the basic procedures that the Constitution mandates to insure the dignity and integrity of the members of our society.[2] The following are two of the rights guaranteed citizens by the Constitution.

SELF-INCRIMINATION

There is a basic presumption in our society that a person accused of a crime is innocent until proven guilty. In order to ensure that the state will gather evidence on its own efforts an accused individual "cannot be compelled . . . to be a witness against himself."[3]

BILLS OF ATTAINDER AND EX POST FACTO LAWS

Article I, Section 9, prohibits the United States from passing any bill of attainder or ex post facto law. A bill of attainder is a legislative act which inflicts punishment without a judicial trial. Although the term ex post facto, meaning simply "after the fact," would prohibit retroactive legislation affecting either civil rights or criminal punishments, it applies only to penal statutes. The Constitution thus prohibits the passing of any statute which by its operation alters the situation of the accused to his disadvantage. This includes any subsequent statute which makes criminal and punishes such act which was innocent when done; any statute that makes a crime greater than it was when committed; and any statute that inflicts a greater punishment than the law annexed to the crime when committed.

POLICE POWER

Every society has certain goals or objectives that are necessary to promote peace and prosperity within that society. Some of the traditionally acceptable goals of our society are prosperity, economic growth, national strength and security, justice, opportunity and anything else that might contribute to the "good life". To aid in the achievement of these objectives, state and the federal governments employ certain powers over property rights which influence people to act in a manner conducive to the public good. These powers of the state governments are referred to as their "police powers". The most important of these social interests are health, morals, safety and order and comfort. Protection against fraud; taking property for public purposes under eminent domain; and the regulation of commerce are legitimate economic interests of society.

Whereas the "police power" of the states is a grant of indefinite power, most of congressional power in this area is defined by reference to specified subject matter, such as "to borrow money" and to "make all laws which shall be necessary and proper."[4]

HEALTH

Wide latitude is permitted by the courts to the legislature in its efforts to safeguard the public health. A state may impose a tax or absolutely prohibit the sale of a product if such product can reasonably be considered detrimental to the public health; it may restrict the hours of labor of children in any employment; it may require vaccination; and it may authorize the destruction of cattle having a communicable disease. If the legislation bears no reasonable relation to protecting the public health it will not be upheld on that ground.

MORALS

The principal subjects of regulation in this area have been gambling, liquor and vice. Gambling includes not only betting but lotteries and other devices that are speculative in character. The sale of liquor may not only be regulated but prohibited, even including liquor lawfully owned before the law went into effect.

SAFETY

There are numerous statutes designed to protect the public against the hazards of inherently dangerous property such as explosives and businesses such as factories, mines, railroads, and building construction. State laws regulating the width and weight of motor trucks using their highways as a safety regulation have been upheld.

ORDER AND COMFORT

Legislation regulating the use of streets and public places in order to secure quiet, especially in the vicinity of hospitals, is quite common. Zoning ordinance provisions as to grocery stores in residential sections are sometimes sustained because of the increase of fire or police hazards.

LICENSING

Where an occupation, such as selling liquors, may be forbidden altogether, the state may require licenses. Licenses may also be required when a special course of study, training, or experience is necessary to qualify one to pursue an occupation with safety to the public interests. On this basis licenses may be required for such occupations as medicine, law, engineering, and dentistry.

In the exercise of its police power, the state may regulate the requirements for marriage and for divorce. It may forbid marriage between persons closely related and it may entirely forbid divorce. It may make the education of children compulsory. It may take care of persons who are dependents or those who have tendencies injurious to the social order, such as truants, habitual criminals and vagrants.

PROTECTION AGAINST FRAUD

In the exercise of its police power, the state may prevent fraud by the use of short weights, imitations or adulterations. To this end it may make and enforce inspection laws and regulate businesses so as to prevent fraudulent practices. However, it may not prohibit the sale of healthful oleomargarine for the mere purpose of protecting the butter industry against competition.

REGULATION OF THE USE OF PROPERTY

The state may forbid long-time leases of agricultural lands or the creation of contingent interests in property which will vest far in the future. It may regulate the appropriation and use of certain kinds of property (such as game, fish, natural gas and oil) and may forbid wanton waste of gas and oil and forest trees, even by private owners of such property.

It may create land irrigation or drainage systems and compel the owners of land benefited thereby to share the cost. It may authorize the development of water power by damming a stream and flooding the upper riparian land, compelling the owner of such land to submit thereto upon being paid therefor by the owner of the dam.

REGULATION OF PUBLIC UTILITIES

Where a business is of such a nature as to be affected with a public interest it may be regulated by the legislature. The most important of these businesses include the furnishing of transportation, telephone service, gas, water and electricity. In these cases the state may prescribe maximum charges for service and the details of the service to be rendered, the public utility being generally entitled to a fair return on the business.

EMINENT DOMAIN

The Fifth Amendment to the Constitution states that private property shall not "be taken for public use, without just compensation." The Fourteenth Amendment places the same restriction upon the states. It is implicit in these amendments that private property may be taken for a public use if "just compensation" is paid the owner of the property.

The power of eminent domain, while it is not given by any constitutional provision, is inherent in all governments as being necessary for the preservation of governmental effectiveness. It may be exercised by the government not only directly but also indirectly through any enterprise that discharges public functions, such as telephone, water, gas and electric companies.

PUBLIC PURPOSE

If a purpose is recognized as public so that public money may be appropriated to it, property may be taken by the exercise of eminent domain. But there must always be the goal of accomplishing some public good. For example, it is clearly within the public good to build a new highway or municipal building. Where the purpose is public, there is no rule limiting the amount taken in cases of necessity. But if the power is authorized to be exercised by a public utility or municipality the courts will construe the authorization strictly.

COMPENSATION

The constitutional requirement is for just compensation. Thus, where only a part of the total property interest is taken, the owner of the land is entitled to the value of the part taken plus any diminution in value of the rest. If the part remaining is enhanced in value, that enhancement must be deducted unless there is an express constitutional requirement providing that there shall be no deduction. Presently, an owner receives "fair market value" for his property. It is argued that "good will" of the business or emotional value of the home should be included in the award. In the exercise of its police power, however, some kinds of private property may be taken for public use without compensation. For example, the sale of liquor already legally manufactured may be prohibited and a brewery already legally in existence may be forbidden to manufacture beer.

REGULATION OF COMMERCE

As we have seen in Chapter 2 the Constitution gives Congress power to "regulate commerce with foreign nations, and among the several states and with Indian tribes." This means that as far as foreign commerce is concerned, the power of Congress is exclusive. In interstate commerce, Congress has exclusive power only where the subject matter requires one uniform plan of regulation; in other areas it is concurrent with the states but subject to preemption. Thus if Congress acts in any field of interstate commerce this has priority over any conflictive state legislation.

TAXATION

A tax is a compulsory payment of money collected from members of society in order to finance the operations of government. All levels of government, national, state and local, levy taxes.

The Constitution empowers the Congress "to lay and collect taxes, duties, imports and excises, to pay the debts and provide for the common defense and general welfare of the United States; but all duties, imports and excises shall be uniform throughout the United States."[5] The taxing power is a concurrent power; state and local governments also may exercise it, with the Federal power being supreme in the event of a conflict.

Although the primary purpose of taxation is revenue raising, Congress has from time to time enacted tax legislation for social and economic reasons. For example, taxes are imposed on liquor to discourage consumption and on stock transfers to lessen speculation. Taxes have been imposed as instruments of economic policy. In order to influence business organization there is a tax advantage enjoyed by the so-called "small" corporation. To encourage corporate financing through the use of borrowed capital, the interest paid on corporate indebtedness is allowable as a deductible business expense. Taxes may be used by government to discourage or to stimulate business concentration. Thus, an indirect effect of taxation may be regulatory if it has the effect of inducing or preventing some action by businessmen.

JURISDICTION

For the taxing power to be validly exercised, under the fifth and fourteenth amendments, the taxing agency must have jurisdiction of the subject matter, the tax must be levied for a public purpose and it must not be arbitrary, unreasonable, or discriminatory. An interest in land may be taxed only in the jurisdiction where the land is located. The same rule applies to chattels having a permanent location; but if, like railroad cars, they are employed part of the time in one state and part of the time in another, the latter state may tax the average number of cars within it during its tax year.

PUBLIC PURPOSE

Taxes may not be levied to a purpose which the courts regard as private. There can be no taxation, for example, to make a donation to a manufacturer planning to establish a factory within a given state. Taxes may be levied to support public charities and to give pensions to soldiers, sailors, firemen, policemen and teachers as part of their compensation for services already rendered or being rendered. The power to make tax exemptions should be treated on the same basis as the power to levy taxes. In some states, however, tax exemptions have been upheld as a means of encouraging the development of some kinds of private industries.

QUESTIONS FOR DISCUSSION

1. Is judicial review necessary?
2. Contrast the use of police power and eminent domain.
3. Discuss the prohibition against the passage of a bill of attainder. Ex post facto laws.

4. Why may land be taxed only in the jurisdiction where it is located?
5. What effect does the taxing power have on business decisions?

ENDNOTES

1. 1 Cranch 137 (1803).
2. See Chapter 5.
3. Fifth Amendment.
4. Article I, Section 7.
5. Article I, Section 8.

THE PRACTICE OF LAW 4

A society's need for lawyers depends to a large extent upon its degree of cultural, social, political, and economic development. In ancient Greece, for example, a speaker was not allowed to appear in court as an advocate for another, unless he had some interest in the subject matter of the case itself.[1] In colonial America there was a need for very little law; therefore, the lawyer exerted little influence. With independence, as we have seen, the young nation was faced with a rapid expansion of commerce and export trade, settlement of western lands, a growth in shipbuilding, and a growing fishing industry. This economic expansion gave rise to many controversies concerning business agreements, the use of commercial paper, conflicting land claims and property rights. The drafting of legal documents, and the interpretation of the newly-won political liberties became more complex requiring individuals with a knowledge of the law.

HISTORICAL BACKGROUND

Individuals seeking a career in law occupied a somewhat inferior social position in the American colonies. The landowners, the merchants, and the clergymen were extremely conscious of their positions in society and viewed lawyers as a threat to their influence. In fact, in many colonies persons acting as lawyers were forbidden to collect fees for the services they rendered in the courtroom.

Numerous other factors contributed to the social stigma attached to individuals who pursued the law as a career. In England, for example, lawyers had long been unpopular because they were viewed as the perpetrators of much evil as a result of their role in enforcing the common law. The people lived with the restrictions and hardships that were imposed by the system, but knew very little of the supposed liberties the law guaranteed. Perhaps this attitude prompted Mr. Bumble in Charles Dickens' *Oliver Twist,* to declare ". . . the law is a ass, a idiot."

In the colonies, interference by the royal governors, their deputies and the general assembly hindered the development of a trained legal profession. In many of the colonies the governor or general assembly were the sole courts of law. Even when an independent judiciary was created, with the possible exception of the Chief Justice, the courts were staffed by individuals who had virtually no familiarity with the law.

The hostility of religious groups in the colonies further hindered the development of a legal profession. The colonists usually looked to their religious leaders for guidance and it was in these individuals that they found all they deemed necessary to establish a government that was righteous, proper and lawful. Perhaps the greatest hindrance to the study of law, however, was the lack of published materials, such as printed law books and law reports, and the slow development of a formal law curriculum in the colleges. Historians report that in the seventeenth century there were no more than fifteen published law books in the colonies, nor more than thirty volumes of law reports in use.[2]

LAW AS A PROFESSION

Generally, the term "profession" is applied to a group of individuals involved in an area that requires advanced training or education. A profession differs from an ordinary business in that it requires this training and has as its primary objective to render a service to society. Lawyers recognized that the successful discharge of their duties required the utmost confidence and trust of the individuals they served. Because of this, the legal profession developed a code of legal ethics, which, reinforced and supplemented by judicial decisions, regulate the practices of those individuals who engage in the practice of law.

The Preamble of the Canons of Professional Ethics of the American Bar Association indicates the purpose and intent in formulating a code of legal conduct. It states:

> In America, where the stability of Courts and of all departments of government rests upon the approval of the people, it is peculiarly essential that the system for establishing and dispensing Justice be developed to a high point of efficiency and so maintained that the public shall have absolute confidence in the integrity and impartiality of its administration. The future of the Republic, to a great extent, depends upon our maintenance of Justice pure and unsullied. It cannot be so maintained unless the conduct and the motives of the members of our profession are such as to merit the approval of all just men . . .

FUNCTIONS OF THE LAWYER

The lawyer functions as a counselor, giving advice to people in the conduct of their daily transactions. As such, he may draft their estate plan, assist them in the purchase of their homes, or he may incorporate their business. The lawyer also acts as an advocate by assisting parties in the litigation or out-of-court settlements of their legal controversies. As an advocate he may represent his client in a court of law or he may appear before a regulatory body, such as a zoning board. His function as an advocate demands a high degree of trust and confidence with his client, the court, and with society in general.

It should be remembered that in our society the lawyer is brought into a legal controversy by one of the parties to that controversy. Once a participant, it is the duty of the lawyer to advance the interests of his client. However, as an officer of the court, the lawyer is bound to assist the court in dispensing society's concept of justice under the law. Consequently, the lawyer does nothing illegal when he attempts to secure for his client by proper means any advantage which the law offers to his client, the so-called "loopholes" in the law. The following excerpts from The Code of Professional Responsibility define clearly the lawyers responsibility to his client.

CANON 5

A LAWYER SHOULD EXERCISE INDEPENDENT PROFESSIONAL JUDGMENT ON BEHALF OF A CLIENT

The professional judgment of a lawyer should be exercised, within the bounds of the law, solely for the benefit of his client and free of compromising influences and loyalties. Neither his personal interests of other clients, nor the desires of third persons should be permitted to dilute his loyalty to his client. . . .

CANON 6

A LAWYER SHOULD REPRESENT A CLIENT COMPETENTLY

Because of his vital role in the legal process, a lawyer should act with competence and proper care in representing clients. He should strive to become and remain proficient in his practice and should accept employment only in matters which he is or intends to become competent to handle. . . .

CANON 7

A LAWYER SHOULD REPRESENT A CLIENT ZEALOUSLY WITHIN THE BOUNDS OF THE LAW

The duty of a lawyer, both to his client and to the legal system, is to represent his client zealously within the bounds of the law, which includes Disciplinary Rules and enforceable professional regulations. The professional responsibility of a lawyer derives from his membership in a profession which has the duty of assisting members of the public to secure and protect available legal rights and benefits. In our government of laws and not of men, each member of our society is entitled to have his conduct judged and regulated in accordance with the law; to seek any lawful objective through legally permissible means; and to present for adjudication any lawful claim, issue, or defense...

Duty of the Lawyer to a Client

The advocate may urge any permissible construction of the law favorable to his client, without regard to his professional opinion as to the likelihood that the construction will ultimately prevail. His conduct is within the bounds of the law, and therefore permissible, if the position taken is supported by the law or is supportable by a good faith argument for an extension, modification, or reversal of the law. However, a lawyer is not justified in asserting a position in litigation that is frivolous. . . .

Duty of Public Prosecutor

The responsibility of a public prosecutor differs from that of the usual advocate; his duty is to seek justice, not merely to convict. This special duty exists because: (1) the prosecutor represents the sovereign and therefore should use restraint in the discretionary exercise of governmental powers, such as in the selection of cases to prosecute; (2) during trial the prosecutor is not only an advocate but he also may make decisions normally made by an individual client, and those affecting the public interest should be fair to all; and (3) in our system of criminal justice the accused is to be given the benefit of all reasonable doubts. With respect to evidence and witnesses, the prosecutor has responsibilities different from those of a lawyer in private practice: the prosecutor should make timely disclosure to the defense of available evidence, known to him, that tends to negate the guilt of the accused, mitigate the degree of the offense, or reduce the punishment. Further, a prosecutor should not intentionally avoid pursuit of evidence merely because he believes it will damage the prosecution's case or aid the accused.

PROFESSIONAL COMPETENCY

In our society the legal process must be put into motion by individuals. Under this system, lawyers can be held responsible for those deficiencies in the dispensing of justice that are caused by their lack of training, moral integrity, or preparation of their client's cause of action. The requirements of postgraduate professional education at an approved law school to qualify for admission to the practice of law, as well as examinations to determine the moral and intellectual qualifications of the applicant have been adopted in all jurisdictions. Therefore, except when an individual acts as his own attorney, lawyers and most judges are graduates of law schools.

The legal profession, in an effort to police its members in the maintenance of professional standards of learning, competency and conduct, has formed bar associations in the various states. These organizations may initiate proceedings to reprimand or remove from their rolls members who fail to recognize and discharge their professional responsibility.

In the case of *In Re Sacher* a disbarment order was appealed. The court stated:

> The purpose of striking an attorney from the rolls of a court is not to punish him but to protect the court itself and relieve the public of a member of the legal profession, who is unfit to serve as such, in order to maintain the respect due the court by insuring that attorneys, who are 'officers of the court,' are of good professional character. Because the consequences of disbarment are necessarily severe, it is a measure to be exercised only for compelling reasons. In the case at bar we think that the proved instances of unprofessional conduct, constantly repeated in the face of the court's admonitions, and continuing during a trial of extended duration, clearly demonstrated a lack of respect for the court and constituted a serious obstruction to the administration of justice. It is evident that the respondent either was unable to comprehend his obligations to a court of law or was unwilling to fulfill them when he felt it inexpedient to do so. Even if a less severe measure of discipline might have been imposed, we do not find any abuse of discretion in disbarring the respondent from practice.[3]

PRIVILEGED COMMUNICATIONS

An attorney is not allowed to disclose a communication made by his client to him, or his advice given thereon, during the course of his professional employment. This duty continues beyond the course of employment or until waived by the client. The reason for the rule is to enable and encourage individuals seeking professional advice to disclose fully all the facts in reference to which they seek advice, without fear that such facts will be made public. Full disclosure will enable the attorney to better perform the function for which he was employed. Consider the court's statement in the case of *United States* v. *United Shoe Machinery Corporation:*

> The rule which allows a client to prevent the disclosure of information which he gave to his attorney for the purpose of securing legal assistance is founded upon the belief that it is necessary in the interest and administration of justice. . . . In a society as complicated in structure as ours and governed by laws as complex and detailed as those imposed upon us, expert legal advice is essential. To the furnishing of such advice the fullest freedom and honesty of communication of pertinent fact is a prerequisite. To induce clients to make such communications, the privilege to prevent their later disclosure is said by courts and commentators to be a necessity. The social good derived from the proper performance of the functions of lawyers acting for their clients is believed to outweigh the harm that may come from the suppression of the evidence in specific cases.
>
> . . . The privilege applies only if (1) the asserted holder of the privilege is or sought to become a client; (2) the person to whom the communication was made (a) is a member of the bar of a court, or his subordinate and (b) in connection with this communication is acting as a lawyer; (3) the communication relates to a fact of which the attorney was informed (a) by his client (b) without the presence of strangers (c) for the purpose of securing primarily either (i) an opinion on law or (ii) legal services or (iii) assistance in some legal proceeding, and not (d) for the purpose of committing a crime or tort; and (4) the privilege has been (a) claimed and (b) not waived by the client.[4]

THE ATTORNEY-CLIENT RELATIONSHIP

The case of *Keenan* v. *Scott* serves as an illustration of the exact time at which the attorney-client relationship is formed.

> An attorney may be employed without formalities of any kind. The contract may be made by parol, and is often largely implied from the acts of the parties . . . as soon as the client has expressed a desire to employ an attorney, and there has been a corresponding consent on the part of the attorney to act for him in a professional capacity, the relation of attorney and client has been established, and . . . all dealings thereafter between them relating to the subject of the employment will be governed by the rule applicable to such relation. It does not require payment of a fee, or an agreement for a fee, to establish such relationship; the law implies a promise of reasonable compensation . . .[5]

TERMINATION OF THE RELATIONSHIP

The client has a right to fire his attorney at any time. Consider the following court opinion:

A client may at any time for any reason which seems satisfactory to him, however arbitrary, discharge his attorney. Even in the presence of a definite agreement the client's right persists. Cancellation by him cannot constitute a breach of contract, for implied in every such agreement is the right to discharge.[6]

The attorney's right to terminate a relationship, once assumed, arises only from good cause. For example, if the client insists upon an unjust course in the conduct of his case, or if he insists over the attorney's objection in presenting frivolous defenses, or if he deliberately disregards an agreement, the lawyer may be warranted in withdrawing on due notice to the client, allowing him time to employ another lawyer. Also, when a lawyer discovers his client has no case and the client is determined to continue it, withdrawal is justified. Upon withdrawing from a case after a retainer has been paid, the attorney should refund such part of the retainer as has not been earned up to the time of withdrawal.

QUESTIONS FOR DISCUSSION

1. What is a profession?
2. Discuss the functions of the lawyer.
3. What is an adversary system?
4. Should the legal profession be self-regulating?
5. Discuss the attorney-client privilege? Is it necessary?

ENDNOTES

1. These persons in many cases were not trained in the law. They were merely acting as lawyers.
2. For an excellent treatment of the early lawyer see: Warren, Charles, *A History of the American Bar* (Boston, Massachusetts; Little, Brown & Company, 1913).
3. 206 F.2d. 358 (1953).
4. 80 F. Supp. 357,358,359 (1950).
5. *Keenan v Scott,* 64 West Va. 137, 142 (1908).
6. *Matter of Krooks,* 257 N.Y. 329, 331 (1931).

THE LEGAL PROCESS 5

A survey of legal history and legal institutions reveals the importance of law in the ancient and modern world. Much of history is legal history and the institutions of many societies remain as contributions to modern jurisprudence. We turn now from a survey of legal history to the workings of the law—to the modern legal process.

A process can be described as a series of interrelated actions that accomplishes certain objectives. The legal process resolves controversies over the applicability of law. The basic elements of this process are trial, appeal, and case decision. The first step in developing a logical approach to the solution of legal problems is to acquire an understanding of the legal process.

LEGAL REASONING

The more cynical among those interested in the law sometimes claim that every case is decided by the gastronomic theory of legal reasoning. That is, each solution rests upon the condition of the judge's intestinal tract, which is dependent upon what he ate for breakfast. They are correct only in one respect. The system of legal reasoning used by the courts to arrive at solutions to legal problems is conditioned by various factors. However, they are more likely to be historic than gastronomic. The factors affecting the legal reasoning in a particular case are explained in the case decision, a written document that embodies the opinion of the court—the end result of the legal process.

Cases may be capable of an easy solution. The appellate courts may dispose of a case by applying some previously established general rule of law to reach their decision. Such an approach is often the simplest and most logical. However, legal controversies do not always present factual situations that lend themselves to solutions based on precedent. For this reason, there are many conflicting approaches to the solution of legal controversies. For example, the question arises whether the courts should always apply the literal meaning of a rule. The difficulty in this approach is evident even in the interpretation of the most basic social laws of the western world, the Ten Commandments, and in American history in the enforcement of one of the nation's earliest laws regulating business, the Sherman Act.

The experience, background, and philosophy of the judge may influence the decision of a court. In the treatment of religious matters in litigation, for example, the outcome may rest on the judge's knowledge of the nature of the faith involved and his concept of the nature of religion itself. Practically speaking, all decisions at least in part reflect the judge's concept of what constitutes the good of society.

Considerations of public policy may be the basis of a court's determination of legal controversy. As the demand for equality for the minority groups has grown, the law has gradually changed. Many legal rules were overturned by the courts in the areas of housing, education, job opportunity, voting rights, and civil rights in general. Actually, judicial pronouncements influenced by social change accomplished reforms in these areas that seemed impossible to accomplish by legislation.

Custom and trade usage have greatly influenced the direction of commercial law. The uniform laws covering business transactions reflect better business practices developed over the years. The merchant's use of a substitute for money in the form of a negotiable document is one example of a custom that received legal sanction as the law developed.

Whatever approach is employed, the application of the principle of *stare decisis,* or *precedent,* theoretically limits the Supreme Court in the ultimate solution of legal controversies. If the law is to function as a means of compelling people to act in a certain manner, individuals must be able to reasonably rely on the present state of the law as a guide to govern future actions. Likewise, where property is concerned the law has established certain rights, and unless the demands of society are overwhelmingly in favor of change, the law will adhere to precedent. However, where there is no precedent to guide a court in the solution of a legal controversy, new law will have to be established. For example, when the first suit involving an airplane crash reached the courts, there was no available precedent on which to base a decision.

In analyzing a case, the reader will notice citations of other court decisions that are set forth in the written opinion. This occurs because so many judicial decisions are precedent-oriented and, whether applying precedent or not, a court will distinguish the cases cited as authorities, accepting similarities and pointing out differences in the factual situations.

STARE DECISIS

The policy of stare decisis[1] reflects a basic adherence of the legal profession to judicial decisions. There is considerable feeling in legal circles that similar cases should be decided by similar solutions, and lawyers and judges spend much time and effort comparing and distinguishing cases to establish the relevance of the principle of stare decisis. However, where old rules are no longer valid, where there is no previous decision, or where the precedents are in conflict, new rules must be created. This caused Justice Roberts to comment that cases were brought "into the same class as a restricted railroad ticket, good for this day and train only."[2] With this in mind, stare decisis has become a matter of policy that might be followed by an appellate court in resolving a legal conflict.

CASE ANALYSIS

In order for an individual to acquire a "feel" for the law he must develop a legal method of analysis. The subject matter of this legal analysis is the reported case. Cases are studied for their decision, the possibility that the decision will have an impact on the solution of future legal controversies, and the impact of the decision on established legal rights.

The reported case records the solution to a legal controversy, resolved at a fixed date, in a particular jurisdiction, and is determined by an application of legal reasoning. The objective of a case study is to help the reader understand law as a dynamic process and appreciate its role in society. The steps in a case study are to analyze:

1. the meaning of the case citation
2. the nature of the controversy
3. the application of the law
4. requested solutions
   (a) the plaintiff's cause of action
   (b) the defense
5. the decision of the court
6. the legal reasoning justifying the decision
7. the implications of the decision

The case of *De Cicco* v. *Schweizer et. al.,* decided on November 13, 1917, is offered as an illustrative case study.

De Cicco v. Schwizer et al.
221 N.Y. 431 (1917)

CARDOZO, J. On January 16, 1902, "articles of agreement" were executed by the defendant Joseph Schweizer, his wife, Ernestine, and Count Oberto Gulinelli. The agreement is in Italian. We quote from a translation the part essential to the decision of this controversy:

> Whereas, Miss Blanche Josephine Schweizer, daughter of said Mr. Joseph Schweizer and of said Mrs. Ernestine Teresa Schweizer, is now affianced to and is to be married to the above said Count Oberto Giacomo Giovanni Francesco Maria Gulinelli: Now in consideration of all that is herein set forth the said Mr. Joseph Schweizer promises and expressly agrees by the present contract to pay annually to his said daughter Blanche, during his own life and to send her, during her lifetime, the sum of two thousand five hundred dollars, or the equivalent of said sum in francs, the the first payment of said amount to be made on the 20th day of January, 1902.

Later articles provided that "for the same reason heretofore set forth," Mr. Schweizer will not change the provision made in his will for the benefit of his daughter and her issue, if any. The yearly payments in the event of his death are to be continued by his wife.

On January 20, 1902, the marriage occured. On the same day, the defendant made the first payment to his daughter. He continued the payments annually till 1912. This action is brought to recover the installment of that year. The plaintiff holds an assignment executed by the daughter, in which her husband joined. The question is whether there is any consideration for the promised annuity. That marriage may be a sufficient consideration is not disputed. The argument for the defendant is, however, that Count Gulinelli was already affianced to Miss Schweizer, and that the marriage was merely the fulfillment of an existing legal duty. For this reason, it is insisted, consideration was lacking. The argument leads us to the discussion of a vexed problem of the law which has been debated by courts and writers with much subtlety of reasoning and little harmony of results. . . . The courts of this state are committed to the view that a promise by A to B to induce him not to break his contract with C is void. *Arend* v. *Smith*, 151 N. Y. 502. If that is the true nature of this promise, there was no consideration. We have never held, however, that a like infirmity attaches to a promise by A, not merely to B, but to B and C jointly, to induce them not to rescind or modify a contract which they are free to abandon. To determine whether that is in substance the promise before us, there is need of closer analysis.

The defendant's contract, if it be one, is not bilateral. It is unilateral. . . . The consideration exacted is not a promise, but an act. The count did not promise anything. In effect the defendant said to him: 'If you and my daughter marry, I will pay her an annuity for life.' Until marriage occurred, the defendant was not bound. It would not have been enough that the count remained willing to marry. The plain import of the contract is that his bride also should be willing, and that marriage should follow. The promise was intended to affect the conduct, not of one only, but of both. This becomes the more evident when we recall that though the promise ran to the count, it was intended for the benefit of the daughter. . . . When it came to her knowledge, she had the right to adopt and enforce it. . . . In doing so, she made herself a party to the contract. Since, . . . it was unilateral, the consideration being performance . . . action on the faith of it put her in the same position as if she had been in form the promisee. That she learned of the promise before the marriage is a legitimate inference from the relation of the parties and from other attendant circumstances. The writing was signed by her parents; it was delivered to her intended husband; it was made four days before the marriage; it called for a payment on the day of the marriage; and on that day payment was made, and made to her. From all these circumstances, we may infer that at the time of the marriage the promise was known to the bride as well as the husband, and that both acted upon the faith of it. The distinction between a promise by A. to B. to induce him not to break his contract with C., and a like promise to induce him not to join with C. in a voluntary rescission is not a new one. The criticism has been made that in such circumstances there ought to be some evidence that C. was ready to withdraw.

Whether that is true of contracts to marry is not certain. Many elements foreign to the ordinary business contract enter into such engagements. It does not seem a far-fetched assumption in such cases that one will release where the other has repented. We shall assume, however, that the criticism is valid where the promise is intended as an inducement to only one of the two parties to the contract. It may then be sheer speculation to say that the other party could have been persuaded to rescind. But where the promise is held out as an inducement to both parties alike, there are new and different implications. One does not commonly apply pressure to coerce the will and action of those who are anxious to proceed. The attempt to sway their conduct by new inducements is an implied admission that both may waver; that one equally with the other must be strengthened and persuaded; and that rescission or at least delay is something to be averted, and something, therefore, within the range of not unreasonable expectation. If pressure, applied to both, and holding both to their course, is not the purpose of the promise, it is at least the natural tendency and the probable result.

The defendant knew that a man and a woman were assuming the responsibilities of wedlock in the belief that adequate provision had been made for the woman and for future offspring. He offered this inducement to both while they were free to retract or to delay. That they neither retracted nor delayed is certain. It is not to be expected that they should lay bare all the motives and promptings, some avowed and conscious, others perhaps half-conscious and inarticulate, which swayed their conduct. It is enough that the natural consequence of the defendant's promise was to induce them to put the thought of rescission or delay aside. From that moment, there was no longer a real alternative. There was no longer what philosophers call a "living" option. This in itself permits the inference of detriment.

The same inference follows, not so inevitably, but still legitimately, where the statement is made to induce the preservation of a contract. It will not do to divert the minds of others from a given line of conduct, and then to urge that because of the diversion the opportunity has gone by to say how their minds would otherwise have acted. If the tendency of the promise is to induce them to persevere, reliance and detriment may be inferred from the mere fact of performance. The springs of conduct are subtle and varied. One who meddles with them must not insist upon too nice a measure of proof that the spring which he released was effective to the exclusion of all others.

Undoubtedly, the prospective marriage is not to be deemed a consideration for the promise "unless the parties have dealt with it on that footing." But here the very formality of the agreement suggests a purpose to affect the legal relations of the signers. One does not commonly pledge one's self to generosity in the language of a covenant. That the parties believed there was a consideration is certain. The document recites the engagement and the coming marriage. It states that these are the "consideration" for the promise. The failure to marry would have made the promise ineffective. In these circumstances we cannot say that the promise was not intended to control the conduct of those whom it was designed to benefit. Certainly we cannot draw that inference as one of law. Both sides moved for the direction of a verdict, and the trial judge became by consent the trier of the facts. If conflicting inferences were possible, he chose those favorable to the plaintiff.

The conclusion to which we are thus led is reinforced by those considerations of public policy which cluster about contracts that touch the marriage relation. The law favors marriage settlements, and seeks to uphold them. It puts them for many purposes in a class by themselves. It has enforced them at times where consideration, if present at all, has been dependent upon doubtful inference. It strains, if need be, to the uttermost the interpretation of equivocal words and conduct in the effort to hold men to the honorable fulfillment of engagements designed to influence in their deepest relations the lives of others.

The judgment should be affirmed with costs.

CASE CITATION

The case citation, sometimes called the cite, is useful for the complete research of a particular case. It consists of the names of the parties, the court that decided the case, and the date of the decision: *De Cicco* v. *Schweizer, et. al.,* 221 N.Y. 431, 117 N.E. 807, (1917)

Reported cases are usually appealed cases, or appellate opinions. Sometimes the name of the party against whom an adverse judgment was rendered at the trial level appears first, while at other times the original order of the names of the parties is continued until the controversy is resolved.

In the instant case De Cicco brought the action against Schweizer and others. If this case were reported at the trial level, De Cicco's name would appear first as the plaintiff. Although Schweizer, the appellant, is appealing the decision and De Cicco is the appellee, or respondent, who is responding to the appeal, the New York court continues the names of the parties in their original order. The court reached its decision in 1917.

State court opinions, as a rule, will list two citations. The original report of this case opinion can be found in the *New York Reports,* Volume 221, page 431, cited as 221 N.Y. 431. It can also be found in the *Northeastern Series,* Volume 117, page 807, cited as 117 N.E. 807. State cases are reported in a *State Reporter System* or in a group of states such as the *Northeastern Series.*[1] Other groups are *Atlantic,* cited as A.; *Northwestern,* cited as N.W.; *Pacific,* cited as P.; *Southeastern,* cited as S.E.; *Southwestern,* cited as S.W.; and *Southern,* cited as S. When these sectional reports reached three hundred volumes, the publisher, instead of labelling the next volume 301, called it Volume 1, Second Series. There are special series for the intermediate and trial courts of New York called the *New York Supplement,* cited as N.Y.S.; and a California series called the *California Reporter,* cited as Cal. Rpts.

The decisions and opinions of the United States Supreme Court are published in the official publication *United States Reporter,* cited as S. Ct., which are published by a private firm. Decisions rendered by the United States Courts of Appeals are published in the *Federal Reporter,* cited as F., and the decisions of the United States District Courts that are accompanied with opinions are published in the *Federal Supplement,* cited as F. Supp.

THE NATURE OF THE CONTROVERSY

The nature of the controversy is presented as a narrative of a situation that resulted in a controversy that ultimately brought the parties to the courts to seek a solution. From this course of conduct, the facts that influenced the decision of the court must be separated from the totality of the evidence.

On January 16, 1902, articles of agreement were executed by the defendant Joseph Schweizer, his wife, Ernestine, and Count Oberto Gulinelli. The agreement is in Italian. We quote from a translation the part essential to the decision of this controversy:

"Whereas, Miss Blanche Josephine Schweizer, daughter of said Mr. Joseph Schweizer and of said Mrs. Ernestine Teresa Schweizer, is now affianced to and is to be married to the above said Count Oberto Giacomo Giovanni Francesco Maria Gulinelli: Now in consideration of all that is herein set forth the said Mr. Joseph Schweizer promises and expressly agrees by the present contract to pay annually to his said daughter Blanche, during his own life and to send her, during her lifetime, the sum of two thousand five hundred dollars, or the equivalent of said sum in francs, the first payment of said amount to be made on the 20th day of January, 1902."

Later articles provided that "for the same reason heretofore set forth," Mr. Schweizer will not change the provision made in his will for the benefit of his daughter and her issue, if any. The yearly payments in the event of his death are to be continued by his wife.

On January 20, 1902, the marriage occurred. On the same day, the defendant made the first payment to his daughter. He continued the payments annually till 1912.

THE APPLICATION OF THE LAW

In each reported case the appellate court must be satisfied with the law as it has been applied by the lower court. For an effective analysis of the case the reader must be able to define this problem. The court's decision will be made in regards to the application of the law. The question to be answered in the instant case is whether there is any consideration for the promised annuity.

REQUESTED SOLUTIONS

Each of the parties to a legal controversy will present his cause to the court and request that relief be granted in his favor. The plaintiff will allege that he has a legal cause of action and that because of certain conduct of the defendant he is entitled to judgment in the manner requested. The defendant will counter with an allegation that the plaintiff has no legal cause of action, or that if he has, the defendant is seeking a denial of the plaintiff's request.

(a) Plaintiff's Cause of Action

This action is brought to recover the installment of that year. The plaintiff holds an assignment executed by the daughter, in which her husband joined.

(b) The Defense

The argument for the defendant is, however, that Count Gulinelli was already affianced to Miss Schweizer, and that the marriage was merely the fulfillment of an existing legal duty. For this reason, it is insisted, consideration was lacking.

THE DECISION OF THE COURT

Since the defendant is appealing a decision of a lower court, the decision of the appellate court will be made with regard to this initial decision. In the case of *De Cicco* v. *Schweizer et. al.,* the final decision was "The judgment should be affirmed with costs." The effect of this decision is to grant the plaintiff's request and place the costs of the appeal on the defendant.

THE LEGAL REASONING JUSTIFYING THE DECISION

The process of legal reasoning is the method used by the courts to arrive at solutions to legal controversies. It is also the method by which courts justify their conclusions.

> Undoubtedly, the prospective marriage is not to be deemed a consideration for the promise unless the parties have dealt with it on that footing. But here the formality of the agreement suggests a purpose to affect the legal relations of the signers. One does not commonly pledge one's self to generosity in the language of a covenant. That the parties believed there was a consideration is certain. The document recites the engagement and the coming marriage. It states that these are the consideration for the promise. The failure to marry would have made the promise ineffective. In these circumstances we cannot say that the promise was not intended to control the conduct of those whom it was designed to benefit. Certainly we cannot draw that inference as one of law. Both sides moved for the direction of a verdict, and the trial judge became by consent the trier of the facts. If conflicting inferences were possible, he chose those favorable to the plaintiff.
>
> The conclusion to which we are thus led is reinforced by those considerations of public policy which cluster about contracts that touch the marriage relation. The law favors marriage settlements, and seeks to uphold them. It puts them for many purposes in a class by themselves. It has enforced them at times where consideration, if present at all, has been dependent upon doubtful inference. It strains, if need be, to the uttermost the interpretation of equivocal words and conduct in the effort to hold men to the honorable fulfillment of engagements designed to influence in their deepest relations the lives of others.

The court hears the case, applies a rule of law, and disposes of the case. This approach makes the law seem very logical and easy to understand. However, situations are not always similar, nor does precedent necessarily produce a decision that is in accord with the presently accepted standards of social conduct or utility. Therefore, there are conflicting approaches to the solution of legal controversies and there are other variables which affect the ultimate solution.

Social Factors

The experience, background, political and legal philosophy of the judge or judges may influence the opinion of the court. In the interpretation of constitutional matters, for example, the decision may rest on whether the judge adheres to a strict or liberal interpretation philosophy. In a sense, each opinion will contain a certain amount of discussion about the court's feelings on the good or welfare of society. In the instant case, for example:

> The springs of conduct are subtle and varied. One who meddles with them must not insist upon too nice a measure of proof that the spring which he released was effective to the exclusion of all others...

> The law favors marriage settlements and seeks to uphold them. It puts them for many purposes on a class by themselves. It has enforced them at all times where consideration, if present at all, has been dependent upon doubtful inference.

Whatever reasoning is employed, the principle of stare decisis, or precedent, may limit the Supreme Court in the solution of a legal controversy. If the law is to function as a means of social control in order to maintain the welfare of society, individuals must be able to reasonably rely on the present state of the law as a guide to act in a socially acceptable manner. There must be a certain degree of predictability in the law. For example, in the area of property law, there has been established certain rights with regard the usage of property. Society demands that the law adhere to precedent. However, where there is no precedent, new law must be established.

Technological Factors

Rules of law must be modified to keep pace with changing technological developments. The first train accident caused by the malfunction of a computer will necessitate a new rule of law, as did the first auto accident or airplane crash. Consider the work done by the courts in the area of defamation of character. Where the defamatory information is uttered orally to a third person, it is considered slander, whereas the written defamation is called libel. However, technology in the form of radio, motion picture and television enabled men to more easily defame one another and the old rules had to be extended.

THE IMPLICATIONS OF THE DECISION

In formulating a decision the court is necessarily influenced by the possible effect it will have on the future welfare and conduct of society. For example, the effect of the reapportionment cases shifted the balance of political power from the rural areas of our country to the rapidly expanding urban centers.

QUESTIONS FOR DISCUSSION

1. Should there be controversies over the applicability of the law?
2. What factors affect the rendering of a decision in a particular legal controversy?
3. What is "stare decisis"?
4. What is the primary objective of case analysis?
5. When does a court decision become final?

ENDNOTE

1. The sectional groups are Atlantic (Connecticut, Delaware, District of Columbia, Maine, Maryland, New Hampshire, New Jersey, Pennsylvania, Rhode Island, Vermont); Northeastern (Illinois, Indiana, Massachusetts, New York, Ohio); Northwestern (Iowa, Michigan, Minnesota, Nebraska, North Dakota, South Dakota, Wisconsin); Pacific (Alaska, Arizona, California, Colorado, Hawaii, Idaho, Kansas, Montana, Nevada, New Mexico, Oklahoma, Oregon, Utah, Washington, Wyoming); Southeastern (Georgia, North Carolina, Virginia, West Virginia); Southwestern (Arkansas, Kentucky, Missouri, Tennessee, Texas); and Southern (Alabama, Florida, Louisiana, Mississippi).

CRIME AND TORT   6

One of the functions of law in the social order is to discourage unacceptable behavior. To minimize this type of activity society provides for the imposition of penalties on those members who indulge in it. The law also provides channels whereby an individual can seek personal remedy when he is the only member of society who has been injured by an unacceptable or negligent activity. Many unacceptable activities demand both punishment by society and payment of compensation to the injured party. For example, assault and battery is both a criminal act and one to which the legal process will award compensation in a civil suit by the victim. Therefore, the legal consequence of unproductive behavior may be both punishment and compensation.

The individual state legislatures have the broad inherent power to define what actions are criminal and to enact laws prescribing punishments for particular criminal actions. In most jurisdictions criminal law is based on the English common law, modified and supplemented by statutory enactments and by judicial decisions. In those states where the common law has been expressly abolished, crime is defined by statute. Even in these states, however, the statutory crimes are interpreted by reference to the common law whose terminology has a well-settled usage.

CLASSIFICATIONS OF CRIME

A crime may be classified as treason, felony or misdemeanor. Treason against the United States is defined by the United States Constitution as: "levying war against them, or in adhering to their enemies, giving them aid and comfort."[1] In some state constitutions treason against the state has a similar definition: "Whoever levies war against this state, or knowingly adheres to its enemies, giving them aid or comfort, is guilty of treason against the State of Indiana."[2]

The common law felonies included murder, mayhem, rape, robbery, burglary, and arson. The most common test of a felony is whether the particular offense is punishable by death or imprisonment in the state's prison. Criminal statutes usually specify whether a crime is felony or a misdmeanor.

A misdemeanor is an offense other than treason or a felony.

INTERESTS PROTECTED BY SOCIETY

A crime is a wrong against society, hence the perpetrator of it is punished by society. Whatever is deemed to be a criminal act will depend upon the particular society at a given time, its tradition, customs and beliefs, and its moral, ethical, or social duties. Society traditionally has an interest in the protection of each member of society; hence the law provides protection against injuries to the person, protects an individual's domestic relations, protects against interference with freedom of movement, and protects property interests.

THE CRIMINAL ACT

In order that there be a punishable offense it is usually necessary that there be both a voluntary act and an intent to commit a crime. It must be shown that those accused willfully intended to commit the crime. In some crimes, such as burglary, there must be a specific intent to commit a felony. However, in the commission of a felony where a death results, no specific intent is required. All that must be shown is a general criminal intent.

COMMON LAW CRIMES

While there are no universal definitions that will fit all criminal behavior, consider the following definitions adopted by the State of Indiana in its statutory enactments.

MURDER

Murder is the killing of a human being with "malice aforethought." Whether or not "malice" is present is determined for each specific case. The term "aforethought" may not require either premeditation or deliberation if there is "malice" at the moment of killing.

> Whoever purposely and with premeditated malice, or in the perpetration of or attempt to perpetrate a rape, arson, robbery or burglary, kills any human being, is guilty of murder in the first degree and on conviction shall suffer death or be imprisoned in the state prison during life.[3]

MAYHEM

"Whoever purposely and maliciously, with intent to maim or disfigure . . . cuts off or disables a limb or any member of another person, is guilty of malicious mayhem, and, on conviction, shall be imprisoned in the state prison not less than two (2) years, nor more than fourteen (14) years, and be fined not more than two thousand dollars ($2000)."[4]

RAPE

"Whoever has carnal knowledge of a woman forcibly against her will, or a female child under sixteen (16) years . . . is guilty of rape, and on conviction shall be imprisoned not less than two (2) years, nor more than twenty-one (21) years: Provided, that in cases where the female upon whom the crime is committed is a child under the age of twelve (12) years the punishment shall be imprisonment for life."[5]

ROBBERY

"Whoever takes from the person of another any article of value by violence or by putting in fear, is guilty of robbery and on conviction shall be imprisoned not less than ten (10) years, nor more than twenty-five (25) years, and be disfranchised and rendered incapable of holding any office of trust or profit for any determinate period."[6]

BURGLARY

"Whoever breaks and enters into any dwelling, house, or other place of human habitation with the intent to commit any felony therein . . . shall be guilty of burglary, and on conviction thereof shall be imprisoned not less than ten (10) years, nor more than twenty (20) years, and be disfranchised and rendered incapable of holding any office of trust or profit for any determinate period."[7]

ARSON

"Any person who wilfully and maliciously sets fires to or burns, or causes the setting of fire to or the burning, or who aids, counsels or procures the setting of fire to or the burning of any dwelling-house, (or other like property) . . . shall be guilty of arson in the first degree and, upon conviction thereof, shall be imprisoned in the state prison not less than two (2) years nor more than fourteen (14) years."[8]

DEFENSES

INSANITY

Insanity is a complete defense to a criminal prosecution. If the individual is unable to formulate the state of mind necessary for liability he should not be convicted. Generally, if the person accused of a criminal act was incapable of distinguishing between right and wrong at the time the act was committed, or if he could not appreciate the nature and consequence of his actions, he will not be held criminally responsible for his actions.

INFANCY

A child is said to be incapable of committing a crime prior to reaching the age of reason. In most jurisdictions a child under seven is said to be incapable of committing a crime, whereas between the ages of seven and fourteen there is a presumption of incapacity. Over the age of fourteen there is a presumption of capacity. If the child does not have the mental capacity to distinguish right from wrong, he is incapable of having a criminal intent.

TORTS

A tort is usually defined as a civil wrong, other than breach of contract, for which the legal system will afford relief in the form of a cause of action for money damages. The state of mind of the wrong-doer is the determining factor in establishing tort liability. Whether the activity will give rise to a cause of action depends on: whether the actor intended the consequences of his actions; whether he behaved in such a manner as to indicate a complete lack of regard for the rights of others; or whether his activity could be defined as extra-hazardous to which attaches liability without fault. In other words, liability is based upon the contacts individual members of society have with each other. Compensation will be awarded for losses individuals suffer because their individual interests are injured by another's conduct.

The theory of the intentional tort is that one individual ought not be allowed to culpably injure another with reckless abandon. If he does so, he will have to make compensation. An individual's conduct in his daily activities must produce foreseeable results, be reasonable under the circumstances, and be carried on with due care. When it is less than this, the person is liable only to those to whom he owes a duty, and for the foreseeable consequences. In a negligent act, therefore, there must be a relationship between the parties, hence the duty owed, and the negligent act must be both the actual and the probable cause of the injury. Negligence might be described as careless behavior that causes harm.

There are situations, however, where liability is imposed without fault. In extra-hazardous activities, such as the use of explosives, the individual or his employer will be responsible for any injuries that result from his activities even if all the necessary precautions have been taken.

The liability-without-fault theory is also applied when a manufacturer sells a defective product, and a person is injured as a consequence of the defect. Even if all reasonable measures have been taken to eliminate the possibility of defect, the manufacturer is held liable because he created the risk and he is also in a position to pass it on as a cost of doing business.

INTENTIONAL TORT

Some activities giving rise to a cause of action in tort involve intentional interferences with the person, freedom from mental disturbances caused by supposed contacts with his person, restraints placed upon his freedom of motion, interference with his property and injury to his reputation. It should be noted that there is a relationship between the intentional tort and criminal activity in that battery, assault, and false imprisonment can carry both criminal and civil liability.

BATTERY

Battery is a direct physical contact which results in physical injury or the offensive touching of a person. How much touching is necessary? The New

Jersey Court in *Rullis* v. *Jacobi,* 192 A.2d 186, 189 (1963), stated ". . . the plaintiff grasped Jacobi's arm. Though Jacobi suffered no bodily harm, it must be concluded that the plaintiff touched him in an offensive way, thus committing a technical assault." *Morrow* v. *Flores*, 225 S.W. 2d 621, 623, 624 (1950), illustrates the concept of transferred intent. Here a third person received a bullet in the foot that was intended for another. The alleged wrong-doer intended injury to one person but injured another by mistake. The court held that intent was the determining factor. As long as one *intends* the consequence of his actions, it is of little concern who is the recipient of such intent. A "battery may be committed though the person actually injured thereby was not the person intended to be injured."

In society a certain amount of personal contact is part of an individual's daily activity. Casual contact, a tap on the shoulder or a grasp of the arm is taken for granted. Any injury that is a reasonable consequence of such activities does not give rise to a cause of action.

ASSAULT

Actionable assault is causing an individual to be put in fear or apprehension of an immediate injurious or offensive contact with his person. The carrying out of the threatened contact is a battery and not assault, contrary to common usage by the news media. To be protected here is one's right to be free from the mental disturbance of the supposed contact.

The manner in which a threat is made is important in determining assault. The individual must have the apparent ability to carry out his threat and the threat must put one in immediate fear and apprehension of offensive contact. *Assault does not include battery.* There are many decisions qualifying this "threat" factor. For example, the threat of an injury that is to take place in the future is not an assault, it must be immediate.[9] There is no threat where the individual is too far away to do any immediate harm.[10] Holding a weapon in a threatening position is an assault because the plaintiff cannot tell if the weapon is loaded.[11]

FALSE IMPRISONMENT

The individual is entitled to be free from the imposition of any restraints upon his movements. False imprisonment is an illegal holding of an individual against his will. There are many ways a person can be held so as to be falsely imprisoned.

In *Hoffman* v. *Clinic Hosp., Inc.,* 213 N. Car. 669, (1938), the plaintiff was told that she was to remain in the hospital until she paid her bill. After staying longer than she had planned, the plaintiff left without paying her bill. It was the opinion of the court that false imprisonment entails at least a threat of force to deprive a person of his liberty. Since she was able to leave, the plaintiff was not restrained in such a manner as to constitute false imprisonment.

Is a person falsely imprisoned when his passage is blocked in one direction? *Martin* v. *Lincoln Park West Corp.,* 219 F.2d 622 (1955), where the plaintiff was locked out of his room, says no. Imprisonment is something more than a loss of freedom to be able to go where one pleases. It is an entire restraint upon the will. However, the existence of an escape route is no defense when the person desiring to leave is unaware of it. A person restrained must have knowledge of the possible avenue of escape. The plaintiff in *Lukas* v. *J. C. Penny Co.*, 318 P.2d 717 (1963) was considered to be imprisoned when her movements were restrained on a street. An employee of the store verbally detained her.

SELF-DEFENSE

Self-defense is a privilege that permits an individual who is attacked to take reasonable steps to ward off the threatened harm to his person. The privilege allows the use of reasonable force to prevent the threatened harmful contact. In *People* v. *Cherry*, 121 N.E.2d 238, 240 (1954), the court stated: "The standard by which defendant must be judged is phrased solely in terms of the physical necessities of the situation presented . . . the victim may not pursue his counterattack merely for the sake of revenge."

Fear of great bodily harm in the future will not justify a "self-defensive" attack. Any act of self-defense must be the result of an immediate attack. There is no liability where the individual believes his opponent to be reaching for a gun. The court, in *Haeussler* v. *De Loretto*, 240 P.2d 654, 655 (1952) said: "defendant ordered plaintiff to leave his premises; plaintiff advanced threatingly toward defendant; defendant struck him once; two of plaintiffs teeth were loosened, necessitating dental care; defendant used reasonable force in defending himself and in removing plaintiff from his premises."

CONVERSION

Conversion is an intentional assumption of property and deprivation of the owner's rights. The intent to deprive another of his property is the key. If there is no intent, there is no cause of action for conversion. In an early English case, the court stated that conversion "rests upon the unwarranted interference by the defendant with the dominion over the property of the plaintiff from which injury to the latter results."[12]

To establish the tort where there has been no wrongful taking, demand for the return of the property in question and a refusal to return it are necessary. Destruction, alteration and excessive use of a chattel will amount to conversion. The same result holds with the purchase of stolen goods.

DEFENSE OF PROPERTY

There is no privilege to take a human life in defense of property except when necessary to prevent an invasion of one's home or to prevent a felony of violence; each of these is an extension of the privilege of self-defense. If one sets spring traps in order to prevent a felony and a would-be felon is injured thereby there is no liability; but if the injured party is rightfully on the land or is a mere trespasser there is liability.

A person in the possession of land is entitled to use a reasonable and appropriate amount of force to eject a trespasser. Generally, the trespasser may be pushed or carried off; it is not proper to strike unless there is resistance to the ejectment. Where the trespasser has entered forcibly there is no need to request him to depart, but if he has entered peaceably he should be asked to leave peaceably.

LIBEL AND SLANDER

The interest protected by society is that of security of reputation. One's reputation depends upon the opinion which others entertain as to his character, and is damaged by the communication of something which is disparaging. Defamation, therefore, consists of a statement or other communication to another which causes a person to be regarded with hatred, contempt, ridicule, or the like or which tends to injure him in his business, trade or profession.

Slander is generally defined as oral defamation. Libel is usually written or printed defamation, but includes all defamation in permanent form, such as painting or caricature. A libel may thus be produced without being communicated, though of course no action would arise until there was communication. Slander, however, cannot exist unless it is communicated.

SLANDER PER SE

Certain classes of slander are actionable per se—that is, without proof of special damage. These include statements imputing crime or loathsome disease or disparaging one in his office, business, trade or profession. In all jurisdictions statements charging an individual with having committed a crime are actionable per se. In order to give rise to a cause of action the offense must be an indictable one, involving moral turpitude or subjecting the offender to infamous punishment. It is not necessary that the individual be guilty of the crime charged or subject to the punishment at the time of the statement; nor is it necessary that the act charged be a crime at the place where the alleged act was committed; the test is furnished by the law of the place where the words were spoken.

A slanderous charge that an individual is suffering from a loathsome disease, such as venereal disorders, is actionable per se. The test is not the moral stigma but the tendency to exclude him from human society. Defamatory charges that the plaintiff lacks a requisite of his trade, business or profession, or that he has been guilty of misconduct or unfair practices in his business dealings are likewise actionable per se. An imputation of insolvency is actionable per se because a businessman must have credit to carry on his business.

LIBEL

No cause of action arises unless the defamation has been published (i.e., communicated) to other than the injured party. Publication may be either intentional or negligent; if a libelous letter is sent to an individual and is opened by his employee, the sender is liable only if he should have foreseen that the letter would be thus opened. Where a person writes a defamatory letter and reads it to a third party there is, of course, publication, but there is conflict of authority as to whether it is libel or slander. The better view is that it is only slander since the third party merely hears the words. Where the defendant dictates a defamatory statement to a secretary who types it and reads it, it would be libel.

TRUTH

Truth is a complete defense in a defamation suit, irrespective of the defendant's intent at the time he published the statement. Lack of malice is not a defense; however, it would serve to limit the damages. Likewise, a retraction is not a defense but may sometimes be shown in mitigation of damages.

NEGLIGENCE IN BUSINESS

The business firm will sometimes employ other parties to help in the implementation of business decisions. In *Ultramares Corp.* v. *Touche, Niven & Co.,* 225 N. Y. 170 (1931), a firm of public accountants was held liable for negligence in conducting an audit. The decision was based in part on the belief that the defendants owed a duty to issue their audit certificate under a standard of care and proper caution. The extent of their duty was determined by their contract of employment.

Lawyers who certify their opinion as to the validity of corporate bonds with the knowledge that the opinion will be used to attract investors will become liable for the consequences of their negligence should their opinion be rendered without proper care. Title companies insuring titles to tracts of land with knowledge that the land will be sold at auction will be liable to purchasers who may wish the benefit of the insurance without the necessity of paying a premium.

PRODUCT LIABILITY

There is a close connection between the negligence concept and the strict liability concept in the area of product liability.

In *Larsen* v. *General Motors Corporation,* 391 F. 2d 495 (1968) U. S. Ct. of Appeals, Eighth Circuit, the driver of an automobile claimed injury as a result of alleged negligent design of the steering assembly. Although the design did not cause the accident, the plaintiff claimed he received injuries he might not have otherwise received. The court held that where the manufacturer causes an unreasonable risk to be imposed upon the user of its products, the manufacturer should be held liable for the resultant injury.

In *Escola* v. *Coca Cola Bottling Co. of Fresno,* 150 Cal. 2d 453 (1944), the plaintiff was injured when a bottle of Coca Cola broke in her hand. The manufacturer was held liable on the theory that he placed the article on the market, knowing that it was to be used without inspection, and a defect in the article causes injury.

QUESTIONS FOR DISCUSSION:

1. Why is the concept of state of mind an important factor in tort action?
2. What is the determining factor in an action for assault?
3. Should a society allow privileged invasions to another's physical integrity?
4. When does conversion take place?
5. Should an individual be responsible for only foreseeable consequences of his actions?

ENDNOTES

1. Article III, Section III.
2. Burns, *Indiana Statutes, Annotated Criminal Code, IV,* Part 2, 10-4401.
3. *Ibid.,* 10-3401.
4. *Ibid.,* 10-407.
5. *Ibid.,* 10-4201.
6. *Ibid.,* 10-4101.
7. *Ibid.,* 10-701.
8. *Ibid.,* 10-301.
9. *Tuberville* v. *Savage,* Cucinotti Ortman, 399 Pa 26 (1960).
10. *Ross* v. *Michael,* 246 Mass. 126, 140 N.E. 292 (1923).
11. *Trogdon* v. *Terry,* 172 N.C.540 (1916).
12. *Hollis* v. *Fowler,* L.R. 7 Q.B. 639 (1874).

THE COURSE OF A TRIAL 7

A study of society's legal system necessitates a discussion of procedural law—the means available for the enforcement of legal rights and/or prevention of any interference with an individual's legal interests. This branch of law includes all legal steps from the first step in starting a suit through the actual litigation to the final satisfaction of the court's judgment. Simply stated, it is the overall plan for resolving a legal controversy.

Each individual has an absolute right to initiate a lawsuit to obtain redress for a legal wrong in a court of law. Therefore, to justify commencing a lawsuit the attorney representing a plaintiff must determine: (1) whether or not his client has suffered an injury; (2) whether or not the legal system will afford a remedy; and (3) what court can properly resolve the controversy.

THE COURTS

Under a dual system of government, a dual system of state and federal courts exists. Article III, Section 1 of the Federal Constitution provides that: "The Judicial Power of the United States, shall be vested in one supreme Court and in such inferior Courts as the Congress may from time to time ordain and establish." Congress has established a federal system made up of district courts and courts of appeal. In addition, special courts such as the Court of Claims, the Court of Customs and Patent Appeals, and the Customs Court have been ordained. The *Federal District Courts* are the trial courts in the federal system where federal cases are initiated. Each state has at least one district court. The *Circuit Courts of Appeal* are exclusively appellate courts, established for the purpose of reviewing cases tried in the district courts. Their sole function is to review cases appealed from district courts and in some instances, decisions appealed from the regulatory commissions.

JURISDICTION

The term jurisdiction designates the extent of a court's power to decide controversies. If a person or a physical object is within the jurisdiction of a court, the court has the right to render judgment and to give effect to such judgment. A court's jurisdiction is usually established by a constitutional or legislative grant of powers, which is limited in application to the court's geographic location. The court's process, therefore, extends normally throughout the territorial boundaries of the state in which it sits, and no farther.

The powers of the federal judiciary are established by Article III, Section 2, of the Constitution of the United States, which states:

> The judicial Power shall extend to all Cases, in Law and Equity, arising under this Constitution, the Laws of the United States, and Treaties made, or which shall be made, under their Authority; to all Cases affecting Ambassadors, other public Ministers and Consuls; to all Cases of admiralty and maritime Jurisdiction; to Controversies to which the United States shall be a Party; to Controversies between two or more States; between a State and Citizens of another State; between Citizens of different States; between Citizens of the same State claiming Lands under Grants of different States, and between a State, or the Citizens thereof, and foreign States, Citizens or Subjects.

This, however, is limited by the Eleventh Amendment to the Constitution, which reads:

> The Judicial power of the United States shall not be construed to extend to any suit in law or equity, commenced or prosecuted against one of the United States by Citizens of another State, or by Citizens or Subjects of any Foreign State.

The Constitution, therefore, does not confer any jurisdiction upon the lower federal courts, it merely prescribes the limits of judicial power that Congress may confer upon them. The District Courts and Circuit Courts of Appeal have only such jurisdiction as is conferred upon them by Congress. However, since the Constitution specifies the original (non-appellate) jurisdiction of the Supreme Court, Congress has no authority in this area. Congress does have the power to limit the appellate jurisdiction of the Supreme Court.

Although the state and federal courts are independent of one other, they enjoy concurrent jurisdiction over many matters. In fact, state courts have equal jurisdiction with the federal courts in all matters in which jurisdiction has not been reserved exclusively to the federal courts. The United States judicial code spells out the classes of controversies in which the jurisdiction of the federal courts is exclusive. These cases include bankruptcy, the patent and copyright laws, antitrust violations, and admiralty and maritime cases. The federal statutes likewise enumerate what cases can be appealed to the Supreme Court from state courts.

There is some variation in the make-up of the court systems of the several states. Basically, each state has courts of original jurisdiction and one or more courts of appellate jurisdiction. The student should become familiar with the court structure and the jurisdiction of the various courts in his state.

A state system is usually organized with one or more trial courts of original jurisdiction. Jurisdiction in each instance is determined by the monetary amount in dispute and, if more than one court exists, by territorial limitations. There is usually an intermediate appellate court and a court of final appeal. State systems follow basically the federal structure in that cases are taken from the trial court to the intermediate court of appeal and then to the court of final appeal. The decision in the highest state court of appeal is final in all controversies not involving federal questions.

PROCEDURAL DUE PROCESS

The rules a court adopts for the conduct of its proceedings must not deny to any party that comes before it his basic rights as guaranteed by the federal Constitution. The due process clause of the Fourteenth Amendment[1] requires that no state can "deprive any person of life, liberty, or property without due process of law." Due process has been defined by the United States Supreme Court to mean "that there shall be a regular course of proceedings, in which notice is given of the claim asserted and an opportunity afforded to defend against it . . . In determining whether such rights were denied, we are governed by the substance of things and not by mere form." [*Simon* v. *Craft*, 182 U.S. 427, 436, 437. (1901)]

THE ADJUDICATIVE PROCESS

The adjudicative process is twofold. First, it involves issues of fact as to the fair appraisal of the allegations of the respective parties based on the evidence presented. Secondly, it involves issues of law as to the application of an appropriate legal principle to the factual situation set forth by the plaintiff and defendant.

PLAINTIFF'S PLEADINGS

The first step in initiating a lawsuit is taken by the attorney for the plaintiff, who files with the court a document, called the petition, which presents the plaintiff's version of the facts that constitute his cause of action and what remedy he is asking the court to award him. (See Figure 7-1) This initial pleading, also variously called the complaint, the statement of claim, or the declaration, is taken to be a complete statement of the plaintiff's case, and evidence is not admissible to establish any omitted facts. In this manner the defendant is made aware of the facts the plaintiff expects to prove during the course of the trial and is able to prepare a defense.

NOTICE

Following the filing of the petition, the court must inform the defendant of the pending legal action by serving him with a summons. (See Figure 7-2) Service may be made through the sheriff's office, by a United States Marshall or by a professional process server, depending upon which court is issuing it and which state is involved. This document informs the defendant that legal proceedings have been instituted against him, the names of the parties involved in the controversy, and the nature of the action, and demands a response from the defendant within a certain period of time. Where *actual* service of a summons to the person of the defendant is not possible, that is by handing it to him, *constructive* service may suffice. In the latter instance a registered letter is sent to the defendant's last known address or

A COMPLAINT

IN THE COURT OF COMMON PLEAS
SUMMIT COUNTY, OHIO

Ernest Student	)	
221 North Street	)	
Akron, Ohio 44304		
and	)	No. _____
Dolly Student		
221 North Street	)	
Akron, Ohio 44304		
	)	
Plaintiffs		
vs.	)	COMPLAINT
Herbert A. Worker	)	
2631 East Market Street		
Kent, Ohio 43204	)	
and		
Worldwide Flush, Inc.		
343 Industry Street		
Kent, Ohio 43204	)	
Defendants	)	

COUNT ONE

1. On May 6, 1970, plaintiff, Ernest Student, was driving an automobile, owned jointly by Ernest Student and his wife, plaintiff Dolly Student, southwardly in the left traffic lane of Exchange Street, a multi-lane public highway in Akron, Ohio.

2. At the same time defendant, Herbert Worker, was driving an automobile, leased by defendant Worldwide Flush, Inc., southwardly in the right traffic lane of Exchange Street.

3. Negligently and without warning, defendant, Herbert Worker shifted from the right traffic lane to the left traffic lane of Exchange Street immediately in front of plaintiff Ernest Student, thus causing plaintiff, Ernest Student, to strike the left rear of defendant, Herbert Worker's automobile.

4. At the time of the impact defendant, Herbert Worker, was the agent of defendant, Worldwide Flush, Inc., and was acting within the scope of his agency and authority.

Figure 7-1

5. As a direct result of the impact plaintiff, Ernest Student, has suffered a rib fracture, a contusion over the sternum, and a rupture of an intervertebral disc at L-5, S-1. To date, he has expended $767.58 in medical expenses and has lost intermittently a total of 23 days of work. He has suffered great pain of body and mind and in the future will continue to do so and in the future will be compelled to expend additional sums for medical treatment and hospitalization and will suffer intermittently loss of wages. In addition, the automobile owned by plaintiffs, Ernest Student and Dolly Student, was damaged in the amount of $411.00. Being deprived of the use of the automobile for three weeks, plaintiff, Ernest Student, was required to expend $60.00 for public transportation.

WHEREFORE, plaintiffs demand judgment against defendant, Herbert Worker, or against Worldwide Flush, Inc., or against both of them as follows:

(a) In behalf of plaintiffs, Ernest Student and Dolly Student, for damage to their automobile in the sum of $411.00.
(b) In behalf of the plaintiff, Ernest Student in the sum of $15,000.00, together with the costs of this action.

COUNT TWO

1. For a second claim plaintiff, Dolly Student, restates all that is alleged in paragraphs 1 through 4 of Count One.

2. Plaintiff, Dolly Student, further states that she is the wife of Ernest Student and that as a direct result of the injuries suffered by Ernest Student as set forth in paragraph 5 of Count One, plaintiff, Dolly Student, has been and will be deprived of the consortium of her husband, Ernest Student.

WHEREFORE, plaintiff, Dolly Student, demands judgment against defendant, Herbert Worker, or against defendant, Worldwide Flush, Inc., or against both of them in the sum of $5,000.00 together with the costs of this action.

Chester Goodfellow, Attorney for Plaintiffs
Goodfellow, Nice & Easy, Attorneys at Law
221 West Market Street
Akron, Ohio 44304

Figure 7-1(Cont)

a legal notice is published in a newspaper of general circulation within the geographical area of the court's jurisdiction. Unless the requirements of notice have been met, the court has no jurisdiction over the defendant. It is this notice that gives the court the right and power to act against the defendant. Without notice, the decision of the court would be without legal effect.

JUDGMENT BY DEFAULT

A petition that states a cause of action must be answered by the defendant. If he fails to respond and plead a defense against the plaintiff's allegations, a judgment will be entered against him by default. This will be in effect a final decision of the court.

DEFENDANT'S PLEADINGS

If the defendant's attorney determines that the plaintiff's allegation of his cause of action will not permit him to recover judgment, he may file a demurrer or motion to dismiss for failure to state a cause of action. This pleading raises the question of whether the petition is sufficient as a matter of law to support the plaintiff's case. In the demurrer, the factual allegations of the petition are admitted, with a statement that they do not provide a basis for awarding judgment. Thus a question of law is raised that must be decided by the court. When allowed, the controversy will be disposed of without trial unless the defects in the petition may be cured by amendment. If the decision is contrary to the demurrer and the defendant does not plead further, judgment is entered against him by default. Although he will usually default at this point and he may decide to challenge the factual allegations made by the plaintiff.

If the controversy is contested, the defense attorney must file with the court, within the allowed time, a document known as an answer, (See Figure 7-3) in which he will deny the basic allegations set forth in the plaintiff's petition. By this denial the defendant raises an issue of fact as to which version of the controversy is correct. The case must be submitted to the jury on these issues.

THEORY OF PLEADING

The parties to the controversy must furnish the information necessary for the court to make its decision. The pleadings serve to set the limits within which the trial will be conducted. Only testimony and evidence on items set forth in the pleadings will be allowed. In cases where the parties have omitted essential facts, the judge may upon due notice, allow the attorney to cure these defects with an amended pleading. Thus, where an issue has been established by the pleadings, the case is ready for trial. If the issue raised is a matter of law, the decision rests solely with the judge. If a question of fact is at issue, the case must be submitted to the jury for a determination in cases involving a jury.

SUMMARY JUDGMENT

After the pleadings have been filed, either party may ask the court for a judgment based on the pleadings. The court, in *Gauch* v. *Meleski,* 346, F. 2d 433 (1956) said:

SUMMONS

IN THE MARINETTE COUNTY CIRCUIT COURT
MARINETTE, WISCONSIN

Eleanor Wood, Plaintiff,   )

)

         vs.   )   Civil Action No. 1960

)

Michael Patrick, Defendant,   )

THE STATE OF WISCONSIN, to the sheriff of Marinette County, Greetings: We command you to summon Michael Patrick, whose address is 53241 Crestview Drive, Wausaukee, Wisconsin, to appear before our Circuit Court within and for the County of Marinette at the Court House in Marinette, in said County, on the 22nd day of November, 1977, then and there before the Judge of said Court, to answer the complaint of Eleanor Wood (a certified copy of said complaint is hereunto annexed). If you fail to do so, thereafter judgment, upon proper hearing and trial, may be taken against you for the relief demanded in the complaint.

Witness my hand as Clerk of said Court, and seal thereof. Done at office, in Marinette, the County aforesaid, on the 22nd day of October, 1977.

                                        ———————————

                                        Clerk of Court

State of Wisconsin   )

)   ss.

County of Marinette   )

I, ... , Clerk of the Circuit Court, within and for said County, do hereby certify that the foregoing is a true copy of the original summons issued in a certain cause in the Circuit Court of said County, where Eleanor Wood is plaintiff and Michael Patrick is defendant.

Given under my hand and seal of said Court at office in the city of Marinette, County and State aforesaid, on this 22nd day of October, 1977.

                                          ———————————

                                        Clerk of Court

Figure 7-2

AN ANSWER
IN THE COURT OF COMMON PLEAS
SUMMIT COUNTY, OHIO

Ernest Student   (
221 North Street
Akron, Ohio 44304   ((No. _____
   and
Dolly Student   (
221 North Street
Akron, Ohio 44304   (

        Plaintiffs   (ANSWER
    vs.   (
Herbert A. Worker
2631 East Market Street   (
Kent, Ohio 43204
   and   (
Worldwide Flush, Inc.
343 Industry Street   (
Kent, Ohio 43204
Defendant Herbert A. Worker:

1. Admits the allegations contained in paragraphs 1 and 2 of Count One of the complaint, and admits these same paragraphs as incorporated by reference in Count Two of the complaint.
2. Denies the allegations contained in paragraph 3 of Count One of the complaint, and denies the same paragraph as incorporated by reference in Count Two of the complaint.
3. Alleges that he is without knowledge or information sufficient to form a belief as to the truth of the allegations contained in paragraph 4 and 5 of Count One of the complaint, and alleges that he is without knowledge or information sufficient to form a belief as to the truth of the allegations contained in paragraph 4 as incorporated by reference in paragraph 1 of Count Two of the complaint, and further alleges that he is without knowledge or information sufficient to form a belief as to the truth of the allegations contained in paragraph 2 of Count Two of the complaint.

                             _____

        William   Williams, Attorney for
        Defendant, Herbert Worker
        Williams, Jones & Smith, Attorneys
          at Law
        225 North High Street
        Akron, Ohio 44304

Figure 7-3

The basic mission of the summary judgment procedure is to allow the court to pierce the pleadings and assess the proof in order to see whether there is a genuine need for a trial. . . . The trial court can, and indeed should, assess the evidence presented . . . to determine its admissibility and to ascertain whether all the admissible evidence creates a genuine, material dispute of facts. The trial court should . . . avoid assessing the probative value of any evidence presented to it, for this . . . is properly the function of the jury. The court can, however, determine whether or not there is a genuine dispute, hence whether a trial is necessary or whether the case should be dismissed.

PRETRIAL CONFERENCE

Courts may rely on the pretrial conference to avoid unnecessary delays, to encourage settlements, and to avoid surprises during the course of the trial. At this conference, the judge may attempt to clarify controversial points or present possible terms of settlement for the parties to consider. Lawyers will present some of their legal arguments and review their evidence for the judge. Other information may be obtained by the use of the written interrogatory questions and answers under oath. These conferences not only narrow the issues by eliminating unnecessary litigation, but they also cut down on the time of the trial. The end result is to promote a just and impartial adjudication of the controversy.

DEPOSITIONS

A common pretrial procedure employed by attorneys in the preparation of their cases is the deposition. It is testimony taken and recorded, under oath, concerning a witness's view of the facts involved in a given controversy. Depositions are used to preserve testimony and to secure testimony from witnesses that might be outside the jurisdiction of the court or in prison.

If the witness is not available at the time of the trial, his deposition may be introduced as evidence in the trial.

CONTINUANCES

A trial may be postponed or continued at the request of one of the parties to the controversy. This is a procedural rule that a court may apply at its discretion. Among the grounds for asking for a continuance are: (1) illness of one of the parties to the controversy; (2) illness of a key witness; (3) illness of one of the attorneys; (4) the inability to secure the presence of a key witness or some vital evidence; and (5) a request by an attorney to secure more time in which to prepare his case.

VENUE

In some instances a number of courts may have jurisdiction over the person or the subject matter of the case. Venue refers to whether or not a court should hear the case. Sometimes, therefore, the defendant may request that the case be heard in a specific court. He generally has the right to be tried in the court located in the county where he is a resident. The motion for a change of venue must be in writing and clearly state the grounds for making the request. Such motions may allege an inability to obtain a fair trial because of a local prejudice or because the judge cannot conduct an impartial trial.

THE TRIAL

The Sixth Amendment to the Constitution of the United States provides:

> In all criminal prosecutions the accused shall enjoy the right to a speedy and public trial, by an impartial jury of the State and district wherein the crime shall have been committed, which district shall have been previously ascertained by law, and to be informed of the nature and cause of the accusation; to be confronted with the witnesses against him; to have compulsory process for obtaining witnesses in his favor and to have the assistance of counsel for his defense.

The Seventh Amendment to the Constitution provides:

> In suits at common law, where the value in controversy shall exceed twenty dollars, the right of trial by jury shall be preserved, and no fact tried by a jury, shall be otherwise re-examined in any Court of the United States, than according to the rules of the common law.

This amendment governs actions brought in the federal courts. It does not apply to state court actions; but the constitutions of most of the states preserve in varying degrees the right to trial by jury. The right to a jury trial is guaranteed, but that right does not have to be exercised. The parties may waive the right, preferring to be tried soley by the judge. In other instances the defendants may prefer to wait for a jury trial, a wait which is almost always longer than for non-jury trials. The first step in a jury trial is to select the jurors from a panel (or venue) of prospective jurors. Each prospective juror is questioned by the judge and the attorneys to determine if there is any reason to prevent him from being seated. Prospective jurors may be disqualified for cause, such as bias, preconceived notions about the results of the controversy, or similar reasons. The attorney usually has an unlimited number of *challenges for cause* because the client is entitled to an impartial jury. The lawyers may also make a limited number of *peremptory challenges*, without revealing their reasons for not wanting a particular juror.

BURDEN OF PROOF

The burden of proof is always with the party who raises a particular issue. He must convince the jury that the facts are as he alleges them to be. In a civil case the plaintiff has the initial burden of proof. He must bring forth enough evidence to sustain the facts in his pleading so that if nothing more were shown to the contrary, he would be entitled to judgment. If the defendant can meet this evidence with equal or greater evidence to the contrary, the party presenting the greatest weight of evidence will receive judgment. In a criminal case the state must prove beyond "a reasonable doubt" that the accused committed the crime.

OPENING STATEMENTS

The plaintiff's attorney makes the opening statement to the court, in which he explains the issues in the case, what he expects to prove and what his client desires as an appropriate remedy. The opening argument is not evidence, but merely an attempt to familiarize the jury with the essential fact of the case. The defendant's lawyer will then make an opening statement of what he intends to present to the court.

THE PLAINTIFF'S CASE

It is also the plaintiff's obligation as moving party in the suit to present his proof first. The plaintiff, through his attorney, will introduce physical evidence, conduct demonstrations, and present legal arguments which tend to support his case. The attorney will also call his witnesses to the stand and conduct direct examinations to persuade the jury that certain facts are true. When the direct examination is finished, opposing counsel may, if he wishes, conduct a cross-examination. The cross-examiner attempts to tear down what the witnesses have built up in direct examination. The manner and extent of cross-examination is largely within the discretions of the trial court. The cross-examiner may want to make the witness appear to be forgetful, confused, or self-contradictory; he may question the credibility of the witness' statements; or he may try to impeach the witness on grounds of his general reputation for veracity. At the time he is presenting his witnesses, counsel will also present his physical evidence in whatever order he thinks best for his case. He must be able to present evidence to support the disputed facts he has alleged in his pleadings. At the conclusion of his presentation, the plaintiff's attorney will "rest" his case.

THE DEFENDANT'S CASE

The order of the defendant's case is approximately the same as that of the plaintiff. His objective is to place doubt in the minds of the jury as to matters the plaintiff must prove and he will try to introduce evidence that will support his version of the alleged facts of the case. He, likewise, will "rest" when he has finished his case.

CLOSING ARGUMENTS

In their closing statements to the jury, the opposing lawyers review the evidence, urge the jurors to look at favorable inferences and conclusions in the presentation of their case, stress the weaknesses of the opposition's offer of proof, and suggest a verdict be returned that is favorable to their client. Closing statements emphasize the important points the jurors should consider when they retire to resolve the legal controversy. In most states the defense sums up first, with the plaintiff having the final word.

THE JUDGE INSTRUCTS THE JURY

The function of the jury is to try fact and to apply the law to the facts. However, the jury has no way of knowing what the law is until the judge tells them. The judge must instruct the jury as to how the various legal principles apply to the choices facing them in arriving at a verdict. Initially the judge details the questions of fact that the jury must answer on the basis of the parties' presentations. The judge then explains the rules of law that apply to these alternative findings of fact.

Counsel may challenge the correctness of the judge's instructions, may assist the judge in preparing the instructions, or request that additional instructions be given to the jury for their consideration. It is within the judge's discretionary powers to determine the appropriateness of counsel's requests. This gives each party an additional opportunity to summarize his legal contentions and to make his point on the record for a later review of the case.

VERDICT

In most states a unanimous agreement must be reached before the jury may return to the courtroom to report their decision. If they are unable to bring in a verdict on this basis, the judge must encourage them to do everything possible to reach an accord. However, if they remain deadlocked, the judge will declare a mistrial, the jury will be dismissed, and the trial will be over.

JUDGMENT

The judgment is a formal confirmation and recording of the jury's verdict. To be effective, it must be entered in the proper docket. On appeal, a judgment may be modified, affirmed, or reversed.

SUPPLEMENTAL MOTIONS

DIRECTED VERDICT

When both parties have rested and all evidence has been presented, either the plaintiff or the defendant may test the sufficiency of the other's case by requesting the court to direct the jury to return a verdict in their favor. The effect of a directed verdict is that the court must decide whether the plaintiff's evidence, if uncontested, is sufficient to support a judgment in the defendant's favor. Where the plaintiff makes the motion for a directed verdict, he is asking the court to decide on the present grounds that a reasonable jury could only find in his favor. Where the court directs a verdict, the action is terminated.

JUDGMENT N.O.V.

When one party is dissatisfied with the jury's verdict, he may move that the court award him the judgment because the verdict is clearly contrary to the

MOTION FOR A NEW TRIAL

IN THE MARINETTE COUNTY CIRCUIT COURT
MARINETTE, WISCONSIN

Eleanor Wood, Plaintiff,　　　　　)
　　　　　　　　　　　　　　　　)
　　　　　　　vs.　　　　　　　　)　　　　Civil Action No. 1960
　　　　　　　　　　　　　　　　)
Michael Patrick, Defendant,　　　　)

Now this day comes the plaintiff (or defendant) and moves the court to set aside the verdict rendered in the said cause, on the 22nd day of November, 1977, and to grant to him a new trial therein, for the following reasons:

1. The verdict in said cause is against the evidence, against the weight of the evidence, and against the law under the evidence.

2. The court erred in admitting incompetent, irrelevant and immaterial evidence offered by the defendant.

3. The court erred in rejecting competent, relevant and material evidence offered by the plaintiff.

4. The court erred in the instructions given to the jury at the instance of the defendant.

5. The court erred in refusing the instructions asked by the plaintiff.

_____
(Attorney for Plaintiff)

Figure 7-4

evidence as a matter of law or because the award is insufficient. The court may set aside the verdict and enter a contrary judgment. The motion for judgment n.o.v. (not withstanding the verdict), like the motion for a directed verdict, raises the legal question whether there was enough evidence to make an issue for the jury. The evidence must be viewed in the most favorable light for the party against whom the motion is made. The motion must be denied if there is any substantial evidence to support a verdict.

NEW TRIAL

The loser may also ask for a new trial because of some irregularity in the trial just completed, such as the verdict being against the weight of the evidence. Either party may request a new trial on the grounds that the damages awarded are excessive or insufficient, that a reasonable jury might have properly reached a contrary verdict, or that there is new evidence available. (See Figure 7-4) A dissatisfied party has a specified number of days in which to appeal. If no appeal is taken, the judgment stands on record as the final disposition of the case.

QUESTIONS FOR DISCUSSION

1. What is the constitutional test of procedural due process?
2. What is the objective of procedural due process?
3. When does a particular court have jurisdiction in a legal action?
4. What is the objective of the pleadings?
5. What is the purpose of the pretrial conference?

ENDNOTE

1. The courts of the federal system are subject to the due process clause of the Fifth Amendment.

APPEALING A CASE   8

Cases can be appealed only from those trial courts that are "courts of record." A court of record is one in which the proceedings are recorded, and it is this record that forms the basis for the court of appeal's review. The record is the basic statement of the case, with the grounds for appeal spelled out, supported by legal briefs on the law. Cases tried in courts that are not courts of record can be retried in some other trial court. For example, a case tried in a small claims court may be retried in a county or district court within the county.

It is not the function of the appellate court to reevalutate the evidence presented in the lower court. In fact, an appellate court will seldom give consideration to any issues not raised during the trial. Appellate courts do not sit with juries, nor do they rehear testimony. A hearing before the appellate court is a review of the legal rulings of the lower court, conducted as an oral argument by the attorneys. It is the function of these courts, therefore, to determine whether a case was handled properly and to make an attempt at obtaining uniformity throughout the jurisdiction by resolving any differences of opinion over the law found to exist among lower courts. When judgment is rendered by an appellate court the legal controversy is usually terminated.

An appeal usually involves:

1. transferring a certified record (an abstract or a transcript) of the proceedings in the lower court to the appellate court;
2. filing written briefs in which the parties to the controversy set forth reasons for the appeal and their respective contentions as to what decision should be rendered by the appellate court, and cite previous case decisions to support their contentions;
3. presenting oral arguments to the appellate court, if such arguments are allowable by the rules of the particular court; in some courts the argument on appeal is confined to the written brief.

The appellate court, after reviewing the record of the lower court proceeding, after listening to the oral arguments of the attorneys, and after due deliberation, will state its decision in the form of a written opinion. It may affirm, reverse, or modify the decision of the lower court. Under some circumstances the court may remand the case to the lower court for a new trial. When the appellate court refuses to hear a case, a judgment is usually final.

Most states have only one appellate court, usually known as the supreme court. The nation's highest appellate court is the Supreme Court of the United States. While it is true that the Supreme Court considers only a limited number of cases, its functions will familiarize the reader with appellate procedure.

THE SUPREME COURT IN THE AMERICAN SYSTEM

The Supreme Court of the United States is somewhat different from the high tribunals of the other nations of the world. In countries that have used the British legal system as a model, the Parliament is supreme. Decisions of the highest courts in these countries can be overruled by legislative statutes. Although the American system of law is modeled after the British in many ways, we have departed from it on this point.

Under the doctrine of judicial review, the Supreme Court can declare state and federal laws unconstitutional, and it can invalidate actions of the president. This practice, which began with John Marshall, has become an integral part of our governmental system.

Generally, a ruling of the Supreme Court with regard to the constitutionality of congressional or presidential actions is final. There are two ways, however, in which a Supreme Court decision can be overruled. The Court can reverse itself, or the Constitution can be amended to alter the effect of the decision. In all other respects, the judiciary is supreme. When the highest court reverses a lower federal court or the highest state court, when it invalidates a federal law, when it rebukes the president for certain conduct, its decision is the law of the land. No other court in the world possesses this degree of power.

SIZE OF THE COURT

The Supreme Court is the only court expressly mentioned by name in the Constitution. The Judiciary Act of 1789 brought this Court into operation by providing for the appointment of a chief justice and associate justices, establishing thirteen federal district courts and the circuit courts on which the justices would sit and providing for appellate jurisdiction from the state courts on questions of federal policy. However, through the years, due to a variety of circumstances, the number of justices has varied. There were five in 1801, seven in 1807, nine in 1837, ten in 1863, seven in 1866. Under the Act of April 10, 1869, the number was again set at nine, and so it has remained down to the present time. The Supreme Court and the district courts continue in existence to the present day. However, the circuit courts (not to be confused with the Federal Circuit Courts of Appeal) were abolished in 1911.

THE JUSTICES

Although justices are appointed for life, they can retire at full pay at the age of 70, provided they have had ten consecutive years of service. All the justices have one vote in deciding cases. The chief justice presides over the Court and assigns the writing of opinions. His unofficial duty is to use his influence in leading the Court and in preventing the division of the justices into opposing positions from which there can be no compromise.

Supreme Court justices, like other federal judges, can be removed from office by impeachment. The House of Representatives brings the charges, and the Senate acts as a trial court. A two-thirds vote of the senators is required for removal from office. There has been only one attempt at impeachment.

Justice Samuel Chase, a Federalist, was impeached in 1803 by a Republican House of Representatives for his intemperate actions and his political partisanship. The vote in the Senate fell four short of the required two-thirds majority.

APPELLATE PROCEDURE IN THE COURT

The term of the Supreme Court begins on the first Monday in October of each year, the day fixed by law, and continues until the end of May or the beginning of June.

The usual procedure is for the Court to be in session for a two-week period, followed by a two-week recess for writing opinions, studying appeals, and reviewing certiorari petitions. When the Court is in session, it meets each Monday afternoon. Since this session involves a review of a decision of some other court, there is no jury and no witnesses are heard. The Court has before it a record of the proceedings in the lower court, with printed briefs containing the contentions of each side. The lawyers handling the case, in addition to submitting written briefs, are required to present oral arguments in order to clarify and develop their contentions. The "argument" sessions are held during the first four days of each two-week period in which the Court sits. At this time, each side is allowed one hour to present its case, unless that time allotment is cut in half because of the nature of the issue.

On the Friday of each "argument" week, the justices assemble in secret conference to discuss the cases that have been presented to them. The chief justice expresses his views on the first of the argued cases; the associate justices then voice their opinions in order of seniority. After this discussion, a vote is taken. The junior justice votes first, and the others follow in order of their appointment. The chief justice votes last. This procedure is followed to prevent the junior justices from being influenced by the votes of their more experienced colleagues. In this way, every justice has a chance to vote on all the business before the Court. Justices may excuse themselves from participating in a case because they have some personal interest in the litigation or are connected with it in some way.

A majority vote is required to decide a case. If all nine justices participate in a case, a vote of five is needed for a decision. Since six justices are required for a quorum, no case can be decided by fewer than four votes. If the justices divide evenly in their opinions, the decision of the lower court is sustained. To grant a writ of certiorari, four justices must support the petitioner.

COURT OPINIONS

After the vote has been taken, the opinions must be written. Making assignments to write opinions is, as indicated, the official duty of the chief justice. If he votes with the majority, he assigns the opinion to one of the justices. If the chief justice votes with the minority, then the senior justice on the majority side makes the assignment. Any justice can write a *concurring opinion* or a *dissenting opinion*. A justice concurs if he agrees with the majority decision but not with the reasoning. He dissents when he disagrees with the decision.

The written opinion is printed, circulated, and studied by all the justices in order to reach agreement on the final wording and the reasoning. These matters are discussed at the Friday conferences until the final form is agreed on. On the Monday afternoon of "opinion day," the decisions are announced and the opinions are read.

The decisions and opinions of the Court are published in the official publication *United States Reporter,* cited as U.S., under the editorial supervision of a reporter appointed by the justices. In addition, cases decided by the United States Supreme Court are found in the *Supreme Court Reporter,* cited as S. Ct., which are printed by a private firm.

THE JURISDICTION OF THE COURT

ORIGINAL JURISDICTION

Article III, Section 2, of the Constitution gives the Supreme Court original jurisdiction in "all cases affecting Ambassadors, other public Ministers and Consuls and those in which a State shall be a party." This provision is apparently based on the feeling that the representatives of foreign governments are entitled to the fullest measure of respect. The same rationale is applied to the governments of the states. It would be beneath the dignity and importance of these foreign representatives and state governments to submit their affairs to any court other than the Supreme Court. While Congress cannot affect this jurisdiction, they have made it concurrent with lower courts in some instances.

APPELLATE JURISDICTION

Most cases are taken to the Supreme Court on appeal from the state courts and the lower federal courts. Article III, Section 2, of the Constitution gives Congress extensive powers to decide what kinds of appeals may be carried to the Supreme Court and under what conditions. In some cases direct appeal is permitted; in others the appeals must go through the lower courts.

There are two main routes by which cases reach the Supreme Court.

1. Cases may arise out of the constitutionality of federal laws and treaties, issues that are generally raised in the lower federal courts.
2. Cases may arise out of the actions of state courts. When a state law is attacked as unconstitutional the issue will be considered first by the courts of the state in question. Eventually, the Supreme Court may be called on to rule on the validity of this state enactment and the legal correctness of the state courts.

OBTAINING REVIEW BY CONSENT OR BY RIGHT

There are two other methods of obtaining review of a case by the Supreme Court. One is a *writ of certiorari,* which the Court at its discretion may grant or deny. The second method is through the *right of appeal,* when the Supreme Court is asked by a lower court to review the facts in a case and the law as applied to the facts. Such action is taken as a matter of right because the Supreme Court must answer federal questions with regard to the Constitution; therefore, it is obligatory for the Court to review the case.

Although Congress decides the types of cases that may be appealed to the Supreme Court, the Court itself has the power to grant specific requests for *certiorari.* The number of requests made for appellate review is much greater than the Court can handle; therefore, the number of cases the Court chooses to review is usually small.

Supreme Court Rule 19, drafted by the Court, provides some guidelines for determining which requests will be considered, such as "an important question of federal law . . . should be, settled by this court; or [when the lower court] has decided a federal question in a way in conflict with applicable decisions of this court . . . " The opposing party may argue that the petitioning party's reasons do not merit discretionary acceptance. After considering the relative merits of the opposing claims the court will announce without opinion whether it will hear the case. Due to the increasing numbers of petitions for certiorari there have been proposals that an intermediate court review these requests.

REVERSING COURT DECISIONS

There are two ways in which a decision of the Supreme Court can be reversed. First, the Court may change its mind and overrule itself. Second, amendments may be added to the Constitution. Two instances of reversal are explained below:

1. In *Corrigan* v. *Buckley,* 271 U.S. 323 (1926), the Court unanimously ruled that private individuals could employ restrictive covenants whereby as owners of property they could agree not to sell or lease their property to persons of race, religion, or national origin. In the case of *Shelley* v. *Kraemer,* 334 U.S. 1 (1948), the Court held that private restrictive covenants could not be validly enforced by the state courts because this would violate the equal protection clause of the Fourteenth Amendment. At the same time, in *Hurd* v. *Hodge,* 334 U.S. 24 (1948), the Court held that enforcement of these covenants was also prohibited by federal law.
2. One of the most famous of these reversals was announced in May 1956 in the public school desegregation case. The Court's decision in *Brown* v. *Board of Education,* 347 U.S. 483 (1954), overruled the "separate but equal" principle that had been established by *Plessy* v. *Ferguson,* 163 U.S. 537 (1896). In the Brown decision the Court concluded that "in the field of public education the doctrine of 'separate but equal' has no place."

SOME LANDMARK CASES

The Supreme Court has handed down a number of decisions that have influenced the nation's economy. The cases cited below are cases in which the decisions of the Court created precedents that have had a pronounced effect on the growth of business in the United States.

FREEDOM OF CONTRACT

Trustees of Dartmouth College v. *Woodward,* 4 Wheat. 518 (1819). This decision reflects Justice Marshall's belief in the sanctity of contracts. This is plainly a contract to which the donors, the trustees, and the Crown (to whose rights and obligations New Hampshire succeeds) were the original parties. It is a contract made on valuable consideration. It is a contract for the security and disposition of property. It is a contract, on the faith of which, real and personal estate has been conveyed to the corporation. It is then a contract within the letter of the Constitution, and within its spirit also.

There is no doubt that Marshall expanded the contract clause beyond the intention of the framers, who had intended it as a limitation on the states alone. However, his interpretation of it reflected the Chief Justice's strong feelings of nationalism. This decision made the contract clause the most powerful instrument for the safeguarding of vested private property rights, which were vital to the economic development of the country. Also, for the first time, a corporate charter was held to be a contract.

IMPLIED POWERS OF CONGRESS

McCulloch v. *Maryland,* 4 Wheat. 316 (1819). One of the most important constitutional questions affecting the future development of American business concerned the interpretation of the "necessary and proper" clause.

> But we think the sound construction of the Constitution must allow to the national legislature that discretion, with respect to the means by which the powers it confers are to be carried into execution, which will enable that body to perform the high duties assigned to it, in the manner most beneficial to the people. Let the end be legitimate, let it be within the scope of the Constitution, and all means which are appropriate, which are plainly adapted to that end, which are not prohibited, but consistent with the letter and spirit of the Constitution are constitutional.

CONTROL OF INTERSTATE COMMERCE

Gibbons v. *Ogden,* 9 Wheat. 1 (1824). Chief Justice Marshall defined the power to regulate foreign and interstate commerce given to Congress under these clauses in the broadest terms possible:

> What is this power? It is the power to regulate; that is, to prescribe the rule by which commerce is to be governed. This power, like all other powers vested in Congress, is complete in itself, may be exercised to its utmost extent, and acknowledges no limitations, other than are prescribed in the Constitution. The power of Congress, then, comprehends navigation within the limits of every state in the Union; as far as navigation may be, in any manner, connected with commerce.

This decision made possible the development of all forms of commerce under federal, rather than state, control. The case itself did not answer the question, however, as to whether the states had concurrent jurisdiction over interstate commerce.

ECONOMIC REGULATION

Munn v. *Illinois,* 94 U.S. 113 (1877). The Court reasoned that it has always been an established principle that when the public has a definite and positive interest in a business, it has a right to regulate the operations of that business. The argument of the Court was

> When . . . one devotes his property to a use in which the public has an interest, he, in effect, grants to the public an interest in that use, and must submit to be controlled by the public for the common good, to the extent of the interest he has thus created. He may withdraw his grant by discontinuing the use; but, so long as he maintains the use, he must submit to the control.

QUESTIONS FOR DISCUSSION

1. What is the function of appellate courts?
2. Why is the Supreme Court unique as a nation's high tribunal?
3. Why does the Supreme Court have original jurisdiction?
4. What is the voting procedure in the Supreme Court?
5. How may a decision of the Supreme Court be changed?

PART II
CONTRACTS

THE BASIC CONCEPT
OF A CONTRACT

The foundation of business activity is the contract. Our personal daily actions involve contracts to such an extent that many of them are taken for granted and not even thought of as involving a legal relationship. Consider the activities of our imaginary Mr. and Mrs. Wiley Wood who live at 2370 Crestview Drive, Everytown, Ohio 44720. On Monday, Mrs. Wood takes clothes to the cleaner, orders a set of dishes by telephone, buys groceries at the market and stops at the gas station for a fill-up on the credit card. In the afternoon, she takes a daughter for a piano lesson, takes another daughter to be fitted for glasses and buys a coat that will be ready in a week. Meanwhile, Mr. Wood calls the plumber to replace a defective toilet bowl, leaves the portable television at the repair shop, transfers his car insurance to a different company, asks the paper boy to start delivery on Sunday and has a tooth filled at the dentist. At work, he engages a painter to redecorate his office.

Each of the above situations involves a contractual relationship of some form or another. Sometimes a paper will be signed, sometimes words may spell out the extent of the obligation, sometimes tickets will be given or sometimes, as in the case of the dentist, very little will be said. It is necessary to examine the basic concept of a contract in order to determine the extent of the obligations, if any, incurred by the parties.

Business agreements come about because individual persons or individual business firms realize that through a cooperative arrangement they can accomplish a business objective that they would be unable to accomplish alone. The arrangement may take the form of a *joint venture,* in which the parties involved pool their skills or facilities (resources) to accomplish a common goal, or it may take the form of a *transaction,* whereby one party exchanges goods or services for the goods or services of another, with each party expecting to benefit by the exchange.

Parties involved in joint ventures or transactions inevitably find that to gain each other's cooperation they must make certain promises that obligate them either (1) to perform an act or (2) to deliver something of value to each other. In effect, each takes on a liability that he would not otherwise take on in order to obtain a benefit not otherwise available. The interests of the parties must be served equally, and the obligations must fall on each equally.

The terms of the agreement will reflect the concessions made by the parties to each other. Depending on the complexity of an arrangement, there will be a certain amount of bargaining before terms are settled. When all parties are satisfied with the arrangement, a business agreement is reached. *The agreement is the expression by each party of his willingness to abide by the terms decided upon.* Thus, *the parties to an agreement obligate themselves to specific terms.*

By obligating themselves to an arrangement's terms, the parties place a liability on their own interest. Thus, it is preferable in most cases that they afford themselves some protection against the default of the other party or parties involved. Our legal system affords this protection in business agreements, provided that *the parties give evidence of their intent to make the agreement a legal relationship,* that is, provided each is willing to make the terms legally binding upon both himself and the other party or parties involved.

When the parties to an agreement decide to create a relationship in which their individual interests will be protected by the law, the agreement is made into a *contract.* Thus, an important aspect of the creation of a contract is that the agreement becomes a legal ralationship; the rights of the parties become legal rights; and their obligations become legal obligations. This means that the rights are protectable and obligations enforceable under the legal system of the society. To merit this protection, of course, the terms of the agreement must conform with the rules the law sets down for the rest of society.

In sum, a contract is a means of forwarding the interests of individual parties through a joint arrangement with other parties; as such, it creates specific rights, eligible for protection under the law.

ELEMENTS OF A CONTRACT

A contract obligation is consensual: it is created by the mutual consent of the parties involved and is enforceable by law according to the actual or presumed intention of the parties. By agreement, the parties are allowed to fix their own terms and to place limitations upon their respective liabilities. The parties are said to be in privity with each other, hence the relationship is sometimes referred to as "privity of contract." Although individuals must usually give clear evidence of their intention to create a contract, the law will, in some situations, presume a contractual relationship because of the *apparent* intention of the parties to create a contract. However, an agreement must meet certain conditions before the parties who enter into it are legally obliged to carry out its terms. The four essential elements in any contract arrangement, in order for it to be legally enforceable, are *agreement, consideration, competent parties,* and *legal subject matter.*

AGREEMENT

The parties to a contract must make an agreement. They must agree with certainty on the same thing, on the same terms, and at the same time. Their agreement must impose legal obligations that are understood to be actionable in a court of law and for which a remedy may be sought if the agreement is breached. However framed, there must be communication of the agreement in terms of a promise offered in exchange for a counterpromise or an act on the part of the offeree. The Uniform Commercial Code, Sec. 1-201, declares that "agreement means the bargain of the parties in fact as found in their language or by implication from other circumstances including course of dealing or usage of trade or course of performance."

CONSIDERATION

Consideration is the evidence of the parties' intent to make their agreement legally binding. If an individual agrees to do something, some inducement must exist for him to make good on his promise. To establish consideration, each party must show in the agreement that he is willing to part with something in return for the act or promise of the other party. *Consideration is whatever of value is bargained for and given in exchange in the agreement.* Whether the consideration given in any particular case is sufficient to make the contract enforceable must be determined by the court.

COMPETENT PARTIES

There must be at least two parties to a contract; a man cannot contract with himself. Furthermore, these individuals or business firms must be capable of voluntarily imposing duties upon themselves and of understanding the nature of their agreement. Also, they must be free to judge the purpose and value of their business relationship. In other words, they must be fully aware of their rights and obligations under the contract.

LEGAL SUBJECT MATTER

Since the parties to a contract intend that theirs will be a legal relationship and that they will have the right to invoke the assistance of the courts for enforcement, the contract itself must be legal with respect to its terms and its objectives. A contract is considered illegal if its terms violate public statutes, public policy, judicial decisions, or legal constitutions.

DEFINITION OF TERMS

The majority of business contracts are *simple* contracts. Simple contracts require consideration but need take no special form. The contracts entered into by Mrs. Wood fall into this catagory. They may exist as enforceable agreements whether oral or written, except as special evidence rules prevail. For example, a contract for the sale of real estate requires the production of written evidence of the agreement to be enforceable.

When both parties to a contract have performed all the obligations imposed on them by their agreement, the agreement is said to be an *executed* contract; if neither party has performed his obligations, the agreement is said to be an *executory* contract. If one side has performed but the other has not, the contract is said to be executed on one side and executory on the other.

An agreement that meets all the legal requirements for a contract is a *valid* contract. If special circumstances give one of the parties to an agreement the right to avoid his obligations under the contract if he so chooses, this condition creates a *voidable* contract. The term *void* describes an agreement that has no legal effect.

A contract is unilateral when only one party promises performance, the promise being in exchange for an *act* by the other party. Unilateral contracts are made either by an offer of a promise for an act or by an offer of an act for a promise. For example, *A* contacts *B,* saying, "Ship me two cars of Idaho potatoes at once, price $10 per bu., C.O.D." *B* ships at once as requested. This is a unilateral contract. A contract is *bilateral* when both parties promise performance, each promise being given in exchange for the other. The following is a simple bilateral contract: *A* says to *B,* "I promise to work for you for one month in return for your promise to pay me $300." *B* answers, "I accept."

An agreement, whether oral or written, in which all the terms are clearly detailed, is said to be an *express* contract. An *implied* contract is an actual contract in which part or all of the agreement has not been expressed in words but may be inferred from the conduct of the parties. This would be a contract *implied in fact.* For example, consulting your dentist implies a promise on your part to pay the price of an office call even though fees are not discussed. A contract may also be *implied in law.* When no definite contract exists between the parties but one party has benefited by the act of the other without the intention that the benefit be a gift, the law will create an obligation to pay fair value for such a gain. This obligation, which is not contractual, but quasi-contractual, may be deemed a contract implied in law.

WHICH LAW GOVERNS

The question of which law is to be applied in the case of contract action cannot always be precisely determined from the face of the agreement. If the parties have specified in their agreement that the contract is to be governed by the law of a particular locale, this directive will be enforced unless contrary to the public policy of the state which suit is brought. Otherwise, the court will apply the law of the place where the contract was made to settle matters of validity or interpretation. The place of contracting is the place where the final act necessary to make the agreement operative as a contract takes place, whether it is the giving of a promise or the performance of an act. However, the law of the state where the contract is to be performed will usually govern questions of performance and damages awarded for breach of performance.

INTERPRETATION OF CONTRACTS

The specific obligations of the parties in the average contract may not be adequately defined. Courts frequently find it necessary to interpret these conditions to determine what the parties have undertaken to do before it is possible to determine whether they have lived up to the terms of the contract. Certain rules of interpretation are used to determine the exact meaning of the words contained in the contract. Although not regarded as conclusive, these guidelines must be considered:

1. The true intention of the parties is the guiding and controlling factor.
2. Obvious spelling and grammar mistakes may be corrected to ascertain the true meaning of the language.

3. Words will be given their ordinary, or popular, meaning in the light of extrinsic evidence introduced to make the court aware of the circumstances to which the word is being applied and which caused the words to be used.
4. In cases where a contract might be interpreted in different ways, the courts will apply the interpretation that will make the contract valid, providing there is evidence that the parties intended to create a legal agreement.
5. Written words will be considered over printed as expressing the true intention of the parties. Typed portions are regarded as written.
6. Contracts will be construed against either the party bringing the action or the party who prepared the contract. If, after applying all the processes of reasoning to determine the meaning of the language, there is still doubt as to its meaning, the terms will be construed in favor of the party who tried to make a valid contract and did not resort to the courts to resolve the controversy.
7. The transaction should be considered as a whole, taking into account both the agreement itself and all the circumstances involved.

THE PAROL EVIDENCE RULE

Upon completion of the oral negotiations, a contract is usually reduced to a written form and signed by the parties. It would seem, therefore, that the parties are in agreement upon the material parts of the contract. The parol evidence rule prohibits the admission of oral statements made prior to or at the time of the signing which would in any way alter, contradict, qualify or change any of these material terms. Exceptions to this rule are made when:

1. the contract is not complete
2. there is ambiguity in the language;
3. there is a mutual mistake;
4. there was fraud, duress, or undue influence present; and,
5. there was a lack of consideration.

It should be sufficient to say, "Never sign a contract, unless you are absolutely certain that it contains all the terms you agreed upon."

LEGAL PRINCIPLES

A contract is an agreement between individual persons or individual business firms in which the rights of the parties are legal rights and their obligations are legal obligations.

The four essentials of a contract are agreement, consideration, competent parties, and legal subject matter.

Simple contracts require consideration but need take no special form.

Contracts may be executed or executory, unilateral or bilateral, and express or implied. Implied contracts may be implied in fact or implied in law.

Unless otherwise specified by the terms of the agreement, questions of validity or interpretation are resolved according to the law of the state where the contract was made. The law of the state where the contract is to be performed will ordinarily govern questions of performance and damages for breach of performance.

The courts will interpret the conditions of a contract when the meaning of the terms is not clear. The courts will not admit oral evidence to alter a contract that is complete on its face.

DOCUMENT FOR REVIEW

CANADIAN FOOTBALL LEAGUE

STANDARD PLAYER CONTRACT

BETWEEN

. . . . a member of the Eastern Football Conference
Western Football Conference
(hereinafter referred to as the "Conference"), and of the Canadian Football League,
hereinafter called the "Club."

—AND—

. . . . of the city/town of . . . .

in the province/state of . . . . hereinafter called the "Player"

In consideration of the mutual and respective covenants and agreements hereinafter contained, the parties hereto hereby agree as follows:

1. The term of this contract shall be from the date of execution hereof until the 1st day of June following the close of the football season commencing in 197...., subject however to rights of prior termination as specified herein.

2. The player agrees that during the term of the contract he will play football and will engage in activities related to football only for the Club and will play for the Club in all its Conference's scheduled and play-off games, and Canadian Football League play-off games and any exhibition games for which the Club may arrange; and the Club, subject to the provisions hereof, agrees during such period to employ the player as a skilled football player. The player agrees during the term of this contract to report promptly for the Club's training sessions and at the Club's directions to participate in all practice sessions.

3. For the player's services as a skilled football player during the term of this contract, and for his agreement not to play football, or engage in activities relating to football, for any other person, firm, Club or corporation during the term of this contract and for the option hereinafter set forth giving the Club the right to renew this contract and for the other undertakings of the player herein, the Club promises to pay the player the sum of $ . . . . .to be payable as follows: 75% of said salary in weekly installments commencing with the first and ending with the last regularly scheduled Conference game played by the Club during such season, and the balance of 25% of said sum at the end of the last scheduled Conference game, unless the Club shall, after its last scheduled Conference game have any Conference or Canadian Football League play-off games to engage in, in which event the remaining 25% shall be paid at the end of the last such play-off games.

A. The above named player shall receive a bonus of $1,000.00 upon receipt of signed contract.

B.   The above named player shall receive an additional $500.00 bonus if he is on the club's active roster as of the first league game in 1972.

4. The Club shall be entitled to deduct from each and every payment made under any of the provisions of this agreement, any amount required for the player's income taxes and any other deductions required or authorized by law.

4A. The player shall participate in the Canadian Football League Pension Plan and the Club is authorized, from time to time, to deduct and remit to the Trustee such sums of money as may be required for the Player's contribution to the Plan.

5. The Club agrees to pay the proper and necessary travelling and reasonable board and lodging expenses whenever the player is travelling in the services of the Club for games in other than the Club's home city, but when not so travelling, the player shall pay his own expenses.

6. Prior to the start of each football season, the player shall attend before the Club's medical committee for a complete physical and medical examination, and, if, in the opinion of the said medical committee, the player is not completely fit to participate in football activities, this agreement and everything herein contained, at the Club's option, shall be void and of no force and effect.

7. The player agrees to comply with all the rules and regulations now, or which may hereafter be, adopted during the duration of this contract, by the Canadian Football League and/or the Conference and/or the Club.

8. The player agrees that should he at any time or times, or in any manner, fail to comply with the covenants or agreements on his part herein contained, or any of them, or should the player at any time be intemperate, immoral, careless or indifferent, or conduct himself in such manner, whether on or off the field, as in the opinion of the Club, endangers or prejudices the interests of the Club, or fails to attain when requested, first class physical condition, or fails to maintain first class physical condition throughout the football season, then the Club shall have the right to discipline, fine, suspend for any period or indefinitely, or cancel the contract in such manner as the Club shall deem fit and proper, and in case of a fine being imposed by the Club, the player agrees to pay such fine or the Club may withhold an equivalent amount from any salary due or to become due in payment thereof.

9. The player agrees to promptly pay any fine levied on him by the Conference or any of its properly authorized officers or the Canadian Football League's Commissioner, and failing such prompt payment the Club is authorized to pay same and deduct such amount from any salary due or to become due to the player.

10. The player represents that he is and will continue to be highly skilled in all types of football team play to play football of the calibre required by the Conference and by the Club, and agrees to perform his services hereunder to the complete satisfaction of the Club and its Head Coach. If, in the opinion of the Head Coach, the player fails at any time during the term of this contract to demonstrate sufficient skill and capacity to play football of the calibre required by the Conference or by the Club, or if, in the opinion of the Head Coach, the player's work or conduct in the performance of this contract is unsatisfactory, or, where there exists a limit to the number permitted of a certain class of player, and in the opinion of the Head Coach, the player, being within that class, should not be included amongst the permitted number, the Club shall have the right to terminate this contract upon notice to the player. It is agreed by both parties that the Club's Head Coach shall be the sole judge as to the competency and satisfaction of the player and his services.

11. Upon termination of this contract during the football season, the player shall only be entitled to receive and the Club shall only be required to pay to the player as compensation for services theretofore rendered hereunder, such portion of the total compensation for the regular season as provided in paragraph 3 hereof, as the number of the regular scheduled Conference games already played bears to the total number of Conference games scheduled for the Club for that season, and upon such termination the Club shall pay to the player the balance of such compensation as then remains owing to the player.

12. The player promises and agrees that during the term of this contract he will not play football or engage in activities related to football in Canada or in the United States of America for any other person, firm, Club or corporation except with the prior written

consent of the Club, and that he will not, during the term of this contract engage in any game or exhibition of baseball, basketball, hockey, wrestling, boxing, or any other sport which endangers his ability to perform his services hereunder without the prior written consent of the Club.

13. The player hereby represents that he has special, exceptional and unique knowledge, skill, and ability as a football player, the loss of which cannot be estimated with any certainty and cannot be fairly or adequately compensated by damages, and therefore agrees that the Club shall have the right, in addition to any other rights which the Club may possess, to enjoin him by appropriate injunction proceedings against playing football or engaging in activities relating to football in Canada or the United States of America, for any person, firm, Club or corporation, and against any other breach of this contract.

14. It is mutually agreed that the Club shall have the right to sell, exchange, assign and transfer this contract and the player's services to any Club of the Conference or to any Club in a Conference affiliated with the Canadian Football League, and the player agrees to accept such assignment and to report promptly to the assignee Club and faithfully to perform and carry out this contract with the assignee Club as if it had been entered into by the player with the assignee Club instead of with this Club, and the player agrees that the assignee Club shall pay to the Club any amount owing by the player at the time of such sale, exchange, assignment or transfer and shall be permitted to deduct such amount from salary due or to become due to the player.

15. On or before the date of expiration of this contract the Club may, upon notice in writing to the player addressed to renew this contract for a further term until the 1st day of June following said expiration, on the same terms as are provided by this contract, except that (1) the Club may fix the rate of compensation to be paid by the Club to the player during said period of renewal, which compensation shall not be less than ninety per cent (90%) of the amount set forth in paragraph 3 hereof, and (2) after such renewal this contract shall not include a further option to renew the contract; the phrase "Rate of Compensation" as above used shall not be understood to include bonus payments or payments of any nature whatsoever other than the precise sum set forth in paragraph 3 hereof.

16. It is mutually understood and agreed that if the operation of the Conference is suspended this contract shall immediately be terminated and the remuneration to be paid to the player shall be on the basis as provided by paragraph 11 herein.

17. The player acknowledges the right and power of the Club and/or of the Conference and/or of the Conference's or the Canadian Football League's Commissioner to fine, suspend for any period or indefinitely, and/or cancel the contract of any player who accepts a bribe or who agrees to throw or fix a game, or who bets on a game, or who is guilty of any conduct detrimental to the welfare of the Conference, or the Canadian Football League, or of professional football; and the player hereby releases the said Conference and its or the Canadian Football League's Commissioner and the Club, jointly, and severally whatsoever he may have arising out of or in connection with the decision of the Conference or its or the Canadian Football League's Commissioner or the Club in any of the aforesaid cases.

18. The player agrees that he will not make any appearances on any program, including radio and/or television, or at any function, nor will he write articles pertaining to football or assist in the coaching of any football team other than the Club without the written consent of the Club first obtained.

19. The parties agree that the Club shall have the exclusive right to permit any person, firm or corporation to display, for publicity or commercial purposes, pictures of the player without the player receiving remuneration therefor, and the player shall not allow either gratuitously or for remuneration, any pictures of the player to be used for any publicity purposes without the consent in writing of the Club first had and obtained.

20. If the player is injured as a result of playing football for the Club, the Club will pay the player's reasonable hospitalization until discharge from the hospital, and his medical

expenses and doctor's bills, provided that the hospital and doctor are selected by the Club, and provided further that the Club's obligation to pay such expenses shall terminate at a period not more than eight weeks after the injury, and the player releases the Club from any and every additional obligation, liability, claim or demand whatsoever in connection therewith.

21. It is further agreed that if the player is injured in the performance of his duties hereunder during or subsequent to the Club's first scheduled Conference game, and the injury or injuries are such as to render him, in the sole judgment of the Club's physician, unfit to play skilled football during the football season or any part thereof, the Club shall pay to the player, so long as in the sole opinion of the Club's physician the player continues to be unable to resume his duties hereunder, 100% of the salary to which the player would be entitled to pursuant to paragraph 3 hereof, if he had played in the scheduled Conference games; it being understood and agreed that this obligation shall not extend beyond the current playing season and does not include bonuses for playoff games. If, after examination by the Club's physician, the player in said physician's opinion is able to resume his duties hereunder, the player may, if he disagrees with such opinion, so notify the Club in writing within 36 hours of the examination and may within 36 hours of such notification submit at his own expense to an examination by a physician of his choice. If the opinion of the physician selected by the player with respect to the player's physical ability to render the services required by this contract is contrary to that of the Club physician, the dispute shall be submitted to a disinterested physician to be selected by the Club's physician and the player's physician or, if they are unable to agree, by the Commissioner and the opinion of such disinterested physician shall be conclusive and binding upon the player and the Club. The expense of obtaining the opinion of such disinterested physician shall be borne by the Club if his opinion agrees with that of the player's physician and by the player if such opinion agrees with that of the Club's physician.

22. The player represents to the Club that he is not under contract or option to play football for any other Club in Canada or the United States of America during the term of this contract and that he has no contractual obligations which would prevent him from entering into the within contract.

23. Should the player become a member of the Armed Forces of either Canada or the United States of America or retire from football prior to the expiration of this contract, or any option contained herein, and subsequently be released from the Armed Forces or return to professional football, then and in either event the time elapsed between the players induction into the Armed Forces and his discharge therefrom, or between his retiring from professional football and his return thereto, shall be considered as tolled, and the term of this contract shall be considered as extended for a period beginning with the player's release from the Armed Forces or his return to professional football, as the case may be, and ending after a period of time equal to the portion of the term of this contract which was unexpired at the time the player entered the Armed Forces or retired from professional football; and the option contained herein shall be considered continuously in effect from the date of this contract until the end of such extended term.

24. This agreement contains the entire agreement between the parties and there are no oral or written inducements, promises or agreements except as contained herein.

25. This agreement has been made under and shall be governed by the laws of the

Province of ....

In event this Club reaches the playoffs, remuneration to the players will be as follows:
$400.00—total compensation for all semi-final games;
$800.00—total compensation for all final games;
Grey Cup remuneration—$1500.00 total compensation for playing in the Grey Cup;
$500.00 additional compensation for winning the Grey Cup.

CLUB RULES AND REGULATIONS

1. All players must be on time for all meetings, practice sessions, meals, and all types of transportation. The curfew must be observed. Players must keep all publicity appointments and be on time.

2. Drinking of intoxicants is forbidden.

3. Players must not enter drinking or gambling resorts nor associate with gamblers or other notorious characters.

4. Players must report all injuries to a coach and the club physician or trainer immediately, and be prompt in keeping appointments.

5. Players must wear coats and neckties in hotel lobbies, public eating places, and on all public conveyances.

6. Players must familiarize themselves with paragraph 17 of their contract.

7. Players shall not write or sponsor magazine or newspaper articles, or endorse any product or service or appear on or participate in any radio or television program without the consent of the club.

IN WITNESS WHEREOF the player has hereunto set his hand and seal and the Club has caused this contract to be executed by its duly authorized officer or officers this day of   A.D. 197

SIGNED, SEALED and DELIVERED

in the presence of:

....

Club

By ....

....

Witness to Player's Signature

Player

....

Player's Address

PLAYER'S COPY

THE AGREEMENT 10

A contract comes into being as the result of an agreement between two or more parties. Each contract is preceded by a series of events; the period in which these events occur is commonly known as the *bargaining period.* During this time the person desiring to enter into a contract will acquaint the other party with the terms of his proposal. Depending on the nature of the contract, the bargaining period may be long or short and the matters discussed either detailed or relatively straightforward. In more detailed contracts, for example, such matters as shipping dates, price ranges, and financing terms may be discussed. In simpler versions, the offeror may state definite terms (e.g., a fixed selling price), in which case no elaborate bargaining is necessary.

The bargaining is successful when it results in the *making of an offer*—a preliminary step to the completion of a contract. An offer may be defined as the communication by one party, known as the offeror, to another party, called the offeree, of the offeror's willingness to act or to refrain from acting in a specific manner if the offeree in turn will act or promise to act or refrain from acting as requested. The offeror for the most part controls the terms of the proposed agreement and the selection of the person in whom a power of acceptance is created.

The bargaining process terminates and a contract is formally created upon the *acceptance of an offer* on the part of the offeree. For the acceptance to be valid, it is essential that the parties shall have reached an agreement as to the nature and extent of the obligations assumed. Furthermore, since there is no adequate manner of determining a man's subjective thoughts, the intention of each party must be effectively communicated to the other. Until such communication is made, neither the offer nor the acceptance is operative.

ESSENTIALS OF AN OFFER

Whether a communication by one party to another is a legal offer is a matter of interpretation that must be determined in light of the circumstances involved. The following factors must be considered:

First, an offer becomes effective only after it has been communicated to the offeree, since the latter must be aware of the offer before he can accept it. No action on the part of the offeree will be construed as an acceptance unless it can be proven that the offer to contract has been effectively communicated. To be effectively communicated, the offer must be made verbally by, or indicated by the actions of the offeror or his duly authorized agent. If the offeree learns of the offeror's intention from some other source, no offer results because no offer has been effectively communicated.

Second, it must be determined whether a proposal is merely a preliminary step in bargaining—an invitation by one party requesting the other party to make an offer—or whether the offeror intends a binding offer to contract. The determining factor will be the language used by the offeror. The offer must be so worded as to lead a reasonable man to believe that the offeror intends to be bound or committed to the stated proposition as soon as the offeree indicates his acceptance, without further negotiation. If a reasonable person would not conclude that the offeror was making such a commitment, no binding offer is made. A request for information as a first step to negotiation does not in itself constitute an offer. There must be a genuine desire to affect the legal relations of the parties. Nor are all statements made to invite or attract persons to act in a certain manner offers. Within this class of communications (those that are not offers) fall most catalogs, circulars, advertisements, estimates, proposals in which major terms are not included, and oral statements of general terms where it is understood that more detailed terms will be put into writing and signed before the agreement is considered binding. The primary reason that these proposals do not qualify as offers is that the parties making them have no intention of entering into a binding agreement on the basis of the terms expressed. The offeree should understand that the offeror never intended his action to have any legal consequences. This is likewise true in the acceptance of rejection of social invitations.

Consider the following advertisement shown in Figure 10-1 from Smith's Food Market. This does not represent an offer to sell the items listed. It is merely an invitation to the customer to make an offer on these terms. There will be a sale if the items listed are still available upon acceptance of the offer to purchase. Thus the advertiser is in a position to accept or reject such an offer.

The question of intent also arises in connection with offers made in jest or in moments of strong emotion, such as anger, along with offers inviting persons to act in a certain manner. Offers clearly made in jest or under emotional stress are usually not enforced, since there is no reasonable justification for relying on them. However, if it is not clear whether the offer was made in jest or under conditions of stress, all circumstances must be carefully considered to determine whether a reasonable man would have been led to believe that the offeror intended to be legally bound by his offer.

Third, an offer must be definite enough so that the offeree will know what obligations are being suggested and what the offeror is promising. It must therefore define with certainty the act or promise that the offeror must give in exchange for what he asks of the offeree.

AUCTIONS

When articles are sold at a public auction, the offer is made by the bidder and accepted by the seller through the auctioneer. The seller may withdraw his item from sale at any time during the auction simply by rejecting all offers that have been made. The purchaser may withdraw his bid at any time before the sale has been completed by the auctioneer. The seller sets the conditions by which the contract is to be completed. However he may not bid at his own sale unless it is announced beforehand that he intends to do so. If the seller were to

Figure 10-1

Source: *Peshtigo Times,* Peshtigo, Wisconsin, March 20, 1974

bid himself or have an agent bid for him without prior notice to the public, the result would be fraud, because the potential buyers have the right to presume that the sale is being held in good faith. When the auction is advertised as an "auction without reserve" the first bid is considered an accepted offer and the article cannot be withdrawn. (See Figure 10-2)

INVITATION FOR BIDS

When one advertises that bids will be received for work (e.g., a construction project), it is the person who submits a bid and not the person asking for bids who is the offeror. The person asking for bids is the offeree; hence he may reject any or all bids. Because this is the case, the bid may be let to the lowest bidder, but it may also be let to a low bidder who is the best in terms of financial responsibility. In the absence of a state statute to the contrary, the bidder may withdraw his bid at any time before it has been accepted. (See Figure 10-3)

AUCTION SALE

Maves Brothers **Sat., March 23**

Starts 12:30 p.m.

Located 3 miles West of Crivitz, Wis., on W.
53 HEAD OF EXCELLENT HIGH PRODUCING HOLSTEIN
DAIRY CATTLE Many cows producing 60 to 75 lbs. milk daily.
Consisting of 50 top notch, large type Holstein milk cows of which
about 25 are just fresh shortly and producing heavy, the balance are
mostly all close up springers due to freshen soon. 3 excellent top
quality Holstein jumper bulls. This is a good young, well marked
herd of Holstein milk cows. All are large type cows that show excellent type and production. Also all cattle are dehorned and from
many years of artificial breeding. Many of these fresh cows are now
producing 60 to 75 lbs. of milk daily. Mr. Farmer: This is one of the
best herds ever to be sold at public auction: Most of these cows are
either just fresh and producing heavy or are close up springers due to
freshen soon. These cows show excellent production and all have
nice attached udders. GRADE A MILKING EQUIPMENT Craft
400 gal. bulk tank, all complete; 4 new De Laval Sterling milker tops,
6 Sterling De Laval milker buckets, 2 50-lb. milker buckets, milk
transfer with approx. 100 ft. of plastic line, large Surge 6 to 8 unit
milker pump and motor, hot water heater, rinse tanks, pails and so
forth. BARN EQUIPMENT Complete stalls and stanchions for 50
cows. Complete milker vacuum line and miscellaneous items too
numerous to mention.
Clerk: K.M. Paulson; Cols. Yoap & Yoap, Auctioneers   **(pd)**

Source: *Peshtigo Times,* Peshtigo, Wisconsin, March 20, 1974

Figure 10-2

TICKETS

Frequently, tickets purchased for entrance into places of amusement or as
evidence of a contract for transportation contain matter in small print that
limits or defines the rights of the holder. It is generally held that this printed
matter is part of the offer and is accepted by the holder if he is aware of it even
though he does not actually read it. However, acceptance of an offer cannot be
inferred from receipt of a ticket that does not purport to be a contract. If a
ticket is received merely as evidence of ownership and is to be presented later
as a means of identification, any written provisions on the ticket are ineffective
unless the recipient's attention is directed to them at the time the ticket is
accepted. For example, suppose Mr. Wood parks his car in a parking lot, pays
thirty-five cents, and receives a ticket which states that the operator of the
parking lot is not liable for the contents of cars left in the lot. Wood does not

---

Bids Wanted
On School Buses

The Board of Education of the United Wausaukee School District No. 1, Marinette County, Wausaukee, Wisconsin, will receive sealed bids for two 1974 model school buses with a seating capacity of 60 and 66 passengers each. The bus body is to be mounted on a factory-built Chevrolet, Ford, or GMC school bus chassis or conventional wheel base and first line body, to comply with the school bus standards as adopted by the said Board of Education and by the State of Wisconsin. Delivery date to be not earlier than July 1, 1974 and no later than November 1, 1974. Detailed specifications may be obtained at the office of the Administrator of the United Wausaukee Schools, Wausaukee, Wisconsin 54177.

Bids are to be sealed and delivered personally or mailed to the office of the Administrator of the United Wausaukee School on or before 7:30 p.m., April 10, 1974 and marked "Bus Bids", at which time the Board will meet to open and consider the bids. The said Board reserves the right to reject any or all bids and to accept the bid that they consider the most advantageous to the United Wausaukee School District.

Trade In: Two buses, a 1966 48-passenger and a 1966 60-passenger.

The buses may be inspected by contacting the School Bus Garage, Village of Wausaukee.

United Wausaukee School District Board
Roger Marquardt, Clerk

C3/20-27

Source: *Peshtigo Times,* Peshtigo, Wisconsin, March 20, 1974

Figure 10-3

notice the ticket provision, and the contents of his car are stolen. Mr. Wood has good cause to take legal action against the parking lot operator because his (Wood's) attention was not directed to the provision on the ticket which said that the operator was not liable for the contents.

DURATION OF AN OFFER

By making an offer the offeror gives the offeree a continuing power to create a legally binding contract, since an offer that has been properly communicated continues until it lapses, is revoked, is rejected, or is accepted. When an offer is terminated in one of these four ways, the offeree's power to create a contract is likewise ended.

LAPSE

The person making a proposal may set whatever time limit he wishes on his offer. If he states that it will remain open for a certain period of time, it automatically lapses at the end of that period. Nothing further need be done to cancel the offer. An attempted acceptance after the specified time period will not amount to an acceptance, but may result in a new offer by the offeree. If the time an offer will remain open is not stipulated, it is held to remain open for a reasonable time—that is, for such a period as a reasonable person might conclude was intended. Defining the reasonableness of the time limit usually involves such items as the nature of the offer's subject matter and the common practices, customs, or procedures of a particular field of business. For example, most sales contracts made through salesmen are not final until approved by the home office. If the price of a property offered for sale is constantly fluctuating, an offer concerning it will remain open a shorter period of time than would an offer involving property that had a more stable price.

Other factors that should be considered in determining a reasonable length of time for an offer to remain open are the conditions under which the offer was made, the relationship of the parties, the language employed, and the manner in which the offer was communicated. An oral offer, made directly or over the telephone, is usually held to lapse when the conversation ends unless the offeror definitely indicates that he is leaving the offer open for further consideration by the offeree.

An offer that is a continuing proposal for the formation of a contract assumes that the offeror is capable of entering into such a relationship. Any act that destroys the offeror's capacity to contract must destroy outstanding offers. If the offeror dies or is declared insane by a court of law, the offer immediately terminates even though the offeree may have no knowledge of the death or insanity of the offeror. However, if a contract has already been formed, the death or insanity of one of the parties does not cause a recision.

REVOCATION

Since an offer is created by an individual, it is subject to his control, and he may withdraw it at any time, terminating the offeree's power of acceptance. The offeror creates a power of acceptance in the other party but he retains a power of revocation. He is free to withdraw his proposal, provided he does so before acceptance and properly notifies the offeree. This is true even if the offeror had promised to keep his offer open for a definite period. However, if the offeree, in reliance on the offer, has substantially changed his position, the offer may not be revoked, especially if the offeror had promised to keep the offer open for a definite period. Take, for example, the following situation: Smith, a subcontractor, submitted a bid for certain construction work to Brown, a general contractor, who in turn used Smith's offer in making his bid for the other job. His legal position is changed; he has incurred a legal obligation he did not have before and would not otherwise have incurred.

An offeror's revocation of his offer does not become effective until it has been communicated to the offeree. For communication to be accomplished, the revocation must be received by the offeree or must reach his place of business, where it will be readily available to him. The revocation is held to be effective as soon as the offeree has had a reasonable opportunity to open and read the notice. An oral revocation is considered effective when the offeree hears of the offeror's changed intention from the offeror himself or his agent. An exception to the rule of actual notice is applied in the case of offers to sell real property. It has been held that actual knowledge by the offeree that the property has been sold terminates his power of acceptance, without a requirement that personal notice of that fact given be made by the offeror.

In the case of public offers that are communicated by newspaper advertisements, over radio or television or by posters, the offeror may revoke the offer by publishing a notice of the same general character as that used to publish it. This is true because the identity of the offerees is unknown to the offeror. In this situation it is possible for the offer to be revoked without the offeree's knowledge. For example, an offer of a reward for information leading to the capture of a criminal is a general offer made by public notice published in a post office, and a power of acceptance is created in all those who read it. It would be impractical to require the offeror to notify all those who have read the offer that it has been revoked. Therefore, courts have held that a general offer by publication may be revoked by publication; this revokes the power of acceptance even though the offeree may never hear or read of the revocation.

If the offeree has furnished consideration to the offeror to keep the offer open for a stated period, the offer cannot be revoked without the consent of the offeree. In this case the offeror has contracted not to revoke the offer for the period of the option. A withdrawal would breach the agreement and render the offeror liable for any damages sustained by the offeree. An option cannot be revoked by the offeror during the option period; not even the offeror's death can cause revocation.

REJECTION

An offer may be terminated by rejection on the part of the offeree. The rejection causes the offer to terminate immediately, even though it was supposed to have remained open a longer period of time. Rejection of an offer contained in an option contract can terminate the option before its normal expiration date. By his rejection, the offeree manifests his intention to refuse the offer; and by communication of this fact to the offeror, the offer is terminated.

Once the offeree has rejected the offer he cannot change his mind and accept; the rejection terminates his power of acceptance. A later attempted acceptance would amount to nothing more than a counteroffer. A proposal by the offeree of new terms that would be acceptable to him or an offer to act on the present terms contingent on certain events is a new proposal. It is, in effect, a counteroffer, which by implication rejects the original offer because the offeror has a right to assume that the offeree is unwilling to agree to the offer as originally proposed. However, when the offeree's reply indicates that he is seeking other terms without rejecting the original proposal, the original offer remains open. For example, suppose Mr. Wood offers to sell his house to

Brown for $50,000. If Brown says, "I will give you $45,500," Wood may refuse to lower the price and seek another purchaser. Brown has no cause to take action against Mr. Wood because Brown rejected the original $50,000 offer when he made the counteroffer of $45,500. However, if Brown says, "Will you take $45,500?" he is making an inquiry, and the original offer remains open for acceptance.

ACCEPTANCE

No agreement can ever be reached without acceptance, for acceptance is evidence of the offeree's consent to the terms of the offer and of his willingness to be bound by them. To accept an offer, the offeree must make some promise or statement or perform some act that shows he agrees to the terms of the offer and is willing to enter into a contract with the offeror. By giving his promise or acting as requested, the offeree also furnishes the consideration that makes his contract with the offeror legally enforceable. The acceptance, while it may take any one of several forms, must fulfill certain prerequisites: it must be absolute and unconditional; it must agree unequivocally to the terms of the offer; it must conform in the manner, at the place, and within the time set forth by the offer; and, finally, it must be communicated to the offeror.

ACCEPTANCE OF UNILATERAL AND BILATERAL OFFERS

A contract is created when an offer is made by an offeror and is accepted by the named offeree. No third person can substitute himself for the offeree and effectively accept the offer. If the offeror stipulates that the only valid form of acceptance for his offer is an outright act, then the offer he is proposing is an offer for a *unilateral* contract.

If, on the other hand, the offeror is willing to accept a promise of an act in return for his own promise as set forth in his offer, the offer he is proposing is an offer for a *bilateral* contract.

The Restatement, Contracts, Sec. 45 states: "If an offer for a unilateral contract is made, and part of the consideration requested in the offer is given or tendered by the offeree in response thereto, the offeror is bound by a contract. . . ." In other words, the offer becomes a binding contract as soon as part of the performance has actually been rendered or a proper tender of performance has been made by the offeree.

Published offers of a reward for desired information are unilateral offers calling for the furnishing of information not already known by the offeror. A request that the other party ship specific goods by a named carrier for a given price is also an offer for a unilateral contract, and shipment of the goods as specified constitutes an acceptance.

Since a unilateral contract is promise for a completed act, the acceptance of such an offer is not effective until the completion of the required act. Less than full performance will not be construed as compliance; hence, the offeror may withdraw his offer at any time before substantial performance of the act has been completed by the offeree. Expenses incurred by the offeree in preparation for performance do not affect this right to revoke. However, if the partial performance of the act has benefited the offeror, he must pay the offeree for the benefit received, although he is under no obligation to permit the offeree to complete performance. Once substantial completion of performance has occurred, the offeror loses the right to revoke his offer.

An offer for a bilateral contract contemplates the exchange of a promise for a promise. The bilateral offer is accepted by a promise to do what is requested in the offer. For example, one who makes an offer to sell real property for a given price is making or comtemplating a bilateral contract and expects notice of acceptance. An employer who offers a contract of employment is bargaining for a prospective employee's promise to go to work. The contract is completed as soon as the employee signifies his acceptance by signing the contract. The promise must be communicated to the offeror and may consist of any conduct that clearly shows the intent of the offeree to be bound by the conditions set forth in the offer. No formal procedure is required for acceptance.

If the agreement takes the form of a written instrument, acceptance is usually not effective until the instrument has been signed and delivered. The exception to this is where the parties intended that an earlier verbal agreement be binding and that the writing should serve merely as evidence of the oral contract.

Silence by the offeree never amounts to acceptance, even if the offeror states in his offer that failure to reply will be considered acceptance. Silence may indicate that the offer was not received or that the offeree gave no thought to acceptance or even to replying. For example, Wiley Wood may write a letter to Baker offering to sell a certain rare book for $300, adding that unless he hears from Baker within the next ten days, he will conclude that Baker has accepted the offer. If Baker fails to reply, there is still no contract because an offeror's assumption that the offeree's silence may be interpreted as an indication of acceptance is not reasonable. There are cases, however, where the past conduct of the parties and the circumstances accompanying the silence of the offeree amount to acceptance. For example, mailing out a fire insurance renewal form to a policy holder constitutes an offer to insure for the new period, and retention of the form by the insured constitutes acceptance if so intended. The company cannot later refuse to renew the policy. Also by using a product knowing its receipt was not intended as a gift may likewise be deemed an acceptance. However, some states (Ohio) have statutes treating unsolicited mailings as gifts.

ACCEPTANCE BY THE OFFEREE

An offer may be accepted only by the party to whom it was made, that is, by the offeree. An offer cannot be assigned to a third party. Sometimes items are ordered from a firm that has discontinued business, and the items are shipped by its successor. In such cases the offeree is not obligated to accept the goods. If he does accept the items knowing that they were shipped by the new concern, his action constitutes an agreement to pay for them. An offer made to the public may be accepted by any member of the public who is aware of the offer.

TIME ACCEPTANCE TAKES EFFECT

Since the acceptance of a bilateral offer becomes effective when it has been communicated by the offeree to the offeror, the question often arises as to when the communication is effected. Is the communication effected when the acceptance is deposited with the medium of communication, or is it effected when it reaches the offeror? The matter is decided by referring to the medium of communication employed by the offeror. For example, the fact that an offer is received by telegram indicates a desire to employ a fast means of communication. If the offeror indicates in the terms of the offer the medium to be used, the acceptance is completed as soon as it is deposited with that agency. For example, if an acceptance by letter is indicated, a contract is made by mailing a letter of acceptance, properly stamped, within a reasonable time.[1] If the offeror does not specify the medium of communication to be used, the assumption is that the offeree is authorized to use the same medium used by the offeror in transmitting the offer.[2] Therefore, the acceptance will be completed as soon as it is deposited with that agency. If no medium is indicated, mail is usually deemed the authorized medium. If the offeree communicates his acceptance by some medium other than that specified or used by the offeror, or by a medium of communication considered unreasonable under the Uniform Commercial Code, the acceptance is not completed until it reaches the offeror or his place of business and may be considered invalid unless it arrives within the time an acceptance would have arrived had it been sent in an authorized manner. If a letter of acceptance is never received, the burden of proof is on the offeree; he must prove to the court's satisfaction that it was actually deposited in the mail.

LEGAL PRINCIPLES

An offer is the communication by one party, the offeror, to another party, the offeree, of the offeror's willingness to act or to refrain from acting in a specified manner if the offeree in turn will act or promise to act or refrain from acting as requested.

An offer becomes effective only after it has been communicated to the offeree by the offeror or his duly authorized agent.

The offeror must intend his offer to be legally binding.

The offer must be definite. It can leave no doubts about what is being offered and what is being requested.

In an auction sale, the auctioneer is empowered to accept offers made by bidders.

When it is advertised that bids will be received from business firms for some type of work, the person calling for bids is not *making* an offer but rather is *calling* for offers. The party who submits a bid is the offeror.

If a ticket is purchased for entrance into places of amusement or as evidence of a contract for transportation, the holder of the ticket is bound by the terms printed on the ticket, even if his attention is not directed to them. If a ticket is received merely as evidence of ownership and is to be presented later as a means of identification, the provisions printed on the ticket are ineffective unless the recipient's attention is directed to them at the time the ticket is accepted.

An offer is terminated when it lapses, is revoked, is rejected, or is accepted. An offer lapses at the end of the definite period if a definite period is stated; if no definite period is stated, the offer lapses after a reasonable length of time.

The offeror may revoke his offer at any time before it has been accepted. An offeror's revocation of his offer does not become effective until it has been communicated to the offeree. However, direct notice of revocation is not always required. An offeree's rejection of an offer is not effective until he or his agent has communicated it to the offeror. Once the offeree has rejected the offer, he cannot later accept it.

An acceptance is an indication by the offeree of his willingness to be bound by the terms of the offer. An attempted acceptance by an offeree who has already rejected the offer once will amount to nothing more than a counteroffer.

A unilateral offer is not accepted until completion of the act required in the offer. A bilateral offer is accepted by a promise to do what is requested in the offer.

A bilateral offer is accepted by a promise to do what is requested in the offer.

Silence, of itself, never constitutes an acceptance.

An offer can be accepted only by the party to whom it was made—that is, by the offeree.

If, in his offer, the offeror indicates the medium to be used in notifying him of the acceptance, the acceptance is completed as soon as evidence of it is deposited with the specified agency of communication.

If the offeree communicates his acceptance by some medium other than that specified or used by the offeror, the acceptance is not completed until it reaches the offeror.

CASE FOR REVIEW

LUCY V. ZEHMER

196 Va. 493, 84 S.E. 2d 516 (1954)

This suit was instituted by W. O. Lucy and J. C. Lucy, complainants, against A. H. Zehmer and Ida S. Zehmer, his wife, defendants, to have specific performance of a contract by which it was alleged the Zehmers had sold to W. O. Lucy a tract of land owned by A. H. Zehmer in Dinwiddie county containing 471.6 acres, more or less, known as the Ferguson farm, for $50,000. J. C. Lucy, the other complainant, is a brother of W. O. Lucy, to whom W. O. Lucy transferred a half interest in his alleged purchase.

The instrument sought to be enforced was written by A. H. Zehmer on December 20, 1952, in these words: "We hereby agree to sell to W. O. Lucy the Ferguson Farm complete for $50,000.00, title satisfactory to buyer," and signed by the defendants, A. H. Zehmer and Ida S. Zehmer.

The answer of A. H. Zehmer admitted that at the time mentioned W. O. Lucy offered him $50,000 cash for the farm, but that he, Zehmer, considered that the offer was made in jest; that so thinking . . . he wrote out "the memorandum" quoted above and induced his wife to sign it; that he did not deliver the memorandum to Lucy, but that Lucy picked it up, read it, put it in his pocket, attempted to offer Zehmer $5 to bind the bargain, which Zehmer refused to accept, and realizing for the first time that Lucy was serious, Zehmer assured him that he had no intention of selling the farm and that the whole matter was a joke. Lucy left the premises insisting that he had purchased the farm.

Depositions were taken and the decree appeal form was entered holding that the complainants had failed to establish their right to specific performance, and dismissing their bill. The assignment of error is to this action of the court . . .

The defendants insist that the evidence was ample to support their contention that the writing sought to be enforced was prepared as a bluff or dare to force Lucy to admit that he did not have $50,000; that the whole matter was a joke; that the writing was not delivered to Lucy and no binding contract was ever made between the parties.

It is an unusual, if not bizarre, defense. When made to the writing admittedly prepared by one of the defendants and signed by both, clear evidence is required to sustain it.

The evidence is convincing also that Zehmer wrote two agreements, the first one beginning "I hereby agree to sell." Zehmer first said he could not remember about that, then that "I don't think I wrote but one out." Mrs. Zehmer said that what he wrote was "I hereby agree," but that the "I" was changed to "We" after that night. The agreement that was written and signed is in the record and indicates no such change. Neither are the mistakes in spelling that Zehmer sought to point out readily apparent.

The appearance of the contract, the fact that it was under discussion for forty minutes or more before it was signed; Lucy's objection to the first draft because it was written in the singular, and [the fact that] he wanted Mrs. Zehmer to sign it also; the rewriting to meet his objection and the signing by Mrs. Zehmer; the discussion of what was to be included in the sale; the provision for the examination of the title; the completeness of the instrument that was executed; the taking possession of it by Lucy with no request or suggestion by either of the defendants that he give it back; are facts which furnish persuasive evidence that the execution of the contract was a serious business transaction rather than a casual, jesting matter as defendants now contend. ...

If it be assumed, contrary to what we think the evidence shows, that Zehmer was jesting about selling his farm to Lucy and that the transaction was intended by him to be a joke, nevertheless the evidence shows that Lucy did not so understand it but considered it to be a serious business transaction and the contract to be binding on the Zehmers as well as on himself. The very next day he arranged with his brother to put up half the money and take a half interest in the land. The day after that he employed an attorney to examine the title. The next night, Tuesday, he was back at Zehmer's place and there Zehmer told him for the first time, Lucy said, that he wasn't going to sell and he told Zehmer, "You know you sold that place fair and square." After receiving the report from his attorney that the title was good he wrote to Zehmer that he was ready to close the deal.

Not only did Lucy actually believe, but the evidence shows he was warranted in believing, that the contract represented a serious business transaction and a good faith sale and purchase of the farm.

CASE PROBLEMS

1. Defendant, the manager of a department store, ran a newspaper ad which stated in part, "Will sell and deliver and install, for any one who purchases from certain well-known standard makes of radios at 25-50 percent reduction from advertised list prices." The makes were named. Among them was a Zenith D12 model which the plaintiff selected. The defendant refused to sell although cash was offered. The plaintiff brought this action for the radio. Decide.
2. In May 1967, New City offered a reward of $2000 for the conviction of any person setting fire to any building within the city limits, publicizing the reward by advertising in the daily newspapers for about a week. There had been numerous fires in 1967, and the city council ordered this published statement in addition to an already existing public ordinance against arson. Shortly thereafter the fires ceased. No specific withdrawal was printed. In January 1971, an extensive fire took place. Plaintiffs, suspecting one Sam Marriot of having set the fire, pursued Marriot to New York, brought him back, and secured his conviction. Plaintiffs then sought the reward offered in 1967. The city refused to pay, claiming that the offer of reward was no longer in force at the time of the fire. Decide.
3. On January 6, 1970, Smith and defendant entered into the following agreement: "The above seller hereby sells and agrees to hold in its storage for the Purchaser, and the above Purchaser hereby buys, the merchandise described below, which shall be shipped to Purchaser at Waseca, Minn. on Aug. 1, 1970.

Quantity	Description	Per Gal.
5000 gals.	Worth Motor Oil SAE 10-70, Base	21-31¢
3000 gals. and	Beter Motor Oil SAE 10-70	26-36¢
others in same manner.		

   As per Price List attached . . ."
   Two weeks after making this agreement, defendant repudiated it. Smith treated the contract as breached, and brought an action for damages. Decide.
4. A petition alleged that plaintiff agreed to buy steel bars from defendant. The answer denied that any contract had been made. The following letters and telegrams were sent:
   December 5. Letter from plaintiff to defendant: "Please quote me prices for 2000 to 5000 tons 50-lb. bars."
   December 8. Letter from defendant to plaintiff: "Your favor of the 5th inst. at hand. For bars, we will sell 2000 to 5000 tons. [Prices stated.]"
   December 16. Letter from plaintiff to defendant: "Please enter our order for 1200 tons."
   December 18. Telegram from defendant to plaintiff, received same day: "We cannot book your order at present at that price."
   December 19. Telegram from plaintiff to defendant: "Please enter an order for 2000 tons, as per your letter of the eighth. Please forward written contract. Reply."
   Was there a contract?
5. Kemp, on January 30, wrote Kohn offering certain real estate. On February 7, Kohn wrote to accept the offer upon the terms proposed. On February 7, before Kemp received Kohn's letter Kemp mailed a letter withdrawing his offer. On

February 9, Kemp received Kohn's letter of acceptance which had been mailed prior to the time of the mailing of Kemp's letter of revocation. Kohn brought an action alleging that he accepted Kemp's offer before it had expired. Decide.

6. Defendant made the following offer: "Gentlemen: I have about 80,000 feet of oak, for which I will take $16 per thous. delivered on rail cars at Bridgewater. I will take $8 per thous. for the mill culls I have at Bridgewater, as that is what it cost me, cut and deliver the same." Plaintiff replied: "Dear Sir: We have received your letter of the 20th and will take your 4/4 oak at $16, mill culls out, delivered on rail cars at Bridgewater. We will handle all your mill culls, but not at the price you are asking. We are buying from A. L. & Company for $4.50 on board the cars." Was there a contract?

7. Plaintiff, a merchant, gave a salesman of defendant an order for shoes to be shipped on June 5, 1970. The order was written, a copy sent the defendant who returned a card to plaintiff acknowledging the order and stating it "shall have our prompt attention." No shoes were sent. Plaintiff brought an action for damages. Decide.

8. Harvey, defendant, owner of a barbershop in Monmouth, on March 21, 1970, wrote plaintiff, a barber in Peoria, offering him a chair in his shop at $160 per week during the season which was to begin on April 5 and end on Labor Day. The offer stated, "You will confer a favor by giving me your answer by return mail." Plaintiff on March 23 answered by letter accepting the offer. The letter was not postmarked until March 25. Defendant made other arrangements when he did not receive plaintiff's answer by return mail. Plaintiff brought an action for breach of contract. Decide.

ENDNOTES

1. Restatement, Contracts, Sec. 67: "An acceptance sent by mail or otherwise from a distance is not operative when despatched, unless it is properly addressed and any other precaution taken which is ordinarily observed to insure safe transmission of similar messages."

2. The Uniform Commercial Code alters this rule in situations that occur between merchants. Section 2-206 (1) invites acceptance "in any manner and by any medium reasonable in the circumstances."

CONSIDERATION 11

Consideration is a term that may be said to defy definition. There is no one correct definition, nor is there one simple, uniform concept that can be correctly applied to all situations. We have learned that a contract is formed on the basis of one or more promises of performance, but we have also seen that not every promise made by one party to another creates a legal duty or provides a legal remedy in the event of nonperformance. No legal remedy exists if one is promised a gift and the promise is not kept; the promisee is in no worse position than he would have been had the promise not been made. The test of a legally enforceable promise is whether it is supported by consideration. To be binding, the promise must be paid for by someone.

The concept of consideration is the concept of a bargain. An offer may be made either for the purpose of economic gain or in order to prevent a loss, whereas acceptance is usually motivated by the prospect of gain. If the offeror bargains for something based on his promise, the offeree must regard the promise as worth whatever is asked of him or he would not accept the exchange. Consideration is what is requested by a promisor in return for his promise; once he receives it his promise is transformed into an obligation. It must be something to which the promisor is not otherwise entitled and something that the promisee is not legally bound for reasons other than the agreement to furnish. As a general rule, one party to an agreement cannot require the other party to perform a promised action unless he can show that he has provided consideration in exchange for the other party's promise.

If a contract is bilateral, each party to the contract is a promisor and must receive consideration to make the contract binding. For example, if Mr. Wood promises to pay Sam $800 for painting the Wood's home. Sam promises to paint the house for $800. Mr. Wood is a promisor; he has received for his promise Sam's promise to paint the house. Likewise, Sam is a promisor; he has received for his promise Bill's promise to pay him for the work.

In a unilateral contract there is only one promisor, and the performance of the act he asks of the other party is the consideration that makes his promise binding. If Mr. Wood promises to pay Sam $100 for a week's work, Mr. Wood is a promisor and receives for his promise the services performed by Sam; Sam, once he has performed the requested services, is entitled to receive $100 from Mr. Wood.

ADEQUACY OF CONSIDERATION

Normally, the courts do not weigh the adequacy of consideration. If the parties have freely entered into an agreement and some consideration is given, the agreement is enforceable, even though one party may have benefited more from the contract than the other. So long as the parties get what they bargained for the courts will not measure value, nor will they attempt to apportion value on a pro rata basis. Consideration is not made insufficient by the fact that its market value is not equal to the market value of what is promised. Only if the requested act is wholly without value in a legal sense, as determined by the court, will the contract be void for lack of consideration. Thus it can be said that the fairness of an agreed exchange is of no consequence, so long as the consideration is of some value.

Suppose, for example, that Mr. Wood owns two farms, one of which is larger and more valuable than the other, and makes separate contracts to sell each to a different purchaser. Purchaser A agrees to pay $9000 for the better farm, and purchaser B agrees to pay $9000 for the poorer farm. A court will not set aside B's promise on the ground that he is getting less than his money's worth simply because A is getting a much better farm for the same price. Since a contract is a voluntary agreement, the contracting parties make their own terms, agree among themselves on what promises are to be exchanged, and set their own values as to the prospective exchanges.

In the absence of fraud or other misconduct, the courts usually will not interfere with an agreement simply to ensure that each side is getting a fair return. The fact that the consideration given may seem small to persons other than the contracting parties or to a reasonable man does not, in the absence of fraud, affect the validity of the contract.

There are two exceptions to this rule. These may be brought to the court's attention during a suit for breach of contract.

1. *Evidence of Fraud*—Smallness of consideration may be evidence of fraud because one would not make the exchange if fraud were not present.
2. *Promise to Exchange Different Amounts of Identical Units*—A promise to exchange a penny for a dollar, or one bushel of apples for ten bushels of similar apples is evidence of an unfair bargain, since the inadequacy of the exchange is readily apparent.

FORBEARANCE AS CONSIDERATION

In most cases, consideration consists of the performance of an act or the making of a promise to act. Consideration may also consist of forbearance or a promise of forbearance. The promisor may desire to bargain for the inaction of the other party or for his promise not to act. For example, an officer of a corporation may ask a creditor of the corporation to refrain from suing the company, promising to pay the debt himself if the corporation does not do so. The forbearance or promise to forbear by the creditor constitutes consideration for the officer's guarantee of payment.

The waiving (giving up) of any right can be used as consideration for the enforceability of the promise of another to act in some manner or to make some payment. The relinquishment of a right in property or of a right to sue for damages will act as consideration for a promise to pay money in return for surrendering the right. The right given up in return for a promise may be a right against a third person or his property, rather than one against the promisor himself or his property. However, there is no consideration when the right given up is known to be worthless by the person surrendering it. A claim must be made in good faith for its surrender to constitute consideration. The following are examples of forbearance from exercising a legal right that constitute sufficient consideration: forbearing to terminate a contract, forbearing to revoke an offer for a specified time, forbearing to bid at an auction, forbearing to bring suit against a wrongdoer. Surrender of these rights makes legally binding a promise to pay for such forbearance.

LEGALITY OF CONSIDERATION

A promise to do something that the law prohibits or to refrain from doing something that the law requires is not valid consideration. For example, a promise by A not to hit B if B will pay him $100 is void for lack of consideration. Also, the performance of a duty imposed by statute will not constitute valid consideration for another's promise. Thus a promise by a public office-holder to do or not to do his job or a citizen's promise to appear as a witness will not support a promise to pay money. A person must promise or do more than the law demands in order to furnish valid consideration.

PERSONS ALREADY BOUND

Since consideration is what the promisor states he must receive for his promise, it must be given after the promisor makes this statement. The performance of a present obligation cannot be offered as consideration, and an agreement based on such performance is unenforceable. In effect, one party receives nothing for his promise, since the other party was already bound to perform the act by a previous commitment. For instance, a promise to pay a reward for the capture of a criminal is unenforceable if the capture is made by a policeman, since the promisor receives only that which he has a right to demand without making any promise—the apprehension of a lawbreaker by an officer of the law. By the same criterion, a person cannot offer as consideration his promise not to do something that he has already committed himself not to do.

UNFORESEEABLE DIFFICULTIES

In some situations, a contractor will refuse to complete a building unless the owner promises him a payment or bonus in addition to the sum specified in the original contract. If the owner does promise to pay, the question arises as to whether his promise is binding. Where the contractor has no valid excuse for not completing performance, the owner is not obligated to make any additional payment. In fact, the owner may insist on complete performance or sue for damages. As a practical matter, however, the owner will often promise the additional sum in order to get the job done. Legally, his promise to pay is unenforceable because he does not receive any new consideration. The contractor is merely promising to furnish a performance he is already bound to furnish.

Those courts which hold that there is no consideration for the second promise make an exception when there are extraordinary circumstances caused by unforeseeable difficulties or mistakes and when the additional amount demanded by the contractor is reasonable for the extra work done by him. This exception is limited strictly to circumstances that are truly unforeseeable, however, and does not extend to factors that the parties should have anticipated, such as strikes, price increases, and variability in the weather.

COMPROMISE OF CLAIMS

In cases where a creditor agrees to accept as full payment from the debtor a sum that is less than the full amount of the debt, the agreement is held to be without consideration. The creditor may recover the balance at a later date because in making payment the debtor was doing only what he was legally obligated to do and the creditor was receiving something to which legally he was already entitled. If A owes B $100, B's promise to accept $50 in full payment is not binding upon him and does not prohibit his demanding the remainder later. However, anything given by the debtor in an agreement of this type which differs in legal value from that which he was already bound to give will be considered sufficient consideration and will release him from further debt.

If a debtor makes a partial payment before a debt is legally due, this is construed as consideration since the creditor was not legally entitled to demand payment at that time. Likewise, if the creditor accepts some article, even one of slight value, in addition to a partial payment in advance of the due date, an agreement to release the debtor from further obligation is held to be binding. Whenever some new or additional consideration is present, however small, the creditor's promise to accept part payment in lieu of full payment is enforceable. The law of consideration is satisfied as long as the negotiated promise includes something that was not within the requirements of a pre-existing duty.[1]

When the amount of a claim or obligation is in dispute, any agreement by the creditor to accept some other amount as a compromise, even if it is less than what he claims is owed to him, is binding on the parties. Examples of this situation are claims for damages for torts or breach of contract. In these cases, an agreement between the parties fixing the amount to be paid in settlement is a valid contract.

Another exception is recognized where a group of creditors of one debtor together agree to accept a lesser sum in full payment of the aggregate debt. This arrangement is referred to as a composition of creditors and is generally held to be binding, even though the creditors are getting less than the sum of the original debts. Such an agreement is made with the understanding among the creditors that they shall all be treated alike, with no preference given. Normally the debtor would have to pay each creditor the full amount of the debt owed him. Where there is a composition of creditors, however, he must pay each the same amount on the dollar. (See Figure 11-1)

A COMPOSITION AGREEMENT

This agreement, made this 14th day of November, 1976, by and between M. T. Wallett, Debtor, and U. R. Stucke ($10,000), I. M. Broke, ($4,000), and Ivan Hade ($3,000), all creditors of the debtor, in the amounts specified after their names, and by and between them as such creditors.

WITNESSETH: That the said undersigned creditors, for and in consideration of $1.00 to them paid, the receipt whereof is hereby acknowledged, and of their own mutual promises and agreements to accept the terms hereof, do hereby agree with the said M. T. Wallett, debtor, and to and with each other respectively to compound and settle their respective claims and demands against the said M. T. Wallett at the rate of seventy cents on the dollar of said claims, to be paid in the following manner:

Thirty per cent (30%) in cash, on or before December 20, 1976,
Twenty per cent (20%) in four (4) months, and
Twenty per cent (20%) in eight (8) months from the date hereof.

The said creditors severally and respectively agree to give the said M. T. Wallett a full release from their respective claims and demands as soon as the said seventy cents on the dollar is paid in the manner above set forth.

Debtor _____

(_____
(
Creditors (_____
(
(_____

Figure 11-1

PAST CONSIDERATION

An act or promise that has occurred in the past does not constitute consideration for a present promise. The theory is that at the time it was given, such an act or a promise was not intended to be in exchange for the later promise by the other side. For example, a warranty not made at the time of a sale is unenforceable, as is a promise to pay for a gift or service given after the receipt of the benefit. However, when benefits are derived by fraud, a promise to compensate is held to be supported by consideration.

The following example illustrates the general rule: An uncle says to his nephew, "Since you've given up smoking during your first year at school, I promise you $100." The promise, even if made "in consideration of" the nephew's past conduct, is not consideration; it does not create a legal obligation to pay the money. This promise would be enforceable had it been made prior to the first school year. Had the uncle at that time said, "If you give up smoking during your first year of college, I'll pay you $100," he would then have received for his promise the nephew's counterpromise to stop smoking. In the second instance, the uncle is buying his nephew's promise to give up smoking rather than rewarding the young man's past conduct.

NEED FOR A BINDING PROMISE

To constitute consideration, a promise made in return for an offer must be binding. The agreement must impose a liability or create a duty on both parties; each party must be bound by his promise or neither is bound. Suppose a coal company promises to sell to a manufacturer all the coal the latter orders at a specific price and the manufacturer in turn agrees to pay that price for any coal he orders from the coal company. Because the manufacturer has not actually obligated himself to purchase any coal at all from the coal company, his promise is not supported by any consideration and consequently has no legal validity. If, however, the manufacturer promises to purchase all the coal he requires for a specified period and the coal dealer agrees to supply it at a specified price per ton, the weight of judicial precedent supports the validity of the contract. Any agreement with the right of cancellation available to either party at any time is unenforceable. However, if the right of cancellation is conditional upon the occurrence or nonoccurrence of an event, the contract is enforceable because neither party may avoid his obligation except under the specified conditions.

EXCEPTIONS TO THE REQUIREMENT OF CONSIDERATION

PROMISSORY ESTOPPEL

Whenever an individual makes a promise that a reasonable man would expect to induce someone to act in reliance thereon, the courts will enforce the promise. Thus, when a charitable organization accepts pledges of money for its operation, the pledgee's promise may be binding if the group has acted in some material way in reliance upon the pledge. However, unless there is actual reliance on the pledge,consideration is deemed not present and the promise is revocable until payment occurs.

A SEAL

At common law, consideration was not necessary to support a promise under seal. The seal was interpreted to mean that the parties intended a gift or a promise to make a gift to be enforceable. However, with the advent of the doctrine of consideration, the use of the seal diminished greatly. As a result, the contract under seal is now treated as a regular contract and is not enforceable without consideration.

DEBTS OF RECORD

Debts such as legal judgments or alimonies do not need consideration to support the obligation. They are enforceable by their nature; it would be against public policy to allow court ordered obligations to be questioned on this ground.

LEGAL PRINCIPLES

Consideration is that promise or performance by the other party demanded by the promisor as the price of his promise. Ordinarily, the law does not weigh the adequacy of consideration, nor will the courts reappraise the value that a person placed upon the consideration at the time of the agreement.

Consideration may consist of forbearance (refraining from doing an act) or a promise of forbearance. Performance of an action prohibited by law or forbearing to perform an action required by law is not valid consideration. To constitute consideration, a promise must impose liabilities, or create duties, binding on both parties.

Performing or promising to perform something that one is already under a legal obligation to do is not consideration, although unforeseeable difficulties in fulfilling a contract may cause a new promise made in return for meeting the existing obligation to be binding.

A partial payment made in satisfaction of an admitted debt is not sufficient consideration for any promise, including a release of the entire debt, since the debtor was under a preexisting obligation to pay.

The requirement of consideration may be waived in cases of promissory estoppel and debts of record.

A negotiable instrument is prima facie evidence of consideration.

CASE FOR REVIEW

GOODMAN v. DICKER

83 U.S. App. D.C. 353, 169 F.2d 684 (1948)

Appellants are local distributors for Emerson Radio and Phonograph Corporation in the District of Columbia. Appellees, with the knowledge and encouragement of appellants, applied for a "dealer franchise" to sell Emerson's products. The trial court found that appellants by their representations and conduct induced appellees to incur expenses in preparing to do business under the franchise, including employment of salesmen and solicitation of orders for radios. Among other things, appellants represented that the application had been accepted; that the franchise would be granted; and that appellees would receive an initial delivery of thirty to forty radios. Yet, no radios were delivered, and notice was finally given that the franchise would not be granted.

The case was tried without a jury. The court held that a contract had not been proven but that appellants were estopped from denying the same by reason of their statements and conduct upon which appellees relied to their detriment. Judgment was entered for $1500, covering cash outlays of $1,150 and loss of $350, anticipated profits on sale of thirty radios.

The main contention of appellants is that no liability would have arisen under the dealer franchise had it been granted because, as understood by appellees, it would have been terminable at will and would have imposed no duty upon the manufacturer to sell or appellees to buy any fixed number of radios. From this it is argued that the franchise agreement would not have been enforceable (except as to acts performed thereunder) and cancellation by the manufacturer would have created no liability for expenses incurred by the dealer in preparing to do business. Further, it is argued that as the dealer franchise would have been unenforceable for failure of the manufacturer to supply radios appellants would not be liable to fulfill their assurance that radios would be supplied.

We think these contentions miss the real point of this case. We are not concerned directly with the terms of the franchise. We are dealing with a promise by appellants that a franchise would be granted and radios supplied, on the faith of which appellees with the knowledge and encouragement of appellants incurred expenses in making preparations to do business. Under these circumstances we think that appellants cannot now advance any defense inconsistent with their assurance that the franchise would be granted. Justice and fair dealing require that one who acts to his detriment on the faith of conduct of the kind revealed here should be protected by estopping the party who has brought about the situation from alleging anything in opposition to the natural consequences of his own course of conduct. ... In *Dickerson* v. *Colgrove,* 100 U.S. 578, 580, the Supreme Court, in speaking of equitable estoppel, said:

> The law upon the subject is well settled. The vital principle is that he who by his language or conduct leads another to do what he would not otherwise have

done, shall not subject such person to loss or injury by disappointing the expectations upon which he acted. Such a change of position is sternly forbidden. ... This remedy is always so applied as to promote the ends of justice. ...

In our opinion the trial court was correct in holding defendants liable for moneys which appellees expended in preparing to do business under the promised dealer franchise. These items aggregated $1150. We think though, the court erred in adding the item of $350 for loss of profits on radios promised under an initial order. The true measure of damage is the loss sustained by expenditures made in reliance upon the assurance of a dealer franchise. As thus modified, the judgment is affirmed.

CASE PROBLEMS

1. Richards gave Hogan an option to purchase, for $8000, an undivided one-half interest in and to all the oil on specified lands. One dollar was given in consideration. Before Hogan completed the contract by the payment of the $8000, Richards withdrew the offer. Hogan brought suit alleging that the option was binding because of the payment of $1.00. Decide.
2. Spence owned a house under which Link agreed to build a basement according to certain specifications and at a contract price of $3000. Upon beginning the work, Link found unusual swamplike conditions under the house which greatly increased the difficulty and expense. Work was stopped, but later the defendant agreed to pay the extra costs, after which Link continued the work. After construction was finished the defendant refused to pay the additional costs and plaintiff sued. Decide.
3. On March 20, 1974, William Story, age 17, agreed to refrain from drinking liquor, using tobacco, swearing, and playing cards or billiards for money until he should become of age. In return, his uncle, Alexander Adams, agreed that he would at that time pay him $8000 for so refraining. Story fully performed his part of the agreement, but the executor of Adams' estate now contends that the contract was without consideration and therefore invalid. He asserts that the promisee benefited by refraining from the use of liquor and tobacco; that what he did was best for him to do, independent of his uncle's promise. The promisor, he claims, benefited in no material way from his nephew's actions; therefore the contract was without consideration. Decide.
4. Plaintiffs entered into a contract with defendants to manufacture and deliver fertilizer. The terms were set forth in detail in a written agreement, which included the following provision: "We [plaintiffs] reserve the right to cancel this contract at any time we deem proper." Plaintiffs manufactured the fertilizer, packed it, and tendered delivery. When defendants refused to accept and pay for it, plaintiffs brought an action to recover damages for breach of contract. Decide.
5. Laski owned a building which was destroyed by fire. He offered a reward for the apprehension and conviction of the suspected arsonist. Hogan, sheriff of Marinette County, arrested the suspect who was convicted of arson. Hogan brought an action for payment of the reward. The fire occurred in Marinette County and the arrest was made in that same county. Decide.
6. Smith, a tenant, made certain repairs for which he claimed his landlord, Jones, had promised to reimburse him. Smith sent checks to Jones, marking them as in "full payment." Jones accepted and deposited the checks, insisting that they were only received on account. An action was brought to collect the disputed amount. Decide.

7. Weber was insolvent and could not pay his creditors in full. He therefore proposed a settlement whereby he would obtain a land bank loan of $15,000 if his creditors would accept a pro rata share of this amount in full settlement of their claims. Plaintiff, a creditor in the amount of $9804.37, together with Weber's other creditors, agreed to the proposed settlement. Under this agreement plaintiff's claim was reduced to $8250. Later plaintiff repudiated the agreement and brought an action to recover the full amount and to foreclose the mortgage that had been given to secure the debt. Decide.

8. Defendant signed a subscription for funds to plaintiff Church "in consideration of the securing by the plaintiff of other pledges for its work." This was presented as a claim in defendant's estate and refused. No payment was made in defendant's lifetime, and there was no evidence that plaintiff had exchanged any value with defendant. Suit was brought to compel payment of the subscription. Decide.

ENDNOTE

1. Restatement, Contracts Sec. 84: "Consideration is not insufficient because of the fact that the party giving the consideration is then bound by a duty owed to the promisor or to the public, or by any duty imposed by the law of torts or crimes, to render some performance similar to that given or promised, if the act or forbearance given or promised as consideration differs in any way from what was previously due."

INCAPACITY   12

We have already seen that to be legally binding, the wording of an agreement must be of sufficient clarity to enable the court to determine its exact meaning and to fix exactly the liability of the parties. A related prerequisite is that the parties themselves be capable of granting the contract legal validity. Whereas it is assumed that in most cases the parties to a contract are fully capable of understanding its terms and obligations, there are certain cases where this capacity is insufficient, in the eyes of the law, to render the contract valid. In these cases, the law makes an effort to afford protection to individuals who cannot protect themselves. Consequently, contracts entered into by such persons are voidable; they are valid, but may be disaffirmed. Those lacking or having a limited legal capacity are infants, the insane, drunkards, aliens, and convicts. Generally, the courts allow them to review contracts to which they are parties at a later date, if at that time they may be presumed to be better able to understand the consequences of their actions, and to accept or reject the agreements after such review.

INFANTS

All persons, male or female, under the age of twenty-one are deemed infants, although in some jurisdictions, females, for purposes of specific statutes, reach their majority at eighteen. Presently about one-half of the states have lowered the age for everyone to eighteen.

The theory behind the law as it applies to infants is one of protection. Presumably, the infant's immaturity of judgment and his inexperience might easily be taken advantage of by older persons. This is particularly true in matters involving contractual rights. Consequently, all contracts of an infant are voidable at his option, although an adult entering into a contract with an infant is bound by the terms of the agreement.

EXECUTORY CONTRACTS

Where the contracts of an infant are fully executory, the fulfillment of the contract depends wholly on the will of the infant. Even should the contract be fully executed or executed in part, the infant can still avoid having to fulfill his part of the agreement by returning the consideration that he (the infant) had been given. For example, suppose Mr. Woods' 17-year-old son, Timothy buys an automobile. He may return the automobile and demand from the car dealer the return of his down payment. As long as Tim is an infant it does not matter whether he had made a number of payments or has paid for the car in full; the contract remains voidable. This would be true even if Tim used false identification to make the purchase. Fraudulent misrepresentation of his age does not cause an infant to forfeit his right to avoid a contract, but the defrauded party may initiate proceedings against the infant in tort.

EXECUTED CONTRACTS

The fact that both parties to the contract have fulfilled their promises does not affect the right of the infant to avoid an agreement. Furthermore, if the minor dies, his personal representative can also avoid it. However, if the minor is in possession of the consideration given him by the other party it must be returned, as he cannot disaffirm the contract and retain the benefits of the agreement. Also, the infant must continue to meet any burdens imposed upon him by the contract until he actually disaffirms it.

If the infant has spent, lost, or squandered the consideration given him and is unable to return it, most courts hold that the infant may nevertheless disaffirm the contract and demand the return of the consideration held by the other party. If the minor has possession of the consideration but it is in a different form, he is bound to return what he has as a basis of his right of disaffirmance.

A provision in the contract that the minor is of legal age does not deprive him of his right to rescind, nor, generally speaking, does the fact that he is in business or has all the appearances of an adult.

A contract cannot be avoided in part. It must be disaffirmed in its entirety or not at all.

TIME OF AVOIDANCE

With the exception of sales of real estate, an infant may avoid his contract and demand the consideration with which he has parted at any time during his minority. This right continues until a reasonable time after he becomes of age (depending on the nature of the article and the circumstances of each case).

A minor must disaffirm the sale of his real estate within a reasonable time after he reaches his majority. This provision is said to result from the fact that the land will always be there and that the minor cannot be materially injured by being forced to wait until he becomes of age. He may, however, prior to disaffirmance, enter into possession of the property, take over its management, and appropriate the income from it to himself.

WHAT CONSTITUTES RATIFICATION

Although an infant may avoid a contract during his minority, he can ratify an agreement only as an adult. Ratification may occur by virtue of a new promise, either oral or written, or it may be implied from the individual's conduct if his actions indicate an intention to accept the benefits of the contract. If the contract is wholly executory, continued silence would imply disaffirmance. Otherwise, any words or conduct that show the newly adult party's willingness or intention to be bound constitutes ratification. For example, an executed contract may be ratified through the retention and use for a reasonable period of time of a purchased article, by acceptance of the benefits incident to ownership, or by any other act of ownership that clearly indicates satisfaction with the contract made during one's minority.

MINORS' LIABILITY FOR NECESSARIES

It is often incorrectly stated that a minor is liable for the contracts he makes involving items considered necessary to maintain his standard of living. As a general rule, unless required by statute, this is not true; he is legally liable in quasi-contract only for the reasonable value of necessaries received by him, after proper consideration is given to his station in life. Furthermore, he is held accountable for the value (which may be more or less than the contract price) of necessaries that he contracts for and that are actually supplied to him by another party.

Before goods can be considered necessaries, it must be established that the infant is in need of them and that they are not already being furnished by anyone. Also, the things furnished must concern the person of the infant and not his estate. Necessaries consist of such things as clothing, food, lodging, medical attention, and the amount of education deemed usual for a person of his station in life. Therefore, should the adult allege that Timothy's car was a necessity, Mr. Wood's life style would be of concern. Contracts relating to the minor's estate, property, or business do not involve necessaries. For example, he would not be liable on contracts made to carry on a business, to build a warehouse, or even on a contract for fire insurance on real property. Finally, the item alleged to be a necessity must be actually furnished to and used by the minor.

PARENTS' LIABILITY FOR INFANTS

Mr. Wood does not become liable for Timothy's purchase. A parent is never liable for an infant's contracts unless he has made the infant his agent (thereby giving the infant the authority to enter into the agreement in the parent's name) or unless he was actually a party to the agreement. However, the parent is under a duty to support his family; whenever he fails or refuses to do so he is responsible for any necessaries furnished to the infant by third parties. At the same time, the parent is entitled to any compensation that the infant earns unless the parent has in some manner surrendered this right. However, as a practical matter, few, if any, parents assert such a right.

An infant is liable for his own torts, and they cannot be disaffirmed. If a minor is old enough to understand and appreciate the consequences of his behavior, he is personally liable for any damage or injury he inflicts on others. The parent is responsible for his children's torts only if they are committed at his direction, if they are committed in his presence when the children could and should have been controlled, or if he actively shares in the minors' conduct. However, some states have inacted statutes making the parent's liable for their children's acts of vandalism.

INSANE PERSONS

Contracts entered into by an insane person before hs is declared insane are generally *voidable* by him or by his representative during the period of his insanity and for a reasonable period after he gains his sanity. He may ratify his contracts upon his recovery and for a reasonable time thereafter.

A person is considered insane only when his will and judgment are so affected that he cannot appreciate or understand the subject of the contract, its nature, or its probable consequences. This degree of incapacity is established when the person is declared insane by a court of law. It should be noted, however, that mental capacity may also be affected by defects such as retardation, senility and the like. Contracts made after such a declaration are *void* unless made by a court-appointed guardian acting in the insane person's name.

An insane person may disaffirm a contract on the ground that his assent was not true or real. The party with whom he has contracted, however, does not have this right of avoidance. In addition, the courts hold that an insane person cannot disaffirm unless he can return the consideration received, provided the contract is reasonable and no advantage has been taken of his condition.

An insane person, like an infant, is liable for necessities in accordance with their fair value. He is also liable for labor and materials furnished for the preservation of his estate, where such were deemed necessary. These are quasi-contractual liabilities, not obligations based on contract.

DRUNKARDS

A contract made by a person who is intoxicated to the point that he does not understand the nature of his undertaking or its legal consequences is voidable at his discretion. He may disaffirm the contract for a reasonable period of time after he becomes sober. Failure to do so will be deemed ratification. When he disaffirms a contract he must return the consideration, unless it is noted that the other party has taken unfair advantage of his condition. If a drunkard is declared by court to be incompetent and incapable of handling his own affairs and a guardian is appointed for him, any contracts made during this period, except by the guardian, are void, not voidable. Like the infant, the drunkard is liable in quasi-contracts for the reasonable value of his necessaries.

ALIENS

An alien is a citizen of a foreign country presently residing in the United States. Aliens have the same right as citizens to make contracts and invoke the protection of the courts to enforce obligations owed to them. They may defend in law suits brought by American citizens. In time of war, however, an enemy alien is generally denied the right to enter into a binding contract. Rights he would normally have are held in abeyance.

CONVICTS

The common law denied convicted felons all rights to enter into or to sue on a contract. In the United States, convicts, for the most part, have full contractual capacity—they can make binding contracts and can use the courts for their enforcement. However, a contract entered into by a convict who is restrained from carrying out his obligations under the agreement because of his detention is void.

LEGAL PRINCIPLES

A voidable contract is valid but may be disaffirmed at the option of the party having grounds for refusing to perform.

A party to a contract must have full legal capacity in order to be legally bound to that contract.

An infant may avoid any contracts, except those involving the sale of real estate, and demand the consideration with which he has parted at any time during his minority and for a reasonable time after reaching his majority.

An infant is liable in quasi-contracts only for the reasonable value of necessaries received by him after proper consideration is given to his station in life. Contracts relating to the minor's estate, property, or business do not involve necessaries.

An infant who, by fraud, induces an adult to enter into a contract may rescind the agreement. However, he will incur tort liability for damages sustained by the adult as a result of the fraud.

A parent is liable for his children's torts if they are committed at his direction or in his presence when the children should have been controlled.

Insane persons may avoid contracts made before they were declared insane, but this action can be taken only during moments of legal sanity. Contracts made while legally insane are void.

Contracts made by persons intoxicated to the point where they are incapable of understanding the effect of their actions are voidable. Contracts made by a drunkard who has been declared legally incompetent and for whom a guardian has been appointed are void.

Contracts of aliens are valid and unvoidable, except in the case of enemy aliens in wartime, whose contracts may be held in abeyance until hostilities are ended.

Contracts made by a convict are valid unless he is restricted from performance by confinement.

CASE FOR REVIEW

STERNLIEB v. NORMANDIE NAT. SECURITIES CORPORATION

263 N.Y. 245, (1934)

Again we have the troublesome question arising from the repudiation by a young gentleman, just under twenty-one, of his contract of purchase. On the

21st day of September, 1929, the plaintiff purchased from the defendant five shares of the capital stock of the Bank of United States and of the Bankus Corporation, for which he paid $990. In his complaint he alleges that he was under twenty-one years of age. After the stock had dropped in value until it was worthless, this young plaintiff further alleges that on the 14th day of September, 1932, he notified the defendant that he rescinded his purchase, and that he was ready to tender and return the certificates.

The defendant as a defense alleges that the plaintiff falsely and fraudulently represented and warranted to the defendant before and at the time of purchase that he was over twenty-one years of age, and that the defendant relied upon these statements in parting with the stock.

At common law a male infant attains his majority when he becomes twenty-one years of age, and all unexecuted contracts made by him before that date, except for necessaries . . . are voidable at his election. In an action upon a contract made by an infant he is not estopped from pleading his infancy by any representation as to his age made by him to induce another person to contract with him. Neither could the infant be sued for damages in tort by reason of any false representations made in inducing or procuring the contract. For his torts generally, where they have no basis in any contract relation, an infant is liable, just as any other person would be, but the doctrine is equally well settled that a matter arising *ex contractu,* though infected with fraud, cannot be changed into a tort, in order to charge an infant, by a change of the remedy. The only difference between an executory and an executed contract appears to be, that in the former the infant may disaffirm at any time short of the period of the Statute of Limitations, unless by some act he has ratified the contract, whereas in the latter, he must disaffirm within a reasonable time after becoming of age, or his silence will be considered a ratification.

This case pertains to an executed contract for the purchase of stock which the plaintiff has disaffirmed within a reasonable time. The fundamental principle is the same, whether the infant be plaintiff or defendant. He may repudiate and rescind his contract upon becoming of age, whether he has made false representations regarding his years or not, and in any instance, the party with whom he had his dealings is entitled to recoup under certain circumstances.

That the false representation regarding age does not prevent rescission, even when the infant be the plaintiff, is the holding of the courts in the majority of our States.

Like so many questions of policy, there is much to be said upon both sides, and the necessities of one period of time are not always those of another. The law, from time out of mind, has recognized that infants must be protected from their own folly and improvidence. It is not always flattering to our young men in college and in business, between the ages of eighteen and twenty-one, to refer to them as infants, and yet this is exactly what the law considers them in their mental capacities and abilities to protect themselves in ordinary transactions and business relationships. That many young people under twenty-one years of age are improvident and reckless is quite evident, but these defects in judgment are by no means confined to the young. There is another side to the question. As long as young men and women, under twenty-one years of age, having the semblance and appearance of adults, are forced to make a living and enter into business transactions, how are the persons dealing with them to be protected if the infant's word cannot be taken or recognized at law? Are business men to deal with young people at their peril? Well, the law is as it is, and the duty of this court is to give force and effect to the decisions as we find them. Some States have met the situation by legislation.

Let us refer to the Iowa Code, as a fair example, taken from the case of *Friar v. Rae-Chandler Co.* (192 Iowa, 427, at p. 428):

> Sec. 3189. A minor is bound not only by contracts for necessaries, but also by his other contracts, unless he disaffirms them within a reasonable time after he attains his majority, and restores to the other party all money or property received by him by virtue of the contract, and remaining within his control at any time after his attaining his majority, except as otherwise provided.
>
> Sec. 3190. No contract can be thus disaffirmed in cases where, on account of the minor's own misrepresentations as to his majority, or from his having engaged in business as an adult, the other party had good reason to believe him capable of contracting.

CASE PROBLEMS

1. The plaintiff sold a horse, harness, and wagon to Carp, a minor, eighteen years of age. Carp had no use for the outfit except driving it for pleasure. Carp sold the harness and wagon, and the horse became so disabled that it had to be destroyed. The plaintiff brought suit for the unpaid balance of the purchase price. Carp disaffirmed the contract and sued for the amount paid on the contract. Decide.
2. Conn, while under age had made a contract with the Text Book Company for a course of study in engineering. Conn paid part of the price and received a set of books and lessons. Three months after he became of age, he made a $10 payment, but he did not work out any of the lessons. A month later he returned the books and the lessons, notifying the company that he was disaffirming the contract. The company sued Conn for the balance on the contract. Decide.
3. Lee, a minor, purchased an automobile on credit. When sued by Easy Credit, Inc., for the purchase price, he raised the defense that he was not liable because he was a minor when he made the contract. He was still a minor when he filed the answer. The court ruled that the automobile was a necessity because Lee used it for transportation to and from his place of employment. Was he responsible for the debt? Decide.
4. Freddie Frosh, a minor, was a student at Yale University. He rented rooms from Gregory for the school term of forty weeks at $30 per week, occupied the rooms for about three months, and then abandoned them and moved elsewhere. Gregory was unable to rent the rooms for the balance of the term and sued Frosh for the rent for the period of abandonment. Decide.
5. Fletcher, while a minor, purchased an unimproved city lot on a land contract that required a down payment and installments each month until a total of $300 was paid. The vendors were to pay the next year's taxes. About two months after he attained his majority, Fletcher wrote defendants asking the amount of taxes due on the lot for the year 1973 and also whether he should remit to them or to the county or city tax collector. Vendors replied that they had paid the taxes and that Fletcher should remit to them, but he never did so. When the first notes fell due, eight months after he had attained his majority, Fletcher disaffirmed the contract and brought an action to recover the money paid to defendants. Decide.

6. Joyce Jordan, minor daughter of defendants, injured her foot which became swollen, discolored, and painful. Her parents, thinking it only a sprain, did not provide medical aid. Garfield, discovering Joyce's plight, sent her to Dr. Green. He discovered that a bone had been fractured and applied a cast which he removed a month later. Her parents were aware of the situation, as Joyce lived at home. Dr. Green submitted a bill of $45 to the parents which they refused to pay. An action was brought to collect the fee. Decide.

7. The plaintiff was injured with a pellet fired from an air rifle by eight-year-old Richard Smith. Richard's father purchased the gun and gave it to his son. The gun was left in the child's room. Richard, while playing in the front yard, fired the gun at an object lying on the sidewalk and the pellet ricocheted and hit Masen as he was walking. Masen brought an action against the child's father. Decide.

8. Cart purchased a number of second-hand articles at an auction conducted by defendant. Cart at the time was actually insane, but he had not been declared incompetent to manage his affairs. Subsequently, a guardian brought this action to set aside the contract. Defendant when dealing with Cart acted in good faith and did not know that he was insane. Decide.

ILLEGALITY   13

A contract is essentially a private agreement between parties, and the subject matter is normally of concern only to the parties themselves. However, because a contract offers a means of protection under our legal system, it is also a legal relationship; its terms must therefore fall within the bounds of the law. They can in no way jeopardize the public interest by creating obligations for the parties the carrying out of which would violate public policy. Any agreement that creates unlawful obligations cannot become a contract, since by definition a contract is legal.

A discussion of illegality involves a consideration of the aspects of an agreement that may keep it from becoming a contract, and thus from being enforceable under the law. For since the legality of the relationship can be voided by the presence of illegal factors, so the rights that would normally be created under a contract agreement are voided also. Moreover, since no legal rights are created, there can be no remedies under the law for injuries sustained to one or more of the parties under an illegal agreement. The law gives no action to a party to an illegal contract, either to enforce it directly or to recover money paid on it after its execution. It will leave the parties where they are with their bargain.

Thus, individuals have the right to enter contracts voluntarily and as a means of forwarding their own interests, but the legal system retains the right to place restrictions on the terms of the contract in order to protect the public welfare from illegal agreements and denies enforcement of any illegal obligations under such agreements. To become a contract, an agreement must be free of illegalities.

WAGERING CONTRACTS

A *wager* is defined as *an agreement between two or more parties whereby they promise to pay money or transfer some other form of property dependant on the occurrence of an uncertain event.* In such transactions, what one party gains the other necessarily loses. For example, Mr. Wood and Mr. Patrick are at a football game. Wood bets Patrick $25 that Alabama will win the game, and Patrick bets $25 that Notre Dame will win. Each has assumed a risk of losing money, depending on the outcome of the game. Wagers are generally deemed contrary to public policy and in most states are contrary to positive law. However, some states have enacted lottery laws which legalize a form of gambling.

Many risks exist even in everyday transactions. When is an agreement a wager? Is Mrs. Wood's monthly church bingo game gambling? The courts indicate that where a party assumes or creates a new risk and promises to pay another person a consideration based upon the outcome of an uncertain event beyond the control of the party, the arrangement is a wager. In the example above the determining event—the outcome of the game—was assumed by the parties. Had Wood and Patrick been playing golf and bet on the outcome of the match, the wager would have involved a creation of risk by the parties.

A contract to purchase corporate securities or stocks, to the extent that it is not forbidden by statute, is legal if the agreement is so drawn that delivery must be accepted if tendered. If, however, the agreement and the transactions between the parties indicate an intention that delivery shall not be made on the future date, but only a settlement based on the difference between the contract price and the market price on that date, the arrangement is illegal. Such an agreement is deemed a wager because it allows the parties to gamble on the future course of the market. Since intention to perform is sometimes difficult to ascertain, the court must, in breach of contract suits, examine all available evidence contracts, business correspondence, past dealings, and anything else that might reveal the intent of the parties.

USURIOUS LOANS

Every state limits by statute the amount of interest that may be charged upon borrowed money or for the extension of the maturity of a debt. Any contract by which the lender is to receive more than the maximum allowed by statute is deemed usurious and is illegal. However, the law is not violated by collection of the legal maximum in advance; by collection, in addition to the maximum interest charge, of a service fee, provided that the fee is no larger than is reasonably necessary to cover the incidental cost of making the loan; or by charging a higher price for goods sold on credit than for goods sold for cash. It is likewise not usury to provide that if the principal is not paid on the due date the debtor must pay a rate higher than the legal rate, since he can avoid the excessive payment by being punctual.

It is usury, however, where the lender requires the borrower to purchase the desired property at an excessive price. Other similar devices are likewise illegal. It is usurious, for example, when the lender, as seller, transfers property to the buyer, who promises to pay at a future date an amount larger than the actual value of the property plus interest during the time period between the transfer of the property and the date of payment.

In some states the penalty for usury is the loss of all interest contracted above the legal rate; in some, all interest is forfeited; and in others the penalty may be a portion of or all the principal. Many statutes make the usurious contract void and without effect.

When a person lends the money of others, he may charge a commission in addition to the maximum rate. A commission may not be legally charged when a man lends his own funds, even though he has to borrow the money with which to make the loan and expects to sell the commercial paper shortly thereafter. An exception to this rule is made for corporations: bonds or notes of incorporated companies may in most states bear any rate a particular industry is willing to pay for money.

LIMITATIONS UPON LIABILITY

The parties to a contract may ordinarily agree upon the nature and extent of their respective liabilities; but where an assignment of liability involves one party dealing with the public, the law does not assume the bargaining position as being equal. Any business that may be considered a public business by reason of its nature, consequence, and effects on the community is not permitted to relieve itself of any liability that might result from its own negligence.

Public utilities and other quasi-public enterprises are denied the right to relieve themselves by contract of responsibility for their own carelessness. A public carrier which in its contract provides that it will not be liable for loss or damage to property entrusted to it, even though the damage is caused by its own negligence, is nevertheless liable. The provision is contrary to public policy and is thus illegal and unenforceable.

RESTRAINT OF TRADE

Contracts that provide for the restraint of trade or the limitation of competition are generally deemed to be illegal. Agreements by companies within an industry not to compete, to divide the market, to maintain prices, to limit production, to pool the business, to divide the profits, for exclusive dealing, or for tie-in sales are contrary to public policy.

Contracts for partial restraint of trade may be valid (1) if such restraint has reference to and is part of the sale of property, a business, or a profession or the discontinuance of employment and (2) if such restraint is reasonably necessary for the protection of the purchaser or the employer. For example, when a seller sells a going business, including its good will, he may promise the buyer that he will not set up a competing business within a certain geographic area for a certain period of time. Such a contract is valid if the limits it sets are reasonable and are needed to protect the buyer. Precautions for the preservation of the good will of a business that does not substantially lessen competition or create a monopoly in any line of commerce are always legal.

AGREEMENTS TO INFLUENCE GOVERNMENTAL ACTION

In certain instances agreements are entered into whereby one of the parties promises to use his personal influence in regard to certain governmental actions. Included in this type of arrangement are contracts intended to influence legislative, executive, or administrative action or to influence the obtaining of public contracts.

Any agreement designed to make use of personal contacts and influence in procuring governmental action if by its nature contrary to public policy and is void because the resultant action is not based upon the merits of the case. All agreements tending to injure the public service by improper influence exerted on an administrative, executive, legislative or judicial officer are contrary to public policy. The question of public policy depends upon the purpose of the agreement and not the amount of actual harm that it inflicts upon the public. In other words, any agreement the purpose of which is to create a situation that is potentially harmful to the public interest is void even though actual injury cannot be shown.

The federal lobbying law is the Federal Regulation of Lobbying Act, 60 Stat. 839-842, 2 U.S.C.A. Sections 261-270 (1946). It provides for the registration of those persons who attempt to influence legislation by Congress, requiring such information as name and business address, name and adress of employer, and salary. Violators may incur fines, imprisonment, or both, and be prohibited from engaging in further lobbying activity for a period of years. State laws attempt to accomplish the same thing as the federal law. However, violations usually do not call for the imposition of criminal or civil charges, but merely for revocation or suspension of their certificate of registration.

One may enter into a valid contract to lobby for the purpose of influencing governmental action as long as such action is taken openly and is done upon the merits of the proposition. For example, one may enter into a valid contract to carry on investigations, assemble data, hire experts to explain the data to the governmental body, prepare arguments to be presented to governmental committees, and to engage in other similar activities to promote the merits of a particular position. It is contrary to the public interest when the contract contemplates the use of threats, bribery, and other improper means of influence. In this area the line between proper and improper action is often a thin one.

CONTRACTS WITH UNLICENSED PARTIES

Frequently contracts are negotiated with unlicensed persons engaged in businesses that require a license from a governmental body. The question of the legality of these arrangements when they are made with a person who does not possess a license depends on the objective of the licensing statute. Where the statute is designed to afford a measure of protection for the public by setting up standards of professional competence, the contract is illegal and unenforceable. On the other hand, if the statute simply establishes a technical requirement whose only purpose is to raise revenue, the contract is generally held to be enforceable.

EFFECT OF ILLEGALITY

If a contract is illegal, it is generally unenforceable by either party, regardless of whether one or both have partially or even fully performed their obligations. They cannot recover damages for breach of their illegal promises, nor for consideration with which they have parted, nor, in quasi-contract, for the benefits conferred or their value. In other words, the courts will leave the parties to an illegal bargain in exactly the position in which it finds them and will simply uphold the status quo. If a contract is for the sale of goods prohibited by statute and one of the parties makes delivery, neither the goods nor their value may be recovered. However, if the facts and circumstances are such that the interests of the public are best served by allowing a recovery, such a recovery will be granted. If the situation is such that one party did not intend an illegal act, he is generally permitted either to recover any consideration paid or to avoid the contract. For example, a broker employed to make contracts for grain futures for a principal who does not intend to deliver if the market price falls may recover a commission if he did not know of his principal's intention to breach the contract.

Sometimes the courts are faced with contracts not wholly illegal but containing some illegal portions. Where it is possible to do so, they will enforce the terms that are legal and refuse enforcement for other portions of the agreement. For example, if an agreement exists to sell x for $50 and y for $20, the sale of x will be enforced even if the sale of y is declared to be illegal. If the agreement is indivisible, none of its terms are enforceable. In the preceding example, an agreement to sell x and y together for $75 will be illegal because the consideration cannot be apportioned between the two items.

LEGAL PRINCIPLES

A contract can be judged illegal if it is explicitly forbidden by statute or if it is contrary to public policy.

Contracts that are wagers, dependent mostly on chance, are expressly prohibited by statute in most states.

Lending arrangements that charge more than the maximum amount of interest set by state statutes are illegal and unenforceable.

Any contract made by a business which is public in nature that by its terms seeks to avoid the legal liability of that business for its own negligence is considered to be contrary to public policy.

A contract that restrains trade or obstructs the workings of government or justice by illegal means is deemed unenforceable by the courts.

An illegal contract is generally unenforceable by either party; neither party may obtain legal relief for nonperformance. An innocent party may be able to avoid the agreement.

If a contract can clearly be divided into legal and illegal portions and if the legal parts can stand by themselves, the contract can be enforced to the extent that it is legal.

CASE FOR REVIEW

WEBB v. FULCHIRE

25 N.C. 485 (1843)

The defendant had three acorn cups and a white ball, which he placed under one of the cups in the presence of the plaintiff. The defendant proposed to bet the plaintiff twenty dollars that he could not tell which one of the three cups the ball was under. The plaintiff bet him that he could, and thereupon staked twenty dollars. The plaintiff pointed to the cup, and bet that the ball was under that one. The defendant raised the cup and the ball was not there. The money staked was then paid over to the defendant as being won by him. In the same way the defendant won twenty dollars more, which was in like manner paid over to him . . .

It is not denied that the law gives no action to a party to an illegal contract, either to enforce it directly, or to recover . . . money paid on it after its execution. Nor is it doubted that money, fairly lost at play at a forbidden game and paid, cannot be recovered in an action for money had and received. But it is perfectly certain, that money, won by cheating at any kind of game, whether allowed or forbidden, and paid by the loser without a knowledge of the fraud, may be recovered. A wager won by such undue means is not won in the view of the law, and, therefore, the money is paid without consideration and by mistake, and may be recovered. That, we think, was plainly this case. The bet was that the plaintiff could not tell, which of the three cups covered the ball. Well, the case states that the defendant put the ball under a particular one of the cups, and the plaintiff selected that cup, as the one under which the ball was. Thus we must understand the case, because it states as a fact, that the defendant "placed the ball under one of the cups," and that the plaintiff "pointed to the cup," that is, the one under which he had seen the ball put, as being that which still covered it. We are not told how this matter was managed, nor do we pretend to know the secret. But it is indubitable, that the ball was, by deceit, not put under the cup, as the defendant had made the plaintiff believe, and under which belief he had drawn him into the wager; or that, after it was so placed, it was privily and artfully removed either before or at the time the cup was raised. If the former be the truth of the case, there was a false practice and gross deception upon the very point, that induced the laying of the wager, namely, that the ball was actually put under the cup. For, clearly, the words and acts of the defendant amount to a representation that such was the fact; and indeed the case states it as the fact. Hence, and because we cannot suppose the vision of the plaintiff to have been so illuded, we rather presume the truth to be that the ball was actually placed where the defendant pretended to place it, that is to say, under the particular cup which the plaintiff designated as covering it. Then the case states that the defendant rai ed that cup and the ball was not there; a physical impossibility, unless it had been removed by some contrivance and sleight of hand by the defendant. Unquestionably it was affected by some such means; for presently we find the defendant in possession of the ball, ready for a repetition of the bet and the same artifice. Such a transaction cannot for a moment be regarded as a wager, depending on a future and uncertain event; but it was only a pretended wager, to be determined by a contingency in shew only, but in fact by a trick in jugglery by one of the parties, practiced upon the unknowing and unsuspecting simplicity and credulity of the other. Surely, the artless fool, who seems to have been alike bereft of his senses and his money, is not to be deemed a partaker in the same crime . . . with the juggling knave, who gulled and fleeced him. The whole was a downright and undeniable cheat; and the plaintiff parted with his money under the mistaken belief that it had been fairly won from him, and, therefore, may recover it.

CASE PROBLEMS

1. Casualty Company carried the insurance on an elevator in the Exchange Building and paid damages resulting when the elevator fell from the third floor of the building to the basement, injuring the passengers. Suit was brought to recover the amount of the loss from the Elevator Company, defendant, which had installed the elevator and had contracted to inspect it regularly and to service and repair it whenever necessary to keep it in condition as a passenger elevator. A provision of the contract provided that the Elevator Company should not be liable for injury resulting from any defects in the elevator. Decide.

2. Jones contracted with the telephone company for a substantial amount of telephone connections. The attorney general of the state requested the telephone company to cancel this contract because the lines were being used to furnish illegal information to "bookies." The telephone company threatened to discontinue their services and cancel their contract to Jones, whereupon a suit for injunction was brought to prevent the threatened breach of contract. Decide.

3. Plaintiff published a newspaper which was generally favorable to Democratic policies. The defendant, Page, was running for the Republican nomination for Congress. The plaintiff agreed to support Page through his paper, it being agreed that the charges would be higher if Page won the nomination than otherwise. Plaintiff brought an action to collect the bill for advertising. Decide.

4. Foco and Magg were in the business of growing, harvesting, and marketing carrots. Foco made a contract with Magg to harvest beans on Magg's land, market them, and divide the profits with Magg. The market price of beans rose greatly above the price at the time of the contract, and Magg refused to allow Foco to harvest the full quantity specified. Magg thereby obtained a $30,000 profit for himself by reselling the beans. When Foco sued for breach of contract, Magg raised the defense that Foco had failed to obtain a license as a "dealer" or "cash buyer" under the state Agricultural Code, and that, therefore, their contract was invalid. Decide.

5. Ricks, a real estate salesman, negotiated a lease for his employers, Backer & Thorp, who were real estate brokers. A broker's commission was charged for securing the lease, and assignment of this amount was made to plaintiff, who brought suit to recover the commission. A state statute required that real estate salesmen be licensed, pronouncing it a criminal offense to act as a salesman without a license. Ricks did not hold such a license when negotiations for the lease were in progress. Defendants refused payment, claiming that since the salesman was not licensed the contract for a commission was unlawful. Decide.

6. Craig paid $2500 for an option to purchase certain property. Because the property was not fully insured, Craig procured fire insurance from defendant company. Thereafter a fire loss was incurred. The insurance company refused to pay the loss and charged as a defense that the policy was void because Craig did not have an insurable interest in the property. This action was brought to collect on the policy. Decide.

7. Defendant operated a restaurant in which he illegally sold alcoholic beverages. He also legally operated a billiard hall in connection with the restaurant. He employed plaintiff to render services in the billiard hall and in selling the liquor. When defendant failed to pay him, plaintiff sued. Decide.

8. Wells was the owner and publisher of a matrimonial journal called *The New Cupid* and he also operated a matrimonial brokerage bureau. Miss Duval paid Wells a fee to find her a husband. She was not willing to marry any of the men to whom she was introduced by Wells and sued to recover the fee paid. Decide.

REALITY OF CONSENT　　　14

Contractual relationships are usually entered into by parties who are acting voluntarily and who fully understand the legal consequences of their actions. A contract is ideally a consensual transaction in which each party has given his unqualified approval, or assent, to the terms of the bargain. Such consent can be based only on a proper meeting of the minds of the contracting parties; in actual business situations, however, the conditions under which a contract was created may have been such that the approval, or consent, of one of the parties was not given on a truly voluntary basis or was given based on some fact not in reality part of the contract. An investigation of the bargaining period may reveal the presence of factors that will undermine the validity of the contractual agreement. Such shortcomings, whether voluntary or involuntary and whether attributable to mistake, misrepresentation, fraud, duress, undue influence, or other factors, have the effect of nullifying the contract, since no true meeting of the minds occurred as a basis for voluntary consent.

No contract will be recognized or enforced unless the parties involved have agreed upon the same thing in the same sense. Moreover, anything that would destroy the basic presumption of voluntary action by the parties is considered grounds for avoiding liability on the contract. A meeting of minds on a contract must be free from mistake, misrepresentation, fraud, duress, and undue influence; otherwise, one of the legal essentials of a contract is not present, and a legal remedy can be employed to avoid liability.

MISTAKE

A mistaken notion of fact or of law that is acted upon by one or both of the parties to a contract will invalidate the contract. The underlying assumption is that had the parties known the true nature of the conditions, they would not have given their assent to the agreement. The mistaken belief may be in the minds of both parties (a mutual mistake) or one party (a unilateral mistake). The mistake may relate to the circumstances of the agreement or to a proper understanding of the legal relationships being created. However, a mistake based on lack of attentiveness to stated facts, as when a party fails to read the fine print of an agreement before giving his consent, will not be sufficient grounds for avoiding a contract.

MISTAKES OF FACT

If both parties act on a mistake of fact regarding an essential element of the contract, such as the identity or quantity of the things they are negotiating about, the contract is voidable by either party. The law, however, will not grant relief merely on the ground that one or both parties thinks that the contract resulted in a bad deal. To be entitled to relief, both parties must have contracted in the mistaken belief that certain material facts were true, although the mistake may relate to existing or past facts. While the courts occasionally grant relief for mistakes pertaining to future events or facts, it is generally held that contracting parties must assume the risk of possible future events.

For example, Mr. Wood agrees to sell his house to Mr. Patrick and Mr. Patrick agrees to buy it. At the time the contract is entered into the house has been destroyed by fire; however, both parties believe it to be in good condition. The contract in this case will be voidable by either party.

If the mistake is unilateral, that is, if only one party is mistaken about a material fact, no relief will be granted. Since such mistakes are usually the result of negligence, the court will hold the mistaken party to his contract. However, when the other party knows or should know of the first party's mistake but remains silent, the court will grant relief to the mistaken party, since it will not allow one party to knowingly take advantage of another's mistake.

MISTAKES OF LAW

Where the contracting parties make a mutual mistake about the legal relationships involved in their agreement, they are usually required to carry out their contract. Everyone is presumed to know the law and ignorance of it is no excuse. However, where the mistake concerns the laws of another state or those of a foreign country, this presumption is not applicable. The parties are responsible only for understanding the legal effect of local contract law.

MISREPRESENTATION

It sometimes happens in contract relationships that one party induces the other to enter into the contract by unintentionally misstating a material fact or by unintentionally failing to disclose a material fact. Either circumstance is closely related to fraud, but each differs in that the untrue statement is made innocently; in cases of fraud, the statement made is known to be false or is made with reckless disregard for the truth. Misrepresentation of a material fact that becomes the basis for a party's entrance into a contractual relationship is grounds for the recission of the contract. Insofar as misrepresentation is an involuntary form of invalidation, both parties to the contract are restored to their original positions and each returns any benefits he has received. Where the consideration used in the contract is in the form of goods, the goods may be returned in kind or their market value may be repaid in the form of currency. If a service has been rendered, the party receiving the service must pay an amount commensurate with the value of the work.

The words "material fact" are most important in misrepresentation cases. A statement of material fact relates to something that exists at present or that has taken place in the past. Moreover, this statement, in a case involving misrepresentation, must have a moving influence upon the conduct of the contracting party. Did it induce the contract? Would the party have made the contract had he known the truth? Statements of *material fact* are to be distinguished from statements of *opinion*. The latter have to do with incidental facts or value judgments and cannot be used as grounds for relief. There is no right to rely on a statement of opinion as an inducement unless it is made by an expert.

FRAUD

Fraud is the *intentional misrepresentation by one party to a contract of a material fact which is relied upon by the other party to his injury.* Before a party to a contract can be held guilty of fraud, it must be established that (1) a false representation has been made or a material fact has been concealed, (2) the misrepresentation has been made knowingly or with reckless disregard for the truth, (3) the misrepresentation has been made with the intent to deceive and for the purpose of inducing the other party to act upon it, (4) the party who is the victim of the misrepresentation has, in fact, acted in reliance upon it, (5) the victim has suffered a loss of injury as a result of his action.

The misrepresentation need not be a direct falsehood for fraud to be present. There is, in fact, no need to make a statement at all to have fraud; failure to reveal defects or confirming false impressions by remaining silent, is sufficient. If one party by his concealment, his actions, or some other means deliberately induces another to enter into a contract he would not have entered into had he known all the facts, fraud is present.

To constitute actionable fraud, the misrepresentation must be of *a material fact.* (This requirement rules out statements of opinion, sales talk, and the like.) A material fact may be defined as *a fact that induced the contract.* The prime test for fraud is to ask, "Would the other party have entered into the contract had he known the truth?" If one party asks no questions about a material fact before entering into a contract and the other party fails to disclose the truth about it, there is no misrepresentation. Expert opinions may lead to fraud if they amount to deliberately false statements made by a recognized professional in the field, whose opinions may reasonably be relied upon in the contract. Opinions, however, must be in regard to an existing or past fact and not to forecasts or predictions.

Before an injured party can claim fraud, he must show that he entered the contract in reliance upon the false statements or misrepresentations of the other party. However, the courts will deny him the right to bring suit if he had the means to determine the truth of the statements. The courts demand that a person use reasonable caution and employ his powers of observation and that he not rely entirely on statements made by the other party. He need not, however, go to any great trouble or expense to ascertain the true facts.

If a party has been induced to enter a contract by fraud, he has a choice of two remedies. He may rescind the contract, return what he has received, and recover what he gave; or he can retain the benefits and bring suit in tort for what he has suffered as a result of the fraud. The measure of damages in the latter situation would approximate the difference between the value of the contract as it was represented to him and its actual value. Finally, the injured party may choose to be bound by the contract even after he becomes aware of its fraudulent nature.

DURESS

It is presumed that the parties to a valid contractual transaction entered into the agreement voluntarily after considering the terms presented to them. If one party forces the other to enter into a contract against his will, the voluntary aspect of the agreement is negated and the injured party may avoid any obligations assumed under the contract. The condition of duress is defined as *a threat to a person's safety, property, or liberty that induces in him such fear or apprehension that he is incapable of exercising free will.* To constitute duress, not only must a threat have been made, but the party threatened must believe that the other party has the present ability to carry out the threat. Examples of duress include: a threat of bodily harm; actual bodily harm; a threat to retain another's property; a threat to destroy another's property; and a threat of criminal prosecution, regardless of the person's guilt. The threat may be to a close relative and still be considered as affecting the person's free will. Whether duress exists must also be determined from the circumstances of the transaction since susceptibility to coercive influence is not uniform. For example, women are considered more susceptible than men, older persons more susceptible than younger ones, and persons of ill health more susceptible than those who are well. These and similar factors will be considered in determining whether duress is present in such form as to negate a person's liability under a contract.

UNDUE INFLUENCE

Undue influence is another instance in which the purportedly voluntary act of one of the parties to a contract is in reality not voluntary. In other words, a contract may be obtained without genuine assent from a weak, dependent party by someone in a dominating position. Whenever the defense of undue influence is raised as grounds for inferring that a contract was not the result of a voluntary act, there must be evidence of a close relationship of trust and confidence between the parties. The situation may be that of an elderly person or a person in the care of another who comes to rely upon that latter for advice in business transactions. Or it may be the result of a confidential relationship, such as that of a guardian and ward, husband and wife, or attorney and client. In these cases, the stronger person may take advantage of the situation to force an inequitable contract on the weaker either by virtue of his influence or by his advice. Undue influence, therefore, is a kind of mental coercion that destroys the free will of one party and induces him to do that which is against his will. Undue influence renders the contract voidable at the option of the person upon whom such influence is exercised.

REFORMATION OF WRITTEN AGREEMENTS

An equity court will correct a written instrument that, through a mistake or oversight of both parties, does not conform with the parties' intentions. The final draft of the contract may omit a provision that was intended to be included or include a provision that the parties had agreed to omit. Normally the parol-evidence rule forbids the introduction of any oral or written evidence that might alter the terms of a written agreement. However, if it can be shown that a mistake has been made in reducing the contract to writing, it will be changed to conform with the original intention of the parties. A court will alter the writing to conform with the agreement, unless the rights of innocent third parties have intervened. This is called reforming written agreements. It is an equitable remedy, the purpose of which is to make a mistaken writing conform to the previous agreement of the parties.

TIME LIMIT ON AVOIDANCE

Whenever the defense of mistake, misrepresentation, fraud, duress, or undue influence gives one party the right to avoid a contract, he must exercise that right within a reasonable time or be obligated on the contract. As in other situations, what constitutes a reasonable time depends on the circumstances of the case. The "limit of avoidance" is the period of time the injured party has either to avoid the contract or to accept the obligation.

LEGAL PRINCIPLES

A material fact is an inducing cause of the contract.

A mistake is an erroneous belief by one or both parties about the existence of some material fact of the contract.

Misrepresentation is the unintentional misstatement or concealment of a material fact.

Fraud is the intentional misstatement or concealment of some material fact that induces another to enter into the contract.

Duress of undue influence exists when one party is coerced into entering a contract by threats or by some other means that prevent him from exercising his free will.

Contracts entered into for any of these reasons are void or voidable.

The courts demand that a person use reasonable caution and employ his powers of observation in entering a contract; ignorance of readily ascertainable facts is not grounds for avoidance.

Before the courts will grant relief in cases of fraud, the plaintiff must show that he suffered a loss.

The injured party must bring his action within a reasonable time in order to avoid the contract.

CASE FOR REVIEW

GEREMIA v. BOYARSKI ET AL.

107 Conn. 387 (1928)

The defendants are carpenters and building contractors, and in April . . . the plaintiff requested them to submit bids for the carpenter work and painting for a house that he was building for himself. The defendants met in the evening of April 25th for the purpose of making their estimates, but did not complete their figures, owing to the lateness of the hour. They wrote their figures on two separate pieces of paper, but did not add the figures. The next morning the plaintiff called upon the defendants, and requested the defendant Boyarsky to stop the work that he was upon and complete the estimate. Boyarsky sat down with the plaintiff at a workbench, and proceeded to add up the various items upon the two sheets. In his haste, he made an error in adding the items on the first sheet, footing them up at $99.10, when the correct footing should have been $859.10. This error, being carried to the second sheet, made the apparent cost of the work $1450.40 instead of $2210.40. The plaintiff thereupon awarded the contract to the defendants, and later the same day they executed a written contract to do the work for the sum of $1450.40. The plaintiff, when the erroneous bid was given, and when he procured the signing of the contract, had good reason to believe and know that there must have been a substantial omission or error in the amount of the bid. That evening the defendants discovered their mistake, and offered to go forward with the work according to the actual prices carried out in their estimate, and as low as any responsible contractor would do it for, if less than $2210.40. The plaintiff refused their offer, and insisted that they complete the work for $1450.40. The sum of $2375 was a reasonable price for the work covered by the defendants' contract, and the plaintiff thereafter let the contract for the work to other contractors for that sum. . . .

The finding discloses a case where the defendants, by reason of an error in computation, have obligated themselves to perform a contract for a sum substantially less than the sum which the actual figures of their estimate totaled, and less than the reasonable cost of the work contracted to be done. It is the contention of the plaintiff that equity should not relieve the defendants from the consequences of their mistake, because (a) it was a unilateral mistake; (b) is was not material to the making of the contract; and (c) it resulted from the defendants' own negligence. While the mistake of only one of the parties inducing him to sign a contract cannot be a ground for a reformation of the contract, it may be ground for its cancellation. . . . Though the mistake was not induced by the conduct of the other party, equity will grant relief, if the latter, when he becomes aware of the mistake, seeks to take an unconscionable advantage of it. . . . The plaintiff, though he is found by the court not to have participated in the mistake, had good reason to believe that one had been made before the contract was signed, was notified of the mistake by the defendants before he had changed his position in any respect, and sought to take unfair advantage of it by insisting upon the performance of the contract at a price upon which the minds of the parties had never met. When the contract is still executory and the parties can be put in statu[s] quo, one party to the contract will not be permitted to obtain an unconscionable advantage merely because the mistake was unilateral. . . .

That a mistake through which the defendants agreed to perform the contract for a price one-third less than the total of the actual figures, of their estimate was of so essential and fundamental a character that the minds of the parties never met would not seem to require discussion. . . .

It may be conceded that the error in addition made by the defendant Boyarsky, when he hastily totaled the items of his estimate at the request of the plaintiff, involved some degree of negligence. It would be inequitable under the circumstances to permit the plaintiff, who had good reason to know, before the contract was signed, that there must have been a substantial omission or error in the amount of the bid, to take advantage of such error while the contract was still executory, and he had been in no way prejudiced, and to require the defendants to do the work for an amount much less than the actual cost. In similar situations when a price has been bid which, because of erroneous arithmetical processes, or by the ommission of items, was based on a mistake, rescission has been allowed where the contract was still executory, and it would be inequitable to permit the other party to gain an unfair advantage from a mistake which has not prejudiced him in any way.

The mistake of the defendants was of so fundamental a character that the minds of the parties did not meet. It was not, under the circumstances, the result of such culpable negligence as to bar the defendants to redress, and the plaintiff, before the contract was signed, had good reason to believe that a substantial error had been made, and, while the contract was still executory, and he had been in no way prejudiced, refused to permit the correction of the error, and attempted to take an unconscionable advantage of it. The defendants were clearly entitled to a decree canceling the contract.

CASE PROBLEMS

1. An action was brought to recover the $480 balance due under a contract for the purchase of a cash register. Smith bought a cash register relying on the seller's statement that its use would save the expense of a bookkeeper and half the clerk's time. Smith alleged that these assertions were false and sought to rescind the sale on the ground of fraud. Decide.
2. The Ranch Company bought a herd of cattle from Stewart, who prevented the purchasing agent from making inquiries on his own account as to the truth of Stewart's representation regarding the number of calves branded. The inquiries would have revealed the fact that a number of the cattle had recently been lost. The Ranch Company sued for fraud. Decide.
3. Pumpper orally agreed to buy a year's supply of gasoline from plaintiff, with the understanding that the agreement was to be put in writing, Plaintiff's agent presented two documents to Pumpper, telling him that they embodied the oral agreement, and defendant signed them without reading them. One of the documents was a lease of Pumpper's filling station to plaintiff at a nominal rent. Plaintiff brought suit, based on the lease, for possession of the premises. Decide.
4. The American National Bank, administrator of decedent's estate, sold her personal effects at auction. At this sale, West bought a box of the decedent's old

clothes for $9.50. It was later discovered that in a pocket of a bathrobe in this box were two rings with a value of $2500. On learning of their discovery the administrator brought suit to recover the rings. Decide.

5. Plaintiff collided with an oil truck driven by defendant. Plaintiff's wife was killed in the accident. Plaintiff sued to recover damages for wrongful death. Defendant pleaded a release from all liability signed by plaintiff. Plaintiff alleged that he signed it because the insurance told him it would settle everything and "we will drop the manslaughter charge." Decide.

6. Kleaner sold Sudds a car wash for $17,000. An action was brought to rescind the sale. Sudds showed that Kleaner made fraudulent representations concerning the income from the business, which he relied upon to his damage of $11,200. Sudds was told that the business had earned $450 to $600 a week during the preceding year. Sudds swore that the record of weekly earnings shown to him covered only part of July and August. He admitted that Kleaner did nothing to prevent him from examining the books. Decide.

7. Defendant gave plaintiff an option to purchase his hotel for $65,000. Plaintiff exercised the option and tendered the proper sum to defendant, who refused it because the land had gone up in value about 50 percent after a decision by the Standard Car Company to locate its plant in that neighborhood. The rumor that some company proposed to establish a manufacturing plant nearby was known to both parties at the time the option was taken. Plaintiff brought an action to enforce the alleged contract. Decide.

8. Francois Valbert executed deeds to two of his children for the purposes of equalizing his property amongst his five children. Francois was eighty-four years old at the time and somewhat childish. His actions were erratic. Franklin, another son, sought to set aside these deeds on the ground of undue influence of the children to whom the property was conveyed. Decide.

Certain classes of contracts, although they fulfill the legal requisites of a valid contract, are not enforceable in the courts unless they are reduced to writing. The written contract has been a general requisite of legal enforceability for certain classes of agreements in Anglo-American law since the passsage by the English Parliament in 1677 of the Statute of Frauds. When a written contract is the subject of a lawsuit, the writing must be produced as evidence of the agreement at the trial or the courts will not grant the relief requested by the injured party. The courts will enforce an oral agreement unless the Statute of Frauds is raised as a defense. If the plaintiff cannot prove with reasonable certainty the terms of the contract, the defendant may claim the protection of the Statute. When a contract, falls within the Statute, oral evidence is not allowed.

WHAT THE STATUTE COVERS

The Statute of Frauds applies to the enforcement of executory contracts. If both parties have fully performed their obligations under an agreement the courts treat the bargain as binding and allow it to stand. It does not cover contracts implied in law or quasi-contracts. Although the law may vary somewhat from state to state, the following kinds of agreements are generally protected by the Statute:

CONTRACTS MADE BY AN EXECUTOR OR ADMINISTRATOR IN A REPRESENTATIVE CAPACITY TO PAY DEBTS OF THE ESTATE OUT OF HIS OWN PERSONAL FUNDS

Usually an executor is a person or a corporation named in a decedent's will to administer the distribution of his estate. An administrator is appointed by the court to act as executor where none is named in the will or where the named executor either refuses to perform or is incapable of performing his duties. Persons having the responsibility of executor or administrator sometimes make promises for the benefit of the survivors of the decendent. Promises made in a representative capacity to answer for the debts or liabilities of the deceased out of his (the representative's) personal assets must be in writing to be enforceable.

CONTRACTS TO GUARANTEE THE DEBTS, DEFAULTS, OR OBLIGATIONS OF ANOTHER

In a contract of this nature, one party promises another that he will be responsible for the debts or obligations of a third person. A promise to pay another's bills or to settle accounts on any of his wrongful acts if he does not settle them himself is a guaranty of payment and must be in writing to be valid. The Statute does not apply if the promisor agreed to be solely liable for the debt in the first place and it was understood that the third party was not liable for payment. Nor does it apply when the promise is made to benefit the promisor and not the third party.

CONTRACTS THAT CANNOT BE COMPLETED WITHIN ONE YEAR FROM THE DATE ON WHICH THE AGREEMENT IS MADE

If the terms of an executory contract make it impossible to fully perform the agreement within one year of the date of the agreement, neither side is obligated to perform unless he has signed a written memorandum as evidence of the contract. If the terms of the contract are such that it is possible, however remotely, to complete performance within the year, an oral agreement is enforceable. For example, it is generally held that a contract of employment intended to continue for the life of an employee need not be in writing. It is possible that such a contract may be completed within one year of its inception. When one party fully performs an agreement that requires longer than a year to complete and the other party accepts the benefit of his performance, an oral agreement is enforceable. The period included by the Statute begins on the date on which the contract is entered into by the parties, not on the date of the start of performance.

CONTRACTS MADE IN CONSIDERATION OF MARRIAGE

The Statute does not refer to the marriage contract itself, the mutual promises to marry, but to agreements made by parties prior to marriage in which they accept obligations not ordinarily included in the implied obligations of marriage itself. For example, a promise of a property settlement for the wife after marriage is within the Statute. Sometimes one person promises to do something for another if the other marries or agrees to marry some third person. When marriage is the consideration for the payment of money or the transfer of property, the promisor is not required to carry out the promise unless he signs a memorandum. Oral premarital agreements are enforceable under the Statute; consequently the wife cannot, after the wedding, seek enforcement on the ground that she has performed her end of the bargain.

CONTRACTS FOR THE TRANSFER OF AN INTEREST IN REAL PROPERTY

All contracts for the sale of real property or an interest therein must be evidenced by a written memorandum. Real property transactions have always been looked upon as formal and of a most serious nature because of the finality of transfer of rights irreplaceable by the owner. These contracts include agreements concerning portions of the surface of the land, the earth below, and the space above. They may refer to buildings and their improvements attached to the land or to the natural products of the land, such as timber and minerals, if title is to pass before serverance.

An exception to thus rule is made where a party occupies real property under an oral agreement and makes substantial changes, or alterations, in the property. The alterations must have been made in reliance upon the oral promise of the seller and before the Statute was invoked by the other party. Where the courts feel that they cannot return the parties to their former position, they will enforce an oral agreement.

CONTRACTS FOR THE SALE OF PERSONAL PROPERTY VALUED AT $500 OR MORE

Due to the great number of sales of personal property, the Statute of Frauds necessitates a written memorandum only when the purchase price is above a figure designated by state statute. The Uniform Commercial Code sets this amount at $500.

The section of the Statute dealing with personal property applies both to contracts to sell and to present sales of goods. It does not apply to articles that are to be altered or specifically manufactured by the seller for the buyer, even if the price exceeds the minimum amount; nor does it apply to agreements for the purchase of items not suitable for sale in the seller's ordinary line of business. These agreements do not require written contracts to make them enforceable where it can be shown that the seller has obligated himself to begin manufacture. Oral agreements, if proved, will be satisfactory. Also, oral contracts will be enforced to the extent that partial payment for delivery of goods has been made.

NATURE OF THE WRITING REQUIRED BY THE STATUTE

Where a written contract is required the Statute demands only that the agreement be in writing and that it state all the essential terms of the contract. No particular form is required; the terms may be contained in one document or a number of letters, telegrams, or other pieces of paper. Whatever documents are offered in evidence, they must be connected, consistent, and complete.

To be complete, the written agreement, or memorandum, should contain the following information:

1. essential terms of the contract;
2. identification of the subject matter of the contract;
3. names and identities of the parties to the contract; and
4. signature of the party to be charged.

The signature of each party to the agreement should be the one he ordinarily uses in business transactions, although the law does not make this requirement. It may be printed. It may be an initial, a mark, or any other symbol, as long as the party intends to authenticate the document. The signature need not appear at the end of the memorandum, but it must appear somewhere and must be readily identifiable. Written evidence of an agreement makes it enforceable only against the party or parties who have signed it. In other words, it must be signed by the defendant or his agent. The writing need not be in existence at the time the contract is make, but it must exist before any legal action can be taken to enforce the terms of the agreement.

EFFECT OF NO WRITING

Any contract that requires a writing dates from the time of the oral agreement but is unenforceable until written evidence is produced. The Statute does not prevent the existence of a valid contract, but requires written evidence to establish it. Anyone who is prevented from enforcing a contract because the defense of the Statute of Frauds is successfully raised may recover from the party who has benefited the value of any services, property furnished, or money transferred under the oral agreement. If the performance consists of goods or services, their value in money must be paid. For the purpose of determining value, the terms of the oral contract are admissible as evidence of what the parties intended. When the party who raises the defense of the statute has performed, most courts hold that he is not entitled to restitution as long as the other party is ready and willing to perform.

LEGAL PRINCIPLES

The Statute of Frauds applies only to executory contracts.

The following types of contracts require a writing to be enforceable under the Statute:

1. contracts made by an executor or administrator in a representative capacity to pay the debts of the decedent's estate out of his personal funds;
2. contracts to guarantee debts, defaults, or settlements for the wrongdoings of another;
3. contracts that cannot possibly be completed within one year from the date on which agreement is made;
4. contracts made in consideration of marriage;
5. contracts for the sale of an interest in real property; and
6. contracts for the sale of personal property valued at $500 or more.

Partial payment or partial delivery of personal property under an oral agreement make the agreement enforceable to the extent of the partial payment or partial delivery.

An oral contract for the sale of real property will be enforced if one of the parties makes such changes in the property that he cannot be returned to his former position.

The sale of specially manufactured items is outside the Statute. A special item is one that is not resalable in the seller's ordinary line of business.

Any contract that requires a writing dates from the time of the oral agreement but is unenforceable until written evidence is produced.

Where the defense of the Statute of Frauds is successfully raised, the plaintiff may recover in quasi-contract anything that he transferred to the other party under an oral agreement. If there is conflict as to the extent of recovery, the oral agreement is admissible in evidence.

CASE FOR REVIEW

MOSEKIAN v. DAVIS CANNING COMPANY

40 Cal. Rptr. 157 (1964)

Defendant Adams called at plaintiff's farm, identified himself as a buyer for defendant Davis Canning Company, and offered to buy plaintiff's peach crop. Plaintiff asked the price per ton, and Adams replied that since the price had not been set, the purchase would be on an "open contract." In the canning peach industry the cannery association sets a price each year when crop and market conditions are ascertained. Customarily canners contract to buy crops before maturity, agreeing to pay whatever price per ton the association thereafter sets; hence the term "open contract."

Plaintiff testified that Adams bought his crop "roadside" on such an open contract, and when he asked for confirmation Adams said he would bring a written contract for signature when the price was set. This Adams did not do. The peaches ripened, and plaintiff went looking for Adams. When he found him, at a neighbor's farm, he asked for picking boxes to "roadside" his fruit, which was dropping. Adams said he hadn't started taking fruit but that he would commence in a couple of days, at which time he would see plaintiff. Adams did not return, so again plaintiff went looking for him and when he found him advised that the fruit was ripening rapidly and falling on the ground. Adams replied, "Sell it to somebody else." Plaintiff, unable to dispose of his fruit at a cannery, sold it to a "dry yard." The trial court awarded plaintiff, as damages, the difference between the canning peach price and the dry yard price.

First, we note that when sold separately a crop of fruit growing upon trees is not considered to be a part of the real property. This rule of law was established in a number of very early cases which are cited by plaintiff, and it was reaffirmed by the case principally relied upon by plaintiff, *Vulicevich* v. *Skinner,* 77 Cal. 239, 240 19 P. 424, often referred to as the landmark case on the question. The court in Vulicevich said: " 'Contracts for the sale of growing periodical crops—*fructus industriales*—are not within the statute of frauds, and therefore need not be made in writing. . . .' "

A reversal does not follow, even though the provisions of Civil Code . . . are applicable, since the trial court found defendants were estopped to invoke the statute. The doctrine of estoppel as applied to the statute of frauds is delineated in *Monarco* v. *Lo Greco,* 35 Cal.2d 621, pages 625-626, Mr. Justice Traynor summarized circumstances under which the doctrine may be invoked:

> It is contended however, that an estoppel to plead the statute of frauds can only arise when there have been representations with respect to the requirements of the statute indicating that a writing is not necessary or will be executed or that the statute will not be relied upon as a defense. However, where either an unconscionable injury or unjust enrichment would result from refusal to enforce the contract, the doctrine of estoppel has been applied whether or not plaintiff relied upon representations going to the requirements of the statute itself. . . . In reality it is not the representation that the contract will be put in

writing or that the statute will not be invoked, but the promise that the contract will be performed that a party relies upon when he changes his position because of it.

Defendants argue that the evidence upon which the court based the finding of estoppel falls short of even the broad language of Monarco. The answer lies in whether there is acceptance of plaintiff's testimony which, standing alone, if believed, sufficiently supports the finding. The trial judge observed this 80-year-old man who is hard of hearing, and to the trial judge belonged the prerogative of believing or disbelieving his testimony, as well as all other evidence. The record reflects testimony of the plaintiff which supports the trial court's finding:

> That the Plaintiff did in fact reasonably rely upon the agreements and representations of the Defendants described in Paragraphs (5) and (6) and was induced thereby to sell his growing crop of peaches to the Defendant DAVIS CANNING COMPANY, in June, 1960, and to hold said crop for the use and benefit Defendant Cannery and seek no other buyers therefore until after Defendants' repudiated their contract of purchase about July 24, 1960, and by which date a portion of the crop had fallen due to overripening and a substantial part of the Plaintiff's peaches had become too ripe for sale to fresh fruit packers, . . .

Plaintiff's change of position brings the case within the rationale of the Monarco case.

CASE PROBLEMS

1. Boeing contracted with Des Moines Steel Company for the latter to construct a supersonic wind tunnel. Freitag Manufacturing Company sold material to Gillespie Company, which subcontracted to do part of the work. In order to persuade Freitag to keep supplying materials on credit, Boeing and Des Moines, the principal contractor, both assured Freitag that he would be paid. When Freitag was not paid by the subcontractor, he sued Boeing and the contractor. They defended on the ground that the assurances given Freitag were not written and therefore unenforceable. Decide.
2. Ann Jones, who was employed in a store owned by William Jones, her brother, was injured in an accident while a passenger in his car on store business. Dr. Pick cared for the injured girl for nearly five months. About a month before her release from the hospital, defendant Paul Simon, called there and is alleged to have told Dr. Pick, "If Bill doesn't take of the bill, I will." When sued by Pick for the amount of Ann's medical expenses, Simon raised the defense of the Statute of Frauds. Decide.
3. Smith, on whose land was a greenhouse, orally agreed to sell the greenhouse to Jones for $600. Jones sent Smith a check for the amount, which he endorsed for deposit, but before depositing it had an opportunity sell his residence to a purchaser who insisted that the greenhouse be included. Jones brought suit for possession of the greenhouse. Decide.
4. Fixit Company took possession of certain real property under an oral agreement. While in possession they built a new building and made substantial improvements to the existing structures. Subsequent to this the seller brought an action to recover the property. Decide.

5. Brogan, who lived with Mr. and Mrs. Sandle, orally promised Mrs. Sandle that he would leave his property to her if she would do his housekeeping. She did so for twenty months, when he died without leaving a will. Mrs. Sandle made a claim against the estate for the value of the services provided the decedent. Decide.

6. Never-Leak Roofing Company orally guaranteed Boggs that they would repair his roof if it should leak at any time during the next four years. When the roof needed repair, Never-Leak refused to honor its guarantee. Boggs brought suit and Never-Leak claimed the Statute of Frauds as a defense. Decide.

7. Smith paid Jones $1000 on an oral agreement to purchase a home and received the following receipt:

> January 5, 1972. Received from: Smith $1000 in cash for deposit on property located at 7305 Starcliff Avenue, North Canton, Ohio. Balance $26,000 to be paid on or about March 7, 1972.
>
> Jones

Smith decided not to proceed with the sale and brought suit for his deposit claiming the absence of an enforceable contract. Decide.

8. This is an action by the buyer against the seller for breach of a contract for the sale of land. The alleged written contract is as follows:

> Ludlow, Mass. March 8, 1967, Received of John B. Andre Five Hundred Dollars first payment on land west side of Miller Street. Balance to be paid on delivery of deed. (signed) Mr. F. H. Ellison.

The Statute of Frauds is raised as a defense. Decide.

THE RIGHTS OF THIRD PARTIES

Just as tangible property can be transferred between people, so too may contract rights and duties be conveyed. A contracting party may assign his right to receive performance to another. For example, he may render services and assign his right to payment for them. A party may delegate to a third person his duty to perform. In a building contract, the general contractor seldom undertakes the duty of personal performance. The situation may even call for an assignment of the entire contract, including all a party's rights and duties. It is important to note, however, that whatever arrangements are made with third parties, the original contract remains in force and the original parties remain bound by it.

Although the most frequent means by which third parties acquire rights in contracts is by assignment, certain persons may be recognized as having enforceable rights created in them by a contract to which they are not parties and for which they gave no consideration. These individuals are called "third-party beneficiaries" and are classified as (1) donee beneficiaries, (2) creditor beneficiaries, or (3) incidental beneficiaries, depending in how the benefits are derived. If A conveys land to B in return for B's promise to pay A's son C $500, C is a donee beneficiary. However, if A gives consideration to B in exchange for B's promise to pay C $500 owed to C by A, C is creditor beneficiary. The term "incidental beneficiary" denotes a person who will benefit only indirectly by the performance of a contract; such persons, unlike donee and creditor beneficiaries, have no enforceable legal rights in the contract. For example, if Destructo Demolition promises to demolish some abandoned buildings for Landowner, this contract may benefit property owners in the immediate area. However, if Destructo breaches their contract with Landowner, these owners will not have the right to sue either Destructo or Landowner for its breach. They are incidental beneficiaries of the original contract in that there is only a possibility of a benefit.

ASSIGNMENT

An assignment is any act that indicates the intention of one party to transfer all or part of his rights under a contract to another party not involved in the original contract relationship. It may consist of any manifestation of intention by the present owner of the right to transfer the right to the assignee; no special form is required. Normally an assignment is effected by a writing, but any act, written or spoken, that gives clear evidence of intent to transfer, or assign, is sufficient. Only situations covered by the Statute of Frauds require writings. Consideration is usually involved in an assignment but is not a requisite. The party who makes the assignment is the assignor; the party who receives the assigned rights is the assignee; the party who must perform the contractual obligation is the obligor. For example, A, in consideration of services rendered by B to A, promises to pay B $500. B (the assignor) assigns the right to receive the money to C. C (the assignee) then has the right to maintain an action for the money against A (the obligor).

RIGHTS THAT MAY BE ASSIGNED

Almost any contract right is assignable, so long as all the contracting parties agree to it and the assignment leaves unchanged the rights and duties of the promisor. Even if the obligor objects, the assignor may assign his contract rights. However, a contract calling for personal services may not be assigned because it involves an element of personal confidence and skill, which would be destroyed by assignment. For example, a contract for an artist to paint a portrait or a contract of insurance against certain risks are non-assignable because they were made upon the character of the contracting party, namely, reputation of the artist and the insured.

When contract rights concern the personal credit, skill, or confidence of the performing party, the right of assignment is usually restricted. Assignment of particular rights may be forbidden by statute, it may be contrary to public policy, or it may be forbidden by the original contract. An example is the prohibition against the assignment of future salaries due public officials or of alimony. Various statutes have likewise declared that claims against the alimony. Various statutes have likewise declared that claims against the government or some branch thereof shall not be assignable. Tort claims for damages are not assignable until they have been reduced to judgment. It is good business practice to include in the contract the fact that the contracting parties are only interested in contracting with each other and that their expectations can not be met by anyone else.

RIGHT TO RECEIVE MONEY

As a rule, a right to receive money under an existing contract is freely assignable, even though the money is not yet due. However, an assignment of a future right to money is not valid if no contract exists or you are not presently employed. It is well settled in law that the mere expectancy or possibility of receiving funds is a future right not owned by the assignor; hence it is not assignable at law. Consequently, wages to be earned in the future where there is not an existing contract or present employment are not assignable. A number of states limit the right of an employee to assign future wages to a maximum percentage and hold that any attempt to assign a larger amount is unenforceable. This limitation is not to be confused with laws regarding garnishment of wages, which specifically exempt certain property and a percentage of wages from attachment.

DELEGATION OF DUTIES

A delegation of duties occurs when one of the parties to a contract enlists someone else to perform his obligation for him. Any contractual duty may be delegated as long as it is routine in nature and may be performed as well by one person as by another. For example, in a construction job the entire task cannot normally be performed by the contracting party. It is common, therefore, for the contractor to delegate tasks to other parties. No delegation is allowed when an obligation is personal in nature; when it involves a special skill, confidence, or trust; or when the contract expressly prohibits delegation.

DUTIES OF THE ASSIGNOR

When the assignor makes an assignment, he implicitly warrants that the right being assigned is legally valid; that it was not obtained through fraud, duress, or the like; and that he knows of no defenses available to the obligor. However, he makes no implied warranty that the obligor will perform.

In the case of delegation of a contractual duty, the assignor remains liable for performance. If the assignee should fail to perform, the assignor is liable for damages caused by the failure of performance. Delegation does not relieve the assignor of his original obligation under the contract. For example, in building contracts the builder may assign his right to payment and delegate the duty of performance to his assignee. If the assignee's performance is not adequate, the builder remains liable just as if he himself failed to perform.

RIGHTS OF THE ASSIGNEE

The assignee steps into the shoes of the assignor when a contractual right is assigned; thus his right to demand performance from the obligor is no greater than the assignor's. Stated differently, whatever defenses are good against the assignor are good against the assignee. For example, suppose A (the assignor) sells to B goods for $1000 and makes an effective assignment to C (the assignee) of his right to collect from B (the obligor). One-half the goods are damaged in transit and are returned by B to A. C may collect only one-half the amount formerly due, or $500; however, he may recover from A the remaining $500.

If the assignee meets a refusal to perform by the obligor, who has no defense, he may recover from the obligor. The assignee cannot recover from the assignor in such a situation. In the example above, should B fail to perform, C has a cause of action against B by virtue of the assignment because A has given up all contract rights against the obligor.

RIGHTS AND DUTIES OF THE OBLIGOR

(The non-assigning party) It is a general rule that a party cannot escape ultimate responsibility for a non-released obligation by assignment. Failure on the part of the assignee to perform his duties gives rise to a cause of action by the obligee. In the majority of states he can elect to sue either the assignor or the assignee. If he elects to sue the assignor, this gives the assignor the right to look to the assignee for a contribution.

NOTICE OF ASSIGNMENT

Once a creditor assigns a claim, the assignee may enforce the contract against the other party as fully as his assignor might have done, subject to any defenses that the other party may have against the assignor. In most states the assignee may sue in his own name.

If a creditor assigns a claim, the assignee should notify the obligor as soon as possible of the assignment. Where he fails to do this and the obligor, without knowledge of the assignment, pays the assignor, the obligor cannot be again required to pay the debt to the assignee, even though the assignor, after collecting, leaves the jurisdiction or becomes insolvent. If the obligor receives notice of the assignment and nevertheless pays the assignor, he does so at his own risk.

Between assignor and assignee the assignment is valid even if the debtor has not received notice of the assignment. If the assignor collects the claim after assignment, he is liable to the assignee for the value of the performance he has received.

SUCCESSIVE ASSIGNMENTS

Occasionally an assignor will make successive assignments of the same right. In this situation the first assignee to notify the obligor is usually entitled to performance. However, some courts hold that priority is determined by the time of the assignment. The remaining assignees may sue the assignor for any damages incurred as a result of the wrongful assignments.

NOVATION

The individual entitled to receive performance may agree to release the original obligor from responsibility and substitute the party to whom the duty has been delegated for performance of the contract. If all three parties agree to this arrangement, the original obligor is discharged, the original contract is discharged, and a new agreement is substituted. This arrangement is referred to as a novation. It is an express agreement that differs from an ordinary delegation in that all the parties agree to release the assignor.

THIRD PARTY BENEFICIARY CONTRACTS

Frequently a contract is negotiated for the benefit of a third person who is not a party to the contract itself. For example, a life insurance policy will name as beneficiary someone other than the policyholder. Problems sometimes arise concerning the rights of such third parties to enforce the obligation to perform. Circumstances to consider in this case are the nature of the benefit conferred and the intention of the parties.

DONEE BENEFICIARIES

A donee beneficiary is a third party to whom the promisee owes no legal obligation. Therefore the benefit to be conferred is strictly a gift. Once the agreement has been made, the donee has an absolute right to enforce this agreement. Nor may the benefit be revoked without his consent, unless the parties expressly reserved the privilege of doing so when they entered into the contract. An example of this type of agreement is a life insurance policy, wherein the original parties are the company and the insured and the third party who receives the specified death benefits is the donee beneficiary. All jurisdictions allow beneficiaries of such contracts to bring suit to enforce the agreement.

CREDITOR BENEFICIARIES

A creditor beneficiary is a third party to whom the promisee already owes a legal obligation at the time the contract is made; the promisor, in effect, agrees to assume the obligation in whole or in part. For example, a person who buys mortgaged real estate and assumes the mortgage debt makes a contract for the benefit of a third party who is a creditor. Such debt makes a contract for the benefit of a third party who is a creditor. These contracts are enforceable by the creditor beneficiary if it is clear that performance is expressly meant to benefit him to discharge the promisee's obligation to him.

INCIDENTAL BENEFICIARIES

An incidental beneficiary is a third party who is to benefit only indirectly from the performance of a contractual obligation. Generally such a beneficiary is not entitled to enforce performance. For example, an agreement to construct a new factory will indirectly benefit the community. The breach of such an agreement would not give the citizens of the community the right to sue either of the contracting parties. In other words, if the parties did not expressly intend to benefit the third person, he is not permitted to take any action. Only the original parties have rights in the contract.

LEGAL PRINCIPLES

Third parties may acquire rights in a contract by assignment or as third party beneficiaries.

Neither writing nor consideration is necessary for an assignment.

Contracts calling for personal services may not be assigned.

The assignor implicitly warrants the assigned right as valid.

The assignor cannot assign away his liability for performance.

The assignee takes the rights subject to any defenses against the assignor.

The obligee may elect to sue either the assignee or the assignor in the event of lack of performance by the assignee.

The obligor must pay the assignee after he has received notice of the assignment. Otherwise he is justified in paying the assignor.

Donee and creditor beneficiaries may sue on a contract made for their benefit.

For a donee beneficiary to recover, the contract must be made expressly for his benefit. Incidental beneficiaries may not recover.

CASE FOR REVIEW

AMERICAN BRIDGE CO. v. CITY OF BOSTON

202 Mass. 374 (1909)

This is an action of contract brought by the plaintiffs as assignees of all "the moneys now due or which may hereafter become due" to . . . Coburn, the assignor under two certain building contracts between him and the defendant, dated respectively July 16 . . . and August 27. . . . It is brought to recover the amount of two architect's certificates, one for $2210 and the other for $3085.50 each dated November 10. . . .

It is contended by the plaintiffs that these sums were due and payable at the time the defendant received notice thereof, that the plaintiffs' rights were fixed at the time of notice and could not be changed by the act of the assignor or of the defendant after notice, and consequently that the damage caused to the defendant by the default of the assignor in leaving his contract unperformed, although without any fault of collusion on the part of the defendant, cannot be recouped in this action. It is contended that the only remedy open to the defendant is by way of an action against the assignor.

Even if it be conceded in favor of the plaintiffs that the sums were due and payable at the time of the notice, and that the rights of the plaintiffs were fixed at that time, still the conclusion which the plaintiffs seek to draw by no means necessarily follows.

The assignment of a chose in action conveys as between the assignor and assignee, merely the right which the assignor then possesses to that thing; but as between the assignee and the debtor it does not become operative until the time of notice to the latter, and does not change the rights of the debtor against the assignor as they exist at the time of the notice.

It becomes necessary to consider the exact relation between the defendant and Coburn, the assignor, at the time of the notice. The auditor has found that written notice of the assignment was given to the defendant on November 13 . . . before the service of any trustee process. At that time there does not seem to have been any default on the part of Coburn. At the time of the notice what were the rights between him and the defendant, so far as respects this contract? He was entitled to receive these sums, but he was also under an obligation to complete his contract. This right of the defendant to claim damages for the non-performance of the contract, existed at the making of the contract and at the time of assignment and of notice, and the assignees knew it, and they also knew that it would become available to the defendant the moment the assignor should commit a breach. Under these circumstances it must be held that the assignees took subject to that right. Coburn, the assignor, abandoned the work in a few days after the notice. This action was not brought until . . . nearly four years after the breach.

Even if the sums were due and payable in November . . . at the time of the notice, still if this action had been brought by the assignor after the default, there can be no doubt that the defendant would have had the right to recoup the damages suffered by his default. And the assignees who seek to enforce this claim can stand in no better position in this respect than the assignor. The defendant is simply trying to enforce a right existing under the contract at the time of the notice, a right of which the assignees had knowledge, and since they have delayed suit for these sums until after default, the defendant may recoup against them as it could have recouped against the assignor. It cannot without its own fault or consent be deprived of rights under the contract. Any other conclusion would make the contract different from that into which the defendant entered.

CASE PROBLEMS

1. Winery contracted to sell and deliver to Gargiulo 750 barrels of wine monthly, with payment to be made thirty days after each shipment. After this contract was made, Gargiulo incorporated his business and assigned the contract to the corporation. Winery refused to deliver the wine, alleging that the contract was not assignable without its consent. Gargiulo brought suit on the contract. Decide.

2. Defendant was the operator of a large department store in Worcester. He leased a portion of the store to the plaintiff for the purpose of running a clothing establishment. Plaintiff agreed to operate his business in such a way as to give the appearance of being one of the departments of the defendant's business. A dispute arose concerning the plaintiff's right to sublet the space leased to him by the defendant. Decide.

3. Dupuy, an attorney, was under contract with Williams by which Dupuy agreed to perfect title to certain real estate owned by Williams. Dupuy assigned his rights under the contract to Sloan who performed the agreed tasks. Sloan brought suit to enforce the assigned contract. Decide.

4. Plain was the assignee of a $8000 bond given under a construction contract issued by the school board to the contractor, the assignor. Plain made no attempt to notify the school board of the assignment until after their settlement with the contractor, but evidence was given to show that the board members did know of the assignment. Was Plain entitled to collect? Decide.

5. Mall was employed by Broadview Company at a salary of $500 per month. He was not working under contract and could have quit or been discharged at any time without liability on the part of either party. In order to secure a loan from Wenham, Mall executed a written agreement, as follows: "I do hereby transfer, assign, and set over to Wenham all salary or wages due or to become due me from Broadview Company." Later, Mall alleged that this assignment was invalid. Decide.

6. Rosier purchased a tank carload each of oil and gasoline from Chanute Company on open account. Chanute assigned $1516.58, the unpaid balance of the purchase price, to the Sinclair Company, which brought an action against Rosier for the money assigned. Rosier refused to pay the assignee because of a counterclaim against Chanute, consisting of $289.70 that Rosier claims to have paid on account and $1477.30 to cover certain state inspection fees that had been collected by Chanute from defendant and that should have been returned after the inspection law was declared invalid. Decide.

7. Plaintiffs leased a tract of land to Mary Kaehler. The lessee agreed "to keep the buildings now erected . . . upon said premises insured against loss by fire." A fire occurred in March, 1970 which resulted in a total loss of a building on the leased premises. The lessee refused to file a proof of loss in regard to that building and to take any action against the Insurance Company. Therefore, the plaintiffs brought an action against the Insurance Company. Decide.

8. The National Theatres Syndicate sold a number of shares of stock to the defendants for the sum of $43,938. The sales contract stated the following: "It is further understood and agreed that . . . we will retain Mr. Homer Ballister, persently employed as your manager, in some suitable position for a period of one year." Defendants terminated Mr. Ballister's employment before the end of the one-year period, and suit was brought for breach of contract. Decide.

PERFORMANCE, DISCHARGE, 17
AND BREACH

Each party to a contract incurs a duty to perform certain obligations. Once a party performs his part of the agreement, his obligation is deemed to be discharged and he has no further responsibility. However, performance is not the only way in which a party may discharge his obligation. Circumstances may arise that legally excuse one of the parties from his obligation, or the other party may fail to perform an obligation under the contract and excuse performance by the injured party because of the breach.

PERFORMANCE

A promise of performance is an undertaking by a party to a contract that imposes upon him an obligation to do or to refrain from doing something. This obligation may be either absolute or conditional. If it is absolute, it must be performed and failure to do so will amount to breach of contract. An obligation is conditional when it is dependent upon the occurrence or nonoccurrence of some future event that will in some manner change the legal relation of the parties in the contract. Whereas every contract contains a promise, not every contract contains a condition.

Three types of conditions may terminate, abate, qualify, or otherwise affect the principal obligation of the other party: conditions precedent, conditions concurrent, and conditions subsequent. A condition is a manifestation of the intent of the parties. It is what the contracting parties expect to accomplish by entering into the particular contract as to extent of liability, when it will occur and what will amount to a termination or suspension of their particular liability. It is, therefore, an essential element of the contract and, as such, should be incorporated into the contract and be understood by the contracting parties.

CONDITIONS PRECEDENT

A condition precedent is a duty that must be performed antecedent to the other party's liability. The parties to a contract are usually free to make any arrangement they wish concerning which is to perform his obligation first. Even where the contract is not specific in this regard, it may be understood that one party must perform his obligation before he can demand performance from the other. For example, a provision in a building contract that the contractor is not to receive final payment until the city engineer has issued a certificate of occupancy stating that the building has been erected according to the terms and specifications of the contract and is suitable for occupancy is a condition precedent. Issuance of the certificate fulfills the condition precedent to the duty of the other party to make final payment to the contractor.

CONDITIONS CONCURRENT

If the contract makes it clear that the parties are to perform at the same time, neither is bound to perform until the other has carried out his part of the agreement. Such conditions are concurrent. In this case, before either party can claim the other is in default, he must make a valid tender of performance (see below). Concurrent conditions may be stated expressly in the contract or implied from usage or custom. For example, in a contract for the sale of real property, the delivery of the deed transferring the property and payment of the purchase price or a specified down payment are concurrent conditions. The ordinary cash sale is another example.

CONDITIONS SUBSEQUENT

The occurrence of a condition subsequent may be specified as necessary to terminate the legal relation between the parties to a contract. For example, a lease may contain a provision stating that it may be terminated by either party by a 30-day written notice to the other party to that effect. This is a condition subsequent that must be performed in order to terminate an existing liability. A condition in an insurance policy that the insured must give timely notice in the event of a loss is a condition subsequent that must be performed to continue the liability of the insurance company. For a condition to be accurately labeled precedent or subsequent, it must be examined in the context of the particular legal relation under consideration.

DEGREES OF PERFORMANCE

Under common law, a party had to render full performance before his obligation was discharged and before he could demand performance from the other party. Full performance meant "precisely according to the terms of the agreement." This has since been modified to allow a party who has substantially performed his obligation and who has been acting in good faith to recover from the other party on the contract. The rule of substantial performance requires the substance of the agreement to be performed and is applicable where literal or complete performance is impossible or would result in great hardship. In such cases, the other party must perform his part of the bargain, but he has the remedy of offsetting any damage sustained by reason of the incomplete performance. If however, wide, material, and significant variations from full performance evidence a disregard for contractual duty, no performance need be tendered in return.

TIME OF PERFORMANCE

If the parties do not provide that performance is to occur upon a certain date or within a specified time, it is implied that performance must take place within a reasonable time. What is a reasonable time will depend on the nature of the subject matter of the contract and whether a delay will result in injury or damage. Time will be considered a condition precedent where it is stated in the contract as being, or may be implied as being, an essential part of the agreement. Suppose Mr. Wood contracts with a photographer to have a portrait ready by November 10 so he can give it to his wife on her birthday November 14. Is time a condition?

TENDER OF PERFORMANCE

A tender of performance is a timely offer to perform his part of the bargain made by a party with the present ability to do so. A tender may involve the payment of money or the performance of an act. It is required as a basis for breach of contract action against the other party where conditions are involved. A valid tender relieves the offering party of any further duty to perform except where money obligations are involved. While it does not discharge a debt, it stops the accruing of interest from the date on which tender was made, and it releases any security given by the debtor for the debt.

PERFORMANCE TO THE PERSONAL SATISFACTION OF THE OTHER PARTY

Occasionally, one party to a contract will agree to perform to the personal satisfaction of the other party. In such cases, the performance must meet reasonable standards where measurable by standards. An exception may be made where the personal taste of the other party is a controlling factor, in which case that party must be individually satisfied. However, if it can be shown that the unsatisfied party is acting in bad faith or solely for the purpose of avoiding payment, the courts will leave the parties with their bargain.

DISCHARGE

A valid contract continues to exist until the happening of some event sufficient to discharge its existence in the eyes of the law. Contracts may be discharged by agreement of the parties, by impossibility of performance, or by the operation of law.

AGREEMENT OF THE PARTIES

Contractual obligations may be discharged or altered by agreement of the parties before or during performance. Several methods may be used by the parties to effect such discharge and alteration:

1. *Mutual rescission.* Since a contract is a voluntary commitment, it is only reasonable that the contracting parties should be permitted to rescind it by mutual agreement. Mutual rescission discharges both parties of their obligations under the contract. Each is restored to his original position by the return of any money or property that has changed hands.
2. *Substituted agreement.* A contract may be discharged by an agreement of the parties to enter into a new contract that is inconsistent with the old one. Since there is inconsistency and since the new agreement is intended

to replace the previous one, the original contract is discharged. If only a few terms of the new contract are inconsistent with the old, the latter is discharged only to the extent that there is no conflict. A new contract created under these conditions must be supported by valid consideration. If valid consideration is not present, the new contract is not enforceable and the first agreement is held to be still in effect.

3. *Novation.* (See Chapter 16, pp. 148)
4. *Waiver.* A waiver is the voluntary relinquishment by one party of some right to which he is entitled under a contract. It may be express or implied. It usually arises where one party accepts minor variations in the performance of the other party. For example, a contract may call for the payment of money between the first and the fifth of the month. A waiver is given if payment is accepted at a later date and if there is no objection to the late payment.
5. *Accord and satisfaction.* Sometimes the parties to contract will make an additional agreement varying somewhat the performance called for in the original contract. This agreement is referred to as an accord. When the new agreement has been fully performed, the original obligation is also satisfied and the first contract is discharged. The original agreement remains in effect until satisfaction occurs and may be enforced by the other party at any time prior to satisfaction.

IMPOSSIBILITY OF PERFORMANCE

Ordinarily, events occurring after a contract is entered into will not affect performance. The following are exceptions that will discharge a party from his obligations under an existing agreement:

1. *Subsequent illegality.* If, after a contract is made, a change in the legal situation renders performance illegal, the contractual obligations are discharged. For example, if A makes a contract with B and the act to be performed by B becomes illegal through a change in the law, his nonperformance is excused unless he expressly assumes the risk of such change. In the latter case B must make compensation since he cannot perform the illegal act. Where a change in the law merely makes performance more difficult, the contract is not discharged.
2. *Death or incapacity of a party.* In a contract calling for personal services, the death or incapacity of the party who is to render the services discharges him or his estate from all liability under the agreement. Whenever an obligation requires special skills or judgment or involves a personal relationship, death or incapacity will excuse performance and terminate the obligation. Where the services are not personal, death or illness does not excuse performance by the estate.
3. *Destruction of subject matter.* In many contracts, the continued existence of the subject matter is essential to performance. If the property involved is of such a nature that it is irreplaceable and it is destroyed through no fault of either party, performance is excused and the obligation is discharged. If, however, the loss results from the negligence of one of the parties, he is liable for damages. If one party has performed, either partially or entirely, by the time the property is destroyed, he is permitted to recover the fair value of any benefit he has conferred on the other. Often a seller or manufacturer must depend on a

particular source of supply in order to perform an obligation. If both parties are aware of this fact and something curtails the supply, the performance of the seller or manufacturer is excused. For example, if A contracts to furnish apples from a certain orchard and the orchard is destroyed, his nonperformance is excused. If, however, he simply promises to deliver certain goods without mentioning any source, he must either fulfill that obligation or pay damages.

DISCHARGE BY OPERATION OF LAW

Contracts may be discharged by operation of law through bankruptcy or by the running out of the statute of limitations.

1. *Bankruptcy.* A discharge in bankruptcy bars any creditors of the debtor from bringing suit against him. It is an effective defense on all debts that have been discharged. However, bankruptcy does not in itself constitute a failure of consideration that will discharge the contract.
2. *State or federal statutes of limitations.* These statutes specify the time in which a party must bring suit on a cause of action. If the injured party does not act within the time specified in the statute, he loses his right to bring the action.

The statutory period begins once a cause of action accrues, that is, when one of the parties has a right to commence action against the other. It stops running when the other party leaves the jurisdiction and starts again when he returns. In other words, the statute applies only while the defendant is within the state and its jurisdiction and does not apply when he is outside that jurisdiction. The statute may be revived after the time period has elapsed if the party who broke the agreement makes a written promise to perform or, in the case of a money obligation, if he makes a voluntary acknowledgment or part payment of the debt.

BREACH

When a contract is made, each party assumes that the other will carry out his part of the agreement. There is always the possibility, however, that one of the parties will fail to perform the obligations required of him. An unjustifiable failure to perform all or part of a contractual duty is a breach of contract when it substantially deprives the other party of that for which he bargained.

A breach of contract is always a nonperformance of duty, but not every nonperformance of duty is a breach of contract. Every executory contract creates a legal duty, but in most cases immediate performance is not required. Not only may performance be required at some time in the future, it may be contingent upon the happening of some uncertain event. In this case, failure to render performance is not a breach of contract unless the time for performance has expired and all conditions precedent have occurred. For example, if an owner has contracted to pay a builder $10,000 as soon as a building is completed, nonpayment is not a breach until after all work is finished.

A breach of contract may be total or partial. A building contractor may fail to start excavation for the foundation or he may fail merely to use the brand of sewer pipe required by the contract. He has breached the agreement in either case. The terms "total breach" and "partial breach" are sometimes used in determining the remedies available to the injured party. A total breach of contract is the nonperformance of a contractual duty that is so *material,* or so essential, that it defeats the justifiable expectations of the injured party to the extent that he may regard the contract as being terminated.

In the case of a total breach, the injured party may immediately obtain a judgment for his loss. If the breach is partial, the injured party can maintain action at once, but he is not permitted to stop further performance. For example, failure to pay an installment of money when due will create a right of action for the money but will not always constitute a total breach.

In every agreement there is an implied condition that neither party will *interfere* with the other party's performance or with his justifiable expectations arising from the agreement. Such interference is a breach of contract. One who is sued for nonperformance has a defense if he can prove that his performance was prevented or substantially interfered with by the plaintiff.

Parties who wish to be relieved of the obligation to perform contractual duties in the event of unusual circumstances must provide for such events in the contract. If they do not and an unusual circumstance arises, they cannot be relieved of performance without a breach. Business contracts often provide that a firm will be relieved of performance in cases of fire or other events over which they have no control (normally referred to as "acts of God"). It is necessary that such provisions be included within the body of the contract to be enforceable. These conditions are never implied.

ANTICIPATORY BREACH

An anticipatory breach is a repudiation by one of the parties of his contractual duty at a date earlier than that fixed by the contract. Repudiation may be made by word or by act. If one party makes a definite statement to the other party that he either will not or cannot perform his end of the contract, it will be deemed an anticipatory breach unless the promisor had some legal justification for his statement. Likewise, an voluntary act rendering performance of the contract impossible is an anticipatory breach of contract. For example, if one who has contracted to sell a certain object to another sells or agrees to sell the same object to a third party, this is a repudiation of the contract. Such action amounts to evidence of intent not to perform the first contract.

In order to have an anticipatory breach of contract. There must be definite and unequivocal evidence of intent on the part of the repudiator not to render the promised performance at the time fixed in the contract. Doubtful or indefinite statements that the performance may or may not take place will not beheld to create an immediate right of action. A mere request for a change in the terms or for cancellation of the contract is not in itself enough to constitute anticipatory breach. For example, if A has an employment contract with B and B states that unless business improves he will have to discharge A, A cannot bring an immediate action for anticipatory breach.

An anticipatory breach may be retracted, provided the other party has not cancelled the contract, has not materially changed his position, and has not indicated that he considers the repudiation final. Also, the rules for anticipatory breach are not applicable to a promise to pay a money debt at a future date. Even though the debtor indicates before maturity that he will not or cannot pay the debt, the creditor must wait until the due date before bringing suit.

LEGAL PRINCIPLES

Failure to perform an absolute obligation amounts to a breach of contract. Failure to perform a conditional obligation may or may not amount to breach of contract.

There are three types of conditions: conditions precedent, conditions concurrent, and conditions subsequent.

A condition precedent must be performed antecedent to the other party's liability.

A condition concurrent must be performed at the same time by both parties.

A condition subsequent may continue, suspend, release, or terminate the contractual liability of the other party to the contract.

Substantial performance may be deemed sufficient where literal or complete performance is impossible or would result in great hardship.

Time is not a condition precedent unless it is so designated or may be reasonably implied.

A tender of performance is a timely offer to perform his part of the bargain made by a party with the present ability to do so. It is necessary order to establish the liability of the other party where conditions are involved.

Contracts in which one party must perform a task to the personal satisfaction of another party will be enforced in the absence of bad faith.

Contracts may be discharged by agreement of the parties, by impossibility of performance, or by operation of law.

The statute of limitations may be revived by a voluntary acknowledgment of the obligation in writing or by part payment of a debt.

A breach of contract is always a nonperformance of a duty. A total breach of contract justifies rescission, whereas a partial breach gives rise to a cause of action for damages.

In every agreement there is an implied condition that neither party will interfere with the other party's performance or with his justifiable expectations arising from the agreement.

Normally, additional hardships that arise after a contract has been entered into do not justify rescission.

An anticipatory breach is clear evidence that the other party does not intend to perform. It gives rise to an immediate cause of action, except in contract for the payment of money. An anticipatory breach may be retracted if the other party has not acted upon it.

CASE FOR REVIEW

LACH v. CAHILL

138 Conn. 418 (1951)

The plaintiff sues to recover a deposit he made with one of the defendants upon a written agreement to purchase a house belonging to the other. The trial court concluded that the agreement never came into existence because it was subject to a condition which had not been fulfilled. It rendered judgment for the plaintiff for the return of the deposit and the defendants appealed.

The finding . . . discloses the following facts: On November 10 . . . the plaintiff signed an agreement with the defendant Cahill, acting through his agent, the defendant Rabbett, to purchase Cahill's house in Windsor Locks for $18,000 and paid a deposit of $1000. A few days later Cahill also signed the agreement and accepted the deposit. The contract contained the following provisions: "This agreement is contingent upon buyer being able to obtain mortgage in the sum of $12,000.00 on the premises, and have immediate occupancy of the premises." The conveyance was to be made by warranty deed within thirty days after acceptance of the agreement by the seller.

The plaintiff had been a practicing attorney for a little more than one year, was married and the father of three small children. Rabbett knew the financial position of the plaintiff and that he contemplated a bank mortgage payable in installments over a reasonable period of time. On November 14, the plaintiff applied to the First National Bank of Windsor Locks for a $12,000 mortgage, which was denied. Thereafter, in the period up to November 21, he unsuccessfully applied for a mortgage loan at five different banks and loaning institutions. He was informed that the banks in Hartford were not interested in placing loans on outlying property. He conferred with the federal housing administration examiners, who advised him that although he was a veteran his income did not meet the requirements for an F.H.A. guaranteed loan. Rabbett informed the plaintiff not later than November 18 that Cahill was definitely not interested in a purchase money mortgage. On December 1, the plaintiff wrote to Cahill that he was unable to secure a mortgage in the amount of $12,000 and requested the return of the deposit. On December 5, Cahill by letter offered to take back a purchase money mortgage payable on demand or to obtain a mortgage from another person, but he specified no terms. The plaintiff had already made a deposit on another house in Newington.

The decisive issues in the case are whether the ability of the plaintiff to secure a $12,000 mortgage was a condition precedent to his duty to perform his promise to purchase and whether he made a reasonable effort to secure the mortgage. Unless both questions are answered in the affirmative the plaintiff cannot recover. A condition precedent is a fact or event which the parties intend must exist or take place before there is a right to performance.

. . . A condition is distinguished from a promise in that it creates no right or duty in and of itself but is merely a limiting or modifying factor. . . . If the condition is not fulfilled, the right to enforce the contract does not come into existence. . . . Whether a provision in a contract is a condition of the non-fulfilment of which excuses performance depends upon the intent of the parties, to be ascertained from a fair and reasonable construction of the language used in the light of all the surrounding circumstances when they executed the contract.

The plaintiff was a young man of limited means, just starting in his profession and under the necessity of finding a home for his wife and their three small children. He required a mortgage payable in reasonable installments over a period of time if he was to complete the prospective purchase of Cahill's house. The court properly concluded that the language used, read in the light of the situation of the parties, expressed an intention that the plaintiff should not be held to an agreement to purchase unless he could secure a mortgage for $12,000 on reasonable terms as to the amount and time of installment payments.

The condition in the contract implied a promise by the plaintiff that he would make reasonable efforts to secure a suitable mortgage. . . . The performance or nonperformance of this implied promise was a matter for the determination of the trial court. The conclusion reached upon the facts was proper.

CASE PROBLEMS

1. Behn agreed to charter his vessel, the *Montaban,* to Burns for a charter to Hong Kong. In the charter agreement it was stated that the ship was "now in the port of Amsterdam," at which port the ship did not . . . arrive until several days later. Burns refused to accept the vessel when ready to load and contended that the representation was a condition of the contract. Decide.

2. Land Company agreed to sell property to Loud under a contract whereby he was to pay a certain amount when the contract was made and a certain amount on other specified dates, and whereby he was to receive no title until after all installments were paid. Land Company sues for the first installment; Loud defends on the ground that the company did not tender a deed as a condition precedent to the recovery of the installment. Decide.

3. In payment for certain shares of corporate stock, defendants gave their note, which contained the provision that "Said units of stock are not to be issued or delivered until this note is paid in full, whereupon the said unit shares of stock are to be issued and delivered." When the note was not paid at maturity, plaintiff brought suit to collect on it, but at no time tendered the stock. Defendants claimed that since the bank did not tender the stock it had no right to recover on the note. Decide.

4. The defendant ordered catalog covers from the plaintiff in accordance with proofs submitted by the plaintiff to the defendant. In printing the covers, the plaintiff put the defendant's firm name at the bottom of the last page, which was a deviation from the proofs. The defendant refused to accept the goods and plaintiff brought suit to recover alleging substantial performance. Decide.

5. Plain contracted to construct a building for defendant according to specifications and plans provided. As an outstanding feature of the interior, the building was to contain a stairway from the center of the main floor. Plain made an error in construction of the stairway, making it only 5′ 7″ instead of 6′ 3″, as specified, and defendant refused to pay, claiming that the stairs, as constructed, were not up to the standards required of plaintiff. When Plain sued for payment, defendant entered a counterclaim, seeking to rescind the contract. Decide.

6. Plaintiff agreed to paint a portrait of defendant's father for $500, the work to be "to the entire satisfaction of all concerned." When the portrait was finished, defendant was not satisfied and refused to accept it. Suit was brought to recover the contract price. Decide.

7. Omar ordered from plaintiff certain men's fall apparel with the understanding that the order was to be shipped by August 25. Shipment was not made until September 28, and defendants did not receive the goods until October 22, at which time Omar refused to accept delivery and immediately returned them. Plaintiff brought an action for $173.25, which he alleged to be due him. Decide.

8. Plaintiff purchased concrete blocks from defendants, who were the manufacturers and distributors of these materials. Defendants failed to make delivery at the time specified in the contract, claiming their failure was due to a gasoline shortage. Plaintiff brought suit for damages. Defendant contended impossibility of performance. Decide.

REMEDIES 18

Various remedies are available to a contracting party injured by the other party's failure to perform. Which remedy is employed will depend upon the circumstances of the case. The injured party may desire to rescind the contract and be restored to his original position, with each party returning any benefits he has received. *Rescission* will relieve the parties of their contractual obligations. Another alternative open to the injured party is to demand performance by the other side. *Specific performance* is asked to force performance as agreed in the original contract. *Monetary compensation* for damages may be sought by the injured party for any unexcused breach of contract where it can be shown that he incurred an actual loss as a direct result of the failure of the other party to perform. A fourth, and less common, remedy is the *injunction*. It may be employed to prevent a breach of contract.

RESCISSION

Rescission, or relief from contractual obligations, may be granted by the courts where the circumstances require it. For example, if A secures B's signature on a contract by fraud, B may ask to have the contract rescinded by a court of equity. When granting relief from contractual commitments, the court will usually restore the parties to their original position.

Rescission is usually granted in the following cases:

1. when the agreement was induced by fraud, duress, or undue influence;
2. when the contractual undertaking resulted from a mistake;
3. when one of the parties lacked contractual capacity, and
4. when a material breach of contract has deprived the plaintiff of what he bargained for under the contract.

SPECIFIC PERFORMANCE

Where the subject matter of a contract is unique, a monetary award to the injured party may be inadequate compensation. In such cases, the court may grant specific performance, an equitable remedy developed at common law. It had long been argued that a party to a contract had a right to break it and pay damages. However, when the damages did not compensate, it was insisted that the other party was entitled to performance. In these latter cases equity forced performance as agreed upon in the contract.

A court will not ordinarily decree specific performance for personal services, since this would be closely akin to involuntary servitude. In cases involving unique or extraordinary services, the courts may enjoin a party to a contract from performing such services for others during the term of the contract. Two contractual situations in which decrees for specific performance may be granted are contracts for the sale of real estate, because no two pieces of land are alike (and therefore every piece is unique), and contracts for the sale of personal property which has a particular value that makes it impossible to duplicate the items on the open market (for example, art objects and stock in a closed corporation).

MONEY DAMAGES

The word *damage* means a "loss" or harm suffered; the plural, *damages,* usually refers to money awarded as compensation for such loss, but it is sometimes used to mean both the harm suffered and the compensation. As a rule, the injured party is entitled to recover enough money to put him in as good a position as he would have been in had the contract been fully performed by the defendant. This sum is referred to as the actual damages, since they are awarded to compensate the injured party for losses actually sustained as a result of the breach. The value of the promised performance less the cost of the plaintiff's performance is the ordinary measure of recovery. In addition, the injured party is usually entitled to interest on the damages and to reimbursement for some of the cost of bringing the action. If at the time of the breach the plaintiff has rendered partial performance, his damages include the cost of partial performance. However, he is not ordinarily permitted to recover attorney's fees, witness fees, or other legal expenses.

In order to recover money damages, the injured party must show:

1. that a breach actually occurred;
2. that the loss is measurable, not speculative;
3. that the loss resulted from the breach; and
4. that he has done his best to mitigate the loss.

DUTY TO MITIGATE DAMAGES

Once a breach occurs, the injured party must do everything within reason to minimize the amount of damage he sustains. In other words, in an action for breach of contract, he cannot recover for damages that, after he was aware of the breach, he could have avoided. For example, suppose A and B enter into a written contract under which A agrees to employ B for two years at a monthly salary of $700. At the end of the first year A fires B without cause. B is not warranted in remaining unemployed for the second year on the assumption that he will be able to recover $8400 in damages from A. The law requires that B make a reasonable effort to find similar employment with another employer in the same locale. He is not allowed to increase his damages willfully, either through action or through inaction.

NOMINAL DAMAGES

Any breach of contract, no matter how slight, gives the injured party a right of action. Nominal damages are awarded the plaintiff where he is able to show a breach of contract by the other party but is unable to prove any actual loss or injury as a result. The nominal sum awarded may be quite small— perhaps one dollar. The court will also assess court costs against the losing party.

PUNITIVE OR EXEMPLARY DAMAGES

Punitive or exemplary damages are usually awarded in tort cases; they may also be awarded in an action for breach of contract to marry. Their objective is to punish the defendant for fraud, malice, or willful misconduct. For example, where the promise is broken under humiliating circumstances and in such a way as to injure the plaintiff's character, the court may award exemplary damages. Exemplary damages are awarded not in place of, but in addition to, actual damages. In fact, a verdict for exemplary damages may be given if a cause of action is proved even though there is no finding of substantial damage.

CONSEQUENTIAL DAMAGES

The limit of liability in breach of contract cases is ordinarily compensation for such losses sustained as the defendant had probable cause to foresee as a result of breach when the contract was made. In most cases, the court will not award damages for loss or injury resulting from unexpected or unusual consequences of a breach. For example, suppose A had a contract to deliver raw materials to B and B had a contract with C for the finished product. If A fails to deliver, this will cause B to breach his contract with C. B cannot recover from A the cost of the subsequent breach unless A was aware that the second contract was dependent on performance of the first. In other words, a party who breaks his agreement is expected to reimburse the other party for any losses that would normally result from his failure to perform his obligation, but he is not expected to pay for losses that are out of the ordinary and are caused by conditions he did not contemplate when he assented to the contract.

MEASURE OF DAMAGES

The amount of damages is usually determined by the jury. The object of the award is to compensate the injured party as much as possible for any losses incurred as a result of the other party's failure to perform. As a rule, the measure of damages is the loss which the injured party can prove he sustained as a result of the breach. Regardless of the situation, the plaintiff must introduce evidence sufficient to afford basis for estimating the loss in money with reasonable certainty. For example, in a contract of sale, the measure of damages is the difference between the contract price and the market price at the time of the breach. In an employment contract the damage is the money that the employee would have been paid had the contract not been breached, less what he earned or should have earned for the balance of the contract period had he been able to obtain another similar position. When the injured party does not incur an actual loss from the breach, he is entitled only to nominal damages. There is no rule of thumb for determining the amount of exemplary damages. This will vary according to the degree of misconduct and other circumstances of the case.

LIQUIDATED DAMAGES

For the express purpose of avoiding the expense of litigation, many contracts stipulate the amount of damages to be paid as the cost of nonperformance in the event of a breach of particular terms. These damages are referred to as liquidated damages, and the injured party has a right to claim the amount specified as the measure of damages. In practice, the reason for providing for liquidated damages is that in certain kinds of contracts it is often difficult to estimate with any degree of accuracy the amount of actual damages that would result from a breach. For example, a typical construction contract will provide that if the contractor has not completed performance by a specified time he must pay a certain amount per day until performance is completed. For liquidated damages to be recovered, the amount stipulated must be reasonable and must bear some relationship to the probable damages incurred by the injured party. Furthermore, it must be evident that the money was intended as compensation for a possible breach and not as a penalty to force performance. Liquidated damages will be construed as a penalty when the amount on the fact of the contract is out of proportion to the possible loss, even if this is contrary to the intention of the parties. However, once the court decides that the amount is reasonable, that amount will be awarded, regardless of the actual damages sustained by the injured party.

INJUNCTION

The principal use of the injunction as a remedy in contract law is to enjoin the other party from breaching a negative covenant of his contract. In the usual situation, the law cannot prevent the commission of an injury and can afford a remedy only after the injury has been suffered. However, a court of equity can prevent the commission of a wrong by an injunction. For example, suppose A had contracted to play basketball for a certain team for one year, with a one-year option; he agreed not to play for anyone else during the second year. If A broke his contract with the team and was preparing to play for a rival team, his original team could file a suit in equity to enjoin him from playing for anyone else. Under such circumstances, an injunction would be issued ordering A to refrain from violating his contract. A would therefore be required to sit out the second year of his contract. In such cases the injured party must prove that the services which the employee contracted to perform were unique in character, requiring special skill and ability, and that it would be extremely difficult to replace him. The injunction is also available to prevent a breach of contract where the seller of a going business agrees not to compete in a given territory for a certain period of time.

LEGAL PRINCIPLES

The nature of the remedy available for breach of contract depends upon the circumstances of each case. Remedies available are rescission, specific performance, money damages, and injunction.

Rescission will normally relieve the parties of their contractual obligation and return them to the position prior to the breach.

Specific performance can be used when the subject matter of the contract is unique and when an award of money damages would be inadequate.

Money damages will be granted when it can be shown that an actual out-of-pocket loss occurred as a direct result of the breach.

Damages may be actual, nominal, special, exemplary or punitive, or liquidated.

Before an award for money damages will be granted it must be shown by the injured party that: (1) a breach has actually occurred; (2) a loss has occurred that is measurable, not speculative; (3) the loss resulted from the breach; (4) there was an attempt by the injured party to mitigate the loss. The measure of actual damages is usually the cost of the breach as an outright dollars-and-cents loss.

CASE FOR REVIEW

CAMPBELL SOUP CO. v. WENTZ

172 F.2d 80 (1948)

On June 21, 1947, Campbell Soup Company (Campbell), a New Jersey corporation, entered into a written contract with George B. Wentz and Harry T. Wentz, who are Pennsylvania farmers, for delivery by the Wentzes to Campbell of all the Chantenay red cored carrots to be grown on fifteen acres of the Wentz farm during the 1947 season. The contract provides . . . for delivery of the carrots at the Campbell plant in Camden, New Jersey. The prices specified in the contract ranged from $23 to $30 per ton according to the time of delivery. The contract price for January, 1948 was $30 a ton.

The Wentzes harvested approximately 100 tons of carrots from the fifteen acres covered by the contract. Early in January, 1948, they told a Campbell representative that they would not deliver their carrots at the contract price. The market price at the time was at least $90 per ton, and Chantenay red cored carrots were virtually unobtainable. The Wentzes then sold approximately 62 tons of their carrots to the defendant Lojeski, a neighboring farmer. Lojeski resold about 58 tons on the open market, approximately half to Campbell and the balance to other purchasers.

On January 9, 1948, Campbell, suspecting that Lojeski was selling it "contract carrots," refused to purchase any more, and instituted these suits against the Wentz brothers and Lojeski to enjoin further sale of the contract carrots to others, and to compel specific performance of the contract.

We think that on the question of adequacy of the legal remedy the case is one appropriate for specific performance. It was expressly found that at the time of the trial it was "virtually impossible to obtain Chantenay carrots in the open market." This Chantenay carrot is one which the plaintiff uses in large quantities, furnishing the seed to the growers with whom it makes contracts. It was not claimed that in nutritive value it is any better than other types of carrots. Its blunt shape makes it easier to handle in processing. And its color and texture differ from other varieties. The color is brighter than other carrots. The trail court found that the plaintiff failed to establish what proportion of its carrots is used for the production of soup stock and what proportion is used as identifiable physical ingredients in its soups. We do not think lack of proof on that point is material. It did appear that the plaintiff uses carrots in fifteen of its twenty-one soups. It also appeared that it uses these Chantenay carrots diced in some of them and that the appearance is uniform. The preservation of uniformity in appearance in a food article marketed throughout the country and sold under the manufacturer's name is a matter of considerable commercial significance and one which is properly considered in determining whether a substitute ingredient is just as good as the original.

. . . We see no reason why a court should be reluctant to grant specific relief when it can be given without supervision of the court or other time-consuming processes against one who has deliberately broken his agreement. Here the goods of the special type contracted for were unavailable on the open market, the plaintiff had contracted for them long ahead in anticipation of its needs, and had built up a general reputation for its products as part of which reputation uniform appearance was important. We think if this were all that was involved in the case specific performance should have been granted.

The reason that we shall affirm instead of reversing with an order for specific performance is found in the contract itself. We think it is too hard a bargain and too one-sided an agreement to entitle the plaintiff to relief in a court of conscience. For each individual grower the agreement is made by filling in names and quantity and price on a printed form furnished by the buyer. This form has quite obviously been drawn by skillful draftsmen with the buyer's interests in mind.

Paragraph 2 provides for the manner of delivery. Carrots are to have their stalks cut off and be in clean sanitary bags or other containers approved by Campbell. This paragraph concludes with a statement that Campbell's determination of conformance with specifications shall be conclusive.

The defendants attack this provision as unconscionable. We do not think that it is, standing by itself. We think that the provision is comparable to the promise to perform to the satisfaction of another and that Campbell would be held liable if it refused carrots which did in fact conform to the specifications.

The next paragraph allows Campbell to refuse carrots in excess of twelve tons to the acre. The next contains a covenant by the grower that he will not sell carrots to anyone else except the carrots rejected by Campbell nor will he permit anyone else to grow carrots on his land. Paragraph 10 provides liquidated damages to the extent of $50 per acre for any breach by the grower. There is no provision for liquidated or any other damages for breach of contract by Campbell.

The provision of the contract which we think is the hardest is paragraph 9.

. . . It will be noted that Campbell is excused from accepting carrots under certain circumstances. But even under such circumstances the grower, while he cannot say Campbell is liable for failure to take the carrots, is not permitted to sell them elsewhere unless Campbell agrees. This is the kind of provision which the late Francis H. Bohlen would call "carrying a good joke too far." What the grower may do with his product under the circumstances set out is not clear. He has covenanted not to store it anywhere except on his own farm and also not to sell to anybody else.

We are not suggesting that the contract is illegal. Nor are we suggesting any excuse for the grower in this case who has deliberately broken an agreement entered into with Campbell. We do think, however, that a party who has offered and succeeded in getting an agreement as tough as this one is, should not come to a chancellor and ask court help in the enforcement of its terms. That equity does not enforce unconscionable bargains is too well established to require elaborate citation.

. . . As already said, we do not suggest that this contract is illegal. All we way is that the sum total of its provisions drives too hard a bargain for a court of conscience to assist.

CASE PROBLEMS

1. Cannon contracted to lease from Gunn two buildings, one at 26-28 West Street and the other, an adjoining building, at 22-24 West Street, for a period of three years beginning February 1. The two buildings were alike in all services and were intended as roominghouses. On February 1, Gunn refused to execute the lease for the building at 22-24 West Street. Cannon brought suit for damages in the amount of the profits that he asserted he would have earned by operation of the roominghouse. Decide.

2. On September 2, plaintiff made a contract with defendants to build a house for $23,850. Plaintiff began work and received payments totaling $18,000, and on November 22, received notice from the defendants advising him of the cancellation of the agreement because of defective workmanship. Defendants engaged another contractor to redo some of the plaintiff's work and paid him $7500 to complete the job. Plaintiff brought suit and defendants put in a counterclaim for the excess they had paid over the contract price. Decide.

3. Bott took out a fire insurance policy with Mutual Globe Insurance Company which contained a clause permitting the company to cancel the policy at its election. Bott was notified of cancellation to take effect the 23rd of November but, although he was told that his money would be refunded upon his calling at the company's office, no premiums were returned to him. The insured property was later destroyed by fire and Bott, claiming that the policy was still in force, brought an action for damages. Decide.

4. Smith and Jones entered into a contract whereby Smith was to sell to Jones his restaurant and bar business with all fixtures and contents, and transfer to him his liquor license if the transfer were approved by the Ohio Liquor Commission. The Commission gave its proposal to the proposed agreement. Smith refused to perform, and Jones brought an action for specific performance. Decide.

5. Plaintiff entered into a contract with defendant whereby the defendant would purchase and take possession of his clothing business on July 1. After taking possession, the defendant abandoned the premises and refused to complete the

transaction. Plaintiff resumed possession of the business and retained the proceeds of the sales made while defendant had possession. Plaintiff brought suit to recover damages for breach of contract. Decide.

6. Dealer entered into a written contract with a distributor whereby the latter appointed him "exclusive wholesale distributor of Berghoff beer" for five years in a designated territory. The distributor breached the agreement by selling their beer to others in the territory within the five-year period. Dealer brought an action for an injunction to prevent these sales. Decide.

7. Builder contracted to place a reinforced concrete floor in a warehouse for the owner of the building. Before the floor was completed, the warehouse was destroyed by a fire, caused by no fault of either party. An action was brought to recover for partial performance of the contract. Judgment was for builder and defendant appealed. Decide.

8. Plain contracted to make certain alterations and additions to defendant's property and to provide the necessary materials. The job included rebuilding a private chapel for which Plain had to order specially designed millwork. In March 1973, a fire, not caused by any fault or negligence of either party, destroyed the chapel. At that time the special millwork had been completed but had not been delivered or approved by the architect. Defendant paid $10,522.08 for the work done and the materials that were installed before the fire. Plain brought suit to collect an additional $4407.84, the price of the millwork. Decide.

PART III
THE AGENCY AND
EMPLOYMENT RELATIONSHIP

THE NATURE OF THE EMPLOYMENT RELATIONSHIP

Employment relationships are normally created by a contract. This agreement may be in writing and recites in some detail the exact terms of the employment relationship. It may also be oral and informal. For example, Mrs. Wiley Wood employs Ellie, her maid, on the basis of an oral agreement. By virtue of her assigned household duties the relationship created is that of employer-employee. The situation is altered, however, on those days that Ellie makes purchases for the Wood household on the credit of her employer. Then she is acting as an agent for the purposes of contracting with the various business firms. On the other hand, Mr. Wood employs an accountant to care for the books of his firm and to prepare his income tax. The basis of this relationship is a formal contract. The accountant will operate as an independent contractor because Mr. Wood is interested only in the end result of his work-product and has no control over the accomplishment of the desired results. Whatever the situation, the laws regulating employment relationships should be consulted to determine their applicability.

EMPLOYMENT RELATIONSHIPS

An *employee* is an individual whose function it is to perform personally a task or a series of tasks for his employer. In the performance of these tasks he is subject to the control and direction of his employer. The tasks themselves are purely mechanical or manual acts and services. There is no direct involvement with third persons. Factory workers, coal miners, and farm hands are typical employees.

An individual need not always use a representative to accomplish results; he may prescribe the end result and obtain the contractual promise of another person to perform the act. The *independent contractor's* function is simply to perform an agreed task for an agreed price. The finished job must meet certain requirements, but the contractor, and not the employer, controls *how* the job is done—in what manner and using what methods and materials. Furthermore, an employer is not liable for the torts of an independent contractor, nor does an independent contractor have authority to obligate an employer on contracts. (See Figure 19-1).

However, employers frequently find it necessary to employ *agents* to act for them in business transactions. The agent carries out the instructions of the principal, but he is granted certain powers and rights, to be exercised for the principal's benefit; these powers and rights constitute authority vested in the agent by the principal.

174

AGENCY-INDEPENDENT CONTRACTOR DIAGRAM

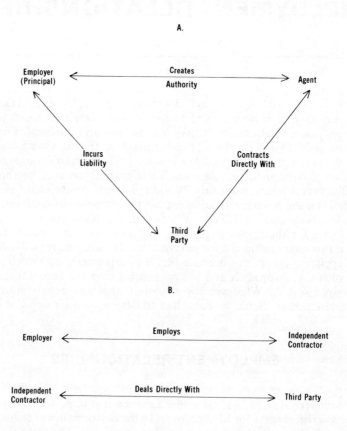

Figure 19-1

CREATION OF AN AGENCY RELATIONSHIP

Agency is a legal relationship, based upon the express or implied consent of the parties involved, that is created when one party, the agent, is employed to represent another, the principal, in contractual matters with third persons. A principal may appoint an agent to conduct any transaction that he may legally conduct himself. With few exceptions, any qualified person may employ an agent to represent him and act on his behalf. The conduct of the parties is evidence of, and determines the nature of, the relationship. In all instances of agency the parties must consent to act in accordance with an agreement, but there need not be a formal, written contract between them. Their relationship is governed by a body of law that defines their rights and liabilities with respect to each other and to third persons.

Agency is basically a relationship between individuals. An agency relationship exists whenever one person is authorized to make a contract for another. The modern corporation employs numerous representatives: management personnel, purchasing agents, salesmen, and lawyers may act in behalf of the corporation. Most business ventures, except the single proprietorship, call for the employment of representatives in various capacities.

An agency is created when one party is given express authority to act for or on behalf of another. A contract detailing the nature of the authority being bestowed may be drawn up, or the authorization may be made orally. (Better business practice dictates that the extent of the agent's authority be detailed in a formal statement.) However the authorization is made, the agency agreement must be entered into with the consent of both the principal and the agent. Consent is held to mean that the parties intended that an agency should exist. This intention must find expression either in the words or actions of the parties. (See Figure 19-2)

Agency may also be created by the conduct of the parties. When the principal's conduct leads the agent to believe that the principal condones his acting as an agent, this in itself may be sufficient to create an agency. The fact that no contract is involved does not affect the agent's power to bind his principal in contracts. Likewise, an agency relationship may exist under an agreement unsupported by consideration. The acts of an agent under a gratuitous appointment are as binding upon the principal as where consideration is present.

CAPACITY OF PARTIES

Since it is not necessary that the relation of the principal and agent be contractual, it is not necessary that the principal have the capacity to contract when he appoints an agent. However, because agency does require the consent of the parties, the principal must have sufficient legal capacity to give valid consent to the agreement.

A person whose legal capacity is limited cannot increase his capacity by appointing an agent. Thus, any appointment of an agent by an infant or an insane person for the purpose of increasing capacity is void, and any agreement entered into by the agent would be ineffective. However, an infant or an insane person can be bound by the acts of an agent to the extent that he would be bound had he himself acted.

Nevertheless, an infant or an insane person may act as an agent for someone else and may make binding agreements for his principal. Any person, regardless of his age or mentality, who understands the nature of the relationship and who has the capacity to perform may serve as an agent. Within this capacity of agency, the infant or insane person has the right to terminate his contract of agency at his will.

Business firms, such as corporations or partnerships, that are able to make contracts must appoint agents in order to conduct business. Although the partnership is not recognized as a legal entity, each partner acts as the agent of his co-partners. Furthermore, if one partner appoints an agent for the partnership, the agent is the agent of all the partners.

176

POWER OF ATTORNEY

KNOW ALL MEN BY THESE PRESENTS that I, Michael John, of North Canton, county of Stark, state of Ohio, have made, constituted and appointed, and by these presents do make, constitute and appoint Timothy David, of North Canton, county of Stark, state of Ohio, my lawful agent and attorney for me, and in my name, and for my use, to ask, demand, sue for, recover and receive all such sum or sums of money, debts, goods, wares and other demands whatsoever, which are or shall be due, owing, payable and belonging to me, in the conduct of my business. Upon the receipt of any such debts, dues or sums of money, or discharges, done in my name, I hereby authorize said agent and attorney, to give proper receipt or release for same. My said agent and attorney is hereby given the authority to perform all things necessary to be done in order to carry out and execute the purposes of this power of attorney.

IN WITNESS WHEREOF, I have hereunto set my hand and seal this 8th day of March, 1976.

WITNESSES:

_____   _____(Seal)

_____

Figure 19-2

Normally, anyone can be an agent who is capable of performing the functions involved. An agent must be capable of carrying out the principal's instructions, but he need not have the capacity to contract, since the contract that is made usually does not bind the agent himself. The legal status of a contract is determined by the principal's capacity to contract, not the agent's. As a rule, a partnership may serve as an agent, but the capacity of a corporation to serve as an agent will depend on the scope of the powers granted it by its charter.

AUTHORIZATION

The authorization of an agent may be made by any actions of the principal which indicate that the agent is to act in his behalf. This authority may be conferred by written or spoken words or by some other conduct of the principal that may reasonably be construed as authorization.

There are three main classifications of authority: (1) express, (2) implied, and (3) apparent.

EXPRESS AUTHORITY

The most common procedure followed in the creation of agency is for the principal to confer express authority upon the agent by virtue of a contract. The agreement may be detailed or quite general; in the latter case the extent of authority is governed by such items as commercial customs and business usages. Another factor affecting authority is the power of other agents in similar positions. However, as the term implies, express authority is an indication that the principal has detailed the extent to which the agent acts on his behalf in contractual relationship with third parties.

IMPLIED AUTHORITY

The courts have generally held that where authority is expressly conferred upon an agent, the agent also has the implied authority to perform any acts necessary to carry out the business he has been authorized to do. It is not essential in giving express authority to spell out every detail. The evidence examined to determine the scope of an agent's implied authority includes those factors upon which the agent bases his justified and reasonable belief as to what authority he possesses.

In cases where the agent is unable to contact the principal for instructions, a special type of implied authority arises that is governed by the personal judgment of the agent. These cases are emergency situations in which the agent's authority becomes implied by virtue of the contingency.

APPARENT AUTHORITY

Apparent authority is that authority which the principal, by his conduct, has led third persons justifiably to believe he had conferred on the agent, when in fact such authority has not been conferred. If a third party mistakenly relies on the apparent authority of an agent, the principal is legally prohibited from denying that such authority exists. This prohibition is an *estoppel*.

Apparent authority may be greater than, less than, or equal to an agent's actual authority. The extent of apparent authority is determined by analyzing the relation between the principal and third persons.

Apparent authority is created by the actions of the principal, as is express authority, except that the impression of conferral created by the principal must be conveyed to a third person rather than to the agent. A principal may be held liable on the basis of apparent authority only if there is willful or negligent conduct on his part which reasonably leads the third person to believe that he could rely on that authority. The objective evidence upon which the third person has based his beliefs may be the words or conduct of the principal, standard practices of trade, or the fact that the principal has appointed the agent to perform a task that implies a certain amount of authority. For example, suppose that an agent is designated as a "manager" and on occasion is left in charge of the business establishment. It would be unreasonable for third persons to believe that his authority has been limited to that of a mere clerk.

TYPES OF AGENTS

There are a number of types of agency relationships that may be created by a principal and agent. These are more commonly identified as general, special, professional, or gratuitous.

GENERAL AND SPECIAL AGENTS

A *general agent* usually possesses a wide grant of general authority to represent his principal in a series of transactions over a period of time. Mr. Wood employs Mr. Brady as his purchasing agent. It is necessary for Mr. Brady to possess this wide grant of authority to function in his position. He likewise possesses a much broader amount of apparent authority than most agents would possess.

Mrs. Wood's use of her maid to make household purchases on credit creates a special agency. A *special agent* is one who is generally employed to conduct a single transaction or perhaps a limited number of transactions. Because of the nature of his employment, his authority is more limited and he has little or no apparent authority.

PROFESSIONAL AGENTS

A *professional agent* is a person who publicly offers to act as an agent for others for a fee. He is subject to the principal's control while handling his business, but he is not under his control with respect to how the business is conducted. For example, you may employ a real estate broker to sell your house. You have control over the business transaction but not over the obtaining of prospects to buy. In general, the laws of principal and agent apply to a principal and a professional agent.

GRATUITOUS AGENTS

An agency relationship may be created when the agent would not be compensated for his services. The promise of the agent who acts without compensation is not enforceable because of lack of consideration. However, where he undertakes performance, he is under a duty to perform properly and reasonably under the circumstances of the situation.

RATIFICATION

Ratification consists of words or conduct by a person that indicate his approval of an unauthorized act done on his behalf. Such action makes the principal liable, just as if he had authorized the act.

Initially, ratification is a matter of intention, when it must be determined whether the principal intended to approve, or ratify, the action of the agent. Ratification is frequently accompanied by reliance by the third party; however, such reliance is not necessary to constitute valid ratification. The following conditions must be present:

1. The person ratifying must have the present ability to do the act himself or to authorize it to be done;
2. The person acting must have acted as the purported agent of his principal;
3. The principal must have been in existence at the time the act was done and must have been competent to do or authorize the act in question;
4. The principal must have had knowledge of all the material facts at the time he ratified the act;
5. The third party must not have canceled the transaction; and
6. The entire transaction must be ratified.

Ordinarily, ratification may be either express or implied. If a person, having full knowledge, accepts the results or benefits of an unauthorized act done on his behalf, he will be bound on the transaction. Silence will not constitute ratification unless, under the circumstances, it very strongly indicates a clear intention to be bound.

Any acts, legal or illegal, that the principal was capable of performing or authorizing at the time the act was done may be ratified. Ratification is irrevocable, and it shifts all responsibility from the agent to the principal for the ratified acts from the time they were completed. It relieves the agent from liability to both the principal and third persons and entitles him to whatever compensation would have been available had the acts been authorized.

SUBDELEGATION OF AUTHORITY

Since agents are usually selected on the basis of their personal qualifications, no agent is allowed to delegate his authority to another without the consent of the principal. If an agent attempts to delegate to a sub-agent any act that involves personal skill, judgment, or trust, without the prior consent of the principal, the sub-agent has no authority to bind the principal. An exception is allowed when the duties delegated are purely ministerial or technical and do not involve the exercise of skill or discretion.

LEGAL PRINCIPLES

Agency is a personal relationship based upon, and requiring, the consent of the parties.

Parties to an employment relationship are classified as employer and employee, employer and independent contractor, principal and agent, or principal and professional agent.

The relationship of employer and independent contractor is closely related to that of employer and employee. The independent contractor however, is not under the control of the employer in regard to the means he uses to achieve the end result.

An agent is entrusted by his principal with the conduct of contractual relations with third persons, subject to the principal's control.

The professional agent is in business for himself. He is subject to the principal's control while he is handling his particular business, but his actions are not otherwise under the control of the principal.

Express authority may be detailed or general, written or oral. In most cases no formalities are required to establish such authority.

Implied authority is that authority which may reasonably and justifiably be considered necessary for the agent to carry out the business he has been authorized to accomplish.

Apparent authority is that authority which the principal has led third persons to believe he has conferred upon his agent.

A person whose legal capacity is limited cannot increase his capacity by appointing an agent. However, such a person may act as an agent for someone else.

A person capable of carrying out his principal's instructions may serve as an agent, even though he does not have the capacity to contract for himself.

Ratification may be express, or it may be implied from the conduct of the principal. Once made, it is irrevocable and shifts all responsibility from the agent to the principal.

In general, third persons may withdraw from unauthorized transactions at any time prior to ratification.

CASE FOR REVIEW

GORTON V. DOTY

57 Idaho 792 (1937)

In September, 1935, an action was commenced by R. S. Gorton, father of Richard Gorton, to recover expenses incurred by the father for hospitalization, physicians', surgeons', and nurses' fees, and another by the son, by his father as guardian ad litem, to recover damages for injuries sustained as a result of an accident.

It appears that in September, 1934, Richard Gorton, a minor, was a junior in the Soda Springs High School and a member of the football team; that his high school team and the Paris High School team were scheduled to play a game of football at Paris on the 21st. Appellant was teaching at the Soda Springs High School and Russell Garst was coaching the Soda Springs team. On the day the game was played, the Soda Springs High School team was transported to and from Paris in privately owned automobiles. One of the automobiles used for that purpose was owned by appellant. Her car was driven by Mr. Garst, the coach of the Soda Springs High School team.

One of the most difficult questions, if not the most difficult, presented by the record is, Was the coach, Russell Garst, the agent of appellant while and in driving her car from Soda Springs to Paris, and in returning to the point where the accident occurred?

Briefly stated, the facts bearing upon that question are as follows: . . . appellant knew the Soda Springs High School football team and the Paris High School football team were to play a game of football at Paris, September 21, 1934; . . . she volunteered her car for use in transporting some of the members of the Soda Springs team to and from the game; . . . she asked the coach, Russell Garst, the day before the game if he had all the cars necessary for the trip to Paris the next day; . . . he said he needed one more; . . . she told him he might use her car if he drove it; . . . she was not promised compensation for the use of her car and did not receive any; . . . the school district paid for the gasoline used on the trip to and from the game; . . . she testified she loaned the car to Mr. Garst; . . . she had not employed Mr. Garst at any time; and . . . she had not at any time "directed his work or his services, or what he was doing."

Specifically, "agency" is the relationship which results from the manifestation of consent by one person to another that the other shall act on his behalf and subject to his control, and consent by the other so to act.

To enable the Soda Springs football team to play football at Paris, it had to be transported to Paris. Automobiles were to be used and another car was needed. At that juncture, appellant volunteered the use of her car. For what purpose? Necessarily for the purpose of furnishing additional transportation. Appellant, of course, could have driven the car herself, but, instead of doing that, she designated the driver (Russell Garst), and, in doing so, made it a condition precedent that that person she designated should drive her car. That appellant thereby at least consented that Russell Garst should act for her and in her behalf, in driving her car to and from the football game, is clear from her act in voluntering the use of her car upon the express condition that he should drive it, and, further, that Mr. Garst consented to so act for appellant is equally clear by his act in driving the car. It is not essential to the existence of authority that there be a contract between principal and agent or that the agent promise to act as such, . . . nor is it essential to the relationship of principal and agent that they, or either, receive compensation . . .

It is vigorously contended, however, that the facts and circumstances bearing upon the question under discussion show appellant loaned her car to Mr. Garst. A determination of that question makes it necessary to quote appellant's testimony. She testified as follows:

"Q. On or about the 21st of September, 1934, state whether or not you permitted Russell Garst to use that car? A. I did.

Q. Under what circumstances? A. I loaned it to him.

Q. When did you loan it to him? Was it that day, or the day before? A. On the day before I told him he might have it the next day.

Q. Did you receive any compensation, or were you promised any compensation, for its use? A. No, sir.

Q. What were the circumstances under which you permitted him to take it? A. Well—"

After having so testified, appellant was then asked:

"Q. You may relate the conversation with him, if there was such conversation. A. I asked him if he had all the cars necessary for his trip to Paris the next day. He said he needed one more. I said that he might use mine if he drove it. That was the extent of it."

While it appears that appellant first testified that she permitted Russell Garst to use her car and also that she loaned it to him, it further appears that, when she was immediately afterward asked to state the conversation she had with the coach about the matter, she stated that she asked him if he had all the cars necessary for the trip to Paris the next day, that he said he needed one more, that she said he might use her car if he drove it, and, finally, she said that that was the extent of it. It is clear, then, that appellant intended, in relating the conversation she had with the coach, to state the circumstances fully, because, after having testified to the conversation, she concluded by saying, "That was the extent of it." Thus she gave the jury to understand that those were the circumstances, and all of the circumstances, under which Russell Garst drove her car to the football game. If the appellant fully and correctly related the conversation she had with the coach and the circumstances under which he drove her car, as she unquestionably undertook, and did, do, it follows that, as a matter of fact, she did not say anything whatever to him about loaning her car and he said nothing whatever to her about borrowing it.

We therefore conclude the evidence sufficiently supports the finding of the jury that the relationship of principal and agent existed between appellant and Russell Garst.

CASE PROBLEMS

1. Plaintiff was one of a group of boys operating motor scooters supplied by the defendant for the sale of ice cream. Each boy operated within a designated area, paying his own expenses, working when he pleased without supervision, selling at prices fixed by him and accounting each evening for sales at the wholesale rate. Plaintiff brought suit against the defendant because of an accident while driving a scooter. Decide.

2. Plaintiff slipped on an icy sidewalk which was the result of water being negligently spilled by defendant's nephew. It was alleged that the nephew was gratuitously carrying the water for the defendant to use in washing his car. Plaintiff brought suit for the injuries. Decide.

3. While Barber was on an extended business trip, his wife traded in his 1973 Buick, which he had left at home for her use, on the purchase of a 1974 automobile from

the Carolina Auto Sales Company. When he returned to the United States, Barber sued the company for the value of the Buick, contending that his wife was not his agent and had no authority to sell his automobile. Decide.

4. The plaintiff and the defendant were owners of adjoining pieces of property. Upon the plaintiff's property there was a house. The defendent's property was vacant, and was covered with a mass of rock, which extended above the curb. The defendant made a contract with Tobin to excavate his plot to the depth of 10 feet below the curb line, preparatory to building thereon. In the performance of the contract, Tobin appears to have proceeded unskillfully and with considerable recklessness, and, in the work of blasting, he caused some damage to the plaintiff's house, both within and without. For the damages the plaintiff brought suit. Decide.

5. On November 10, 1976, the accountant employed by defendant corporation, under express direction of one of its officers, signed for one typewriter, which was delivered by plaintiff and paid for. On December 1, 1976, the same accountant, on his own initiative, signed a second order for an additional typewriter. When the second typewriter was delivered, defendants disclaimed it and asked plaintiff to remove it. Plaintiff sued for the price of the second typewriter. Decide.

6. Reco's farm was operated by his agent, Berry. The latter hired Wagner to bale hay in 1973, telling him to bill Reco for his work. Wagner did so and was paid by Reco. By the summer of 1974, Reco had terminated the agency, but, as Berry remained in possession as tenant of the farm, nothing appeared changed. In 1974, he again asked Wagner to bale hay and bill Reco. When Reco refused to pay, on the ground that Berry was no longer his agent, Wagner brought suit to enforce payment. Decide.

7. Dahl was a typewriter sales agent for plaintiff with authority to collect for machines sold. Defendant, Davis, operated a casino where Dahl lost several hundred dollars of plaintiff's money. To make up his shortage, Dahl borrowed $125 from Davis and gave two of plaintiff's typewriters as security. Dahl sent the $125 to plaintiff, who credited it to his account. Plaintiff then brought an action to recover the two typewriters. Defendant claimed the right to hold the machines until the loan is repaid, on the ground that plaintiff's retention of the $125 was ratification of the transaction. Decide.

8. In February, 1976, plaintiff received from defendant company, in which he was insured against disability, a letter stating that the company cancelled the insurance, and an enclosed check for premiums paid. In July, plaintiff's wife, without authority, cashed the check, which fact plaintiff learned three months later. The next year he brought suit on the policy. Decide.

PRINCIPALS AND AGENTS   20

Certain rights and obligations are created by the agency agreement and are inherent in the agency relationship. They arise upon the establishment of the agency and may continue after its termination. The duties binding upon the agent remain binding even when he receives no compensation for them. The obligations the principal in turn owes his agent may be in contract or tort liabilities.

PRINCIPALS' OBLIGATIONS TO AGENTS

Contract liabilities of principals are classified as compensation, reimbursement for expenses, or indemnity for losses sustained.

COMPENSATION

It is the duty of the principal to employ the agent in accordance with the terms of their agreement and to pay him the agreed compensation. Where no definite compensation has been agreed upon, the principal must pay the agent a sum equal to the reasonable value of the agent's services. Where relatives or friends work for each other and no express agreement has been formulated, the services may be deemed gratuitous. An agent's claim to compensation is based on the performance of his task or, in the event of his improper discharge before the end of a preestablished period, his claim for damages.

REIMBURSEMENT (TO AGENT FOR HIS EXPENSES)

The principal must reimburse the agent for expenses incurred in performing duties on his behalf. The agent is not entitled to reimbursement for expenses caused by his own neglect or incurred through actions that were not within the scope of his authority.

INDEMNITY (TO AGENT FOR THIRD PARTY LIABILITY)

The agent is justified in presuming that instructions given by the principal are instructions that he has a legal right to give. Where this is not the case and the agent incurs a liability to some third party because of trepass or conversion, the principal must indemnify the agent against loss.

The principal is charged with notifying third parties of any limitations upon his agent's authority that would not be reasonably assumed by the third party.

AGENTS' OBLIGATIONS TO PRINCIPALS

Anyone who serves as an agent acts in a representative capacity. His obligations to his principal include loyalty, obedience, care and skill in handling the principal's affairs, a complete accounting of his actions, and the full reporting of information.

LOYALTY

An agent has a definite obligation to be loyal to the interests of his principal. He can undertake no business venture that competes with or interferes in any manner with the business of his employer, nor can he make any contract for himself that he should have made for his principal. Thus a sales agent cannot sell his principal's property to himself, unless the principal agrees to the sale. Similarly, a purchasing agent cannot buy his own property or property in which he has an interest.

If an agent does buy from or sell to himself, either directly or indirectly, without the consent of the principal, the principal has the right to have the transaction set aside. Such contracts are voidable at his election even when the price received was the best obtainable, the transaction was free from fraud, and the agent honestly believed that he was pursuing a course that would be most beneficial to his principal.

As a rule, an agent is not permitted to represent both parties to a transaction. However, if the agent is acting as a middleman, whose duty it is to bring the parties together so that they may negotiate their own transaction, he may represent both parties, provided they have both been informed of his dual role. The law states that if, after this disclosure has been made to the principal, he is willing to allow his agent to continue representing both sides, the agent may resume his dual role. The law *does not presume* approval of such a role by the principal. There must be an express agreement to the dual representation.

In the course of the employment, the principal may reveal to the agent a great deal of information concerning his (the principal's) business. The agent has a duty not to disclose confidential information to a third person or to use such secrets for his own benefit to the detriment of the principal.

The agent is permitted, however, to use general information acquired during the term of his employment. In transacting his principal's business, he may well acquire a great deal of general knowledge about the business in which his principal is engaged. When the employment is terminated, he is free to acquire similar employment and thereby benefit by his knowledge of that particular type of business.

All profits made by an agent from transactions conducted for his principal or resulting from violation of his loyalty to his principal belong to, and may be recovered by, the principal. The contract involved may have been favorable to the employer; nevertheless, the agent is not permitted to make any personal monetary gain or profit as a result of the agency relationship other than the fee paid him by the principal for his services.

OBEDIENCE

The agent must follow lawful instructions given him by the principal that are within the scope of the duties he has been hired to perform. Even where the agent feels that the instructions are a burden or an inconvenience, he must obey them if they are reasonable. If he fails or refuses to follow legitimate instructions, he will be liable to the principal for any damages suffered by the principal as a result.

In some situations the agent may be justified in deviating from instructions. When an emergency arises and the agent is unable to consult his principal, he may be justified in using his own judgment, especially where following his instructions would clearly result in injury to the principal. If an emergency does not exist, the agent must follow instructions even though his course of action seems clearly injurious to the principal.

When the agency is general and the principal has not given the agent detailed instructions, the agent must use his own judgment and follow that course of action which he feels will best further his principal's interest.

SKILL AND DILIGENCE IN HANDLING PRINCIPALS' AFFAIRS

Agents are presumed to exercise that degree of skill and diligence ordinarily expected of persons engaged in the same business. However, an agent need exercise only a reasonable degree of care; he is not liable for a failure to use the highest degree of care possible. Nor, unless he warrants the success of his performance, does he assume the risk of success or satisfaction in negotiations. Of course, an affirmative act to commit a wrong makes the agent liable to the principal.

COMPLETE ACCOUNTING

It is assumed that the agent will keep his property separate and distinct from that of his principal and that agency transactions will be recorded carefully. Money or property entrusted to an agent must be accounted for to the principal. The agent is required to keep records showing receipts and expenditures, and money collected by an agent for his principal should not be commingled with his own funds. If funds are deposited in a bank, they should be kept in a separate account and so designated that a trust is apparent. Otherwise, any loss resulting from an insolvent bank must be borne by the agent. In this situation even the good faith of the agent will not excuse his liability.

DUTY TO COMMUNICATE

The agent has a duty to tell his principal all facts pertinent to the subject matter of the agency that he obtains in the course of his activities as an agent. This rule extends beyond the obligation to inform the principal of conflicting interests of third parties in a particular transaction. It imposes upon the agent a duty to keep the principal fully informed on all matters that materially affect the principal's business. Failure to communicate to the principal notices received in the transaction of the business or to disclose pertinent information will render the agent liable for any resulting injury.

LEGAL PRINCIPLES

The principal has a duty to pay the agent any compensation due him by the terms of the contract of employment. If no contract exists, the principal must pay the reasonable value of the agent's services.

The principal must reimburse the agent for all money advanced and all expenditures made in the course of the performance of his duties. Likewise, the agent must be indemnified for any losses incurred as a result of the agency relationship.

The agent owes a duty of undivided loyalty to his principal. He must not disclose any confidential information gained in the transaction of his principal's business.

An agent authorized to buy or sell for his principal must not buy from or sell to himself unless all the pertinent facts are disclosed to the principal and the principal consents to the transaction.

As a rule, an agent will not be permitted to act as agent for both parties to a transaction.

The agent has a duty to follow and obey the instructions of his principal. Only in emergencies, where following the instructions of the agency agreement would result in injury to the principal, may he disobey his instructions.

The agent has a duty to communicate to the principal all notices received in the course of the transaction of the principal's business.

The agent has a duty to keep a true and accurate account of all property and money of the principal in his possession. If he fails to do so he is liable for any and all losses that may result.

The agent must exercise the degree of care and skill expected of agents performing similar services.

CASE FOR REVIEW

DE PASQUALE v. SOCIETA DE M. S. MARIA

173 A. 623 (1934)

Francesco Loporchio, the president of the defendant society, brought a suit in equity in the name of the society against the vice president, the financial secretary, the corresponding secretary, and the treasurer thereof. The bill alleged that said officers left a meeting of the society taking with them the records and bank books; that they kept the records, correspondence, and bank books of the society; that the vice president issued a call for a special meeting of the society, the secretary sent out notices for this meeting, and said officers threatened to usurp the powers of the president and of the corporation. The bill prayed that these officers be temporarily and permanently enjoined from holding any meeting in accordance with the aforesaid notice and from collecting any dues or money in the name of the society, and further prayed that they be ordered to turn over to the society any money belonging to it. The respondent officers took the subpoenas to plaintiff and engaged him to take charge of the case.

The power of an officer or agent of a corporation to bind the corporation is governed by the general law of agency. . . . As a general rule, an agent or an officer of a corporation must act within the scope of his authority to bind the corporation. But if by reason of an emergency or by necessity it becomes impossible for an agent to protect his principal's property or interests by a strict compliance with his usual or regular authority, the scope of his authority is extended or varied to fit the circumstances. The officer or agent who then acts in good faith and with reasonable discretion, in so acting, is still held to be acting for his principal with authority to bind him by his acts.

The principle of law applicable to the case at bar is stated in American Law Institute, Restatement, Agency, vol, 1 § 47, as follows: "Unless otherwise agreed, if after the authorization is given, an unforeseen situation arises for which the terms of the authorization make no provision and it is impracticable for the agent to communicate with the principal, he is authorized to do what he reasonably believes to be necessary in order to prevent substantial loss to the principal with respect to the interests committed to his charge."

The society was, by decree of the court, for the time being incapable of taking any formal action for its own protection. Its administrative officers were intrusted with the general conduct of the business of the society. It was their duty, in the emergency which had been created by the action of the president, to protect its property and to prevent, by all lawful means, the impending danger to the corporate life. To deny them the authority to protect the corporation by the employment of counsel would be unreasonable and inconsistent with the general authority intrusted to them by the society and would tend to frustrate the purpose for which the society was incorporated.

In the circumstances we are of the opinion that the respondent officers had implied authority to act for the society in the employment of counsel.

CASE PROBLEMS

1. Donald MacArthur was employed by the Gibbs Steel Company as a traveling salesman. His territory included nearly the entire state of Wisconsin and northern Michigan. The employer paid all of his expenses at motels and gave him an allowance of $75 a month for the upkeep and maintenance and operation of his car. The selection of lodgings was left to MacArthur's discretion. In the course of one of his trips he arrived in Madison and stayed at the Madison Club. In the evening he went to a tourist camp on the outskirts of Madison, selecting the cabin because it would be convenient in enabling him to get an early start for Stoughton the next morning. He had a room with a shower bath adjoining and while stepping under the shower he slipped on a small rug, fracturing his femur. He claimed reimbursement for the injury. Decide.
2. Hurte took out hospitalization insurance with the Instant Insurance Company, paying premiums to Krook, Instant's agent, who was authorized "to sell Hospitalization, forms D and R." When Hurte sued on the policy, the insurance company claimed that the policy had lapsed because the last premium due had not been paid. Hurte showed that he had paid the premium to the agent; the company showed that it had never received payment from Krook. Decide the liability.
3. Defendant contracted to pay plaintiff a commission of $750 "in consideration of services rendered in connection with the sale" of defendant's premises, "one-half

of said commission to be paid on signing the agreement for sale of property and the balance on delivery of the deed." The agreement of sale was signed the same day and $3,000 of the purchase price paid on account. At the same time, defendant paid plaintiff $375, one-half the stipulated commission. Two and one-half months later—time having been made of the essence—defendant tendered the deed but the buyer failed to pay the balance of the purchase price, stating that he did not have the money. Thus there was no "delivery of the deed." What will be the decision when plaintiff sues for the balance of his commission?

4. One of defendant's depositors became insane and a trustee was appointed for him. The defendant's trust officer, one of its directors, learned of this in the course of his private affairs. Thereafter, the depositor drew out most of his account. The trustee brought suit to recover the sums drawn out. Decide.

5. Defendant, as broker for plaintiff, obtained a purchase order for a carload of beans from Lexton, who later canceled the order by giving notification to the agent before shipment of the beans was made. The agent failed to communicate this information to plaintiff, who proceeded to ship the beans from Colorado to Kentucky. Because there was no purchaser in Kentucky, the beans had to be returned, at a loss of $500. Plaintiff brought suit against the agent for damages. Decide.

6. Plaintiff brought an action to recover the $300 lost because of defendant's alleged disobedience of instructions. Defendant in Louisiana possessed $300 due plaintiff in North Carolina. Plaintiff instructed "You can send enclosed in letter in $50 or $100 bank drafts." Defendant purchased eighteen drafts, chiefly in denominations of $5, $10, and $20 but one of $100 and enclosed them in a letter carefully folded, sealed, and properly addressed and stamped. The letter never reached its destination. Decide.

7. Plaintiff brings suit for breach of contract to employ him as manager of a building. Defendant ordered plaintiff to bring proceeding for the eviction of tenants. Plaintiff thought that the eviction was unjust and refused. The defendant discharged him. Decide.

8. Schipper & Block contracted to employ plaintiff, Doherty, for a period of eighteen weeks at $125 per week, payable weekly. Plaintiff was discharged before the contract had expired, and at the end of the first week following discharge brought suit, winning a judgement for $125 for the week's wages. The judgment was paid. At the expiration date of the contract he again brought suit, this time to collect the balance that would have been payable under the contract. Defense claimed that the first suit and judgment barred plaintiff from prosecuting the subsequent suit. Decide.

THE ACCOUNTANT 21

Ordinarily an accountant rendering services to clients is considered an independent contractor in that the client bargains for the product of his work. While the services offered vary, it is primarily the area of auditing that raises the various degrees of legal responsibility. It is here that accountants review, investigate, examine, and consider the representations of others, and issue a report in the form of a considered opinion that the representations examined fairly represent the financial position of the business firm. Due to the nature of their services, accountants might incur a liability to their clients, or to non-clients that might make a decision based on his work-product.

DUTY TO CLIENT

The accountant enters into a contractual relationship with his client with respect to the nature of the services to be rendered. It is this agreement that defines and limits the scope of legal responsibility. The accountant is responsible for his opinion of the financial representations. He is not a guarantor of their accuracy, nor is he responsible for the content of the representations. However, his opinion must be the result of professional competency and integrity. His examination must be made in accordance with the generally accepted principles of accounting and standards of auditing.

The accountant must exercise.the same degree of skill and accuracy expected of any prudent accountant with an ordinary degree of competency. The problem in assessing legal responsibility arises because of a difficulty in measuring what amounts to lack of skill. Until a universal definition of acceptable auditing standards is formulated, the contract should be drawn in fairly precise terms. If the accountants are to conduct a cash audit, a balance sheet audit, or a detailed audit, or if they are to produce an unaudited document the contract should plainly state the facts. In some cases, lack of skill may be of no consequence whereas in others it may amount to a breach of contract.

Although the accountant is not an insurer of the accuracy of his work, he must be able to discover whether the financial representations are a statement of actual conditions. He must do more than merely determine mathematical certainty. If he fails to make an investigation when it was indicated, or if his investigation fails to disclose, irregularities that should be reported he will be responsible if he did not use the care of a reasonably prudent accountant. When he exercises this skill, he will not be held liable for errors in judgment that he might make in reporting his opinion. In other words, negligence results from a failure to do, or not to do, that which a reasonable and careful accountant would, or would not, have done under similar circumstances.

When an examination of financial materials has not produced sufficient competent evidence to enable him to form an opinion on the financial statements taken as a whole, an independent auditor should state in his report that he is unable to express an opinion on such statements. The necessity of disclaiming an opinion may arise from a limitation on the scope of his examination, from the existence of uncertainties concerning the amount of an item, or the outcome of a matter materially affecting the financial position of the firm. (See Figures 21-1 and 21-2)

A DISCLAIMER OF OPINION

The accompanying balance sheet of Destructo Toy Company as of December 31, 1976, and the related statements of income and retained earnings and changes in financial position for the year then ended were not audited by us and accordingly we do not express an opinion on them.

December 31, 1976

Figure 21-1

A DISCLAIMER OF OPINION

We are not independent with respect to Destructo Toy Company, and the accompanying balance sheet as of December 31, 1976, and the related statements of income and retained earnings and changes in financial position for the year then ended were not audited by us; accordingly, we do not express an opinion on them.

December 31, 1976

Figure 21-2

DUTY TO THIRD PERSONS

In the usual contractual relationship, the client owes his duty of performance to his client and not to any non-client who might rely on his work. Because there is no privity relationship between the accountant and the non-client, there can be no recovery for negligence.

NEGLIGENCE

The usual exception is the liability of the accountant to the non-client who is the *intended beneficiary* of the accountant's work-product. In order to establish the liability of the accountant it must be shown that he is aware of this intended use of his work-product, that he was negligent in rendering his opinion, and that this negligence was the cause of the damage. Since third party investors are placing ever increasing reliance upon the accountant's work-product, reliance is becoming more foreseeable.

FRAUD

The accountant will be responsible to the person who relies upon his financial statement when it is obvious that the accountant intended to influence that person's conduct. The court must decide when this influence is fraudulent. Usually when there is a misstatement or an omission of a material fact which causes damage to a third person, the accountant is liable to that injured third person. The rationale for such determination is that the accountant is guilty of constructive fraud in falsely representing unqualifiedly that the financial statements fairly represent the firm's position when in fact he really does not know, that this is true. This is known as gross neglect of duty.

In order to establish fraud other than that arising from gross negligence, there must be fraudulent intent. The accountant may be liable for fraud if (1) he is guilty of making a statement known to be untrue or without reasonable grounds for believing it to be true, (2) made with the intent that another person shall act in reliance thereon, (3) if that person relies on the statement, and (4) if the act causes injury to the person relying thereon.

ACCOUNTANT'S STATUTORY LIABILITY

Congress enacted the Securities Act of 1933 to assure that full and fair disclosures are made about the financial condition of most companies selling securities in interstate commerce. To accomplish this purpose, the act specifically requires that all covered companies planning to issue securities must file registration statements with the Securities and Exchange Commission. Section 11 of the act requires that the accountant exercise a high degree of care in the performance of his duties by imposing upon him extensive liability for negligence. It provides that third parties may sue the accountant for damages if the registration statement contains an untrue material fact or omits a material fact that would cause the financial statement to be misleading. The third party need only prove that he incurred a loss; he need not prove that his loss was caused by the falsehoods in the registration statement. The accountant, therefore, has the burden of establishing his freedom from negligence and fraud, not only at the time he makes his statements, but also at the time the registration statement becomes effective.

A "due diligence" defense against liability is available to accountants if they neither knew of deficiencies in the registration statement nor had reason to know of them despite their exercise of due diligence. Due diligence will be determined by how far the accountant should have gone under the circumstances. In other words, the accountant can claim due diligence if after a reasonable investigation, he had no reasonable ground to believe that any statements were untrue or that there was an omission of a material fact or that there were misleading statements intentionally included.

The Securities Act of 1934 is concerned with purchasers or owners of securities issued by registered companies who suffer damages because of reliance on financial statements which contain a false or misleading statement. The accountant may disclaim liability on the grounds that he acted in good faith and had no knowledge that the statements were false or misleading. Thus, he may be negligent but not liable if he acted in good faith.

The federal statutes also impose criminal liability of a fine of not more than $10,000 or imprisonment for not more than five years, or both, if there is a willful falsification or willful omission of any material fact in a registration statement.

PRIVILEGED COMMUNICATION

Ordinarily the relationship between the accountant and his client is dependent upon trust and confidence. At the common law, however, communications between the accountant and his client were not entitled to the status of a privileged communication because the accountant's services were not deemed as indispensible as those of an attorney or a physican. As a result of this, and in absence of case law or a statute to the contrary, the accountant may be compelled to testify against his client on matters arising out of their business relationship.

THE WORK PAPERS

Ownership of the work papers used by the accountant to prepare his work product is basically custodial. Since the accountant is an independent contractor, and not an employee, the work papers of the accountant are solely his property. The client is interested in the end result of his services, namely the work product. However, the possession of a property right in the papers does not give the accountant the legal right to refuse to disclose their contents to parties other than his client, when such disclosure is ordered by the courts. Court decisions have further reduced this property right by not allowing the accountant to reveal their contents except on a court order or to transfer them to a third party without the client's consent. Thus the work papers are preserved as evidence of services rendered and their confidentiality is retained.

LEGAL PRINCIPLES

An accountant is liable for failure to follow recognized, professional standards. The accountant should have a detailed, written agreement with his client specifying the scope of the work to be done.

An accountant can be liable for negligent misrepresentation only to the person who hired him or to a person whom the accountant, at the time he prepared his report, should have known would rely upon it.

An accountant is liable to a relying third party when he fraudulently prepares a financial statement. Negligence, when not equivalent to fraud, is nonetheless evidence to sustain constructive fraud.

The accountant is liable to third parties for gross negligence or fraud if it is shown that they suffered injury by relying upon his opinion.

The accountant has a valid defense if the misrepresentation was not material or constituted ordinary negligence, if the party did not rely on the misrepresentation, or if he had a reasonable basis for his opinion.

The accountant is liable to purchasers of securities if he did not act in good faith or did not have a reasonable basis for his opinion or if the purchaser relied upon his misstatements and this reliance caused his injury.

Valid defenses of the accountant are proof that he had no intention or knowledge that the statements were to be used in connection with the registration statement and proof that he acted in good faith.

CASE FOR REVIEW

STANLEY L. BLOCH, INC. v. KLEIN

258 N.Y.S.2d 501 (1965)

It appears that in or about March 1955, plaintiff, by oral retainer, had employed defendants, a firm of certified public accountants, to perform usual and required audits of its books and records. Pursuant to such retainer, the credible evidence shows that defendants, by their employees, undertook to verify the accuracy of plaintiff's ledger entries, to prepare interim financial reports, to audit the books of account and to verify the amount of plaintiff's inventory, its most significant business asset. Accordingly, employees of defendant who attended plaintiff's premises at least several days a month supervised those employees of plaintiff who made the original entries in its books and records.

On August 7, 1957, defendant issued a balance sheet of the financial position of the corporate plaintiff as of April 30th of that year. This financial statement was prepared by one of defendants' senior certified public accountants. The subject financial statement, significantly, appears on defendants' letterhead and, unlike other statements prepared and issued by them, it failed to carry the usual disclaimer stamp to the effect that such statement was based upon *unaudited* figures in their client's books and records. The complaint alleges that this balance sheet erroneously represented plaintiff's surplus at $8152.79 and an inventory of $196,646.23, whereas there was, in fact, a deficit of $53,540.87 and an inventory of only $134,952.57.

Proper auditing procedure, as is necessarily involved in the preparation of an unqualified financial statement, must be distinguished from accounting or mathematical procedures, despite the fact that defendants' witness claimed there is no such distinction. On the contrary, unlike accounting or mere mathematical calculating, in auditing procedures, accepted professional standards require a certified public accountant to set forth clearly and unambiguously in his report a statement to the effect that a physical inventory was not observed. While there are legal precedents for holding that it was not negligent for an accountant to accept the report or work of a responsible employee of his client without independent verification, these, generally, are old and outmoded cases. . . . It is apparent that contemporary professional standards now require verification by an independent check or sampling process, or a clear statement by the accountant limiting, qualifying or disclaiming the affected portion of the issued financial report. . . .

The certified public accountant, by virtue of his attained position and his contract of employment, must exercise the care and competence reasonably expected of persons in his profession to ascertain the facts on which his financial report is made. While his retainer agreement may set forth only the duties to be performed, applicable law governs such performance and requires, in addition to reasonable care, adherence to accepted professional standards. . . . If he fails to perform in accordance therewith, the accountant . . . may be liable either for breach of his contract or, in tort, for failure to exercise due care.

In this respect, it is to be noted that . . . Rule 2.03 of the American Institute of Certified Public Accountants . . . also requires that a certified public accountant, when he associates his name with a financial statement, (1) express an unqualified opinion; or (2) disclaim an opinion; or (3) express a qualified opinion; or (4) *when unaudited financial statements are presented on his stationery without comment, disclose prominently on each page of the financial statement the fact that they were not audited.* Defendants' failure to place any qualification notice on the subject balance sheet, therefore, clearly constituted a violation of the emphasized portion of the cited rule which, without any doubt, fixes the existing and accepted standards of the profession.

In view of these recognized standards, therefore, the balance sheet here involved, issued under defendants' professional letterhead, must be deemed to be an unqualified and, in effect, an audited financial statement upon which plaintiff had the right to rely in order to determine and evaluate its financial condition as of April 30, 1957. It is clear that in order to relieve themselves of any liability for errors contained in this April 30, 1957 balance sheet, defendants could have and *should have* indicated on its face all items that were not independently verified. Having failed to do so, they must assume any attendant liability.

Thus, giving due consideration to all of the evidence before me, I find that in issuing the subject balance sheet, defendants failed to conduct the required audit and, in effect, improperly represented on their professional letterhead, that the figures taken by them from plaintiff's books and records, were verified and audited computations. . . .

In addition to this failure to conduct a proper audit or to qualify their statement accordingly, the proof also indicates that defendants arbitrarily set up at least two accounting adjustments affecting the surplus and sales returns figures, thereby arriving at their "finished goods" value of $53,407.47 in the April 30 balance sheet. Significantly, no reconciliation of the surplus account accompanied the delivery of this financial statement to advise plaintiff properly of these adjustments, nor did defendants, in any manner, qualify or otherwise explain these accounting manipulations in the subject balance sheet. Similarly, while the proof clearly establishes that defendants had facts available to them at the time they delivered this balance sheet to plaintiff to indicate that this financial statement was, or, at the very least, might be inaccurate, they did not, as they contend, advise plaintiff of any such possibility until after delivery of their unqualified financial report. In my opinion, all of this proof, coupled with the subsequently revealed substantial inaccuracies in the balance sheet, must be deemed to constitute actionable negligence.

Upon the evidence before me, therefore, I find plaintiff is entitled to recover from defendants only (1) the accounting and auditing fees paid to defendants for the one year of services rendered by them immediately prior to the issuance of the erroneous balance sheet, to wit, $3600 (twelve months at $300 per month) and (2) the accounting and auditing fees necessitated by the review of this erroneous statement, to wit, $2500.

CASE PROBLEMS

1. Plaintiff brought action against the defendants for breach of contract in their capacity as public accountants. Defendants were employed on the express agreement that they should frequently check the plaintiff's cash account in one branch of its business and verify the items thereon. Because of their failure to do so a cashier was able to embezzle large sums of money. Decide.
2. Plaintiff brings suit for damages against defendant auditors for negligence in not discovering the presence of an embezzlement by an employee of the plaintiff. Plaintiff contends that the defendants were negligent because of a failure to detect employee's wrongdoing. The defendant alleged that the plaintiff was negligent in failing to properly supervise his employee's acts or to learn the true condition of his own business and to detect wrongdoing. Decide.
3. Plaintiff brings suit for damages resulting from malpractice by defendant as to representations of the financial condition of a corporation which the plaintiff was induced to purchase. There was not sufficient evidence to substantiate fraudulent intent on the part of the defendant. The plaintiff alleged, however, the unqualified certification of the financial statement and the method of preparation is sufficient to sustain a claim of malpractice. Decide.
4. The defendants, independent auditors holding themselves out as expert accountants, failed to detect, during the course of their audits for two years, the embezzlement by a city clerk of $1984.26 during the year 1968 and $5339 during the year 1969. Plaintiff contended that the embezzlements were not discovered because of lack of competence and negligence on the part of defendants. Decide.
5. Ace Construction Company built bowling alleys. With the introduction of automatic pin setting, its business flourished. To secure funds for expansion, it made a public offering of common stock. Suit was brought under the Securities Act of 1933 by a purchaser of stock claiming material omissions in the prospectus that was issued by Ace to induce sales. Decide.
6. On April 2, 1969 the defendant sent to Green a certified balance sheet, with ten additional copies knowing that it was to be used to obtain credit. Thirty days later the defendant sent a letter of explanation of this balance sheet. Although the balance sheet attached to the covering letter was substantially identical with the original balance sheet, it contained the following notation, which did not appear on the original balance sheet, released thirty days earlier: "This balance sheet is subject to the comments contained in the letter attached to and made a part of this report." Suit was brought alleging malpractice. Decide.
7. Auditors for Express Company during the course of making some special studies for their client unrelated to their auditing function discovered that the statements which they had certified contained material errors. They failed to communicate this information to anyone. A purchaser of Express Company securities brought suit for damages. Decide.
8. The plaintiff is a purchaser of securities, distant from the company and the auditor. The only thing foreseeable was that investors would buy and that they

would rely upon the financial statements. The complaint charged that the earnings and assets were "fictitiously" presented. Decide.

AGENTS AND THIRD PERSONS 22

An agent who undertakes to represent a principal implies thereby that the principal has the legal capacity to contract. If an agent purports to act for a principal who is in fact nonexistent or who is contractually incompetent the agent himself becomes liable to the third party for any resulting loss. Minors, corporations not yet formed, and unincorporated associations are examples of incompetent principals. However, if the third party knows that the principal is incompetent at the time the contract is made, the agent is relieved of liability.

An agent acting for an undisclosed principal renders himself personally liable to third parties even after the third parties learn the identity of the real principal. When the third party discovers the existence of the principal, he may elect to hold either the principal or the agent liable, but not both. The agreement was made on the agent's credit: however, the principal is likewise liable because the contract is for his benefit. If the principal later breaches the contract, the third party may seek satisfaction from the agent: if it is the agent who breaches the agreement, he may seek satisfaction from the principal.

An agent should exercise care in his execution of contracts. If he signs a negotiable instrument with his own name and does not indicate that he is acting in a representative capacity, he is personally liable on the instrument. An agent is also solely liable if, after an undisclosed principal has supplied him with funds for payment to a third party, he fails to relay these funds. The third party in this situation may sue only the agent. There is conflict in this area, however. Some courts hold that the principal remains liable to the third person even where he has paid the agent prior to disclosure.

If a person without proper authority purports to act as an agent, the contract is not binding on the principal unless he ratifies it. The third party's only recourse is to sue the supposed agent. The agent may escape personal liability if he makes known all the facts relating to his agency at the time a contract with the third party is made. The agent may also avoid liability if, unknown to him, the principal has died. The liability of the agent for damages rests on the theory of a breach of implied warranty of authority to represent the principal.

Sometimes a third party will overpay or mistakenly pay an agent. If the agent is aware of the mistake he must return the money; he will be liable for damages if he turns the money over to the principal. If the agent is unaware of the mistake when he receives the payment but learns of it before he has turned the money over to the principal, he must still return it to the third party. If, however, he receives the money in good faith, unaware that the third party is in error in making payment, and turns it over to his principal before finding out about the mistake, he is relieved of all liability to the third party. The third party's only course of action in such a situation is against the principal, since the agent has acted in good faith.

An agent may voluntarily assume certain obligations to third persons. His liability will depend largely on the promises he has made during the negotiations. For example, an agent may personally guarantee the payment of the principal's debt in cases where he receives property from a third party for the principal on the assumption that the property will be returned if certain conditions are not met by the principal. Also, a contract may be executed on the strength of the agent's credit where it is evident that the agent intends to assume the obligation and is aware that credit is being extended to him personally.

TORT LIABILITY OF AGENTS

Where the agent commits a tort wholly outside the scope of his employment, he alone is liable. If the tort is committed in the course of the agent's authorized transactions on the principal's behalf, both are liable.

An agent is personally liable for any tort that he commits, whether in the course of his employment or not. The fact that his principal may also be responsible does not diminish his liability. In some instances, should the principal be held liable, he may sue the agent. If the tortious act is committed at the principal's direction, however, and if the agent is not aware of the illegality of the act, he may recover from the principal any damages he is required to pay the third party.

CONTRACT LIABILITY OF THIRD PERSONS

In a general agency, the third party is not liable to an agent on contracts the agent makes on his principal's behalf. A third party is liable to the agent, however, when the agent, intentionally or otherwise, makes himself a party to the contract. It should be noted that either the principal or the agent may bring suit against the third party for breach of contract. When both wish to sue, the principal's right of action takes precedence.

The agent of an undisclosed principal always binds himself and may sue the third person in his own name in the event of nonperformance. As in the situation above, the right of the agent to sue is secondary to that of the principal whenever the principal asserts his rights under the contract.

The third party may also render himself liable to the agent when he defaults on a contract in which the agent had a beneficial interest or on which he anticipated a commission. An auctioneer, for example, may sue for the purchase price of the goods in the event of default by the buyer.

TORT LIABILITY OF THIRD PERSONS

An agent may bring an action to recover damages for personal injuries caused by the tortious acts of third persons, irrespective of the agency relationship. Actually, tort liability is connected with agency only in a few instances. The agent has a right to carry out his duties unhindered by other persons. Therefore, when a third party has influenced the principal to terminate the agent's employment, the third party is liable in tort to the agent. Likewise, if a third party influences another to breach a contract in which the agent has an interest, the third party becomes liable to the agent. The liability of third persons to the agent for tortious conduct in connection with agency may also arise because of interference with the agent's possession of chattels.

LEGAL PRINCIPLES

The two general areas of an agent's liability to a third party are contracts and torts.

If an agent acts for a nonexistent or incompetent principal, he is liable for any loss incurred.

An agent acting for an undisclosed principal is personally liable on contracts made and may be sued by a third party.

An agent is liable on documents he signs for his principal if he fails to indicate that he is signing in a representative capacity.

An agent may be liable on an implied warranty of authority where he misrepresents the scope of his authority.

An agent may voluntarily assume liability on contracts he executes for his principal.

Where an agent commits a tort outside the scope of his agency, he is liable to third parties. If the tort is committed within the scope of his agency, both the agent and principal are liable.

The third party becomes liable to the agent for performance of a contract only where the agent is liable on the contract.

Third parties are liable to an agent for any torts they commit against the agent.

Any tort liability connected with the agency relationship may be enforced by the agent, as when the third party influences the principal to discharge the agent.

CASE FOR REVIEW

FIRST NATIONAL BANK OF DAVIDSVILLE v. ST. JOHN'S CHURCH, WINDBER

296 Pa. 467 (1929)

The defendant, St. John's Church, Windber, Pa., is an unincorporated . . . church organization, located in Somerset county, of which Rev. J. A. Figlewski was pastor . . . and such as gave the plaintiff bank a note as follows:

2,500.00/100   Davidsville. Pa., Nov. 30, 1925
On demand after date, we or either of us promise to pay to the order of the First National Bank, Davidsville, Pa., at the First National Bank, Davidsville,

Pa., two thousand five hundred and no/100 Dollars without defalcation, value received. [Containing power of attorney to confess judgment, waiving inquisition, exemption, etc.]

Witness our hands and seals

St. John's Church, Windber, Pa. [Seal.]

Rev. J. A. Figlewski, Pastor. [Seal.]

. . . In the summer of 1923, the church membership, at a properly convened meeting, decided to repair their school building and erect a convent and to secure a loan of $15,000 for that purpose. Under the rule of the church, a parish like the defendant could not incur an indebtedness exceeding $500 without the consent of the bishop. . . . Hence the pastor sought and obtained a permit, as follows:

Chancery 1211 Thirteenth St., Altoona, Pa., July 7—23
Rev. J. Figlewski, St. John's Church, Windber—
. . .At a meeting of the Diocesian Consultors you were granted permission to contract a debt of $15,000 for masonry repairs & changes to school & convent. By order of . . . Bishop Bernard Conley

Sec'y Consultors.

Some two years and four months after the permit was issued, the pastor presented it to the plaintiff and obtained thereon a loan of $2500, for which he gave the note in suit. There was oral testimony that he told the bank the permit was not nearly exhausted. So far as appears, he made no representations to the bank as to the action taken by the congregation. The evidence for the defendant was that the church had obtained loans to the amount of the $15,000 from two local banks shortly after the date of the permit, with which, and some $10,000 additional raised by the congregation, the specified improvements were made during 1923 and 1924. The loan in suit was the only one made by the pastor from plaintiff for defendant, although he was known to the bank and had previously done business with it. The proof tends to show that soon after making the loan in suit the pastor absconded with the $2500. From the church funds the succeeding pastor paid the interest on this note for two years, but testified that he did so in ignorance of the true situation and without the knowledge or approval of the lay members. . . .

The trial court erred in treating the mere permit and assurance of the pastor that it was not exhausted as warranting the loan. The age of the permit, nearly two and a half years, was such as to require inquiry of the congregation. The plaintiff bank and the church were close neighbors, and slight inquiry by the former would doubtless have disclosed the fact that the improvements stated in the permit had been completed and paid for, inter alia, by funds secured from other banks, to the full amount of the permit, and that the congregation had refused to request a further permit. . . .One who gives credit to a pastor on the faith of an old permit without inquiry from the congregation does so at his peril. Otherwise a pastor might bankrupt the church for his own purposes despite the limit in the permit. Happily, it is rare that a priest or pastor betrays his church. That the pastor had possession of the old permit proved nothing as to its vitality. The money having been secured from different banks, there was nothing strange in his retention of the permit, especially as it was his warrant for executing the notes. That it had been fully exhausted shortly after its date, quite clearly appeared by the evidence for the defense; yet the proof as to that, being oral, was probably for the jury.

Here the agency of the pastor was to borrow $15,000 for the church; when that was done and obligations given therefore, the permit was exhausted and the agency terminated. . . . Furthermore, he who relies upon the act of an agent must show his authority to do the thing relied upon. . . . The authority cannot be proven by the words or acts of the agent . . . but of course it may by his testimony.

A person dealing with an agent must not act negligently, but must use reasonable diligence to ascertain whether the agent acts within the scope of his power. He is not authorized under any circumstances blindly to trust the agent's statements as to the extent of his powers. 21 R.C.L. p. 853.

If this loan was valid, one for the entire $15,000 would have been. So the bishop's express limit, and the like limit of the congregation would go for nought.

Had the church received the $2500, the case would present a different aspect . . . but there is no evidence or even averment that it received the money or any part of it, and the burden as to that was upon the plaintiff.

CASE PROBLEMS

1. An action was brought by plaintiff to recover the purchase price of a carload of paper shipped to Peerless Paper Company under a contract of purchase by the company and guaranty of payment signed "Last National Bank, by Will Dagge, V.P." It was discovered that the bank could not be held responsible on the guaranty because it had no power under its charter to make such a contract. Plaintiff sought to hold Dagge on the ground that he warranted his authority. Decide.

2. A group of telephone users in and around North Canton, Ohio, organized themselves into what was known as the "North Canton Telephone Users." At one of their meetings some of the members authorized Walter Taylor to engage a rate expert to represent them and said Users at a hearing in regard to telephone rates to be held before the Public Utilities Commission of the State of Ohio. Walter Taylor employed the plaintiff to represent the Users. The members ratified and approved the contract made by Walter Taylor after the plaintiff performed the agreed services. This action was brought for compensation for his services. Decide.

3. Plaintiffs, a partnership, sue defendants, a building committee for an unincorporated church association, for payment for lumber furnished to erect a church and charged to the church association. Defendants allege that credit was extended to the association and not to the defendants personally. Plaintiffs had agreed, it was claimed, to take payment out of funds to be raised by church subscriptions and donations. Decide.

4. J. Lewis, principal of Hapeville High School, rented two station wagons from Dixie Drive-It-Yourself System to be used in transporting students on school activities. The contract was signed "Hapeville High School, J. Lewis, Principal." The terms of the contract stated that the customer would pay for any damage which might occur to the vehicle while in his possession. While on school business, a wreck occurred and damaged one of the wagons to the extent of $400.

Dixie Drive-It-Yourself System sued Lewis and he alleged that he signed the contract as agent for Hapeville High School. Decide.

5. Defendant leased certain premises from plaintiff under the name Food Shops, Inc., which he represented to be a corporation, claiming that he, as president of the corporation, had been authorized to execute the lease. The corporation was later found to be nonexistent. In an action brought on the lease, defendant claimed that his only liability would be for damages because of breach of implied warranty or deceit. Decide.

6. Roberts purchased wheat from defendants on his own account, but with the intention that Keigh & Company, plaintiffs, should have the benefit of the contract on joint account with him if they so chose. After plaintiffs had agreed to take a part of the purchase on joint account with Roberts, he became unable to fulfill his contract. Suit was brought against defendants as undisclosed principals. Decide.

7. In 1975 Canning Corporation sought financing from Busch. Busch requested certified financial statements to determine the financial condition of the company. The corporation employed Debbitt to prepare the statements. He represented the corporation to be solvent by a substantial amount. In fact, the corporation was insolvent. Relying on the certified statements, Busch loaned the corporation $500,000. Subsequently, the corporation went into receivership, resulting in a loss to Busch of $300,000. Busch brought an action against Debbitt. Decide.

8. Walter Williams was physically and mentally incapacitated prior to his death and his wife Ester, acted in his behalf by authority of his power of attorney. In such capacity, she signed for herself and for her husband a contract for the sale of certain land which they owned as tenants by the entirety. The power of attorney, however, did not authorize her to enter into this contract. The buyer was ready, able, and willing to perform, but his wife, upon learning that the power of attorney was insufficient, announced that she was "not going through with the deal." Buyer brought an action for damages for breach of contract. Decide.

PRINCIPALS AND THIRD PERSONS   23

It is a fundamental concept of the law of agency that the authorized act of an agent is deemed the act of the employer-principal. In all situations, therefore, to ascertain the liability of the principal, the third person must first establish the existence of an agency relationship. The principal acquires rights and liabilities only from those transactions performed by his agent in an authorized capacity. Even when the existence of an agency is established, the question remains as to what type of agency it is and what powers are possessed by the agent. In the final analysis, the problem of determining the principal's rights to, and liabilities for, the actions of his agent is one of determining the limits of the agent's scope of employment.

LIABILITY OF DISCLOSED PRINCIPALS

A principal is disclosed when the third party is aware both of the agency and of the principal's identity. In general, the disclosed principal is liable to third persons only for actions of the agent that fall within the actual or apparent scope of the agent's authority. This liability is based on the fact that he is using another person to carry out his transactions *in the manner he himself would carry out* the same transactions. He is further liable if notice is given to the agent of affairs that concern the principal and should be brought to his attention and he fails to act on this notice or does not receive it. In localities and areas of business where it is customary for the agent to have certain authority incidental to his particular business, this authority is considered part of the agent's actual authority.

Secret limitations placed upon the authority of an agent do not bind third parties unless their attention has been directed to them. In other words, the third party is not bound to search out unexpected or unusual restrictions, and he is justified in assuming that the agent possesses those powers that similar agents customarily have under normal circumstances.

Where unusual circumstances arise (such as an existing emergency that necessitates immediate action on the part of the agent), the principal or his representative may add sufficiently to the agent's powers to enable him to meet the situation. If time permits and the principal is available, any proposed remedy for the problem should be presented to him for approval; but when he is not available, the agent's powers are extended sufficiently to cover the difficulty involved.

SPECIAL CIRCUMSTANCES

A real estate broker possesses no authority, implied or apparent, in the absence of an express agreement, to enter into a contract for the sale of property. At the time the broker presents his prospective buyer, the owner has the right to contract or not, as he sees fit. The same is true of salesmen whose authority is limited to obtaining orders for merchandise that are subject to approval by the principal. If such a limitation conforms to custom and usage, the buyer's contract is ineffective until it has been approved by the seller.

The power of an agent to collect a bill owed to his principal may not be readily implied. Clearly, an agent behind a counter who sells goods has the power to collect for them at the time of the sale (but not at a later date). Likewise, the agent who delivers goods that have been sold for cash has a right to collect all payments due at the time of delivery, but not at a later date.

Authority to collect gives the agent no right to accept anything other than money in payment unless he is expressly authorized to do so. An agent is not usually permitted to borrow money for use in the agency or to buy goods on the principal's credit. The principal will not be liable in this situation unless he has given the agent an expressed or implied capacity to borrow or to buy on credit.

The principal is liable upon all written contracts made by the agent as long as they relate to matters within the scope of the agent's authority and are properly executed. However, since there is a rule of law regarding commercial paper to the effect that an individual cannot be held liable on instrument unless his name appears thereon, the agent should take care that any negotiable instrument executed by him clearly indicates his representative capacity.

LIABILITY OF PARTIALLY DISCLOSED PRINCIPALS

A principal is partially disclosed when the third party is aware of the existence of the agency but does not know the identity of the principal. For example, Mr. Wood employs Gallery Realty to rent houses for him. Third persons deal with the realtor, knowing they represent someone although they are unaware of his identity. In such situations both the principal and the agent will be liable to the third party (who, since he does not know the principal, will be contracting with the agent's credit reputation in mind). The agent may, however, shift the liability to the principal by making it clear to the third party at the outset that he is not and will not be a party to the contract.

UNDISCLOSED PRINCIPALS

The principal is undisclosed when the third party is aware neither of the identity of the principal nor the existence of the agency—that is, when the third party believes the agent is the only other party.

All contracts involving an undisclosed principal are entered into on the strength of the agent's credit and in his name. The third party, upon learning of the principal's identity, may elect to enforce the contract against the principal rather than the agent. In these cases, the principal is liable for any act that would have been within the scope of the agent's authority had he been a disclosed principal.

Election of the principal as responsible for performance becomes possible only when the third party learns of the existence of the principal. If a settlement has taken place, no election is possible. Otherwise, the third party may look to either the agent or the principal for performance until such time as he definitely elects to hold one or the other to the contract. No conduct on his part that precedes the disclosure of the principal can constitute an election. After disclosure, he may evidence his election either by obtaining a judgment against one of the parties or by making a definite declaration of his intention. The third party is usually free at any time to sue the party whose credit is best, and he is not held to have elected until a judgment is obtained.

LIABILITY OF PRINCIPAL FOR AGENTS' TORTS

The principal becomes liable to third parties for damage incurred by them through the negligence of the agent so long as the latter is acting within the scope of his employment. If the agent is engaged in his own business venture when the tort is committed, having temporarily left his principal's business, the principal is relieved of any liability. (This is true even when damage results from an automobile accident and the employee was driving his employer's car.) As long as the agent is attempting to follow his principal's business, the principal is liable for the actions of the agent.

Clearly, the principal is in no respect liable for the willful misconduct of an agent that has nothing to do with the principal's business and is motivated entirely by the agent's personal feelings toward the third party. However, where the agent's predominant motive is to advance his principal's interest, it has been held that the principal is liable. The principal cannot escape liability because he has hired an agent who is overly enthusiastic about his duties to the point where he does more than is desirable in his principal's behalf.

LIABILITY OF THIRD PARTIES

A disclosed principal may sue a third party upon any contract made by an agent in the principal's name and for his benefit. Furthermore, any contract made for the benefit of the principal, even though the agent may have acted outside the scope of his authority, entitles the principal to performance.

An undisclosed principal is entitled to performance by third parties of all simple contracts made for his benefit by an agent. However, if a contract is such that it cannot be assigned or its duties delegated, an undisclosed principal cannot demand benefits. In taking over the performance of contracts made for him, the undisclosed principal is subject to all defenses that the third party could have established against the agent.

LEGAL PRINCIPLES

In order to establish the liability of the principal, the third person must first establish the existence of an agency.

A principal is liable only for acts that fall within the expressed, implied, or apparent scope of his agent's authority.

A principal is disclosed when a third party knows of both his identity and the existence of the agency.

An agent can act outside his authority only when his powers are enlarged by virtue of an emergency.

To avoid liability, principals must designate the instances where an agent's normal authority is not applicable.

The principal is bound by the warranties of his agent, provided they are of the nature usually made in the trade. He is not bound to unusual warranties made by his agent.

A principal is partially disclosed when the third party is aware of the existence of the agency but does not know the identity of the principal.

Both principal and agent are liable if the principal is partially disclosed.

The principal alone is liable if he is partially disclosed and his agent makes it known that he was not a party to the contract.

A principal is undisclosed if both the existence of the agency and the identity of the principal are unknown to the third person.

If an undisclosed principal is disclosed and the third party elects to bring suit against him, he is liable.

If an undisclosed principal is disclosed and the third party elects to bring suit against the agent, the principal generally will be liable to the agent if he (the principal) had not made the necessary payment to the agent allowing him to perform on the contract.

The principal is liable for the torts of his agent if they are committed within the scope of the business.

A willful tort by an agent against a third party in no way binds the principal if it is not related to the principal's business.

CASE FOR REVIEW

MILLER v. FEDERATED DEPARTMENT STORES, INC.

294 N.E.2d 474 (1973)

In this action for tort, the plaintiff Bertha Miller seeks recovery for personal injuries sustained from an assault by an employee of the defendent., Federated Department Stores, Inc. Her husband also seeks recovery for consequential damages for the injuries so sustained by his wife. Originally the action was in four counts against the defendent. Later, two counts by the wife and husband against the individual employee were added. The jury returned verdicts for the plaintiffs against the individual employee, and against the corporate defendent on two of the four counts against it. The case comes before us on the defendant's exceptions to the denial of its motion for directed verdicts on the counts against it for the assault by the employee and for consequential damages to the husband. The counts against the employee are not before us. The plantiff Bertha Miller, while shopping in the defendant's store and standing at a counter, had been brushed at her ankle by a cart pushed by the employee, who was a porter in the defendant's store. A short time later when she left the counter she saw the employee waiting for an elevator. She said to him "If you would say 'excuse me,' people could get out of your way." The employee then pushed her an when she remonstrated with him he punched her in the face knocking her to the floor. It is well-settled that the critical test of liability on the part of the employer for a tortious assult on a third person by the employee is whether the act was done within the scope of employment and was in furtherance of the employer's work.

If an assault is committed by an employee, not in the course of his employment but outside the scope of his duties, or in a spirit of vindictiveness or to gratify personal animosity, or to carry out an independent purpose of his own, then the employer is not liable. In our examination of the evidence in its aspect most favorable to the plaintiffs, we are unable to find that the unprovoked assault by the employee on the plaintiff Bertha Miller was within the scope of his employment and in furtherance of the employer's work.

CASE PROBLEMS

1. Builder listed certain property for sale with a real estate agency While being shown the property, Acke asked the agents whether there was a good septic tank. They replied that there was "a mighty good one" and, relying on this statement, plaintiff purchased the property. It later appeared that the septic tank was wholly inadequate, at times backing up into the basement. Acke brought suit for $3000 damages against the former owner of the property as principal. Decide.
2. Steinhaus was the owner of a trucking business. He supplied the Adams Express Company, the defendant, with a motor van and a chauffeur at the rate of $5 an hour. The defendant did the work of loading at its station and unloading at the railroad terminal. It sealed the van at the point of departure and unsealed at the point of destination. Between departure and destination, the truck remained without interference or supervision in charge of the chauffeur. While on this route, it struck and killed the plaintiff's son. The plaintiff brought an action against Steinhaus for damages. Decide.
3. Indemnity Insurance rejected the application for a policy by Sam Samson, who had a record of a previous accident and three traffic tickets. Samson, therefore, arranged to transfer the title of the automobile to his brother who was carrying insurance with Indemnity. It was alleged that the insurance agent, Walters, suggested or at least approved the suggestion of the change of title. The policy was issued to Sam's brother and forwarded to Sam, who paid the premiums. Three months later Sam was involved in an accident with the auto which resulted in the death of Anderson. Indemnity voided the policy upon learning of the facts concerning the issuance of the policy. Decide.
4. Poretta sold wood to Young, who was in fact acting for Superior Dowel Company, an undisclosed principal. When Poretta learned this, he brought suit for the purchase price against Dowel, who defended on the ground that he had paid the amount to Young. Dowel appealed a judgment in favor of Poretta. Decide.
5. Howe sold petroleum products to Martin, trading as United Oil. Martin sold the business to Smith, who was introduced to Howe as the purchaser of the business, and Howe continued to sell to Smith. Smith incorporated the business but failed to notify Howe. He continued to carry the account as United Oil. Several checks

given in payment of invoices were signed "United Oil Inc., Smith." When sued, Smith set up as his defense that he was acting as agent for United Oil, Inc.

6. Supply Company purchased from a local dealer ten General Motors trucks guaranteed for ninety days as to material and workmanship, all of which proved to be defective. After several unsuccessful attempts to settle plaintiff's claim, O'Connor, Eastern Regional Manager for General Motors Truck Company, defendant, met with local branch manager of General Motors, the president of the sales agency, and the president of Supply Company to discuss the matter. At the meeting O'Connor agreed to accept return of the trucks and to pay Supply $7823.06. General Motors Truck Company refused to carry out this agreement, contending that O'Connor did not have authority to make a binding contract of that scope. Supply Company brought an action to enforce the contract. Decide.

7. Defendant claimed to have a security interest in a television set that plaintiff had purchased from a third party. Plaintiff and defendant orally agreed that plaintiff would pay $100 at the rate of $15 a week. When he failed to remit, defendant sent its agent to collect the account or repossess the set. Approached by the agent and two detectives, plaintiff told them not to enter since his wife was ill and very nervous. Nevertheless, they walked in, threw a small radio and lamp on the floor, breaking them, slammed a door so hard that the glass in it broke, and took the television. Plaintiff sued for trespass and damages sustained. Decide.

8. Samuel Plotkin was driving from Spring Park to Minneapolis. Following was a bus operated by defendant company and driven by its employee. The bus had trouble passing Plotkin's car. Plotkin did not hear the bus' horn and failed to make room for the bus to pass on the left, as required by law. After a time, the bus did get ahead. In Crystal Bay, the bus stopped at an intersection. Its driver walked back to Plotkin's car, stopped at the same crossing, and after words about Plotkin's previous failure to let the bus pass, struck Plotkin on the mouth. The plaintiff alleged that the bus driver was within the scope of his employment by trying to make schedule time. Decide.

TERMINATION OF THE AGENCY RELATIONSHIP   24

Since the agency relationship is created at will, it may be terminated at will by either party. Neither party may compel the other to continue the arrangement on other than a voluntary basis.

The termination of an agency relationship will affect the interests of the employer—principal, the agent, and those third persons with whom the agent has business dealings. It is in the best interests of the principal to know how and when the agent's authority can effectively be brought to an end. To an agent, the termination of the relationship may result in a breach of his contract of employment. Third persons ought to be aware of the extent to which they deal with agents at their own risk.

TERMINATION BY ACT OF THE PARTIES

Termination by the parties may occur at a time specified by their original agreement or may be caused by the later actions of one or both of them. When the agency relationship is created, the parties to the agreement may specify the duration of the relationship. For example, P will tell A that he has the authority to act on his behalf until January 1, 1969; accordingly. A's authority to act for P will terminate on that date. Where no time is stipulated, the agency will terminate at the end of a reasonable time. (A "reasonable time" is interpreted by the courts according to the nature and purposes of the agency.)

The original agreement may terminate the relationship upon the accomplishment of the purpose called for, it being obvious that the parties to the agency came together only for the purpose of accomplishing that end. When this end is reached, the relationship terminates as a matter of course. The original agreement may also provide that the agency shall terminate upon the happening of a specified event.

Nonaccomplishment of the act for which the two parties were brought together may also terminate the agency. If within a reasonable time after the agency's creation the object of the arrangement has not been accomplished, the parties may mutually agree to terminate before the original termination date. Neither party is liable when the agency is terminated in this fashion.

Usually the agency relationship is revocable at will by the principal without liability for the act of revocation. However, when the principal enters into a valid contract where he binds himself not to revoke, he is liable for the damages caused by the revocation. In other words, a principal possesses a "right to revoke" when his agent has an appointment for no specific period of time, terminable by the principal without liability. A principal has a "power to revoke" in those situations where, because of the nature of the relationship, he may revoke the agent's authority even though he (the principal) has contracted not to revoke the authority within a limited time. However, the principal is subject to liability in damages for the act of termination. These situations occur most frequently when the principal has agreed to employ the agent for a specific period. (There are some irrevocable agencies that will be discussed below.)

Either party has the "power" and the "right" to terminate for cause. A termination for cause carries no right to damages. Disobedience, dishonesty, or any conduct on the part of the agent that will prevent him from properly and effectively representing the principal is sufficient cause for termination.

The agency can also be terminated by the action of the parties for a legal cause. For example, in every service contract it is implied that the employee shall obey the lawful orders of the employer to the extent that they are reasonable and not arbitrary. Disobedience justifies discharge by the employer without liability. Likewise, permanent disability gives an immediate right to the *able* party to terminate the agency. In the case of temporary disability, which does not in itself constitute grounds for termination, the contract continues in force until the employer elects to terminate it. Also, when an employee violates a term of the employment contract, the employer is privileged to terminate the contract, irrespective of the relative importance of the breached positions.

Finally, an agency may be terminated by a renunciation or abandonment of agency by the agent. Just as a principal may revoke the agency, either rightfully or wrongfully, according to the circumstances, the agent likewise may renounce his agency either rightfully or wrongfully. If he has a justifying cause for his renunciation, he may be legally allowed to terminate the agency. However, if he simply breaches the contract for no good reason, he will be held liable to the principal for any resultant loss or damage to him.

TERMINATION BY THE OPERATION OF LAW

There are a number of events which will terminate an agency instantly, regardless of the intent of the parties. The general rule of law is that authority is terminated on the death, bankruptcy, or insanity of either the principal or the agent.

The principal's death will ordinarily terminate the agency relationship even though the agent and the third party subsequently act in ignorance of his demise. For example, suppose that A and T were operating in a city far removed from P. They might carry on a business transaction unaware that P had died. The death of the agent will have the same effect.

If either party becomes bankrupt, the agency is terminated unless the bankruptcy has no effect on the operation of the agency.

Because of the general concession that war suspends all commercial transactions between residents of the belligerent countries, the rule is that agency is terminated as a matter of law upon the outbreak of war whenever the principal is a citizen of one country and the agent is a citizen of the other.

Destruction of the subject matter or of the principal's interest in the subject matter terminates the agency as a matter of law, if not as a matter of necessity. For example, if A is selling P's house and the house is destroyed by fire, the agency is terminated. However, if a principal himself sells a chattel when he has appointed an exclusive agent to handle the sale, the agency is terminated but the principal is liable for damages caused by his wrongful act.

A change in the law may terminate an obligation and the resulting agency relationship, since implied in every contract is the understanding that the obligations imposed are within the law.

AGENCY COUPLED WITH AN INTEREST AND AGENCY COUPLED WITH OBLIGATION

In certain types of agency relationships the agent has a legal or equitable interest in the subject matter. This type of relationship is called *agency coupled with an interest* and cannot be terminated without the consent of the agent. Therefore, death of the principal will not constitute a termination of a true agency coupled with an interest. For example, a mortgagee whose mortgage includes the right to sell in case of default could not have this right taken away during the lifetime of, or by the death of, the principal.

Agency coupled with an interest is often confused with *agency coupled with an obligation*. The latter type of agency is created as a source of reimbursement to the agent because of an obligation owed him by the principal. Although it cannot be terminated by the principal during his lifetime, it is terminated by his death. For example, an agent who is given the right to sell a certain automobile and to apply the proceeds to a claim against the principal has his authority terminated by the death of his principal.

EFFECT OF TERMINATION ON THIRD PARTIES

The agent's actual authority to represent his principal ceases as soon as the relationship is dissolved and the agent is notified to that effect. For example, if an agent is fired, his authority immediately terminates. Third persons who are not informed of the agency's termination, however, may continue to deal with the agent on the assumption that he still possesses authority to act for the principal.

Specific notice of termination need not be given to third parties when the termination results from the operation of the law, because this type of termination is considered public and third parties are deemed to be aware of it without the necessity of additional information. If the death of the principal occurs before an agent contracts with a third party, the third party has no cause of action against either principal or agent, unless the agent is acting for an undisclosed principal. In the latter case, the agent is liable to the third party, since he makes the contract in his own name.

When the agency is terminated by an act of the parties, the principal has a duty to third parties who have dealt with the agent or who rely on his appearance of continuing authority to notify them of the termination of the agent's authority. To those who have relied upon the agency by dealing with the agent, the principal's duty can be satisfied only by the receipt of actual notice by the third party. To those who have never dealt with him but who have learned of the agency, the principal satisfies his duty to third parties by giving "constructive" notice. This is accomplished by placing a public notice in a newspaper of general circulation, a trade journal, or a similar publication.

LEGAL PRINCIPLES

An agency relationship may be terminated by an act of the parties, the expiration of a stated period of agency, or by the mutual agreement of the parties. It may also be terminated by the operation of law in the event of death, insanity, bankruptcy, war, destruction of the subject matter, or a change in the law. The liability of the principal and the agent will depend on the facts of each situation.

Agency coupled with an interest cannot be terminated without the consent of the agent, even in the event of the principal's death. Agency coupled with an obligation, however, although it cannot be terminated without the agent's consent during the principal's lifetime, will terminate at his death.

When an agency is terminated by the operation of law the principal is not required to give public notice to third parties. However, in agencies terminated by acts of the parties, the principal is obligated to notify third parties who may have knowledge of the agency. Failure to give proper notice may make the principal liable for future dealings to which the agent may for any reason subject him.

CASE FOR REVIEW

BURCH v. AMERICUS GROCERY CO.

125 Ga. 153 (1906)

The manager of Burch's store . . . assuming to act as Burch's agent ordered goods from the Grocery Company after his discharge, of which the Grocery Company had no notice. Burch did not receive the goods, as the manager kept them himself.

Whenever a general agency has been established for any purpose, all persons who have dealt with such agent, or who have known of the agency and are apt to deal with him, have a right to presume that such authority will continue until it is shown to have been terminated in one way or another; and they also have a right to anticipate that if the principal revokes such authority, they will be given due notice thereof. It is a general rule of law, therefore, upon which there seems to be no conflict of authorities, that all acts of a general agent within the scope of his authority, as respects third persons, will be binding on the principal, even though done after revocation, unless notice of such revocation has been given to those persons who have had dealings with and who are apt to have other dealings with the agent upon the strength of his former authority. The obligation resting upon the principal of giving notice of the revocation of the authority conferred upon his agent has been analogized to the duty which the law imposes upon the members of a partnership to give due notice of its dissolution to creditors and the public at large. Where there is no attempt at all to comply with this duty, a retiring partner is to be held liable for debts of the partnership, created after he ceased to be a member thereof, unless he shows that notice of his retirement had been brought home to the persons who subsequently became its creditors. Actual notice alone will affect creditors of the firm. And like notice must be shown before one who has revoked the authority conferred upon his general agent will be at liberty, relatively to persons who have dealt with such agent upon the faith of his authority as recognized by his principal in the past, to repudiate a contract made in behalf of the principal by the agent after his authority has been revoked. The term "actual notice" is intended to be understood in its strictly legal, technical sense, and is not to be confounded with actual knowledge. Notice is actual when one either has knowledge of a fact or is conscious of having the means of knowledge, although he may not use them; it may be either express notice, or simply implied notice—notice communicated by direct and positive information from persons cognizant of the fact, or notice such as arises when the party to be charged is shown to have had knowledge of such facts and circumstances as would lead him, by the exercise of due diligence, to a knowledge of the principal fact. In the present case no express notice was shown, and the controlling issue was whether or not the plaintiff had "implied notice."

The jury, after considering all the facts and circumstances brought to light at the trial, found against the contention of the defendant that due caution and prudence on the part of the plaintiff's drummer ought to have suggested to him the propriety of making inquiry, if he did not divine the truth. The burden of proof was upon the defendant to establish his defense that the plaintiff was affected with implied notice.

CASE PROBLEMS

1. Mrs. French purchased a large cemetery plot from the Kensico Cemetery. On the plot Mrs. French erected a mausoleum in which she interred some members of her family. In 1961 she paid the cemetery $8000 under an agreement by which the cemetery agreed to invest the money and apply the income to the maintenance of Mrs. French's lot and mausoleum. The agreement contained a statement that the provision for perpetual care was beneficial to the cemetery and to other lot owners because it prevented the deterioration of the lot and mausoleum and protected adjoining lot owners from damage from such deterioration and enhanced the value of their lots. In 1969, Mrs. French delivered to the cemetery a written demand for the return of the $8000. The cemetery refused and Mrs. French brought suit. Decide.

2. An action was brought on a note for $36,000 that the owner, Burr, had acquired from an insolvent bank for $82. Burr granted plaintiff the power to sell, dispose of, or collect the instrument, and to retain half the proceeds. Burr later released the claim against defendant. It was alleged that he was without power to surrender the claim because plaintiff had an agency coupled with an interest. Decide.

3. Plaintiffs, stockbrokers, sold stock short for Brokker and borrowed the stock to make delivery for him. While the transaction was pending, Brokker died, and plaintiffs continued to protect the account. After defendant had been appointed administratix of the estate, plaintiffs required additional margin, which was not

forthcoming; they thereupon brought in the stock and charged Brokker's estate. They then sought to recover the losses incurred thereby. Defense was that plaintiff's agency was revoked by Brokker's death and that plaintiffs should have covered the stock immediately upon learning of his demise. Decide.

4. Julius asked a notary public to prepare two deeds, but he left blank the name of the person to receive the property. He executed the deeds without filling in the blanks and left the deeds with the notary. Subsequently, Julius died. After his death, the notary inserted the names of Julius' grandchildren. His sons brought an action to have the two deeds set aside. Decide.

5. Will held a promissory note executed by Puck. He assigned the note to Writt, an attorney, as agent to collect the note. Writt began a suit against Puck, but nothing more was done. After two years, Will went to Puck's office, obtained the note, and said that he "was taking it to someone else." Will thereupon started a second suit against Puck and this was known by Writt. Subsequently, Writt took action in the suit that he had brought against Puck, who then raised the defense that Writt's authority to sue had been revoked. Decide.

6. As defendants' purchasing agent, Rose had often bought junk for them from Power Company. When Rose was discharged from his job, defendants neglected to notify Power Company. Following his discharge, and without authority, Rose purported to order junk for defendants from plaintiff, Reservoir and Irrigation Company, which was a subsidiary of Power Company and closely connected to it by common management. Defendants received the junk and paid Rose for it, on Rose's affirmation that he was the owner, having purchased it on his own. Plaintiff sued defendants for the price of the junk, on the ground that Rose still had apparent authority to bind them. Decide.

7. On September 9, 1973, defendant authorized Wheeler, his agent, to sell certain real property and to execute a contract for its sale. On the same day, he empowered Fairchild to sell the same land, the authority of the agent being limited in each instance to the particular transaction named. That afternoon, Wheeler effected a sale of the land, consummated by a conveyance. On September 10, Fairchild, having received no notice of the previous sale made by Wheeler, contracted to sell the same land to plaintiff, who, upon defendant's refusal to perform on his part, brought an action for damages for breach of contract. Decide.

8. Goldsmith was the owner of a shirt factory. He hired Turner as a salesman for five years under a written agreement which stated that Turner would sell goods in accordance with samples of goods manufactured or sold by Goldsmith. After the agreement had been in force for about two years, Goldsmith's factory was destroyed by fire. He refused to continue the employment, claiming that the agreement was indefinite and also that the destruction of the factory had caused a termination of the employment. Decide.

REGULATION OF THE EMPLOYER-EMPLOYEE RELATIONSHIP

25

Prior to 1932, the law of labor relations was for the most part the product of court decisions. If an employer complained of the picketing of his business or if a union complained when an employer fired a man to discourage unionization, only the courts could resolve the controversy. During this period, extending roughly from 1870 to 1930, the injunction became a widely used instrument for the suppression of such union activities as strikes, pickets and boycotts. However, no comparable judicial relief was available to keep employers from discriminatory treatment of union members or to coerce employers to bargain with unions.

Today national labor policy is expressed in the provisions of the major federal labor relations statutes; the Railway Labor Act, the Norris-LaGuardia Act, the National Labor Relations Act, the Fair Labor Standards Act, the Taft-Hartley Act, the Labor-Management Reporting and Disclosure Act and the Occupational Safety and Health Act.

RAILWAY LABOR ACT

The Railway Labor Act of 1926 applied originally to the railroad industry, but has since been extended to the airlines. Its purpose was to avoid work stoppages by employees and lockouts by employers through establishment of negotiation, mediation, and arbitration procedure, enforced by legal sanctions. Major power of administration was vested in a nonpartisan Board of Mediation appointed by the President. Disputes were to be settled as follows:

1. In the event of a labor dispute, the Mediation Board was to attempt to get the parties to negotiate.
2. If the first step failed, the next step was to induce the parties to submit the difficulty to arbitration. If arbitration was agreed to, the awards became binding and legally enforceable. The agreement to arbitrate was, and remains, voluntary.
3. If arbitration is refused by either party, the Board of Mediation was to recommend that the President create an emergency board of investigation. (a) If the President created such a board, it was required to submit a report to the President on the controversy within thirty days. The parties were required to maintain the status quo until the board submitted its report and thirty days thereafter. At the expiration of a maximum of sixty days, if the parties still did not agree to abide by the findings of the emergency board, they were free to engage in a strike or a lockout. (b) If the President did not appoint an emergency board as recommended by the Board of Mediation, the disputants were required to maintain the status quo for thirty days.

217

In 1934, 1936, and again in 1951, the Railway Labor Act was amended to include:

1. criminal penalties for violations by unions, carriers and their officers of certain of the Act's provisions;
2. the right of employees to organize and bargain collectively through representatives of their own choosing;
3. a provision that no carrier shall require any person seeking employment to sign any contract or agreement promising to join or not to join a labor organization.
4. a provision that provided a method for the designation of bargaining representatives by certification and that "upon receipt of such certification the carrier shall treat with the representative so certified as the representative of the craft or class for the purposes of this Act."

NORRIS-LAGUARDIA ACT

The Norris-LaGuardia Act was passed in 1932. It provided that the jurisdiction of the federal courts to issue injunctions in labor disputes should be limited. Its key sections are as follows:

1. Section 3 provides that a federal court cannot enforce or grant any relief based upon a "yellow dog contract" by which an individual agrees that during his employment he will not join a labor organization.
2. Section 4 reiterates the worker's right to strike, assemble, and peacefully picket and identifies specific situations protected from injunctive process. It prohibits the issuance by a federal court of an injunction restraining reasonable conduct "in any case involving or growing out of a labor dispute," and thereby protects all peaceful union activity from restraining orders.
3. Section 6 defines a stringent rule of agency liability, requiring, before liability for unlawful acts of others may attach to an officer or agent of any organization in a labor dispute case, that there be proof of actual participation, actual authorization, or ratification after actual knowledge of the commission of unlawful acts.
4. Section 7 provides that the complainant in a "labor dispute" case will be denied injunctive relief unless he can prove to the court's satisfaction all of the following:
   a. Unlawful acts have been threatened or committed.
   b. Injury to property will result.
   c. Injury to complainant will be greater than injury to defendant unless the unlawful acts are enjoined.
   d. Complainant has no adequate remedy at law.
   e. Police or other public officers are unable or unwilling to furnish adequate protection to complainant's property.
5. Section 8 further requires that the complainant show that he made reasonable efforts to negotiate the existing difference.
6. Section 9 requires the injunction to restrain only specific complaints.
7. Section 13 defines "labor dispute" to include "any controversy concerning terms or conditions of employment, or concerning the association or

representation of persons in negotiating, fixing, maintaining, changing, or seeking to arrange terms or conditions of employment."

NATIONAL LABOR RELATIONS ACT

The original National Labor Relations Act (the Wagner Act.) passed in 1935, provided positive protection for employee self-organization against employer interference and made it an unfair labor practice for an employer to refuse to bargain collectively.

Section 7 set forth the following:

> Employees shall have the right to self-organization, to form, join, or assist labor organizations, to bargain collectively through representatives of their own choosing, and to engage in other certain concerted activities for the purpose of collective bargaining . . . and shall also have the right to refrain from any or all of such activities.

The National Labor Relations Act declares it to be an unfair labor practice for an employer:

1. to interfere with guaranteed rights;
2. to dominate or interfere with the formation or administration of a labor organization or contribute financial support to it;
3. to discriminate in regard to hire or tenure to discourage membership in a union;
4. to discharge or discriminate against an employee because he has filed charges or given testimony under the Act;
5. to refuse to bargain collectively with representatives selected by the majority of employees; or
6. to enter into a hot-cargo agreement with a union.

FAIR LABOR STANDARDS ACT

The Fair Labor Standards Act of 1938 has three broad objectives: (a) the establishment of minimum wages, reflecting concepts of a "rudimentary minimum standard of living;" (b) the encouragement of a ceiling upon hours of labor which was to result in an increase in the scope of employment by increasing the cost of overtime work, defined as work in excess of forty hours per week; and (c) the discouragement of "oppressive child labor." Several amendments have been made to the 1938 Act increasing the minimum hourly wage rate and enlarging the scope of the Act by expanding its coverage.

NATIONAL LABOR RELATIONS BOARD

To enforce employee rights, the National Labor Relations Act established the National Labor Relations Board. This administrative agency has a general counsel who functions as its chief enforcement officer. He is in charge of the regional offices of the agency, to which private parties can initiate complaints, and through which investigations are conducted, settlements arranged, and litigation is originated. Litigation, conducted before a trial examiner, proceeds in a manner similar to what would take place in a federal trial court. A panel of the board, or the full board, composed of four members and a chairman, serves as a reviewing tribunal. Its judgments are subject to review by the Federal Circuit Courts of Appeal. A violation of a board decree carries no sanction until enforced by a court.

The National Labor Relations Board also determines the proper selection of the "election" units. Section 9 of the statute provides that: "Representatives designated or selected for the purpose of collective bargaining by the majority of the employees in a unit appropriate for such purposes, shall be the exclusive representatives of all the employees in such unit for the purposes of collective bargaining." This means that there will be collective bargaining if the majority of employees want it, and one means of determining the will of the majority is through the Labor Board. The board's function in part, is to determine the "unit appropriate", to umpire the pre-election campaign between the union (or unions) seeking representation and to conduct the election itself and determine its outcome.

TAFT-HARTLEY ACT

In 1947 the NLRA was amended by the Taft-Hartley Act, which restates the policy in favor of collective bargaining and stresses a public interest in all labor affairs. Its policy statements and provisions emphasize that four major groups are involved in every labor dispute: employees, unions, employers, and the public. The major changes introduced by Taft-Hartley were:

1. the outlawing of the closed shop;

2. recognition that employers need not recognize or bargain with unions formed by supervisory personnel:

3. provision that employers and unions may both maintain suits in federal courts for damages for breach of collective agreements;

4. provision that employers may sue unions for damages arising out of secondary boycotts and strikes for unlawful purposes;

5. definition of union unfair labor practices as:

   a. causing an employer to discriminate against his employees except where the employee, under a valid union arrangement, fails to pay periodic dues or initiation fees;
   b. refusing to bargain in good faith with an employer;
   c. engaging in certain strikes and secondary boycotts;
   d. requiring payment of excessive initiation fees;
   e. engaging in featherbed practices.

6. provision that national Emergency Strikes be subject to an eighty-day "cooling-off period;"

7. provisions that labor organizations and employers may not make contributions or expenditures in federal elections.

REPORTING AND DISCLOSURE ACT

The Labor-Management Reporting and Disclosure Act of 1959 reaffirms the national policy favoring collective bargaining and the national interest in maintaining a free flow of commerce. It finds that these objectives are jeopardized by the failure of employers, unions, and their officials to observe standards of responsibility and ethical conduct in administering the affairs of their organizations.

Thus, the Discloure Act of 1959 was drafted requiring reporting to the government on various union affairs and on certain transactions between union and management. Who must report, what must be reported, and how the reporting requirements are carried out are detailed in the Act. Likewise, the law aims at preventing irresponsible fiscal considerations, such as misappropriation of union assets and loans, and abuses in pension and insurance plans, by requiring a reporting of fiscal information concerning dues, fees, loans and the like.

OCCUPATIONAL SAFETY AND HEALTH ACT

Congress enacted the Occupational Safety and Health Act in 1970 to assure, as far as technologically possible, safe and healthful working conditions to every employee in America. Commonly called OSHA, this legislation authorizes the Department of Labor to formulate safety and health standards for businesses engaged in interstate commerce. Where specific standards cannot be developed, the employer is held to a high degree of care in his general duty to maintain a safe workplace free from recognizable hazards and to refrain from actions which might cause harm to others.

Enforcement of OSHA is the duty of the Secretary of Labor. He is responsible for inspecting and investigating conditions at the workplace. The act provides for the imposition of both criminal and civil penalties. A willful or repeated violation may be assessed a civil penalty of not more than $10,000 for each violation. A serious violation calls for an assessment of up to $1000 for each violation, Thus, if the secretary (acting through an area OSHA director) finds a violation, he may issue a citation to the employer in which he proposes a penalty. An employer has fifteen working days to contest the secretary's action before it becomes final. If an employer is convicted of willfully violating the act and thereby causing death to any employee, he shall be punished by a fine of not more than $10,000 or by imprisonment for not more than six months, or both. The act also makes mandatory certain record-keeping, reports and surveys.

The Occupational Safety and Health Act exempts nonprofit and charitable organizations, churches and church-related activities, domestic employers, agricultural employers and federal and state governments as not being employers in the traditional sense of the term.

WORKMEN'S COMPENSATION LAWS

Since 1910, all states have provided insurance against occupational accidents and diseases. Such insurance is more commonly referred to as workmen's compensation. The theory of this insurance is that these costs are a proper part of the cost of production and should properly be counted along with other costs.

The original workmen's compensation laws were designed to cover only "accidental" injuries—injuries caused by some unexpected or exceptional happening or exposure arising out of and in the course of the employment. Later, specified diseases of gradual contraction, termed occupational diseases, were included. In some states, the limitation to accidents has been entirely eliminated. But, even where such limitation is retained, it is generally held that it is not necessary that the injury be *caused* by an accident. It is sufficient that the injury itself is accidental—that it results unexpectedly, although from fully expected and intended results incidental to the employment. Therefore, all the consequences of a fall on the job, though the fall be due to an illness, are now deemed to be an "accidental injury arising out of the employment," if anything in the conditions or at the place of work can possibly have contributed to or aggravated such consequences.

The courts are now also rapidly discarding the principle that an accidental injury must be incurred somewhat suddenly. For example, an attack of arthritis, "lit up" by being jolted and jarred while riding five days on a trailer drawn over bumpy ground by a tractor has been held to be an "accidental injury."

It was the purpose of the original compensation laws to follow the common law so far as to limit liability for compensation to cases of "traumatic injury." But the compensation laws are now being construed to go indefinitely beyond that. Thus paralysis, for example, suffered by a chauffeur through fright caused by brake failure is a compensable accident. A similarly liberal construction is now being given even to those statutes which provide expressly that, to be compensable, the injury must be one of "violence to the physical structure of the body."

Our courts and commissions are also departing from the original compensation law doctrine that to be compensable, an accident must arise out of "a risk of the employment" and not be caused by an "added peril"—by a risk incurred by doing something clearly not contemplated by the employment. For example, where a driver whose truck was stalled on the road by a blizzard was forced to leave the shelter of a neighboring house and spend the night in his truck with the consequence that his feet were frozen, the resultant injuries were held to have arisen "out of and in the course of the employment."

Most states have laws permitting an action for damages for injuries to survive the death of an injured person and laws permitting a new cause of action for the wrongful death caused by the injury. However, these laws have many limitations as to who can bring suit, when the action must be brought, and the amount of damages. Workmen's compensation laws are interpreted to provide the exclusive means of compensation for injuries, diseases, or deaths which are covered by the law. A worker or his dependents can sue for damages in court only if he is not covered by the workmen's compensation law for that injury or disease.

The methods of financing workmen's compensation awards are insurance with a private insurance company, insurance with a state fund, or self-insurance. If self-insurance is permitted, the state agency usually must approve a particular employer. The agency may also require a bond or deposit of securities from the employer. Most states provide penalties of fines and imprisonment if an employer fails to meet the financing requirements.

Benefits to the worker accidentally injured in the course of his employment include medical benefits (unlimited in most states), indemnity benefit payments during the period of disablement and for permanent disabilities, vocational rehabilitation, death benefits to members of his family, and burial expenses. If a worker is injured during the course of his employment by the negligence of a third party (not his employer or a fellow employee) he may usually collect benefits under the workmen's compensation law and his right of action against the third party is assigned to the workmen's compensation agency. If the worker elects to sue the third party, he cannot collect any workmen's compensation benefits for the injury.

A worker is usually required to complete a claim form, which is completed by his doctor and employer before any payments are made. Claims must usually be made within one year after an injury. Most states have an "agreement system" in uncontested cases where the worker and his employer or the employer's insurance carrier agree upon a settlement before payments are made. Approval of the agreement by the administrative body may be required before payments start. A few states have a "direct pay system" in which the employer (in uncontested cases) may begin making payments immediately, before the worker is required to sign any papers. Nearly all states provide for a few days' waiting period before payment of benefits is required.

In contested cases, a hearing is usually held before an administrative officer, who usually has exclusive jurisdiction to determine facts. Appeals to state courts are limited to questions of law or to determining whether there was "substantial evidence" to support the facts found by the agency.

LEGAL PRINCIPLES

There are seven basic statutes regulating labor relations: the Railway Labor Act, the Norris La Guardia Act, the Wagner Act, the Fair Labor Standards Act, the Taft-Hartley Act, the Labor-Management Reporting and Disclosure Act, and the Occupational Safety and Health Act.

The Wagner Act established the National Labor Relations Board, composed of four members and a chairman, whose two main functions are: (1) to review unfair labor practices and (2) to umpire union elections and campaigns.

An employer is forbidden to discriminate against an employee as a way of encouraging or discouraging union membership.

It is the duty of the employer to bargain in good faith with the representative of a majority of the employees in an appropriate bargaining unit.

It is unlawful for an employer to discriminate against an employee because of any testimony he may have given in an NLRB hearing.

The Fair Labor Standards Act has helped set standards for minimum wages and maximum hours.

The Taft-Hartley Act seeks to bring unions as well as employers under government regulation to help eliminate the imbalance of the Wagner Act. It prohibits the closed shop.

The Labor-Management Reporting and Disclosure Act brought about a new concept in labor law—the direct intervention by the federal government into the internal structure and affairs of labor unions.

An employer commits an unfair labor practice if he interferes, restrains, or coerces employees in their right to organize or join a union.

A union commits an unfair labor practice if it restrains or coerces employees for any reason and to any end.

The Occupational Safety and Health Act promotes safe and healthful working conditions in businesses involved in interstate commerce.

To be compensable, it is not necessary that the injury be caused by an accident, merely that it be accidental.

Injuries due to traumatic experiences, and those due to risks which are added perils of employment are compensable.

Progressive diseases that are "lit up" or accelerated while in employment are compensable.

Infections and weakening of resistance to other illnesses due to injuries while in employment are compensable.

Prompt notice of injury or death is not necessary to satisfy the compensation laws. Evidence to the effect that the injury was indeed sustained is sufficient.

CASES FOR REVIEW

N. L. R. B. v. FRUIT PACKERS

337 U.S. 58 (1963)

Under . . . the National Labor Relations Act . . . it is an unfair labor practice for a union "to threaten, coerce, or restrain any person" with the object of "forcing or requiring any person to cease using, selling, handling, transporting, or otherwise dealing in the products of any other producer . . . or to cease doing business with any other person. . . ." A proviso excepts, however, "publicity, *other than picketing,* for the purpose of truthfully advising the public . . . that a product or products are produced by an employer with whom the labor organization has a primary dispute and are distributed by another employer, as long as such publicity does not have an effect of inducing any individual employed by any person other than the primary employer in the course of his employment to refuse to pick up, deliver, or transport any goods, or not to perform any services, at the establishment of the employer engaged in such distribution." The question in this case is whether the respondent unions violated this section when they limited their secondary picketing of retail stores to an appeal to the customers of the stores not to buy the products of certain firms against which one of the respondents was on strike.

Respondent Local 760 called a strike against fruit packers and warehousemen doing business in Yakima, Washington. The struck firms sold Washington State apples to the Safeway chain of retail stores in and about Seattle, Washington. Local 760, aided by respondent Joint Council, instituted a consumer boycott against the apples in support of the strike. They placed pickets who walked back and forth before the customers' entrances of forty-six Safeway stores in Seattle. The pickets—two at each of forty-five stores and three at the forty-sixth store—wore placards and distributed handbills which appealed to Safeway customers, and to the public generally, to refrain from buying Washington State apples, which were only one of numerous food products sold in the stores. Before the pickets appeared at any store, a letter was delivered to the store manager informing him that the picketing was only an appeal to his customers not to buy Washington State apples, and that the pickets were being expressly instructed "to patrol peacefully in front of the consumer entrances of the store, to stay away from the delivery entrances and not to interfere with the work of your employees, or with deliveries to or pickups from your store." A copy of written instructions to the pickets—which included the explicit statement that "you are also forbidden to request that the customers not partronize the store"—was enclosed with the letter. Since it was desired to assure Safeway employees that they were not to cease work, and to avoid any interference with pickups or deliveries, the pickets appeared after the stores opened for business and departed before the stores closed. At all times during the picketing, the store employees continued to work, and no deliveries or pickups were obstructed. Washington State apples were handled in normal course by both Safeway employees and the employees of other employers involved. Ingress and egress by customers and others was not interfered with in any manner.

A complaint issued on charges that this conduct violated § 8 (b) (4) as amended . . . that "by literal wording of the proviso (to Section 8[b][4]) as well as through the interpretive gloss placed thereon by its drafters, consumer picketing in front of a secondary establishment is prohibited."

. . . All that the legislative history shows in the way of an "isolated evil" believed to require proscription of peaceful consumer picketing at secondary sites, was its use to persuade the customers of the secondary employer to cease trading with him in order to force him to cease dealing with, or to put pressure upon, the primary employer. This narrow focus reflects the difference between such conduct and peaceful picketing at the secondary site directed only at the struck product. In the latter case, the union's appeal to the public is confined to its dispute with the primary employer, since the public is not asked to withhold its patronage from the secondary employer, but only to boycott the primary employer's goods. On the other hand, a union appeal to the public at the secondary site not to trade at all with the secondary employer goes beyond the goods of the primary employer, and seeks the public's assistance in forcing the secondary employer to cooperate with the union in its primary dispute.

. . . There is thus nothing in the legislative history prior to the convening of the Conference Committee which shows any congressional concern with consumer picketing beyond that with the "isolated evil" of its use to cut off the business of a secondary employer as a means of forcing him to stop doing business with the primary employer. . . .

Peaceful consumer picketing to shut off all trade with the secondary employer unless he aids the union in its dispute with the primary employer, is poles apart from such picketing which only persuades his customers not to buy the struck product. The proviso indicates no more than that the Senate conferees' constitutional doubts led Congress to authorize publicity other than picketing which persuades the customers of a secondary employer to stop all trading with him, but not such publicity which has the effect of cutting off his deliveries or inducing his employees to cease work. On the other hand, picketing which persuades the customers of a secondary employer to stop all trading with him was also to be barred.

In sum, the legislative history does not support the Board's finding that Congress meant to prohibit all consumer picketing at a secondary site, having determined that such picketing necessarily threatened, coerced or restrained the secondary employer. Rather, the history shows that Congress was following its usual practice of legislating against peaceful picketing only to curb "isolated evils."

We come then to the question whether the picketing in this case, confined as it was to persuading customers to cease buying the product of the primary employer, falls within the area of secondary consumer picketing which Congress did clearly indicate its intention to prohibit. . . . We hold that it did not fall within that area, and therefore did not "threaten, coerce, or restrain" Safeway.

RUSSELL v. PHARR YARNS, INC.

196 S.E.2d 571 (1973)

Plaintiff-employee was a "doffer and creeler", which job consisted of hanging cones of yarn on defendant-employer's machines. At about 8:00 p. m. on 15 July 1971 plaintiff was removing cones of yarn from a box on wheels, which she rolled in front of her, and placing the cones of yarn on the machines. As she reached down into the box for two cones, she felt a severe pain in her back. A physician testified that she had been treated after the date of the unjury for a herniated disc.

Plaintiff testified that she had been performing this type of work for about three years, and usually emptied the boxes of cones four to five times a workday. The boxes usually contain about 50 to 60 cones when full.

Plaintiff was uncertain about the cause of the injury. She did state that, "[a]s I was bringing the bobbins up, the only thing unusual that happened from the way that I normally do it is that I felt a slight tug." When asked by the Deputy Commissioner to testify as to what she knew happened, she stated, "I was coming up out of the box . . . and I felt this jabbing pain in my back."

The Commission found:

> She had most of the yarn hung when she reached down into the bottom of the cart, grasped two cones, and began to raise up. Upon raising up to the point that

her upper torso was horizontal with the floor she felt a jabbing pain in her back. The pain was intense enough to cause her to scream and drop the cones.

. . . Up to the time that claimant felt the stabbing pain in her back nothing unusual or out of the ordinary occurred which caused the pain. She was performing her regular duties in the usual manner.

. . . Claimant was not injured by accident within the meaning of the North Carolina Workmen's Compensation Act because no unusual event, constituting an interruption of her usual routine of work, caused the back injury."

The words "accident" and injury" are not synonymous.

Thus, an accident has occurred only where there has been an interruption of the usual work routine or the introduction of some new circumstance not a part of the usual work routine. A hernia or back injury suffered by an employee does not arise by accident if the employee at the time was merely carrying out his usual and customary duties in the usual way. . . . Injury arising out of lifting objects in the ordinary course of an employee's business is not caused by accident where such activity is performed in the ordinary manner, free from confining or otherwise exceptional conditions and surroundings.

Countless cases of back or hernia injuries can be cited in which the plaintiffs did not recover an award because there was no unusual circumstance about the performance of the job which showed that an accident had occurred. See for example, Lawrence v. Mill, 265 N.C. 329 (plaintiff reached into a tool box to retrieve an object weighing about 47 pounds, as he had done on other occasions); Byrd v. Cooperative, 260 N.C. 215 (lifting 100-pound bags of fertilizer); Harding v. Thomas & Howard Co., 256 N.C. 427, (truck driver unloading 12 one-pound packages of coffee in the usual manner); Turner v. Hosiery Mills, 251 N.C. 325 (plaintiff leaned over back of hosiery machine to make an adjustment to the machine); Hensley v. Cooperative, 246 N.C. 274, (Plaintiff twisted his back when picking up a basket of chickens).

Hernia or back injuries, of course, have been compensable in other cases. In Keller v. Wiring Co., 259 N.C. 222. . . . the plaintiffs were injured when lifting objects while in an unusually twisted, cramped, or awkward position.

In Davis v. Summitt, 259 N.C. 57, . . . (1963) . . . the plaintiffs were performing physically strenuous tasks without the assistance from other workmen which was normally used.

In Harris v. Contracting Co., 240 N.C. 715, (1954), the plaintiff's feet slipped, and he fell injuring his back.

Upon review of an order of the Industrial Commission, this Court does not weigh the evidence, but may only determine whether there is evidence in the record to support the finding made by the Commission.

If there is any evidence of substance which directly or by reasonable inference tends to support the findings, the court is bound by such evidence, even though there is evidence that would have supported a finding to the contrary.

In the instant case there was competent evidence upon which to base a finding that the plaintiff was performing her regular duties in the usual manner, and that "up to the time that the claimant felt the stabbing pain in her back nothing unusual or out of the ordinary occurred which caused the pain."

CASE PROBLEMS

1. Plaintiff brought suit for the defendant's alleged violation of the Fair Labor Standards Act. The defendant denied the act applied to his business since it was shown that he was engaged in the manufacture and supply of artificial ice in a single city, though ice was supplied to trains at the terminal which was used in both freight and passenger service on trains operating into other states. This amounted to a very small portion of the business. Decide.

2. The National Labor Relations Board conducted an election in Brooks Car Agency on April 12, 1971. Union Local No. 727 won by an 8 - 5 vote and was certified as exclusive bargaining representative. The day before certification the defendant Brooks received a letter signed by nine of the thirteen employees in the bargaining unit stating that they were not in favor of being represented by Union Local No. 727. The defendant refused to bargain with the union and was cited for an unfair labor practice. Decide.

3. The respondent company had executed an exclusive bargaining contract with the union. The contract provided for a minimum wage scale; but no provision was made for merit increases. The subject was not mentioned in the agreement. After the contract was executed, the company, in line with past practices, gave out a number of merit raises. The union requested information concerning the merit raises as a basis for future collective bargaining. The request was denied. The NLRB ordered the company to bargain on this matter. Decide.

4. Since 1952 ASB Company has engaged in collective bargaining with a group of eight unions. Prior to the negotiations, ASB had contracted with the unions on five occasions, each agreement having been preceded by a strike. On May 1, 1961, the union said they intended to seek a modification of their current contract, due to expire on August 1. In light of the failure to reach an agreement and a lack of available business, the ASB decided to lay off certain employees. Due to this layoff the union filed charges with the NLRB. Decide.

5. DMC was a South Carolina corporation operating one textile mill. In March, 1956, the Textile Workers Union initiated an organizational campaign at the mill which the corporation resisted vigorously, including threats to close the mill if the union won a representative election. The board of directors voted to liquidate on September 12 and this action was approved by the shareholders on October 17. The Union claimed this was a violation of the Wagner Act. Decide.

6. In 1964, Marl, working for Eclipse Lumber Company, refused to pay a union political assessment and thereupon left the union and paid no more dues. Under Union rules he remained a member until he was "dropped by some affirmative act of the Union," which was not taken. In 1972 he returned to work with Eclipse. He was told by the Union that he could be reinstated if he paid back dues. Marl protested. At the end of thirty days the Union notified the Company to dismiss Marl. Marl protested to NLRB. Decide.

7. A strike was called in June, 1969; but before the strike was terminated some of the employees, including Melvin Finch, returned to work. One of the terms in the new contract was that the union would take no disciplinary action against any employee who had returned to work early. However, the union advised the company that charges were pending against all employees who had returned to work during the strike. In June, 1971, Finch was informed that he was denied a promotion because of the pending charges. Finch filed charges against the union and his employer. Decide.

8. In March, 1972, after failing to agree upon a contract, the union called a strike against Carrier. During the course of the strike the union picketed the several

entrances to the plant, including one used by an independent railroad and which was accessible only to railroad employees. Carrier alleged that this was not primary picketing, and hence, it was illegal. Decide.

PART IV
PARTNERSHIPS

DEFINITION AND FORMATION

26

The most effective form of organization must be determined from the needs of the particular firm. A form suitable for one type of business activity may not be appropriate for another. The factors that must be considered include the type of business, the availability of capital, tax considerations, continuity of the organization, and the extent of government regulation of the industry. Although no two firms are ever exactly alike or have identical requirements, the corporate form seems more suitable for very large undertakings because high capital requirements can most easily be met by a large number of shareholders. General partnerships, on the other hand, are most often formed in the conduct of small scale enterprises. A partnership usually involves a coming together of persons with similar interests or skills who need the advantages of organization without the complexities and formalities of the corporation.

ADVANTAGES AND DISADVANTAGES OF PARTNERSHIPS

A partnership has the following advantages over a corporation:
1. The organization involves less formality at the initial stages. A partnership is formed simply by a contract between the members of the firm, whereas incorporation requires a number of statutory steps to be taken by the incorporators.
2. Less formal procedures may be used in transacting company business, compared with the legal requirements for voting and meetings of shareholders faced by corporations.
3. There is relative freedom from public supervision and no need for annual reports such as those made by corporations to shareholders.
4. The tax burden is lighter since income is taxed only once, as the individual partner's income, whereas corporate dividends are subject first to corporate income tax and then to individual income tax when distributed to shareholders.

A partnership has the following disadvantages:
1. Each partner is responsible for the acts of all other partners within the scope of the business. The individual shareholder, on the other hand, is not held liable for actions of the corporation.
2. Each partner has unlimited financial liability for the obligations of the firm. In a corporation the shareholder is liable only to the extent of his capital contribution.
3. The firm is subject to immediate dissolution by the death or bankruptcy of any of the individual partners. Any change in membership causes dissolution, whereas the corporation's life is usually perpetual.

233

HISTORICAL BACKGROUND

The development of partnership law in England, and later in the United States, was characterized by a great deal of uncertainty and confusion. Merchants and other businessmen treated the firm as a legal entity, while the common law courts refused to do so, considering it merely an association of individuals. The need for uniform legislation soon became obvious.

The Uniform Partnership Act was drafted and recommended to the various states in 1914. Section 6 of the Act defines a partnership as "an association of two or more persons to carry on, as co-owners, a business for profit." Although the word "persons" suggests living individuals, a partnership may also include other partnerships among its members; where it is permitted by local law, corporations can become partners. Although the Act adopts the common law theory of partnership, it does recognize the entity theory for some purposes, which will be discussed later. (For example, a partnership may acquire property in the firm name.) The Act has helped to establish uniformity, but it does not resolve all previous disputes, nor does it attempt to cover all aspects of partnership law.

A partnership may also be defined as a contract of mutual agency, each partner acting as a principal on his own behalf and as an agent for his co-partners. Each partner is individually liable for all the obligations of the organization created in pursuit of the partnership business because each partner is an agent both for the partnership and for each individual partner. Creditors who have difficulty in collecting from the partnership may turn to any one of the partners and demand payment from his personal financial resources (assuming that he has sufficient financial resources).

ESSENTIALS OF A PARTNERSHIP

Unlike a corporation, a partnership is not a legal entity. (A legal entity is "in being," or "exists" for legal purposes and is recognized by the law as a "person.") Whereas a corporation is in fact an entity created by an act of the state, a partnership is not; it results from an agreement between two or more parties. Thus a partnership is not treated as a "person" in regard to such matters as the payment of taxes. It is not a taxable entity; rather, the partners are taxed individually on their incomes. Nor can the separate entity concept be used to protect partners personally from liability for claims of the partnership's creditors. However, as we have mentioned, the Uniform Partnership Act does treat a partnership as an entity for some purposes. The partnership may hold title to property and enter into contracts in its own name, and in some states it may sue or be sued. Also, a partnership may be viewed as an entity for the purpose of changes in partnership membership.

A partnership is created by the voluntary agreement of the parties, expressed by words, either written or oral, or by their conduct. For a new member to join an existing partnership, this voluntary agreement is necessary as a matter of law. A person cannot be forced to enter a partnership, and existing partners may not be forced to accept a new partner whom they do not want.

A partnership is a joint venture in regard to capital contributions, power of management, and profits and losses. This is not to say that all partners necessarily have an equal investment in terms of capital contributions. The size of the investment, as well as the profit and loss ratios of the partners, may vary widely. However, every member of a partnership has some ownership interest in the profits.

COURT RULES FOR DETERMINING THE EXISTENCE OF A PARTNERSHIP

If two or more parties intend their relationship to be a partnership, and if their relationship includes the essential elements of a partnership as set down by the Uniform Partnership Act, their relationship will be considered a partnership. In addition, some business that may not have been intended to be partnerships are treated as such by the courts, if the essential elements of a partnership are present. If the parties agree upon an arrangement that is a partnership in fact, it is immaterial that they call it something else or that they declare themselves not to be partners; they will still be treated by the courts as partners. On the other hand, the mere fact that the parties to an agreement call their relationship a partnership will not make it one if they have not, by their contract, agreed upon an arrangement that conforms with the legal definition of a partnership.

The presence or absence of profit sharing is important in determining whether a business is a partnership. The practice of profit sharing is considered prima facie evidence that a business is a partnership. However, not every organization in which profit sharing exists is a partnership. Between two people or among a small group of people, profit sharing usually is an indication of partnership. In a large business venture involving many people, profit sharing may not necessarily indicate a partnership. When profits are distributed to employees as payment of a debt, to a landlord as rent, or to the widow of a deceased partner as an annuity, the recipient is not considered a patner. Unless there is co-ownership of the business and a right to common control, profit sharing in itself is not sufficient evidence to establish the existence of a partnership.

PARTNERSHIP AGREEMENT

In order to enter a partnership, an agreement, either oral or written, must be established. In cases where the Statute of Frauds is involved the partnership agreement must be in writing. However, it is good business practice to have the agreement in writing to avoid any conflicts that may arise among the partners later. The following points should be included in a partnership agreement:

1. the names of the partners;
2. the name of the partnership;
3. the nature of the partnership business;
4. the duration of the agreement;
5. the capital to be invested by each partner and the penalties for failure to contribute and maintain the agreed amount of capital;

6. the managerial powers to be vested in each partner and the rights and duties of each;
7. the accounting procedures to be used—the nature of accounting records and financial statements and the timing of periodic audits;
8. the plan for sharing profits and the time of distribution;
9. the partners' share of losses;
10. the salaries and drawing of funds allowed to partners;
11. the causes and methods of dissolution; and
12. the distribution of partnership property upon dissolution.

Any revision of the articles of partnership requires the agreement of all the partners.

TYPES OF PARTNERS

A partnership may have many different types of partners. All partners do not necessarily have the same rights and powers. Some members may have more authority than others, or greater liability, and some may enter the partnership in different ways than others.

A partner is not necessarily an individual. According to the Uniform Partnership Act, Sec. 2, "individuals, partnerships, corporations, and other associations" may become partners. Essentially, anyone legally capable of forming a contract may become a partner; therefore, the partnership must be an association of competent parties. It is presumed that all persons are capable of entering into a partnership without restriction, with the exception of infants, the insane and the intoxicated. A partnership between an infant and an adult can be voided only by the infant and may be disaffirmed by him against the adult. The infant can regain his capital contribution without loss upon disaffirmance. This right is granted to minors as protection against those who would be inclined to take advantage of their inexperience and immaturity. Some courts, however, subject an infant's capital contribution to the claims of unpaid creditors and to whatever losses have been sustained by the firm prior to his withdrawal.

There are various types or kinds of partners:

1. *General partners,* who have a voice in management and unlimited liability; their individual assets are subject to partnership losses.
2. *Special partners,* who have no voice in management; their losses are sometimes limited by statute to the extent of their contributions.
3. *Secret (or silent) partners,* whose connection with the firm is not disclosed to outside sources but who are nonetheless partners and subject to liability for partnership obligations in much the same way as undisclosed principals are liable for contract obligations.
4. *Nominal partners,* who, by words spoken or written or by their conduct, represent themselves or consent to another's representation of them as partners in an existing partnership or partners with other persons not in a partnership. Nominal partners are liable to any party to whom such representation has been made. They become partners by estoppel.

PARTNERSHIP BY ESTOPPEL

If two or more persons manifest by their conduct that they are partners and if their relationship includes the essential elements of a partnership, they are to be thought of and treated as partners. According to the Uniform Partnership Act, Sec. 16, "When a person by words spoken or written or by conduct, represents himself, or consents to another representing him to anyone as a partner in an existing partnership or with one or more persons not actual partners, he is liable to any party to whom such representation has been made." Liability created by estoppel arises when the third party gives credit to the actual or apparent firm in reliance upon the representation of partnership that has been communicated to him.

Two requirements are necessary to establish partnership liability by estoppel. First, the party alleged to be a partner must either have represented himself as a partner or have knowingly consented that others make this representation. Second, there must be a reliance upon the representation by the party who extended credit to the firm. If the creditor knew, or reasonably should have known, that no partnership existed, no partnership liability can be established.

PARTNERSHIP NAME

In the absence of a statute to the contrary a partnership may operate under any name it desires. The firm name may designate either the persons involved or the nature of the business. In the latter case, many states require that a certificate be filed giving both the name under which the partnership operates and the names of the partners conducting the business. Failure to register the partnership does not make contracts with third parties void. However, failure to register is a crime, and as a penalty the unregistered partnership is denied access to the courts.

The firm name is an asset of the firm and will be protected by law. Care must be taken in choosing a name not to adopt the name of an established firm since the first user is protected by law from infringement on its name. Partners may even be prohibited from using their own names for the business if they are identical or very similar to an already existing business and may mislead the public. In some states partnerships are forbidden to use the words "and company" lest they lead the public to believe that the firm is a corporation.

GOOD WILL

Good will is an asset of the firm because of the expectation of continued patronage from old customers and the probable patronage of new customers due to the firm's good name. In short, good will is the commercial value of the firm's reputation. Where this intangible factor arises from professional services, it is held to be nontransferable and is generally not regarded as a partnership asset. In all other cases good will is an asset that accrues for the benefit of the partners.

The partnership agreement will usually contain a negative covenant clause to protect good will. This clause states that in the event of retirement from the firm each partner agrees not to compete with the firm for a reasonable time.

LEGAL PRINCIPLES

A partnership is a voluntary association of two or more persons to carry on, as co-owners, a business for a profit.

No formal expression of the arrangement is necessary. Intent will be evidenced by the agreements and the conduct of the parties.

Profit sharing is prima facie evidence of the existence of a partnership. Other indicators are a community of interest and common control of the firm.

It is good business practice to have the partnership agreement in writing. It is a legal requirement to do so when the Statute of Frauds is involved.

Anyone capable of making a contract may enter into a partnership agreement.

All partners do not necessarily have the same rights and powers nor the same liability and authority.

A partnership by estoppel is created by statements or conduct that justify in others the belief that one is a partner.

In the absence of a statute to the contrary, a firm may operate under any name it desires, whether that of the partners or one indicative of the type of business to be transacted.

The firm name and the good will that accrues to it are assets of the firm and will be protected by law.

CASE FOR REVIEW

ROSENBERGER v. HERBST

232 A.2d 634 (1967)

On January 1, 1957, defendant Julius Herbst and one Eugene Parzych entered into a formal agreement relating to the operation of a farm owned by Herbst, located in Bucks County. The agreement, which is long and complex, recites Herbst's contribution of certain assets, principally the use and occupancy of the farm. It further acknowledges Parzych's indebtedness to Herbst in the amount of $6000, repayable with interest of five per cent per annum.

The actual farming operation is stated to be "under the full control of Parzych." Herbst is entitled to receive one-half of the net profits, and is bound to indemnify Parzych for one-half of any losses sustained.

In a key paragraph, the agreement recites: "Since any remuneration due hereunder to Herbst is a payment in return for his investment in the business and his capital contribution thereto, as well as in return for his leasing the Herbst Farm to Parzych without further rental payments, *the parties do not intend by this agreement to establish a partnership of any kind or type, but rather [a relation] of Debtor and Creditor and Landlord and Tenant."* [*Emphasis supplied.*]

Between February, 1957 and June, 1960, the plaintiffs, trading as "Clover Leaf Mill" (hereinafter "Clover Leaf") sold and delivered to Parzych large quantities of grain, feed, and fertilizer for use on the farm.

In July of 1961, Clover Leaf, for the first time, formally demanded payment from defendant Herbst for certain debts contracted by Parzych in connection with farming operations. Herbst disclaimed all liability, and this suit followed.

In relying on the profit sharing provision of the Herbst-Parzych agreement, the lower court clearly erred. The Uniform Partnership Act, . . . specifically provides: "The receipt by a person of a share of the profits of a business is prima facie evidence that he is a partner in the business, *but no such inference shall be drawn if such profits were received in payment:* (a) As a debt by installments or otherwise, (b) As . . . rent to a landlord . . . (d) As interest on a loan, though the amount of payment vary with the profits of the business . . ." [Emphasis supplied.] As previously noted, Parzych's indebtedness to Herbst was to be repaid from the proceeds of the farming operation. Furthermore, the agreement specifically provided that Herbst's remuneration was to be considered "a payment in return for his leasing the . . . Farm to Parzych without further rental payments. . . ." Accordingly, no inference of partnership may be drawn from Herbst's receipt of a fractional share of the proceeds of the farming operation.

The construction of this contract must, ultimately, be determined by reference to the intent of the parties. Paragraph Nine of the agreement clearly states that " . . . the parties do not intend to establish a partnership of any kind or type. . . . " Our Supreme Court has held: "[W]here [the parties] expressly declare that they are not partners this settles the question, for, whatever their obligations may be as to third persons, the law permits them to agree upon their legal status and relations [as between themselves]."

In light of the parties' express statement of intention, coupled with the inconclusive nature of the remainder of the agreement, we hold that defendant Herbst and Eugene Parzych were not partners.

CASE PROBLEMS

1. Defendants, members of an Elks' lodge, an unincorporated body, appointed a committee to erect a lodge building, adopting a motion which authorized them to borrow money for this purpose. The committee borrowed various sums, giving the lenders certificates of indebtedness in the name of the lodge, signed by the officers and sealed with a seal usually used by the secretary for authenticating communications to other lodges. This seal had never before been attached to a monetary obligation. Suit was brought by plaintiff, an owner of one of the certificates, against the members of the lodge, who were joined as defendants and alleged to be partners. Decide.
2. The creditors of the Pittston Tire Company filed a petition to put William Ganaposki in bankruptcy as a partner of the company. Ganaposki denied that he was a partner. It was alleged that his name appeared on various checks, drafts, and financial statements of the company and that one of the financial statements

was in his handwriting; but there was no evidence that he made any contribution to the capital, shared in the profits, or had any control over the management of the business. Decide.

3. Hicks sued defendants as partners under the name of Cram & Hutchinson. Hutchinson contended that he was not a partner and had no interest in the concern, but he had allowed Cram to state in business transactions that he was a partner and had made no denial of this. Decide.

4. Call contracted with Dever to sell 5100 head of cattle to Linn and Dever, who were doing business under the name Linn & Dever. Subsequently, in an action against Linn and Dever to recover damages for breach of contract, Call contended that the defendants were partners. Linn objected that no partnership existed, claiming that the transaction was simply a joint venture between himself and Dever. Decide.

5. Fox, owned, and Beason operated, a farm on which plaintiff, Florence, an employee, injured her hand. Plaintiff sued Fox and Beason as partners. Beason and defendant had an agreement in writing in the nature of a "share crop" lease: Fox was to furnish the farm and cows; Beason and Fox were to furnish hogs and chickens, "share and share alike," and to divide equally the cost of threshing; Fox was to supply the gasoline engine and Beason the cane mill; and each was to pay one-half the expense of operation. Each was also to get one-half of the proceeds, Fox as rent and Beason for his work. Decide.

6. Rocco Rizzo, Sr. operated a wastepaper business at 612 West Taylor Street, Chicago, Illinois. Michael, the oldest son, went to work for his father in 1910, Joseph in 1913, Rocco, Jr., in 1916, and John in 1920. Michael was the general manager, Joseph the receiving clerk, and John and Rocco, Jr. were truck drivers. The name of the business was originally "Rocco Rizzo & Company," later it was "Rocco Rizzo Son & Company," and still later "Rocco Rizzo Sons & Company." Michael, Joseph and John admitted on examination that they all worked in the business, shared equally in the profits, and went without pay if there were no profits. In 1929 the father, who had retired from active participation in the business, deeded the business property to Michael. On June 27, 1931, Rocco Rizzo, Jr. died. The plaintiff thereafter brought this action against the three brothers as surviving partners of Rocco Rizzo Sons & Company, claiming that the estate of the decedent should be awarded a one-quarter share in the partnership as of the date of his death. Decide.

7. Taylor carried on business under the name of Taylor & Company, but "& Company" did not represent the additional or separate interest of anyone else. This was contrary to the law. He sued Lord for damages for breach of a contract to purchase goods, and defendant set up the defense that Taylor had been carrying on business in violation of the law. Decide.

8. A father and son formed a partnership for the purpose of manufacturing and selling alcoholic beverages. The son obtained federal and Ohio licenses to run the business under his own name, without stating that the father had any interest. Both the federal and state statutes required that the holder of such licenses disclose the names of all persons interested in the firm, imposing criminal penalties for failure to do so. Subsequently, the father sued the son for an accounting of the profits of the partnership. Decide.

THE GENERAL NATURE OF A PARTNERSHIP

27

The scope of a partner's authority to impose liability on the partnership is determined by the laws of agency, since every partner is an agent of the partnership for the purpose of its business and is limited in some respects by the terms of partnership agreement.

Limitations on the partner's authority must be stated in the partnership agreement and conveyed to third parties. The partnership is bound by the action of any partner so limited if the third party had no knowledge of the limitations. However, the partner may be held liable to the partnership for damages occuring as a result of such unauthorized action. Where the third party was aware of the limitation, the firm would not be bound.

TYPES OF AUTHORITY

Express authority in the partnership comes from the partnership agreement; however, special authority not mentioned in the agreement may be granted to a particular partner, which authority may be limited to a particular act or similarly restricted.

In the absence of an express agreement describing the powers of the partners, each partner has the implied power to perform all legal actions necessary for carrying on the partnership business. The nature and scope of the business and what is usual in a particular industry—that is, the business customs and usages of the area in which the firm operates—determine the extent of the implied powers.

TRADING AND NONTRADING PARTNERSHIP

The courts make a distinction between a trading partnership and a nontrading partnership in judging the extent of a firm's implied authority. A trading partnership is one created primarily for the purpose of buying and selling commodities. In a trading partnership, each partner has the implied power to borrow money, to lend the credit of the firm, and to sign negotiable papers in the firm's name.

A partner's power to borrow money on the firm's credit will depend primarily on the nature of the partnership's business and whether it is standard practice in such business to use borrowed money to cover operating expenses. The power to borrow money on the firm's credit will carry with it the power to pledge firm assets to secure the repayment of the borrowed money. A partner has the power, ordinarily, to endorse for deposit or for discount negotiable instruments drawn payable to the order of the partnership. A partner's power to issue negotiable instruments in the name of the partnership is dependent upon his power to borrow money on the firm's credit. If he can do one, he can do the other.

A partnership engaged in the production of commodities or in providing service is a nontrading partnership. In this situation, a partner's powers are more limited, and he does not have the implied power to borrow money or to bind the firm on negotiable paper. Doctors, lawyers, and dentists are associated in partnerships of this type.

As a rule, a partner does not have the authority to do any acts that will defeat the purposes of the partnership, that are illegal, or that impose an unreasonable burden on the partnership, such as selling all the partnership assets or obligating the partnership as surety or guarantor for third persons.

NOTICE

Notice to any partner of any matter relating to partnership affairs is considered notice to the partnership. The partnership is held to have received notice even if the partner does not communicate this knowledge to the firm. An exception is made by the courts only when the partner receiving notice and a third party have intentionally combined in committing a fraud upon the partnership.

This concept of notice is like that of the law of agency which states that notice to an agent is notice to the principal.

LIABILITY OF PARTNERS

CONTRACT LIABILITY

The Uniform Partnership Act provides that partners are jointly liable on all debts and contract obligations of the partnership made by a partner for the firm within the scope of his authority. The distinction between *joint and several liability* and *joint liability* should be emphasized. In a suit upon a joint obligation, each living joint obligor must be made a party defendant to the action or the action will fail. Where an obligation is joint and several, the parties may all be joined as defendants in one suit or each may be sued in a separate suit. Whatever the situation, execution may be made only against the assets of those partners who were actually sued and served.

Some states have enacted legislation changing this procedure for bringing suit against a partnership. These jurisdictions have made partnership contract obligations joint and several, thus allowing suit against less than all the partners. The same result has been obtained in other jurisdictions in the absence of statute where not all of the partners were within the jurisdictional reach of the court. This is true only when the partnership is being sued. The courts and legislatures are not willing to relax the rules when the partnership is bringing the suit. In these situations, all the partners must be joined as parties in the suit.

A judgment based upon a joint obligation must be against all the obligors or none of them. The death of an obligor ordinarily terminates his general partnership liability. However, his assets are subject to any debts incurred prior to death. A judgment upon a joint and several obligation against one of the obligors, until and unless satisfied, does not release the others, nor does it bar a subsequent suit against them; whereas a release of one joint obligor releases all. Therefore when a partner makes a contract for the firm, all members become liable, and all members must be joined in any litigation concerning the contract.

TORT LIABILITY

A partnership is liable, and the partners are jointly and severally liable, for the wrongful act or omission of a partner while acting within the scope of partnership business if it results in loss or injury to any person not a partner. For example, where a partner, in the transaction of partnership business, induces a person to enter into a transaction by misrepresentation and fraud, both the partnership and the co-partners will be liable.

The partnership and all the partners are liable for a willful and malicious tort of a partner if it is committed in the interest of the partners and within the scope of partnership business. The partners are jointly and severally liable to injured third persons. However, if the tort is personally motivated, the partners and the co-partners are not liable. When a judgment is entered against the firm, each member is individually liable, regardless of the amount of his capital contribution.

CRIMINAL LIABILITY

When a partner commits a crime in the transaction of partnership business, the co-partners are not criminally liable unless they have directly participated in the criminal act. If the firm carries on an illegal activity, all the partners will be criminally liable. However, as a practical matter, their liability is usually limited to the payment of fines, since it would be impossible to imprison the firm.

PARTNERSHIP PROPERTY

The Uniform Partnership Act, Sec. 8 states:
1. All property originally brought into the partnership stock or subsequently acquired by purchase or otherwise, on account of the partnership, is partnership property.
2. Unless the contrary intention [is apparent,] property acquired with partnership funds is partnership property.

Thus, each case dealing with partnership property must be decided by weighing all its pertinent facts and circumstances. Whether property used in a partnership business arrangement belongs to the firm or to an individual partner has been the subject of much litigation. In the absence of an express agreement, the court will attempt to ascertain the intent of the parties through their conduct with respect to the general purpose and use of the property in the business. However, the mere use of the property by the partnership is not proof that the property is an asset of the firm.

To avoid any confusion, those items that constitute partnership property should be identified in the partnership agreement. The amount of property that the firm may acquire is not limited unless restrictions are imposed by statute or by the partnership agreement. The partnership may own real as well as personal property unless it is prohibited from doing so by statute or by the partnership agreement.

PARTNERSHIP CAPITAL

Partnership capital includes all money credited to the capital accounts of the various partners, provided these funds are for use in carrying on the business. It is this amount that the partnership is obligated to return to each partner at the time of dissolution, and it can be varied by an agreement between the partners. Any monies paid into the firm or any profits used to aid in carrying on the business are not considered capital, since they may be withdrawn at any time and must be repaid prior to the return of capital.

TITLE TO PARTNERSHIP PROPERTY

All partnership property originally contributed to the firm or subsequently purchased in the ordinary course of business is held in the firm name. Consequently, any transfer of this property must be in the firm name.

Section 8 of the Uniform Partnership Act recognizes the partnership as a legal entity for the purpose of taking, holding, and conveying title to real property in the partnership name. In jurisdictions that have not adopted the Uniform Partnership Act, the partnership is not recognized as a legal entity for such purposes. Since the title to real property must rest in a person, either natural or artificial, title must be held in the name of a member of the business in such areas.

PROPERTY RIGHTS OF PARTNERS

The Uniform Partnership Act, Sec. 24, defines the extent of the property rights of a partner as "(1) his rights in specific partnership property, (2) his interest in the partnership, and (3) his right to participate in the management." The Act states that a partner has an equal right with his partners to possess specific partnership property for partnership purposes but has no right to possess such property for any other purpose without the consent of his partners. A partner's right in specific partnership property is not subject to attachment or execution, except on a claim against the partnership. On the death of a partner, his right in specific partnership property vests in the surviving partner or partners, except where the deceased was the last surviving partner, whereupon his right in such property vests in his legal representative.

POWERS WITH RESPECT TO PROPERTY

Each partner has the implied authority to sell to purchasers personal property held for the purpose of resale in the ordinary course of business and to execute any documents necessary to make an effective conveyance thereof. A partner has no power to sell assets used in the business unless he has been authorized by the other partners to do so. The sale of assets is not considered to be in the ordinary course of business, and a prospective purchaser should make certain that the partner he is dealing with has been given the authority to sell them.

When the firm is in the real estate business, a partner has the implied power to sell firm real estate. If title to realty is held in the firm name, the sale of it without the consent of all partners may be set aside unless the property has been conveyed to an innocent third party, in which case the third party takes good title.

If firm property is held in the names of one or more of the partners, the sale of it by these partners conveys good title unless the purchaser knows or should know that title was held for the firm.

TENANCY IN PARTNERSHIP

The determination of the rights and interests of individual partners in partnership property perplexed common law jurists. They did not consider the partnership a legal unit, separate and distinct from its members; therefore, the property of the firm could not belong to the partnership as such but must belong to the individual members as co-owners, and any conveyance by the firm had to contain the name of an individual partner to be effective. Since the common law recognized joint tenancy and tenancy in common as forms of co-ownership, the question arose as to which of these applied to partnership property. The majority of jurists favored a tenancy in common, while the business community, on the other hand, looked on the firm as a legal unit and claimed that partnership property belonged to the firm. These opposing views produced many conflicts relating to the ownership of firm assets.

The Uniform Partnership Act embodies both the common law views in that, while the entity theory is rejected, the firm is vested with the ownership of firm assets. The Act rejects the common law arguments for co-ownership and creates a new type of ownership called tenancy in partnership, by which specific partnership assets, both real and personal, are held by the partners. The Act confers on the partners an equal right to the possession and use of specific partnership property for partnership purposes. No right to possess such property may be granted to any person without the consent of the partners. The right to specific property is not assignable, nor is it subject to attachment or execution except on a claim against the partnership. Also, this property is not subject to dower, curtesy, or allowances to widows, heirs, or next of kin. Unlike a tenancy in common, the firm assets are subject to the claims of partnership creditors and cannot be partitioned or distributed between or among partners unless the firm debts are first paid and firm claims satisfied.

LIMITED PARTNERSHIPS

A limited partner is one who contributes money or property, but not services, and who runs the risk of losing his contribution but does not assume personal liability for the obligations of the partnership. His rights are limited to receiving profits or a return of capital upon dissolution. Every limited partner must have at least one general partner who will be liable for the partnership obligations. The special or limited partner may be held liable for partnership obligations if he acts as a general partner by participating in the conduct of partnership business.

According to Section 2 of the Uniform Limited Partnership Act, a limited partner must file with the designated state office a sworn certificate setting forth detailed information concerning the relative rights of the members of the limited partnership. If he fails to do so or misrepresents information in this form, he will be judged a general partner and held personally liable for partnership obligations.

The rights, powers, and liabilities of a general partner in a limited partnership are defined by Section 9 of the U.L.P.A. as being subject to the same liabilities and restrictions as those of a general partner in a partnership without limited partners,except that without the written consent of, or ratification by, all limited partners, general partners have no authority to:

(a) Do any act in contravention of the certificate,
(b) Do any act which would make it impossible to carry on the ordinary business of the partnership,
(c) Confess a judgment against the partnership,
(d) Possess partnership property or assign their rights in specific partnership property for other partnership purposes,
(e) Admit a person as a general partner,
(f) Admit a person as a limited partner, unless given the right in the certificate,
(g) Continue the business with partnership property on the death, retirement or insanity of a general partner, unless given the right in the certificate.

LEGAL PRINCIPLES

Each partner is an agent and a principal of his fellow partners; each partner binds the partnership on any act performed within the scope of partnership business.

Express authority in a partnership comes from the partnership agreement.

Implied authority is that which is necessary to implement express power . . . . There are no implied powers in a nontrading partnership.

Any limitations imposed upon the partner must be specified in the partnership agreement, and notice of the limitations must be given to any third party dealing with the partnership.

Notice to one partner of any matter relating to partnership affairs is considered notice to the firm.

Partners have joint liability on all contracts made for the partnership.

All the partners are liable for a tort committed by one partner within the scope of partnership business. If the tort is personally motivated, only the partner performing the act is liable.

Even though a crime is committed by a partner in the course of business, the rest of the partners are not liable unless they have directly participated in the crime.

What is firm property will be determined by the intent of the parties and their use of the property.

Partnership capital is the sum of all the partners' permanent investments in the business.

Title to property may be held in the firm name.

All partners have an equal right to the possession of partnership property for partnership purposes.

Each partner has the authority to sell firm assets held for resale. Where the sale of assets in not done in the ordinary course of business, express authority must be given by all partners to such a sale.

Tenancy in partnership is a form of ownership created by the Uniform Partnership Act.

CASE FOR REVIEW

BOLE v. LYLE

287 S.W.2d 931 (1956)

John Bole, Jr., instituted this suit against B. Frank Lyle, Homer S. Peters and W.J. Barton, Jr., partners formerly operating under the name and style of Cherokee Box and Handle Company to recover $738.60 alleged to have been advanced to defendants for the purchase of lumber which was never delivered.

The primary question . . . is whether or not W. J. Barton, Jr., in executing the contract of sale was acting within the apparent scope of his authority as a partner.

On April 15, 1946, the date of the alleged contract, the Cherokee Box and Handle Company owned and operated a manufacturing business in Johnson City, Tennessee where it made packing crates, insulating pins and "dimensional stock," the last under a contract with the United States Government. All of these products were made from wood and, to supply the needs for lumber, defendants had previously purchased a boundary of timber which they were in the process of cutting and manufacturing into lumber at the time in question. The defendant, W. J. Barton, Jr., was the managing partner.

On a trip to Chattanooga, Barton became acquainted with A. E. Darling of the Darling Lumber Company of Big Rapids, Michigan. Darling was, apparently, in some way connected with the Lakeview Lumber Company of Lakewood, Michigan, which latter company the bill alleges was owned and operated by complainant Bole.

The bill is predicated upon a letter dated April 15, 1946, from A. E. Darling Lumber Company addressed to Cherokee Box and Handle Company and written by A. E. Darling, purporting to confirm a telephone conversation of that date between Darling and Barton for the purchase of certain specified types and amounts of lumber and enclosing Darling's check for $1500. The letter bears the following acceptance:

> "It is understood and agreed by the Cherokee Box & Handle Company, Johnson City, Tennessee, that the above is agreed to and fully understood and

the money is to be used and the title vested in Lakeview Lumber Company and A. E. Darling Lumber Company as above noted. . . .

(Signed) Cherokee Box & Handle
Company
by Wm. J. Barton, Jr.
Gen. Mgr.

After endorsing the check "Cherokee Box and Handle Co. by Wm. J. Barton, Jr. Gen., Mgr.", Barton opened a bank account in the name of "Wm. J. Barton, Jr., Agent", endorsing the check in his name as agent. He explained to the bank official that he was trading in his individual name and for that reason desired a separate account from that of Cherokee Box and Handle Company. The partnership received no part of the proceeds of the check and the other partners knew nothing of the transaction until claim was made after the dissolution of the partnership.

While the record is not clear, it is perhaps inferable that that part of the lumber which was shipped by Barton came from the tract of timber owned by the partnership. No other lumber was ever sold in this manner by Barton or by the partnership and the undisputed proof shows that neither this timber nor any other was ever bought for sale. The partnership was not a trading partnership but solely engaged in the business of manufacturing.

The act of Barton was not done "for apparently carrying on in the usual way the business of the partnership". On the contrary, the act was entirely outside the only business ever conducted by the partnership and there is no showing that his act "apparently" had a connection with the manufacturing business. This was not surplus or defective lumber such as a business engaged in the manufacture of wood products might find it desirable to sell from time to time, in which case the sale might conceivably have the appearance of being incident to the business of the partnership.

The general rule is that each partner is a general agent of the firm but only for the purpose of carrying on the business of the partnership. Any sale by a partner to be valid must be in furtherance of the partnership business, within the real scope of the business or such as third persons may reasonably conclude, from all the circumstances, to be embraced within it. If the act is embraced within the partnership business or incident to such business according to the ordinary and usual course of conducting it, the partnership is bound regardless of whether the partner, in performing the act, proceeds in good faith or bad faith toward his copartners.

Sales made by a partner in a trading firm are, or course, not viewed with the same strictness as in nontrading firms such as here involved because in trading firms sales are usually within the scope of the business while in nontrading firms they are exceptional and only incidental to the main business. A priori, in determining whether an act is within the scope of the business it is of importance, first, to determine the character of the partnership operations.

We think the case here presented is simply that of a nonresident, unfamiliar with the partnership operations, being defrauded by one of the partners acting in a matter beyond both the real and apparent scope of the business and beyond the real or apparent scope of the agency. There was nothing in the firm name to suggest that it was in the business of selling lumber. Complainant chose to deal with one of the partners without knowing anything of the nature of the partnership operations and that the nonparticipating partners were in no way responsible for his loss and that recovery should be against Barton alone.

CASE PROBLEMS

1. Winship and two others were partners in the business of making and selling soap and soap products. Winship, without the knowledge of his partners, borrowed money from the bank and signed the firm name to a promissory note. His co-partners denied liability on the note. Decide.
2. Joe and Sam Smith were partners in a manufacturing firm. Sam, without the knowledge of Joe, wrote a libelous letter to plaintiff in an attempt to induce payment for goods sold to him. Plaintiff brought suit against the partners for libel. Joe argued that he had not authorized or ratified it and therefore should not be held liable. Decide.
3. Petrikis, Ellis, and Keith, partners, signed an agreement: "We, the undersigned, hereby agree to sell our interests in the partnership business. If and when the sale takes place, and after all bills are accounted for, the remainder of the money it to be divided according to the share each partner now attains in the said business." Petrikis then began negotiations with Hanges and contracted to sell him the business for $17,500. Ellis refused to accept the terms of the contract. Hanges then notified the partners that he was calling the deal off, whereupon Petrikis and Keith brought suit against him for breach of contract. Decide.
4. Elsbury was convicted for grand larceny on an indictment charging him with stealing $1000 from S. L. Corsino. It was alleged that Elsbury and Corsino were general partners in operating a cafe and that the $1000 in question had been deposited in the bank under the firm name. Elsbury appealed on the ground that the $1000 for the theft of which he was charged was not the property of another and therefore could not be stolen by him. Decide.
5. Plaintiff bought from defendant, his former partner, the entire interest in the partnership, including goodwill. When defendant thereafter solicited business from customers of the old partnership, plaintiff sought to enjoin such solicitation. The trial court dismissed the action and plaintiff appealed. Decide.
6. Plaintiff seeks to recover possession from defendant of office space on which plaintiff's father had secured a ten-year lease. Plaintiff was called into military service, and during his absence the father entered into a partnership agreement with defendant that gave the latter an option to purchase an interest in the office equipment, but which did not mention the lease on the office space. The office space was actually used for partnership purposes. When plaintiff's father died, the executrix assigned all interests in the lease to plaintiff, but defendant continued in possession, claiming under the right of a surviving partner. Decide.
7. Plaintiff and defendant, Leidinger, took out insurance on their respective lives in order to obtain loans for continuing their partnership. They used partnership funds to pay the premiums. When the insurance agent informed them that the partnership could not be made a beneficiary, they named their respective estates as beneficiaries. The broker who wrote the policy on plaintiff's life testified that, when the partners discussed the form of the policy, plaintiff said, "We want this insurance so if anything happens to either one of us, the one who is left will have the money to wind up the business, or to carry on as he sees fit." When Leidinger died, was his estate entitled to the proceeds of the policy?
8. Azeve, in partnership with six others, owned and operated a dairy business. In 1964, acting as agent for the partnership, Azeve purchased with partnership

funds six shares of Gustin Creamery stock "for the company." He afterwards purchased one additional share. Without the knowledge of his six partners, these shares were issued in the name of the partnership, Azeve & Company. Sequeri, a partner, testified that seven shares were purchased so that each of the seven partners might separately own one share. The purchase price of the stock was originally taken from the proceeds of the business and subsequently charged to each partner in the final accounting. Were the shares partnership property?

THE LEGAL RELATIONSHIP OF PARTNERS

28

In the partnership relationship there are a number of rights and duties that one partner has with regard to the other partners in the firm. The provisions in the partnership agreement drawn up on the formation of the business usually specify the extent of these rights, duties, and remedies. For example, the rights of the individual partner in regard to sharing in profits and losses, participation in management, compensation for services, the right to inspect the books of the firm, the right to an accounting, and rights to interest are defined in the agreement. When no mention of these rules is made, the Uniform Partnership Act controls in the jurisdictions in which it has been adopted.

SHARING IN PROFITS AND LOSSES

Each partner has the right to share in the profits of the partnership. Unless there is a previous agreement to the contrary, the profits are shared equally. The same will hold true if there are losses. If on dissolution there are not sufficient assets to repay each partner his capital contribution, the difference is considered a loss to be met like any partnership loss.

Suppose in the ABC partnership A contributed $100,000 to the firm, B contributed $80,000 and C, $20,000. On dissolution, there remains $65,000 after payment has been made to creditors. Since the total capital contribution to the firm was $200,000, the loss is $135,000; and since losses must be shared equally, each partner suffers a $45,000 loss. Since C paid only $20,000 and his share of the loss is $45,000 he must pay an additional $25,000 to the firm. A's share of the remaining capital is $55,000, and B's share is $35,000. The $90,000 necessary to repay A and B is made up of the remaining $65,000 and the $25,000 owed by C.

PARTICIPATION IN MANAGEMENT

Partners have an equal voice in the management of the business. Regardless of the amount of his capital contribution, each partner has one vote in all business decisions made by the firm. An agreement may be made to vest the powers of management in a single individual. When there is no such agreement, the opinion or vote of the majority of the partners is controlling. Where the partners cannot reach a decision, their only recourse is dissolution of the partnership.

A simple majority is not always sufficient to effect change. According to Section 9 of the Uniform Partnership Act, a unanimous vote in favor of the action is necessary in the following situations:

1. in assigning firm property to a trustee for the benefit of creditors;
2. in confessing a judgment;
3. in disposing of business goodwill;
4. in committing an act that would make impossible the conduct of the partnership business;
5. in admitting a new partner; and
6. in undertaking a new business.

FIDUCIARY RELATIONSHIP OF PARTNERS

A partner is not liable to the partnership for losses caused by honest errors of judgment on his part. However, he is liable to the co-partners for losses resulting from his negligence of lack of reasonable care and skill in conducting firm business. He is also personally liable for exceeding the authority granted or specified in the partnership agreement. Suppose, for example, that in the partnership of Smith, Jones, and Smith, the articles of partnership state definitely that the firm shall not deal in office equipment and Jones commits the firm to the purchase of a carload of filing cabinets upon which the firm suffers a loss. Jones is liable to the co-partners for the loss because he violated the articles of partnership, regardless of any good intentions he may have had.

RIGHT TO INTEREST

Ordinarily, partners are not entitled to draw interest from the firm on their capital contributions because the share of profits they withdraw constitutes earnings on capital. This rule stands even in the absence of an agreement to that effect in the articles of the partnership.

Where a partner makes a payment or an advance to the firm over the amount of capital he agreed to contribute, interest will be paid on these payments. If a partner decides not to withdraw his profits, these funds are not considered advances and will not draw interest. However, in some jurisdictions, these amounts may qualify as loans, and as such, they may be subject to interest payments.

INDEMNIFICATION

The Uniform Partnership Act states that the firm must indemnify every partner with respect to payments made and personal liabilities reasonably incurred by him in the ordinary conduct of business or for the preservation of firm assets. For example, when a partner makes a business trip, he is entitled to indemnification for travel expenses.

COMPENSATION FOR SERVICES

A partner is not entitled to compensation for his services, regardless of the time he spends on partnership business, unless there is an agreement to pay wages. Each partner owes a duty to devote the necessary time and energy to the business. However, the partnership agreement may specify that active partners shall receive a salary in addition to their share of the profits. Also, under the Uniform Partnership Act, when partners devote time to winding up the firm's affairs in the event of dissolution, they are entitled to a reasonable compensation.

Every partner must account to the partnership for any benefit and hold as a trustee for the firm any profits gained by him without the consent of the other partners from any transaction connected with the partnership. He must also account for any use he might have made of partnership property. Representatives of deceased partners engaged in the liquidation also owe these two duties to the firm.

INFORMATION AND INSPECTION OF THE BOOKS

Each partner has a duty to disclose to the other partners and to the legal representatives of any disabled or deceased partners all information relative to partnership business. It is not a breach of duty not to inform a partner of matters that are on the books, since he has access to this material. However, any notice of other partnership rights acquired by an individual that is not on the books must be communicated to all members of the firm.

Each partner has the right to inspect the books at any time, providing he is not doing so to secure an advantage over other firm members or for fraudulent purposes. He may not remove them without the permission of the other partners, however, since each partner has the right to have in his possession all information concerning the conduct of the business. He may make copies or take notes from them but the books must remain at the firm's principal place of business.

RIGHT TO AN ACCOUNTING

When partners cannot voluntarily settle firm disputes and where the disputes are so serious as to make the continuance of the partnership impossible, the partners may apply to a court of equity for an accounting in order to determine each member's share of the firm's assets. Likewise, a partner is entitled to an accounting upon dissolution. A partner may ask for a formal accounting in the following situations:

1. if an agreement is reached for an accounting at a definite date;
2. if it is learned that one partner has withheld profits arising from a secret transaction;
3. if an attachment execution has been levied against the interest of one of the partners;
4. if one of the partners has not had proper access to the books;
5. if the partnership is approaching insolvency and all parties are not available; and
6. whenever the court deems that an accounting is just and reasonable under the circumstances.

LEGAL PRINCIPLES

All partners receive an equal share in the profits and losses of the firm unless a previous arrangement is made to the contrary.

On dissolution, each partner will receive his capital contribution, but he is not allowed interest unless he has made a contribution over and above his initial investment. The entire partnership must indemnify every partner for personal expenses in connection with firm business.

All the partners in a partnership have an equal voice in partnership affairs. Usually a simple majority can make decisions, but in some cases a unanimous vote is required.

Unless an agreement is made in advance, no partner is entitled to a salary.

All benefits from a partnership must be accounted to the firm.

All information concerning partnership business must be given to the partners. A partner may inspect the firm's books at any time.

A partner may ask for an accounting when the business is in jeopardy.

CASE FOR REVIEW

HURTER v. LARRABEE ET AL.

224 Mass 218 (1916)

This is bill for accounting by two retiring members of a partnership against three remaining general partners, who hereafter will be referred to as the defendants. The firm carried on a wholesale dry goods business of considerable magnitude. The articles of co-partnership provided amongst other matters, that upon the termination of the partnership two or more of the general partners having a majority interest therein might continue the business under the firm name, and in that event should

> pay to the retiring general partners for their interest in said business the amount standing to the credit of each of the retiring general partners on the books of the firm January 1, 1913, after the stock taking of that date and after the interest and profit has been placed to each general partner's credit.

The three defendants elected to continue the business, and the two plaintiffs, to retire. Disagreement as to how much should be paid to the plaintiffs caused this suit. . . .

The plaintiff's first exception is to the refusal of the master to make a finding upon the negligence of the defendant Brady in supervising the accounting department of the firm. The duties of the several partners were not defined by the partnership articles, but by common consent Brady, in addition to having charge of a special department, exercised a general oversight over the conduct of the business and over the office and bookkeeping and accounting department. But the bookkeeping was in charge of one Ferguson until just before the dissolution of the partnership, when he left. Ferguson was generally trusted by all the parties. But the bookkeeping and accounting was done on a rather complicated system and was found to be full of mistakes and errors, resulting apparently from lack of care and diligence. All the partners, including Brady, believed the business to have been prosperous and were deceived as to its real condition until it was revealed by the report of an expert accountant. The master refused to make a finding as to the negligence of Brady because, although there was some evidence tending to show that he ought to have known that the books were badly kept and exhibited defects and errors, there were other facts which made that question irrelevant. The relation of Larrabee and Chandler, the other defendants, is the same as that of the plaintiffs to the books. They ought not to be made to pay to the plaintiffs for Brady's negligence. Moreover, the main duty of the master was to ascertain the actual facts as to the assets and liabilities of the firm at its dissolution, so far as these could be determined with reasonable certainty from the books of the firm. Negligence of one partner had no bearing on this issue. The basis of the accounting fixed by the agreement is the share of each partner, after interest and profit and each if found, as shown by the books. There is no general principle of partnership which renders one partner liable to his co-partners for his honest mistakes. So far as losses result to a firm from errors of judgment of one partner not amounting to fraud, bad faith, or reckless disregard of his obligations, they must be borne by the partnership. Each partner owes to the firm the duty of faithful service according to the best of his ability. But, in the absence of special agreement, no partner guarantees his own capacity. Where one assumes the duty of keeping the books, reasonable presumptions are made against him when he disputes their accuracy. But when there is good faith throughout, he is not estopped to show the truth about the books even though he may have been inefficient. . . .

The basis of settlement established by the partnership articles in the present case was what was shown by the books of the partnership. But this means a set of books which were a reasonably correct representation of the firm's affairs. It did not mean books so full of palpable mistakes and grave errors as to be manifestly untrustworthy and incapable of showing justly the affairs of the firm. Under the circumstances disclosed, the only course open was to correct the errors so far as possible, and from all credible evidence ascertain the true condition of the firm. This was the course pursued by the master.

CASE PROBLEMS

1. Louis Mitchell and Charles Brewer were co-partners doing business under the name of Mitchell and Company. Brewer brought an action for an accounting, contending that Mitchell was in possession and control of the books and refused to allow him to inspect them; and that Mitchell was fraudulently disposing of those books. He also claimed that Mitchell excluded him from all control of the business, and had carried away the books from the place of business, refusing to disclose their whereabouts. Decide.

2. In 1968, Lentz and Pearson formed a partnership. Their agreement provided that they should be paid salaries in such amounts as should be "determined by both from time to time, as the profits warrant." Later a dispute arose, and Pearson brought suit to recover the salary he claimed was due him, offering oral evidence that he was to receive $100 a week. Decide.

3. Holmes and Darling were partners in operating a sales agency for the White Rock Mineral Springs Company. Holmes demanded an accounting by Darling of profits realized by him in selling wine and whiskey. It was alleged that Darling and his son, an employee of the firm, took orders for wine and whiskey at the office and on the road while selling White Rock water, and that the wine and whiskey business was contemplated under the partnership articles as the selling of goods that might conveniently be sold along with the mineral water. Decide.

4. Plaintiff and Fred Doll and Luther Harre organized a partnership for producing a crop of potatoes. Harre was to receive half the profits, and the remaining half was to be divided equally between plaintiff and Doll. The crop brought a profit of $36,000, half of which Harre paid to Doll, who paid plaintiff $7345.00. Plaintiff had previously advanced $1000 to Doll for the purchase of farm machinery, one-half of which he agreed to pay. When plaintiff brought suit for his full share of the profits, Doll filed a counterclaim alleging that he was entitled to $1155 compensation for his services as general manager of the business. Doll also asked some contribution from plaintiff for the money that he had paid in settlement of an automobile accident that occurred while he was acting within the scope of the partnership business. Decide.

5. Metcalf seeks an accounting against Bradshaw, showing that they were partners in the practice of law under an agreement that each should give his time and talents to prosecuting the interests of the firm. Within the term of the partnership, defendant received certain fees for acting as executor of several estates. Plaintiff claimed that these fees were partnership income. Decide.

6. Mitchell and Reed were co-partners operating the Hoffman House in New York. The partnership by its terms expired on May 1, 1961, the lease on the property also terminating at this time. The firm expended large sums of money in improving the property, thus greatly increasing the rental value. In 1959 Reed obtained a new lease on the Hoffman House in his own name for a term commencing when the old lease expired. In June of 1961 Mitchell, who had learned of the new lease only after the expiration of the partnership, brought an action to have the lease declared partnership property, claiming that the lease should be deemed for the firm's benefit and that defendant should be held as trustee for the firm. Decide.

7. Plaintiff and defendant entered into a partnership agreement under which, with minor exceptions, defendant was to exercise unlimited control of the business. Plaintiff, becoming dissatisfied with some of defendant's actions, brought suit seeking dissolution of the firm, contending, among other arguments, that he had been denied his proper share in the management of the business. Decide.

8. Jackson and Caldwell were partners in the public accounting firm of Missina, Jackson, Caldwell & Company. Beginning in January, 1961, meetings were held in an effort to solve management problems, but to no avail. Jackson gradually withdrew from active partnership participation. Caldwell gave formal notice of termination of the partnership as of March 31, 1962, and the parties agreed that clients and accounts were to be allowed to follow the accountants of their choice without solicitation by either party. Immediately upon termination of the partnership, Caldwell and Jackson agreed upon a division of the assets, and both proceeded to establish new firms to service the old accounts. Jackson sought an accounting for purposes of obtaining his share of the good will of the partnership. Good will had not been mentioned in either the partnership or dissolution agreements. Decide.

TERMINATION OF A PARTNERSHIP   29

The usual procedure in terminating a partnership is to sell assets, pay liabilities, and distribute the remaining cash to the partners. In some situations, the firm is sold as a unit; in others, it is sold in separate parts. In either case, a partnership that is terminating its business is said to be in liquidation, or winding up. This process may take a short time, or it may take several months or even years.

It is necessary to distinguish between dissolution, winding-up, and termination. *Dissolution is a change in the relationship of the partners caused by any partner ceasing to be associated in the carrying on of the business.* It may lead to termination, but it may also result in little or no interruption of the firm business. The firm may continue in operation by the enjoining of a new partner or by the continuance in business of the other partner or partners; a purchaser may carry on the business; or the firm may be incorporated. If termination is desired or necessitated, the intermediate stage, or winding up, is begun. This *entails the completion of business, the sale of assets, the payment of liabilities, and the distribution of cash and the settlement of all partnership affairs.* During this process, the partnership still exists. *When the winding-up period is completed, the partnership is said to be terminated.* Until that time, the firm continues to exist.

CAUSES FOR DISSOLUTION

The causes for dissolution of the firm are many and varied. Dissolution may be voluntary or involuntary. The firm may be dissolved in violation of the agreement, without any violation, or by the operation of law.

VOLUNTARY DISSOLUTION

The following will dissolve the firm but will not breach the partnership agreement: (1) expiration of an agreed time period set forth in the agreement; (2) accomplishment of the purpose for which the business was organized; (3) acts of a partner,where neither term nor purpose is specified in the agreement; and (4) expulsion of a partner from the firm in accordance with the terms of the agreement.

A partnership can also be dissolved by an act of a partner that violates the partnership agreement. There exists between the partners a principal and agent relationship. Each partner has the power to withdraw from this relationship, but withdrawal may result in breach of contract if a definite time has not elapsed or if a specified purpose is not accomplished. A partner then becomes liable for damages sustained by the other partners because of his withdrawal.

OPERATION OF LAW

A partnership is dissolved by the operation of law (1) by the death of a partner, (2) by the bankruptcy of a partner or the partnership, or (3) by an event that makes the subsequent conduct of the partnership business illegal.

Since a partnership is a voluntary association of individuals, the death of one or more of the partners dissolves the personal relationship between them. The winding-up and termination may be postponed, and the remaining partners may carry on business. This means, however, that the old firm has been dissolved and replaced by a new one. Provisions for continuation of a partnership in the event of the death of a partner may be found in the partnership agreement. The reason for this is to avoid an untimely liquidation of assets of a successful business arrangement. It is customary to provide that the surviving partner or partners shall purchase the share of the deceased partner from the proceeds of life insurance taken out by the partnership on the lives of the individual partners. An alternative provision might allow the personal representative of the deceased partner to operate as a member of the firm for a limited time. At the same time, the surviving partners are given an opportunity to purchase the share of the deceased partner.

The bankruptcy of a partner will dissolve the partnership because the bankrupt partner no longer has control over his assets. Likewise, bankruptcy of the partnership results in dissolution because the partners no longer have control over firm assets.

Conditions may arise that make continuation of the business impossible and dissolution necessary. If a law is passed that makes the partnership's operation illegal, the firm must dissolve. When a partnership is composed of residents of different countries, war between the two countries will make the partnership illegal, and it must dissolve.

COURT DECREE

A partnership may encounter circumstances that make its operation both impossible and unprofitable to continue for the specified term. By application by one of the partners to a court of equity, the partnership may be dissolved for any of the following reasons: (1) a partner has been declared legally insane; (2) a partner has become totally incapacitated to perform the duties required of him under the agreement; (3) a partner is guilty of misconduct and neglect of duty to such an extent that the partnership operations are impeded; and (4) a partner has willfully persisted in breaching the partnership agreement or has committed a fraudulent act. These circumstances in themselves will not dissolve a partnership. They will, however, provide the basis for a court of equity to decree a dissolution.

LIABILITIES AFTER DISSOLUTION

Although dissolution means the termination of the personal relationship between the partners, it does not terminate a firm's existence for the purpose of concluding its affairs. The obligation of continuing the partnership during this winding-up period normally falls on the surviving partners. They must perform this task as trustees for the interests of all partners.

The surviving partners cannot elect to operate the firm and force the estate of the deceased partner to leave his capital contribution in the partnership. The estate can be held liable only for debts incurred before his death. The Uniform Partnership Act requires that the other partners assume their proportionate shares of a contract entered into after dissolution.

CONTINUANCE OF BUSINESS AFTER DISSOLUTION

If a partnership is dissolved by the wrongful withdrawal of a member, the remaining members may continue the partnership in operation after settling with the withdrawn partner. Under the Uniform Partnership Act, Sec. 38, if no accounting is made at the time of the partner's withdrawal, the remaining partners can continue the business for the agreed period and for that purpose may possess partnership property, securing the payment of the withdrawing partner's interest by posting a bond approved by the court, covering not only the partner's interest at the time of withdrawal but also indemnifying him against future liabilities of the firm.

NOTICE OF DISSOLUTION

Under the Uniform Partnership Act, notice of dissolution is required even though the dissolution is caused by the operation of law, except when a partner becomes bankrupt, dies, or when the operation becomes illegal. A retiring partner who fails to give notice of dissolution to those who have extended credit to the old firm, if the creditors have not acquired knowledge of the dissolution in some other manner, will be liable on contracts of the new firm.

Notice must be given to old customers because they are justified in assuming that the firm will continue in business. Notice of the dissolution to potential customers should be made by publication of this fact in a newspaper of general circulation in the area of the firm's business.

If a partner has not been actively engaged in the firm's operations and creditors are not aware that he is a partner, he is under no duty to give notice of his withdrawal. However, where he has been an active member, his liability will continue until notice has been given in proper form.

LIABILITY OF INCOMING PARTNERS

At common law, when a new partner was admitted to membership in an existing firm, he did not thereby become liable on old obligations of the partnership. Under the Uniform Partnership Act, Sec. 17, a person admitted as a partner is liable for all obligations created before his admission, to the extent of his investment. His personal estate, however, is not liable for such obligations. The incoming partner may, of course, assume liability by a novation or by contracting with his co-partners or with a retiring partner that old creditors will be paid.

CREDITORS OF THE OLD FIRM AND THE NEW FIRM

Under the Uniform Partnership Act, creditors of the dissolved partnership continue as creditors of a new partnership formed if the partnership affairs are not liquidated. They also remain creditors if the partnership is assigned to a single partner or to one or more third parties. A similar situation occurs when all partners assign their rights in partnership property to one or more persons who promise to pay firm debts and to continue the operation of the business.

DISTRIBUTION OF FIRM ASSETS

The assets of a partnership consist of all its tangible property, its goodwill, claims against third parties, and claims against the partners individually for contributions necessary for the payment of firm obligations. If the firm is solvent and business is terminated, firm creditors are the first to be paid. Next, each partner who has made advances to the firm must be repaid. Each partner is then entitled to a return of his capital. Any remaining profits are distributed in a predetermined ratio; if there are losses, they are settled by contributions.

MARSHALLING ASSETS

Priority regarding claims in the liquidation of firm and individual assets may be given to one class of creditors over another where both the firm and the partners are insolvent. Firm creditors have priority regarding firm assets, whereas personal creditors have priority regarding individual assets. The process of ranking assets to meet these priorities is called marshalling assets.

Firm creditors are not entitled to payment out of individual assets until individual creditors have been paid unless (1) there are no firm assets and no living solvent partners or (2) a partner has fraudulently converted firm assets into personal assets.

LEGAL PRINCIPLES

Any change in the membership of a firm causes its dissolution.

A partnership may be dissolved voluntarily, by the operation of law, or by court decree.

Winding-up is the settlement of partnership affairs.

Termination occurs when the firm ceases to exist after the winding-up period is completed.

The obligation of continuing the partnership during the winding-up period normally falls on the surviving partners.

Unless notice of dissolution is given, a withdrawing partner may become liable for additional obligations of the firm.

Marshalling assets gives firm creditors priority over firm assets and individual creditors priority over individual assets where both the firm and the members are insolvent.

CASE FOR REVIEW

LYON ET AL. v. JOHNSON ET AL.

28 Conn. 1 (1859)

The defendants, Johnson and Signor, previous to the ninth day of March. . . had been in partnership in the town of Danbury under the name of R. Johnson & Company, and as such partners had in the fall . . . purchased coal of the plantiffs, who also did business in Danbury as partners under the name of Lyon & Burr. On the 9th day of March . . . the firm was dissolved, and the business was thereafter carried on by Signor alone. Notice of the dissolution was published for three successive weeks in the Danbury Times, a weekly newspaper published in Danbury; but no other notice was given to the plaintiffs. In the fall . . . Signor bought a quantity of coal of the plantiffs, which they sold and delivered upon the credit of the firm of R. Johnson & Company, and in the belief that he bought it for that firm. The advertisement of the dissolution of the partnership of the defendants was inserted in the newspaper next after an advertisement of the plantiffs; but the plaintiffs did not take the paper, and had not seen the notice of the dissolution, and had no knowledge that the partnership was dissolved. The sale of coal by the plantiffs to the defendants . . . was the only previous dealing of the firm of Lyon & Burr with the defendants; but for some years before the defendants had bought coal of the firm of Lyon & Bates, a firm of which the plaintiff Lyon was a member, and which was dissolved in the summer . . . Bates retiring from the business, and Lyon forming a new partnership with Burr, who had been a clerk of Lyon & Bates, and the new firm taking and continuing the business of the former firm. . . .

. . . Once existing, and publicly known. . . the continuance of the connection will be presumed by the public till the contrary appears. If a dissolution takes place by operation of law, as by death or bankruptcy, no notice is required. The operations of law have a notoriety which all are bound to regard. But a dissolution by limitation, or the voluntary and mutual assent of the partners, is a matter of private arrangement, which cannot be presumed to be known to others unless they are informed of it. Until such information is given, actually or constructively, therefore, the continuance of the connection, and of the powers and liabilities of each partner, may well be presumed by every one who has occasion to deal with either on account of the firm. It follows upon the principles of justice and policy, and in conformity with the perfectly well settled rule of law, that upon such a dissolution of the partnership a retiring partner, who wishes to do justice to others and terminate his own responsibility, is under the obligation to give information of the fact to all who have dealt or are dealing with the firm, and to the public at large, with whom new attempts to deal may be made. It is equally clear that the notice so given by a retiring partner should be coextensive with the obligation assumed and as particular and specific as can be reasonably required of him under the circumstances of the case. He knows or may know who the persons are who have dealt with the firm, and he can, without unreasonable effort, give each of them actual notice, and therefore the law requires that he should do so. He cannot, without more effort or expense than can reasonably be demanded of him, give actual notice to every other member of the public, and therefore the law does not require it; but it does require him to discharge his obligation if he would terminate his liability, and to give some, and reasonable, notice to the public at large. Ordinarily a publication in one of the newspapers published in the place or county where the partnership business was conducted, as it is the customary mode of giving such information, will, as to all who have not had previous dealings with the firm, be deemed sufficient. That is the least that can be required of him in an ordinary case in respect to the public, and even that may not in all cases be sufficient, and whether it be or not will depend on the circumstances of the particular case. But in relaxing the rule as applicable to those who have not dealt with the firm, and considering a general notice, operating as a constructive notice, to be sufficient as to them, because of the difficulty of giving actual notice to everybody, the courts have not intended to relax, and have not relaxed, the rule in respect to those who have dealt with the firm. As to them there is no reason for such relaxation, and a publication is never sufficient, unless, indeed, it can be shown that the publication was seen by them, and therefore that they in fact had actual knowledge.

In this case the dissolution of the firm of R. Johnson & Company was voluntary, and not by operation of law. The plaintiffs had previously dealt with the firm, and upon the facts found they may well be considered as regular dealers. No actual notice of the dissolution was given them, and it is found that they had no actual knowledge of it.

The publication, unless it came to their knowledge, was not as to them sufficient. The character of their previous dealing and the circumstances attending the publication of the notice, including the contiguity of the advertisements, were proper matters of evidence to be taken into consideration by the court in the question whether the plaintiffs actually knew of the dissolution or not. Doubtless the court considered them. But having found that no actual notice was given to the plaintiffs, and they did not see the publication, and had no actual knowledge of the dissolution, and that there had been previous dealing between the parties, the court correctly rendered judgment for the plaintiffs.

CASE PROBLEMS

1. Davis and Russell formed a partnership in 1954 under the name of Russell & Davis Lumber Company. On September 20, 1955, the partnership was dissolved by written agreement. A notice of dissolution was published in a newspaper of general circulation in the county where the business was conducted but no actual notice of dissolution was given to the firms which had extended credit to the partnership at the time of dissolution. After the dissolution, several firms which had previously extended credit to the partnership continued to extend credit to the continued business. Their claims were not paid. Suit was brought against Russell and Davis. Decide.

2. Bland and Will signed a formal partnership agreement to run for a stipulated period. Shortly thereafter Bland became dissatisfied and published notice that the partnership had been dissolved. Later Will purchased goods from plaintiff, giving a note signed with the partnership name. When plaintiff brought an action

to collect on the note, Bland denied liability on the argument that the partnership had been dissolved. Plaintiff argued that the partnership could not be dissolved until the expiration of the period agreed upon. Decide.

3. Plaintiff sued upon a promissory note made by Brady & Company of Detroit in which Holland was alleged to be a partner. Defendant showed that he was not a member of the firm when the note was given and that a notice of dissolution was published in the Detroit papers. He claimed that a copy of this notice was mailed to plaintiff in Chicago, but plaintiff denied ever receiving it. Decide.

4. When plaintiff was adjudged temporarily insane, defendant, his partner, carried on their business without change or notice of change until after plaintiff's recovery, then excluded him from the firm's operation. Plaintiff sued for dissolution and an accounting of profits, including those earned during the period of his temporary insanity. Defendant contended that the partnership had been dissolved when plaintiff was declared insane. Decide.

5. Barclay sought a judicial dissolution because his partner, Barrie, had been totally incapacitated for three years and eleven months as a result of a stroke. At the end of that period, when the trial was taking place, Barrie was recovering, with the prospect of being able to resume his work within another nine months, which would be three months from the end of the five-year partnership term. Decide.

6. Coal Company was a partnership owned by two brothers. On the death of one, the survivor began, but did not complete, the liquidation of the business. Lee brought suit to compel the surviving partner to make an accounting. In addition to delaying the liquidation, the liquidating partner used some of the partnership funds, and took a partnership truck, for his own use, never accounting for them. He claimed that he was entitled to compensation for his services under the Uniform Partnership Act.

7. Plaintiff and defendant were law partners. After the firm was dissolved, defendant attended to its unfinished business, including the collecting of outstanding fees and the trial of several cases then in progress. When all such business had been cleared up, plaintiff sued for a share of the profits thereby realized. Defendant argued that, as he had performed all services necessary, he should be entitled to the entire amount. Decide.

8. On February 15, 1965, Maude Crocker and Grace Buchner, as a partnership engaged in retail merchandising, made a contract with plaintiff to act for one year as its resident New York buyer to render services in buying, merchandising, and supplying market information about styles, available merchandise, and prices, and in sending out bulletins, etc. Mrs. Crocker died in August, 1965. Plaintiff sued Mrs. Buchner as surviving partner for one year's compensation under the contract. Decide.

PART V
CORPORATIONS

DEFINITION AND FORMATION

The corporation is the most common form of business organization. Its popularity is partially explained by the limited liability of corporate stock-holders. A shareholder is liable only to the extent of his original investment—the amount he spent to purchase his shares of stock. Corporate enterprises also attract investors because the corporate entity is better able to raise the large sums of money necessary to carry on an extensive business enterprise. Another advantage is the corporation's relative permanence as a legal entity, which enables the business to continue when there is a transfer of ownership of shares or upon the death of shareholders.

A corporation is a legal entity created by the consent of the government and endowed with certain powers to enable it to carry on as a legitimate business enterprise. As an artificial, or legal being, it is seperate from the people who create, own, and manage it. Thus, it may own, control, and convey property, make contracts, sue or bring suit, and generally carry on business transactions in its own name. Any debts or other obligations incurred are owed by the corporate entity and not by the owners of the corporation. Finally, it continues to exist, despite changes in its membership, as long as it continues operation as a legitimate business.

TYPES OF CORPORATIONS

Basically, there are three types of corporations: corporations for profit; corporation not for profit; and governmental corporations. *Corporations for profit* usually issue stock and are owned by the shareholders who invest in hopes of receiving dividends. The objective of *nonprofit corporations* is generally religious, charitable, social, or educational. *Governmental, or public, corporations* are organized for governmental purposes—many cities and towns are corporate entities. This chapter will concern itself primarily with corporations organized on a profit basis.

THE ENTITY CONCEPT

The corporation is recognized as an entity for the purpose of carrying on corporate activities and, as such, is considered a person under the due process clause of the federal Constitution. As an entity, it is a legal resident for purposes of taxation and court jurisdiction of the states where it does business. It is a citizen of its state of incorporation as well as of the state of its principal place of business for the purpose of suit. It becomes a citizen of other states when it is admitted to do business there and at that time is entitled to the protection of the "privileges and immunities" clause of the federal Constitution. As an entity, it may be punished for any violation of criminal laws and any torts committed by its agents within the scope of corporate business.

FORMATION OF A CORPORATION

Each state has general incorporation statutes that define the purposes for which corporations may be formed and detail the steps to be taken for incorporation. In applying for corporate recognition by the state, it is usually necessary to list: (1) the name and address of each incorporator; (2) the purpose or purposes for which the corporation is being organized; (3) the name of the corporation; (4) the kind of stock it intends to issue, the number of shares, and other relevant information; and (5) the period of corporate existence, which may be perpetual. The application, signed by all the incorporators and acknowledged by a notary public, is forwarded to a state official, usually the secretary of state. The secretary issues a charter that sets forth the powers, rights, and privileges of the corporation as prescribed by the general incorporation act. This charter is filed in the proper recording office in the county in which the principal office of the corporation will be located. When the charter has been received and filed, a meeting of incorporators is held at which the board of directors and the officers of the company are elected and the bylaws drafted. Corporate life begins when the charter has been recorded with the county clerk, when the minimum amount of capital has been subscribed and paid, and when public notice has been given of the corporation's intention to commence its business operation.

PROMOTERS' CONTRACTS

A promoter is one who does the preliminary work necessary to bring a corporation into existence. He initiates the business, negotiates all contracts and leases, purchases supplies, prepares advertising, and performs any other task necessary for the proposed venture to begin operations. In this function, however, the promoter cannot act as an agent of the corporation since the corporation is not legally in existence and he cannot be an agent for a nonexistent principal. The corporation, once it comes into existence, cannot be held liable on contracts made in its behalf by the promoter, since it was not in existence at the time the contracts were made.

Once corporate life begins, the corporation is free to adopt or reject the contracts made by the promoter. In order for the corporation to adopt a promoter's contract, the contract must be a valid, subsisting contract that is within the legal authority of the corporation. The corporation must adopt the contract in its entirety, either expressly or impliedly. However, unless a provision in the contract specifically exempts them from personal liability, or unless they are released by the third party's consent to a novation, promoters themselves continue to be liable on pre-incorporation contracts and are not relieved from liability by the corporation's adoption of a contract.

DE JURE AND DE FACTO CORPORATIONS

Incorporation statutes as set forth by the various states include both mandatory and directory provisions. If the incorporators comply with the mandatory requirements of the statute and fulfill in a substantial manner all the statutory prerequisites for the organization of the corporation, they create a de jure corporation e.g., valid by law. The existence of this type of corporation cannot be successfully questioned even in a direct proceeding brought by the state for that purpose. It is, as the name implies, a corporation in law, entitled to exist and operate for the period specified in its charter. Directory provisions deal with matters of form and procedure; however, if the incorporators choose to proceed in a different manner and can do so while still complying with the mandatory provisions of the statute, there is no adverse effect on the corporation's existence.

Where the incorporators fail in some material respect to comply with the mandatory provisions of the incorporation statutes, there can be no corporation in the true legal sense. However, in certain circumstances, the courts will recognize the organization as a de facto corporation—a corporation in fact although not in law. The courts hold that if (1) there is a valid statute under which the corporation could be organized, (2) the parties have made an honest effort to organize under the statute, and (3) they have done business as a corporation, their corporate existence cannot be collaterally attacked by a third party. In the event of a suit by or against the corporation, neither the corporation nor the other party can defend on the grounds of defects in the corporation's organizations.

The state can attack the legitimacy of a de facto corporation by bringing a quo warranto proceeding. If the incorporators do not comply with the conditions set by the state, the state may enjoin the organization from the exercise of corporate powers. Unless the state takes such action to dissolve the corporation or to force compliance with the law, no third party can avoid his liabilities with the corporation on the ground that it was improperly formed.

SERIOUSLY DEFECTIVE CORPORATIONS

Where no corporation is formed either in law or in fact, although those who organize the business hold that it is a corporation, the organizers are usually treated as partners with unlimited liability for the firm's contracts. Statutes in some states impose unlimited liability upon officers of seriously defective corporations for failure to comply with corporate requirements pertaining to organization.

CORPORATE POWERS

The corporation is a creation of the state and has only those powers conferred upon it by the state of incorporation. It is authorized to do whatever is necessary to accomplish its legitimate business, or any purposes otherwise permitted by law. The state may grant any power that does not violate the federal Constitution or its own constitution and statutes of incorporation. In addition, the implied and incidental powers of the corporation allow it to do those things which are incident to, and reasonably necessary to, the carrying out of powers expressly granted. Powers possessed by a corporation are divided into three categories: (1) express powers, (2) incidental powers, and (3) implied powers.

EXPRESS POWERS

In applying for a charter, the incorporators usually describe the powers they wish to exercise in very general terms. The word "power" connotes a legal capacity, and only powers specifically enumerated are deemed to exist. In a power is not mentioned, it cannot be exercised unless it is implied by, or incidental to, the powers granted. The state enabling statute and the corporate charter are thus a measure of the power of a corporation.

The charter is a contract between the state and the corporation. It cannot be cancelled by the state unless the corporation violates its terms or requests that it be terminated. The charter is also a contract between the corporation and its shareholders. It describes the nature of the corporation, the kind of business activity the corporation will pursue, and the form of ownership the shareholders have. It serves also to inform third persons of the extent of the corporation's legally authorized power.

INCIDENTAL POWERS

A corporation ordinarily possesses those powers that are deemed essential to its operation. Those powers are, in effect, inherent in each corporation as a legal entity. Corporations generally have unwritten, incidental powers in the following areas:

1. *Corporate name.* A corporation may adopt any name that is not the same as that of an existing firm or similar enough to that of an existing firm to confuse the public.
2. *Corporate seal.* A company seal may be used to formalize corporate documents.
3. *Corporate existence.* The corporation continues in existence even when some of its members die or become incapacitated.
4. *Property rights.* Corporate charters usually provide authority for the acquisition, holding, and transfer of any property necessary for the corporate business.
5. *Corporate regulations.* Corporations may make their own bylaws or other regulations necessary for the internal management of their affairs. These bylaws are binding on the shareholders unless they conflict with the charter, with state statutes, or with public policy.
6. *Legal action.* The corporation may initiate and defend in legal actions.

7. *Financial ability.* A corporation has the power to finance its authorized business. It may issue or execute negotiable instruments, bonds, or other secured transactions. Generally, a corporation may also mortgage, lease or transfer its property to raise funds or pay obligations that have been incurred in accomplishing corporate objectives.

IMPLIED POWERS

In addition to the powers expressly granted in the corporate charter and the recognized incidental powers, a corporation also possesses those powers necessary for carrying out its express powers. In general, therefore, the implied powers are those powers that will aid in the achievement of the purposes for which the corporation was organized. Frequently a court decision is necessary to determine the validity of implied powers.

LEGAL PRINCIPLES

There are three types of corporations: corporations for profit, corporations not for profit, and governmental corporations.

The corporation is a citizen, a resident, and a person, under different circumstances.

Each state defines the purposes for which corporations may be formed and details the procedure for incorporation within its territory.

Corporate existence begins when the charter is recorded, capital is subscribed, and notice given.

Promoters are liable on contracts made in behalf of a corporation unless the contracts specifically exempt them from liability or unless they are relieved of liability by third parties.

A de jure corporation has successfully fulfilled the requirements of the corporate statutes of the state; the legality of its existence cannot be questioned.

A de facto corporation has the same rights and privileges as a de jure corporation in dealing with third parties, other than the state of incorporation. It will exist so long as its right to exist is not challenged by the state of incorporation in a direct action.

Where a corporation is defectively organized, the organizers may have unlimited personal liability.

The corporation holds those powers that are conferred upon it by the state. These powers must be in accord with the federal Constitution and the statutes of the state of incorporation.

Corporate powers are divided into three categories: express powers, incidental powers, and implied powers.

Express powers are those found in the corporate charter, the corporate articles, and the state enabling statute.

Incidental powers are those which are essential to the operation of any corporation and are deemed to inhere in a corporation as a legal entity. The power to have a corporate name and a corporate seal, to have continuous existence, to buy, sell, and hold property, to make bylaws and regulations, and to take legal action are recognized as incidental powers.

Implied powers are those which are necessary to carry out the express powers. They include the power to acquire stock in other corporations, the power to acquire the corporation's own stock, the power to own stock in subsidiary corporations, and the power to sell corporate assets.

Court decisions are frequently necessary to determine whether an implied power may be legally exercised.

CASE FOR REVIEW

PEOPLE v. FORD

294 Ill. 319, 128 N. E. 479 (1920)

Information in the nature of quo warranto by the People against E. E. Ford and others to determine the legality of the organization of a corporation. . . .

The . . . General Corporation Act. . . . Section 4 provides that:

Whenever three or more adult persons, citizens of the United States of America, at least one of whom shall be a citizen of this state, shall desire to form a corporation under this act, they shall sign, seal and acknowledge before some officer, competent to take acknowledgment of deeds, a statement of incorporation setting forth the following: [Here follow thirteen paragraphs stating the facts to be contained in the statement.]

The section closes with the sentence that:

Such statement shall be filed in duplicate in the office of the secretary of state on forms prescribed and furnished by the secretary of state.

Section 5 provides that

Upon the filing of such statement, the secretary of state shall examine the same, and, if it is in conformity with the provisions of this act, he shall indorse thereon the word 'Filed' followed by the month, day and year of such filing. Upon such filing the corporation shall be deemed fully organized and may proceed to business.

On September 5 . . . a certificate of incorporation of the Washer Maid Company was filed in duplicate in the office of the secretary of state. The Attorney General afterward . . . filed in the circuit court of Cook county an information in the nature of quo warranto against E. E. Ford, A. J. Fisher, and C. R. Gilbert, charging them with having unlawfully usurped, intruded into, held, and executed the office of directors of a pretended corporation known as the Washer Maid Company, under color of a void and illegal certificate of incorporation, and calling upon them to show by what warrant they exercised such privileges.

The question presented was whether the requirement that the incorporators shall seal the statement is mandatory or directory. It was argued on behalf of the people that the requirement of the seal is a condition precedent to the legal existence of a corporation. A somewhat similar question arose early in the history of the state in the case of *Cross v. Pinckneyville Mill Co.*. . . . The act . . . to authorize the formation of corporations for manufacturing, agricultural, mining or mechanical purposes, provided that any three or more persons desiring to form a company for such purpose should make, sign, and acknowledge, and file "in the office of the clerk in the country in which the business of the company should be carried on and a duplicate thereof in the office of the secretary of state, a certificate in writing," in which should be stated the name of the company and other facts mentioned in the statute. It was further provided that when the certificate should have been filed as aforesaid the persons who should have signed and acknowledged, and their successors, should be a body politic and corporate. In the case mentioned the duplicate certificate of organization had not been filed in the office of the secretary of state, but the court held that fact unimportant to defeat the organization or rights growing out of it; that there is a well settled distinction between mandatory and directory provisions, and that carrying out of the true intention of the Legislature and effectuating the object of the law would not be promoted by strict technical constructions, converting every direction and detail of power into a mandatory prerequisite of corporate existence.

More recently a question arose as to the effect of the failure to mail notices of the meeting of subscribers of the capital stock to elect officers, as required by section 3 of the Corporation Act. . . . We said:

> The statue prescribes a certain course to be pursued in organizing a corporation in this state. It does not necessarily follow, however, that any departure from that course will prevent a corporation from becoming one de jure. Whether or not such departure will have that effect depends upon the nature of the provision which is violated. If it is a mandatory provision, a failure to substantially comply with its terms will prevent the corporation from becoming one de jure; but if the provision is merely directory, then a departure therefrom will not have that consequence.

It was held that it was immaterial whether or not notice had been given in the manner directed by the statute; the persons entitled to notice having waived it and actually attended the meeting, so that the purpose of the statute in requiring the notices to be given was accomplished. . . .

The requirement of a seal in the execution of documents by individuals has become a mere formality. It means nothing. Private seals no longer exist as a means of execution of specialties, for even an individual scrawl is not required. In most deeds the word "seal" is printed on the blank form which is used, and the grantor does not know whether he has used a seal or not. It depends upon whether the word was printed on the paper or not. The solemnity of the sealed instrument is purely Pickwickian and no longer represents an idea. While courts of law in this state cannot disregard the legal quality of the sealed instrument, courts of equity frequently relieve parties from the difficulties arising from the application of the rigid rules of the common law to such instruments.

We may look to the intention of the statute in determining the effect of an omission to add the seal. The purpose is to make a public record of the corporation, the definition of its powers, the amount of its stock, the names of its stockholders, its location, and other facts in connection with it, which are of interest to the public to know, and of the state in its supervision over corporations to be acquainted with. The addition of a seal is of no importance for these purposes. It is not of the essence of the thing to be done, and no prejudice can result from its omission. The essential act of making the statement, though not in the precise manner indicated, accomplishes the substantial purpose of the statute, and that is sufficient. It would not be carrying out the intention of the Legislature to hold that the addition of a scrawl by the signers of the statement is mandatory and its omission invalidates the incorporation.

CASE PROBLEMS

1. Button brought an action to obtain possession of property belonging to Machine Corporation. Hoffman contested Button's title to the property. Button testified, "I bought all the stock. I own all the stock now. I became the absolute owner of the mill. It belonged at that time to the company and I am the company." Decide.
2. Bridge Corporation owned a toll bridge which was part of the highway system of Ohio. The bridge was not kept in proper repair to carry traffic. The state legislature enacted a statute providing that the stockholders of Bridge Corporation would have no further right to vote for the directors of the corporation and in the future the directors would be appointed by the governor of the state. A stockholder sought to enjoin the enforcement of such statute on the ground that it took property without due process of law under the 14th Amendment to the U. S. Constitution. Decide.
3. Lynch and Beane undertook to form a corporation. All the steps required by the statute for the creation of a corporation were taken except that the articles of incorporation were not filed with the county recorder. The corporation entered upon the performance of its duties in the business of constructing houses and other buildings. At the end of six months the corporation was forced into bankruptcy. One of its creditors sued Lynch and Beane, as though they were partners, on the theory that the corporation had never been formed because there had been a substantial failure to comply with the statutes when there had been no filing of the articles with the county recorder. Decide.
4. Plaintiff was incorporated in 1907 under the name "Osborn Paper Company." Owned and operated by the Osborn family, it had in half a century built up a large and profitable general wholesale and retail paper business. Defendant, which was incorporated on January 1, 1959, was engaged in the same business and had a place of business located within 100 yards of plaintiff's place of business. Carrold Osborn, after whom defendant company was named, was only a minority stockholder. He was a grandson of the founder of plaintiff company and at one time was in its employ. Plaintiff sought to restrain defendant from using the name "Osborn" on the theory that by its use defendant is guilty of unfair competition. Decide.
5. Minner purchased property for the purpose of mining coal. He then formed the Digger Corporation and posted on his land this sign, "Digger Corporation Mines." Neither Minner nor any other person paid any money into the capital stock of Digger Corporation. There was issued to Minner all of the stock of the corporation except one share which was issued to his wife. Neither Minner nor his wife paid any money for such stock. There was no meeting of stockholders, no directors were elected, no corporate control was exercised and no corporate books were kept. One of the employees in the mine, Hurte, was killed by

negligence in the mining operations. His executor sued both Digger Corporation and Minner for the wrongful death. Decide.

6. Steele Corporation was authorized to "manufacture all forms of rough and finished metal products." It built a large steel mill in which to carry on its business. It also purchased a section of land near the steel mill and planned to build houses for its employees. A stockholder sued to enjoin Steele from diverting funds for that purpose. Decide.

7. Dowel Corporation was authorized to "cut lumber, and mill and manufacture a full line of finished wood products." The company bought 10,000 acres of land covered with virgin pine timber which was not easily accessible. The company built a lumber mill and other buildings on the land. It also proceeded to build 100 houses for its employees near the mill. Shook, a stockholder, sued to enjoin the building of the 100 houses. Decide.

8. Hill made a contract for the sale of plants to the Denver Nursery, Inc. The contract was signed by Parr as Denver's president. Hill knew, and the contract stated, that the corporation was not yet formed, but Hill insisted that the contract be executed in this manner rather than delayed until the corporation was organized. The corporation was never formed, and Hill sued Parr and its other promoters. Decide.

CORPORATE SECURITIES   31

The Uniform Commercial Code defines a security as

> an instrument which is issued in bearer or registered form; and is a type commonly dealt in upon securities exchanges or markets or commonly recognized as a medium for investment; and evidences a share, participation or other interest in property or in an enterprise, or evidences an obligation of the issuer.

The Model Business Corporation Act states, "Shares means the units into which the proprietory interests in a corporation are divided." A share of stock, therefore, represents a contribution to the capital of a corporation and is evidence of a contract between the holder and the corporation.

CERTIFICATES OF STOCK

A corporation ordinarily issues a certificate of stock as evidence of the ownership of the firm by shareholders. The issuance of such certificates is not essential either to the existence of a corporation or to the ownership of its stock; however, it is common practice to issue these certificates because the shareholder's interest cannot easily be transferred without them.

According to the Model Business Corporation Act, the certificate representing shares must include: (1) the state of incorporation; (2) the name of the person to whom it is issued; (3) the number and class of shares and the designation of the series, if any, represented; and (4) the par value of each share or a statement that there is no par value. (See Figure 31-1)

The type of stock a corporation may issue is described in the charter or bylaws of the organization. If they are "silent" on the matter (if no details are given), the state incorporation statutes will be controlling. The certificate may be endorsed and transferred. Legal ownership changes from seller to buyer when the new owner's name is entered on the corporation's books, after the firm has been notified of the sale. A new certificate is then issued and the old one voided.

Shares of stock, in the absence of valid provisions to the contrary, are freely transferable. Any restraint upon the transfer of the stock must be described on the stock certificate. However, the limitations and restrictions the law places on transfers need not be stated since whoever deals in certificates of stock is charged with notice of such limitations. To be valid, stock transfer restrictions must be adopted for a lawful purpose. Restrictions cannot be unreasonable and should be definite and clear to ensure their enforcement.

278

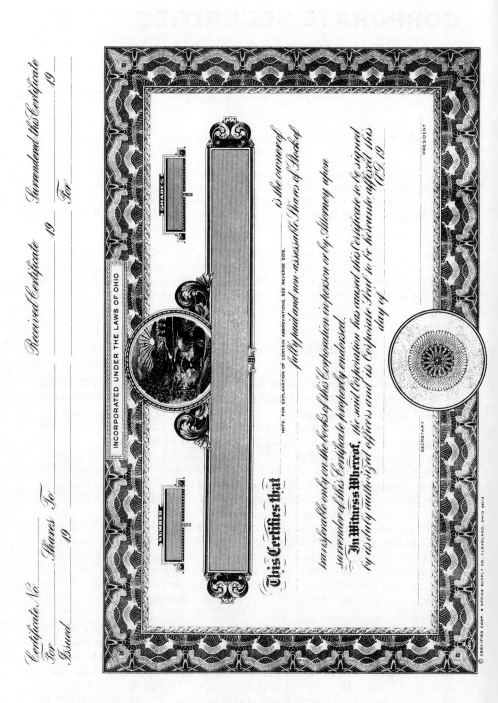

Figure 31-1   Side 1

For Value Received,_____ hereby sell, assign and transfer unto

_____ *Shares represented by the within Certificate, and do hereby irrevocably constitute and appoint*

_____ *Attorney to transfer the said Shares on the books of the within named Corporation with full power of substitution in the premises.*

Dated_____ 19___

In presence of

Figure 31-1 (cont) Side 2

KINDS OF SECURITIES

Corporate securities are classified as common stock, preferred stock, stock warrants, and bonds.

COMMON STOCK

The ordinary stock of the corporation is known as common stock. A share of common stock is considered personal property and confers on the shareholder the right to vote for members of the board of directors and on certain specific corporate decisions, to share proportionately in declared dividends, and to share in the distribution of net assets upon dissolution. Holders of common stock have no special rights or privileges and no preference of priority over other types of shareholders in the distribution of dividends.

PREFERRED STOCK

As its name suggests, this type of stock assures its holders prior claim over common stock holders with regard to funds available for annual dividends and for all assets, after all debts have been paid, should the company be forced to dissolve. (This fact is usually set out in the articles of incorporation.) The preferred stock issue offers a fixed rate of return to the stockholder. For example, the designation "6 percent preferred stock, $100 par value," on the stock certificate indicates that the shareholders are entitled to receive six dollars in annual dividends on each share they own before any dividends are paid to holders of common stock.

Preferred stock may be either participating or nonparticipating and either cumulative or noncumulative; it is usually nonvoting stock. *Participating preferred stock* means that if corporate earnings for the year are sufficient to pay the preferred dividend and an equal percentage dividend to all the common shareholders and funds are still available for distribution, the preferred shareholders have the right to share equally in these remaining funds with the common shareholders. *Nonparticipating preferred stock* indicates that once the preferred shareholders have received their contract dividend, they are entitled to no further share in the distribution of earnings, no matter what percent return the common shareholders earn on their investment.

Cumulative preferred stock means that if earnings are insufficient to meet the annual liability to the preferred shareholders in a given year, this liability is carried over, and these dividends in arrears must be paid out of future earnings before any dividend to the common stockholders is declared or paid. If dividends are to be paid out of current profits only, the preferred stock is *noncumulative*. Where the issuing contract is silent on this matter, preferred stock is deemed cumulative.

Preferred stock may be created only if it is provided for in the corporate charter or, in the absence of such a provision, when consented to by the common stockholders. Preferential rights must be stated on the stock certificate in order to be effective; otherwise, the stock will have no rights other than those of common stock.

Preferred shareholders usually do not have a vote in the management of the corporation. This privilege is reserved for the common shareholders. In some instances, the state statutes provide that if the corporation fails to pay dividends to the preferred shareholders for a certain period, the common shareholders may lose their voting privilege to the preferred shareholders.

STOCK WARRANTS

When a new issue of stock is brought out, present shareholders may have the right to purchase additional shares in order to maintain their proportionate ownership in the corporation. One method of giving effect to this preemptive right is by issuing stock warrants to existing shareholders. The stock warrant is a certificate that guarantees the holder the right to buy a given number of shares of stock at a given price for a given time. It may be issued in connection with the sale of a share of stock or a bond or it may be issued alone. To avoid a dilution of their percent of ownership in the corporation, the corporation offers the new issue to the current shareholders, usually in the form of warrants that give the current shareholders an opportunity to buy at a cheaper price than the stock would sell for on the open market. Warrants are available for sale on the open market and are usually bearer instruments, endorsed over by the one to whom the warrant was issued.

BONDS

The bond is another type of corporate security, but the bondholder is essentially a creditor of the firm rather than a participant in ownership. He has no say in the management of the firm but has preference over the owners in the distribution of assets upon dissolution.

A corporate bond is an unconditional promise to pay, in writing and under seal, a specific sum of money to the bearer or registered owner at a designated time and to pay a specified rate of interest upon the face value. Bonds may or may not be secured by specific assets. They may be *callable* and *convertible*. The callable feature gives the corporation the option of paying off the bonds at an agreed value, whereas the convertible feature gives the bondholder the option of converting the bond to stock at an agreed value. An *issue of bonds* is an issue of many promises to pay with identical terms. They may be issued at a premium or discount. Issuance is governed by the articles of incorporation and state law.

CAPITAL AND CAPITAL STOCK

Business corporations have both capital and capital stock. Although sometimes used synonymously, the terms do not mean the same thing.

Capital refers to the net worth of the corporation. It is the aggregate of the sums subscribed and paid in by the stockholders, together with all gains or profits arising from the business, less any losses that have been incurred.

Capital stock refers to the declared money value of the outstanding stock of the corporation. A corporation that has issued 1000 shares of $100 par value stock has a capital stock valued at $100,000. Modern corporation statutes usually provide for changing the amount of the authorized capital stock. The Model Business Corporation Act provides that the capital stock may be reduced by a two-thirds vote of the shareholders. Similar provisions govern increases in the capital stock.

AUTHORIZATION AND ISSUANCE OF STOCK

The right of a corporation to issue stock is controlled by the state. Corporate laws require that the articles of incorporation clearly indicate: (1) whether the corporation will issue only one class of stock or two or more classes; (2) how many shares of a single class or of several classes will be authorized; (3) whether the stock will have a par value; (4) what the par value will be; and (5) the amount that must be paid in upon stock subscriptions before the corporation will commence business. According to the New York State Stock Corporation Law, the corporation has a choice of including in the articles all pertinent information regarding the "designations, preferences, privileges, and voting powers of the shares of each class, and the restriction of qualifications thereof" or stating that the board of directors shall have power to fix these details before issuance. If the latter is the case, the board of directors must exercise this power by adopting formal resolutions to be filed with the secretary of state and the county office where the principal place of business is located. The corporation's charter may permit additonal issues to be authorized by an amendment to the articles filed with the secretary of state and approved by the state of incorporation.

Once the corporation complies with the conditions described above, its stock is authorized. It may issue all, part, or none of the stock, as it chooses. Stock it does not issue remains authorized unissued stock, not to be confused with the treasury stock of the corporation.

LEGAL PRINCIPLES

A certificate of stock is evidence of ownership in a corporation.

Any restraints on the transfer of stock must be enumerated on the stock certificate.

Corporate securities are classified as common stock, preferred stock, stock warrants, and bonds.

Common stock is the ordinary stock of a corporation.

Preferred stock has a prior claim over common stock in regard to dividends and distribution of assets upon dissolution.

A stock warrant allows a present shareholder to maintain his relative percentage of ownership in a corporation.

A bond is an obligation of the firm; it may be secured or unsecured.

Capital refers to the net assets of the corporation.

Capital stock is the declared value of the outstanding stock of a corporation.

Stock may have a par value, no par value, or a stated value, in addition to its book and market value.

The right of a corporation to issue stock is controlled by the state.

CASE FOR REVIEW

GENERAL INV. CO. v. BETHLEHEM STEEL CORP.

100 A. 347 N.S. (1917)

This is an application for a temporary injunction to restrain Bethlehem Steel Corporation from increasing its capital stock. The present capital stock is $30,000,000 divided one-half preferred and the other common, with equal voting rights. The plan is to increase the capital stock by $45,000,000, the additional to be called common, class B. Of this, $30,000,000 is to be put out as a stock dividend; $15,000,000 is to be sold. The stock is to have all the characteristics of common , except that it will have no vote.

The situation therefore is that over 99 percent of the present stock desire that the plan should go forward, and opposition is made by only 125 shares. Of these, 100 were actually bought after the promulgation of the plan, and I think for the sole purpose of bringing this suit. . . .

Whether the corporation has the legal power to issue this class of stock depends upon the construction to be put upon the eighteenth section of the Corporation Act. . . . From a casual reading of that section it would seem that stock of any kind, nature, or description, common or preferred, or whatever it may be called, may be created with or without voting privileges. Counsel for complainant insists that . . . the privilege of voting is necessarily incidental to common stock.

The question is . . . whether a stockholder is entitled to require that any new stock issued should be vested with the privilege of voting. . . . I have examined in the short time I have had all the cases that I could locate, and I have failed to find any statement of such public policy . . .

It is almost impossible to get a definition of "common stock" or a statement of what classes of stock may be issued, and the necessary rights and privileges of the classes, that is satisfactory. Thompson, § 3426, in referring to common stock, says that the name itself indicates its nature, and it is so called because it is the common stock, or the stock which private corporations generally issue; and is usually the only kind authorized. He says the universal rule is that the owners of common stock are entitled to a pro rata dividend of profits, and to a pro rata participation in the management of the corporation; that the holders of common stock sometimes have a preference in the management of the corporation. In section 3425 with reference to classes of stock he states: "The first general division of stock is into common or preferred stock; and these two classes are again subdivided into almost an infinite variety."

[And in Section 859:]"The rule that a right to vote follows the ownership of stock means only that in the absence of any common restriction upon all the stock, or upon a class of stock, this right prevails. That is, the right of a stockholder to vote cannot be arbitrarily abridged and is not subject to universal restriction. But the rule is equally emphatic, if not so general, that restrictions may be placed upon the right to vote; or, as sometimes stated, the right to vote may be separated from the ownership of stock. It must be remembered, in this connection, that stockholders can make any agreement respecting their stock, or the voting of it, that they may see fit or deem wise, except agreements that are void as against public policy."

Turning to the statute:

Every corporation organized under this act shall have power to create two or more kinds of stock, of such classes, with such designations, preferences and voting powers or restrictions or qualifications thereof as shall be stated and expressed in the certificate of incorporation or any certificate of amendment thereof.

No broader language could have been used, and, unless the usual meaning of these words is to be restricted by reason of the existence of some public policy, it is inconceivable to me that a corporation may not issue this class of common stock, or call it what you will. I have failed to find the existence of any such public policy. The matter is one for the stockholders to determine by their contract. If the public does not want to buy, it does not have to. The legal rights of the present stockholders are not affected; they contracted at the time they went in that they would have the advice, consultation with, and action by (or rather the opportunity of securing such advice, consultation, and action) of the then existing stock (and this subject to its reduction in accordance with law); but there was no contract that the corporation would, if it created further stock, give that further stock the voting privilege, so that the present stockholders might have the opportunity of securing advice by and consultation with and action by the new stockholders.

The essential elements of common stock are that the holders have an opportunity to make profit if there is any and participate in the assets after all other claims are paid, and bear the loss if there be such.

By common stock is meant that stock which entitled the owners of it to an equal pro rata division of profits, if any there be; one stockholder or class of stockholders having no advantage, priority, or preference over any other shareholder or class of stockholders in the division. Cook, § 12, p. 62.

That the purpose of the plan is to retain control in the present stockholders does not vitiate it. The question is one of good faith. There is no charge of bad faith in the present case.

There are many cases in other states not necessary to cite holding that it is within the power of stockholders to combine for the purpose of maintaining a management in control, and if done in good faith there is no legal objection to it. The mere fact that one of the results of the plan may be to perpetuate the control in the hands of its present stockholders does not vitiate the plan. The stockholders were entitled to vote as their selfish interests dictated.

CASE PROBLEMS

1. Railroad Company sued to recover from Hyde an assessment on stock originally subscribed for by Creighton and transferred to Hyde, who registered the transfer upon the books of the corporation. Hyde defended on the ground that prior to the action brought against him he had transferred his stock to a third party. Decide.
2. This was an action to require defendant to transfer to plaintiff on the corporate books six shares of stock in the oil company on surrender of certificates held by him. Plaintiff had purchased the stock in the open market. A request for its transfer was refused. The corporation alleged that the plaintiff was a competitor and rival of parties to the trust agreement and had a hostile intent in demanding the transfer. Decide.
3. Carol obtained a divorce from Ted. The divorce court, declaring that shares of stock in certain companies held in Ted's name were community property, decreed that Carol owned half the shares. She took the decree to the corporations to request new stock certificates in her name for the shares. The corporations refused to issue them, on the ground that the existing share certificates held by Ted had not been surrendered. Carol then sued her husband and the corporations to compel the issuance of new certificates. Decide.
4. Klassy Duds, Inc., adopted a bylaw which provided that no person should be allowed to hold more than five shares of its stock at one time. Miller bought 64 shares of the stock, which the directors refused to transfer to him. Miller brought an action to enforce his rights as a stockholder. Decide.
5. By perpetrating a fraud upon the decedent, Shultz obtained the assignment and delivery of certain stock certificates. Decedent's executor, seeking to enjoin transfer of the stock or payment of dividends thereon to Shultz brought an action to compel payment of dividends to the estate and issuance of certificates to himself as executor, in lieu of those held by Shultz. Decide.
6. ABC Corporation made no profits for a period of five years and during that period has paid no dividends on either its common or preferred shares. Its preferred shares provided for 5 percent preferred dividends but nothing was said about such shares being cumulative. In the sixth year a 5 percent dividend was declared for the preferred shareholders and a 6 percent dividend for the common shareholders. A preferred shareholder sued for and on behalf of himself and other preferred shareholders to enjoin the payment of any dividend to the common shareholders until the preferred shareholders were paid 5 percent for each of the past five years and for the current year. Decide.

7. Builder, Inc., built up a large surplus which was available for dividends. It paid the preferred shareholders their preferred 6 percent dividend and a similar amount to the common stockholders. The directors decided to divide the rest of the surplus proportionately among the common and preferred shareholders. There was nothing on the certificates of the preferred stock which provided for their being "participating" shares. Rooke, a common stockholder, sued the corporation on behalf of himself and other common stockholders, to enjoin the proposed division of surplus. Decide.

8. Spear, a minority stockholder, sought by a bill in equity to compel the declaration of a 7 percent dividend, claiming priority over payments made to the holders of debenture bonds. Decide.

FEDERAL SECURITIES REGULATION   32

The original need for federal regulation of securities was due largely to the inadequacy of state regulation, dramatized by the stock market crash of 1929. This created a distrust of corporate securities and those who dealt in them. The aftermath of the crash occasioned a number of Congressional investigations which revealed many undesirable and deceptive practices in the marketing of securities. From these investigations came recommendations for governmental controls. The first of these was the Securities Act of 1933, followed by the Securities Exchange Act of 1934, the Investment Company Act of 1940 and the Investment Advisors Act of 1940.

SECURITIES ACT OF 1933

This act is concerned largely with the initial distribution or sale of securities rather than with subsequent trading. Its objective is to protect investors in new security issues from fraudulent sales and to provide them with all material information necessary to make a sound investment decision. It provides that securities which are offered to the public through the mails or other channels of interstate commerce must be registered with the Securities Exchange Commission by the issuer. The registration statement must contain specific information about the security and the issuer: size of business, capitalization, earnings, financial statement, etc. The commission has no authority to approve any security or to pass on its merits. Its sole function is to assure that the registration statement is complete. It is in no way an approval or guarantee of a security issue. A prospectus and advertisement of sale containing the basic information in the registration statement must be given to all prospective buyers.

The method of enforcement of the Securities Act is the SEC's veto power. The registration statement becomes effective twenty days after filing, unless within that period the Commission refuses to permit its effectiveness or issues a stop order with regard to the sale of the security. It can be issued, after notice and opportunity for hearing, if the registration statement contains any untrue statement of a material fact or omits any material fact that makes the statement misleading.

Exempt from registration requirements are securities issued by governments, issues of securities in small amounts if exempted by SEC rules, securities sold to persons within a state by persons within that state, private rather than public offerings, and securities being issued in exchange for other securities.

SECURITIES EXCHANGE ACT OF 1934

This Act deals with trading of securities. It has as its basic objectives: (1) to afford a measure of disclosure to people who buy and sell securities; (2) to prevent fraud and deception in securities trading and manipulation of the markets; (3) to regulate the securities markets; and (4) to control the amount of credit which goes into the securities markets. The act denies the use of the mails and other instrumentalities of interstate commerce to stock exchanges unless they register with the SEC or unless that agency exempts them from registration. The registration subjects the exchanges to agency regulations. Under amendment (12g), coverage of the 1934 Act is extended to corporations having total assets exceeding $1,000,000 and a class of equity securities held by 500 or more shareholders. It provides that these corporations must register that security even if it is not traded on a public stock exchange.

ISSUERS

No security may be listed on an exchange unless its issuer files an application for registration with both the exchange and the SEC containing much the same information as is required for new issues by the 1933 act. Securities which are not listed on an exchange do not subject the issuer to the registration, reporting, and other provisions. Over-the-counter brokers and dealers must also register with the SEC. There are general provisions outlawing fraud and manipulation in both the exchange and over-the-counter markets, and the registered exchanges and their members must abide by the rules set down in the act and by the regulations of the SEC issued under authority of that act. The credit provisions of the act give the board of Governors of the Federal Reserve System authority to set margin requirements on all exchanges and grants the SEC the task of enforcing them. Other rules of the act include:

1. Brokers must not commingle the securities of different customers as collateral for a loan without the consent of the customer. Also Brokers may not pledge customer's securities for more than the customer's debt.
2. No broker shall execute any sell order unless the order is marked either "long" or "short."
3. No broker shall employ any device, scheme, or artifice to defraud.
4. No member of a national securities exchange, while on the floor of that exchange can participate, directly or indirectly, in any transaction in any security for any account in which that member has an interest (specialist is an exception).
5. Titles of securities must include such information as par or stated value, rate of dividends (if fixed), indication of preference, (if any), convertibility and whether the stock is cumulative or noncumulative.
6. If proxies are solicited on behalf of management relating to the annual meeting at which directors are elected, each proxy request shall be accompanied by the annual report.
7. Profits realized by "insiders" (officers and directors who own 10 percent or more of a stock) as a result of inside information not disclosed to the public may be recovered in actions brought by the issuing corporation or by any of its security holders.

THE SECURITIES AND EXCHANGE COMMISSION

The SEC was created by the Securities Exchange Act of 1934. It consists of five commissioners appointed by the president with the advice and consent of the Senate. The commission administers the Securities Act of 1933, the Investment Advisors Act of 1940, the Securities Exchange Act of 1934, the Investment Company Act of 1940, and other acts of Congress. The commission also has advisory functions in corporate reorganization proceedings under Chapter X of the Bankruptcy Act.

INVESTMENT COMPANY ACT OF 1940

The Investment Company Act requires registration of all investment companies which make use of the mails or other interstate facilities of communication. Besides information contained in the registration statements filed under the 1933 and 1934 acts, this registration must also contain the registrant's intent with respect to such specific subjects as diversification, issuance of senior securities, borrowing and lending money, underwriting, and investing in real estate or commodities. The regulatory provisions which attach to all registered companies (not exempt) are designed to accomplish five main objectives: (1) to regulate the selling practices of investment companies; (2) to seek honest and unbiased management; (3) to obtain greater participation in management by security holders; (4) to ensure adequate and feasible capital structures; and (5) to ensure the availability of financial statements to security holders and the SEC.

INVESTMENT ADVISERS ACT OF 1940

This act requires registration with the SEC of persons engaged for compensation in giving advice or issuing analyses or reports concerning securities. It outlaws fraudulent or deceptive practices on the part of registered advisers, prohibits profit sharing arrangements, and prevents assignment of any advisory contract without the consent of the client. The Act applies to those persons whose primary business enterprise is advising on investments.

LEGAL PRINCIPLES

All publicly distributed securities must be registered with the SEC except exempt issues and transactions.

Registration of a security requires full disclosure of the material facts and circumstances of a primary distribution.

The Securities Act of 1933 is concerned with the initial distribution of securities.

A prospectus containing the basic information in the registration statement must be given to all prospective buyers.

The Securities Exchange Act of 1934 deals with post-distribution trading.

The Investment Company Act of 1940 requires all investment companies using the mails or interstate facilities to register with the SEC.

The Investment Advisers Act of 1940 requires registration with the SEC of persons engaged in the business of rendering advice or issuing analyses or reports concerning securities.

Corporations are required to follow prescribed channels in soliciting votes by proxy.

Officials of corporations are restricted in their activities in trading their own company stock and are required to report such dealings.

Brokers and dealers trading through an exchange must make full disclosure to their customers of the capacity in which they are acting and segregate those activities as far as is possible.

No one may engage in trading to manipulate the market.

CASE FOR REVIEW

SECURITIES AND EXCHANGE COMMISSION v. MACON

28 F. Supp. 127 D. (Colo. 1939)

The development of oil wells, like mining, is highly speculative, and, as has been well said, the opinion of the best geologists is at most . . . a guess. Nevertheless the Congress has seen fit to enact this law which contains quite definite definitions of what fraud is, and what shall or shall not be stated in promoting oil wells, especially in campaigns to raise money for their development. We must test the allegations and the evidence and base our result upon those definitions.

The government charges the defendants have employed devices, schemes and/or artifices to defraud, and . . . that they have obtained money or property by means of untrue statements of a material fact or have omitted . . . a material fact necessary . . . to make the statements made . . . not misleading.

. . . We have an exhibit, No. 19, which would seem to indicate the state of mind of Mr. Macon during the course of or at the outset of this enterprise. He cannot be condemned solely upon the statements made therein, but they should be considered as a circumstance in deciding the intent or lack of intent to violate the statute.

Another question that has been argued is the right of a promoter or a stock salesman to rely upon statements made by so-called experts without any checking, investigation, or determination of the correctness of the same before putting them out to the public. I do not believe a salesman has the right to pass the opinion of someone else on to the public, and derive benefit therefrom in selling stock and receiving the proceeds, without being in some way responsible for such statements. Any other construction would open the way to a great many abuses, and permit people to derive profit from letters of experts irrespective of the merits or their standing in their profession, without any responsibility. That is contrary to fundamental principles applicable to actions of this kind, which, as has been well stated, are actions for fraud. Counsel have emphasized that most of the statements complained of are mere opinions. In a strict sense that is true. In a sense it is not true. Mere opinion or expression of the writer's views as to a future situation, or as to conditions which necessarily cannot be stated definitely, if relied upon by the purchaser of stock, is at his own risk. On the other hand, the expression of opinion, coupled with other statements, may amount to a statement of a material fact, although it is disguised and framed technically to be nothing more than a mere opinion. This statute requires that a full disclosure of all facts pertinent to a situation known to the seller must be made. A very vicious form of deception may consist of lifting a part of an opinion of an expert and omitting to state other parts of it. There is evidence that that was done in this case in several instances.

It is true the circular defendants filed with the Securities and Exchange Commission is innocuous so far as containing any fraudulent statements. If that were all the defendants used in their sales campaign, there would be no cause of action. That I assume was a censored document, and it had to satisfy the Exchange Commission before the defendants could register or proceed with the sale of this stock. But they did not stop there. The prospectus when sent out to their customers was accompanied in most, if not all, cases by circulars and other literature that had not been censored or submitted to the Commission. It is those circulars in most instances the government complains of.

Mr. Macon . . . gave an explanation in defense of every statement . . . that the government complains of. I was impressed as I listened to his testimony that most of it was based upon hearsay. . . . He said crowds of people on one or two occasions rushed out to see the well come in or to see the gas burn, or matters of that kind, all trivial, unsubstantial, and sufficient only to excite curiosity. Certainly phenomena of that kind cannot justify the positive statements as to what has been developed in a particular oil well, or what the prospects are. He may have been convinced in his own mind, but certainly all this was not sufficient . . . to justify him making the statements he did in the circulars. He cannot pass such information on and escape responsibility by saying "I believed it." It would be an insult to the intelligence of any business man of experience.

Something has been said about the use of the word "may" and the word "might"; that there "might" be a well, or it "may" develop into a gusher. Language of that kind standing alone, could not be objectionable, that is, come within the statutory definition. But the trouble in this case was that it was always coupled with other statements which, considered as a whole, constituted a statement that the writer was confident of the truth of what he said. It would impress the ordinary man in the street that he sincerely believed the statements he was making were true, and that what he said could be relied upon, especially as it was intended to be relied upon by the purchaser.

The most objectionable feature of this literature is not so much what was said, but that, as counsel once wrote . . . of his opponent's brief, it is full of omissions. In all fairness, the writer of this literature should have set out other statements in the opinions he quotes from, which would tend to negate the quotations set out.

CASE PROBLEMS

1. Five securities salesmen petition to review an order of the Securities and Exchange Commission which barred them from further association with any broker or dealer. The commission found that the salesmen represented that a certain stock would increase in value, that the company would have good earning prospects, and that the company was about to enter into very lucrative contracts when, in fact, the company was insolvent and had no profits since its inception. Decide.

2. Chasins brought an action against his broker alleging a violation of the Securities Act. It appears that the broker failed to inform Chasins that he was making a market in the over-the-counter market for securities he sold in that market to Chasins. Decide.

3. Plaintiff alleged fraudulent statements were made by a director and principal investor concerning optimistic reports of earnings for the future of the corporation. The principal stockholder had failed to qualify his statement that the corporation would "have earnings" with the fact that much of this income would relate to a change in accounting method that had taken place five months earlier. Decide.

4. Plaintiffs' brought suit against the defendants, directors of a credit company who were responsible for a fraudulent proxy solicitation issued pursuant to a merger agreement. The first director, a professional architect, never attended a board of directors' meeting until twelve days before the proxy solicitation was mailed and did not know of any wrongdoing. The second director, a successful surgeon, whose family had invested over one-half million dollars in the company, fully relied on the company's accountants for information and did not know of any wrongdoing until well after the issuance of the solicitation. Decide.

5. A purchaser of certain manufacturing equipment paid for with bills of exchange sufficiently claimed fraud in connection with the transaction. He charged that the equipment did not and could not perform as represented, that the sellers intended to and did misrepresent their capacity to perform in order to induce the purchase, that the purchaser relied on the misrepresentations and was damaged. The allegations made a claim for fraud within the purview of the securities laws. Decide.

6. Plaintiff filed his complaint against a broker-dealer in securities charging defendant with a scheme to defraud plaintiff by selling to him short-term commercial paper not owned by defendant. Defendant claimed commercial paper is exempt from the Securities Act. Decide.

7. The SEC requested that the defendants be permanently enjoined from selling securities without complying with the registration requirements of the Securities Act. The SEC contended that the Minnesota corporation's earnings consisted entirely of interest on loans and receivables invested outside Minnesota. This made the corporation ineligible for the Securities Act intrastate exemption for its sales of unsecured installment promissory notes in Minnesota residents. In effect, the strength of the installment notes, which were registered under Minnesota law, depended on land developments outside Minnesota and outside the jurisdiction of the Minnesota courts. Decide.

8. The government brought an action against an underwriter and its president for antifraud violations of the Securities Act. The defendant-president devised a scheme whereby fictitious orders for shares were entered to make it appear that the offering was completely sold out before the deadline specified under terms of the offering. This would permit over-the-counter trading in the shares. Purchases in the after-market were then generated so that the fictitious orders could be "crossed out" or offset by subsequent purchases. Decide.

MANAGEMENT OF THE   33
CORPORATE BUSINESS

Corporate management involves the functions of three groups within the corporations: shareholders, directors, and officers. Their roles are defined and limited by the corporation's charter, its bylaws, and the state's incorporation statutes. General management of the corporate business—making and implementing policy decisions—is delegated almost exclusively to the board of directors. However, the power to amend the corporate charter, sell corporate assets, change the makeup of the corporation, and terminate corporate power remains with the shareholders. Making bylaws is also a shareholder function, unless this power is modified by statute.

The shareholders' principal control over the actions of the directors is through their voting power. The state incorporation statutes give the shareholders the right to remove a director, with or without cause, and to elect a new director or board of directors. In large corporations, exercise of this right is hampered by the large number of shareholders and by management's control over proxy solicitation.

Because of the complexities of the modern corporation, the board of directors does not handle the daily activities of corporate business, delegating instead much of its authority to the officers of the company. The board retains a measure of control through its power of removal; it may remove an officer whenever it feels inclined to make a change.

SHAREHOLDERS

A shareholder, or stockholder, is an individual whose name appears on the books of the corporation as the owner of shares of stock and who is entitled to participate in the management and control of the corporation. The majority vote of the shareholders binds the corporation and all its members in any transaction or proceeding within the scope of corporate business as authorized by the corporate charter. They are limited in the action they may take in that they may not pursue a policy detrimental to the corporation.

Action by the shareholders normally binds the corporation when it is taken in a regular meeting or a properly called special meeting. A regular meeting is one prescribed by the charter or bylaws, whereas a special meeting is usually called by the directors. At common law no notice was required for the annual meeting because information regarding it was usually set forth in the articles or bylaws. Where statutes, articles, or bylaws do not provide a time and place for this meeting, personal notice must be given to all shareholders. When giving special notice, the directors must include a statement detailing the matters to be acted upon. Any actions taken at the special meeting other than those described in the notice will be illegal.

VOTING

Each shareholder in a corporation has the right to vote at shareholders' meetings, unless he owns a nonvoting stock. A company usually allocates one vote per share. Statutes frequently require corporations to keep stock books or other records giving the names and addresses of all shareholders and the number and class of shares held by each. In addition, statutes sometimes require the preparation of a voting list before each shareholder meeting. The person to whom the vote is given is the individual whose name last appears on the stock register before notice of a meeting is given. A shareholder can, however, delegate his vote to a qualified representative, called a proxy. (See Figure 33-1) In such cases, the law of principal and agent is binding.

In electing the board of directors, where a cumulative voting right has been given to shareholders by statute, charter, or bylaw, each shareholder is entitled to as many votes as he has shares of voting stock, multiplied by the number of directors to be elected. For example, if three directors are to be elected and a shareholder has 300 shares of voting stock, he may cast 900 votes. A shareholder may give his total votes to one or more nominees in any proportion he desires. Cumulative voting is confined to the election of directors; its purpose is to improve the minority shareholders' opportunity to gain representation on the board of directors.

VOTING POOLS AND TRUST AGREEMENTS

In order to institute changes or special programs, minority shareholders must band together. A frequently used procedure is to form a voting pool in which minority members desiring the same results vote along the same line. A second method is the voting trust, in which minority shareholders delegate their votes to a single proxy who acts as a trustee and is given full voting power according to minority policy. Voting trusts are limited by law to a ten-year time period unless extensions are granted.

The weakness of the proxy as a practical device for maintaining control for any length of time is that it is revocable at any time unless it is coupled with an interest. This is also true of the pooling agreement. However the courts are satisfied if the interest is the manner in which the shares are to be voted and the end to be accomplished. Use of the trust to exclude minority shareholders is outside the legitimate purposes for which trusts have been created and is against public policy.

BYLAWS

The bylaws are the rules of conduct adopted by the corporation to govern its internal affairs. Under the proper circumstances, the corporation enacts rules designed to facilitate the performance of corporate activity. Such bylaws are regarded as allowable under the incidental powers of a corporation. They cannot be repealed, amended, or added to in any way that will utlimately affect the vested rights of the shareholders, unless, of course, the shareholders are in agreement. Similarly, the directors cannot delegate their power to amend the bylaws.

Figure 33-1

🄰 **AT&T**

PROXY

American Telephone and Telegraph Company
195 Broadway, New York, N.Y. 10007

Side 1

**This proxy
is solicited by
management for
the annual meeting
on April 21, 1976
at 2:00 P.M.**

Philadelphia Civic Center—
Convention Hall
Civic Center Boulevard
at 34th Street
Philadelphia,
Pennsylvania

The undersigned hereby appoints John D. deButts, Edward B. Hanify and
J. Irwin Miller, and each of them, proxies, with the powers the undersigned would possess if personally present, and with full power of
substitution, to vote all Common Shares of the undersigned in American
Telephone and Telegraph Company at the annual meeting of its shareholders to be held on April 21, 1976, and at any adjournment thereof,
upon all matters that may properly come before the meeting, including
the matters described in the proxy statement furnished herewith, subject
to any directions indicated in the boxes on the reverse of this card. **If
no directions are given, the management proxy committee intends
to vote the shares represented by this proxy as recommended by
the directors on the matters described on the reverse.**

If you do not sign and return a proxy, or attend the meeting, your shares
cannot be voted.
Please sign on reverse

Please use an "X" if you wish to indicate your vote in the boxes below. **Side 2**

The directors recommend a vote "For"			The directors recommend a vote "Against"					
	For	Withheld		For	Against		For	Against
A. Election of Directors (Pages 2–8)			D. Shareholder Proposal I (Pages 12–13)			G. Shareholder Proposal IV (Pages 18–20)		
	For	Against		For	Against		For	Against
B. Ratification of Auditors (Page 9)			E. Shareholder Proposal II (Pages 14–16)			H. Shareholder Proposal V (Pages 20–21)		
	For	Against		For	Against		For	Against
C. Sale of Shares to Employees' Savings Plan (Pages 9–11)			F. Shareholder Proposal III (Pages 16–17)			I. Shareholder Proposal VI (Pages 21–24)		

Account No   025 526 351 76   025 526 351 76

MICHAEL P LITKA & MRS ELEANOR R
LITKA JT TEN
2370 BEECHMOOR DR N W
NORTH CANTON OHIO 44720

**Sign here as
name(s)
appear above** X _____

X _____ Date _____ 1976

Please sign this proxy and return it promptly whether you plan to attend the meeting or not. If signing for a corporation or
partnership or as agent, attorney or fiduciary, indicate the capacity in which you are signing. If you do attend the meeting and
decide to vote by ballot, such vote will supersede this proxy.   2 304 214

The bylaws are subordinate to the incorporation statutes of the state and to
the charter of the corporation. They must be reasonable, conform to public
policy, and not discriminate against shareholders of the same class. Valid
bylaws are binding on all shareholders regardless of whether they know of the
existence of those bylaws or were among the majority that consented to their
adoption. Bylaws are not binding upon third persons, unless these persons are
aware of the bylaws' existence.

The bylaws normally control the appointment of officers, their duties,
powers, and compensation; the time and manner of holding shareholders'
meetings; the fiscal year of the corporation; the issuance and transfer of stock;
the power of, and limitations on, directors in corporate management; the
handling of funds and declaration of dividends; and the amendment of the
bylaws. They are generally authorized to adopt bylaws for the corporation,
subject to the bylaws, if any, adopted by the shareholders.

DIRECTORS

The ultimate control of the corporation lies with the shareholders; however,
the actual conduct of a corporation's affairs is delegated by the shareholders

to the directors, who guide the basic policies of the corporation and who in turn delegate to the officers the task of actual management.

Requirements regarding the number and qualifications of directors vary from state to state, but most states require a minimum of three directors. All directors must be of legal age and at least one must be both a citizen of the United States and a resident of the state of incorporation. Most states require directors to be shareholders unless the articles of incorporation or the bylaws provide otherwise. The original board of directors is generally designated in the certificate of incorporation. Their successors are chosen by vote of the shareholders.

In the exercise of their duties and powers, directors are guided and limited by the corporation's charter and bylaws and by the governing statutes. They must exercise their authority collectively and not individually. Individual directors have no power to act as agents of the corporation. The principal function of the directors is to establish and guide the policies of the corporation in the transaction of ordinary business activities. To accomplish these policies, the board elects the officers of the corporation, delegates authority for their functions, and supervises their conduct. It is the duty of the directors to determine whether dividends should be declared and to approve all major actions initiated and negotiated by the officers.

The board cannot delegate authority to sell major assets, to issue stock, or to declare dividends. Its relationship to the corporation and its shareholders is fiduciary; in managing corporate affairs the directors must exercise that degree of care which men of prudence exercise in the management of their own affairs. This standard cannot be exactly defined and necessarily varies with the size and type of the corporation. Nevertheless, by reason of this standard, the directors are personally liable for ultra vires acts and for the illegal declaration and payment of dividends. They are liable to creditors for losses resulting from fraudulent conduct. Directors are not liable for accidents, mistakes of judgment, or losses, if they have acted in good faith and have exercised ordinary care, skill, and diligence. Occasionally a defense against liability is put forth by directors who attempt to distinguish themselves from the "managing" directors. They allege that since shareholders elected them in "name" only that they should not be held to the same degree of care as the "managing" directors. However, the courts are still of the opinion that one who accepts a position on a board of directors must make himself aware of the responsibility he assumes as a director and exercise appropriate care and judgment.

The tenure of office of directors is fixed by the charter or bylaws. The stockholders can remove a director with cause, but one director cannot remove another. The directors elect and may remove the company's officers and adopt their own bylaws.

The board of directors enjoys broad discretionary powers in managing the corporation. However, in carrying out this function, the members of the board must act as a unit. No director may cast his vote by proxy; in order to vote he must be present at the directors' meeting. The bylaws usually provide for the method of calling directors' meetings and for the time and place of the meetings. They also normally require that a record be kept of all activities of the board, and the evidence of the exercise of its powers is usually kept in the corporate record books.

In the absence of a stipulation in the charter or bylaws to the contrary, directors receive no compensation for their services as such. Their reward is essentially social and business prestige. They are given a nominal honorarium for their attendance at meetings. They may also recover for the reasonable value of services performed for the company other than their duties as directors.

OFFICERS

State statutes usually provide that a corporation must have certain officers—a president, a vice-president, a secretary, and a treasurer. In some instances the officers are elected by the shareholders, but generally they are appointed by the board of directors. No particular formality is observed in making such appointments, nor are particular qualifications required of officers. Unless prohibited, a director may hold an executive office; there is rarely any prohibition against this kind of dual service.

The officers of a corporation are its agents. As such, their powers are controlled by the laws of agency, subject to limitations imposed by the charter and bylaws or by the instructions of the board of directors. Management positions usually carry broad authority to act on behalf of the corporation. Delegation to the officers involves two concepts: (1) basic policy implementation and (2) ordinary policy implementation. Basic policy involves those matters which require board approval, whereas ordinary policies may be acted upon by the chief executive officer alone.

Generally, the president is the presiding officer of both the board of directors and the corporation. The treasurer, or controller, keeps corporate records and receives and disburses corporate funds. The secretary keeps the minutes of corporate meetings.

Where the officer performs solely an internal function, there are generally no incidental or inherent powers. The problems relating to the authority of the officers arises in transactions with persons outside the corporation. This usually involves the chief executive officer who is presumed to be able to do all things that are within the everyday business activity of the company. However, the third person must be aware of the usual limits of the authority of the officer with whom he is dealing and is responsible for his actual knowledge of the internal practices of the corporation and the customs of the trade.

The relation of the officers to the corporation, like that of the directors, is fiduciary. For this reason, the officers are liable for any secret profits made in connection with the business of the corporation. They are liable for willful or negligent acts resulting in damage to the corporation. On the other hand, they are not liable for mere errors in judgment committed while exercising their discretionary powers, provided they have acted with reasonable prudence and skill.

ULTRA VIRES ACTS

Any action of the corporation that is beyond the authority given to it by the state, or beyond its incidental or implied power, is said to be an ultra vires act (literally, "beyond power") and is subject to challenge by the state or the shareholders. The state can object to ultra vires acts by enjoining the corporation from committing them or by bringing quo warranto proceedings to demand forfeiture of the charter. The shareholders can enjoin the corporation from performance of future ultra vires acts or set aside current ultra vires acts on the grounds that the corporation is subjecting the capital to risks not called for in the charter. However, a third party cannot object to ultra vires acts.

When an ultra vires contract has been fully executed, the courts will let it stand. If executed on one side, it will be enforced as to the other party. If executory, the defense of ultra vires will be allowed. If it has been partially or wholly executed on one side, the general view is that the recipient of the benefit is not permitted to deny (estop) the existence of the contract.

TORTS

The corporation is liable for officers' torts, even ultra vires torts. Also, the courts have often held a parent company liable for torts committed by its subsidiary when the parent so completely dominated the activity of the subsidiary that it became purely an agent or arm of the parent corporation. In cases of excessive dominance by the parent company, close scrutiny will be given to the financial structure of the corporations to determine whether two corporations actually exist. When there is some indication that the corporate device is being employed for fraudulent purposes, the courts may justifiably disregard the subsidiary's claim to a separate corporate identity.

LEGAL PRINCIPLES

Corporate management rests with the stockholders, directors, and officers of the company.

A shareholder whose name appears on the corporate register is entitled to vote for the directors.

A regular meeting is called yearly. Whenever special meetings are called, notice, including a statement of purpose, must be given.

The bylaws are the internal rules of the corporation and are binding on all who have notice of them.

The directors must act as a unit; each director must vote personally and not by proxy.

Directors may be personally liable for actions resulting in damage to the firm when they fail to act with reasonable prudence.

Officers are appointed agents of the corporation and as such are governed by the laws of agency.

Ultra vires actions are actions beyond the scope of the corporation's authority. They may be challenged by the state or by shareholders.

CASE FOR REVIEW

CHICAGO CITY RAILWAY CO. v. ALLERTON

18 Wall. 233, 21L.ED. 733 (1931)

The applellant in this case is a corporation owning a street railroad in the city of Chicago. The directors of the company, without consulting or calling a meeting of the stockholders, resolved to increase the capital stock of the company from $1,250,000 to $1,500,000. To this the appellee, who is a stockholder, objected and filed the bill in this case, praying for an injunction to prevent the increase. . . .

Without attempting to decide the constitutional question, or to give a construction to the act of the legislature, we are satisfied that the decree must be affirmed on the broad ground that a change so organic and fundamental as that of increasing the capital stock of a corporation beyond the limit fixed by the charter cannot be made by the directors alone, unless expressly authorized thereto. The general power to perform all corporate acts refers to the ordinary business transactions of the corporation, and does not extend to a reconstruction of the body itself, or to an enlargement of its capital stock. A corporation, like a partnership, is an association of natural persons who contribute a joint capital for a common purpose, and although the shares may be assigned to new individuals in perpetual succession, yet the number of shares and amount of capital cannot be increased except in the manner expressly authorized by the charter or articles of association.

Authority to increase the capital stock of a corporation may, undoubtedly, be conferred by a law passed subsequent to the charter; but such a law should regularly be accepted by the stockholders. Such assent might be inferred by subsequent acquiescence; but in some form or other it must be given to render the increase valid and binding on them. Changes in the purpose and object of an association, or in the extent of its constituency or membership, involving the amount of its capital stock, are necessarily fundamental in their character, and cannot, on general principles, be made without the express or implied consent of the members. The reason is obvious.

First, as it respects the purpose and object. This may be said to be the final cause of the association, for the sake of which it was brought into existence. To change this without the consent of the associates, would be to commit them to an enterprise which they never embraced, and would be manifestly unjust.

Second, as it respects the constituency, or capital and membership. This is the next most important and fundamental point in the constitution of a body corporate. To change it without the consent of the stockholders, would be to make them members of an association in which they never consented to become such. It would change the relative influence, control and profit of each member. If the directors alone could do it, they could always perpetuate their own power. Their agency does not extend to such an act unless so expressed in the charter, or subsequent enabling act; and such subsequent enabling act, as before said, would not bind the stockholders without their acceptance of it, or assent to it in some form. Even when the additional stock is distributed to each stockholder pro rata, it would often work injustice, because many of the stockholders might be unable to take their respective shares, and might thus lose their relative interest and influence in the corporate concerns.

These conclusions flow naturally from the character of such associations. Of course, the associates themselves may adopt or assent to a different rule. If the charter provides that the capital stock may be increased, or that a new business may be adopted by the corporation, this is undoubtedly an authority for the corporation (that is, the stockholders) to make such a change by a stockholders' vote, in the regular way. Perhaps a subsequent ratification or assent to a change already made, would be equally effective. It is unnecessary to decide that point at this time. But if it is desired to confer such a power on the directors, so as to make their acts binding and final it should be expressly conferred.

Where the stock expressly allowed by a charter has not been all subscribed, the power of the directors to receive subscriptions for the balance may stand on a different footing. Such an act, might, perhaps, be considered as merely getting in the capital already provided for the operations and necessities of the company and, therefore, as belonging to the orderly and proper administration of the company's affairs. Even in such case, however, prudent and fair directors would prefer to have the sanction of the stockholders to their acts. But that is not the present case, and need not be further considered.

CASE PROBLEMS

1. Smith was a director and Abbott a director and president of Concrete Corporation, of which there were four directors in all. At a meeting at which one director was absent, Smith and Abbott presented claims that they held against the corporation for special services rendered by them. As directors, they voted in favor of paying their claims; the remaining director present voted against the claims. After a new board of directors was elected the next year, the corporation sued Smith and Abbott to recover the money paid on the claims. Decide.

2. Plaintiff founded, and later incorporated, a business of which his son was president and he was secretary and treasurer. The father and son held all the outstanding shares. The son, as president, gave his father notice that a special shareholders' meeting was called "for the purpose of electing directors of the corporation for the ensuing year, or for such action or further business as may arise at said meeting." The father did not attend the meeting and the son, by voting his shares, elected himself and his wife directors. They then held a directors' meeting, at which they voted to terminate the father's employment by the corporation. The father brought suit to declare the election of directors and the action of the directors' meeting void on the ground that the notice to the shareholders did not indicate that the object of the meeting was to terminate his employment. Decide.

3. Waters, on behalf of himself and other creditors of Minneapolis Mechanical, Inc., brought a proceeding in equity to cancel a deed given by the corporation to Phillips. The deed had been signed by all of the directors, but they signed separately and at different times. No meeting had been held to authorize the transfer of the property. Decide.

4. Fresh Foods Inc., was a corporation organized under the Ohio corporation statute and engaged in the business of buying and selling agricultural products. Two-thirds of the stockholders voted to convert the corporation into a coopera-

tive and to allow dividends upon a patronage basis. The corporation then possessed undistributed profits that might have been paid to stockholders. Suit is brought by plaintiffs, who are stockholders, to prevent the distribution of the corporation's profits as provided by the amended articles and bylaws, on the ground that, under the original articles, stockholders are entitled to dividends that they will be deprived of by the amendments. Decide.

5. Borsh, Waters and Moore are the directors of Oil, Inc., which is authorized by it's charter "to engage in the oil business, drill oil wells, lease and purchase land, build and operate refineries and build and operate oil pipe lines." The directors of Oil decide to invest all the surplus funds of the corporation in a new mining venture. Pokey, a stockholder brought suit to enjoin the making of such investment. Decide.

6. Electric Power's charter stated that it was incorporated "for the manufacture, supply, and sale of electricity for light, heat, and power to the public and to municipalities." It maintained salesrooms and salesmen for selling all kinds of electric appliances. The state where E. P. was incorporated brought an action to enjoin the corporation from carrying on this business, on the ground that it was ultra vires. Decide.

7. Paper Products Inc., sues NoNews, which was in the business of operating newsstands, for the price of a quantity of small cellophane bags sold to the defendant. The latter contended that it had no power under its charter to purchase cellophane bags because they had no direct connection with the operation of newsstands. The charter provided, in part, that the corporation had the right "to act as agents, general or special, and to buy and sell newsstand and/or soda fountain supplies of all kinds, and any and all other similar or kindred lines and the right to buy, hold, sell, and deal in real estate and personal property." Decide.

8. The directors of Fresh Foods, Inc., which operated a chain of retail grocery stores decided to sell three of the stores in the chain. These three stores were not doing well financially and the directors determined it would be better if they were sold and the proceeds were used to relocate stores in other areas. Pokey, a stockholder, sued the corporation and its directors to enjoin this proposed sale, contending that such action required stockholder approval because it involved a sale of the corporate assets. Decide.

SHAREHOLDERS' RIGHTS, LIABILITIES, AND REMEDIES

A share of stock represents an investment in a corporation. It is intangible personal property that confers neither the right to share in the active management of the firm (although it does confer voting rights) nor a right to any specific assets. Basically, the share of stock is evidence of a profit sharing contract between the owner and the corporation. However, in addition to the voting franchise, the shareholder obtains protection for his investment through his right to inspect the corporate books and records and by virtue of his right to bring a derivative suit for certain types of injury suffered by the corporation at the hands of third parties as a result of mismanagement.

PURCHASE AND SUBSCRIPTION

Ownership of stock is most commonly acquired through a transfer of the stock from a shareholder desiring to sell to an individual wishing to purchase the stock. An individual may also purchase shares when they are first issued, by a stock subscription either prior to the formation of the corporation or shortly after incorporation.

A purchaser has the right to have issued to him a certificate of ownership for the number of shares of stock he has purchased from the former owner. This is accomplished by the endorsement and delivery to him of the old certificate and subsequent delivery of the certificate to the corporation for the transfer to be noted on the corporate books. A transferee becomes a shareholder when his name is registered on the corporate stock book.

To ensure that the corporation will have a minimum amount of capital, it is often necessary to obtain subscriptions to its stock prior to incorporation. Agreements to subscribe for stock of corporations to be formed in the future usually may be rescinded or revoked at any time before the corporation is formed. Prior to incorporation, such agreements are merely offers. They are accepted by the corporation and become enforceable at the time that corporation is actually formed. The investor has a degree of protection because certain conditions are implied in this type of agreement—namely, that the corporation will be completely organized, that the full amount of the capital stock will be subscribed, and that the articles and bylaws will be as stated at the time of the subscription. Otherwise, the subscriber will not be liable on his agreement.

A subscription to stock made after incorporation is a contract between the subscriber and the corporation. The contract may come into existence by virtue of either an offer made by the corporation and accepted by the subscriber or an offer made by the subscriber and accepted by the corporation. The subscriber becomes a shareholder from the moment his offer is accepted by the corporation, regardless of when the stock certificate is executed and delivered.

SHAREHOLDERS' RIGHTS

Shareholder's rights are determined by state statutes, articles of incorporation, and bylaws. In general, they are designed either to induce or to protect the investment. Three basic rights of all shareholders are: (1) the right to share in such dividends as may be distributed; (2) the right to have a claim against the assets of the corporation; and (3) the right to vote.

RIGHT TO DIVIDENDS

As a rule, shareholders have no claim to dividends until they are declared. Once declared, dividends cannot be rescinded, and the shareholder assumes the vested rights of a creditor. A court of equity may, upon appeal by the shareholders of a corporation, order the directors to make a dividend distribution where it is shown the directors have, without justification, refused to declare a dividend.

The majority of states consider a dividend proper when it does not impair the capital stock of the corporation. A declaration that reduces the net assets of the corporation below the outstanding capital stock is illegal. Earned surplus, therefore, is generally the basis for declaring a dividend. Surplus created by the appraisal of fixed assets usually can be used only for stock dividends. Some states require that dividends be declared only out of net profits. Capital surplus and appraisal surplus cannot be used for dividends in these states. In general, dividends can be declared only when provision has been made for all expenses. Dividends cannot be declared on the mere expectation of profits, nor if the corporation is insolvent or will become insolvent as a result of the dividend. Dividends customarily are paid in cash, but may also be in the form of stock. The amount received depends on the number of shares held by the individual.

CLAIM TO ASSETS

Upon the winding up of corporate business, the shareholder has a right to his proportionate share of corporate assets remaining after all debts have been paid. If there are classes of stock outstanding, each shareholder within a class will share pro rata with others in his class, but the rights of the class will be determined from the state statutes, the articles of incorporation, and the bylaws.

RIGHT TO VOTE

As stated, shareholders participate in management by attending stockholders' meetings and by voting their stock to elect a board of directors who, in turn, appoint officers to carry on the everyday business of the corporation. Unless otherwise stated in the articles of incorporation, the state statutes, or the bylaws, each share of stock entitles the holder to one vote. Shareholders may vote by proxy; proxies are revokable unless coupled with an interest.

PROTECTION OF THE INVESTMENT

The following rights are of primary importance in protecting the investor's basic rights to dividends, assets, and participation in management:

Right to a stock certificate. Since a shareholder must be in a position to prove his ownership of his shares, corporate law stipulates that shareholders must be given a stock certificate as evidence of ownership. Where this evidence is lost or destroyed, he may demand a new certificate from the corporation.

Right to transfer stock. As a rule, a shareholder is entitled to transfer his stock whenever and to whomever he desires. However, restrictions are sometimes placed upon transfer. For example, if a shareholder wishes to sell shares, he may first have to offer them for sale to the corporation or to the present shareholders. This practice is more common in the smaller closely held corporations. It is rather impractical in the large manufacturing corporations. All rights that accompany the ownership of shares remain with the original holder until a transfer of ownership has been completed on the books of the corporation.

Preemptive rights. When the corporation issues new stock, existing shareholders usually have the right to subscribe to a percentage of these shares equal to the percentage their present holdings constitute of the former total of capital stock. This right enables each shareholder to maintain his relative interest of ownership in the firm. However, he does not have to exercise this right. It may be sold, transferred, or merely not used. Preemptive rights apply only to new issues of an existing class of stock and not to past issues. They may be denied to shareholders by the articles of incorporation or by the state statute.

Right to inspect the corporation's books. A shareholder of a corporation has the right to inspect the books of the corporation for a proper purpose, at a proper time and place. Most courts hold that this right cannot be exercised where its purpose is improper or unlawful or merely to satisfy idle curiosity.

Right to prevent wrongful actions. A shareholder may bring a suit in equity to enjoin the officers of a corporation from entering into ultra vires contracts or from any action that would impair the shareholder's rights in corporate assets.

SHAREHOLDERS' LIABILITY

One of the most attractive features of the corporate form of enterprise is the limited liability of shareholders. Generally, shareholders are liable only to the extent of their investment, although there are exceptions to this rule.

A shareholder's liability to the corporation for the purchase price of the stock depends upon the contract between the corporation and the shareholder. Once the corporation accepts a subscription contract and delivers the shares of stock, the shareholder is liable for the price agreed upon. If, at the time the stock is issued, the full agreed price is paid and the stock is issued as fully paid and non-assessable, the corporation cannot collect any additional amount from the shareholder. Nor, if a shareholder holds fully paid, non-assessable stock, is he personally liable to the creditors of the corporation.

Any liability of the shareholder to creditors must be based on: (1) an obligation owed to the corporation; (2) a liability created by statute; (3) a wrongful withdrawal of assets from the corporation that causes injury to creditors; or (4) a wrongful failure to contribute to the capital of the corporation. For example, when the corporation becomes insolvent or is adjudged bankrupt, a shareholder is liable for any unpaid balance on the subscription price of his stock. If the stock is assessable, the shareholder is liable for any lawful assessment made on his stock. Holders of par value shares that were issued at a discount are liable to the corporation's creditors for the amount of the discount. Any debt owed by the shareholder to the corporation is an asset of the corporation available for the payment of creditors.

Where dividends are paid unlawfully, the shareholders are liable to the corporation's creditors in case of bankruptcy for the amount paid out unlawfully, or as much thereof as is necessary to satisfy the claims of creditors. Some states provide that in order for a shareholder to be liable on unlawful dividends, he must know that they were unlawfully declared and must have accepted them in bad faith. Generally, all shareholders of record are liable to creditors if the circumstances are such that liability for the benefit of creditors is imposed.

SHAREHOLDERS' REMEDIES

Shareholders have four basic means of remedying corporate weaknesses or mismanagement: (1) they may elect new directors if they feel that the existing management is not adequate; (2) they may bring an individual suit if their individual rights are impaired; (3) they may enjoin management from illegal activities; or (4) they may bring a derivative suit in equity to enforce a corporate cause of action.

A shareholder may sue the corporation in his individual capacity as a shareholder if the corporation has deprived him of any rights that naturally accrue to him as a shareholder. For example, he may bring suit if his voting rights are denied or in any way impaired. He may also bring suit if the corporation has failed to carry out an agreement to repurchase or redeem his shares.

The shareholders have the right to demand that the capital of a corporation not be subjected to risks not provided for in the charter. An individual shareholder may bring suit to enjoin the directors, officers, or agents of a corporation from engaging in conduct that would impair the corporate assets, if the directors, officers, or agents are acting outside the scope of their authority, are guilty of negligent conduct, or are engaging, or about to engage, in fraudulent activities with other shareholders that would be injurious to the corporation.

Such a suit is said to be "derivative" because the shareholder has no individual rights against these persons for neglect and mismanagement resulting in damages to the corporation. It is a corporate cause of action.

If the directors refuse to follow up on a breach of contract action in favor of the corporation, shareholders may file a derivative suit in equity, claiming that the corporation has a cause of action and the directors refuse to act on it. The first step is to request that the directors bring the action. This step may be dispensed with if it would be meaningless because all the directors or a majority of them are involved in the alleged wrongful conduct. The basis of the suit is an action for specific enforcement of an obligation to protect their interests as shareholders of the corporation. Whether there is a cause of action will depend on whether the corporation's assets have been wasted or its business is being interfered with because of a wrongful act. In order to be a party to the suit, a shareholder must have been a shareholder at the time the events that are alleged to have given the corporation a cause of action against a third party occurred. Since it is a corporate cause of action, any judgment received is for the benefit of the corporation; a shareholder usually is permitted to recover only expenses involved in the litigation.

LEGAL PRINCIPLES

A share of stock is evidence of a profit sharing contract between the owner and the corporation.

The most common method of acquiring ownership is through purchase.

Pre-incorporation subscriptions are regarded as continuing offers to purchase.

The basic rights of a shareholder are the right to share in dividends, to have a claim against the corporate assets, and to vote.

A dividend that will render the corporation insolvent is illegal.

A shareholder may be liable for the unpaid purchase price of his stock.

The basic remedy of the shareholder is a derivative suit.

CASE FOR REVIEW

STOKES v. CONTINENTAL TRUST CO.

78 N.E. 1090 (1906)

. . . The question presented . . . is whether according to the facts found the plaintiff had the legal right to subscribe for and take the same number of shares of the new stock that he held of the old?

. . . If the right claimed by the plaintiff was a right of property belonging to him as a stockholder he could not be deprived of it by the joint action of the other stockholders and of all the directors and officers of the corporation.

What is the nature of the right acquired by a stockholder through the ownership of shares of stock? What rights can he assert against the will of a majority of the stockholders and all the officers and directors? While he does not own and can not dispose of any specific property of the corporation, yet he and his associates own the corporation itself, its charter, franchises and all rights conferred thereby, including the right to increase the stock. He has an inherent right to his proportionate share of any dividend declared, or of any surplus arising upon dissolution, and he can prevent waste or misappropriation of the property of the corporation by those in control. Finally, he has the right to vote for directors and upon all propositions subject by law to the control of the stockholders, and this is his supreme right and main protection. Stockholders have no direct voice in transacting the corporate business, but through their right to vote they can select those to whom the law intrusts the power of management and control.

A corporation is somewhat like a partnership, if one were possible, conducted wholly by agents where the co-partners have power to appoint the agents, but are not responsible for their acts. The power to manage its affairs resides in the directors, who are its agents, but the power to elect directors resides in the stockholders. This right to vote for directors and upon propositions to increase the stock or mortgage the assets, is about all the power the stockholder has. So long as the management is honest, within the corporate powers and involves no waste, the stockholders can not interfere, even if the administration is feeble and unsatisfactory, but must correct such evils through their power to elect other directors. Hence, the power of the individual stockholder to vote in proportion to the number of his shares, is vital and can not be cut off or curtailed by the action of all the other stockholders even with the cooperation of the directors and officers. . . .

We are thus led to lay down the rule that a stockholder has an inherent right to a proportionate share of new stock issued for money only and not to purchase property for the purposes of the corporation or to effect a consolidation, and while he can waive that right, he can not be deprived of it without his consent except when the stock is issued at a fixed price not less than par and he is given the right to take at that price in proportion to his holding, or in some other equitable way that will enable him to protect his interest by acting on his own judgment and using his own resources. . . .

The remaining question is whether the plaintiff waived his rights by failing to do what he ought to have done, or by doing something he ought not to have done. He demanded his share of the new stock at par, instead of at the price fixed by the stockholders, for the authorization to sell at $450 a share was virtually fixing the price of the stock. He did more than this, however, for he not only voted against the proposition to sell to Blair 9 Company at $450, but as the court expressly found, he "protested against the proposed sale of his proportionate share of the stock and again demanded the right to subscribe and pay for the same, which demands were again refused," and "the resolution was carried notwithstanding such protest and demands." Thus he protested against the sale of his share before the price was fixed, for the same resolution fixed the price and directed the sale, which was promptly carried into effect. If he had not attended the meeting, called upon due notice to do precisely what was done, perhaps he would have waived his rights, but he attended the meeting and before the price was fixed demanded the right to subscribe for two hundred and twenty one shares at par and offered to pay for the same immediately. It is true that after the price was fixed he did not offer to take his share at that price, but he did not acquiesce in the sale of his proportion to Blair & Company, and unless he acquiesced the sale as to him was without right. He was under no obligation to put the corporation in default by making a demand. The ordinary doctrine of demand, tender and refusal has no application to this case. The plaintiff had made no contract. He had not promised to do anything. No duty of performance rested upon him. He had an absolute right to the new stock in proportion to his holding of the old and he gave notice that he wanted it. It was his property and could not be disposed of without his consent. He did not consent. He protested in due time, and the sale was made in defiance of his protest. While in connection with his protest he demanded the right to subscribe at par, that demand was entirely proper when made, because the price had not then been fixed. After the price was fixed it was the duty of the defendant to offer him his proportion at that price, for it had notice that he had not acquiesced in the proposed sale of his share, but wanted it himself. The directors were under the legal obligation to give him an opportunity to purchase at the price fixed before they could sell his property to a third party, even with the approval of a large majority of the stockholders. If he had remained silent and had made no request or protest he would have waived his rights, but after he had given notice that he wanted his part and had protested against the sale thereof, the defendant was bound to offer it to him at the price fixed by the stockholders. By selling to strangers without thus offering to sell to him, the defendant wrongfully deprived him of his property and is liable for such damages as he actually sustained.

CASE PROBLEMS

1. Smyth was a promoter of a corporation about to enter the grain business. Davis in a telegram to Smyth promised to subscribe for $20,000 in shares of stock in the corporation yet to be formed. The directors met, accepted the subscription after the corporation was formed, and sued Davis on his subscription promise. Davis set up a defense that before the corporation was formed he told Smyth that his offer to subscribe for stock was withdrawn. Decide.
2. Hansen, a stockholder of the Marble Corporation, applied for an order granting him an inspection of the books and the corporate records. The application was contested on the ground that Hansen was not entitled to the relief because he was engaged in a competing business. Decide.
3. French, appointed receiver of Manufacturing Company in an action to establish its insolvency and force stockholders to pay for unpaid stock, sued Harding on the ground that his shares had never been fully paid. Harding shows that he is not an original subscriber, having bought the stock on the market through a broker. He states further that he did not know it was unpaid. Decide.
4. Miners' Bank, plaintiff, brings an action against the Gustin Company to require payment of a debt by contribution on defendant's alleged stockholder's liability. The bank was aware, when it loaned the money, that some stock was issued at one-tenth of par value, and some for nothing. Defendants deny that a creditor can enforce stockholders' liability in full where the underpayment of stock was known when the debt was created. Decide.
5. Cagey Corporation had been in business for several years and was in need of cash. It decided to issue new stock for sale to the public. The par value of each share of the new issue was $10 but this stock was given to brokers to be sold at whatever

the market would bring. The entire issue was sold for an average of $5 per share. Cagey became insolvent and Farrell was appointed receiver. Farrell sued all the shareholders of this new issue of stock, contending that the stock was watered and that they were liable to make up the difference between what they paid and the $10 par value per share. Decide.

6. The stockholders of Blocke, Inc. passed a bylaw which required that all stockholders, as a condition precedent to a right to inspect the books of the corporation, give at lease three months notice before the proposed inspection. It also provided that the purpose of such inspection must be approved by the board of directors. Pokey, a stockholder, demanded the right to inspect the books within two weeks and stated that his purpose for inspection was a proper one. The demand was refused by the directors under the above bylaw. Pokey sought a writ of mandamus to compel the officers and directors to permit his inspection of the books. Decide.

7. The stockholders of Fixit Corporation passed a bylaw providing that "the shares of stock held by a stockholder, Miller, shall have no voting rights." Miller was the owner of one hundred shares of common stock. Prior to the above bylaw all such common stock had voting rights. Miller had been a constant troublemaker in stockholders' meetings and the stockholders thought he would not attend such meetings if his voting rights were taken away. Miller sued to enjoin the stockholders from denying him the right to vote at stockholders meetings. Decide.

8. Plaintiff, a stockholder in Madison Company, brought an action to obtain a grant of proportionate right to an increase in capital stock and to enjoin defendants, the directors, from completing sale of the increased stock to others without offering it to him. Decide.

A corporation is considered a "domestic" corporation in the state or country that has granted its charter; it is a "foreign" corporation in all other jurisdictions. It is a citizen and a resident of the state of its incorporation and has no legal existence beyond the state's boundaries. A corporation cannot change at will either its residence or its citizenship.

A corporation has a right to transact intrastate business in the state of its incorporation. What powers it may exercise in other states will depend on whether its corporate activities are interstate (between the several states) or intrastate (within the state) in nature. Under the commerce clause of the federal Constitution, Congress is given exclusive jurisdiction over "commerce between the several states" and over foreign commerce. Consequently, a corporation engaged strictly in interstate commerce has the right to transact such business in the several states without undue interference from the states. These corporations are, however, subject to the police power regulations in the states in which they conduct their business. They must comply with any laws concerning public health, public morals, public safety, and public welfare.

The right of a foreign corporation to carry on business that is wholly intrastate is left entirely with the states. The right to do business as a corporation is a privilege granted by the state creating the corporation. A state cannot grant privileges beyond its territorial jurisdiction. Jurisdictional limitations do not ordinarily affect citizens of the United States, who are protected by the privileges and immunities clause of the federal Constitution, which guarantees that their rights as citizens of one state will be recognized in all other states. However, the Supreme Court has held many times that a corporation is not a "citizen" in the sense in which the term is used in this context in the Constitution. Thus the privileges and immunities clause does not apply to corporations. Their rights, such as the right to do business, will not be recognized in any state other than the state of incorporation unless the state expressly grants such recognition. A corporation is recognized, or licensed, to carry on intrastate business in the foreign state usually by obtaining a certificate from the secretary of state and paying a stipulated fee. The states also have the power to impose conditions upon foreign corporations, even though domestic corporations are not similarly burdened. These regulations are designed to ensure that domestic corporations will not be put at a competitive disadvantage by the foreign corporations.

CONSTITUTIONAL LIMITATIONS

There are constitutional limitations on the states' power to exclude foreign corporations or impose conditions on them. For example, under the commerce clause, state laws cannot unduly burden interstate or foreign commerce. They cannot impose discriminatory taxes on capital stock, nor can they, as a privilege of admission, prohibit access to federal courts, deny due process or equal protection of the law, regulate the making of contracts, or take property without due process. In general, a state cannot impose any restrictions on a foreign corporation it has admitted to do interstate business that violate the corporation's constitutional rights. Once it is licensed by the state to carry on business, it is fully protected by the Constitution.

A state has the right to deny foreign corporations the right to carry on within the state types of business in which domestic corporations are not permitted to engage, even though such businesses are within the chartered powers of the foreign corporation. The state can require that foreign corporations obtain a license and pay a reasonable franchise fee. It can require that foreign corporations post a bond with a state official to ensure performance of its contracts; and it can require foreign corporations to designate a resident agent upon whom service of summons may be made until the statute of limitations has run on all business done in the state. Again, the only limitation imposed on a state in this regard is that it cannot exact conditions that would arbitrarily interfere with rights guaranteed a corporation by the federal Constitution.

Because state incorporation statutes vary, a firm may find it to its advantage to incorporate under the laws of a state in which it has no intention of conducting business. For example, a group of men desiring to manufacture and sell swimwear might incorporate in Delaware, a state known for its liberal incorporation laws, although they intended to manufacture and market their product in California. The corporation would be bound under California statutes regarding foreign corporations and would be a domestic corporation in Delaware.

DOING BUSINESS

No exact definition can be given the term "doing business." There are no precise requirements as to the nature or extent of the business that must be done, although the Model Foreign Corporation Act can be used as a guide to determine whether a corporation is in fact "doing business" within a state. According to the Act, a foreign corporation is "doing business" when "some part of its business substantial and continuous in character and not merely casual or occasional" is transacted within a state. The Act further states that a corporation is not "doing business" in a state merely because it is involved in a single transaction, is prosecuting or defending lawsuits, is collecting debts or accepting evidence of security of debts, has a resident agent, owns property, or is doing anything related to the management or control of internal affairs. The Act also states that a foreign corporation shall not be required to obtain a license to do business or to file amended articles by reason of the fact that it has a mail-order house or has salesmen within or offices within the state.

A corporation can engage in interstate commerce without obtaining permission from the state. It can buy goods in another state to be shipped to its own state and it can sell goods in its own state to be shipped into another state.

It can solicit business in another state either by mail or by resident salesmen so long as the contract to sell or the sale is made in the home state. A corporation does not conduct business in the jurisdictional sense in the absence of continuous and systematic solicitation within a state. For example, the borrowing of money from a local bank is a transaction that constitutes business for the lender but not for the borrower.

Any preliminary act or act that leads toward future business transactions in the state is not considered "doing business." Where a foreign corporation acquires the stock of a domestic corporation and exercises the rights of stockholders, it is not considered to be "doing business," unless through stock ownership the domestic corporation is controlled by the foreign corporation and in reality is acting as its agent. To be "doing business' implies corporate continuity of conduct, evidenced by the investment of capital, maintenance of an office to transact business, and those incidental circumstances that attest the corporation's intent to carry on business.

FAILURE TO COMPLY WITH
REQUIREMENTS FOR ADMISSION

States have been given the authority to impose conditions on foreign corporations in order to protect their citizens from dishonest and fraudulent corporations. A state may deny the privilege of conducting business to a corporation that refuses to comply with these conditions.

A corporation that conducts business within a state without complying with its regulations for foreign corporations may be denied access to the local courts as a plaintiff and yet be subject to suit. This prevents enforcement of contracts made with local residents in matters in which the corporation acted as a local business. However, a third party may hold the corporation who has failed to comply with state requirements but has done business within the state liable on executory contracts. Neither party may bring action on a completed contract. Suits brought by stockholders against directors regarding the internal management of the corporation must be brought in the courts of the state in which the corporation is classified as a domestic corporation.

In addition, personal penalties may be imposed upon shareholders, directors and officers of a foreign corporation doing business without a license. These include personal liability for corporate obligations, fines, and in some instances, arrest and imprisonment.

LEGAL PRINCIPLES

A corporation is a domestic corporation in the state of its incorporation; it is a foreign corporation in all other jurisdictions.

States may exclude or impose limitations on foreign corporations, subject to constitutional limitations.

Once admitted to do business, a corporation may not be unduly burdened by legal requirements in competition with domestic corporations.

The definition of "doing business" varies with situations, although the stipulations of the Model Corporation Act are generally used as a guide.

Foreign corporations who fail to comply with the regulations of the state where they are doing business may be denied access to local courts as plaintiffs, although they may be subject to suit.

CASE FOR REVIEW

ULMER v. FIRST NATIONAL BANK OF ST. PETERSBURG

55 S. 405 (Fla. 1911)

Sections 1 and 4 of chapter 5717, [the Corporation Act], provide:

> that no foreign corporation shall transact business, or acquire, hold or dispose of property in this state until it shall have filed in the office of the Secretary of State a duly authenticated copy of its charter or articles of incorporation, and shall have received from him a permit to transact business in this state.
>
> Every contract made by or on behalf of any foreign corporation affecting its liability or relating to property within the state before it shall have complied with the provisions of this act shall be void on its behalf and on behalf of its assigns, but shall be enforceable against it or them.

While a state may not impose conditions upon the right of corporations legally authorized by Congress to do business in the state or may not place unlawful burdens upon the interstate business of a foreign corporation lawfully in the state, yet the state may exclude foreign corporations or impose upon them conditions for doing business in the state where it does not conflict with federal laws. A corporation is not a "citizen" within the provision of section 2, art. 4, of the federal Constitution that "the citizens of each state shall be entitled to all privileges and immunities of citizens in the several states," or within the provision of the fourteenth amendment that "no state shall make or enforce any law which shall abridge the privileges or immunities of citizens of the United States."

It is within the power and duty of the state to prevent imposition or injustice from being practiced within its territory, and to provide for the general welfare of its people. To this end it may require all foreign corporations to file their charters and to get a permit before they can do any business, or acquire, hold, or dispose of any property in the state. This does not deny to such foreign corporations any right secured to them by the state or federal organic law, since it is not an unjust discrimination, is not a denial of due process of law or the equal protection of the laws, and is not an unlawful regulation of or burden upon interstate or foreign commerce.

The statute above quoted is within the police power of the state. It does not conflict with federal regulations of or impose unlawful burdens upon interstate or foreign commerce. It does not deny to the foreign corporation any right secured to it by the state or federal Constitution; and it does not appear to have been enacted in violation of organic law.

A corporation existing under the laws of another state is a foreign corporation in Florida within the meaning of the statute.

If the statute has been violated by the foreign corporation in acquiring the note or in making a contract of which the note is a part, the corporation cannot enforce the payment of the note in the courts of the state; and if the note was taken by the indorsee bank with notice of and subject to its infirmities under the existing laws, the bank cannot recover through the courts.

It is admitted that the note was given to the payees as agents for a foreign corporation for shares of its capital stock, that the foreign corporation had not complied with the laws of this state, in that it had not filed in the office of the Secretary of State a duly authenticated copy of its charter or articles of incorporation, and had not received from the said Secretary of State a permit to transact business in this state, when the promissory note sued on was given to its agents for the purchase of its capital stock, and that the plaintiff bank took the note with notice of its imfirmities. It is further admitted that the note was executed in Florida as part consideration for a contract entered into in Florida on behalf of the foreign corporation to deliver certain shares of its capital stock. This shows a contract made in the state on behalf of the foreign corporation affecting its liability, if it does not also show a transaction of business in this state and the acquisition and disposal of property in this state within the meaning of the statute. The making of such contract in the state on behalf of the foreign corporation violates the statute, and the note, a part of the contract or transaction, will not be enforced by the courts of the state. . . . The transaction is not covered by any federal regulation of interstate or foreign commerce, and the statute forbidding it is not an unlawful burden upon interstate or foreign commerce; therefore no question of regulating or imposing a burden upon interstate commerce is presented, since the state may regulate the terms on which a foreign corporation may contract or do business in the state where no federal regulation is interfered with, and no unlawful burden is put upon interstate or foreign commerce.

CASE PROBLEMS

1. Automotive Material Company, an Illinois corporation, acquired some stock in Fixit, Inc., a Wisconsin firm. AMC made loans and took mortgages in Wisconsin. It maintained an office in Wisconsin to pay debts and to adjust claims and appointed an agent to conduct future business. It was alleged that the bank was doing a local business. Decide.

2. U.S. Rubber Company, plaintiff, is a New Jersey corporation that shipped merchandise to its agent, Butler Shoe Company, a Colorado corporation engaged in the wholesale shoe business. Butler, defendant, was to receive goods, assume the risk, and advance funds against the goods in stock, but to keep a separate account as a "consignee account." Upon Butler's defaulting in large sums and refusing to remit, plaintiff sued for an accounting and a receiver to take over the property. Defendant claimed, that plaintiff has not qualified to do business in Colorado as a foreign corporation and consequently has no right to sue in the courts. Decide.

3. Mulford Company, a foreign corporation, petitioned the court to order Curry, secretary of state, defendant, to accept and file its petition for a license to do business in the state. Defendant refused the petition because it was not accompanied by the fee required by statute, a license tax based on the total authorized capital stock of the corporation. Plaintiff claimed that the levying of a license tax upon a foreign corporation imposes a direct burden upon interstate commerce, in violation of the Constitution of the United States. Decide.

4. Plaintiff corporation sued defendants for rental payments on its lease of a linotype machine. The defense was that plaintiff was not entitled to sue because it had not obtained a license to do business in Missouri. Plaintiff did not have an office or place of business in Missouri but did have a traveling salesman there, who had obtained from defendants a lease of a linotype machine with an option to purchase. The lease was approved and executed by plaintiff at its home office in New York. Plaintiff furnished a competent machinist to set up the machine in defendants' shop in Missouri and to instruct defendants' employees in the method of operation. However, the lease expressly provided that the machinist, while so employed, was to be an employee of defendants and that they were to pay his salary and expenses. Decide.

5. Plibrico, an Illinois corporation manufacturing and selling firebrick, marketed this product in New England through the Wilder Company, a Massachusetts firm, under contract as a marketing agent. The latter was to solicit sales and supervise at its own expense installations of firebrick furnished by Plibrico; carry that company's name in the telephone directory and on the office door; send orders to Plibrico for acceptance as to terms; have all orders billed directly to the customer by Plibrico and collected by it; receive from that company remittances from customers minus the price of the firebrick; and correspond with customers on Plibrico stationery. In defense to suit by Plibrico for work and materials, it was urged that Plibrico was doing local business without compliance with the Foreign Corporation law. Decide.

6. Fannie Speed, by her will, gave certain real estate in Chicago to the Kentucky Methodist Episcopal Church, a Kentucky corporation, with authority to begin an educational fund for education and religion promotion in Kentucky. According to the Illinois Inheritance Tax Law, property devised to the use of religious, educational, or charitable corporations is exempt from inheritance tax. The estate claimed that the gift came within the law. The state of Illinois alleged that this exemption did not apply to gifts to foreign corporations, and that the estate should pay the inheritance tax. Decide.

7. In Alabama a statute provided that all contracts made by a foreign corporation within the state without first procuring a license to do business therein, are void. Builder Corporation, a Mississippi corporation, without first obtaining a license to do business in Alabama, made a contract to put a new roof on Cagey's house in Alabama. The roof was put on but Cagey refused to pay for it. Builder sued and Cagey alleged that the contract was void.

8. In order to obtain permission to transact business in South Dakota, Meridian Insurance Company, an Indiana corporation, agreed that in any action brought against it in South Dakota, service of process could be made upon the South Dakota insurance commissioner with the same effect as if the corporation were actually served. Thomson, beneficiary of a policy issued by the company in Texas to a Texas resident, sued on the policy in South Dakota and made service on the insurance commissioner. The company then objected that a state could not constitutionally compel a foreign corporation to appoint the insurance commissioner as its agent for service with respect to lawsuits brought on foreign causes of action. Decide.

TERMINATION, CONSOLIDATION, AND MERGER

36

If the articles of incorporation specify that a corporation is to exist for a certain period, the life of the corporation terminates automatically at the end of that period. An extension may be granted upon application to the state, where such extensions are authorized by statute. In the absence of a provision limiting corporate existence, most corporations have perpetual duration— they continue until dissolution or their charters are annulled by the states of incorporation. Unlike a partnership, a corporation cannot merely sell its assets, pay its creditors, distribute the proceeds to its members, and consider itself dissolved. Procedures for dissolution are authorized in the state statutes. Dissolution may be authorized by formal resolution of the board of directors, by vote of the shareholders, or both. In all authorized terminations, the corporation must file a certificate of dissolution, cease business, wind up its affairs, and publish notice of its dissolution.

INVOLUNTARY DISSOLUTION

A quo warranto proceeding may be employed by the state of incorporation, to test the right of a corporation to continue its corporate life. The state attorney general may dissolve a corporation by ordering a forfeit of its charter for the following reasons: (1) misconduct or defects incident to the formation of the corporation; (2) failure to comply with an express condition in its charter; (3) any abuse or misuse of corporate powers after incorporation; (4) abandonment of the principal place of business; or (5) ceasing to do business.

VOLUNTARY DISSOLUTION

A minority shareholder or group of shareholders can ask for quo warranto proceedings to dissolve the corporation on grounds of: (1) abandonment of the corporate functions by the directors (the failure of the officers to begin or to continue business activities); (2). failure to make a profit; (3) failure on the part of management to establish working relations between management and the shareholders; (4) any fraudulent activities by the officers, such as willful withholding of dividends or an attempt to "freeze out" minority shareholders (forcing them to sell their shares). It should be noted that the courts will usually apply a test of "fairness" with respect to the actions of the majority shareholders when there is a complaint of this type. If the action of the majority affects voting and preemptive rights, rights to dividends and percentage of ownership, the courts will consider that there are valid grounds for the action taken by the minority.

INSOLVENCY

Insolvency does not automatically dissolve a corporation. At the request of corporate creditors, a receiver may be appointed to liquidate the firm's assets and distribute the proceeds to creditors to pay off corporate debts. However, until a formal dissolution is ordered by the court, the corporation continues in existence and the creditors may pursue other remedies to compel payment.

EFFECTS OF DISSOLUTION

Dissolution has the following effects on a corporation: (1) its legal existence is terminated; (2) it becomes a de facto corporation during the winding-up period; (3) any litigation in which it is involved is abated (although the power to be sued may be reinstated against trustees appointed to wind up the business).

Dissolution does not terminate any liability of the corporation to creditors. Creditors, and then bondholders, have first claim on firm assets upon dissolution; shareholders receive the remaining assets (normally, perferred shareholders are paid before common shareholders). If the corporation does not have enough money to pay creditors, the shareholders, because of their limited liability, are under no obligation to pay off the debts. However, anyone who purchased stock from the corporation at a discount might be required to repay the amount of the discount. Ordinarily, the full purchase price of the stock is the limit of the shareholders' liability.

CONSOLIDATION AND MERGER OF CORPORATE POWER

Corporations may combine in two ways: (1) *consolidation,* in which the original corporations cease to exist and a new corporation is formed; and (2) *merger,* when one corporation absorbs another corporation but retains its corporate identity.

PROCEDURE FOR MERGER AND CONSOLIDATION

Authorization for a merger or consolidation must come from the same state that created the constituent corporations. Without this authorization an attempted consolidation or merger is ultra vires and without effect. The procedures for accomplishing a consolidation or merger are detailed in the state statutes. The corporations involved in a merger must prepare a proposal. For consolidation new articles must be drawn up by the directors (or possibly by representatives of the stockholders) of the respective corporations. The articles or the proposal must be submitted to the stockholders of the constituent corporations, who vote separately on the combination. The decision must be accepted by a majority of the shareholders at a properly called shareholders' meeting; a union cannot be effected merely by the action of the board of directors. Creditors of the constituent corporations have no voice in the decision to consolidate or merge.

A new corporation does not result from the transfer, sale, or lease of the assets from one corporation to the other. Nor does a transfer of all its property and franchises dissolve the corporation because a corporation can exist without assets or franchises. Likewise, the fact that one corporation own: all the stock of another corporation does not constitute a consolidation or merger.

RESULTS OF CONSOLIDATION AND OF MERGER

The corporation resulting from a consolidation or merger acquires all the property, rights, powers, franchises, and debts and obligations of the constituent corporations. Any mortgaged property passing to the new or continuing corporation makes that corporation liable for its payment. The rights and powers of the new corporation include: (1) the right to charge a certain price for goods or services or a certain rate for transportation; (2) the right to sue the officers of the consolidating or merging corporations; and (3) the right to the benefits of a patent licensed to one of the constituent corporations.

Consolidation or merger gives the shareholders of the former companies the right to become shareholders of the new firm by surrendering their old shares in return for new ones at a predetermined ratio. When a shareholder will not accept stock in the new corporation, he must be paid compensation for his stock equivalent to its fair market value before the consolidation or merger took place. In other words, shareholders normally have the right to dissent and refuse to join in the proposed transaction and to have their shares valued and paid out in cash. Since the procedure is statutory, the modes of valuation differ among the states. A dissent of a substantial number of shareholders, however, may defeat the proposed merger or consolidation. For example, if the amount required to pay the dissenting shareholders would result in a drain of cash that would prevent one of the companies from carrying out its agreement, a proposed merger or consolidation would be defeated.

LEGAL PRINCIPLES

A corporation will last indefinitely if its duration is not limited by its articles of incorporation.

Procedures of dissolution are authorized by the state statutes. A formal resolution by the board of directors or a vote of the shareholders or both may be required.

The state attorney general may bring quo warranto proceedings to challenge the existence of the corporation.

A consolidation occurs when old corporations are dissolved and a new corporation is formed.

A merger occurs when one corporation absorbs another without either losing its identity.

A majority vote of shareholders may accomplish consolidation, merger, or termination of corporate power.

A substantial number of shareholders may defeat a proposed merger or consolidation.

CASE FOR REVIEW

BOWDITCH v. JACKSON CO.

76 N.H. 351 (1912)

Bowditch and other minority stockholders of the Jackson Company seek to enjoin a sale of its assets to the Nashua Manufacturing Company. The question arises whether a majority of the stockholders have a right to sell the corporate assets, and consequently dissolve the Company against the protest of the minority.

The main question in this case is whether a going business corporation can be closed out and dissolved upon the motion of the majority of its stockholders and against the protest of the minority. The plain common sense of the matter is that this is a business venture, to be carried on as such so long as it appears to be good business judgment to do so. When the time comes that a majority in interest believe that their affairs should be wound up and the proceeds distributed, the rational rule is that this should be done. And since the question here is of a business nature, and the limitations of the power of the majority are fixed by the understanding of the business men who made the original compact, business considerations have more than ordinary weight in determining what the contract was. It is admitted on all sides that the majority may sell out if the corporation is insolvent. If insolvency is imminent, action may be taken. And the same is true if it is imprudent to continue. One reason only is given why the power exists in these cases; it is reasonable to suppose that such authority was contemplated, because this is what sound business judgment dictates should be done. The difference between these cases and the present one is of degree only, not of kind.

If the majority may sell to prevent greater losses, why may they not also sell to make greater gains? Bearing in mind that this is purely a business proposition, with no public rights or duties involved, there seems to be no substantial difference between the two cases, as a matter of principle. In each case, the sale is made because it is of advantage to the stockholders. Whether the profit to be made is a reasonable one must be a relative matter. Three percent when others make two might be reasonable; but 3 percent when a sale could be made which would yield the stockholder ten could hardly be thought an investment a reasonable person would retain. The loss to the stockholder by a failure to sell out on a basis which would yield him 10 percent instead of the three he is receiving is in fact much greater than it would be if a concern went on neither making nor losing when the investment would earn four percent elsewhere. It does not seem reasonable that the majority should have power to make a sale in the latter case, and not in the former. In neither case would the sale prevent positive loss, but in each it would result in positive gain. And the question is one of future prospects. Its decision requires the exercise of business judgment, sagacity, and power to forecast coming events. It is not an issue appropriate for trial and decision in courts, but rather one to be settled by the judgment of the men conducting the business in question. In a limited sense, the majority act as trustees, for all the stockholders. When their acts are impugned by the minority, it is not the function of the court to set its judgment against theirs in settling the wisdom or policy of proposed action. By the contract of association, all questions of this nature were committed to the majority for final decision.

CASE PROBLEMS

1. The Newark Telephone Company's charter expired in 1968 and McCarter was appointed receiver. To wind up its affairs, he sold the property to the Friendship Telephone Company. The city of Newark attacked this conveyance on the ground that the court had no power to direct a sale after the termination of the charter. Decide.
2. Defendant corporation entered into a merger agreement never consented to by plaintiff, owner of one hundred shares of defendant's stock. Plaintiff brought suit, seeking a restraining order and a decree that, if plaintiff was paid the full market value of the stock, the restraint would be discontinued. Defendant replied that the agreement was submitted to a properly called meeting attended by holders of more than half the stock, who unanimously adopted the resolution. Decide.
3. When the stockholders of American Can Company, defendant, voted to transfer the assets of the corporation, plaintiff dissented and exercised his statutory right to be bought out by being paid the "full and fair value" of his shares. Plaintiff appealed the determination of the value of the shares given by an appraiser, claiming that he should be paid the market value of the stock. Decide.
4. Plaintiff brought an action to test whether a going business corporation can be closed out and dissolved upon the motion of the majority of its stockholders, but against the protest of the minority, including plaintiff. Decide.
5. Mining, Inc. was authorized by its charter to engage in the business of mining. It had surplus capital and the directors invested it in buying trucks for rental purposes. This business was ultra vires, however, the trucks were in good condition and were rented for standard prices. The attorney general brought suit against the corporation to compel forfeiture of its charter for doing ultra vires business. Decide.
6. Plaintiff instituted this action in 1971 against Streator Company, an Illinois corporation, to recover for an action arising in Illinois. It was shown that in 1963 the state of Illinois moved to dissolve the Streator Company, and the decree was entered. The defendant claimed the dissolution as a defense against the 1971 action. Decide.
7. Plaintiff trust company brought an action to foreclose a mortgage on the Orient Railroad. The Western Union company intervened, seeking a hearing on general claims that it held against the railroad. Western Union alleged that the stockholders and bondholders planned a sale at foreclosure, and had arranged that a new corporation they had organized would purchase the property, thus leaving nothing for distribution to the general creditors. Decide.
8. Plaintiffs, stockholders of Arms Company, alleged that the directors and officers of the company, by lending out money, taking a mortgage, and foreclosing upon all the properties, caused certain valuable patents owned by the corporation, to

be transferred to defendant. Plaintiffs sought to have the patent assignment made void, to restrain production thereunder, and to have a receiver account for the profits already made. Defendant protested that Arms Company was not a party; that, having been dissolved ten years previously, it had power only to wind up its affairs. Decide.

FEDERAL REGULATION OF CORPORATIONS

37

The basis of the federal regulation of business is found in four important federal statutes; the Sherman Act, the Clayton Act, the Federal Trade Commission Act, the Robinson-Patman Act, and subsequent amendments to these regulations.

The basic objective of the federal antitrust regulations is to foster a competitive economy and to prevent conduct which weakens or destroys competition. The regulations are designed to curb monopoly power which can control prices and exclude competitors from a given market. They encourage competition by allowing free bargaining which, of itself, should prevent the existence of the discretionary market power of monopoly over price and output.

THE SHERMAN ACT

The Sherman Act contains only eight sections, with its major provisions embodied in the first two sections.

> Section 1. Every contract, combination in the form of a trust or otherwise, or conspiracy, in the restraint of trade or commerce among the several states, or with foreign nations, is hereby declared illegal. Every person who shall make any such contract or engage in any such combination or conspiracy, shall be deemed guilty of a misdemeanor . . .
>
> Section 2. Every person who shall monopolize, or attempt to monopolize, or combine or conspire with any other person or persons, to monopolize any part of the trade or commerce among the several states, or with foreign nations, shall be deemed guilty of a misdemeanor. . .

The act adopted the common law concepts of restraint of trade and monopolization without attempting to define them. The first section applies only to agreements involving two or more people. The second applies to monopolies created by individual effort. Its basic contribution was to make restraint of trade and monopolization offenses against the federal government, to require federal enforcement, and to provide for the imposition of penalties.

THE RULE OF REASON

According to the Sherman Act, "every" contract or combination in restraint of trade is illegal. A literal interpretation means that all trade contracts are illegal, because contracts by their nature limit the rights of the contracting parties, which restrains their free exercise of trading privileges. Almost immediately, the courts began to modify this approach. In *U.S. v. Addyston Steel and Pipe Corp.*, 175 U.S. 211 (1899) Judge Taft, Sixth Circuit Court of Appeals, announced what has come to be known as the "rule of reason." Taft stated that at common law, "no conventional restraint of trade can be enforced unless the covenant embodying it is merely ancillary to the main purpose of an otherwise lawful contract, and necessary to protect the convenantee. . . ." Such an ancillary agreement would be a limited agreement whereby the seller of an ongoing business would promise not to compete with the buyer for a limited period of time and/ or in a specific geographical area, as long as such restraints are "reasonable." The "rule of reason" was adopted by the Supreme Court in the case of *Standard Oil Co. of New Jersey v. U.S.* 221 U.S. (1911).

In antitrust proceedings the "rule of reason" is most frequently applied to those restraints incidental to the main agreement and to determine if the latter affect competition to a significant degree. Direct restraints of trade are per se illegal, and are therefore not subject to the rule of reason.

The Supreme Court has also applied the "rule of reason" to the requirements or exclusive dealing contracts. The Court has looked to such items as business necessity and the reasonableness of certain business practices in determining whether or not a violation exists. In other words, if these arrangements are motivated by a legitimate business objective, and if they extend no further than is necessary to achieve this objective, they may be interpreted as not having an effect on competition.

PER SE VIOLATIONS

Per se rules are applied whenever a specific type of practice has been found to be a direct restraint of trade without regard to its reasonableness. A price fixing agreement, for example, cannot be regarded as an ancillary restraint of trade. The government need only show that a price fixing agreement exists and judgment against the parties must follow. A defense can be raised that price fixing did not exist, or that the uniformity of pricing came about as a result of price leadership. It is not a defense, however, that the public was not harmed by the agreement or that the prices so fixed were reasonable prices.

THE CLAYTON ACT

The importance of the Clayton Act was not in its content, for the practices declared illegal could have been attacked by the Sherman Act. Its value was in its attempt to *prevent* monopolies and restraints which were punishable under the Sherman Act. This act was also designed to remedy specific abuses which had arisen under the Sherman Act and to substantially lessen the burden of proof for the prosecution of the alleged violations. Under Sherman, it must be shown that the practice in question has involved a restraint of trade, while under Clayton the practice in question becomes unlawful when its effect "may be" to substantially lessen competition.

Section 2 of the Clayton Act provides in part: "That it shall be unlawful for any person engaged in commerce. . . . . to discriminate in price between different purchases of commodities . . . . where the effect of such competition may be to substantially lessen trade or tend to create a monopoly. . . ." The objective of this provision is to prevent large businesses from selling below cost to drive their competition out of business.

Section 3 of the Clayton Act deals specifically with exclusive contracts, namely, the exclusive dealing contract, the requirements contract, and tying contract. This section applies only to domestic commodities for sale or lease. The Sherman Act can reach service agreements and foreign sales, but the Clayton Act applies only when the receiver actually takes title to the goods. Exclusive dealing contracts are those by which a supplier explicitly forbids a buyer (or lessee) to deal in the goods of another supplier. A tying contract allows the buyer to purchase the product of primary interest (the tying product) if another (the tied product) is also purchased. The classic example of a tie-in sale is where a salt crusher could not be purchased unless a requirements contract for salt was also designed. (International Salt Co. v. United States, 332 U.S. 392, 1947)

Section 7 of the Clayton Act is concerned with the acquisition by a corporation engaged in the interstate commerce of another corporation engaged in interstate commerce "where in any line of commerce in any section of the country, the effect of such acquisition may be to substantially lessen competition to tend to create a monopoly." Probable effect is all that is necessary to determine a merger's illegality. The relevant geographical and product markets determine the probable effect, and the definition of these is often the main concern in a merger case. For the product market, the court considers cross-elasticity of demand and the interchangeability of substitute products. The geographic market is determined after the product market as the area in which the product represents effective competition.

Section 7 of the Clayton Act was designed to prevent corporations in any industry from growing into a type of monopoly by buying up stock in competing concerns and exercising industry-wide control through a holding company. This prohibition extends to the acquisition of stock in a number of companies so that competition between all those acquired might be substantially lessened. It does not apply to purchases of stock purely for investment nor to the formation of subsidiary companies intended to carry on the legitimate business of the parent company. This section as originally enacted did not cover the acquisition of the physical assets of a competing company. However, in 1950 Congress passed Celler-Kefauver Act which amended the original Section 7 and prohibited transactions of this type where the effect may be to lessen competition substantially or to tend to create a monopoly in any line of commerce in any section of the country.

Section 8 of the Clayton Act forbids any person to be a director of two or more corporations, one of which has an equity of more than $1,000,000, if the corporations are competitive in the sense that elimination of competition by agreements among them would constitute a violation of any of the provisions of any of the antitrust laws.

THE FEDERAL TRADE COMMISSION ACT

The Federal Trade Commission Act established the Federal Trade Commission to enforce the act and, in conjunction with the Antitrust Division of the department of Justice, the Clayton Act. The commission was also given power to make investigations, to require reports, and to publish information.

The Federal Trade Commission Act is not strictly an anti-trust act. Its main substantive provision, Section 5, simply declares unlawful any unfair methods of competition in commerce. This section was later amended to make unlawful "unfair or deceptive acts or practices in commerce." Competitive methods are attacked on grounds that all competition should be ethical and fair.

If the commission finds its charges warranted, its usual practice is to issue a cease and desist order against the company or companies involved. However, two other procedures supplement the standard practice. They are the stipulation and the trade practice conference procedures.

STIPULATION CONFERENCE

A stipulation is a signed statement of the facts involved and an agreement to discontinue unlawful practices as specified. If the agreement is broken, a cease and desist order is issued and enforced in the courts with the stipulation as proof.

TRADE PRACTICE CONFERENCE

This involves a meeting of the FTC with representatives of an industry to determine what constitutes fair and unfair practices in that industry.

THE ROBINSON-PATMAN ACT

Congress passed the Robinson-Patman Act in 1936. This Act had a twofold purpose: (1) to prevent suppliers from discriminating in pricing among buyers; and (2) to prevent large buyers from exerting economic pressure to force suppliers to grant discriminatory price concessions.

Section 2 (a) forbids direct price discrimination by the seller. A price discrimination has been defined simply by the courts as any price differential, usually in the form of either volume or quantity differentials. A quantity discount usually is given because of the size of a specific order. A volume discount, also known as an aggregate discount, is a discount given on a specific sales volume over a specific period of time.

The courts have interpreted Robinson-Patman violations in terms of primary-line injury at the seller's level and secondary-line injury at the buyer's level. Most primary-line violations occur in directly competitive situations which involve geographic or territorial price discrimination. For example, if two companies are competing in the same market place for sales, and one of them also has other markets, the latter company is able to cut its price where it is in direct competition while making up its losses in its other markets.

A secondary-line injury occurs in situations where two buyers are competing in the same market and a manufacturer-supplier lowers his price for one but not the other. There is a secondary-line injury if the one company is significantly less able to compete because of price discrimination.

A violation requires proof of a discrimination in price between different purchasers of commodities of like grade and quantity. There must be at least two sales of a commodity to two different purchasers at points reasonably close in time. At least one of these sales must have been in interstate commerce. The agreement must be one of sale; consignments and leases are exempt. Finally, there must be a finding that the discrimination has the "probable effect" of substantially lessening competition or of tending to create a monopoly. The act does allow a seller to price-discriminate between non-competitors. (This legal discrimination may involve different prices to wholesalers versus retailers, for example.)

The Act allows the seller the right to grade his goods and to establish price differentials for different grades. These differences in grades must be substantial and made in good faith. The use of a brand name in conjunction with goods generally sold under "private label" (seller's product, buyer's brand name) does not justify a price differential if the goods are of the same quality under each label.

Price discounts are allowed for short periods to enable the seller to raise cash under distressing financial conditions, to avert a total loss of perishable goods, or to dispose of an overstock of durable goods. American firms are allowed to price-discriminate in foreign trade, although foreign firms are subject to the act when selling their goods here. Leases, consignments, and the sale of services are exempt. A seller is allowed to discriminate in the license of a patent or copyright.

Section 2 (a) allows price differentials that make only due allowance for differentials in the cost of manufacture, sale, or delivery resulting from different methods or quantities in which commodities are sold. This defense is difficult to prove, however, because cost accounting is inexact and because what cost data is available is usually not kept in a form readily adaptable to a defense of a charge of a 2(a) violation. In addition to this, the standards of proof have varied from case to case and, therefore, provide a rather hazy set of guidelines.

One defense to a charge of a 2 (a) violation is found in Section 2 (b) which allows price discrimination for the purposes of meeting competition. The burden of proof is on the seller to show that he responded only to the lawful lower price of a competitor, and that he merely attempted to meet it, not beat it. In addition, the seller must show that he made an effort to find out who the competitor was and the price, and that it was not the buyer who dictated the terms of the deal. The emphasis of 2 (b) has been on individual competitive situations and not on a general system of competition.

Section 2 (c) provides "that it shall be unlawful for any person engaged in commerce . . . to pay or grant, or to receive or accept anything of value as a commission except for services rendered . . ." This provision was designed to stop the payment of ficticious brokerage commissions that were used as a cover for secret price discrimination. Direct or indirect payments of commissions or allowances are prohibited, as are discounts in lieu of brokerage. Where a true brokerage exists, the broker cannot accept a lower commission on a sale and pass the savings on to the buyer. This would constitute a violation of Section 2 (a) of the Robinson-Patman Act. The fact that a buyer was unaware that its favored price was based in part on a discriminatory reduction in brokerage does not constitute a defense. Knowledge of the reduced price is sufficient to establish a violation of 2 (a).

Section 2 (d) declares it is unlawful for a supplier to make any payment to a buyer in consideration of services or facilities provided in promoting the sale of goods, unless similar payments are made available on proportionately equal terms to other buyers.

Section 2 (e) makes it unlawful for the supplier himself to provide promotional services and facilities to a buyer unless he provides facilities on proportionately equal terms to other buyers.

Section 2 (f) forbids the knowing receipt or inducement of a discriminatory price by the buyer; this section is applicable only to buyers.

LEGAL PRINCIPLES

The Sherman Act prohibits combinations in restraint of trade and makes it illegal for persons to monopolize or attempt to monopolize.

The Clayton Act prohibits price discrimination, tying and exclusive contracts, corporate acquisitions, and interlocking directorates, if the "probable effect" is substantially to lessen competition. The Robinson-Patman Act prohibits unjustified price discrimination which would tend to lessen competition.

The Federal Trade Commission Act declares to be unlawful "unfair methods" of competition in commerce.

Stipulation and trade practice conferences often supplement the common practice of cease and desist orders by the FTC.

A price differential is illegal if the probable effect is either a tendency to monopolize, a substantial lessening of competition, or a prevention of competition with the recipient of a special price.

Differences in grades must be substantial and made in good faith.

Price differentials may be justified by cost savings or when used to meet competition in good faith.

Generally, a seller may not give a buyer a special price cut to enable the buyer to meet his own competition.

Direct or indirect commissions are illegal, unless paid to an independent broker for services actually performed.

A broker may not accept a lower fee and pass the savings along to the buyer.

Buyers are forbidden to induce or knowingly secure a discriminatory price.

Sellers are not allowed to sell below cost for the purpose of destroying competition, or to sell at a lower cost in one particular market to destroy competition, even if the "lower" price is above cost.

CASES FOR REVIEW

INTERNATIONAL SALT CO. v. UNITED STATES

332 U.S. 392 (1947)

The Government brought this civil action to enjoin the International Salt Company, appellant here, from carrying out provisions of the leases of its patented machines to the effect that lessees would use therein only International's salt products. The restriction is alleged to violate § 1 of the Sherman Act, and § 3 of the Clayton Act.

International Salt Company is engaged in interstate commerce in salt, of which it is the country's largest producer for industrial uses. It also owns patents on two machines for the utilization of salt products. One, the "Lixator," dissolves rock salt into a brine used in various industrial processes. The other, the "Saltomat," injects salt, in tablet form, into canned products during the canning process. The principal distribution of each of these machines is under leases which, among other things, require the lessees to purchase from appellant all unpatented salt and salt tablets consumed in the leased machines.

The appellant's patents confer a limited monopoly of the invention they reward. From them appellant derives a right to restrain others from making, vending or using the patented machines. But the patents confer no right to restrain use of, or trade in, unpatented salt. By contracting to close this market for salt against competition, International has engaged in a restraint of trade for which its patents afford no immunity from the anti-trust laws. Not only is price fixing unreasonable, *per se,* but also it is unreasonable, *per se,* to foreclose competitors from any substantial market. The volume of business affected by these contracts cannot be said to be insignificant or insubstantial and the tendency of the arrangement to accomplishment of monopoly seems obvious. Under the law, agreements are forbidden which "tend to create a monopoly," and it is immaterial that the tendency is a creeping one rather than one that proceeds at full gallop; nor does the law await arrival at the goal before condemning the direction of the movement.

Appellant contends, however, that the "Lixator" contracts are saved from unreasonableness and from the tendency to monopoly because they provided that if any competitor offered salt of equal grade at a lower price, the lessee should be free to buy in the open market, unless appellant would furnish the salt at an equal price; and the "Saltomat" agreements provided that the lessee was entitled to the benefit of any general price reduction in lessor's salt tablets. The "Lixator" provision does, of course, afford a measure of protection to the lessee, but it does not avoid the stifling effect of the agreeement on competition. The appellant had at all times a priority on the business at equal prices. A competitor would have to undercut appellant's price to have any hope of capturing the market, while appellant could hold that market by merely meeting competition. We do not think this concession relieves the contract of being a restraint of trade, albeit a less harsh one than would result in the absence of such a provision. The "Saltomat" provision obviously has no effect of legal significance since it gives the lessee nothing more than a right to buy appellant's salt tablets at appellant's going price. All purchases must in any event be of appellant's product.

Appellant also urges that since under the leases it remained under an obligation to repair and maintain the machines, it was reasonable to confine their use to its own salt because its high quality assured satisfactory functioning and low maintenance cost. The appellant's rock salt is alleged to have an average sodium chloride content of 98.2 percent. Rock salt of other producers, it is said, "does not run consistent in sodium chloride content and in many instances runs as low as 95 percent of sodium chloride." This greater percentage of insoluble impurities allegedly disturbs the functioning of the "Lixator" machine. A somewhat similar claim is pleaded as to the "Saltomat."

Of course, a lessor may impose on a lessee reasonable restrictions designed in good faith to minimize maintenance burdens and to assure satisfactory operation. We may assume, as matter of argument, that if the "Lixator" functions best on rock salt of average sodium chloride content of 98.2 percent, the lessee might be required to use only salt meeting such a specification of quality. But it is not pleaded, nor is it argued, that the machine is allergic to salt of equal quality produced by any one except International. If others cannot produce salt equal to reasonable specifications for machine use, it is one thing; but it is admitted that, at times, at least, competitors do offer such a product. They are, however, shut out of the market by a provision that limits it, not in terms of quality, but in terms of a particular vendor. Rules for use of leased machinery must not be disguised restraints of free competition, though they may set reasonable standards which all suppliers must meet.

F.T.C. v. COLGATE-PALMOLIVE CO.

380 U.S. 374 (1965)

The basic question before us is whether it is a deceptive trade practice, prohibited by § 5 of the Federal Trade Commission Act, to represent falsely that a televised test, experiment, or demonstration provides a viewer with visual proof of a product claim, regardless of whether the product claim is itself true.

The case arises out of an attempt by . . . Colgate-Palmolive Company to prove to the television public that its shaving cream, "Rapid Shave," out-shaves them all. . . . Ted Bates & Company, Inc., an advertising agency, prepared for Colgate three one-minute commercials to show that Rapid Shave could soften even . . . sandpaper. Each of the commercials contained the same "sandpaper test." The announcer informed the audience that, "To prove RAPID SHAVE'S super-moisturizing power, we put it right from the can onto this tough, dry sandpaper. It was apply . . . soak . . . and off in a storke." While the announcer was speaking, Rapid Shave was applied to a substance that appeared to be sandpaper, and immediately a razor was shown shaving the substance clean.

The Federal Trade Commission issued a complaint . . . charging that the commercials were false and deceptive. The evidence before the hearing examiner disclosed that sandpaper of the type shown in the commercials could not be shaved immediately following the application of Rapid Shave, but required a soaking period of approximately eighty minutes. The evidence also showed that the substance resembling sandpaper was a simulated prop made of plexiglass to which sand had been applied. However, the examiner found that Rapid Shave could shave sandpaper, even though not in the short time represented by the commercials, and that if real sandpaper had been used in the commercials the inadequacies of television transmission would have made it appear . . . to be nothing more than plain, colored paper.

In reviewing the substantive issues in the case, it is well to remember the respective roles of the Commission and the courts in the administration of the Federal Trade Commission Act. When the Commission was created by Congress in 1914, it was directed by § 5 to prevent "(u)nfair methods of competition in commerce." Congress amended the Act in 1938 to extend the Commission's jurisdiction to include "unfair or deceptive acts or practices in commerce" a significant amendment showing Congress' concern for consumers as well as for competitors. It is important to note the generality of these standards of illegality; the proscriptions in § 5 are flexible, "to be defined with particularity by the myriad of cases from the field of business."

The Court of Appeals has criticized the reference in the Commission's order to "test, experiment or demonstration" as not capable of practical interpretation. It could find no difference between the Rapid Shave commercial and a commercial which extolled the goodness of ice cream while giving viewers a picture of a scoop of mashed potatoes appearing to be ice cream. We do not understand this difficulty. In the ice cream case the mashed potato prop is not being used for additional proof of the product claim, while the purpose of the Rapid Shave commercial is to give the viewer objective proof of the claims made. If in the ice cream hypothetical the focus of the commercial becomes the undisclosed potato prop and the viewer is invited, explicitly or by implication, to see for himself the truth of the claims about the ice cream's rich texture and full color, and perhaps compare it to a "rival product," then the commercial has become similar to the one now before us. Clearly, however, a commercial which depicts happy actors delightedly eating ice cream that is in fact mashed potatoes or drinking a product appearing to be coffee but which is in fact some other substance is not covered by the present order.

The crucial terms of the present order—"test, experiment or demonstration . . . represented . . . as actual proof of a claim"—are as specific as the circumstances will permit. If respondents in their subsequent commercials attempt to come as close to the line of misrepresentation as the Commission's order permits, they may without specifically intending to do so cross into the area proscribed by this order. However, it does not seem "unfair to require that one who deliberately goes perilously close to an area of proscribed conduct shall take the risk that he may cross the line." Boyce Motor Lines, Inc. v. United States, 342 U.S. 337, 340. In commercials where the emphasis is on the seller's word, and not on the viewer's own perception, the respondents need not fear that an undisclosed use of props is prohibited by the present order. On the other hand, when the commercial not only makes a claim, but also invites the viewer to rely on his own perception, for demonstrative proof of the claim, the respondents will be aware that the use of undisclosed props in strategic places might be a material deception. We believe that respondents will have no difficulty applying the Commission's order to vast majority of their comtemplated future commercials. If, however, a situation arises in which respondents are sincerely unable to determine whether a proposed course of action would violate the present order, they can, by complying with the Commission's rules, oblige the Commission to give them definitive advice as to whether their proposed action, if pursued, would constitute compliance with the order.

CASE PROBLEMS

1. The Union Oil Company required all lessees of its stations to sign product consigment agreements for a one-year period. The station leases were also for one year. Under the consignment agreement Union retained the title to the gasoline delivered and controlled the retail prices charged. Simpson, a lessee, however, had the burden of risks, except for acts of God, for gasoline in his possession. Simpson sold gasoline below the price set by Union and Union subsequently refused to renew his lease and consignment agreement. Simpson sued, alleging that the consignment arrangement violated Section 1 of the Sherman Act. Decide.

2. Over a period of several years the Schwinn Bicycle Company suffered a decline in its share of the market. To reverse its trend, Schwinn adopted a selective franchising system which included assigning exclusive territories to dealers and distributors. Franchised outlets were obligated not to sell outside of their assigned territories. Under this plan Schwinn retained title to all goods sold. The distributors acted as agents for the company. The government alleged a violation of Section 1 of the Sherman Act. Decide.

3. Theatre Enterprises owned the Crest Theatre, located in a neighborhood shopping district some six miles from the downtown shopping center in Baltimore, Maryland. The Crest, with the most modern improvements, opened on February 26, 1949. Before and after the opening, Theatre Enterprises through its president, repeatedly sought to obtain first-run features for the theatre. Theatre Enterprises approached the defendants, a group of motion picture distributors, separately, initially requesting exclusive first-runs and later asking for first-runs on a "day and date" basis. But the defendants uniformly rejected Theatre's requests and adhered to an established policy of restricting first-runs in Baltimore to the eight downtown theatres. Theatre alleged a conspiracy among the distributors. Decide.

4. American Greetings Corporation manufactured greetings cards and related products in Cleveland, Ohio, and distributed them throughout the United States. Ludwig was in the business of purchasing greeting cards from manufacturers and reselling at wholesale in Ohio. Ludwig alleged that in order to induce retailers to offer its cards, American bought and destroyed Ludwig's cards in the hands of retailers; offered to repurchase the retailer's greeting card display cabinets and to furnish new ones free of charge; offered to pay a cash bonus on condition that the retailers switch their business to American; and offered to place American's cards with them on a consignment basis. Ludwig alleged that he has been injured in his business by such acts. Decide.

5. Moore owned a bakery in Santa Rosa, New Mexico. His business was wholly intrastate. His competitor, Mead's Fine Bread Company, participated in interstate baking business. Mead cut the price of bread by half in Santa Rosa but made no other price cuts in any place in New Mexico or in any other state where it

conducted business. As the result of this action, Moore was driven out of business. Moore sued Mead for damages for violation of the Clayton and Robinson-Patman acts. Mead defended that the price cutting was purely intrastate and did not constitute a violation of the federal statutes. Decide.

6. In 1959 United Biscuit Company sold its cookies and crackers in the midwest to retail grocery store customers. United used graduated monthly discount schedules which allowed discounts up to six percent based on the volume of purchases made by each retail store customer. The discount was calculated on the basis of the aggregated purchases of the store operated by the customer. The larger chains received larger discounts than did the independents. As a result of this policy the Federal Trade Commission issued a cease and desist order. Decide.

7. The Federal Trade Commission brought an action under the Federal Trade Commission Act against Mary Carter Paint Company and issued a cease and desist order. Mary Carter was ordered to stop representing in their advertisements that each customer would be given a can of paint "free" for every can of paint purchased. Decide.

8. The Government brought this action against Pabst Brewing Company, a Wisconsin Corporation, that Pabst violated Section 7 of the Clayton Act when it acquired Blatz Brewing Co., also a Wisconsin firm, in 1958. The Government alleged that the effect of the acquisition ". . . may be substantially to lessen competition or to tend to create monopoly in the beer industry, in the three-state area of Wisconsin, Illinois, and Michigan as the relevant geographic market." Decide.

PART VI
INSURANCE AND SELLING

INSURANCE   38

Every contract of insurance is a device for spreading over a large number of persons a possible financial loss too great to be conveniently absorbed by an individual. Such a loss may result from a destruction of property, an illness necessitating expenditures, or an elimination of earnings caused by a temporary or permanent disability or death. The primary objective of an insurance plan is the cooperation of a large number of persons who, in effect, agree to share the particular risk against which insurance is desired. It is essential that "large" numbers of persons participate so that an individual's share of any loss will be relatively small and violent fluctuations in the loss experience from year to year may be divided. It is this characteristic, primarily, that distinguishes insurance from gambling.

Most of the legal aspects of the insurance contract arise from the fact that it is an aleatory agreement as distinguished from the ordinary business agreement, in which the parties contemplate a fairly even exchange of values. For example, in a sale, the seller believes that the price paid is about equal to the value of the goods, and the buyer expects to get goods about equal to his price. In making an insurance contract, the insured knows that he is paying a sum far less than the insurer is obligated to pay him under certain conditions that hopefully will not occur. As an aleatory contract, the conditions are an essential part of the bargain. They define the risks that the insurer agrees to bear for a group of persons exposed to similar risks and paying similar contributions. If the insurer were compelled by law to pay losses for which it had never agreed to assume the risk and for which it had collected no corresponding premiums from those who sustain the losses, the insurance enterprise could not be maintained and would be tantamount to a charitable institution. Therefore, an insurer is granted the normal protection of contract law that his losses are to be limited to the risks assumed in the contract.

Moreoever, the definitions, concepts, rules, and principles of contract law generally are used in the analysis of facts and the solution of controversies over insurance contracts.

The essential function of a contract is to create expectations and impose duties upon the parties by virtue of the promise or promises that the contract contains. The requirements for creating a legally enforcable contract may be summarized as follows:

1. a manifestation of assent to its terms by the parties to the agreement;
2. a sufficient consideration for each promise;
3. legal capacity of the parties to make a contract; and
4. lawful subject matter in the contract.

PARTIES TO THE CONTRACT

The parties to a contract of insurance are the *insurer*, who assumes the risk, and the *insured*, whose risk is assumed. Insurers are sometimes referred to as *underwriters*.

MUTUAL ASSENT

The offer in the contract of insurance takes the form of an application for insurance, signed by the insured, with information necessary to enable the insurer to make a sound judgment on the request. An unconditional acceptance of the application completes the contract. Sometimes, however, the acceptance may be conditional; for example, where it provides that the contract shall not be deemed effective until a condition is performed such as the premium is paid or the policy is delivered.

CONSIDERATION

The consideration for the insurer's promise to indemnify the insured against a particular loss is the payment or promise of payment, by the insured, of a premium which is a sum of money agreed to be paid periodically to the insurer for assuming the risk.

SUBJECT MATTER

The subject matter of an insurance contract is the insurer's assumption of a risk and promise of indemnification against loss that may be suffered by the insured in exchange for the premium payments by the insured. The law places little limitation upon the character of the risk assumed, except to require a risk to the person insured—an insurable interest.

INSURABLE INTEREST

Regardless of the nature of the insurance or the subject matter of the policy, the person who is insured must have an insurable interest in the subject matter of the insurance. If this interest is not present the transaction amounts to a wager or gambling contract which is void and hence unenforceable. Generally, one has an insurable interest in the subject matter if he stands to gain by its preservation and to lose by its loss, damage or destruction. Some examples are:

1. *Insurable Interest in Life.* If a person is so related by blood, marriage or business to another as to justify a reasonable expectation of benefit or advantage from continuance of the latter's life and loss or detriment from its termination, he has an insurable interest in such life. Also, an individual has an unlimited insurable interest in his own life, which will validate a policy purchased by him in favor of himself or his estate or in favor of another person as beneficiary, even though the beneficiary has no insurable interest in his life.

2. *Corporations.* A corporation has an insurable interest in the life of its president, general manager, principal stockholder or any person or officer on whose efforts the success of the corporation's business is dependent.
3. *Insurable Interest in Property.* A person has an insurable interest in property when he has such right, interest or relation to it that he will be benefited by its preservation and continued existence and will suffer a direct out-of-the-pocket loss from its destruction or injury by reason of the peril insured against.

EXISTENCE OF SUBJECT MATTER

A contract of insurance is invalid where the subject matter is not in existence at the time the risk attaches and such fact is known to one of the parties. For example, if a vessel is lost at sea and the owner, knowing it, insures the vessel with an insurer who has no knowledge of this fact, the policy is void. But, if both parties were ignorant of the loss, the policy would be valid.

COVERAGE EFFECTIVE

Ordinarily, life insurance is not effective until the policy is delivered and the premium paid. In fire insurance, however, if there has been a complete meeting of the minds on the terms of the risk, the insurer becomes liable even if the fire breaks out before the policy is delivered. This may be evidenced by a written memorandum or oral commitment in the form of a "binder."

MARINE INSURANCE

Marine insurance protects against hazards known as perils of the sea—fire, shipwreck or piracy. The term *perils of the sea* does not include the ordinary action of wind and wave, wear and tear, or loss due to delays occasioned thereby. The amount of loss for which an insurer is liable is fixed in the policy. However, where goods are thrown overboard in an effort to save the ship, such loss works to the benefit of the owners of the ship and the rest of the cargo not lost. It is therefore customary to incorporate into marine policies a general-average provision whereby the insurer attempts to collect from owners of the vessel and from cargo saved by the loss caused by throwing other goods overboard and thus averages the loss between all parties concerned. Payment of loss will not be made without actual proof of loss. Evidence of loss must show full particulars of the nature, amount and cause of damage, attested to by the master and crew of the vessel.

FIRE INSURANCE

In many states, a standard fire policy is prescribed by statute or by an insurance commissioner with statutory authority. The purpose of such legislation is: (1) to protect the insured against ambiguous language offering the insurer an escape from liability in case of loss; (2) to secure uniformity in

MEMORANDUM OF HOMEOWNERS POLICY

No. H 14 84 14

New (HCA688445)
RENEWAL OF NUMBER

A STOCK COMPANY

RFI REPUBLIC-FRANKLIN INSURANCE COMPANY
COLUMBUS, OHIO

DECLARATIONS

Named Insured and P.O. Address (Number, Street, Town or City, County, State, Zip Code)

ALL FORMS OF INSURANCE
JAMES J. McGRAW AGENCY
4925 Cleves Pike – 471-5915
CINCINNATI, OHIO
LIFE • FIRE • AUTO • ACCIDENT • LIABILITY

Policy Term: Three (Years) 6/26/74 (Inception) 6/26/77 (Expiration)

The described residence premises covered hereunder is located at the above address, unless otherwise stated herein (No., Street, Town or City, County, State, Zip Code)
2370 Beechmoor Drive, North Canton, Stark County, Ohio

Insurance is provided only with respect to the following Coverages for which a limit of liability is specified, subject to all conditions of this policy.

Coverages and Limit of Liability	Section I				Section II		
	A. Dwelling	B. Appurtenant Structures	C. Unscheduled Personal Property	D. Additional Living Expense	E. Personal Liability (Bodily Injury and Property Damage) Each occurrence	F. Medical Payments to Others Each person	F. Medical Payments to Others Each accident
	$ 46,000	$ 4,600	$ 23,000	$ 9,200	$ 100,000	$ 500	$ 25,000

Premium	Basic Policy Premium	Theft Extension	Additional Premiums		Total Prepaid Premium	Premium if paid in installments	Payable: At Inception (and)	[X] At each anniversary [ ] six months
	$ 477.00	$	$	$	$ 477.00	$477.00	$ 159.00	$ 159.00
			Premium for Scheduled Personal Property		$	$	$	$
			Combined Premium		$	$	$	$

Form and Endorsements made part of this Policy at time of issue: Insert Number(s) and Edition Date(s)
Form HO- 2S (9/70)
Endorsement(s) HO-206 (8/72) HO-181 (2/70) RF EXT 1 (5/71)

DEDUCTIBLE—SECTION I: Any loss by perils insured against under Section I of this policy is subject to a deductible. Exceptions, if any:
[X] Deductible applicable only to loss caused by the peril of windstorm or hail (Clause No. 1)
[X] Deductible applicable to loss caused by other perils (Clause No. 2)
[ ] Deductible not applicable
[ ] Special Loss Deductible Clause $ ______ (Amount)

Section II—Additional residence premises, if any, located: (No., Street, Town or City, County, State, Zip Code)

Mortgagee(s) Citizens Savings Bank, 100 Central Plaza, South Canton, Ohio 44702 (NAME AND ADDRESS)

Countersignature Date June 26, 1974 Agency at CINCINNATI, OHIO
5/8/74 vb

JAMES J. McGRAW AGENCY Agent

In Consideration of the Provisions and Stipulations Herein or Added Hereto and of the Premium Above Specified (or specified in endorsement(s) made a part hereof), this Company, for the **term shown above** from **inception date shown above** at noon (Standard Time) to **expiration date shown above** at noon (Standard Time) at location of property involved, to an amount not exceeding the limit of liability above specified, does insure **the Insured named in the Declarations above** and legal representatives, to the extent of the actual cash value of the property at the time of loss, but not exceeding the amount which it would cost to repair or replace the property with material of like kind and quality within a reasonable time after such loss, without allowance for any increased cost of repair or reconstruction by reason of any ordinance or law regulating construction or repair, and without compensation for loss resulting from interruption of business or manufacture, nor in any event for more than the interest of the Insured, against all DIRECT LOSS BY FIRE, LIGHTNING AND OTHER PERILS INSURED AGAINST IN THIS POLICY INCLUDING REMOVAL FROM PREMISES ENDANGERED BY THE PERILS INSURED AGAINST IN THIS POLICY, EXCEPT AS HEREINAFTER PROVIDED, to the property described herein while located or contained as described in this policy, or pro rata for five days at each proper place to which any of the property shall necessarily be removed for preservation from the perils insured against in this policy, but not elsewhere.

Assignment of this policy shall not be valid except with the written consent of this Company.

This policy is made and accepted subject to the foregoing provisions and stipulations and those hereinafter stated, which are hereby made a part of this policy, together with such other provisions, stipulations and agreements as may be added hereto, as provided in this policy.

This memorandum is for information only; it is not a contract of insurance but attests that a policy as numbered herein, and as it stands at the date of this certificate, has been issued by the Company. Said policy is subject to change by endorsement and to assignment and cancellation in accordance with its terms.

OKM 1001-(2)XC (Ed.10-68 Standard)

Figure 38-1

insurance contracts; and (3) to protect insurers against fraud and the possible imposition on the insured of the perils of alleged oral waivers by their agents. (See Figure 38-1)

DEFINITION AND COVERAGE

Fire insurance protects the insured against property loss by fire and lightning. The usual coverage is not only from a direct loss due to fire, but includes losses resulting from a fire, such as damage by smoke, water or chemicals. A fire kindled for ordinary purposes, such as for lighting and heating, is said to be of friendly origin; unless otherwise provided in the policy, loss or damage resulting from such a fire is not recoverable. A hostile fire is either a fire that breaks out where not desired or intended or a fire intended for a legitimate purpose that becomes uncontrollable.

BINDERS

A fire insurance contract may take effect before the policy is delivered where the agreement is evidenced by a "binder," which consists of a written memorandum or oral commitment giving temporary protection pending delivery of the policy. The binder sets forth the essential terms of the contract and is subject to the conditions to be later incorporated into the policy.

VALUED OR OPEN POLICIES

A valued policy specifies the value of the property insured. An open policy leaves the value open, to be determined at the time of the loss. Policies may be both valued and open. Policies may be valued to the extent that the insurer agrees to pay a specific amount in case of total loss and open to the extent that it agrees to pay, in the event of a partial loss, the value of that loss.

CO-INSURANCE

The co-insurance clause is designed to induce owners to insure their property at a higher percentage of its value. It provides that if the owner will insure his property up to a given percentage of its value, he will be given the benefit of a lower premium, and if he insures for less than the fixed percentage, he must bear a proportion of any loss, that is, he must be a coinsurer on such loss with the insurance company. In the latter case, he may recover only such percentage of the loss as the amount of insurance bears to the fixed percentage in the policy.

CONCURRENT INSURANCE

Where property is insured by more than one insurer and the total concurrent insurance exceeds the general loss, a pro rata clause applies, which means the insured can collect from each company only its proportionate liability to the total amount of coverage.

OCCUPANCY OF PREMISES

The standard policy provides that if a building described in the policy, intended for occupancy by the owner or the tenant, becomes vacant or unoccupied for 60 (sixty) days, the policy, unless otherwise provided by agreement endorsed on the policy or added to it, shall be suspended. It does not matter that the fire occurred after occupancy was resumed; the policy is still suspended.

ASSIGNABILITY

Fire insurance involves a personal relationship in that the insured's character, habits, experience, background, and so on may be material to the risk. Fire policies generally provide, therefore, that the entire policy shall be void upon assignment without the insurer's written consent endorsed on the policy. However, once a fire loss has occurred, the policyholder has a specific claim against the insurer which he may assign, subject to defense by the insurance company. The insured may not, however, assign any excess of insurance over the loss. To that extent, the policy remains personal and non-assignable.

CANCELLATION

Both insurer and insured have the right to cancel a fire policy at will. A standard cancellation clause usually reads: "This policy shall be cancelled at any time at the request of the insured; or by the company giving five days' notice of such cancellation." Where the company elects to cancel, it must offer to pay on demand the amount of the unearned portion of the premium paid by the insured or the policy will remain in force.

LIFE INSURANCE

Life insurance is a contractual arrangement whereby the insurer, for a premium paid annually or at stated intervals, agrees to pay a larger sum at the insured's death. Thus, the purpose of life insurance is for the insurer to assume the risk of loss caused by the insured's death and to make compensation for such loss to a person designated by the insured, known as the beneficiary.

TYPES OF LIFE INSURANCE

Among the more common types of life insurance are the following:
1. *Ordinary Life.* An ordinary or straight life policy calls for payment of premiums throughout the life of the insured, with the payment of a fixed sum to the beneficiary on the insured's death.
2. *Limited Payment Life.* A limited payment life policy requires a limited number of premium payments with the insured being fully protected not only during the period of payments but for the remainder of his life.
3. *Endowment.* An endowment policy provides for payment of a fixed sum to the insured upon conclusion of a given period of premium payments. The sum is payable either to the insured himself or, if he dies before the period of premium payment expires, to his beneficiary.
4. *Term.* Term policies provide for insurance for a fixed term of years. In consideration of a low premium, the policy does not provide for any cash accumulations or permit the owner to take out a paid-up policy at the end of the term.

STANDARD PROVISIONS

Standard provisions are generally incorporated into life policies. A common provision is that no policy may be delivered or issued for delivery unless it contains provisions for the following:

1. a grace period;
2. incontestability after two years;
3. making the policy the entire contract between the parties;
4. adjustment of payment in accordance with the insured's true age, if his age was misstated;
5. loan privileges; and
6. the privilege of reinstatement under certain conditions and upon certain terms.

NOTICE OF PREMIUM DUE

Under the standard policy, notice must be given policyholders when a premium is about to become due. Such notice must be given in writing not less than fifteen nor more than forty-five days prior to due date, or the policy will remain in force for at least a year after default. The notice must also state the penalty for failure to pay the premium on due date or within the stated grace period.

ASSIGNABILITY

Life insurance differs from property insurance in that the loss insured against is one that is certain to happen. Part of the value of life insurance is the inherent right of the owner to certain benefits in the policy. For example, where the insured has named himself as beneficiary and has paid the premiums, all the value in the policy is his. If the owner has named another as beneficiary, with right of revocation, he has a right to assign the policy. If he has not reserved the right of revocation, he needs the beneficiary's consent in order to assign the policy. Generally, all life policies contain a clause to the effect that: "No assignment of this policy shall take effect until written notice thereof shall be given to the company."

TERMINATION OF RISK

A life insurance policy may be terminated: (1) by expiration, as with a term policy; (2) by lapse, through default in premium payment; (3) by payment of the loss; or (4) by forfeiture.

CASUALTY INSURANCE

The term *casualty* is applied to all forms of insurance covering loss or damage resulting from accident or unanticipated contingency, except fire and the elements. Although generally understood to designate health and accident insurance, the term is also applied to insurance that protects against accidents that result in injuries to property.

ACCIDENT AND HEALTH INSURANCE

Accident policies insure against accidental injury or death. Many policies combine accident and health insurance. It is immaterial to recovery that the accident insured against was due to the insured's negligence, so long as it was not deliberate.

LIABILITY INSURANCE

Liability insurance affords indemnity against injury sustained by persons other than the insured, for which the insured might become liable. Originally, it related only to an employer's liability for injuries or accidental death of employees that occurred during the course of their employment. Liability insurance now provides coverage for many forms of liability that the insured may incur toward others. The insurable interest is the loss that the insured may sustain because of his liability toward the person or persons who may suffer the damage or injury in question.

AUTOMOBILE INSURANCE

Automobile insurance protects the insured against hazards inherent in the ownership and operation of an automobile. These include: (1) fire and theft; (2) collision; (3) liability for death or bodily injury; (4) property damage caused by negligent driving on the part of the insured or his agent; (5) medical payments for occupants; and (6) uninsured motorist coverage. These forms of insurance are usually combined in a single policy. (See Figure 38-2)

FIRE AND THEFT

Policies insuring the owner against fire damage to his car or loss of it through theft normally cover both the car and its usual equipment, but not personal belongings that may have been in the car unless specifically stated. Such coverage also excludes loss during the course of illegal or extra-hazardous use.

CARS PURCHASED ON INSTALLMENT PLAN

Purchasers of a car under a secured transaction are usually required to protect the holder of the security interest (see Chapter 56, The Security Interest) by keeping the car insured against loss by fire, theft or collision. Loss, damage or destruction of the car before it is paid for thus protects the security interest, but not the purchaser, unless the latter is also covered by the policy.

COLLISION INSURANCE

Collision insurance protects the owner for loss to his car from a collision with another car or with any other obstacle. Negligence is usually not material. Thus, if the owner of a car sustains damage by contact with another car, or an obstacle, he is indemnified for such damage through collision insurance, whether he was negligent or not.

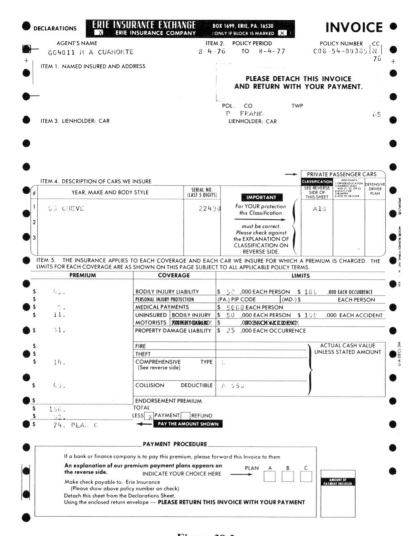

Figure 38-2

DEDUCTIBLE CLAUSES

Most collision policies contain "deductible clauses." If the policyholder agrees to deduct or make no claim for collision damage up to a specified figure, such as $50 or $100, he is given the benefit of a lower premium.

NOTICE OF ACCIDENT AND RIGHT TO CONDUCT LITIGATION

All liability and property damage policies contain a provision fixing a time period for notifying the company of any accident. Failure to do so relieves the insurance company of its liability under the policy. The company may also reserve the right to defend in any suit brought on the policy. If the policyholder insists on the right of defending himself, he relieves the insurer of its liability under this clause.

RIGHT TO SUE THE INSURER

Generally, a person injured in an automobile accident must seek recourse against the owner of the other car, not the company with which he may be insured. Only where the injured party obtains a judgment against the insured owner and such judgment is not paid, may the injured party sue the insurer. Where the insurance company wrongfully refuses to defend the insured and he thereby sustains loss by way of judgment or the cost of defending, the insured may sue the company for such loss.

NO-FAULT AUTOMOBILE INSURANCE

The trend today in automobile insurance is toward providing insurance coverage for the person on whom the loss falls. This provides that part of the costs to a person injured in an automobile accident, such as for medical expenses and income losses, will be compensated by insurance purchased by himself on himself. Advocates of this concept draw on workmen's compensation for an analogous situation in that auto accidents are as inevitable as on-the-job accidents and there is no useful purpose served in trying to place the blame on the respective parties. They will argue further that some people are not compensated because their injuries are not directly traceable to the fault of a third party.

In August, 1970, Massachusetts became the first state to enact a no-fault insurance law. Under this law an insurer must pay, regardless of fault, the first $2000 of economic bodily injury losses sustained by its insureds. Pain and suffering will be considered under a tort claim only if the injured party's medical expenses exceed $500 or if the injury causes death, permanent and serious disfigurement, loss of sight or hearing or a fracture. An injured person can still bring suit on his claims; however, any recoveries are reduced by the amount paid under the no-fault provision. Several other states have enacted no-fault plans since then.

NONDISCLOSURE AND MISREPRESENTATION

A party induced to enter into any contract (including an insurance contract) by fraud has the right, when the knowledge of the fraud comes to his attention, to elect whether or not he shall continue to be bound by it. Mere non-disclosure does not convey the right of recision unless it amounts to fraud. For example, if the insured conceals something he knows to be material (as where he insures a ship which he knows to have been sunk) he is guilty of fraud. The disclosure of misleading information, however innocently done, also gives the misled party the right to void the contract. Thus, if a material fact which the insured states to the insurer turns out to be untrue, the policy is voidable, whether the insured knew his statement to be untrue or not. It will not be a defense that he acted in good faith. This applies only to marine insurance. In most casualty policies it is *not* a warranty.

SUBROGATION

A surety, upon satisfying a debtor's obligation, is said to be subrogated to the creditor's claim against the debtor. Similarly, a fire, marine or indemnity insurer is said to be subrogated to the rights of the insured to the extent that it has made payment to the insured on any claim that it was obligated to satisfy. (See Figure 38-3)

SUBROGATION CLAUSE

This company may require from the insured an assignment of all right of recovery against any party for loss to the extent that payment is made by this company. This insurance shall not be invalidated should the insured waive in writing prior to a loss any or all right of recovery against any party for loss occurring to the party described herein.

Figure 38-3

LEGAL PRINCIPLES

Every plan of insurance is merely a method of spreading over a large number of persons a possible financial loss too serious to be borne by an individual.

Most of the legal aspects of an insurance contract arise from the fact that it is aleatory as distinguished from an ordinary business contract.

Requirements for the legal validity of a contract are (1) manifestation of assent, (2) consideration, (3) legal capacity of the parties and (4) capacity.

One has an insurable interest in the subject matter insured if he stands to gain by its preservation and to lose by its loss, damage, or destruction.

A premium is a periodical sum of money paid to the insurer as consideration for assuming the risk.

A corporation has an insurable interest in the life of its president, general manager, principle stockholder or any officer on whose efforts the success of the corporation's business depends.

A contract of insurance is invalid where the subject matter is not in existence at the time the risk attaches and such fact is known to one of the parties.

A contract is not assignable if it creates a personal relationship or if its terms prohibit assignment.

The amount of loss for which a marine insurer is liable is fixed in the policy.

Payment of loss will not be made without proofs of loss.

A fire insurance contract insures the insured against property loss by hostile fire.

A valued policy specifies the value of the property insured.

Both insurer and insured have the right to cancel a fire policy at will.

Accident policies insure against the contingency of the accidental injury or accidental death.

Liability insurance is most widely resorted to in connection with the ownership and operation of automobiles.

Automobile insurance protects the insured against the hazards incident to the ownership and operation of an automobile.

Where the insurance company wrongfully refuses to defend the insured who thereby sustains loss by way of judgment or the cost of defending, he may sue the company for such loss.

No-fault automobile insurance provides coverage for the person on whom the loss falls rather than for the person who can be held responsible for the loss.

Subrogation gives the insurer the rights of the insured after payment by the insurer to the insured for his loss sustained.

CASE FOR REVIEW

FIDELITY & GUAR. INS. UNDERWRITERS, INC. v. GREGORY

387 S.W. 2d 287 (Ky. 1965)

Fire destroyed appellee's dwelling on August 2, 1962, while a fire insurance policy issued by appellant was in force. The loss was total; the face value of the policy was $7000. The policy is a "valued policy" within the purview of KRS 304.905.

Appellee was out of Kentucky when the fire occurred. When he returned the next day he learned of the fire and reported it to the insurance agent from whom he had obtained the policy. That agent, Pruett, transmitted the information to appellant forthwith.

Under date August 6, 1962, appellant's general agent referred the fire loss to General Adjustment Bureau at the latter's Madisonville office. A copy of the transmittal letter from the general agent to General Adjustment was furnished Pruett, and is in evidence. The letter to the adjustment agency, on a prepared printed form, contained this language: "We have received notice of loss in connection with the above [the instant claim] and are taking the following action: Referring loss to you for adjustment. Forward completed loss papers to this office."

Shortly after receiving the adjustment instructions General Adjustment Bureau sent its employee, Wedding, to investigate the matter. Wedding met with the appellee at the fire scene, and made certain measurements. Wedding asked appellee to furnish a photograph of the residence as it had appeared before the fire; appellee did mail to Wedding such a photograph. Indeed, it is conceded that appellee fully "cooperated" with Wedding.

Wedding testified that he concluded that "as the fire was of undetermined origin and the house was vacant—and appeared to be over insured I made a report to Mr. Bracey." (Bracey is employed by the National Board of Fire Underwriters.) Wedding said that Bracey investigated the fire, as did an investigator for the State Fire Marshal.

Wedding further said that when the investigation case within the investigative jurisdiction of the Fire Marshall "there was nothing I could do until they were through." Accordingly, Wedding said that about two weeks after the fire he informed appellee that the matter was in the hands of the Fire Marshal, and that Wedding could do nothing until the Marshal's investigation had been concluded. Wedding testified that "the proof of loss was never mentioned" as between him and the appellee.

Appellee made one further communication with his own insurance broker, Pruett, at which time he indicated to Pruett that the claim had not been setteld. On October 15, 1962, appellee consulted and retained Raymond Dycus as his attorney to enforce payment on the policy. The attorney testified that on that date he had a telephone conversation with adjuster Wedding, and that Wedding said that the insurance company had waived proof of loss.

Our cases recognize the validity of provisions of insurance policies requiring proof of loss. In some instances the cases have dealt with such clauses which incorporate a provision for forfeiture of the insurance claim; in others, as in the present case, the provision does not impose forfeiture but makes the proper filing a condition precedent to maintenance of a suit upon the policy.

It is well established also that the filing of proof of loss may be waived.

We have held that an adjuster may waive such proof of loss. We believe the insurance company is estopped here to rely on failure to file proof of loss.

The insurance company can become bound by the activities of its agent, even though it may be said that the agent lacked actual authority to waive the filing of the proof of loss. We hold that Wedding's actions, in the sixty-day period, were sufficient as a matter of law to estop the appellant company from insisting on a proof of loss.

It is our view that Wedding's conduct, without respect to what he may or may not have said to attorney Dycus, was of that nature as "would naturally induce delay or lead an ordinarily prudent person to believe that the requirement of the policy respecting proof was waived by the company."

CASE PROBLEMS

1. Plaintiff, a builder, had completed several buildings on which he had not collected his payments, but he had recorded a mechanic's lien. He notified defendant's agent that he wanted to insure the premises and a policy was prepared with a mortgage clause but no other description of the interest of the plaintiff. Defendant denied the agent's right to insure lienholders. Decide.
2. The beneficiary sued on a policy of life insurance, the terms of which stipulated that it would not be effective unless delivered while the insured was in good health. The policy had been mailed to the local agent, who failed for three days to turn it over to the insured. An employee called for the policy and when asked if the insured was ill answered no, but after he had received the policy the agent was told that the insured had died the previous day from a bullet wound. Defendant contended that recovery was barred. Decide.
3. Plaintiff purchased a fire insurance policy covering his store and its contents from the defendant's agent. When a loss was claimed, defendant alleged that the plaintiff had other insurance of which defendant had no notice as required in the policy. Plaintiff showed that this information was given in the application received by the agent. Decide.
4. Plaintiff brought suit on his automobile policy and defendant alleged that the provisions on exclusions covered the circumstances of the claim. The policy

provided: "It is a condition of this policy that it shall become null and void (a) If the automobile described shall be used for carrying passengers for compensation." It was shown that the plaintiff had undertaken to carry a passenger for compensation, though payment had never been received, and while making the alleged trip the passenger had driven away with the auto. Decide.

5. A beneficiary brought suit against the insurance company. It was shown that the application for a $20,000 life insurance policy left a blank for the amount of the premium because the agent did not know "what the premium would figure". On April 7, 1969 the insurance company determined the rates issued a policy and mailed the policy to its agent, who received it Saturday, April 9. Before it was delivered to the insured he was killed. Decide.

6. A beneficiary brought an action claiming accidental death of the insured. It was alleged that he was killed in an encounter in which he was the aggressor. He attempted to force a man who he had previously beaten and abused through a kitchen window opening upon a court some sixteen feet below. Decide.

7. The insurance commissioner of the state of New York charged the defendant with issuing an insurance agreement without a license. The defendant watch company offered with the sale of its watches a certificate in which the company agreed to replace the watch if lost by burglary or robbery within a year from the purchase date. No charges were added to the sales price of the watch for the certificate. Decide.

8. The insurance commissioner of the state of Minnesota brought an action against ABC Automobile Association. That association prepared a contract wherein it agreed to furnish each member up to $100 to communicate with friends or relatives if he was physically unable to do so himself; to provide a limited bail bond if a member were arrested for a traffic violation; and to defend a member or any one of his family against criminal or civil litigation resulting from the use of his automobile. Decide.

THE SALES CONTRACT   39

Commercial transactions involving the sale of goods are as old as recorded history. In the earliest days, such dealings were very simple, usually involving only a buyer and seller in an across-the-table transaction. But as trade and commerce expanded, moving goods from the manufacturer to the ultimate consumer became complicated and middlemen became part of the marketing process. Modernization in transportation meant that goods could be shipped from one section of a country to another and from one nation to another in a relatively short time. However, while in transit, the goods were subject to local trade usages that varied from one jurisdiction to the next. The growing complexity of sales transactions, accompanied by an expanding use of credit, brought about the use of more detailed commercial contracts. The risk of loss in shipment, questions of warranty, and varying interpretations of statutes were only some of the new problems faced by buyers and sellers.

The law of sales consists primarily of statutes and statutory interpretations by the courts. Since rules developed by the courts in various jurisdictions were often conflicting and the resulting confusion was a hindrance to trade, the demand has grown for more uniformity in laws governing the sale of goods. Recently the United States made its most serious effort to obtain national uniformity, with the adoption in all states of the Uniform Commercial Code.

CONTRACT LAW AND THE LAW OF SALES

Since a sales transaction is evidenced by a legal contract, all the basic rules of contract law are applicable: there must be a legally binding agreement between the parties, the parties must have the legal capacity to act; the agreement must be supported by consideration; and the contract must have a legal object. Where any one of these requirements is lacking, the contract is not enforceable.

The Uniform Commercial Code has made some significant changes in the application of contract law to sales transactions in the areas of agreement, revocability of offers, additional terms in acceptance, and modification of existing agreements.

AGREEMENT

Sales and contracts to sell, like other commercial contracts, involve a manifested offer and acceptance. Under the common law of contracts, there must be a meeting of the minds, a definite agreement on all important terms. The U.C.C., Sec. 2-204(3) provides that:

even though one or more terms are left open, a contract for sale does not fail for indefiniteness if the parties have intended to make a contract and there is a reasonably certain basis for giving an appropriate remedy.

Sec. 2-207(3), further provides that:

conduct by both parties which recognizes the existence of a contract is sufficient to establish a contract for sale, although the writings do not otherwise establish a contract. In such case the terms of the particular contract consist of those terms on which the writings of the parties agree, together with any supplementary terms incorporated under any provisions of this Act.

REVOCABILITY OF OFFERS

According to contract law, an offer or option given to keep an offer open must be supported by consideration; otherwise, it is revocable by the person making the offer. The U.C.C. takes the opposite view. According to Sec. 2-205,

An offer by a merchant to buy or sell goods in a signed writing which by its terms gives assurance that it will be held open is not revocable, for lack of consideration, during the time stated or if no time is stated for a reasonable time, but in no event may such period of irrevocability exceed three months; but any term of assurance on a form supplied by the offeree must be separately signed by the offeror.

It should be noted that this rule applies to merchants who deal in goods or who have a peculiar skill or knowledge of the goods they are purporting to deal with in the transaction. Thus, an operator of a lumber yard, a clothing store, or any similar type of business would be considered a merchant under the U.C.C.

ADDITIONAL TERMS

Basic contract law holds that for an acceptance to be binding it must be an absolute and unconditional assent to the offer and must not propose new terms. If new terms are proposed, the acceptance becomes a counteroffer, which in effect terminates the original offer. The U.C.C., Sec. 2-207(1), modifies this rule somewhat:

A definite and reasonable expression of acceptance or a written confirmation which is sent within a reasonable time, operates as an acceptance even though it states terms additional to or different from those agreed upon, unless acceptance is expressly made conditional on assent to the additional or different terms.

These new terms proposed by the offeree are interpreted as proposals for additions to the existing contract that will not affect its validity unless the new terms materially alter the agreement. However, if the terms of the original offer demand an unqualified acceptance, no new terms may be proposed. (U.C.C. 2-207(2))

MODIFICATION OF EXISTING AGREEMENTS

Under basic contract law, no agreement to alter or modify an existing agreement is binding unless it is supported by additional consideration. However, the U.C.C. enforces agreements to modify existing sales contracts even in the absence of new consideration. These changes relax the rules of offers and acceptances as well as the rule of consideration. As a result, more bargains are held to be legally enforceable. (U.C.C. 2-209)

ACCEPTANCES

In a sales contract, acceptance of an offer may be made in any manner and by any medium that is regarded as reasonable under the circumstances and that signifies the offeree's assent to the terms of the offer in a manner requested or authorized by the offeror. (U.C.C. 2—204) When the offer calls for the performance of conditions, the offeror must be notified of the offeree's compliance within a reasonable time. Otherwise, the offeror may treat the offer as having lapsed. For example, where the buyer offers to purchase goods in return for prompt delivery, the seller has the option of making immediate shipment or of promising the offeror that he will make prompt delivery, depending on whether the parties contemplate a unilateral or a bilateral contract.

PRICE TERMS

The parties to a sales contract may agree on a fixed price or they may leave the price open, to be fixed at a future date on the basis of some definite external criteria. Four rules of the U.C.C. (2-305) are applicable:

1. The buyer must pay a reasonable price, usually the current market value, at the time of delivery if nothing is said regarding price in the contract.
2. If the price is to be fixed by either party, the seller or buyer must act in good faith in setting the price.
3. When the price is to be fixed in some manner other than by agreement but it is not fixed through the fault of one of the parties, the other party has the option of treating the contract as cancelled or of fixing a reasonable price himself.
4. If the intent of the parties is that there should be no contract if the price is not fixed in the manner agreed on, then no contract exists.

THE STATUTE OF FRAUDS

Under the Statute of Frauds, (U.C.C. 2-201) certain transactions must be reduced to a written agreement in order to be enforceable in court. Generally speaking, any contract for the sale of goods where the amount in question is $500 or more must be evidenced by a written memorandum. If the price to be paid is over the minimum amount, the sales contract is unenforceable unless the party seeking enforcement can show (1) part payment, (2) receipt and acceptance, or (3) admission of the existence of the contract by the other party.

The U.C.C. does not clarify the part payment or receipt and acceptance requirement in respect to the entire contract. Sec. 2-201 (3)(c) states only that the agreement is enforceable "with respect to goods for which payment has been made and accepted or which have been received and accepted."

According to the U.C.C., Sec. 2-201(1), "unless there is some writing sufficient to indicate (that) a contract for sale has been made between the parties and signed by the party against whom enforcement is sought," the contract is unenforceable.

As a rule, the Statute of Frauds does not apply to oral contracts if the goods are to be specially manufactured for the buyer and are not suitable for sale to other customers in the regular course of the seller's business. This is true in the absence of part payment, receipt and acceptance, or an admission of the existence of the contract. However, the seller must show that a substantial start has been made on the manufacture of the goods in question or that an agreement has been made for their procurement for the contract to be enforceable.

TRANSFER OF TITLE

The Uniform Commercial Code provides that, in a sales contract with no agreement to the contrary, the title to goods passes when the seller has made physical delivery of the proper goods in accordance with the contract. The rights, remedies, and obligations of the parties to the contract are governed by the provisions of the Code without respect to title and regardless of whether title has passed. It deals with problems between the seller and buyer in terms of step-by-step performance or nonperformance under their agreement.

Title to goods cannot pass under a contract for sale prior to their identification to the contract. The U.C.C. provides that "goods must be both existing and identified before any interest in them can pass." For example, if the seller agrees to sell the buyer 500 pairs of shoes and the seller has the shoes in his inventory, title will not pass to the buyer until the 500 pairs of shoes are selected and set aside as the shoes sold to the buyer.

SHIPPING TERMS

If documents of title are to be delivered instead of goods, title passes to the buyer at the time and place of delivery of such documents. (U.C.C. 2-401 (3)(a))

When shipping terms are employed, the U.C.C. refers to transfer of risk. For example, if an agreement is F.O.B. (free on board) shipping point, the seller bears the risk of loss or damage until the goods have been delivered to the carrier. If an agreement is F.O.B. destination, the risk is with the seller until the goods reach their destination. A similar result is reached in a F.A.S. (free alongside ship) agreement. (U.C.C. 2-319)

The Code provides that the terms C.F. or C.I.F. (cost, insurance, and freight), when employed, place an obligation on the seller to ship the goods, to pay insurance and freight charges, and to forward the shipping documents within a reasonable time. (U.C.C. 2-320) In this instance the risk of loss is with the buyer during shipment of the goods. The Code continues the use of C.O.D. (collect on delivery), which tells the carrier not to deliver the goods until the purchase price has been paid. Although the seller retains control over the goods, title passes upon delivery to the carrier. With regard to shipments "to arrive" or contracts on the basis of "no arrival, no sale," the seller is not responsible for the goods' failure to arrive if he has not been negligent, but the buyer may avoid the contract. In an agreement "ex ship" (from carrying vessel), the risk of loss does not pass to the buyer until the goods are properly unloaded.

DELIVERY

Delivery of goods is usually made at the point of shipment or at the time of arrival at their destination, depending on the conditions of the sales agreement. If the goods described in the contract are to be delivered without being moved, title will pass at the time and place of sale unless the seller is required to deliver a document of title, in which case title will pass at the time and place of delivery of the title document. In other words, the title passes whenever the seller completes his performance with reference to the physical delivery of the goods. [U.C.C. 2-401(3)]

CASH SALES

If the contract calls for delivery of the goods and payment of the purchase price to occur simultaneously, the transaction is generally a cash sale, and the goods must be paid for before title passes. (U.C.C. 2-507) Ownership as well as possession of the goods is here exchanged for a payment made at the same time. No portion of the deal is left to be completed later. If the buyer pays by check, the check is usually considered conditional payment only; however, title will vest in the buyer subject to seller's remedies if the check does not clear. (U.C.C. 2-511)

SALE ON APPROVAL

In a sale on approval, the goods are delivered to the buyer to use, but the title and risk of loss remain with the seller until the buyer indicates that he intends to keep the goods. The buyer's use of the goods, in accordance with the trial offer, does not constitute acceptance; but failure to inform the seller before the completion or termination of the trial period (or within a reasonable time if there is no set trial period) that he elects to return the goods is deemed an acceptance. The buyer has title and is responsible for loss of the goods. Until acceptance, goods sold on approval cannot be subject to the claims of the buyer's creditors. (U.C.C. 2-326)

SALE OR RETURN

In a sale specified as "sale or return," when the buyer receives the goods, the title and risk of loss pass to him, as do all incidents of ownership. The buyer does have the option of returning the goods instead of paying the purchase price. If this is done, the returned goods again become the property of the seller. The option of returning the goods must be exercised by returning or tendering the return within the time fixed in the contract or within a reasonable time if no time has been fixed. However, the return of the articles is at the buyer's own risk and expense. The goods, as long as the buyer possesses them, are subject to the claims of his creditors, and he must pay taxes on them. (U.C.C. 2-326)

RISK OF LOSS

The risk of loss of goods offered for sale is determined by the contract. Ordinarily, the risk rests with the buyer as soon as the seller delivers the goods to the carrier. If, however, the contract requires that the seller deliver the goods to a specific place, the buyer does not assume the risk until the goods are tendered there by the seller. The rules regarding risk of loss assume that the requirements of the contract have been correctly followed by the seller. (U.C.C. 2-509)

If a merchant is the seller and the buyer is to receive the goods at the seller's place of business, the buyer does not assume the risk of loss until he receives the goods. The seller is able to protect himself, while still in control of the goods, with suitable insurance. If the seller is not a merchant, the risk of loss passes to the buyer when he is tendered delivery, whether or not he has received the goods. (U.C.C. 2-509(3) These rules may be altered by agreement between the seller and buyer.

LEGAL PRINCIPLES

The law of sales consists primarily of statutes and statutory interpretations. The Uniform Commercial Code provides statutory uniformity in those states where it has been adopted.

Sales contracts do not fail for indefiniteness if it can be shown that the parties intended a contract.

An agreement by a merchant to hold an offer open is irrevocable, even in the absence of consideration, for the time stated or for a reasonable time if none is stated, but in any event for a period not exceeding three months.

An acceptance calling for additional terms is not considered a counteroffer unless it radically alters the basic agreement. Contracts may be modified without furnishing additional consideration.

Acceptance may be made in any reasonable manner.

Consideration may be determined at a time after the agreement. Contracts for the sale of goods valued at $500 or more must be in writing unless the goods are to be specially manufactured for the buyer.

Under the U.C.C., with no agreement to the contrary, title to goods passes when the seller has made physical delivery of the goods.

The rights, remedies, and obligations of the parties involved in a contract for sale in the United States are governed by the provisions of the U.C.C.

Title in goods cannot pass prior to their identification to the contract.

Under an F.O.B. or F.A.S. agreement, risk of loss is with the seller until the goods reach the specified point.

Under a C.F. or C.I.F. agreement, risk of loss is with the buyer as soon as the seller pays the shipping costs and forwards the shipping documents to him.

In a C.O.D. sale title passes to the buyer upon delivery of the goods to the carrier.

Delivery of the goods is made at the point of shipment or at their destination, depending upon the sales agreement.

In a cash sale, title passes when payment is made.

In a sale on approval, title passes when the buyer indicates his approval.

A "sale or return" condition indicates a present sale with an option to return both goods and title to the seller.

A good-faith purchaser obtains a valid title to goods purchased from a seller who has a voidable title.

Who bears the risk of loss is determined by the agreement between the parties.

CASE FOR REVIEW

COOK GRAINS, INC. v. FALLIS

395 S.W.2d 555 (Ark. 1965)

Cook Grains, Inc., filed this suit alleging that it entered into a valid contract with Paul Fallis, whereby Fallis sold and agreed to deliver to Cook 5000 bushels of soybeans at $2.54 per bushel. It is alleged that Fallis breached the alleged contract by failing to deliver the beans, and that as a result . . . Cook has been damaged in the sum of $1,287.50. There was a judgment for Fallis. The grain company has appealed.

Appellant introduced evidence to the effect that its agent, Lester Horton, entered into a verbal agreement with appellee whereby appellee sold and agreed to deliver to appellant grain company 5000 bushels of beans; that delivery was to be made in September, October, and November 1963. Fallis denied entering into such a contract. He contends that although a sale was discussed, no agreement was reached. He also contends that the alleged contract is barred by the statute of frauds.

Following the discussion or sale, whichever it was, between Horton and Fallis, grain company prepared and mailed to Fallis a proposed contract in writing which provided that Fallis sold to the grain company 5000 bushels of beans. The instrument was signed by the grain company and it would have been bound thereby if Fallis had signed the paper, but Fallis did not sign the instrument and did not return it to the grain company. Later, Fallis refused to deliver the beans and the grain company filed suit.

The . . . grain company concedes that ordinarily the alleged cause of action would be barred by the statute of frauds, but contends that here the alleged sale is taken out of the statute of frauds by the Uniform Commercial Code. . . .

(1) Except as otherwise provided in this section a contract for the sale of goods for the price of $500 or more is not enforceable by way of action or defense unless there is some writing sufficient to indicate that a contract for sale has been made between the parties and signed by the party against whom enforcement is sought or by his authorized agent or broker. A writing is not insufficient because it omits or incorrectly states a term agreed upon but the contract is not enforceable under this paragraph beyond the quantity of goods shown in such writing. (2) Between merchants if within a reasonable time a writing in confirmation of the contract and sufficient against the sender is received and the party receiving it has reason to know its contents, it satisfies the requirements of subsection (1) against such party unless written notice of objection to its contents is given within ten [10] days after it is received. . . .

The solution of the case turns on the point of whether . . . Fallis is a "merchant" within the meaning of the statute [which] provides:

Merchant means a person who deals in goods of the kind or otherwise by his occupation holds himself out as having knowledge or skill peculiar to the practices or goods involved in the transaction or to whom such knowledge or skill may be attributed by his employment of an agent or broker or other intermediary who by his occupation holds himself out as having such knowledge or skill. . . .

There is not a scintilla of evidence in the record, or proffered as evidence, that appellee is a dealer in goods of the kind or by his occupation holds himself out as having knowledge or a skill peculiar to the practices of goods involved in the transaction, and no such knowledge or skill can be attributed to him.

The evidence in this case is that appellee is a farmer and nothing else. He farms about five hundred fifty acres and there is no showing that he has any other occupation. . . .

Our attention has been called to no case, and we have found none holding that the word "farmer" may be construed to mean merchant.

If the General Assembly had intended that in the circumstances of this case a farmer should be considered a merchant and therefore liable on an alleged contract to sell his commodities, which he did not sign, no doubt clear and explicit language would have been used in the statute to that effect. There is nothing whatever in the statute indicating that the word "merchant" should apply to a farmer when he is acting in the capacity of a farmer, and he comes within that category when he is merely trying to sell the commodities he has raised.

Notes 1 and 2 under Ark. Stat.Ann. § 85-2-104 (1961 Addendum), (Uniform Commercial Code), defining merchant indicate that this provision of the statute is meant to apply to professional traders. In Note 1 it is stated: "This section lays the foundation of this policy defining those who are to be regarded as professionals or 'merchants'. . . ." It is said in Note 2: "The term 'merchant' as defined here roots in the 'law merchant' concept of a professional in business . . . ."

> A merchant is defined to be, in one sense, a trader, by Webster, and by Burrill and Bouvier in their Law Dictionaries, and a person who is engaged in farming and stock raising is not a merchant. *In re Ragsdale,* 20 Fed.Cas. 175.
>
> The term "merchants" includes those only who traffic, in the way of commerce, by importation or exportation, who carry on business by way of emption, vendition, barter, permutation, or exchange and who make it their living to buy and sell by a continued vivacity or frequent negotiations in the mystery of merchandise, and does not include a farmer who sells what he makes. *Dyott v. Letcher,* 29 Ky. (6 J. J. Marsh.) 541, 543.

In construing a statute its words must be given their plain and ordinary meaning.

CASE PROBLEMS

1. Evans gave the plaintiff's agent an order for merchandise of the value of $686. The latter made a memorandum which he sent to the plaintiff. This memorandum had not been signed by defendants. A few days later, defendants wrote to plaintiff acknowledging that they had "placed an order for a few skirts on December 7" and requesting plaintiff to delay shipment. However, the plaintiff shipped the goods. Defendants refused to accept them. Plaintiff sued for the purchase price, and the defendants pleaded the Statute of Frauds. Decide.
2. Defendant bought hay in the mow at an auction sale of plaintiff's stock and farm produce. The arrangement was that defendant could leave the hay in the mow and that it was to be weighed as taken away. Before any of the hay was removed, it was destroyed by accidental fire. Plaintiff sued for the estimated price, and defendant contended that title had not passed because weighing was necessary to determine the exact purchase price. Decide.
3. Mrs. Chyrchel purchased a mobile home which was delivered and installed. The sewer and gas lines were attached, but the electricity had not been turned on, when fire destroyed the mobile home. When sued for the purchase price, Mrs. Chrychel alleged that since the trailer had not been prepared for occupancy, the risk of loss was still with the seller. Decide.
4. A New Hampshire jewelry dealer purchased two diamonds on a "sale or return" agreement. While they were in his possession, he was informed that the diamonds were stolen property. He, therefore, refused to pay the contract purchase price. The seller brought this action. Decide.
5. Dickinson owned 6249 bushels of wheat that were stored in a warehouse in two piles. Shuttle agreed to purchase 6000 bushels, signing a memo to attest to the purchase. Shuttle left the wheat in the warehouse and later sold it to Patchin, defendant, who obtained possession of it. In the meantime. Dickinson sold both piles of the wheat to a person from whom Kimerly, plaintiff, derived his claim. Kimberly brought suit on the grounds that title to the wheat had never passed to Shuttle and so could not have been passed on to Patchin. Decide.
6. Plaintiffs contracted to purchase defendant's entire output of absorbent paper, which was to be manufactured and stored in defendant's warehouse, and cut into sizes as directed by plaintiffs before delivery. Plaintiffs advanced $36,000, and about $5000 worth of paper had been packed and shipped, when a receiver was appointed for defendant. Plaintiffs brought suit to claim the paper in defendant's warehouse that was already rolled, and the receiver insisted that title to the goods had not passed. Decide.

7. Brown was a local distributor for Storz Brewing Company. Under the distribution contract, sales were made at prices set by the company, "all f.o.b. Storz Brewing Company's plant, from which shipment is made. Distributor agrees to pay all freight and transportation charges from Storz Brewing Company's place of business to the delivery point designated by the distributor, and all delivery expenses." Brown wrote instructing the company to deliver a quantity of beer to his trucker, Stein, as soon as the latter would accept the goods. The company delivered the goods to Stein, but the trucker was later delayed en route by snow, and prolonged exposure to subzero temperatures caused the beer to freeze. Brown rejected the shipment and was sued by the company for the purchase price. Decide.

PRODUCTS LIABILITY AND   40
WARRANTY

"Products Liability Cases" are those involving the liability of the seller, manufacturer, processor or supplier, for injuries caused to the person or property of another by a defect in the product sold. A court recently concluded in one of these cases that they could "see no rational . . . basis for differentiating between a fly in a bottle of beverage and a defective automobile." This statement is indicative of the transformation that has taken place in the area of product liability law in the United States. In no other legal area has change been more rapid and more pronounced. The result has been to increase the liability of the seller, manufacturer, processor, and supplier of goods and to increase the classes of injured parties who may seek recovery in court actions.

Initially, products liability was restricted to the sale of foodstuffs for human consumption. It has been expanded to include almost any product that might cause injury to the physical well-being of a person. This liability may be predicated on several legal principles. The most obvious of these is the violation of a statute which imposes a strict liability for selling or supplying a product that is either defective or contaminated (i.e., pure food and drug statutes). Other principles are negligence, warranty, or strict liability. Each of these latter principles will be examined in terms of the facts that must be present for the imposition of liability, the quality of the proof that must be offered, defenses avilable, and injured parties who may be entitled to recover damages in court actions.

NEGLIGENCE

A minority of jurisdictions still adhere to the use of negligence as a form of recovery in the products liability cases—the theory being: "Assuming that the product was defective or dangerous, can this condition be traced to the manufacturer of the product?" It is the conduct of the defendant that is the determining factor in each situation.

In these cases, the plaintiff who obtained the product and is injured has the burden of establishing: (1) a duty owed by the manufacturer to the plaintiff with regard to the condition of the product; (2) the failure by the manufacturer to satisfactorily discharge that duty; and (3) injuries to the plaintiff received as a direct result of this breach of duty. The non-privity plaintiff, or the person who obtained the product from someone other than the manufacturer, would have to prove that the product was either inherently or imminently dangerous to the well-being of his person when it left the control of the manufacturer.

The basic difficulty in these situations is in proving the allegation of negligence in the manufacturing, processing, inspecting or testing processes involved in the production of the finished product, regardless of how slight the defect may have been when it left the control of the manufacturer. Even if the plaintiff is able to sustain the burden of proof, he may be defeated by the defense of contributory negligence in his own use of the product or by the defense that the product was put to an abnormal or unintended use.

WARRANTY

At common law the seller had no obligation with regard to the quality of the goods sold (caveat emptor). Sales were infrequent, and the buyer usually had ample opportunity to inspect the goods prior to purchase. Any statements that were made were treated as opinions and the only way a buyer could impose an obligation on the seller was by asking him for an express guaranty regarding the goods.

Today, in most sales contracts, the seller undertakes certain obligations incidental to the transaction concerning the nature and quality of the goods sold. When these obligations arise by virtue of an express statement or conduct on his part and relate the title, nature, or quality of the goods he is selling and when they actually induce the sale, the obligations are called *warranties*. (See Figure 40-1) Where a sale is based on a description of the goods or on a sample, the seller is under an obligation to furnish goods that conform to the description or the sample. A warranty, therefore, is a guaranty by the seller with respect to the goods he sells. Moreover, certain obligations are imposed upon sellers by law. These obligations are made part of the transaction in absence of any express contractual arrangements. They are determined by the type of business, product involved, and by the motive of the transaction. Such obligations are known as implied warranties.

The problems for the plaintiff are: (1) was there privity of contract with the manufacturer, processor, or supplier of the product; and (2) was the warranty made a part of the bargain.

EXPRESS WARRANTIES

An *express warranty* is an affirmation of fact or a promise made by the seller to the buyer concerning the nature of the goods. A promise of this sort becomes the basis for the contract. It usually takes the form of a written or oral statement but may sometimes result from the seller's conduct. No particular language or conduct is required, as long as the seller represents facts to the buyer to induce him to buy the goods. It is not even necessary to use the term "warranty." Exceptions to this rule are made, however, when dealers engage in exaggerations about their goods that should be obvious to the buyer. Although they are made to induce the sale, such obvious exaggerations are not treated as warranties because both parties are considered to be entitled to an opinion about the value of the goods. (U.C.C. 2-313)

Where the goods are sold by description, number, or grade, any identifying mark that is made an essential element of the bargain creates an express

Guaranty Against Moth Damage 49269

This Guaranty is insured by THE EMPLOYERS' LIABILITY ASSURANCE CORPORATION, LTD. Boston 7, Massachusetts

Identification of Chest

212604 464030

(Style Number) (Serial Number)

Term of Guaranty

From ____________, 19______ to ____________, 19______

The Lane Company hereby agrees to reimburse the Owner for all Moth Damage to the contents of the above-designated chest in an amount not exceeding One Thousand Dollars ($1,000.00) subject to the conditions set forth below.

1. This Guaranty applies to property owned by the Owner of said chest or by any permanent member of his or her household who does not pay board or rent or by a relative of said Owner permanently residing with him or her, but it does not apply to property owned by a domestic servant or employee of said Owner.

2. (a) The Owner shall take all reasonable means of precaution and ascertain that all property stored in said chest is free of damage caused by moths prior to storing in said chest; (b) the lid of said chest shall be kept closed except when opened to deposit property therein or remove property therefrom; in no event shall the lid be left open longer than absolutely necessary for such deposit or removal of property; (c) the Chest Style Number and Chest Serial Number above shall agree with those of the chest; if the numbers do not agree this Guaranty shall be null and void; (d) this Guaranty applies only to the contents of the chest, designated above, excluding drawer compartments.

3. The Lane Company, Inc., shall not be liable under this Guaranty beyond the actual damage caused by moths to the contents of the chest at the time of discovery of the damage and in no event beyond (a) the actual cash value of the contents, with a proper deduction for depreciation, or (b) One Thousand Dollars ($1,000.00). The Lane Company, Inc., may, at its option, repair any damaged property or replace it with property of like quality and value.

Owner's Name and Address:
Mr & Mrs M P Litka
602 Emerald Ln
Carbondale Ill

4. Upon discovery of Moth Damage the Owner shall give immediate notice thereof to The Lane Company, Inc., at Altavista, Virginia, and also, shall, within thirty (30) days of said discovery, give under oath to The Lane Company, Inc., all the particulars of said Moth Damage requested by The Lane Company, Inc.

5. This Guaranty does not apply if the interest of the Owner in said chest (a) is other than unconditional and sole (except when being purchased on a deferred payment plan), or (b) is transferred, sold or terminated other than by death of said Owner.

6. This Guaranty shall be in lieu of all other Guaranties, express or implied.

7. This Guaranty shall be deemed to have been made in the Commonwealth of Virginia and shall be governed by its law.

This Guaranty is fully insured by a policy issued to The Lane Company, Inc., by The Employers' Liability Assurance Corporation, Ltd., Boston, Massachusetts.

E 8001-6 PART 1

The Lane *Company, Inc., Altavista, Va.*

Figure 40-1

warranty that the goods shall conform to the description. The same is true where the sale is based on samples or models; the seller warrants that all the goods will conform to the sample or model.

If the buyer, by his words or conduct, indicates that he is relying on his own judgment or knowledge in purchasing the goods, no express warranty can be claimed. Likewise, where the goods are made available for inspection prior to the agreement, an express warranty will not cover defects that should have been apparent to a buyer who inspected the property with reasonable care. Where a defect is known to the buyer at the time he agrees to purchase, he may not claim the benefit of an express warranty, since it obviously was not made a basis of the bargain. However, the U.C.C. does not require that the buyer prove his reliance upon an express warranty in actions for breach of warranty. He must merely show that the warranty was made in connection with the transaction.

IMPLIED WARRANTIES

Certain warranties are considered part of the bargain even though the parties themselves say nothing about them. The U.C.C. recognizes two classes of implied warranties: *warranties of title* (which include warranties against infringement) and *warranties of merchantability* (which include warranties arising out of normal trade usage). The parties may agree to exclude any or all implied warranties from their agreement. Such a provision, if its language is clear and unequivocal, will usually be enforced by the courts. (U.C.C. 2-316)

Usually, when the seller sells goods to the buyer, he not only implicitly warrants that he has a right to sell the goods and can pass good title, he warrants that the goods will be free of any encumbrance unknown to the buyer at the time of the sale. In addition, the seller makes an implied warranty against infringement. Sec. 2-312(3) of the U.C.C. provides that the goods "shall be delivered free from any rightful claim of any third person by way of infringment or the like, but a buyer who furnishes specifications to the seller must hold the seller harmless against any such claim which arises out of compliance with the specifications." This implies that the goods will be delivered free of such claims to title as patents, trademarks, or trade names. "Specifications" refers to blueprints, plans, or other similar directions to be followed by the seller.

In addition, a seller whose business it is to sell goods of a certain type is responsible under an implied warranty for the merchantability of the goods at the time of the transaction, that is, for their salability in the market as goods of the kind ordered by the buyer. To be merchantable, goods must be free from defects and reasonably suited for the purpose for which they are ordinarily intended. Also, the goods must be even in quality. The quantity within each unit of goods and among all units involved in the transaction must also be even. The U.C.C. requires that goods be adequately contained, packaged, and labeled, also according to the conditions of the agreement. If any promises are printed on the package, the goods must conform to such promises. Sec. 2-314(1) of the Code goes on to state that "the serving for value of food or drinks to be consumed either on the premises or elsewhere is a sale" and hence is subject to the warranty of merchantability. In other words, when a person is in the business of selling food, the food must be sufficiently wholesome to be suitable for eating.

FITNESS WARRANTIES

The Uniform Commercial Code in 2-314 (1) and 2-315 imposes so-called "fitness" warranties on each sale made by a merchant as:

> Unless excluded or modified, a warranty that the goods shall be merchantable is implied in a contract for their sale if the seller is a merchant with respect to goods of that kind. . . .
> Where the seller at the time of contracting has reason to know any particular purpose for which the goods are required and that the buyer is relying on the seller's skill or judgment to select or furnish suitable goods, there is unless excluded or modified . . . an implied warranty that the goods shall be fit for such purpose.

The warranty of merchantability and fitness for a purpose limit the various defenses that were available to the seller, manufacturer, processor and supplier of goods. For example, the Code's definition of merchantability indicates that products placed in the stream of commerce will pass without objection; they are of fair average quality; are fit for the ordinary purposes for which such goods are used; are adequately packaged, and fulfill the promises made on the container. Thus, according to the decisions of the various courts the question in a warranty liability case is, "Are the goods reasonably fit for the ordinary purpose for which they are sold."

The seller was formerly able to defend on the grounds that he had nothing to do with the packaging or processing, therefore, he was without fault. The use of the implied warranty of merchantability has eliminated this defense.

Another defense that has been virtually eliminated for the seller is that there was a failure of the buyer to make known the specific purpose for which the product was going to be used. The courts' reasoning in these cases is that where the particular purpose or use made of a product is no different than its ordinary use, the seller is presumed to know the purpose by reason of the very nature of the product sold. Actual communication of purpose, therefore, is not needed. This is true even if the product in question was a brand name item.

ADVERTISEMENTS

In warranty cases the injured plaintiff must show that he was in that class of persons covered by privity of contract with the manufacturer. Recent decisions have altered the strict application of this concept by finding express warranties in the manufacturers' use of advertising in various media. Today, manufacturers are showing an increasing reliance on outdoor advertising, radio, television, newspapers and magazines to attract prospective purchasers to the quality of their products. Therefore, these cases hold that certain statements of fact, where relevance is properly shown, can constitute an express warranty despite the fact that the purchaser is not dealing directly with the manufacturer (i.e., privity of contract is not present.)

The New York Court of Appeals expressed this concept:

> The world of merchandising is . . . no longer a world of direct contract; it is rather, a world of advertising and, when representations expressed and disseminated in the mass communication media . . . prove false and the user or consumer is damaged by reason of his reliance on those representations . . . it is highly unrealistic to limit a purchaser's protection to warranties made directly to him by his immediate seller. The protection he really needs is against the manufacturer whose published representations caused him to make the purchase. [*Ranky Knitwear, Inc.,* v. *American Cyanamid Co.,* 181 N.E.2d 399, 402 (1962)]

Since warranty liability arises out of the contract between the parties and is imposed upon the sale of each product, the manufacturer need not make any warranties. He is also in a position to limit the warranty as far as remedies available to the injured party and to whom these remedies are applicable. Its application has likewise been restricted to products intended for personal use or consumption and recovery has been limited to the purchaser, family members of the purchaser, guests in his home, and employees.

The injured plaintiff, therefore, to sustain his case must prove: (1) that the warranty exists, (2) that he is a beneficiary of the warranty; and (3) that the resultant injuries caused the alleged breach of warranty.

EXCLUSION OF WARRANTIES

The buyer and seller may modify or exclude the implied warranties of merchantability or fitness for a particular purpose by an express provision in the sales contract. To accomplish this, the language employed must be clear and unequivocal, because any ambiguity in the contract will be construed against the seller. The Code, Sec. 2-316(1), states:

> to exclude or modify the implied warranty of merchantability or any part of it the language must mention merchantability and the case of a writing must be conspicuous, and to exclude or modify any implied warranty of fitness, the exclusion must be by a writing and conspicious.

For example, the following statement would exclude warranties of fitness: "There are no warranties that extend beyond the description on the face hereof."

The warranty of title and the warranty against infringement may also be modified or excluded by specific wording to that effect. Modification may similarly be accomplished by circumstances indicating an intention on the seller's part to sell without warranties. For instance, all implied warranties are excluded by terms like "as is" or "with all faults" or by other similar language. Also, an examination of the goods or samples, or a refusal to examine them, will preclude an implied warranty with regard to a defect that an examination would have disclosed to the prospective buyer. Business practice and trade usage may also exclude implied warranties.

EXTENSION OF WARRANTIES

At common law it was long established that the warranty obligation extended only to the parties to the contract and not to any other person, even those who might use or come in contact with the goods. Under the U.C.C., Sec. 2-318, however, the application of the seller's warranty extends to "any natural person who is in the family or household of his buyer or who is a guest in his home, if it is reasonable to expect that such person may use, consume, or be affected by the goods, and who is injured by breach of the warranty." It states further that "a seller may not exclude or limit the operation of this section"—which is interpreted to mean that the seller has absolute liability on any such warranty. It might be argued on this basis that the warranty obligation runs with the goods.

STRICT LIABILITY

Strict liability is liability imposed on the seller even though he exercised reasonable care. For example, in *Henningson* v. *Bloomfield Motors Inc.,*[1] Chrysler and the car dealer were held liable for injuries to the passenger due to a defective automobile, without evidence of negligence. "An implied warranty that it is reasonably suitable for use as such accompanies it into the hands of the ultimate purchaser. Absence of agency . . . is immaterial."

This decision refuted the concept of privity and extended liability beyond food and drink. The risks resulting from the use of defective products is shifted to the seller, manufacturer, processor and supplier of goods. *Henningson* has been approved in over 30 jurisdictions and in more than 200 cases. It has been applied to hair tint, polio vaccine, champagne, a glass door, shotgun, electrical cable, bar stool and hula skirt. Liability has been extended to lessors, builders, licensors, and suppliers of services. The manufacturer may incur liability not only by allowing his finished product to enter the stream of commerce but also as a supplier of component parts to other manufacturers. He may incur liability even if he purchases component parts for his own finished product from a supplier.

A purchaser of a power tool sued the manufacturer, not because of a defect, but because the design of the tool was such that it was able to hurl a piece of wood through the air, hitting and injuring the user. In another case an earthmoving machine while backing up killed a workman. It was alleged that because of a huge rear engine box, the driver could not see a man six feet in height as far as forty-eight feet behind the earthmover. The manufacturer was held liable for neglecting his "duty" to reduce this potential hazard, even though it was shown that rearview mirrors extending four feet would not completely eliminate the blind area, and even though the hazard may have been obvious to the workman. The term user has been extended to include passengers in automobiles, and those doing work upon the product such as an employee of the buyer. In another case the plaintiff, a bystander was allowed to recover when he was injured by an exploding shotgun.

Under the concept of strict liability the plaintiff must allege and prove that the defect existed when the product was delivered by the seller and that the defect was the proximate cause of the injury. The conduct of the defendant, therefore, is not an essential element of the transaction it is in a negligence case.

A final item that should be pointed out is that in a contract the Statute of Limitations runs from the time of the contract, whereas in strict liability it is measured from the time of the injury.

LEGAL PRINCIPLES

The term "product liability" is relatively new in American law.

An express warranty is an affirmation of fact or a promise made by the seller to the buyer concerning the goods in a sales transaction that becomes a basis for the sales contract. No particular language or conduct is required to create an express warranty.

A seller's conversation with respect to the goods he is selling is not considered an express warranty because it represents only his opinion as to the goods. Reliance on the seller's opinion is not justified in law in matters upon which the buyer may make a personal judgment.

Where goods are sold by a description, sample, or model, there is an express warranty that the goods shall conform to the description, sample, or model.

Usually, when the seller sells goods to the buyer, he not only implicitly warrants that he has a right to sell them and can pass good title but also that the goods will be free of any encumbrance unknown to the buyer at the time of the sale. This includes the implicit warranty that the goods are free from the rightful claim of any third person.

The implied warranty of merchantability means that the goods are salable in the seller's ordinary line of business.

Where the seller knows the purpose for which the buyer intends the goods and it is apparent that the buyer is relying on the seller's judgment as to their suitability, there is an implied warranty of fitness for the particular purpose.

Where warranties are to be excluded, the language employed in the exclusion statement must be clear and unequivocal.

Warranties extend to guests and members of the buyer's household who could be expected to use the goods.

Those who may be held to answer for injuries has been expanded to include not only the manufacturer and the dealer, but also the manufacturer of component parts, repair and reconditioning firms, assemblers, and lessors of products.

Beneficiaries of this extended coverage include even the casual bystander.

CASES FOR REVIEW

LOOMIS BROS. CORP. v. QUEEN

46 Del. 79 (1958)

This is a petition to open confessed judgment based upon a contract wherein plaintiff was to install fourteen storm and screen windows in defendants' home. Defendants allege the windows were defective, useless as storm windows and not fit for the purpose intended, and that they did not fit snug and tight and did not keep out the rain, snow and wind, and shook and rattled and were not air tight. Plaintiff admits that the storm windows did not fit the aluminum frames snug and tight and that they may let in air and they may rattle.

The windows were purchased from an operating sample consisting of the storm window in miniature, mounted in a frame. They are known as "No. 7 triple track storm and screen windows and tilt features". Admittedly this was a low-priced commodity. Both petitioner and plaintiff knew this. At the hearing, there was a general accord in the matter of the circumstances surrounding the sale and the sample was produced. It was explained, and it seemed apparent from an examination of the same, that the trouble comes about because of the tilting device. It is to be borne in mind that this tilting device is a feature usually found on the more expensive storm windows. It permits interchange of screen and window and self-storage of the part not in use easily from inside the house. In order to provide this desirable feature and keep the price down, this window is ingeniously devised, providing three tracks for the window and screen sections, but none of these tracks have protection on the inside. If they did, they could not tilt when the locking device was released, nor can this inside feature be provided at the price of these storm windows. Therein lies the principal difference between these cheaper windows with the tilting device and the better type. Here is demonstrated the old axiom which I misquote as follows: "There is no quality article made but which some competitor may copy, cheapen and substitute therefor." When one examines the sample and relates its construction to the full-size window, the defect is apparent. Since there is no inside support, the narrow cross member does not bear tightly against the sash. This seemingly makes little difference in the sample, but in the full-size window this lost contact is increased proportionately, and it is here that the wind and rain enter.

Legally we have here presented a very close question. The goods were purchased by sample, the goods conformed to the sample. Query; Must the goods also do the job for which they were designed and, if not, who bears the risk? Section 2-313 of the Uniform Commercial Code of April 6, 1953, "Express Warranties by Affirmation, Promise, Description, Samples", provides: "(c) Any sample or model which is made a basis of the bargain creates an express warranty that the whole of the goods shall conform to the sample or model."

It would seem from a precise interpretation of this section that substantial conformity to the model constitutes performance, but a reading of the cases both before and since the present Uniform Commercial Code indicates that something more is required and that is "fitness for the purpose intended" and "merchantability". All agree that here was conformity and merchantability. It is this fitness for purpose intended that presents the problem, and the philosophy of the law seems to indicate that this principle is basic and must be present in the article supplied regardless of the limitations surrounding a sale by sample or by description.

This was a sale by description and there seems to be little or no difference between a sale by description and a sale by sample with respect to the fitness for purpose intended.

The purpose of storm windows is to keep out wind and weather. These windows conformed to the sample. They are merchantable, but they did not keep out wind and weather. It is conceivable that these windows, installed in a city residence, might have worked satisfactorily. The buyer here had built a new house in a rural section, without the protection of other dwellings and exposed to the full velocity of wind and weather, so even on the question of fitness for purpose intended, these windows cannot be unqualifiedly condemned.

The Commercial Code under discussion here is intended to be a uniform code and that means not only should it be uniformly adopted in the Nation, but that it should be uniformly interpreted. Perhaps in the nature of things, interpretation by the various State courts might vary, although we find no variation as yet, but it seems that a good source of uniformity in interpretation to follow would be that adopted by the Federal courts, if sound. In the case of *John E. Smith's Sons Co.* v. *Lattimer Foundry & Machine Co.,* 19 F.R.D. 379, 389, a case in the middle district of Pennsylvania, interpreting the Pennsylvania statute, the court said: "There was an implied warranty of fitness for the purpose intended that the castings would be the same as the sample."

We are therefore of the opinion that . . . under . . . the Uniform Commercial Code, where the seller submitted sample of goods to the buyer, there was implied warranty of fitness for the purpose intended *and* that goods would be same as sample. Therefore, we think that fitness for purpose intended is the basic ingredient in every item sold, no matter by what type of bargaining the contract is reached, where the seller at the time of contracting has reason to know any particular purpose for which the goods are required and that the buyer is relying on the seller's skill or judgment to select or furnish suitable goods.

GRECO v. BUCCICONI ENGINEERING CO.

407 F.2d 87 (1969)

Frank G. Greco, an employee of the Jones & Laughlin Steel Corporation (hereinafter "J. & L.") suffered serious personal injuries when a magnetic sheet piler malfunctioned at the J. & L. Pittsburgh mill.

The piler in question was delivered to J. & L. in three sections and assembled by J. & L. employees. Its funciton in J. & L.'s new sheet coating line was to collect and pile sheet metal in preparation for shipment to J. & L.'s customers. Sheets of steel came into the piler by means of an overhead magnetic conveyor. Magnets in the conveyor would deactivate when the sheets were directly over the piling area and the sheets would drop between parallel side guides and end stops onto a lift or hoist which was lowered by an operator after a certain number of sheets had settled on it. When this hoist was being lowered to carry the piled sheets to a conveyor system, two strips of metal called "fingers" would protrude from the side guides of the piler to catch and hold the newly arriving steel sheets. When the hoist returned, the fingers would retract into the side guides of the piler, and those sheets that had been collected by the fingers would settle onto the hoist.

Soon after the piler went into operation its fingers began to retract erratically without activation from the operator at the control panel. Four days prior to appellee's injury, J. & L. inserted two "pins" in the fingers in an attempt to prevent this retraction and the resultant spilling of the steel sheets to the floor. Neither appellee nor the other employees were instructed in the use of these pins. It was appellee's belief, based upon his limited experience with the pins during the short time they were in use, that the fingers could not malfunction as long as one of the pins remained inserted; he was not told otherwise. On the day of the accident, with one pin in and the other out, appellee reached beneath the sheet-catching fingers to straighten and center wrapping paper on the hoist as it rose to collect a new pile of steel; without any activation from the control panel, one of the fingers retracted causing the sheets above to tumble down atop appellee's outstretched hand.

Since appellee did not introduce substantial evidence relevant to appellants' negligence in the manufacture or design of the piler, we must first determine whether it is the law of Pennsylvania, as appellee asserts, that a plaintiff in a strict liability case can establish a "defective condition" by proving that the product functioned improperly in the absence of abnormal use and reasonable secondary causes.

The test we must apply is whether reasonable and well balanced minds would be satisfied from the evidence adduced that the defective condition existed when the machine was delivered.

The record discloses that four J. & L. employees testified that they had personally observed the piler malfunction. One of the employees, Victor H. Santoro, . . . testified that there were a "lot of bugs in the machine then, and we were running slow." One of these "bugs" was a malfunction of the fingers. . . . After the line had started into operation the fingers began releasing on their own without any activation from the control panel; . . . this happened often. . . . Santoro was operating the piler on the day of the mishap and he denied causing the sheets to fall by activating the fingers. He stated that he looked at the control panel after the sheets had fallen on appellee's hand, and the switches indicated that the fingers were extended rather than retracted.

Another employee . . . stated that a malfunction in the piler caused the sheets to fall on Greco's hand. He further testified that for approximately six months he had been telling the various foremen on that shift that someone was going to get hurt because of the sheets dropping from the piler.

[W]e think there was indeed sufficient evidence to satisfy reasonable and well balanced minds that a defect existed at the time of sale. We also think that there was ample evidence for the jury to find that the piler was not abnormally used; and that appellee negated all reasonable causes for the malfunction, except manufacturing defect.

It is our opinion, too, that the purported "changes" in the piler by J. & L. employees were not intervening superseding causes relieving appellants of liability.

. . . There is absolutely no evidence that the piler was changed in any way by J. & L. upon assemblage. Concededly, the piler was changed to a small extent when J. & L. inserted pins in the fingers, but this alteration came about because of a defect attributable to appellants. And it was this very defect, namely, the releasing of the fingers without activation, not the insertion of the pins, that caused the amputation of appellee's fingers.

Here . . . the evidence permits the inference that the manufacturer knew that employees would have to reach under the fingers of the piler to properly perform their job. . . . Furthermore, in its erection and instruction manual for the piler, [it] states that "[s]kids must be placed properly on the machine," and after the skids are loaded with steel and lowered, an employee "must then place on a new set of skids—making sure they are well centered and that they will move up between the fingers." Testimony of J. & L. employees established that it was impossible to center the skids automatically; the centering had to be done by an employee who went beneath the fingers and then signaled the operator that the skids were properly positioned. Uncontradicted testimony also established that this was the normal practice of centering the skids at the J. & L. mill and that the company's foremen expected the employees to go beneath the fingers. It is true, of course, that appellee had been present on previous occasions when the machine malfunctioned; however, he said that he had never seen the sheets spill with one pin in and the other out. Inasmuch as appellee had never been instructed in the use of the pins, we are unable to say on the facts before us that he assumed the risk . . .

Since there is ample evidence in the record to support a finding that the errant fingers constituted the defective condition, the judgments in favor of appellee can and will be sustained solely on that basis.

CASE PROBLEMS

1. An Oregon laundryman was concerned about the water in his city. It stained the clothes and left a black residue on the machines. The city put a special filter on his water line and the tar particles ruined the filter. The laundryman gave up and closed his laundry. Later, he brought suit against the city alleging the water was not up to normal warranty standards. Decide.
2. Plaintiff purchased from a broker "500 cases one-fourth oil sardines and 200 cases three-fourths mustard." The order was sent to Packaging Company, a firm that packed such goods and stored them in a warehouse for the broker. The goods were shipped to plaintiff, who, finding upon their arrival that they were not salable, brought an action for breach of warranty. Among other things, defendant points out he did not pack the goods. Decide.
3. Eli Gamel purchased a number of lamps from another dealer who was using them as samples in his retail trade. Gamel, also a furniture dealer, looked the lamps over before he made the purchase. His examination was not thorough, however, for when he got them back to his business, he discovered that some of the lamps were damaged and others were defective. Gamel claimed a warranty of merchantability. Decide.
4. A play "Ladies Night" had been a hit on Broadway. After negotiations, the plaintiffs agreed to sell the motion picture and television rights to defendant for $150,000. Before the formal contract was drawn, defendant, claiming that plaintiffs' title to the motion picture rights was defective, refused to proceed further. Plaintiffs sued for $50,000. Decide.
5. The seller inserted bulky automobile parts in long rectangular cardboard cartons without any covering or sheathing. The ends of the carton were sealed with tape and there was no warning on the carton. The parts had edges which were uneven and sharp. When the buyer slit the tape and reached inside, he severely injured his thumb. The purchaser brought suit against the seller. Decide.
6. Plaintiff was severely burned by a household detergent that she had purchased from a retailer. She sued the seller and its manufacturers, who had extensively promoted the product by television, radio, and newspaper, stating that it could be safely used for household and cleaning tasks and that it was "the all-purpose detergent—for all household cleaning and laundering." The manufacturers defended on the ground that plaintiff had not purchased the detergent from them. Decide.

7. A scaffolding collapsed, causing two workmen who were using it at the time to be seriously injured. Their employer had purchased the scaffold planking and this contract contained a clause to the effect that the lumber was sold "as is." In fact, it contained rot which was not discovered until after it had snapped. The workmen sued for damages alleging that they were not barred by the disclaimer. Decide.
8. Two bottles of Sprite exploded in a supermarket while a shopper was carrying them to the check-out counter. The shopper brought suit on a breach of warranty. Decide.

ENDNOTE

1. 161 A.2d 69, 83 (1960).

PERFORMANCE OF SALES CONTRACTS   41

When two parties enter into a contract for the sale of goods, each assumes a duty to perform certain conditions for the other. The seller obligates himself to transfer and deliver the quality and quantity of goods specified in the contract. (U.C.C. 2-301) The buyer undertakes to accept and pay for the goods if they conform to the agreed specifications. It is generally understood that neither party is obligated to perform his end of the agreement until the other has performed his part or has made a valid tender of performance. (U.C.C. 2-507) If the seller puts the goods at the buyer's disposal in accordance with an agreement for sale and the buyer refuses to accept them, the seller has a cause of action. The order of performance may be varied by the terms of the sales contract.

PERFORMANCE BY THE SELLER

The U.C.C. provides a number of rules to govern performance by the parties to a sales contract. It specifies that unless the parties agree to the contrary all goods must be tendered in a single delivery and payment is required only on such tender. However, according to the circumstances of each case, either party may acquire the right to make or demand delivery in units. If this situation arises, the price, if it can be apportioned, may be demanded for each unit. (U.C.C. 2-307)

When the contract does not mention the place of delivery, the goods are to be delivered to the seller's place of business; if he has none, his residence becomes the delivery point. When documents of title are to be used, they may be delivered through customary banking channels, unless otherwise agreed. (U.C.C. 2-308)

The Code adopts the rule that delivery must be made within a reasonable time when no specific time is provided in the contract. Sec. 2-309(2) states that "when the contract provides for successive performances but is indefinite in duration it is valid for a reasonable time but unless otherwise agreed may be terminated at any time by either party." The agreement may state that notice of termination is not necessary; however, if this provision works an undue hardship on the other party, it will be considered invalid. (U.C.C. 2-309)

Tender of delivery is a condition precedent to the buyer's duty to accept the goods and, unless the contract states to the contrary, to his duty to pay for them. A valid tender entitles the seller to performance from the buyer according to the agreement. This is accomplished by the seller's putting the goods at the buyer's disposal and giving him notice to enable him to take delivery. Unless otherwise agreed, tender must be at a reasonable hour and for a long enough time for the buyer to take possession. Also, the buyer must furnish whatever facilities may be reasonably required to complete the delivery. (U.C.C. 2-503)

According to the Code, the seller who is required to send the goods to the buyer, but not to deliver them to a specified destination, is to deliver to the carrier and make a reasonable contract for their transportation, considering the nature of the goods and the circumstances of the case. (U.C.C. 2-504) When the seller is required to make delivery by use of a specific carrier, the obligation of the seller is determined by whether the agreement is an F.O.B. shipment or destination contract. In the absence of an agreement, a shipment contract will employ the terms "shipping point," "C.I.F.," "F.A.S.," and "C.F." Destination contracts commonly employ such terms as "F.O.B. destination," "ex-ship," and "no arrival, no sale." A valid tender requires that the seller complete his obligation under the terms of the contract. Validity is not affected by who is to pay the shipping charges.

When, without the fault of either party, the agreed facilities for delivery or the agreed type of carrier becomes unavailable or commercially impracticable, a commercially reasonable and available substitute may be used if it is tendered to and accepted by the buyer. (U.C.C. 2-614)

The seller will be excused from his obligation if a government regulation changes the nature of the contract, as, for example, when a change in the law makes the contract invalid. However, if such a regulation affects only a part of the seller's capacity to perform, he must allocate production and deliveries among his customers, although he may at his option include regular customers not then under contract. His allocation may be in any reasonable manner under the circumstances. (U.C.C. 2-615)

PERFORMANCE BY THE BUYER

The buyer's obligation is to pay at the contract rate for any goods accepted. (U.C.C. 2-301) According to the Code, Sec. 2-606, acceptance occurs when the buyer, after inspecting the goods, responds in one of the following ways: (1) he notifies the seller that the goods conform to the contract; (2) he notifies the seller that the goods do not conform to the contract but that he will take them in spite of this fact; (3) he fails to reject the goods after a reasonable opportunity to inspect them; (4) he does any act inconsistent with the seller's ownership, such as having defects in the goods repaired, although ratification of the acceptance by the seller is necessary. Acceptance of any part of a commercial unit is deemed an acceptance of the entire unit. (U.C.C. 2-606)

When the buyer discovers a defect in the goods after acceptance, he must notify the seller within a reasonable time if he intends to revoke his acceptance. A revocation is possible only when the defect impairs the value of the goods.

The Code allows the buyer to inspect the goods on arrival except where they are shipped C.O.D., or for payment against delivery of documents of title. The place of inspection is fixed by the contract; any expenses in connection with the inspection are borne by the buyer. For example, the buyer may test the strength of the goods, their wholesomeness, or other similar qualities. These tests may result in the consumption of some of the goods. If he rejects the goods, the buyer may recover expenses incurred in inspecting them from the seller. Unless otherwise specified, inspection must be at a reasonable place and time and must be carried out in a reasonable manner. (U.C.C. 2-513)

Tender of payment is valid when made by any means or in any manner current in the ordinary course of business. An exception is made when the seller demands payment in legal tender that differs from that used in ordinary business transactions and gives the buyer an extension of time reasonable to obtain such tender. The time and place of payment is the time and place of delivery of the goods.

LEGAL PRINCIPLES

Under a sales contract, the seller obligates himself to transfer and deliver the quality and quantity of goods specified in the contract. Similarly, the buyer undertakes to accept and pay for the goods if they conform to the contract.

Usually, goods are to be delivered in a single delivery, made at the seller's place of business or his residence.

Delivery must be made within a reasonable time.

Payment for goods should be made at the time and place of delivery unless the terms of the sale specify otherwise.

A valid tender of delivery is made when the goods are put at the buyer's disposal.

A valid tender under a destination or shipping contract is determined by the agreement and not by who pays the shipping charges.

The seller will be excused from performance when a governmental regulation changes the nature of the contract.

The buyer's obligation is to pay at the contract rate for any goods accepted. Prior to acceptance, the buyer is allowed a reasonable time to inspect the goods, except where they are shipped C.O.D. or for payment upon delivery of documents of title.

Acceptance may be revoked if a defect is discovered that impairs the value of the goods.

CASE FOR REVIEW

INTERNATIONAL MINERALS & METALS CORP. v. WEINSTEIN

236 N.C. 558, 73 S.E.2d 472 (1952)

The plaintiff and defendants entered into a written contract dated 1 May, 1948, by the terms of which the defendants agreed to sell and ship one carload of scrap metal, consisting of ten tons of assorted scrap copper and ten tons of automobile radiators, to the plaintiff within thirty days. Specifications were agreed upon, and the price the plaintiff was to pay . . . was set out in the contract.

The contract also provided that if the defendants failed to ship the materials . . . within the time prescribed, . . . the plaintiff should have the right to buy like materials in the open market at any time within sixty days after delivery was due, and to charge the defendants with the difference in cost in the event it was compelled to pay a higher price in the open market than that agreed upon in the contact. Delivery was due 31 May, 1948, but was not made.

Thereafter, it is alleged by the plaintiff that the plaintiff's agent and the defendants entered into a supplemental oral agreement on or about 11 June, 1948, whereby the defendants agreed and promised to ship the materials contracted for in accordance with the terms of the original contract as soon as the defendants could dispose of certain other matters of business in which they were then engaged; that the plaintiff relied on said promise and agreement and did not buy in the materials contracted for within the sixty-day period set by the terms of the original contract; that during the summer and early fall of 1948 the defendants continued to promise and agree to ship the materials contracted for, and not until 25 October, 1948, did the defendants, notify the plaintiff through its agent that they would not ship the materials.

Plaintiff offered testimony tending to support the allegations of its complaint including the amendments thereto. On 25 October, 1948, the plaintiff notified defendants by registered letter that unless shipment of the materials called for in the original contract was made by 15 November, 1948, the plaintiff would buy such materials in the open market and charge the defendants with the difference between the contract price and the price it had to pay. The defendants did not ship the materials and the plaintiff went into the open market on 17 November, 1948, and purchased such materials at a cost of $1075 greater than the contract price.

. . . The defendants contend that the "supplemental oral agreement" left the delivery date indefinite, and converted the original contract into one for the purchase and sale of materials at a stated price, delivery to be made at the convenience of the seller. We do not concur in this view.

We construe the supplemental oral agreement to do nothing more than to extend the time of delivery temporarily and to assure the defendants that during the time of such extension, the plaintiff would not exercise its right to go into the open market and purchase the materials. The plaintiff's evidence tends to show that each time the defendants were contacted prior to 25 October, 1948, they promised to make shipment. But, on the above date, the plaintiff's agent was informed by the defendants that shipment would not be made until the market went down to where it was when the contract was made. There is nothing in the alleged supplemental oral agreement, or in the testimony of the defendants, to indicate that the time for delivery was in any way made dependent upon the status of the market. Neither is there anything in the evidence offered by the defendants to indicate that the failure to make delivery was due to the other business matters in which the defendants were engaged when the time for delivery was extended.

Manifestly, it was the duty of the defendants to act with reasonable promptness and diligence to comply with the terms of their contract. And when the plaintiff extended the time for delivery for the reasons stated, it was under no obligation to wait any longer than was reasonably necessary under the existing circumstances for the defendants to comply with their agreement. "If no time for the performance of an obligation is agreed upon by the parties, then the law prescribes that the act must be performed within a reasonable time." . . .

We hold that when the defendants informed the agent of the plaintiff that they would not ship the materials described in the contract until the market fell to where it was when the contract was made, such action constituted a breach of the original contract and of the supplemental oral agreement. And the fact that the plaintiff notified the defendants that the materials contracted for would be accepted if shipped prior to 15 November, 1948, did not constitute a waiver of the breach, if the materials were not shipped, so as to prevent the plaintiff from going into the open market at any time within sixty days from and after 25 October, 1948 and purchasing the materials as it was authorized to do under the terms of the original contract.

The case was submitted to a jury . . . and the issues answered against the defendants.

CASE PROBLEMS

1. A representative of the Chrysler Credit Corporation called on Mrs. Barnes one evening about a missed first installment payment on her car. She explained, to no avail, that she had mailed a check earlier in the week. "Cash or the car" was the response. Mrs. Barnes offered to write another check but the representative refused and took the car. Mrs. Barnes tendered cash the next morning, but the company said she was in default. Mrs. Barnes brought suit for repossession of the car. Decide.

2. Grain Company contracted with Simpson Feed Company, a grain elevator company, to purchase approximately five carloads of soybeans, delivery to be made from October 1 to November 30 at seller's option, with the buyer to furnish the seller shipping instructions as each of the cars was loaded. The first car was loaded on October 30, and shipping instructions given by the buyer the same day. The next day a second car was loaded, but instructions were not given until after forty-eight hours. The seller refused to accept such delayed instructions and canceled the contract. Was the contract properly cancelled?

3. Meat Packers, Inc. purchased a shipment of frozen pork roasts. The shipment arrived at 6 p.m.; an hour and a half later, at 7:30 p.m., the inspection was complete. The meat did not conform to the contract and it was decided to reject. The seller was notified of the intended rejection at 10:20 p.m. The seller claimed the notice of rejection came too late. Decide.

4. The purchaser of a mobile home moved in on the day after its delivery by the seller. Defects appeared in the mobile home and the buyer informed the seller, but buyer remained unsatisfied. On September 10, he notified the seller that he intended to cancel the sale and reject the merchandise. The buyer attempted to move out immediately but, due to housing problems, was unable to find housing until November 1. The seller claimed the purchaser's continued use amounted to acceptance of the goods. Decide.

5. An order of calendars was supposed to arrive on November 15. They came on November 21 and the buyer refused to take them. The buyer alleged that the calendars had been specially designed to accommodate the advertising needs of the buyer. The buyer claimed nonconformity with the contract. Decide.

6. A purchaser ordered three reels of type A cable. One reel of type A and two of type B were delivered instead. The buyer accepted type A and so informed the seller. He further agreed to locate a trucker, if possible, to get the rejected reels back to the seller. When three truckers turned down the job, the buyer informed

the seller it was up to him to pick up the reels. Before the seller was able to reclaim his goods, they were stolen. He sued the buyer for the loss. Decide.

7. Trucson Steel Company, claimed to be entitled to certain steel bars as against the Trustee of the J. F. Growe Construction Company, bankrupt. The plaintiff in selling the steel relied on certain favorable financial statements which the construction company had given to the Dun & Bradstreet Commercial Agencies. These statements were materially false because the construction company was actually insolvent when the statements were made. The steel bars were in the railroad freight house at destination when the construction company was declared bankrupt and the receiver appointed. Plaintiff claimed the property from the trustee. Decide.

8. A buyer received in a single shipment four sets of valves which conformed to the contract and one set of flanges which did not conform. The buyer accepted the valves and rejected the flanges. The seller claimed that this was the breaking up of a commercial unit. Decide.

REMEDIES 42

Basically, contracts for the sale of goods are governed by the same rules as are other types of contracts. If one party, by his failure to perform, denies to the other party the benefits due him under the contract, certain remedies are available to compensate the injured party. The objective of these remedies is neither to penalize the party breaching the sales contract nor to enrich the injured party. Rather, it is to allow the injured party to realize his expectancy interest under the original contract. Generally, the nature of the remedy applied will depend on whether the buyer has accepted possession of the goods.

SELLERS' REMEDIES

BREACH BY THE BUYER

When the buyer will not accept the goods, the seller's course of action will depend on the validity of the rejection. If the rejection is invalid, he may sue for money damages. The measure of damages is the difference between the market price of the goods at the time and place of tender and the unpaid contract price, together with incidental damages, less expenses saved in consequence of the buyer's breach. (U.C.C. 2-706) The U.C.C., Sec. 2-710, states that incidental damages include "any commercially reasonable charges, expenses, or commissions incurred in stopping delivery; in the transportation, care and custody of goods after the buyer's breach; in connection with return or resale of the goods; or otherwise resulting from the breach." If the buyer refuses to accept goods that have been identified to the contract (or goods manufactured especially for the buyer), the seller is entitled to the full purchase price, after he has made an honest effort to resell the goods and has not been able to do so or if it is reasonable to believe that the goods cannot be resold. (U.C.C. 2-709)

The unpaid seller who is in possession of the goods or any part of them is entitled to retain possession as security for the price, although title may have passed to the buyer, when: (1) the buyer defaults in payment of the purchase price in cases where the goods are to be paid for when delivered; (2) the period of credit has expired; or (3) the buyer has become insolvent. The seller may resell the goods within a reasonable time after any of these events or he may bring an action to recover damages. When he elects to resell the goods, he is entitled to recover as damages the difference between the resale price and the contract price, together with any incidental damages, provided the resale is made in good faith and in a commercially reasonable manner. The resale must be reasonably identified as referring to the broken contract. If the goods are resold at a private sale, the seller must give the buyer notice of his intention to resell. If the sale is a public sale, only identified goods may be resold. These goods may be sold as one sale or as units or lots, and the seller is not accountable to the buyer for any profit made on the resale. (U.C.C. 2-703 2-706 2-702)

On the buyer's breach of the sales contract, the seller is not obligated to resell the goods. However, if the goods are perishable, it may be necessary for the seller to resell them as soon as possible. Rescission will be considered as having taken place when he has given notice to the buyer in some way of the time and place of the resale. (U.C.C. 2-706)

An unpaid seller who has given over the goods to some transportation agency may, in the event of the buyer's insolvency, repudiation of the contract, or failure to make payment due before delivery, stop the goods in transit, even though title may have passed to the buyer. The Code, Sec. 2-705, gives the seller the right to "stop delivery of carload, truckload, planeload, or larger shipments of express or freight when the buyer wrongfully repudiates or fails to make a payment due before delivery, or if for any other good reason the seller has a right to withhold or reclaim the goods." However, the seller must notify the carrier in time so that by the exercise of reasonable diligence it may prevent the delivery of the goods. (See Figure 42-1) He is liable to the carrier for any expenses or damages incurred in complying with his order to stop delivery. The right of stoppage of delivery is terminated (1) when the buyer receives the goods, (2) when a carrier holds the goods for the buyer as warehouseman or reships them, or (3) when a bailee other than the carrier holds the goods for the buyer.

Where the seller discovers that the buyer has received goods while insolvent, he may reclaim them upon demand made within ten days after their receipt; he need not actually repossess them. If the buyer has misrepresented his solvency to the seller in writing within three months before delivery of the goods, the ten-day limitation on the seller's right to reclaim the goods does not apply. (U.C.C. 2-702-2) However, his right to reclaim the goods is subject to the prior rights of purchasers in the ordinary course of the buyer's business, other good faith purchasers for value, lien creditors, or the bankrupt's trustee.

When breach of contract occurs after acceptance of the goods, the seller may recover the price of the goods accepted by the buyer, or he may recover the price of the goods lost or damaged after the risk of lots has passed to the buyer. In this situation, if the seller has obtained a judgment against the buyer on the breach, he must hold for the buyer any goods still under his control. If resale becomes possible, however, he may resell them at any time prior to the collection of the judgment. The net proceeds of such a resale must be credited to the buyer upon payment of the judgment, and the buyer is entitled to any goods still in the seller's possession. (U.C.C. 2-709)

VALID REJECTION BY THE BUYER

Even when the buyer's rejection of the goods is valid, the buyer has certain obligations: (1) he must hold the goods; (2) he must exercise reasonable care while they are in his possession; and (3) he must allow the seller a sufficient time to reclaim them. (U.C.C. 2-603) If the rejected goods are of a type usually handled by the buyer, he must obey any reasonable instructions from the seller as to their disposition. When the seller fails to give any instructions and the goods are such that rapid fluctuations in their market value may be expected, the buyer is required to sell them on behalf of the seller.

NOTICE OF STOPPAGE IN TRANSITU

To Rapid Railway Company.

Gentlemen: Pursuant to the right of stoppage in transitu vested in me by law, I hereby as an unpaid seller give you notice to stop delivery of the goods hereinafter mentioned, and, consigned by me, through you, to Destructo Toy, Inc. You are hereby requested to retain possession of the said goods and merchandise and deliver safe to 2370 Beechmoor Drive, N. W., North Canton, Ohio 44720.

The goods are ten (10) carton boxes of model airplanes.

_____ (Seal)

Figure 42-1

BUYERS' REMEDIES

The buyer's remedies, like those of the seller, will depend on whether he has accepted the goods. Two types of remedies are available when the goods have not been accepted or delivered: those relating to the goods and those relating to monetary damages.

Remedies relating to the goods are specific performance and replevin (a common law action that asks that the goods be returned). Where the goods are such that other goods with the same or similar characteristics cannot be obtained elsewhere, the courts will, as a rule, allow specific performance. The buyer has a right to replevin for goods identified to the contract if, after a reasonable effort, he is unable to obtain other goods of the same character or if circumstances indicate that efforts of this sort would be futile. (U.C.C. 2-716)

If the seller fails or refuses to deliver the goods or repudiates the contract, the buyer is entitled to cancel the contract and recover as damages the difference between the contract price and the market price, in addition to any incidental and consequential damages. The buyer has the right to cover—that is, to purchase in the market goods of the same characteristics as those contracted for in order to mitigate his losses. If the buyer covers, the measure of his compensatory damages is the difference between the cost of covering and the contract price, in addition to any incidental and consequential damages. (U.C.C. 2-713 U.C.C. 2-711 U.C.C. 2-712)

Unless there is an agreement to the contrary or the goods are shipped C.O.D., the buyer always has a right to inspect the goods upon receipt before acceptance. If the inspection discloses that they do not conform to their description or the samples or that the quantity is greater or less than that ordered, the buyer may reject them. If he accepts defective goods and wishes to hold the seller liable in damages, he must give the seller notice of the breach within a reasonable time after he discovers it or he will be barred from any remedy. If the goods are not as warranted and the buyer has given the required notice, he can recover as damages the difference at the time and place of acceptance between the value of the goods accepted and the value they would have had if they had been as warranted, together with incidental and consequential damages when proper, unless special circumstances show proximate damages of a different amount.

The buyer may, on notifying the seller of his intention to do so, deduct from the price still due under the contract all or any part of the damages resulting from a breach of that contract. (U.C.C. 2-717)

If the buyer, after he has paid part of the purchase price of the goods, rejects them or revokes his acceptance, he may retain possession of the goods and may claim a security interest in them for the amount paid on the purchase price and for incidental and consequential damages. (U.C.C. 2-711)

While rejected goods are still in the buyer's possession, he must take reasonable care of them and hold them until instructions arrive from the seller. If the seller does not furnish instructions within a reasonable time, the buyer may store the goods for the seller's account or reship them. He has a right to be reimbursed for any expenses incurred.

LEGAL PRINCIPLES

Where the buyer wrongfully rejects or revokes acceptance of goods, fails to make a payment due on or before delivery, or in any other manner breaches the contract, the aggrieved seller may: (1) withhold delivery of such goods; (2) stop delivery of goods in the possession of a carrier or other bailee; (3) identify goods to the contract notwithstanding the breach or salvage unfinished goods; (4) resell the goods and recover damages; (5) recover damages for nonacceptance or repudiation; or (6) cancel the contract.

Where the seller fails to make delivery or repudiates his duties under the contract or the buyer rightfully rejects the goods or justifiably revokes acceptance, the buyer may cancel the contract and recover any portion of the purchase price he has paid. He may choose to (1) cover and, in addition, recover damages for all the goods affected whether or not they have been identified to the contract; or (2) recover as damages for nondelivery the difference between the market price at the time when the buyer learned of the breach and the contract price.

Where the seller fails to deliver or repudiates the contract, the buyer may also (1) recover the goods, if they have been identified (replevin); or (2) in an appropriate case—for example, where the goods are unique or are not purchasable in the market—obtain specific performance.

On rightful rejection or justifiable revocation of acceptance, a buyer has a security interest in goods in his possession or control for any payments made on their price or any expenses reasonably incurred in their inspection, receipt, transportation, care, and custody. He may hold such goods and resell them in a like manner as an aggrieved seller.

CASE FOR REVIEW

ERDMAN v. JOHNSON BROTHERS RADIO & TELEVISION CO.

271 A.2d 744 (Md. 1970)

It has been said that "the seller's warranty is a curious hybrid, born of the illicit intercourse of tort and contract, unique in the law." A further reading of this opinion will show why.

On June 24, 1965, the appellants (Erdman and Pfaff) purchased a color television-radio-stereo console from the appellees (Johnson Brothers) for approximately $1000. As events unfolded this proved to be a most unfortunate investment. The set was put into operation by one of Johnson Brothers' repairmen, and Erdman and Pfaff looked forward with great expectations to many hours of pleasant viewing. Their joy soon turned to consternation, however, as they began experiencing difficulty with the set almost from the outset. In an act of great foresight, the appellants had purchased a service policy from Johnson Brothers; they had many occasions to avail themselves of its benefits.

Approximately one month after the purchase, the set was sent back to Johnson Brothers for repairs, and was returned to the appellants' home about a week later. Sometime after that, Erdman noticed a "crackling sound" in the television; the noise was often accompanied by a "tear" in the picture. This, of course, precipitated complaints by the appellants to Johnson Brothers, and resulted in some two dozen service calls to the appellants' house. Sometime in September, 1966, Erdman and Pfaff for the first time noticed sparks and heavy smoke shooting out of the back of the set and the smell of burning rubber, wire, or some other substance. Another complaint was made. Johnson Brothers' serviceman examined the set on September 30, 1966, and stated that whatever had happened had "fused itself together again," and that if anything serious developed he would be able to fix it.

For the next few months the television operated in its usual (cantankerous) manner and there was no difficulty serious enough to warrant another complaint, at least not until December 7, 1966, a Wednesday. On that date Erdman called Johnson Brothers and for the second time complained about having seen actual sparks and smoke emanating from the rear of the television. The person taking this complaint ventured no opinion as to the cause of the trouble, and merely noted that there would be a serviceman out to the appellants' house on Saturday, December 10, 1966. (Inasmuch as Erdman and Pfaff both worked during the week, the usual practice of the parties was to have the set serviced on Saturdays, as a matter of convenience to the appellants. The very fact that it was necessary to establish a "policy" for making service calls to the plaintiffs' residence perhaps describes the condition of the set more eloquently than this Court ever could.)

On the fateful evening of Thursday, December 8, 1966, (after the second complaint and prior to the day on which the repairs were to be performed) Erdman and Pfaff watched television from approximately 11:20 P.M. until 1:30 A.M. of Friday, December 9, 1966, at which time they observed for the third time that there were sparks and smoke coming from the set. They turned off the television, and retired for the night. About half an hour later they were awakened by the barking of one of their eleven dogs, and discovered that a fire was very much in progress in the vicinity of the television set. The fire spread rapidly, and by the dawn's early light Erdman and Pfaff saw, tragically, that their residence had been completely destroyed. The total loss in real and personal property was $67,825.91.

The Uniform Commercial Code . . . governs the sale of the television in this case, and it provides that anyone who sells goods and who is a merchant with respect to that kind of goods, impliedly warrants in his contract for sale that the goods sold are "merchantable." . . . It would appear that Johnson Brothers most assuredly is a merchant within the meaning of the U.C.C. (§ 2–104) and that they gave an implied warranty to the appellants that the television in question was fit for the ordinary purposes to which a television might be put. . . .

Section 2–714 of the U.C.C. indicates that a buyer may recover not only normal damages from a seller in case of breach, but in a "proper case" the buyer may also recover incidental and consequential damages. Section 2–715 provides that consequential damages may include any "injury to person or property proximately resulting from any breach of warranty." . . .

The U.C.C. view of the question of warranty in terms of principles of causation is in harmony with the view of the text writers who have addressed themselves to the problem. . . .

At this juncture it is appropriate that we review the rationale upon which the trial judge predicated his opinion. Judge Turnbull stated: . . .

> . . . You have a man of high intelligence, who purchased this television set, who continued to use it, even though he knew and had complained that it was arcing, smoking, with actual sparks and a burning odor. Now using a set which is in that condition is certainly not, in my opinion, a use in the normal manner. So that it is my opinion, and I so hold that, even assuming the fire came about as a result of a defect in the set, that the warranty did not extend to the point, under the circumstances of this case, of covering the Plaintiff's damages resulting from the fire. So that I find, and hold that, under the warranty, the Defendant is not responsible to the Plaintiffs. . . .
> . . . [I]t is inescapable to me that the Plaintiffs were guilty of contributory negligence in failing to act as an ordinarily prudent person would act under the circumstances then and there existing, in that, knowing that the set was sparking, arcing, burning or there was an odor of burning, nonetheless, they used the set for a period of, according to the testimony, somewhere in the general neighborhood of two hours, on the late evening and early morning of December 8th and December 9th. I believe that that constitutes negligence. . . .
> . . . So that, sitting as a trier of the facts sitting as a jury, gentlemen, I find that it is inescapable that, even if you assume primary negligence, any trier of the facts must find that there was glaring contributory negligence on the part of the plaintiffs [appellants].

Judge Turnbull . . . makes it abundantly clear that he was of the opinion after hearing all the facts that the appellants used the television set after discovering the defect (when they noticed the burning and sparks and made their second complaint on December 7, 1966), and that therefore the implied warranty of merchantability did not apply.

Our reading of the U.C.C. in light of the record supports this interpretation. It would appear that an individual using a product when he had actual knowledge of a defect or knowledge of facts which were so obvious that he must have known of a defect, is either no longer relying on the seller's express or implied warranty or has interjected an intervening cause of his own, and therefore a breach of such warranty cannot be regarded as the proximate cause of the ensuing injury. Such an interpretation gives effect to the true nature of the action involved and the intention of the U.C.C. without needlessly involving the courts in a discussion of whether the implied warranty is founded in contract, tort, or both.

CASE PROBLEMS

1. On November 8, 1966, Busick contracted to sell Rosenberg one hundred tons of raisins at $350 a ton. On November 13 he tendered delivery and Rosenberg refused to accept the raisins. Busick later sued for damages. Evidence was offered that the market price remained at $350 for at least two weeks after November 13. Busick testified that he was in no hurry to sell as he thought the price was going up. Instead the price declined, and he sold several months later at $235 a ton, for a loss of $115 a ton. Busick claimed damages of $11,500. The trial court fixed the resale value at $335 per ton and allowed Busick only $1500 damages. Was the decision correct?

2. Defendant, a retailer, ordered 100,000 cellophane bags from plaintiff, accompanying his order with a sample bag. The order had been filled and about 25,000 bags used when Lynch noticed that they did not conform to the sample he had given plaintiff. He attempted to return the unused portion along with payment for the used portion, but plaintiff refused them, contending that defendant, by using a substantial quantity of the goods without complaint, had accepted the entire quantity and bringing suit for the full contract price. Decide.

3. A lady in Kentucky bought a package of starch from a local grocery store. It was defective and caused injury to her person. She immediately complained to the manufacturer, Colgate-Palmolive Company, but did not complain to the local grocer until a year later. He refused to do anything, which resulted in a suit for damages. Decide.

4. Omar contracted to sell Rubin four pieces of goods suitable for manufacture into suits. Rubin accepted two pieces and rejected the other two, which concededly did not comply with the order. Omar brought an action for the price of the four pieces, contending that the contract was indivisible and accordingly that Rubin's acceptance of two pieces obliged him to accept the remaining pieces, less any claim for damages because of inferior quality. Decide.

5. Marks contracted with and paid defendant to cover the outside of his house with a material known as "castle stone." Some time after the work had been done, the stones faded in color and cracked; some started to fall off. Notice was given to defendant, who tried without success to remedy the defects. Marks brings an action to rescind the contract. Decide.

6. Ogden sold under a credit arrangement a quantity of apples to Stern, who took an option to leave the apples in cold storage with Ogden until May 1. Before the option had expired, Ogden noticed signs of deterioration in the apples and urged Stern to take and pay for them, but Stern refused. Ogden then resold the apples to other parties at less than the price contracted for with Stern and sued Stern for the difference. Decide.

7. In 1962 Mr. and Mrs. Cummings conferred with Smith about wall-to-wall carpeting for their apartment. It was finally agreed that he would furnish custom-made carpeting of a particular color not available in regular carpeting at a cost of $2327.50. The carpet was laid in June, 1962 and final payment thereon was made on July 2. A week or two thereafter Mrs. Cummings noticed marks in the carpeting and called Smith. He went to the apartment and saw the lines and marks in the carpet which he described as "pass marks." A representative from the manufacturer, who examined the carpet at Smith's request, also testified that the lines were "pass marks" that are inherent in any custom-made carpet made on a small loom. Mrs. Cummings asked Smith to take back the carpeting and replace it, but was told this could not be done. On January 12, 1963 an attorney for Mr. and Mrs. Cummings wrote Smith requesting that he remove the carpet and refund the full purchase price. This request refused, and in October 1963 Mr. and Mrs. Cummings brought this action. Decide.

8. Defendant company sold a car to Smith, who procured an insurance policy on it from plaintiff company. Soon after purchasing the car, Smith had difficulty in starting the motor and noticed that the motor and other parts under the hood were saturated with gasoline. He nevertheless continued to drive the car regularly until about a month later, when it caught fire and was destroyed. Plaintiff company paid him $2000 under the terms of his policy, then sold the car for scrap, realizing $50.50 on the sale. Plaintiff company, assuming Smith's rights, brings suit to recover $1950 from defendant company for breach of warranty. Decide.

PART VII
COMMERCIAL PAPER

REQUISITES OF NEGOTIABILITY

Commercial paper is basically a type of contract. It is a written contract that calls for the future payment of money by one of the parties, either directly or through another party designated to make payment. It may also be described as a contract that evidences a right to receive money, which right may be transferred by negotiation.

The primary function of commercial paper is to serve as a substitute for money. As such, it furnishes the means by which and the basis on which the greater part of commerce and business in the United States is conducted. (Consider how many commercial transactions are settled by the delivery of a check.) Another function of commercial paper is as a medium for the extension of credit. For example, in the purchase of real estate the buyer makes a down payment and a promise in writing to pay the balance of the purchase price over a period of years.

In order to enable commercial paper to efficiently perform these functions, certain rules were devised to identify the negotiable contract and distinguish it from other contracts. The rules governing commercial paper are set out in Article 3 of the Uniform Commercial Code. They deal with types of instruments and the formal requirements for negotiability, negotiation, contract of the parties, holders in due course, establishing secondary liability, defenses, and termination of liability. Because of this codification, we shall be primarily concerned in the succeeding chapters with Article 3 of the U.C.C. and its interpretation.

TYPES OF INSTRUMENTS

The U.C.C. identifies four types of negotiable instruments that are employed as commercial paper: drafts, checks, certificates of deposit, and promissory notes.

A *draft* is a negotiable instrument by which one individual or firm orders another individual or firm to pay a sum of money to a third party. The person who draws up the instrument and orders payment is the drawer, the person to whom the instrument is addressed is the drawee, and the person to whom payment is made is the payee. (See Figure 43-1)

A *check* is a draft drawn on a bank and payable on demand. As in the draft, three original parties are involved: the drawer, the drawee bank, and the payee.

A *certificate of deposit* is an acknowledgment by a bank of its receipt of money with a duty to repay it. It is usually used to evidence a time deposit with a bank. (See Figure 43-2)

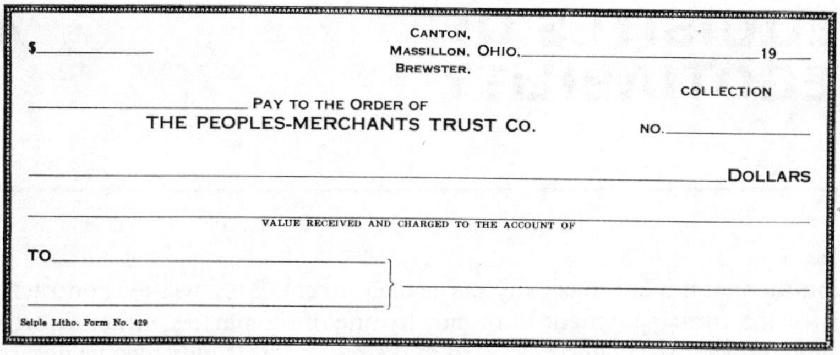
$ ______

CANTON,
MASSILLON, OHIO, ______ 19___
BREWSTER,

COLLECTION

______ PAY TO THE ORDER OF
THE PEOPLES-MERCHANTS TRUST CO.

NO. ______

______ DOLLARS

VALUE RECEIVED AND CHARGED TO THE ACCOUNT OF

TO ______

Seiple Litho. Form No. 429

Figure 43-1

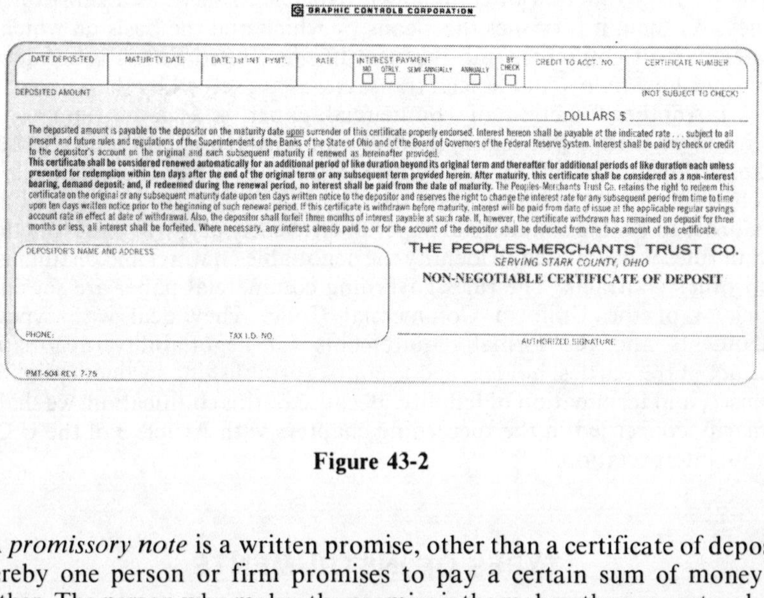
GRAPHIC CONTROLS CORPORATION

DATE DEPOSITED | MATURITY DATE | DATE 1st INT. PYMT. | RATE | INTEREST PAYMENT: MO. QTRLY. SEMI ANNUALLY ANNUALLY | BY CHECK | CREDIT TO ACCT. NO. | CERTIFICATE NUMBER

DEPOSITED AMOUNT (NOT SUBJECT TO CHECK)

______ DOLLARS $ ______

The deposited amount is payable to the depositor on the maturity date upon surrender of this certificate properly endorsed. Interest hereon shall be payable at the indicated rate . . . subject to all present and future rules and regulations of the Superintendent of the Banks of the State of Ohio and of the Board of Governors of the Federal Reserve System. Interest shall be paid by check or credit to the depositor's account on the original and each subsequent maturity if renewed as hereinafter provided.
This certificate shall be considered renewed automatically for an additional period of like duration beyond its original term and thereafter for additional periods of like duration each unless presented for redemption within ten days after the end of the original term or any subsequent term provided herein. After maturity, this certificate shall be considered as a non-interest bearing, demand deposit; and, if redeemed during the renewal period, no interest shall be paid from the date of maturity. The Peoples-Merchants Trust Co. retains the right to redeem this certificate on the original or any subsequent maturity date upon ten days written notice to the depositor and reserves the right to change the interest rate for any subsequent period from time to time upon ten days written notice prior to the beginning of such renewal period. If this certificate is withdrawn before maturity, interest will be paid from date of issue at the applicable regular savings account rate in effect at date of withdrawal. Also, the depositor shall forfeit three months of interest payable at such rate. If, however, the certificate withdrawn has remained on deposit for three months or less, all interest shall be forfeited. Where necessary, any interest already paid to or for the account of the depositor shall be deducted from the face amount of the certificate.

DEPOSITOR'S NAME AND ADDRESS

PHONE: TAX I.D. NO.

THE PEOPLES-MERCHANTS TRUST CO.
SERVING STARK COUNTY, OHIO
NON-NEGOTIABLE CERTIFICATE OF DEPOSIT

AUTHORIZED SIGNATURE

PMT-504 REV. 7-75

Figure 43-2

A *promissory note* is a written promise, other than a certificate of deposit, whereby one person or firm promises to pay a certain sum of money to another. The person who makes the promise is the maker; the person to whom the note is payable is the payee. (See Figure 43-3)

FORMAL REQUISITES

To be negotiable (to qualify as negotiable paper), an instrument must meet certain requirements over and above those of a simple contract. It must:

1. be written,
2. be signed by the maker or drawer,
3. contain an unconditional promise or order to pay,
4. be certain as to the sum of money,
5. be payable on demand or at a definite time, and
6. be payable to order or to the bearer. (U.C.C. 3—104)

No. _____

DEMAND PROMISSORY NOTE

$_____
Amount financed

ON DEMAND, for value received, I, we, or either of us, promise to pay to the order of THE PEOPLES-MERCHANTS TRUST COMPANY

_____DOLLARS

in lawful money of the United States, at its office in _____, Ohio, with interest payable _____

at the rate of _____ per cent per annum, or at such other rate that the Bank might establish provided that Bank shall give the undersigned prior written notice of each change in rate.

And we consent and agree that after this obligation shall have become due, the time of payment thereof may be extended from time to time, by any one or more of us, without even the knowledge or consent of the other or others of us, and in case of such extension and not withstanding the same, we shall and will remain and continue liable thereon as if no extensions had been so made. And we jointly and severally hereby authorize any attorney-at-law to appear in any court of record, situated in the county where the maker resides or in the county where the maker or any one of us sign this note and being in the United States, after the above money becomes due, and waive the issuing and serving of process, and confess judgment and against us or any of us in favor of the holder of this note, for the amount appearing due and the costs of suit, and thereupon to release all errors and waive all right of appeal and stay of execution in our behalf. I, or we, hereby authorize the holder to apply hereon at anytime after maturity any moneys owing by such holder to us or either of us, and further agreeing that in the case of insolvency, bankruptcy, business failure or default on this or any obligation to the holder, then, at the option of the holder, this and all such other obligations shall at once become due and payable, without demand or notice. If the holder obtains such a judgment by confession against any Debtor, then, so long as such judgment exists, such holder, and the successors and assigns thereof, hereby waive any right to file a Certificate of Judgment for Lien thereunder or to take any other court action thereon, if either would result in the acquisition of a security interest in the principal residence of such Debtor.

Interest	$_____	Payment due on demand.
Other charges (describe)		
_____	$_____	Total of payment $_____ plus interest.
FINANCE CHARGE	$_____	Late payment charge: ____ interest until paid.
ANNUAL PERCENTAGE RATE _____%		Unearned Finance Charge: Interest will be charged only upon unpaid balance for period outstanding.

Executed at_____, Ohio, this_____day of_____, 19_____

WARNING — By signing this paper you give up your right to notice and court trial. If you do not pay on time, a court judgment may be taken against you without your prior knowledge, and the powers of a court can be used to collect from you or your employer regardless of any claims you may have against the creditor whether for returned goods, faulty goods, failure on his part to comply with the agreement, or any other cause.

Name	Name	Name
Residence Address	Residence Address	Residence Address

PMT425   BORROWER ACKNOWLEDGES RECEIPT OF A COPY OF THIS NOTE WITH APPLICABLE BLANKS COMPLETED.

Figure 43-3

WRITTEN INSTRUMENT

Early traders needed something physical to transfer when they negotiated the right to receive money. Oral promises were fraught with the possibilities of misunderstanding and fraud; it was difficult to prove a person's liability on a contract that was unwritten and unsigned. Requiring the promise to be written provided tangible evidence of the obligation to make physical delivery of something and was an early requirement of the law.

The courts have placed a broad construction on the word "writing," and no limits are set forth in the U.C.C. regarding the writing instrumentality. Under Sec. 1—201(46) of the U.C.C., writing is defined to include "printing, typewriting, or other intentional reduction to tangible form."

SIGNATURE

To be negotiable, an instrument must be signed by the drawer or maker. However, what constitutes a signature, according to Sec. 1—201(39) of the U.C.C., "includes any symbol executed or adopted by a party with present intention to authenticate a writing." Usually, the full name of the party is added to the instrument. When the identity of the party can be shown by extrinsic evidence or testimony, authentication may be printed or stamped; it maybe accomplished by making an "x," by signing initials, or by a thumbprint. The signature may be on any part of the document.

UNCONDITIONAL PROMISE OR ORDER TO PAY

To qualify as a negotiable instrument, a promissory note must contain a clear, unequivocal promise to pay (as contrasted with language that merely acknowledges the existence of the debt but not the promise to pay it). The word "promise" itself need not appear; but if it does not, the meaning of the words used must be clear.

For a draft or check to qualify as a negotiable instrument, it must contain an unmistakable order to pay, and this order must be addressed to a clearly designated drawee. The terminology used must be strong enough to indicate the drawer's right to order payment and the duty of the drawee to pay. A mere request or authorization is not sufficient.

To ensure negotiability, payment of a note must not be conditioned upon the happening of any event. If the event takes place after the making of the note but before it is presented for payment, the impediment of a conditional promise still exists, since at the time of the making it could not be certain that the event would occur.

Additional wording on the face of the note indicating payment from a certain account does not affect negotiability as long as it is clear that payment will be made in any event. Sec. 3—105 of the Code provides that an instrument is not conditional merely because it "indicates a particular account to be debited or any other fund or source from which reimbursement is expected." If the promise is such that a particular fund or account *must* be used, the instrument is no longer negotiable (except in two very technical situations) since there may be insufficient funds in the account at the time payment is demanded.

Statements to the effect that a note is secured by a mortgage or other security do not in themselves make the note conditional. The Code makes it clear that the negotiability of an instrument is not affected by a mere reference in the instrument to a separate agreement. However, if the note states that it is subject to the terms of the mortgage that secures it, it is no longer unconditional and therefore is nonnegotiable.

SUM CERTAIN

In order to satisfy the requirement of a sum certain of money, the amount to be paid must be determinable at some time during the life of the instrument. Negotiability is not affected by whether the instrument is to be paid with interest, in installments, or with attorney's fees in cases where means of recovery involving employment of a lawyer are necessary. If no interest rate is stated on face of the instrument, the legal rate is assumed. Attorney's fees can be considered part of a security contract, apart from the primary purpose of the note. (U.C.C. 3—106)

PAYABLE IN MONEY

For an instrument to be negotiable, it must be payable in money. Sec. 1—201(24) of the U.C.C. defines money as "a medium of exchange authorized or adopted by a domestic or foreign government as a part of its currency." By "money" or "current money" is meant the medium of exchange of a domestic or foreign government circulating as legal tender, or circulating at par with legal tender, *at the time the instrument is made* (not when it is to be paid). The test of money, therefore, is governmental sanction. An instrument payable in "currency" or "current funds" is payable in money. (U.C.C. 3—107)

When foreign currency is designated for use in the payment of a debt, the Code, Sec. 3—107(2); provides that unless otherwise agreed the debt may be satisfied "by payment of that number of dollars which the stated foreign currency will purchase at the buying sight rate for that currency on the day on which the instrument is payable or, if payable on demand, on the day of demand." From the language of the Code, it would seem that the rate of exchange is determined at the place of payment. Of course, if an instrument specifies that a foreign currency must be used as the medium of payment, the instrument must be paid in that currency.

Instruments that are payable in merchandise, or other than legal tender, may be transferred by endorsement, but they are not negotiable since the value of the goods may fluctuate and may not be certain at all times. If the payee is given the option of taking payment in money or merchandise, negotiability is not affected. However, the choice must rest with the payee and not the maker.

ON DEMAND OR AT A DEFINITE TIME

The requirement that an instrument be payable at a time certain is designed to promote certainty in determining the present value of the instrument. When the primary party can be compelled to pay, when the obligation of the secondary parties may be established, and when the statute of limitations will begin to run must be ascertainable from the face of the instrument.

To be negotiable, an instrument must be payable on demand or at a definite time. Sec. 3—108 of the Code defines instruments as including those "payable at sight or on presentation and those in which not time is stated." When an instrument is to be payable at a fixed or definite time, the time may be stated either as a certain date or as a period before or after a certain date. However, the instrument may not be made payable on the happening of some event that, while certain to occur, will do so at an uncertain future date. (U.C.C. 3—109) For example, an instrument is not negotiable if it is made payable "thirty days after the settlement of my uncle's estate."

A problem area clarified by the U.C.C. is that of the acceleration clause. Negotiable instruments may contain clauses to the effect that the holder is entitled to demand payment before the due date if he considers payment on the due date uncertain. The date of payment may also be accelerated upon failure to make an interest payment or to pay an installment on the principal when due. Sec. 3—109 of the Code provides that the certainty of time of payment is not affected by any acceleration clause, whether acceleration is at the option of the maker or holder or is automatic. Upon the occurrence of any event that would make the instrument payable in full before the due date, the instrument simply becomes a demand instrument. In any case, it still has a time-certain due date.

The U.C.C. also deals with so-called extension clauses that allow the maker of a note to pay all or part of the principal after maturity. For example, a note may be payable in four years, with the maker having the option to extend the time of payment for a two-year period. Sec. 3—109 of the Code provides that an instrument is payable at a definite time if it is payable "at a definite time subject to extension at the option of the holder." This is true as long as the extension is also for a definite time.

WORDS OF NEGOTIABILITY

The U.C.C. requires that negotiable instruments contain words of negotiability. The words "to order," "to bearer," or language to that effect, must appear on the instrument for it to be negotiable and to serve as a proper substitute for money. Such language evidences the intention of the original parties that the instrument be negotiable.

An order instrument may be payable to an individual (payable to the order of A, in which case A's endorsement would be required to make the instrument negotiable); payable to two individuals jointly (payable to the order of A *and* B, in which case the endorsements of both would be required); or payable to either of two individuals (payable to the order of A *or* B, in which case the endorsement of either is sufficient). It may also be payable to an officer as holder of a particular office, in which case the successor or successors to the office may act as the holder. (U.C.C. 3—110) For example, a check payable to the order of "the Secretary of State of the United States" is negotiable.

An instrument may be payable to the bearer when it states that fact, when it is payable to "specified person or bearer" or when the payee is not the name of any person (for example, a check payable to "cash"). (U.C.C. 3—111) A negotiable instrument is also payable to the bearer when it has been endorsed in blank (See Chapter 44 Negotiation.)

IMMATERIAL PROVISIONS

Certain terms may appear on a negotiable instrument that do not affect its negotiability; however, they may affect how the instrument is interpreted. The instrument may recite the consideration, state the place payable, or indicate when it was drawn without affecting its negotiable character. It may state the collateral given or authorize a confession of judgment without changing its negotiability. (U.C.C. 3—112) If the date is omitted, the instrument carries the date it was executed and delivered to the payee. An instrument may be antedated or postdated, providing this is not done with intent to defraud. (U.C.C. 3—114)

RULES FOR INTERPRETATION

1. Where there is doubt as to whether the instrument is a note or a draft, the holder may elect to treat it as either.
2. A draft drawn on the drawer is considered a note.
3. Handwritten terms control typewritten and printed terms. Typewritten terms control printed terms.
4. Where there is a conflict between the amount written and the figures, the words control. If the words are ambiguous, the figure controls.
5. Where interest is provided but the rate is omitted, the rate is the judgment rate at place of payment. The amount is computed from the date of the instrument, or the date of issue.
6. A signature is considered an endorsement if the instrument does not clearly indicate the capacity in which the signature was made.

LEGAL PRINCIPLES

Negotiable instruments were developed as vehicles to substitute for money and to aid in the extension of credit.

The U.C.C. identifies four types of negotiable instruments as commercial paper: drafts, checks, certificates of deposit, and promissory notes.

To be negotiable, an instrument must be written, must be signed by the maker or drawer, must contain an unconditional promise or order to pay a sum certain in money, must be payable on demand or at a definite time, and must be payable to order or to the bearer.

CASE FOR REVIEW

MEES v. CANINO

503 P.2d 1036 (Colo. 1972)

Plaintiff, Carl Mees, alleged . . . that on March 11, 1970, defendant executed a note in the principal amount of $27,000, payable $225 per month and that defendant had made no payments and was in default. Plaintiff demanded judgment for $27,000 plus interest. . . .

At the trial, plaintiff appeared and identified Exhibit No. 1 as "[a] promissory note from Louis G. Canino to me in the amount of $27,000." He testified that demand had been made on the note but that no payments had been made. Defendant did not personally appear at the trial, and no evidence was presented in his behalf. However, his attorney asserted in his defense that the principal amount of the note was $225 rather than $27,000. The note in question is a printed form and provides in part as follows:

No. 922B.   INSTALLMENT NOTE   [Printer's name and address]

$27,000.00   March 11, 1970

___LOUIS G. CANINO___   for value received,   __does__   promise to pay
to the order of   __CARL MEES__   the sum of __Two Hundred__
Twenty-Five ------------------------- Dollars at __Lakewood, Colorado,__
said principal payable   __on the first day of each and every month__
__commencing April 1, 1970__   with interest at the rate of   __8__   per cent
per annum.

[*Default provisions and acceleration clause*]

                                        /s/   Louis G. Canino

The words and figures appearing in the blank portions of the printed note are typewritten, and, below defendant's signature, a memorandum of payments schedule is provided.

At the conclusion of the trial, the court ruled that the principal amount of the note was $27,000; that the note was payable in monthly installments of $225; and that the full amount of the note was due. Judgment was accordingly entered for $27,000 plus interest.

On appeal, defendant argues that the court's construction is erroneous as a matter of law because the words "Two Hundred Twenty-Five" should control over the figures of $27,000." He argues that such construction is required by C.R.S. 1963, 155—3—118(c), which provides: Words control figures; except, that if the words are ambiguous, figures control." This section of the code is applicable where a single amount, such as an amount of principal, is intended to be expressed both in figures and in words, and there is a conflict between the figures and the words or an ambiguity in either the figures or the words used.

In the present case, there is no ambiguity in either the figures "$27,000" or the words "Two Hundred Twenty-Five." Rather, the ambiguity arises because the words "Two Hundred Twenty-Five," when considered in the context within the note, may refer either to the principal of the note or to the monthly payments due on the note. The section of the code, C.R.S. 1963, 155—3—118(c), does not provide a solution to this problem, and resort must be had to other rules of construction. As between the parties, the note must be construed so as to give effect to the manifest intention of the parties. The note should be construed as a whole and effect given to all the provisions thereof. So construing the note, it is obvious that the trial court was correct in finding that the principal of the note is $27,000 and that said principal is payable in monthly installments of $225.

CASE PROBLEMS

1. Chrismer executed and delivered a promissory note, payable to his son, and a carbon copy duplicate. After the father's death, the son brought suit against Chrismer's estate on the carbon copy. The estate contended that the carbon copy was not a negotiable instrument and could not be sued upon without proof of the loss or destruction of the original. Decide.

2. Plaintiff obtained from his sister-in-law the following note, the italicized portions of which were in her handwriting:

> $13,070.86   August 30, 1960
>
> *I, Cecelia W. Donohoe,* after date, *August 30th,* promise to pay to the order of *Richard Donohoe, thirteen thousand seventy and 86/100* dollars without defalcation, value received, *with interest at six percent.* Witness *my* hand and seal.
>
> (Seal)   Hester Johnson
>   Notary Public

Payment was refused by Mrs. Donohoe's estate, defendant, on the ground that the note was not signed by Cecelia Donohoe and was therefore unenforceable. Decide the liability.

3. Plaintiff, White, holder of an instrument, sued defendant, Cushing, its maker. The question in the suit was the negotiability of the instrument, which read:

> 120   Dover, October 27, 1963
>   Savings Bank
>   Pay to James Lawlor, or order, one hundred and twenty dollars and charge same to my account on Book No. 12.
> Witness: (Signed) J. N. Cushing

The bank book of the depositor must accompany this order. Decide.

4. In an action by P. Moore against D. Clines, the instrument sued upon was in the following form:

> $1100.00   Louisville, Ky., May 1, 1974
>   Four months after date, for value received I promise to pay to the order of C. P. Moore Eleven Hundred Dollars. Negotiable and payable at the Citizens Union National Bank, Louisville, Ky. It is agreed by the parties hereto that this note shall bear interest at the rate of _____ per cent per annum until paid.
>   It is agreed that this note is to paid in Elks Club #8 Second Mortgage real estate bonds.
>
>   Thos. D. Clines

Is the instrument negotiable? Decide.

5. A note dated May 25, 1963, obligates Sylvia to pay to Ferri or her order $3000 "within ten (10) years after date." Sylvia argues that the instrument is not negotiable because of the uncertainty of the time of payment. Decide.

6. On July 10, 1969 Rick Strong signed a promissory note for $20,000 payable on or before July 10, 1970. Mr. Strong died two weeks later, and Will Weake, the holder of the note, brought suit against Strong's estate alleging Strong's death caused acceleration of the note. Decide.

7. A promissory note was dated June 15, 1967 and recited a principal sum of $70,400 at an annual rate of 7 percent to be "payable in equal annual installments of principal and interest in the sum of _____ Dollars each on the 15th day of June, 1968 and on each anniversary date thereafter until said entire indebtedness of $70,400 and interest shall be paid in full." The maker argued that the note was unenforceable until completed. Decide.

8. The following instrument was sued upon:

Chemical Products Incorporated
Salt Lake City, Utah

No. *687*   *October 5, 1962.*

On *November 10, 1962* Pay to the order of Chemical Products Inc.
Two Thousand Four Hundred Thirty-two and no/100 Dollars
($2,432.00). The transaction which gives rise to this instrument is the
purchase of goods by the acceptor from the drawer.

Chemical Products Inc.

By *Bob Chron*

Accepted at *Conway, Ark.* on *October 5, 1962.*
Payable at *First National Bank*
Bank Location *Conway, Ark.*
Buyer's Signature *Joe Wellbanke & Richard J. Martin*

Is the instrument negotiable? Decide.

NEGOTIATION 44

A negotiable instrument is incomplete and revocable until it has been issued, or put into circulation. The drawer of a draft or the maker of a promissory note is said to have issued the instrument when he delivers it to another party with the intention of making it effective as negotiable paper. (U.C.C. 3—102(a))

The transfer of the legal title to commercial paper requires *delivery*. Handing over possession of an instrument by an individual to his agent is not a delivery because it is still within the principal's control. However, when a properly endorsed instrument is sent to the payee by mail, at his direction, title passes upon mailing.

Once an instrument has been issued, it may be negotiated from one individual to another until it is presented for payment. The manner of negotiation is determined by the kind of instrument issued. An instrument may be payable either to the order of a given person or to the bearer of the instrument. When it is payable to order, it must be endorsed by the person to whom it is payable and transferred by delivery to the next holder. If it is payable to the bearer, it may be negotiated by delivery, without the necessity of an endorsement. In order to complete a negotiation, the transferor must indicate his surrender of ownership to another and actually deliver control to the other person. However, when the holder surrenders an instrument to a drawee for payment, this is not considered a negotiation requiring an endorsement. (This is true even where the drawee requires a signature as a receipt for payment.) Every other transfer creates a new contract on the instrument between the immediate parties to the transfer, and the rights and liabilities that arise will be somewhat influenced by the type of endorsement used to effect the transfer. (U.C.C. 3—202)

An endorsement must be written by or on behalf of the holder; it must appear on the instrument or, when necessary, on a paper firmly affixed to the instrument, called an *allonge*. (U.C.C. 3—202(2)) To effect an endorsement, the person to whom an instrument is payable, as stated on the face of the instrument or in the special endorsement, or the person in possession of bearer paper merely signs his name on the instrument, thereby indicating his intention to make it negotiable. Usually, an endorsement is made on the back of an instrument, and the endorsee has the right to add qualifying words or statements as part of his endorsement.

In order to have a valid endorsement, a payee must write his name as it appears on the instrument. Where an instrument is made payable to a person under a misspelled name or a name other than his own, he may endorse in that name, in his own name, or in both. Signature in both names may be required by a person paying or giving value for the instrument. It is necessary also that the name used identify the payee and endorser as the same person.

An endorsement is effective for negotiation only when it conveys the entire instrument or any unpaid residue. (U.C.C. 3—203) For example, A cannot endorse to B $100 of a $500 draft; he must endorse the whole amount to B or the negotiation is invalid. However, if it is an installment note and $100 remains unpaid, this $100 of unpaid residue may be endorsed to B.

TYPES OF ENDORSEMENT

Endorsements may be special, blank, qualified, or restrictive. (U.C.C. 3—204)

SPECIAL ENDORSEMENT

A special endorsement specifies the person to whom or to whose order it makes the instrument payable. An instrument specially endorsed becomes payable to the order of the special endorsee and may be further negotiated only by his endorsement. For example, if William is the payee of a negotiable instrument and he endorses it "Pay to the order of Charles, William" Charles must endorse the instrument in order for it to be further negotiated. It is not necessary to include the words "order" or "bearer" in the endorsement. It may read simply "Pay to Charles, William."

BLANK ENDORSEMENT

A blank endorsement occurs when the party to whom the instrument is payable merely signs his name, without making the instrument payable to another person. An instrument payable to order and endorsed in blank becomes payable to the bearer and, like money, may be negotiated by delivery alone, until a holder makes the instrument order paper again by a special endorsement. (U.C.C. 3—204—2)

A holder may convert a blank endorsement into a special endorsement by writing over the signature of the endorser any contract consistent with the character of the endorsement. (U.C.C. 3—204—3) This is referred to as *completing the endorsement*. For example, if George Fleer endorses an instrument in blank and delivers it to Gola Waters, Waters may protect himself by writing "Pay to Gola Waters" over the blank endorsement. This converts the blank endorsement to a special endorsement specifying Waters as the endorsee. This has the same effect as if Fleer, the endorser, had named Waters as the endorsee.

QUALIFIED ENDORSEMENT

A qualified endorsement qualifies the liability of the person making the endorsement. Usually, anyone who endorses a negotiable instrument commits himself to pay the instrument if the maker or drawee fails to do so. However, where any type of endorsement, except a restrictive endorsement, is qualified by adding the words "without recourse" or any other words that indicate an intention not to be liable for payment in the event of nonpayment by the maker or drawee, the endorsee cannot be held liable on his contract. He still has warranty liability though it is somewhat qualified. (U.C.C. 3—414)

The qualified endorsement while limiting the liability of the endorser, does not affect the passage of title or the negotiable character of the instrument. It is often used in situations where the holder of the instrument is merely a trustee for others entitled to the beneficial interest, as, for example, when trust deeds are used as security for loans. It may be used in an agency situation when the agent has no personal interest in the transaction.

RESTRICTIVE ENDORSEMENT

A restrictive endorsement either makes payment conditional or purports to prohibit further transfer of the instrument. It usually specifies a purpose for the endorsement or the use to be made of the negotiable paper. For example, "for deposit only" indicates the endorsee's intention that the instrument be deposited. "For collection only" indicates a receipt of payment by the endorsee." "Pay to Gola Waters upon completion of contract" indicates a condition attached to the endorsement. The first taker under a restrictive endorsement must take with the endorsement in mind, or as the U.C.C. states, "consistently with the endorsement." Such endorsements are not effective against later parties who take without knowledge that the restriction has been ignored.

NEGOTIATION OF BEARER PAPER

A negotiable instrument is deemed bearer paper when (1) it is drawn "payable to bearer" or (2) when the last endorsement on the paper is a blank endorsement. Where an instrument is drawn payable to the bearer, it may be changed to order paper by a special endorsement. Thus, the last endorsement determines the nature of the instrument. Bearer paper may be negotiated by delivery alone, without the necessity of a further endorsement. (U.C.C. 3—202)

TRANSFER BY ASSIGNMENT

Occasionally, an order instrument may be negligently transferred without the endorsement of the payee or special endorsee. This is called transfer by assignment and the person who holds the instrument is designated a transferee of unendorsed order paper. This transferee occupies the same position in regard to the instrument as did the transferor and acquires whatever title the transferor had. However, he has the right to demand the unqualified endorsement of the transferor; at the time of such endorsement the transferee becomes a holder by proper negotiation.

REACQUISITION

When a person reacquires an instrument in a commercial transaction or has it returned to him by a prior party, he may cancel any endorsement not necessary to his title and may reissue or further negotiate the instrument. In this situation, any person whose endorsement follows that of the reacquiring party is discharged as against the reacquiring party and subsequent holders not in due course. If a party's endorsement has been cancelled, he is discharged as against subsequent holders in due course as well. (U.C.C. 3—208) For example, suppose an instrument contained the following endorsements: B, A, D, M, A, N. If A were held liable, he could recover from B, but not from D or M because they could in turn enforce the instrument against A.

NEGOTIATION OF CHECKS

A check is a particular kind of draft. Its distinguishing features are:

1. A check is drawn on a bank.
2. A check is payable on demand.
3. The bank is under a contractual duty to pay all of the checks drawn by the drawer to the extent of funds deposited to the drawer's credit. (See Figure 44-1)
4. The drawer must notify the bank with reasonable promptness of any errors in his monthly statement with regard to checks drawn.

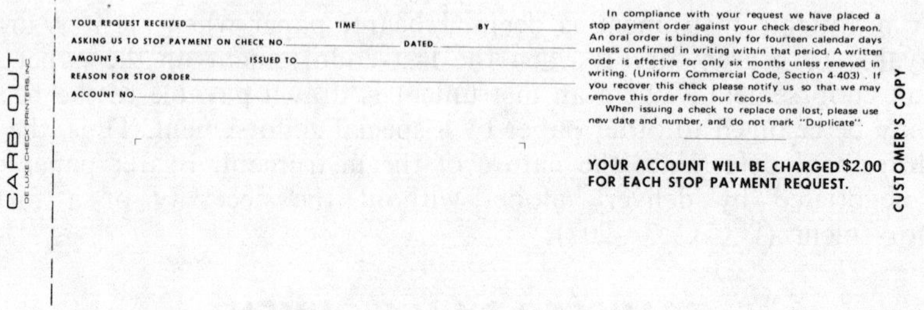
CARB-OUT
DE LUXE CHECK PRINTERS, INC

PEOPLES–MERCHANTS TRUST COMPANY
CANTON, OHIO 44702

YOUR REQUEST RECEIVED ____ TIME ____ BY ____
ASKING US TO STOP PAYMENT ON CHECK NO. ____ DATED ____
AMOUNT $ ____ ISSUED TO ____
REASON FOR STOP ORDER ____
ACCOUNT NO. ____

PLEASE CONFIRM THIS STOP PAYMENT REQUEST BY SIGNING COPY 2.

DELUXE
N 2922

In compliance with your request we have placed a stop payment order against your check described hereon. An oral order is binding only for fourteen calendar days unless confirmed in writing within that period. A written order is effective for only six months unless renewed in writing. (Uniform Commercial Code, Section 4-403). If you recover this check please notify us so that we may remove this order from our records.

When issuing a check to replace one lost, please use new date and number, and do not mark "Duplicate".

YOUR ACCOUNT WILL BE CHARGED $2.00 FOR EACH STOP PAYMENT REQUEST.

CUSTOMER'S COPY

Figure 44-1

It has become common practice to indicate on the face of the check the purpose for which it is drawn. This also serves as an additional receipt for the payment of obligations. A number of checks are presented in Figure 44-2 which illustrate the common practice of using rubber stamp endorsements.

Figure 44-2

THE IMPOSTOR DOCTRINE

Section 3—405(1)(a) of the Uniform Commercial Code—Commercial Paper provides:

> An endorsement by any person in the name of a named payee is effective if (a) an impostor by use of the mails or otherwise has induced the maker or drawer to issue the instrument to him or his confederate in the name of the payee. . . .

In application the statute provides that an an endorsement by any person in the name of a named payee is effective if an impostor by use of mails or otherwise has induced a maker or drawer to issue an instrument to him or his confederate in name of the payee. The courts find no reason to distinguish between a drawer who is duped by an impersonator communicating directly with him through the mails and a drawer who is duped by an impersonator communicating indirectly with him through third persons. The reason for the doctrine is that the courts want to place the burden on the party who could have prevented the loss through the exercise of due care.

LEGAL PRINCIPLES

Ownership of commercial paper is transferred from one person to another by endorsement in the case of "order" paper and by delivery in the case of "bearer" paper.

An endorsement must be written on the instrument itself or on a paper attached to the instrument, called an allonge.

Endorsement must be for the entire instrument.

Endorsement can be made to two persons jointly.

An endorsement should be written on the back of the instrument in the same form in which the endorsee's name appears on the face of the instrument.

Endorsement in blank names no endorsee and is usually the signature of the payee or endorsee. It converts negotiable paper into a bearer instrument.

A special endorsement names a payee; a specially endorsed instrument must be endorsed by the person named before it can be negotiated.

A qualified endorsement qualifies or limits the liability of the endorser. The negotiability of an instrument is not affected by a qualified endorsement.

A restrictive endorsement does not prevent the further negotiation of the instrument, but it does impose restrictions on the rights of the holder.

No endorsement is needed for the negotiation of bearer paper.

The face of the instrument coupled with the last endorsement on an instrument determines whether it is to be negotiated as order paper or bearer paper.

One who reacquires an instrument does not imporve his former position.

An endorsement by an impostor is effective to transfer title to an instrument.

CASE FOR REVIEW

AMERICAN NATIONAL B. & T. CO. v. SCENIC STAGE LINES

276 N.E.2d 420 (Ill. 1971)

On May 12, 1970 defendants-appellants Scenic Stage Lines of Savanna, Inc. and Roger J. Crow executed and delivered to Hausman Bus Sales, Inc., their confession note for $80,000,000 made payable in one installment on June 26, 1970, to secure the purchase of certain used buses. The note bore the following printed words on the reverse side thereof, with the exception of the signature of "Eugene Tarkoff, Sec-Treas.", which was handwritten:

ENDORSEMENT

Pay To the Order of

American National Bank
and Trust Company of Chicago

_____
(Endorser)

_____
(Endorser)

_____
(Seller)

By /s/ Eugene Tarkoff Sec-Treas.
_____
(Title)

The note was placed in judgment on July 24, 1970 by appellee-plaintiff American National Bank & Trust Company of Chicago who alleged in their complaint ownership of said note.

The initial question here, however, is whether or not a note made payable to a corporation by its corporate name can be legally endorsed by the signature of an individual followed by a description of his position but without reference in the endorsement itself to the entity for which he purports to act. The Illinois Uniform Commercial Code does not deal directly with this issue. Article 3 of the Code dealing with liability of parties does provide in Sec. 3—403—Signature by Authorized Representative—that where the instrument names the person represented and the representative signs in a representative capacity, the representative is not liable. In the Code comment on this section . . . the commentator points out that the unambiguous way to make the representation clear is to sign "Peter Pringle by Arthur Adams, Agent" but that any other definite indication is sufficient as where the instrument reads "Peter Pringle promises to pay" and it is signed "Arthur Adams, Agent." There is a strong inference to be drawn from Sec. 3—403 that where the note names the corporation as payee that an endorsement signed by its agent in his own name, followed by a description of his position, is a sufficient indication that the individual signer is acting as agent for the named payee and that such an endorsement is legally sufficient. To hold otherwise would place the plaintiff Bank in the anomalous position of not being able to bring suit against Scenic Stage Lines, the maker of the note, because the endorsement is legally insufficient to convey any rights to the Bank against the maker, and also to deny the plaintiff Bank any rights against Tarkoff as an individual endorser because of the terms of Sec. 3—403. . . . Such a result would seem to be untenable.

Admittedly, there is not a great deal of case law on this particular form of endorsement. Probably, because an endorsement is seldom made in this manner, and it obviously is not the recommended method of doing so. Such case law as there is in Illinois would suggest the holding that the endorsement in this case is legally sufficient to pass title to the plaintiff Bank.

The court cites with approval Daniel on Negotiable Instruments (4th Ed. Vol. 1, Sec. 416):

> Where a note is payable to a corporation by its corporate name, and is then endorsed by an authorized agent or official, with the suffix of his ministerial position, it will be regarded that he acts for his principal who is disclosed on the paper as payee and is therefore the only person who can transfer the legal title.

CASE PROBLEMS

1. Atlanta Federal Savings & Loan Association, Inc. drew a check in the amount of $2000 on Fulton National Bank as drawee, naming Mrs. Obie as payee. Mrs. Obie transferred the check, without endorsement and for consideration, to Jett. The drawee bank refused to pay the check on the ground that it was not endorsed by the payee. Jett sued Atlanta and Mrs. Obie on the check. Decide.

2. In 1965 and 1966 defendants, Cooper and his wife, executed four notes payable to Elliott in the sum of $2500. When plaintiff, Cartwright, brought suit to obtain payment of them, defendants admitted the execution of the notes and their obligation but denied that the notes were the property of Elliott, alleging that they belonged to White by virtue of Elliott's endorsement and delivery of the notes to him. Elliott had told Cooper that after his death he wanted White to have the Cooper notes. He was advised that he should endorse the notes and make them payable to White. Cooper thereupon wrote on each note, "Pay within note to White without recourse," and Elliott signed them but retained possession. When Elliott died his agent had the notes but had received no special instructions to hold them for White. Decide.

3. A promissory note made to Wheeler was sold to plaintiff, Farnsworth. On the back appeared the following words: "I hereby assine [sic] this note over to E. H. Farnsworth, this Nov. 1, 1960. J. A. Wheeler." Suit is brought on the note, and defendant, Burdick, claims that plaintiff has only an assignment and is subject to the defense of failure of consideration. Decide.

4. An action was brought concerning a series of thirty-six promissory notes. Each note contained the typewritten corporate name, "S.R.S. Second Avenue Theatre Corp." in the lower right-hand corner, below which were two signatures, "Harold Segal" and "George Schavan." These signatures were in blank. The holder contends that Segal and Schavan were liable on the notes. Decide.

5. Defendant's son made a note to Riley and Jones, jointly. Later, when partial payment had been made, Riley endorsed the note on the back and delivered it to Karsner for the balance of the value, $835. After the sale to Karsner, Riley fraudulently persuaded defendant to sign the paper as a joint maker. Karsner subsequently negotiated the note, by delivery, to plaintiff, Smith, who paid value for it. The other payee, Jones, had not endorsed the note

until long after it was due. Smith brings an action to collect on the note. Decide.

6. Mr. and Mrs. E. D. Tamas had a joint account with defendant, National Bank. E. D. Tamas also had an individual account there. On October 17, 1967, Mrs. Tamas acquired a check for $2120 payable to Mrs. E. D. Tamas. She endorsed the check in blank, the endorsement reading "Mrs. E. D. Tamas," and gave it to her husband. She alleges that she instructed him to deposit it "to credit of Mr. and Mrs. E. D. Tamas." Tamas endorsed the check "Mr. E. D. Tamas, Martin Hotel," and deposited it in his individual account, later withdrawing the money. On April 3, 1968, Mrs. Tamas received a statement of the joint account and learned that the value of the check had not been deposited. She brought suit to hold the bank liable, contending that it knowingly participated in the diversion of the money. Decide.

7. Manufacturers Hanover Trust provided in its deposit that "unless the depositor shall notify the bank in writing within thirty days of the delivery or mailing any statement of account and cancelled vouchers that the signature upon any returned voucher was forged, the said statement of account shall be considered correct for all purposes and the bank shall not be liable for any payment made and charged to the depositor's account." A depositor sued alleging the thirty day restriction was invalid. Decide.

8. Edmund and Paula Jezemski were husband and wife but were separated. Paula and another man who claimed to be Edmund borrowed money. A check drawn by the Philadelphia Title Insurance Company was made payable to the order of Edmund and Paula Jezemski. The check was endorsed with Edmund's forged signature. The check was paid by the Fidelity-Philadelphia Trust Company, the drawee. When the forgery was discovered, the Philadelphia Title Insurance Company claimed that the Fidelity-Philadelphia Trust Company was liable for the amount of the check because the latter company had made payment on a forged endorsement. Decide.

Every transfer of ownership interests in commercial paper creates a contract between the parties affecting the transfer and in certain cases binding subsequent holders. No individual is liable on an instrument unless his name appears thereon as the result of his signing it or by appropriate action by his agent. Rights and liabilities arise that may be expressed or implied. Other persons who may acquire contractual liability through the negotiation and transfer of commercial paper include:

1. *Endorsers.* An individual (or a business firm) who owns negotiable paper may transfer ownership of it to another individual (or firm) by affixing his signature to the back of the paper and delivering it to the new owner.

2. *Endorsees.* The individual (or firm) to whom an endorsement is made is called an endorsee until he further negotiates the instrument. At that time he becomes an endorser.

3. *Holders.* An individual (or a firm), in possession of negotiable paper which is payable at that time to him (or to the firm), either as payee, bearer, or endorsee, is a holder.

4. *Holders for Value.* When the holder gives consideration for an instrument or takes it in discharge of an obligation, he is deemed a holder for value.

5. *Holders in Due Course.* Under certain circumstances, a holder who qualifies as a holder in due course will take an instrument free from personal defenses.

6. *Accommodation Parties.* An individual (or firm) may add his name to commercial paper for the purpose of assuming liability for and in behalf of another person. (U.C.C. 3—415) Such a party is *a surety.* Whether or not he is paid for his action, he is called an accommodation party. His endorsement is usually required to enable another person to receive credit or a loan of money. Any endorsement that shows it is not in the chain of title is deemed an accommodation endorsement.

7. *Guarantors.* An individual (or a firm) who signs commercial paper and adds "payment guaranteed" or equivalent words guarantees that if the instrument is not paid when due he will pay it according to its terms, without resort by the holder to any other party. (U.C.C. 3—416)

LIABILITY IN GENERAL

There are two principal kinds of liability on a negotiable instrument: primary and secondary. A party is said to have *primary liability* when he is bound absolutely to pay the instrument. The maker of a promissory note and the acceptor of a draft are primary parties. A party has *secondary liability* if he is required to pay the instrument only in the event that it is not paid by the individual from whom payment is initially requested.

PRIMARY LIABILITY

When a maker executes and issues a promissory note, he becomes absolutely liable for payment according to the terms of the note when it comes due, unless he has acquired a valid defense. This liability continues as long as the instrument is in circulation or until a statute of limitations bars an action on it. (U.C.C. 3—413)

When a draft is first drawn and issued, no one has primary liability for its payment. Although it is drawn on the drawee, he has no absolute obligation to pay it. Thus, when a person draws a check on a bank, the bank incurs no liability to the payee or subsequent holder of the check. But by failing to pay the check when funds are available, the bank may incur liability to its customer, the drawer of the check. However, if the holder asks the drawee to accept it or to agree to pay it, the drawee assumes, by such an affirmative action, primary liability for its payment.

Acceptance is the drawee's signed guaranty to honor the draft as presented to him. It must be written on the draft and may consist of the drawee's signature alone or words signifying an intent to assume primary liability. The acceptance is not complete until the instrument has been delivered to the drawee or notice has been given by the person presenting it for acceptance. (U.C.C. 3—414)

There are three types of acceptances: general, qualified, and implied. A *general acceptance* is unqualified; that is, the instrument is accepted as drawn. A *qualified acceptance* can be conditional; it can be for part of the amount (partial); it can be for a particular place only (local); and it can be for a certain time. The holder is not required to take a qualified acceptance, and if he does not, the drawee's withholding of unqualified acceptance may be treated as a *dishonor,* or a refusal to pay. If the holder agrees to a qualified acceptance, the endorsers and the drawer are released from liability unless they expressly or impliedly assent to such acceptance. Silence on their part for a reasonable time after notification is deemed implied authorization. An *implied acceptance* may be presumed by the acts of the drawee. For example, if the drawee keeps the instrument for more than twenty-four hours and refuses to return it to the holder, an acceptance may be implied. However, his liability will be in tort for conversion, and not on the instrument itself.

SECONDARY LIABILITY

All parties not classified as primary parties—specifically, endorsers, accommodation endorsers, and drawers of drafts—have what is termed secondary liability because their liability usually arises only when the primary party fails to pay. Endorsers may be unqualified or qualified.

When a person endorses an instrument without using words of qualification, he is deemed an *unqualified endorser*. By his endorsement, the unqualified endorser guarantees the payment of the instrument if certain conditions precedent are met. These conditions are presentment, dishonor, and notice of dishonor. (See Chapter 47 "Establishing Secondary Liability," for a definition of these terms) Every unqualified endorser incurs this secondary liability; if forced to pay, however, he in turn may collect in the same way from any unqualified endorser who endorsed the instrument before him.

If a person endorses an instrument with the words "without recourse," he is deemed to be a *qualified endorser* whose liability is limited to warranty liability to the endorsee and other parties who may become holders of the instrument.

Where negotiation is accomplished by delivery alone, an endorser's warranties extend in favor of the immediate transferee only and to no other holder. However, even where negotiation is accomplished by delivery alone, the transferor makes the presentment warranties discussed below to the person who pays or accepts the instrument. Another point to be considered in connection with a negotiation by delivery alone that such a transferor, who by definition does not endorse, makes no endorsement contract and therefore does not make any guarantee of payment as does an endorser under Section 3—414 of the Code.

If a person endorses an instrument for the purpose of lending his credit to some other party, he is deemed an *accommodation endorser*. His endorsement is almost always unqualified and he is liable accordingly.

A drawer of a draft has the same conditional liability as the unqualified endorser. He guarantees that, upon refulsal to pay by the drawee, he will pay the amount of the draft to the holder or to any endorser who takes it up. His contract is set forth in Section 3—413 of the Code. He may disclaim this liability by drawing without recourse.

Occasionally, an individual will sign a negotiable instrument without consideration solely for the purpose of "accommodating" another party to the instrument—in order to enable him to negotiate a loan. The status of such an individual is different from that of other types of endorsers in that he never acquires title to the paper. He becomes the owner of the instrument only if it is not paid and he pays it. Nevertheless, he is liable to the holder for the value of the instrument, even though the holder is aware that the accommodation party is acting in that capacity. If the accommodation party is forced to pay the instrument, he is entitled to collect from the party he is accommodating.

ORDER OF LIABILITY OF ENDORSERS

Usually, the endorsers on a negotiable instrument are liable to the present holder of the document in inverse order. (U.C.C. 3—414) The original payee or person negotiating the instrument to the holder is the first person liable, and he remains ultimately liable since the liability of each endorser is to the subsequent or following endorsee.

WARRANTY LIABILITY

Any person who receives consideration upon transfer of an instrument warrants the existence of certain facts. The unqualified endorser, in effect, guarantees that the following facts are true:

1. He has good title to the instrument or is authorized to obtain payment or acceptance on behalf of one who has good title, and the transfer is otherwise rightful.
2. All signatures on the instrument are genuine or executed by authorized agents.
3. The instrument has not been materially altered.
4. No defense of any party is good against him.
5. He has no knowledge of any insolvency proceedings, instituted with respect to the maker or acceptor or the drawer of an unaccepted instrument. These warranties pass to any subsequent holder who takes the instrument in good faith. (U.C.C. 3—417(2)

The qualified endorser makes the same warranties as the unqualified endorser except that the warranty concerning defenses is limited to a warranty that the endorser does not have knowledge of any defense, rather than the absolute warranty that no defense exists. These warranties run to the same person as those of the unqualified endorser.

The warranties made by an individual or a business firm who transfers an instrument by delivery alone are the same as those made by an unqualified endorser. However, such warranties extend only to the immediate transferee. On the other hand, when a person transfers by endorsement, such transferor's warranties extend to any subsequent good faith holder.

In addition to the above warranties on transfer, any person who obtains payment or acceptance, and all prior transferors, make the following warranties under Section 3—417(1):

(1) Any person who obtains payment or acceptance and any prior transferor warrants to a person who is good faith pays or accepts that
  (a) he has a good title to the instrument or is authorized to obtain payment of acceptance on behalf of one who has a good title; and
  (b) he has no knowledge that the signature of the maker or drawer is unauthorized, except that this warranty is not given by a holder in due course acting in good faith
    (i) to a maker with respect to the maker's own signature; or
    (ii) to a drawer with respect to the drawer's own signature, whether or not the drawer is also the drawee; or
    (iii) to an acceptor of a draft if the holder in due course took the draft after the acceptance or obtained the acceptance without knowledge that the drawer's signature was unauthorized; and
  (c) the instrument has not been materially altered, except that this warranty is not given by a holder in due course acting in good faith
    (i) to the maker of a note; or
    (ii) to the drawer of a draft whether or not the drawer is also the drawee; or

(iii) to the acceptor of a draft with respect to an alteration made prior to the acceptance if the holder in due course took the draft after the acceptance, even though the acceptance provided "payable as originally drawn" or equivalent terms; or

(iv) to the acceptor of a draft with respect to an alteration made after the acceptance."

It should be noted that these presentment warranties under 3—417(1) are more limited than the transferor warranties under 3—417(2).

LEGAL PRINCIPLES

No individual is liable on a negotiable instrument unless his name appears thereon as the result of his signing it or his agents having affixed his signature.

There are two kinds of liability on a negotiable instrument; primary and secondary.

Primary parties, the maker of a note and the acceptor of a draft, have absolute liability.

Acceptance must be written on the instrument.

A qualified acceptance may be treated as a dishonor.

Parties with secondary liability guarantee payment if certain conditions are met.

Endorsers are liable in the inverse order of their endorsement.

Each person transferring an instrument (either by endorsement and delivery or solely by delivery) warrants the existence of certain facts with regard to the instrument.

CASE FOR REVIEW

FIRST BANK & T. CO. OF BOCA RATON v. COUNTY NAT. BANK

281 So.2d 515 (Fla. 1973)

Appellant plaintiff seeks review of a final judgment rendered in favor of appellee defendant in a suit to compel appellee to honor certain endorsement guarantees.

A Mr. Donald Hill, a depositor of appellant, wrote two checks on his account to "Firebird International, Inc.", and the checks were delivered to the individual intended. No such corporate entity existed. Nonetheless, the checks were endorsed by one Bill Johnson as president of Firebird International and Firebird International, Inc. and both checks were made payable to the account of a Mr. Charles Moskowitz in the County National Bank of North Miami Beach, appellee herein. County National then endorsed the checks by stamping thereon the following:

PAY TO THE ORDER OF ANY BANK, BANKER OR TRUST CO.,
All Prior Endorsements Guaranteed

"April 7, 1969,

"63—724	COUNTY NATIONAL BANK	63—724
631	OF NORTH MIAMI BEACH	631

[Emphasis supplied.]

Appellant, relying on said endorsement, duly honored the checks. A few months thereafter Hill brought suit in the Circuit Court of Palm Beach County against appellant alleging an improper payment by the drawee to a fictitious entity since no corporate status existed for Firebird International, the payee. That suit resulted in a judgment rendered in favor of Hill for $5,000.00, and is the basis claimed by appellant as its damages herein.

Upon careful consideration of the record, briefs and arguments of counsel, we are of the opinion that the trial judge erred, as a matter of law, in not finding that an endorsing bank is liable to a drawee bank relying upon that endorsement. Fla.Stat. § 673.3—414(2), F.S.A. states:

> Unless they otherwise agree, endorsers are liable to one another in the order in which they endorse, which is presumed to be the order in which their signatures appear on the instrument.

Moreover, any person, customer or collecting bank transferring such an item to another, who has received consideration therefor warrants to the transferree or subsequent collecting bank that all signatures therein are genuine or authorized. . . . It was shown in the case sub judice that such warranty or guaranty from appellee to appellant was not met and as a result the appellant suffered damage. Under the foregoing statutes it clearly appears that the appellant was entitled to recover judgment from appellee.

CASE PROBLEMS

1. John Alden was the maker of a promissory note, due December 29, 1974, and payable to the order of "himself" that he endorsed in blank and discounted at Last Bank, where it was payable. The bank re-discounted it at First National Bank, which made no presentment. On and after the due date the maker had sufficient funds on deposit at the Last Bank to have paid the note until January 7, 1975, when the bank failed. The makers contend that the failure of the holder to make presentment for payment discharged them. Decide.

2. Brown made a ninety-day promissory note payable to Green, who endorsed it to plaintiffs. Before maturity, Brown disappeared. On the last day of grace the plaintiffs notified Green by mail that the note had not been paid, but made no inquiry for, or demand on, the maker. They then brought suit on the note against Green. Decide.

3. Defendant sold furniture to a customer who gave his name as Norton, receiving in payment a note, secured by a mortgage on the furniture, that he endorsed "without recourse" and sold to plaintiff. When the maker of the note later defaulted, it was discovered that his name was actually Morton, and that he had a

very bad credit rating and a prison record. Plaintiff brought an action to recover the money paid to defendant for the note. Decide.

4. The makers gave Ward a promissory note for $10,000 due March 1, 1966, securing it by a mortgage on some farmland. Ward endorsed the note to plaintiff, "Pay to the order of Eleanor H. Leek without recourse on me." The makers defaulted in the payment of an installment and interest, whereupon Leek declared the entire amount due under the terms of the note and brought suit against Ward to collect it. Plaintiff asserts that the real worth of the property was no more than $6500 and that Ward knew of this invalidity and is therefore liable on an implied warranty as a qualified endorser. Decide.

5. Plaintiff sued defendant on a promissory note as follows:

$500.00   January 11, 1974
John Johnson after date does promise to pay to the order of Mrs. Frank O'Dess five hundred dollars at 7 percent interest for _____ Value received.

                                                   John Johnson
                                                   Mike Gunter
No. _____   Due April 11, 1974

Defendant Gunter pleaded he was an endorser and received no notice of dishonor for a period of four years. Decide.

6. A note dated March 5, 1954, payable in three years to the order of William Bell, Jr., was signed as follows:

	Menna M. Good	
(CORPORATE SEAL)	Chet B. Earle, Inc.	(SEAL)
	James G. Dornan	(SEAL)

On the date of the note, Bell was a vice-president and treasurer of Chet B. Earle, Inc. and actively interested in the operation and management of the used car business of the corporation. James G. Dornan was the secretary and Menna M. Good was another of its vice-presidents. William Bell, Jr. died on March 6, 1960; and on April 26, 1963 his executrix brought an action on the note against James G. Dornan. Dornan alleged that the loan was made by Bell to the corporation, that his signature and that of Menna M. Good were affixed in their representative capacity as secretary and vice-president of the corporation, that their titles following their signatures were omitted by inadvertence, and that Bell was fully aware of the fact that the sole obligation was that of the corporation. Decide.

7. Herbert U. Moore executed and delivered to the plaintiff a promissory note in the principal sum of $15,000 with interest at 6 percent. At the time of the execution and delivery of said note, the defendant, Lois Moore, signed her name on the back thereof under the following endorsement:

For value received the undersigned and each of them hereby forever waives presentment, demand, protest, notice of protest and notice of dishonor of the within note and the undersigned and each of them guarantees the payment of said note at maturity and consents without notice to any and all extension of time or terms of payment made by holder of said note.

The complaint alleged that the note was presented to Herbert U. Moore for payment but payment was refused. On July 18, 1963 the note was presented to Lois Moore for payment but she also refused payment. The defendant in her answer admitted the execution of the note but denies that she knew in what capacity she signed the note or the reason for her signing. Decide.

8. An agent of Accident & Guarantee Corporation, authorized to draw drafts on the corporation, drew a $600 draft payable to Johnson, then forged Johnson's

endorsement and sold the draft to defendant, Lincoln National Bank. Defendant presented the draft to Accident, plaintiff, which accepted and paid it but subsequently having discovered the forgery, sued defendant to recover the $600. Decide.

HOLDERS IN DUE COURSE   46

The U.C.C. defines a holder as "a person who is in possession of a document of title or an instrument or an investment security drawn, issued or endorsed to him or to his order or to bearer or in blank." (U.C.C. 1—201) A person can be a holder, therefore, only by showing that he is in possession of a negotiable instrument and that its order or promise "runs" to him. A holder has the right to transfer or negotiate an instrument and, on payment or satisfaction, to discharge it or enforce payment on it in his own name. A "holder in due course" is a special status of holder as defined in U.C.C. 3—302.

The concept of holders in due course was evolved to better enable commercial paper to circulate as money. If a holder is a holder in due course, a presumption of consideration and delivery arises in his favor, and he takes the instrument free from any claims and certain defenses that might have arisen from the transaction that gave rise to the instrument. Because of the somewhat secure position of such a holder, commercial paper is able to circulate freely in various business transactions. To qualify as a holder in due course, a holder must be lawfully in possession of an instrument drawn, issued or endorsed to him, or to his order or to bearer or in blank. Consequently, in the case of "order" paper, any necessary endorsements must be present. He must also (1) have given value for the instrument; (2) have received it in good faith; and (3) have taken it without notice that it is overdue, that it has been dishonored, or that there is any defense against it or claim to it on the part of any person. (U.C.C. 3—302) The Code also makes it clear that a payee may be a holder in due course. (U.C.C. 3—305)

THE REQUIREMENT OF VALUE

To qualify as a holder in due course, the holder must give "value" for the instrument. Thus someone who receives a negotiable instrument as a gift does not receive the same protection as one who acquires an instrument by purchase in a commercial transaction. Value, as used here, means any consideration that will support a simple contract. However, the U.C.C. makes it clear that "value" and "consideration" are not to be used in the same context. An instrument is taken for value when it is taken "in payment of or as security for an antecedent claim against any person whether or not the claim is due." (U.C.C. 3—303(b)) Therefore, if the instrument is given as security for a preexisting debt the holder has given "value," even though, under the common law, there might be no "consideration."

A person who merely promises to pay for an instrument does not give "value" until he actually parts with the consideration, unless he "gives a negotiable instrument for it or makes an irrevocable commitment to a third person." (U.C.C. 3-303(c)) In the first instance, value is given when A accepts a check from B and in turn surrenders a promissory note given by B. A common example of an irrevocable commitment is a letter of credit given by a bank under which the person to whom it is issued may obtain credit up to a stated amount. Some complications do arise, however, when commercial banks accept negotiable instruments for deposit or collection. Generally, the courts have held that a bank becomes a holder for value as soon as it credits the depositor's account, available for withdrawal as of right even though it has the right to charge the account if the instrument is dishonored. (U.C.C. 4—209 4—208)

The fact that the holder of an instrument has paid less than its face value does not in itself prevent recovery of the full amount. However, payment of a sum substantially less than the face value may be considered evidence of bad faith in that it may indicate a suspicion by the purchaser that something was wrong with the instrument. If a holder who has paid only some fraction of the agreed consideration learns of a defense, he is a holder for value only to the extent of the amount that has been paid. In like manner, if a person accepts a negotiable instrument for another debt, he is a holder for value only to the extent of that debt. Finally, a holder may give "value" for the unpaid portion of an installment note.

THE REQUIREMENT OF GOOD FAITH

A holder in due course must purchase the negotiable instrument in good faith (honesty in fact). If an inspection of the instrument fails to show any defects (such as alterations or erasures) and if the purchaser has no knowledge of defects in the title of the instrument or of any rights or defenses against the instrument, the purchase can be made in good faith.

THE REQUIREMENT OF LACK OF NOTICE

According to the U.C.C. Sec. 1—201(25):

A person has 'notice' of a fact when (a) he has actual knowledge of it; or (b) he has received a notice or notification of it; or (c) from all the facts and circumstances known to him at the time in question he has reason to know it exists.

A holder in due course must have purchased the instrument before the due date. The law assumes that a person who does not settle a debt on the date of maturity does so because he has some defense or reason for not paying. As a result, any purchaser of the instrument after maturity is presumed to have known that some defense must exist and therefore cannot be a holder in due course. If the draft or note is payable on demand, it is said to be overdue after an unreasonable time has elapsed. Determination of what length of time is reasonable is based on the facts of each case, mainly the nature of the instrument and normal business practice. For example, Sec. 3—304(3)(c) of the U.C.C. states that the normal amount of time after which a check becomes overdue is thirty days.

Some negotiable instruments that are due on a fixed date also have an acceleration clause and are subject to an early maturity at the option of the holder. In such cases the instrument is overdue after this accelerating option is exercised. However, if a purchaser is unaware that the option had been exercised and the original maturity date has not been reached, he may still be considered a holder in due course.

If the instrument is subject to installment payments, failure by the maker to meet an installment on its due date bars a holder from becoming a holder in due course in the same manner as does failure to meet the maturity date. This does not apply to past-due interest. Again, the holder will not suffer if he did not know of the unpaid installment or could not be expected to know of it.

Sec. 3—304(1) of the Code states,

> The purchaser has notice of a claim defense if the instrument is so incomplete, bears such visible evidence of forgery or alteration or is otherwise so irregular as to call into question its validity, terms of ownership or to create an ambiguity as to the party to pay.

RIGHTS OF HOLDERS IN DUE COURSE

The status of a holder of negotiable paper does not become important until the holder brings suit against an individual or a business firm and the defendant raises against him a defense that can be asserted against an ordinary holder but not against a holder in due course. The law protects the good faith purchaser who takes an instrument in the due course of a commercial transaction.[1] Therefore, to the extent that holder is a holder in due course he takes the instrument free from all claims to it on the part of any person and secure from all defenses of any party to the instrument with whom the holder has not dealt, except infancy and any real defense that nullifies the obligation of that party. (U.C.C. 3—305)

LIMITATIONS OF THE STATUS OF
A HOLDERS IN DUE COURSE

A continuing business transaction involving commercial paper exists between a seller of consumer goods and a finance company which regularly purchases commercial paper from that seller. Commercial paper executed by the customer, is almost immediately negotiated to the finance company who is not aware of any defects in the particular product purchased by the consumer. Since the finance company pays value and the instrument is not overdue, the company qualifies as a holder in due course.

Recently there has been a number of cases questioning the closeness of the relationship of the seller and the finance company and denying the finance company status as a holder in due course. This is especially true where it can be shown that the forms used by the seller were supplied by the finance company. This "close participation" doctrine has been used in non-consumer cases to rebut the good faith requirement.

States are presently enacting laws denying holder in due course status in the above situation.

Some states are limiting the waiver of defense clause in retail installment contracts and California has totally abolished it. The proposed Uniform Consumer Credit Code limits the use of commercial paper and waiver of defense clauses in retail selling situations except where the selling has an agricultural purpose. Thus where the commercial paper has a consumer origin only remote good faith purchasers who have no knowledge of this origin will qualify as a holder in due course when the UCCC is adopted.

SUCCESSORS TO HOLDERS IN DUE COURSE

Sec. 3—201(1) of the U.C.C. (Shelter Doctrine) provides:

Transfer of an instrument vests in the transferee such rights as the transferor has therein, except that a transferee who has himself been a party to any fraud or illegality affecting the instrument or who as a prior holder had notice of a defense or claim against it cannot improve his position by taking from a later holder in due course.

A holder who receives title to a negotiable instrument from a holder in due course, therefore, possesses all the rights of a holder in due course even though he does not satisfy all the legal requirements. The reasoning here is that once a negotiable instrument passes through a holder in due course, all the personal defenses of the primary party or other parties have been cut off, provided that the holder in due course was not a party to any original fraud or illegality concerning the execution and issuance of the instrument. This rule assists the free transferability of commercial paper by allowing the holder in due course to sell the instrument to whomever he desires. Without this protection and the assurance of a free market, commercial paper would not be able to function as a medium of exchange in commercial transactions.

When a negotiable instrument passes back into the hands of a person who formerly held the instrument, the holder is said to be a *reacquirer*. Under the U.C.C., Sec. 3—208, a reacquirer of an instrument reverts to the position he held at the time of the first negotiation of the instrument to him. Also, he is not entitled to enforce payment against any holder of the instrument during the time of negotiation and repurchase. The courts usually apply this rule to the maker of the instrument also, holding that if the maker reacquires his instrument before maturity he may reissue it, but receiving it after maturity amounts to discharge of the instrument.

LEGAL PRINCIPLES

Owners of commercial paper are classified as (1) original parties and their successors or (2) holders in due course.

Commercial paper is intended for the use of the original payee; hence it is subject to any defenses or claims of ownership by the original parties to the transaction that gave rise to the instrument.

The concept of holders in due course was evolved to encourage the free transferability of commercial paper.

To qualify as a holder in due course, a holder must be lawfully in possession of an instrument payable to himself or to the bearer. He must have (1) given value in exchange for the instrument, (2) received it in good faith, and (3) taken it without notice that it was overdue or had been dishonored or had any defense against or claim to it on the part of any person.

According to the U.C.C., "value" differs from "consideration" in that the holder gives "value" only when the instrument is given in settlement of a preexisting debt.

A transfer to a holder in due course cuts off claims of ownership to and personal defenses against the instrument.

A payee may qualify as a holder in due course.

A successor to a holder in due course acquires all the rights of a holder in due course.

A reacquirer cannot improve his position by reacquiring the instrument.

CASE FOR REVIEW

MOFFAT COUNTY STATE BANK v. PINDER

11 Utah 2d 89, 355 P.2d 210 (1960)

. . . R. J. Pinder, appeals from a summary judgment awarding plaintiff, The Moffat County State Bank of Craig, Colorado, a judgment for $2216.03 as the holder in due course of a check for that amount made by Pinder to Bill Arnn. The check was dated October 12, 1956. It was drawn on the Midvale Branch Bank of Sandy, Utah. On October 15, 1956, Arnn endorsed the check in Craig, Colorado, and deposited it with the plaintiff bank in that city.

The deposit slip contains the following provisions: "This bank acts only as depositor's collecting agent and assumes no responsibility beyond its exercise of due care. . . . This bank may charge back at any time any item drawn on this bank which is ascertained to be drawn against insufficient funds or otherwise not good or payable. . . ." The consideration for the check failed, and in accordance with Pinder's directions, the Sandy bank refused payment on October 20, 1956, and the Moffat County received notice of such refusal on October 22, 1956.

Notwithstanding the provisions of the deposit slip, the Colorado bank extended Bill Arnn credit for the full amount of the check, and between the date of the deposit and notice of dishonor, that bank actually paid on checks made by Arnn $2216.03 against the credit resulting from the deposit of this $2500 check.

We have held [in other cases] that, where a check is drawn on one bank and unconditionally deposited in another, the latter becomes merely an agent of circumstances, if the bank of deposit extends credit and permits the depositor to withdraw the amount of the check, the bank becomes the owner thereof. . . .

From the foregoing we conclude that there is no conflict between the laws of this state and the state of Colorado on this subject, and under the facts of this case both in the state of Colorado and in the state of Utah, the Colorado bank became a holder in due course of this check and is entitled to recover the amount which it paid out in reliance on this check without notice. . . .

We conclude that the banking company is a bona fide holder for value in due course, and as such it is entitled to recover the amount of money which it paid in reliance upon the deposit of this check before it had notice of dishonor.

The judgment of the trial court is affirmed, with costs to respondent.

CASE PROBLEMS

1. The defendant, a reputable used car dealer, maintained a place of business in Boston to which a person purporting to be one Therrien came on October 23, 1946. He offered to sell the defendant an automobile and showed the defendant some papers identifying himself as Therrien and a bill of sale for the automobile. The defendant purchased the automobile with a check for $1200 which was dated ahead to October 25, to give him an opportunity to investigate the title to the automobile. On the next day, he discovered that the person from whom he purchased the automobile was an imposter who had stolen the automobile and the identifying papers. The defendant stopped payment on the check on either October 24 or October 25. . . . The imposter drew a line through the numeral '5' in the date of the check to make it resemble the numeral '8'. On October 29, he met the plaintiff, a used car dealer, and purchased an automobile for $764 which he paid for with the $1200 check, receiving the balance in cash. The plaintiff deposited the check on October 30, 1946 but, payment having been stopped by the defendant, the plaintiff received nothing. Plaintiff claimed to be a holder in due course. Decide.
2. The pertinent facts were that a signed check was delivered by the defendant Gravitt to Mrs. Moore, the payee, with the amount left blank. Mrs. Moore took the blank check to Cannon & Company and discussed her account with Cannon with one of its agents. The agent saw that the check was blank as to the amount, and Mrs. Moore in the presence of the agent filled in the check in the amount of $1275. The agent did not make any inquiry as to Mrs. Moore's authority to fill in the amount of $1275. Cannon claimed to be a holder in due course. Decide.
3. This action is brought on two trade acceptances. Evers and Chance took the trade acceptances given by Wigley, Inc. to Manufacturing Corporation. The trade acceptances were transferred to Evers "as a retainer for services to be performed." The two trade acceptances had been obtained by fraud and Wigley set up the fraud as a defense. Evers claimed that he was a holder in due course. Evers and Chance did some work but there was no testimony offered as to the value of the work. Evers did not know that the instruments had been obtained by fraud. Decide.
4. Defendant purchased common stock through stockbrokers, giving his note, payable to them, for $1000. The brokers endorsed the note "without recourse" and delivered it to Simon Cheese Company. Simon endorsed it to First National Bank, plaintiff, and the bank gave credit for the note on the company's checking account. On the date of the endorsement Simon's credit with plaintiff bank

opened at a balance of over $20,000. Deposits totaling over $84,000 were made, with payments on checks of the company amounting to over $90,000, leaving a balance at the end of the day of more than $14,000. The company's balance with the bank exceeded the amount of the note at all times until the date of maturity, when its balance showed $899.15. Plaintiff brought an action on the date. Defendant claimed that the note was obtained by fraud and that plaintiff was not a holder in due course. Decide.

5. Suit was brought on a note dated September 23, 1969 and payable on demand. This note was negotiated to City Bank & Trust Company on June 10, 1970. The Bank claimed that it was a holder in due course of the note. The maker and endorsers claim that the Bank took the note after it was overdue and that it is not a holder in due course. Decide.

6. This was an action by Savings Bank against W. Bentley to recover on a $500 check. Bentley issued the check dated July 18, 1967, payable to the order of General Trucking, Inc. The check was drawn on a bank other than Savings Bank. On July 26, 1967, General Trucking, Inc. endorsed the check and Savings Bank paid the face amount of the check. Bentley stopped payment on the check. Bentley claimed that since Savings Bank took the check eight days after the date of issue, it was not a holder in due course. Decide.

7. The payee obtained a note for $1000 from defendant by fraud. The note was payable in Nome, Alaska, within three months, but the payee offered it for sale in Oregon. The buyer, knowing that the payee was solvent but in need of money, gave him $500 for the note but made no inquiry of the maker, although he was available to give information. In a suit to collect on the note it is denied that plaintiff can be considered an innocent purchaser. Decide.

8. Plaintiff, the holder, sued the maker on a note due January 1, 1974. Plaintiff bought the note from a bank in February 1974, the bank having previously acquired it from a holder in due course. Defendant contends that plaintiff is not a holder in due course since he bought the instrument after its maturity. Decide.

ENDNOTE

1. All but a few states have passed laws eliminating the holder in due course doctrine in consumer transactions

ESTABLISHING SECONDARY 47 LIABILITY

Chapter 45 distinguished the liabilities and obligations of those parties to a negotiable instrument who are primarily liable and those who are only secondarily liable. When the holder is unable to collect payment from the primary parties, he must preserve whatever rights he may have by following legal procedures to sue parties who are secondarily liable. Unless he follows the prescribed procedures, his claims against secondary parties may be denied.

The liability of the unqualified endorser and drawer of a negotiable instrument is not fully established until certain conditions are met. First, the holder must properly present the instrument to the maker or drawee and request payment or acceptance. Second, the maker or drawee must refuse to pay or accept the instrument, thereby dishonoring it. Finally, the holder must give proper notice of the dishonor to secondary parties and demand payment from them.

PRESENTMENT FOR PAYMENT

In order to enforce secondary liability, the holder must present the negotiable instrument for payment at the proper time, at the prescribed place, to the right person, and in the proper manner. When an instrument shows the date on which it is payable, presentment for payment must be made on that day. If the instrument is accelerated, presentment must be made within a reasonable time after the acceleration. In other words, in order to charge a secondary party with liability, presentment must be made within a reasonable time after such party becomes liable. The U.C.C., Sec. 3—503(2), states that a reasonable time "is determined by the nature of the instrument, any particular usage of banking or trade, and the facts of the particular case." With respect to a check, Sec. 3—503(2) (a) of the Code allows "thirty days after date or issue whichever is later" to fix the liability of the drawer and "seven days after his endorsement" to fix the liability of an endorser.

Where an instrument is due on a day that is not a full business day for either the person making presentment or the party obligated to pay, presentment should be made on the following full business day for both parties. It must be made at a reasonable hour or, if at a bank, during the banking day.

Presentment must be made to the person or firm named in the instrument. It may be made to any one of two or more parties named or to any person who has the authority to make payment. Proper presentment can be made by a simple demand for payment; it is not necessary that the holder exhibit the instrument. However, the person to whom presentment is made may in turn demand that the instrument be shown to him, and, once it is paid, the holder must offer to surrender the instrument. The party to whom presentment is made can require the holder to show identification or evidence of his authority. He may demand a signed receipt on the instrument for any full or partial payment and its surrender upon full payment. (U.C.C. 3—505) Presentment will be excused if the holder is unable to locate the proper party after making a reasonable effort to find him. If the holder is unavoidably delayed in making presentment, the delay will be excused providing he presents the instrument as soon as he can. (U.C.C. 3—506)

PRESENTMENT FOR ACCEPTANCE

Presentment for acceptance relates to drafts and is necessary only in the following cases: (1) where the instrument so provides; (2) where it is payable elsewhere than at the residence or place of business of the drawee; or (3) where its date of payment depends upon such presentment. (U.C.C. 3—501(1)(a)) Proper presentment requires that a draft be presented to the drawee so that he may write his acceptance on the instrument. Although the word "accepted" is commonly used, any suitable word or phrase, or merely a signature, is sufficient. Where an instrument is required to be presented for acceptance and the acceptance is refused, the instrument is deemed to have been dishonored, and no presentment for payment is necessary to hold those parties conditionally liable. However, the holder must proceed to give proper notice to the secondary parties immediately to comply with the conditions precedent.

DISHONOR

An instrument is deemed to be dishonored (1) when it has been duly presented for acceptance or payment and acceptance or payment cannot be obtained or refused or (2) when presentment is excused and the instrument is overdue and unpaid. (U.C.C. 3—507) If the necessary notice or protest has been given after the instrument is dishonored, the holder has an immediate right of recourse against the secondary parties, the drawers and the endorsers.

NOTICE

Notice of dishonor may be given in any reasonable manner, oral or written. It must clearly identify the instrument and state that it has been dishonored. Written notice must be sent to the address given on the instrument or, if there is none, to any address at which the party might reside. If a party is dead or incompetent, notice may be sent to his last known address. Once the notice is properly mailed, it is considered given.

Notice must be given as soon as the instrument is dishonored, and if given by a bank, by midnight of the first banking day after dishonor. If given by any other party, it must be given by midnight of the third business day after dishonor.

Notice may be given to any person liable on the instrument by the holder, by an agent acting in the holder's behalf, or by any other party who has received notice or can be compelled to pay. For example, any secondary party who is notified of dishonor has the right to notify any prior secondary party that he intends to hold him liable in the event he (the party first notified) is forced to pay on the instrument. Such notice must be given within the same length of time after notice is received as the original holder had to give notice after the dishonor. (U.C.C. 3—508)

If the holder makes a reasonable effort to give notice but is unsuccessful through no fault of his own, he is still entitled to collect. Also, notice need not be given if the instrument expressly waives it. (U.C.C. 3—511) In the case of a draft or check, no notice to the drawer is necessary if the drawer should realize without notice that the drawee will not accept or make payment on the instrument.

PROTEST

A protest is a sworn statement declaring that the instrument described was presented for payment or acceptance on a certain date and that it was subsequently dishonored. It may be made upon information given to a United States consul or vice-consul, to a notary public, or to any person authorized to certify dishonor by the law of the place where the dishonor occurs. The protest may also certify that notice of dishonor has been given to all parties or to specified parties.

Protest provides a method for proving that a negotiable instrument has been dishonored and that the conditions precedent have been met. The U.C.C., Sec. 3—509, requires a protest with respect to drafts drawn or payable outside the United States. It may be given in any case where the holder feels it is warranted.

LEGAL PRINCIPLES

The conditional liability of secondary parties does not arise until the conditions precedent—presentment, dishonor, and notice of dishonor—are met.

Presentment assumes that the instrument is exhibited at the proper time, in the proper manners, and at the proper place to the person who is supposed to make payment or acceptance of it.

An instrument is dishonored when (1) it has been presented for acceptance or payment and acceptance or payment has been refused or cannot be obtained or (2) when presentment is excused and the instrument is overdue and unpaid.

Notice of dishonor must be given to secondary parties in a reasonable manner within a reasonable time after the instrument has been dishonored.

CASE FOR REVIEW

PERLEN v. WISHNOFF

34 Misc.2d 234, 225 N.Y.S.2d 839 (1962)

The plaintiffs, as payees, sue the defendant Nathan Wishnoff, the third endorser on a $21,000 negotiable promissory note, dated December 14, 1955, which is payable "on demand after date".

. . . The maker of the note is "L. Schwartz Wood Products Corporation of New Jersey". It was endorsed by Louis Schwartz and Robert O. Kleefeld who are respectively the President and Secretary of the maker corporation as the first and second endorsers. The defendant Wishnoff is the third endorser. Robert O. Kleefeld has not been made a party defendant in this action nor has he been sued by virtue of his endorsement of the note, and although the second endorser Louis Schwartz is a named defendant he has not been served with process. Thus, the only endorser who has been sued is the defendant Nathan Wishnoff.

Simulteously with the making of the note, the maker corporation gave a chattel mortgage to the plaintiffs as collateral security for the payment of the note.

It is contended by plaintiffs that on April 18, 1957, demand was made upon the defendant Wishnoff for the payment of said promissory note. Assuming that to be the fact, sixteen months elapsed from the time of the making of this promissory note to the time of its presentation and demand for payment. In the interim, the plaintiffs, without consideration, had released the chattel mortgage which they had on the maker's personal property.

Whether presentment for payment of a demand note has been made upon an endorser within a reasonable time after the issuance of the note may sometimes be determinable as a matter of law, but it is more often a factual issue to be decided in light of the relationship of the parties, the equities of the situation and any other pertinent factors.

After a most careful scrutiny of the facts in this record the Court finds as a fact that demand for payment in this case was not made within a reasonable time after delivery of the note. In coming to this conclusion the Court is mindful of the relationship of the parties, and the fact that the defendant Wishnoff has been damaged by the plaintiffs' delay in presentment of the note for payment. If the note had been timely presented for payment the defendant Wishnoff could have made good on his endorsement by paying the promissory note and he then would have been subrogated to the rights of the plaintiffs in the chattel mortgage. The plaintiffs deprived him of those rights by releasing the collateral which they had.

Having voluntarily, and without consideration, stripped themselves of their lien on the chattels which could have been used either wholly, or at least in part, to satisfy the maker's obligation on the note, the plaintiff's have lost their right, by reason of undue delay in presentment, to recover upon the defendant Wishnoff's endorsement.

In *Commercial National Bank* v. *Zimmerman,* 185 N.Y. 210, 218, 77 N.E. 1020, 1022 . . . the Court said:

The burden is on the holder of a note, when seeking to charge an endorser, to prove due and timely presentment, and the giving of notice to the endorser of its dishonor. The obligation of the endorser is conditional upon all the steps having been taken by the holder, which the statute has prescribed as to presentment, and as to notice of nonpayment, etc. The negotiable instruments law is to codification of the law merchant upon the subjects treated, and in setting forth what is required of the holder of a note it casts upon him the burden to prove that the requirements were all complied with. They were necessary conditions of his right to recover. Presentment of a demand note within a reasonable time is a requirement of the statute, and the liability of the endorser to make good the contract of the maker, unlike that of a guarantor, is conditional and depends upon the holder's having made a case under the statute of an obligation, which he has caused to mature and, by appropriate legal steps to become an indebtedness of the contracting parties. . . .

The plaintiffs, under all the circumstances, have failed to sustain the burden of proof which is theirs.

Judgment is therefore directed in favor of the defendant.

CASE PROBLEMS

1. Smyth signed a note that specified the place of payment as a bank. On March 5, 1967, plaintiff notified a bank officer that he was sending a notary with the instrument that day to enter the demand and, if the instrument was not paid, to have it protested. The notary took plaintiff's notice, showed it to Smyth, and demanded payment, but he refused to pay. When suit was brought on the note, Smyth claimed that the note had not been displayed when presented. Decide.
2. The maker of a note was telephoned at his place of residence by the bank which had the instrument for collection. The bank requested, and the maker refused, payment. The holder of the instrument thereupon sued defendant, the note's endorser. The note was payable at a particular place, the maker's home. Defendant claimed that the instrument was not properly presented for payment. Decide.
3. Sam and Henry Smith were makers on a promissory note payable to Amos and Andy Brown. The payees endorsed the note to George Stevens. The Smith brothers had moved, leaving no forwarding address. Therefore the holder was unable to make a presentment for payment. Despite this fact, notice of dishonor was given to the endorsers. When Stevens sued the Browns, it was alleged that Stevens was not excused from making presentment because the payee was aware of the whereabouts of the Smith brothers. Decide.
4. Jurgens, the holder of a draft, sued Wichmann as the payee and endorser. Wichmann claimed that he had not received notice in time to make him liable as endorser. Jurgens deposited the check in his bank for collection on July 28, and on the twenty-ninth the bank notified Jurgens of the dishonor of the check, and the following day he notified Wichmann by phone of the dishonor. Decide.
5. In an action on a note, Smith's accountant testified that he had dictated a letter notifying Jones that a note which he endorsed had been dishonored. It had been signed by an officer of the corporation, placed in an envelope and handed to the mailing clerk to be stamped and dropped in the mail chute. This was alleged to be the usual procedure for mailing letters. Jones alleged that unless the mailing clerk could testify that he had mailed the letter, notice had not been given. Decide.
6. Defendant was sued as an accommodation endorser on notes given by a corporation of which he was an officer. The notice of protest was left in the customary

place for postal collection. Defendant claimed that notice of presentment was not properly mailed. Decide.

7. In an action on a note, the defendant, the endorser, claimed that the notice of dishonor was not sufficient. The notice that he received was informal and failed to state the dates of the making of the note and the maturity of the note and the name of the payee. Decide.

8. Defendant, an endorser, was sued by plaintiff, who at maturity presented the note and was refused payment. Plaintiff sent defendant a letter stating in part: "A note for $669.08, given us by Yeager & Myers on May 28, 1974, was due today, and, as you are endorser on this note, we are writing to advise you that the same is due and that you are liable for the payment of the note, in lieu of having it protested." Defendant denied that this letter is sufficient notice of dishonor. Decide.

DEFENSES AND DISCHARGE 48

Occasionally, when called upon to pay on a negotiable instrument, the parties involved may raise defenses to avoid payment. Two classes of defenses are available to an individual from whom payment is requested: personal defenses and real defenses. Personal defenses are based on circumstances collateral to the instrument itself. They may be raised to avoid payment to any holder except a holder in due course or a successor to a holder in due course. A real defense exists if it can be shown that no legal instrument was ever created or that liability on an instrument has been destroyed. Real defenses may be successfully raised against all holders. (U.C.C. 3—305)

Real and personal defenses are available to secondary as well as primary parties in suits brought by the holder. For example, an endorser may interpose a real defense against any holder subsequent to him and may raise a personal defense against his immediate endorsee or against subsequent parties who are not holders in due course.

PERSONAL DEFENSES

Personal defenses relate to the transaction for which the instrument was given and to losses resulting from negligence on the part of the primary party in creating and executing the instrument. They include fraud in the inducement; lack, failure, or illegality of consideration; set-offs, or counterclaims; nondelivery of a complete or an incomplete instrument; prior payment; and unauthorized completion of an incomplete but signed instrument.

FRAUD IN THE INDUCEMENT

This defense may be raised where there is fraud involving the consideration for which the instrument is given. The primary party did intend to create an instrument but was fraudulently induced to do so. For example, when an instrument is given to cover the purchase of property that has been fraudulently overpriced, the maker has a good defense against the other party to the transaction.

LACK, FAILURE, OR ILLEGALITY OF CONSIDERATION

Sometimes an individual who is otherwise liable for the payment of an instrument may raise the defense that he never received consideration for the instrument or that the consideration promised to him was never delivered. Likewise, where the consideration for the instrument arises out of an illegal transaction, the fact that the consideration is illegal gives rise to a personal defense. Lack, failure, or illegality of consideration are good defenses against any holder except a holder in due course, just as they could be employed as defense in any suit on a simple contract. (U.C.C. 3-305(2)(b)) However, if the above illegality makes the contract a nullity, the defense is real.

SET-OFFS

A set-off, or counterclaim, may arise from a transaction between the holder of an instrument and the primary party when the primary party raises a claim against the holder that must be balanced, or "set-off" against his (the primary party's) original liability on the instrument. For example, if A sues B for the purchase price evidenced by a promissory note and B rightfully counterclaims that some of the goods were damaged and that he is entitled to reimbursement, B will have to pay on the promissory note, but the amount of the damages will be deducted.

NONDELIVERY

An individual may fully execute an instrument without intending that it be negotiated immediately. However, if, despite his intent, the instrument comes into the possession of a holder in due course, that holder may require payment, because delivery is conclusively presumed. Since a person can qualify as a holder in due course without concerning himself with the question of delivery, a completed instrument that has been lost or stolen and can be negotiated without a forged endorsement can pass good title to such a holder. Likewise, an instrument that is neither completed nor delivered can be collected by a holder in due course. The fact that the maker or drawer was careless or unfortunate enough to let such an instrument get into circulation is not considered a sufficient defense.

PRIOR PAYMENT

If, for some reason, a person pays an instrument without insisting it be surrendered to him, he may be forced by a subsequent holder to make a second payment. Also, if payment is made before maturity on an unsurrendered instrument and it is subsequently negotiated to a holder in due course, such a holder may enforce payment a second time. Payment to the wrong person is a personal defense because the burden is on the primary party to locate the instrument prior to making payment.

UNAUTHORIZED COMPLETION

In some situations a maker or drawer will employ an agent for the purpose of completing a negotiable instrument and delivering it to the payee. The maker or drawer may sign the instrument without filling in the name of the payee or the amount and deliver it to his agent with instructions for its completion. If the maker's instructions are disobeyed by the agent, this fact cannot be used as a defense against a holder in due course.

REAL DEFENSES

Real defenses arise in cases where no instrument or liability was ever created, or, of an instrument or liability was created, something has since destroyed its legal effect. Since no qualified instrument exists, no right or title passes to a holder in due course, or, indeed, to any holder. Real defenses include forgery, fraud in the execution, lack of contractual capacity, illegality, duress, and material alteration.

FORGERY

An individual or firm whose signature on an instrument is neither genuine nor authorized is not liable on the instrument if there was no negligence involved. This rule applies regardless of whether the party is a maker, drawer, or endorser. The U.C.C., Sec. 3—404, states: "Any unauthorized signature is wholly inoperative as that of the person whose name is signed unless he ratifies it or is precluded from denying it." Therefore an instrument negotiated by means of a forgery not only fails to pass title but gives the person whose name was forged a real defense against all subsequent parties. The party ultimately responsible for a forged instrument is the one who dealt directly with the forger. (U.C.C. 3—406)

FRAUD IN THE EXECUTION

A person who unknowingly executes or signs a negotiable instrument has a real defense against payment. Since he did not intend to create an instrument, none exists. For example, if a person is signing a number of papers and, unknown to him, one of the papers is a negotiable instrument, he will not have to pay on it. However, ignorance is not an acceptable defense if the person had an opportunity to obtain knowledge of the instrument's character or its essential terms. For example, if a person could not read and didn't have it read to him before signing, he would probably be held liable on that instrument. The same would be true of a literate person who simply failed to read an instrument before signing.

INCAPACITY

A minor, an insane person, or any other person without legal capacity who executes a negotiable instrument may avoid liability at his election or that of a legal guardian. Likewise, any such person who negotiates an instrument may elect to avoid the negotiation and recover the instrument from a subsequent holder. However, if no defense is asserted, good title passes to the endorsee.

ILLEGALITY

If a state statute specifically declares an instrument void, as in the case of instruments given in connection with gambling and usurious transactions, no holder can demand payment on it. Where the law merely declares the transaction that gave rise to the instrument illegal, without voiding the instrument itself, a holder in due course may demand payment.

DURESS

A person who executes a negotiable instrument under a threat has a personal defense. However, where the compulsion is excessively forceful, such as a threat to his life, the person threatened would be permitted to assert a real defense against a holder in due course.

MATERIAL ALTERATION

Any person who alters the terms of an instrument without permission and changes the contract of the parties discharges any party whose contract is changed. Changes in the number of relations of the parties or adding to or removing any part of the writing as signed will have this effect. However, a subsequent holder in due course may enforce the original tenor of the instrument. For example, if a check is raised from $50 to $550 and negotiated to a holder in due course, the holder in due course may enforce the check against the drawer for $50. This defense is available on any alteration except if the drawer was negligent and contributed to making the alteration easier. In these cases, he will have to pay the full amount.

DISCHARGE

A negotiable instrument is discharged when all rights and liabilities of all the parties to the instrument have been terminated. The U.C.C., Sec. 3—601, distinguishes between the discharge of all parties and the discharge of a single party and provides that no discharge of any party is effective against a subsequent holder in due course unless he has notice thereof when he acquires the instrument.

A negotiable instrument is discharged by any act or agreement that would discharge a simple contract for the payment of money. The extent of the discharge of any party is further determined by reference to the Code.

PAYMENT OR SATISFACTION

Most negotiable instruments are discharged by payment, which is made by the maker or drawee in the usual course of business upon the due date. When the maker pays the instrument and acquires it prior to the due date, he may negotiate it further and keep it in circulation. However, if the instrument is paid before maturity and the primary party does not get possession of it, it may be negotiated to a holder in due course, who can enforce payment again. Therefore, the liability of any party is discharged to the extent of his payment and on adequate notification to a subsequent holder in due course.

TENDER OF PAYMENT

Although the U.C.C. does not define the term "tender," it is generally held to mean a readiness and an ability to pay the instrument according to its tenor. Sec. 3—604(3) of the Code states that an ability and a readiness to pay at every place of payment specified in the instrument when it is due is equivalent to tender.

Specifically, any part making tender of full payment to a holder who refuses payment when or after payment is due is discharged to the extent of all subsequent liability for interest, costs, and attorney's fees. The holder's refusal of such tender wholly discharges any party who has a right of recourse against the party making the tender.

CANCELLATION AND RENUNCIATION

The holder of a negotiable instrument may, without consideration discharge any party by crossing out the terms of the instrument or by destroying it in some way. To accomplish this, he must intend that this be the consequences of his conduct. Where it can be shown that the instrument was cancelled accidentally, without intent, or by someone without authority, no discharge occurs and the parties remain liable thereon.

The holder may at any time renounce his rights against any or all parties to an instrument by a writing signed and delivered or by surrender of the instrument to the party to be discharged.

IMPAIRMENT OF RECOURSE OR COLLATERAL

The U.C.C. Sec. 3—606, states that the surety is discharged by (1) release of the debtor by the creditor, (2) a surrender by the creditor of any collateral given for the instrument, and (3) an agreement by the creditor and debtor to extend the time of payment. These rules apply to sureties, accommodation makers, and acceptors, providing the holder has knowledge of their status, since an individual who undertakes to assume another's liability acquires a right to be reimbursed if he makes payment. A surety assumes an obligation for a definite period and is entitled to the collateral: anything affecting this obligation releases him unless the creditor reserves his rights against him by giving him notice and thereby obtaining his consent to the transaction.

REACQUISITION

Wherever a prior holder reacquires an instrument, intervening parties are discharged as against the reacquiring party and subsequent holders not in due course. The reacquirer may cancel any endorsements not necessary to his title, thereby discharging the liability of such parties. If the reacquirer has no rights against any other party to the instrument, all parties are discharged.

MATERIAL ALTERATION

The material alteration of an instrument discharges all parties except those who know of the alteration and assent to it and subsequent endorsers who, by their endorsements, warrant the genuineness of the instrument. However, a holder in due course may enforce the original tenor of an altered instrument. An immaterial alteration has no effect on the liability of parties to an instrument. (U.C.C. 3—407)

CERTIFICATION OF CHECKS

Certification of a check is acceptance. Although the bank is liable to the drawer, it may obligate itself to pay the holder by certifying the check. Once the bank has certified the instrument, the drawer and all prior endorsers are discharged and the bank has absolute liability for payment. (U.C.C. 3—411) If, on the other hand, the drawer rather than the holder requests certification secondary liability remains and the holder may look to endorsers and the drawer if the check is not paid by the bank.

ACCEPTANCE VARYING DRAFTS

Where the drawee offers to accept a draft in any manner other than as presented, the draft is dishonored. If the holder assents, each drawer and endorser who does not assent to the change is discharged. (U.C.C. 3—412)

DELAY IN CONDITIONS PRECEDENT

Where, without excuse, any necessary presentment or notice of dishonor is delayed beyond the time it is due, any endorser is discharged irrespective of any injury to him. However, drawers are discharged on the instrument only to the extent of the injury caused by the delay. Their liability therefore remains, except insofar as they can show that the delay caused them a loss. Where, without excuse, a necessary protest is delayed beyond the time it is due, any drawer or endorser is discharged. (U.C.C. 3—502)

LEGAL PRINCIPLES

Personal defenses relate to the transaction for which the instrument was given and to losses resulting from negligence by the primary party in creating and executing the instrument. Personal defenses include fraud in the inducement; lack, failure, or illegality of consideration; set-offs, or counterclaims; nondelivery of a complete or an incomplete instrument; prior payment; and unauthorized completion of an incomplete but signed instrument. They may be asserted against the immediate party to the transaction or against any holder who had knowledge of them.

Real defenses mean that no instrument was ever created or, if an instrument was created, that liability thereon has since been destroyed. Real defenses include forgery, fraud in the execution, lack of contractual capacity, illegality, duress, and material alteration. Real defenses may be raised against all holders.

Payment or satisfaction discharges the liability of any party to the extent of his payment and on adequate notification to a subsequent holder in due course.

Any party making tender of full payment to a holder when or after payment is due is discharged from all subsequent liability for interest, costs, and attorney's fees.

Valid cancellation or renunciation by the holder is an effective discharge of the instrument.

A surety is discharged by any impairment of the collateral or recourse by agreement between the debtor and creditor.

When a prior holder reacquires an instrument, intervening parties are discharged as against the reacquiring party and subsequent holders not in due course.

Material alteration discharges all parties who do not know of and assent to the alteration.

Certification at the request of the holder discharges the drawer and all prior endorsers.

If the drawer offers to accept a draft in any manner other than as presented, the draft is dishonored.

An unexcused delay in presentment or notice of dishonor will discharge drawers to the extent of any injury caused by the delay.

An unexcused delay in protest will cause discharge.

CASE FOR REVIEW

DLUGE v. ROBINSON

204 A.2d 279 (1964)

This is an appeal from a judgment for the plaintiffs in an action against J. Robinson as endorser of two checks, brought by Isaac Dluge, the endorsee. The checks were dishonored by the drawee bank because of insufficient funds in the maker's account. Dluge died after instituting suit and the executors of his estate have been substituted as plaintiffs. . . .

If the plaintiffs were holders in due course, they would have to prove only (1) that the defendant endorsed the checks and delivered them to Dluge, and (2) that they had been presented to the endorser for payment within a reasonable time. . . . In the case of an uncertified check this is presumed to be within seven days after the endorsement. . . .

"Presentment is a demand for acceptance or payment. . .by or on behalf of the holder." U.C.C., § 3—504(1). The only evidence of any demand was the admission by defendant that he received a letter from Dluge's attorney demanding payment. The defendant did not state when he received this letter. The plaintiffs did not offer the letter in evidence and there is no way to determine from the record when it was sent except that it was presumably sent before the complaint was filed on September 12, 1960, seven months after the checks were dishonored by the drawee bank. Since the defendant denied any demand at the time the checks were returned to him, and the record is otherwise barren of any evidence of demand within seven days, or any reasonable time, after endorsement, the plaintiffs did not establish any right to recover even if they had been holders in due course.

The plaintiffs are not holders in due course. Dluge gave the checks to the defendant without any demand for payment, so far as the record shows, and was not in possession of them when the suit was brought. Therefore he was not the holder. "Holder means a person who is in possession of a document of title or an instrument or an investment security drawn, issued or endorsed to him or to his order or to bearer or in blank." U.C.C., § 1—201(20). A fortiori, he was not a holder in due course. . . .

The plaintiffs argue that they may nevertheless recover from the defendant, as the endorser of a "lost" check owned by them, under § 3—804 of the Uniform Commercial Code. This section provides: "The owner of an instrument which is lost whether by destruction, theft or otherwise, may maintain an action in his own name and recover from any party liable thereon upon due proof of his ownership, the facts which prevent his production of the instrument and its terms. . . ."

There is, however, neither allegation nor proof that the checks were destroyed, stolen or otherwise lost. If the plaintiffs had proved that Dluge had returned the checks with a demand for payment, or that they later demanded that defendant return the checks, they might argue that his failure either to pay or return them constituted a theft or a conversion. . . . There was no evidence of such demand and therefore no proof of conversion or theft. The maker, Wapner, testified that he paid Dluge and then destroyed the checks. This testimony was stricken from the record, following the plaintiffs' objections. Therefore there is no evidence in the record of the destruction of the checks. Finally, there is no evidence that they were otherwise lost. . . .

"An article is 'lost' when the owner has lost the possession or custody of it, involuntarily and by any means, but more particularly by accident or his own negligence or forgetfulness,and when he is ignorant of its whereabouts or cannot recover it by an ordinary diligent search." Black's Law Dictionary, 4th ed., p. 1096. . . .

Moreover, to recover under § 3—804 of the code, the plaintiffs must prove ownership of the checks. Such proof of ownership must be clear and convincing. . . . In the absence of possession, ownership would usually depend upon proof that the holder did not voluntarily surrender possession unless he did so conditionally upon payment of the checks. Surrender of the checks to a prior party, without payment, and without even a demand for payment, tells against the retention of ownership, and indicates, if anything, an intention not to hold such party liable on the instrument. . . .

The plaintiffs did not prove that the checks were "lost" as that word is used in § 3—804 of the code, or that they were still the owners of the checks when suit was brought. More importantly, there is no proof of demand for payment by the plaintiffs when the checks were returned to the defendant. Plaintiffs have therefore, failed to prove their right to recover against Robinson whether they are holders or owners of the checks.

The burden upon one not a holder who seeks to recover on a negotiable instrument is a heavy one. The plaintiffs have not sustained it. They must recover, if at all, upon the underlying obligation for which the checks were given.

CASE PROBLEMS

1. Carter, Ealey, and Dinwiddie purchased materials in St. Louis from Sterling Company, a New York corporation not legally qualified to do business in Missouri. By Missouri law the act of selling without having qualified to do business was illegal, and a seller could not bring suit on any contract until it had so qualified. In payment for the goods, Carter accepted a draft naming Sterling as the payee. Sterling sold the draft to Salitan and Jacobs, operators of a finance company, who were holders in due course. When suit was brought on the draft, the defense of illegality was raised. Decide.

2. Dawley drew a check for $1079.48 on the Last Bank. When it arrived at the bank for collection the check had been altered to read $1059.74, a change made without the consent of the drawer. The bank refused payment and the holder sued, seeking the balance of the account, but defendant, though not paying the check, held the amount in the account. Decide.

3. The holder sued on this commercial instrument:

    $1300.00   Kewanee, Ill., October 4, 1974
       One year after date I promise to pay to the order of ourselves thirteen hundred dollars at Kewanee, Ill. Value received, with interest at the rate of seven percent per annum.
    Endorsed: Signature
          L. Silver   L. Silver
          H. Clay   H. Clay

    Plaintiff, a bona fide purchaser, paid the face of the note. Material alteration is set up as a defense on two counts: First, the note when delivered contained the figure $100 in the margin and, written, "one hundred" in the body of the note. The figure was altered to $1300, and the word "thirteen" inserted in place of "one." Second, there was a blank space in which the word "thirteen" had been inserted. Decide.

4. An Illinois businessman made certain that he locked his doors and windows at the end of each business day. His blank checks and check printing machine were left in the office, readily accessible to anyone in the office. A burglar with business acumen entered the office and made out thirty checks, each for $186.34 drawn on the defendant. The defendant refused to make good on the checks. Decide.

5. A Nebraska attorney discovered that his secretary was drawing checks on his account and using an ancient rubber signature to accomplish her embezzlement. Since she reconciled the monthly bank statements, it took some time for the attorney to uncover the shortages in his account. By that time the secretary had absconded with the money on forty-four checks. The attorney brought suit contending the bank was negligent in paying out the money. Decide.

6. Construction, Inc. enclosed a certified check along with their bid on a construction project for the board of education. The bank had stamped the check as being

certified, but had forgotten to fill in the signature blank in the certification stamp. Although the bid was the lowest, it was rejected for lack of a certified check. Construction brought suit against the board of education. Decide.

7. Plaintiff notified defendant that his check had to be certified by the bank before plaintiff would accept it. Defendant presented the check for certification, and the bank certified it as follows: "National Bank, pay only through clearinghouse, J. W. Work, Cashier, A. C. J., paying teller." A second check from defendant was also certified upon plaintiff's request. Two days later the bank closed its doors. The checks were duly presented for payment and notice of dishonor sent. Plaintiff brought an action against the drawer for the sum of the checks. Decide.

8. The president of Fly-By Nite Realty Company, with its authority, made its promissory note to his order for $750 due in four months from date. He endorsed and discounted the instrument with Broad National Bank. The note was reduced to $700 and paid by another note for that amount. When the second note was due, the president of Realty gave his check on the holder bank in payment and received the note stamped "Paid." His check, although charged to his account, was not fully paid because a check for $550 drawn on a bank in Bangor, Pa., remained uncollected. In an action brought by Broad National against Realty to collect the amount of the note, the maker contended that the note had been discharged. Decide.

PART VIII
PROPERTY

Real property consists essentially of land and the space above it. The term "land" includes the ground itself and everything in it (minerals), growing on it (naturally occurring vegetation), or otherwise permanently attached to it (buildings and other similar structures that cannot be carried away). A problem arises with regard to crops. Although all vegetation is attached to the land, the law generally distinguishes between crops, which are planted and cultivated by man, and trees and shrubs growing naturally on the land and requiring no expenditure of labor. The former are considered personal property. (See Chapter 54, Personal Property.) The latter are deemed real property. Questions sometimes arise also about the space above the land. Airplanes are generally conceded the right to free passage through the airspace unless injury can be proven to the property holder.

In its most technical legal sense, property is an intangible concept, signifying the rights, privileges, and powers that the law recognizes as vested in an individual in relation to things tangible or intangible, as distinguished from the things themselves. It includes every interest anyone may have in anything that may be the subject of ownership, including the right to freely possess, use, enjoy, and dispose of the same. The sum of these proprietory rights is designated as "title" to property. In its popular usage the term "property" refers to objects that may be the subject of ownership —both physical objects capable of being reduced to possession and such intangible items as goodwill.

Proprietory rights are exclusive rights of the individual owner and are protected against infringement by others. In the last analysis, these rights represent a relationship between the owner and other individuals with respect to objects that are capable of being owned.

Property in land is traditionally dealt with in terms of estates. The extent to which an owner may enjoy his ownership of real property is described as his *estate*. The quality, nature, and extent of an interest in real property will depend on the type of estate held. From this arises the interchangeable use of the terms "real property" and "real estate." Although, technically, the former refers to the land itself and the latter to an interest in the land, the distinction is seldom observed.

FREEHOLD ESTATES

Historically, estates in land are divided into freehold estates and nonfreehold estates. The freehold classification is based on its quantity or duration. A freehold estate will last for an indefinite period. These estates are listed as fee simple estates, fee simple defeasible estates, and life estates. Fee estates carry the highest degree of ownership; they can be inherited, transferred, and mortgaged.

FEE SIMPLE

A grant in fee simple, fee simple absolute, or an estate in fee conveys all the rights incident to the land. For example, a conveyance "To A and his heirs and assigns forever" is a grant in fee simple. The essential elements of this estate are that it has potential infinite duration and is inheritable by both the collateral and the lineal descendants of A. At common law the conveyance creating this estate had to use the words "to A and his heirs," denoting general inheritance. Today this strict adherence to form has been abolished by statute as well as by court decisions.

In summary, the grant of a fee simple conveys to the owner the unlimited power to dispose of the property during his lifetime; at his death, the property is inheritable by his heirs. It may be used for any lawful purpose that is not contary to public policy or social expediency, however, its use is restricted by society only to the extent that it interferes with the right of adjoining property owners or with the general welfare.

FEE SIMPLE DEFEASIBLE

A grant of fee simple defeasible has potentially infinite duration, but it may contain a condition by which the estate may be defeated. It takes two basic forms: (1) fee simple determinable and (2) fee simple subject to a condition subsequent. Both are classified as fee estates because of the possibility that they will last forever.

When the grantor inserts a determinable feature into a conveyance, it is essential that the instrument manifest his specific intention to make such a conveyance. Effective and proper words must be employed; those most often used are "until," "during," "so long as," and similar expressions. If these words are not used, language meaning the same thing must be found. A conveyance to a municipality for "so long as the land shall be used and occupied as a recreation area" is a grant of a fee simple determinable. If the land is always used as a recreation area, the town's ownership will last forever. If, however, the land is ever put to some other use, ownership reverts (automatically, in theory) to the original grantor or his heirs. The distinguishing feature of a grant in fee simple determinable is that the estate ceases upon the happening of the stated event.

A conveyance to a municipality "on the condition that the land shall be used and occupied as a recreation area" is the conveyance of a fee simple subject to a condition subsequent. If the land is not used as directed or ever devoted to another use, the original grantor or his heirs have the privilege of terminating the estate. The distinguishing feature of the fee simple subject to a condition subsequent is that it continues until the power of termination is exercised.

LIFE ESTATES

Life estates may be created by deed or by will. An estate for life is not terminable at any fixed or determinable time; rather, its duration is measured by the life or lives of one or more persons. A grant "to my widow, A, for her lifetime, and at her death to my children, X, Y, Z, and W," creates a life estate in the wife, who is the life tenant. This grant carries with it the right to possession and use of the land. As long as the value of the property is maintained, the taxes are paid, and the property is not wasted, the life tenant may use, possess, and enjoy the property. Although a life tenant can convey his interest to a third person in the absence of a valid restraint in the granting instrument, a life estate is not a very marketable commodity since it ends with the death of the tenant, even if it is in possession of an innocent third party.

FUTURE INTERESTS

The above estate created in A terminates on her death and, regardless of any grant made by A to a third party, all rights to the property are held by the children, X, Y, Z, and W, who are called *remaindermen.* Their estate is called a *remainder,* an estate of expectancy which will come into existence at the end of the life estate. It is a future interest that will come into existence upon the termination of an intervening estate. It is contingent upon X, Y, Z, and W surviving the widow and it becomes vested in them at her death.

A remainder must be created by the same instrument that created the estate or estates preceding it. If the grant had been only "to my wife, A, for her life" the grantor would not have given away a complete estate; hence A's title would have seen subject to the life estate. Whenever the grantor conveys anything less than a fee, he retains a reversionary interest in the property. Upon the death of the life tenant, the property would revert to the grantor or his heirs. The estate is classified as a *reversion.*

The courts will treat an ordinary grant of property as a fee simple unless a contrary intention appears. The tendency among judges is to encourage free and unlimited alienability of real property wherever possible.

NONFREEHOLD ESTATES

The grant of a nonfreehold estate is an executory contract and represents a conveyance of a limited estate in land. It is a grant to another of an exclusive right to the use and possession of property for a definite period of time. It is classified as an estate less than a fee, hence nonfreehold, because the owner of such an interest is entitled only to the use of the property. These agreements, also referred to as *leasehold estates,* are characterized by certainty of duration. (See Figure 49-1)

When a landowner leases land to a tenant, the tenant's right to occupy the land for the duration of the lease is a leasehold estate. Title remains in the owner, but his rights of use and possession are qualified. If the owner sells his interest in the property, the buyer takes it subject to the leasehold. The tenant's rights will fall to the new owner on the termination of the tenant's right of possession. The characteristics of this form of ownership are (1) a contract between the parties, (2) consent of the owner to the legal relationship. (3) the creation of a lesser estate in the person possessing the property, and (4) the retention of a superior estate by the owner of the property. Leasehold estates

F.A.R. Standard Form No. 5, Revised May 1959

Lease Agreement

THIS AGREEMENT, entered into this_____ day of _____, A. D. 19____

between _____

hereinafter called the Lessor, and_____

hereinafter called the Lessee, and_____

hereinafter called the Rental Agent.

WITNESSETH, That in consideration of the covenants herein contained, on the part of the said Lessee to be kept and performed, the said Lessor does hereby demise and lease to the said Lessee that certain property:

_____, Florida

To hold the said premises hereby demised unto the said Lessee from the _____ day of

_____, A. D. 19____, to the_____ day of _____, A. D. 19____,

the said Lessee paying therefor the rent of_____Dollars as follows:

The Lessor covenants with the Lessee that the Lessee paying the rent when due as aforesaid, shall peaceably and quietly use, occupy and possess the said premises for the full term of this lease without let, hindrance, eviction, molestation or interruption whatever, except as provided below, and the said Lessee covenants with the Lessor:

1. To pay said rent here inbefore reserved at the times at which the same is made payable.

2. To pay all water, electric, gas, and telephone charges which may be assessed upon the demised premises during the term hereof.

3. Not to suffer or commit any waste of the premises, nor make any unlawful, improper or offensive use of same.

4. Not to assign this lease or underlet the said premises or any part thereof without the previous consent of the said Lessor being first obtained in writing.

5. That this lease shall terminate when the Lessee vacates the said premises, providing all payments have been made hereunder or a sub-lease agreement has been executed.

6. At the termination of said tenancy to quietly yield up the said buildings and grounds in as good and tenantable condition in all respects (reasonable wear and use and damage by fire and other unavoidable causes excepted) as the same now are:

IT IS HEREBY AGREED that all expenses in connection with upkeep of the grounds including all water used for

irrigation purposes will be paid for by_____

PROVIDED ALWAYS that if the rent hereby reserved, or any part thereof, shall be in arrears, or in event of any breach of any of the covenants and agreements on the part of the Lessee herein contained, the Lessor may at his option declare the entire rent for the term for which said premises are leased, due and payable, and/or may declare this lease terminated and re-enter upon the said demised premises.

PROVIDED ALWAYS that if the premises or any part thereof shall at any time during the said term be destroyed or rendered uninhabitable by fire or storm then the payment of the rent hereby reserved, or a proportionate part thereof, according to the extent of the damage incurred, shall be suspended until the premises shall have been reinstated and rendered fit for habitation.

1. COMMISSION AGREEMENT:

Lessor acknowledges that Lessee was procured by_____and agrees to recognize said Rental Agent as the procuring cause of any further rental agreement entered into with Lessee, and agrees to pay said Rental Agent the Standard Board of Realtors Commission on such extensions or renewals when made. On month-to-month extensions, commission shall be paid monthly or quarterly.

If the property of which the premises are a part is sold by Lessor to Lessee during the term of this lease, or during the term of any further extension or renewal agreement, (any continued occupancy of the premises by the Lessee after the expiration of this lease shall be considered a further extension or renewal agreement), the Lessor will pay said Rental Agent a commission on the selling price, said commission to be based upon the Board of Realtors Commission Schedule in effect at the time of sale, deducting from such sales commission any unearned leasing commission previously paid by Lessor from date of expiration of lease.

WITNESS OUR HANDS AND SEALS, in triplicate, on the day and year first above written. Signed, Sealed and Delivered in the presence of

_____   _____(Seal)

_____   _____(Seal)

(Witnesses to Lessor)

_____   _____(Seal)

_____   _____(Seal)

(Witness to Lessee)

_____   By:_____(Seal)

(Witness to Rental Agent)

Figure 49-1

may be classified according to the duration of tenancy as (1) tenancy for a term of years, (2) periodic tenancy, (3) tenancy at will, or (4) tenancy at sufferance.

TENANCY FOR A TERM OF YEARS

A tenancy for a term of years runs for a fixed period of time. Actually, the term "years" is misleading because the duration may be fixed in units of a year or multiples or divisions thereof. All tenancies for a definite period, whether it be a day, a week, a month, a year, or several years, are included in this category. An estate in A "for six weeks, from January 1 of next year," is a tenancy for a term of years. The most common are the monthly and yearly terms. However, it is sufficient merely to create a tenancy for a term of years; the duration need not be precisely stated and can be exactly computed at the time the tenant takes possession of the property.

A tenancy for a term of years ends without notice on the last day of the term and is renewable only by express agreement. However, the parties may stipulate the need for notice, unless this is prohibited by statute. If the tenant continues in possession after the expiration of the lease, he is termed a *holdover.* In the absence of an agreement to the contrary, acceptance of rent by the landlord from a holdover is usually construed as a renewal of the lease for one year, regardless of the number of years specified in the original lease.

PERIODIC TENANCY

A tenancy may continue for successive periods of a year or successive periods of a fraction of a year, unless terminated. Various kinds of periodic tenancies take their names from the period that serves as the unit of duration. The most common is the tenancy from year to year, although a grant may be for an indefinite term running from month to month, week to week, or day to day. Periodic tenancies may be terminated upon the giving of proper notice by one party to the other. At common law the required notice was one full period in advance where the period was less than one year. If at the end of the period the tenant holds over and pays rent and the landlord accepts the rent, the lease is renewed for the term of the rental period specified in the original agreement. For example, A may lease land to B for a period of three years from a certain date. After the expiration of the three years, if B continues to occupy the land with the consent of A but without any agreement as to the duration of his occupancy, B is a tenant from year to year.

In this category fall all tenancies that are stated to be for fixed periods with the understanding that they will be renewed automatically. Also, a periodic tenancy arises where no definite time is agreed upon and the rent is fixed on a periodic basis. The landlord must give notice of intention to terminate the agreement, although in some states the tenant may vacate the premises without giving notice. In many states notice of termination is subject to regulation by statute.

TENANCY AT WILL

The concept of tenancy at will derives from British law. When an agreement is not for a fixed period but is terminable at the will of the landlord or tenant, it is said to be a tenancy at will. The agreement may be express or it may arise by implication. Tenancies usually arise by implication when a person occupies premises by permission of the owner for an indefinite period and without any reservation of rent. They may also be created by a lease containing a provision that either party may terminate the tenancy upon giving proper notice. for example, a prospective tenant who moves in and occupies the premises of the landlord while the parties are negotiating to fix the terms of the lease would be a tenant at will. A tenant who stays on after the expiration of a lease, but with the understanding that his occupancy is only temporary, is a tenant at will. Many jurisdictions have adopted statutes requiring a thirty-day notice to terminate. The death of either party automatically terminates the tenancy.

TENANCY AT SUFFERANCE

This type of tenancy results when a person who had possessory interest in land by virtue of an effective conveyance wrongfully continues in possession of the land after the termination of his interest. Where a tenant holds over without right after the expiration of his lease, the landlord may treat him as a tenant at sufferance. (This is not to be confused with a periodic tenancy that arises by holding over.) For example, suppose A leases Whiteacre to B for a period of three years and B enters into possession. If B continues in possession after the expiration of the three years, he has a tenancy at sufferance. Likewise, a tenant who breaks his lease by failing to pay rent or by breaching some other condition of the lease yet continues to stay on is in wrongful possession and is a tenant at sufferance. A tenant at sufferance cannot legally regard himself as a tenant; the landlord may treat him as a tenant or as a trespasser. He is technically a trespasser until the landlord makes his election. If the landlord accepts the payment of rent, the acceptance is evidence of his intention to treat the party in possession as a tenant and creates a new tenancy for the period for which the rent was received. If the landlord elects to hold the tenant for another term, he cannot thereafter rescind such election. No notice is required to terminate a tenancy at sufferance.

LEGAL PRINCIPLES

Real property is land and anything permanently attached to it.

Property includes intangible rights of ownership.

The extent to which an owner may enjoy the possession and use of land is termed his estate.

A fee estate is the highest degree of ownership.

An estate in fee simple defeasible may last forever or may be defeated by a condition subsequent.

A life estate is terminable upon the death of the named life tenant or tenants.

Nonfreehold estates are limited with regard to duration of use and possession.

CASE FOR REVIEW

BAILEY v. KRUITHOFF

280 So.2d. 262 (La. 1973)

Convie D. Bailey, II, brought this suit to recover the sum of $688.77 from defendant, Neal Kruithoff, for the alleged wrongful removal of 1500 feet of four-strand barbed wire fence, with one hundred and fifty creosote posts, eight of which were embedded in concrete, and an iron sucker rod gate from plaintiff's property. . . .

The facts relating to the removal of the fence are undisputed. Defendant leased the seven and one-half acres of pasture land in Bossier Parish from Mrs. Sandy on November 27, 1970, for $15 per year. As part of their agreement, Mrs. Sandy in a separate written instrument, gave defendant permission to remove, at the termination of the lease, a fence and hay shed he might construct on the property. This agreement was never recorded. Defendant erected a four-strand barbed wire fence consisting of approximately one hundred and fifty fence posts and an iron sucker rod gate on the property and used the land to graze several head of cattle.

On January 27, 1972, plaintiff purchased the seven and one-half acres from Mrs. Sandy, his sister. The deed contained no reservations and made no mention of the agreement between defendant and Mrs. Sandy concerning defendant's right to remove the fence. Plaintiff's uncontradicted testimony at the trial was that he had negotiated for some time by phone with his sister who lived in El Paso, Texas, before the sale was finalized and at no time during these negotiations did she ever mention the written agreement with the defendant concerning his right to remove the fence. He stated she merely told him of the lease to the defendant and that it was to terminate in December, 1971.

Approximately three weeks after the sale defendant came onto the property and physically removed the fence, except for about eight of the posts which he had to break off just above the ground because they were embedded in concrete. In addition, during this three-week period following the sale defendant continued to graze twelve to fifteen head of cattle on the property.

The issue is whether defendant had the right to remove the fence. The decision depends on whether the fence is classified as a movable or an immovable.

Article 464 of the Louisiana Civil Code defines an immovable by nature as follows: "Land and buildings or other constructions, whether they have their foundations in the soil or not, are immovable by their nature."

The resolution of the issue . . . depends on the interpretation of the term "other constructions". . . . Some of the various objects which have been included within the definition of "other constructions" under Article 464 are: railroad trackage, . . . a brooder for beagle puppies 25x5x4 feet and a chicken brooder 10x5x4 feet, each set on 4x4 inch posts in the ground and a gas tank. . . .

Immovability by nature has been characterized as a creation of the law based on practical considerations and on inherent characteristics of the things concerned. What is a building or other construction qualifying as an immovable under Article 464 is left for judicial determination according to prevailing notions in society. Two criteria that are often mentioned in decisions of the courts are some degree of integration or attachment to the soil and some degree of permanency.

In this case, the fence was embedded in the ground—a few of the posts were in concrete—and thereby integrated with the soil. Pasture fences are generally regarded as permanent in nature.

The nature of a movable is generally such that its identity is not lost if it is moved from one location to another. Ordinarily, all that is necessary is to detach the object from its present location and move it elsewhere with no apparent diminution of its identification in the process. Certainly this is not true of a fence which has no identity as a fence until it has been *constructed*. Once constructed the fence becomes a component part of the land on which it is placed and as such must be regarded as an "other construction" and as an immovable by nature under Article 464. In order to move a fence it must be dismantled and its identity destroyed, which is inconsistent with any reasonable concept of a movable. . . .

We conclude that the fence involved in the case before us is an "other construction" under Article 464 and an immovable by nature. The fence was a "construction" under the ordinary, common sense meaning of that word. It was embedded in the soil, incorporated into the ground, and was a component part of the land. A fence is ordinarily regarded as having a degree of permanency —not to be readily moved about.

The agreement under which defendant retained the right to remove the fence was not recorded. The fence, together with the land, passed to plaintiff free and clear of defendant's unrecorded rights. Defendant had no right to come on the property after the sale to plaintiff and remove the fence, ownership of which was then vested in the plaintiff. Defendant is thus liable for the reasonable replacement cost of the fence he removed from plaintiff's property. The evidence shows this amount is $542.30

CASE PROBLEMS

1. The granting clause of a deed to Hunter Church School read in part, "so long as said real estate shall by said society or its assigns be devoted to uses, interests, and doctrines of a religious nature." Plaintiff sought to enforce a sale to an individual investor; defendant refused to go through with the sale, raising the question of a defect in title since the possibility of reversion existed. Decide.
2. On August 7, 1973, Green agreed to sell Strain his waterfront home on Mercer Island for $35,000. On August 20, 1973, Green and wife executed a warranty deed to Strain and wife, which they delivered to the purchasers on August 27, receiving the purchase price in full. Some time thereafter, they left the premises, taking with them, from the basement, the hot water tank and enclosed electric heater, the Venetian blinds from the windows, certain lighting fixtures, and three mirrors, two of which were rather firmly attached to the walls. It was also claimed, in the ensuing lawsuit, that they unlawfully carried away a fireplace screen, a tool house, and certain chicken wire, with the posts which supported it. The total value of the articles removed was alleged to be $1105. This action was brought to compel defendants to return or pay the value of these articles. Decide.

3. Mr. Cane, in his will, devised his sister his "home and contents" and in a later portion of the will stated "at my sister's death my homestead is to be given to Julia Conant Thompson." Upon his sister's death, the sister's heirs claimed ownership of the home. Decide.
4. The controversy here is over the construction of a clause in the last will and testament of Lewis B. Conger, late of Fulton county, deceased, which reads as follows:

> My beloved wife, Hannah, is to have and to hold the two above described pieces of land during her lifetime; at her decease, I will, devise and bequeath the same to my son, Samuel M. Conger, during his natural lifetime; *Provided,* He will live on and occupy the same; at his death, or his refusal to live on or occupy the same, then and in that case, as well as at the said Samuel M. Conger's death, I will, devise and bequeath the same to the said Samuel M. Conger's lawful heirs.

Decide.
5. Defendant cut timber from a portion of a sixty-six acre tract granted to her as the widow of the deceased. Plaintiff is remainderman of the premises. The willed land originally had twenty acres in cultivation, but times were difficult, and defendant used from ten to fourteen acres, which were not good land for farming, to supply standing timber for saw logs. The timber cut was in excess of normal farm use. In addition, defendant made no repairs on the building and fences. Plaintiff brings suit for the waste and the value of the timber. Decide.
6. By a written lease, Thompson rented residential property in Albert Lea, Minnesota to Baxter at an agreed monthly rental of $122 for "the full term for which he shall wish to live in Albert Lea." Thompson later gave Baxter notice to leave and when he refused to go, brought an action to recover possession of the property. Baxter claimed that a life tenancy had been created that could not be terminated by notice. Decide.
7. A paper or "memorandum," given by the defendant to Homsey read as follows: "This is to certify that the rent at 294 Lawrence Street is $25.00 a month and that immediate occupancy may be had by Mr. Homsey, and rent to begin December 1, 1945, and after a period of two years rent $35.00." The defendant claimed a lease on the premises. The defendant alleged that an essential element in a lease for a term is that there be a demise for a period definitely fixed or at least capable of definite ascertainment. Otherwise, only a tenancy at will results. Decide.
8. Snyder leased a dwelling from Keens for a period of one year at a rental of $75 a month. After the year was up, Snyder remained in possession of the premises against Keens' wishes. At the end of the first month of the second year, Snyder tendered $75 to Keens, who accepted it with the statement that he expected Snyder to vacate the premises immediately. Snyder contended that he had another one-year lease. Discuss the rights of the parties.

CO-OWNERSHIP OF REAL PROPERTY 50

English common law recognized at a very early date the right of two or more persons to own concurrent interests in the same estate in real property. Each co-owner was deemed entitled to an undivided interest in the entire parcel, and neither could claim any specific portion of it. In some instances the co-owners held equal undivided interests, while in others some owners held larger shares than the rest. Because of the possible legal problems that may arise concerning the rights of co-owners, it is essential in all instances of co-ownership to distinguish the form of ownership and the interrelationship among the owners. Estates are classified, according to the number and relation of the owners, as (1) joint tenancies, (2) tenancies in common, (3) tenancies the entireties, or (4) community property.

JOINT TENANCY

Usually, real property is owned by one person, who is said to own the property in severalty (The word "several" was used to mean "separate" at common law.) Joint tenancy makes it possible for more than one person to have the same rights in the same property at the same time. It is a form of co-ownership whereby two or more persons own the one property together, each having exactly the same rights in that property. Blackstone described a joint tenancy as having the four unities of interest, title, time, and possession. It is a single estate in land owned by two or more persons who are not husband and wife. It must be created by one and the same conveyance, executed and delivered at one and the same time, and convey equal interests to the grantees, who must hold undivided possession.

To create a joint tenancy, the conveyance must state that the grantees are acquiring title as joint tenants. A grant "to A and B as joint tenants, with right of survivorship and not as tenants in common" creates a joint tenancy. (In some states, the use of the word "jointly" is sufficient to create a joint tenancy, while in others the right of survivorship must be clearly stated.) The right of survivorship is a distinguishing characteristic of this type of tenancy. All rights of the deceased joint tenant pass to the surviving tenant or tenants, since title is in the group and not in the individuals who make up the group. On the death of the last surviving tenant, the estate passes to his heirs or devisees.

There is no assurance that a joint tenancy will continue in existence until the death of one of the tenants. A joint tenancy will be destroyed if any one of the essentials described above—unity of interest, unity of title, unity of time, or unity of possession—is destroyed. If one of the joint tenants conveys his interest to an outsider, the joint tenancy is severed and the transferee holds title as a tenant in common with the other joint tenants. For example, a conveyance by one of three joint tenants severs the joint tenancy with respect to the undivided third interest so conveyed; however, the joint tenancy remains in effect as to the other two-thirds interest.

Joint estates in land were favored under the common law of England. Conveyances to two or more persons were construed to create a joint tenancy unless a contrary intent was apparent from the wording of the instrument. As time passed, however, the presumption of a joint tenancy lost its validity. Today many state statutes provide that no joint tenancy will be recognized unless the right of survivorship is expressly mentioned in the conveyance. A few states have abolished the joint tenancy in land; others have done away with the characteristic of survivorship, reasoning that ownership should not ultimately depend on the accident of a long life.

TENANCY IN COMMON

A conveyance to two or more persons without other designation will be regarded by most courts as creating an estate in common, with each party having a proportionate undivided interest in the property so conveyed. Like joint tenants, no one of these owners possesses a specific part of the property, but each owns an undivided interest in the entire title. Unlike joint tenants the co-owners are not required to have equal portions of the property, although they do have equal rights to the possession and enjoyment of the property. For instance, A may own an undivided one-half interest, B may own an undivided one-quarter interest, and C and D may own undivided one-eighth interests. The estate of each co-owner passes to his heirs or devisees; no co-owner can acquire rights in the common property by right of survivorship.

The tenancy in common can be created by separate grants, executed at different times and conveying different interests in the property. One co-owner may have acquired his interest in a will read five years previous and another co-owner could acquire his interest in a deed executed two years hence. A tenancy in common may come into being as the result of a statutory enactment that a grant to two or more persons is to be regarded as such unless it appears that the intention was otherwise. Most states provide for the presumption of a tenancy in common unless the parties clearly manifest their intention to create a joint tenancy. The only unity present in this type of tenancy is the unity of possession. Inasmuch as each tenant has an undivided share in possession, the tenancy is terminable at the will of each tenant. Each co-owner may sell, pledge, or, upon his death, pass on to his heirs his share of the property. If a co-owner dies intestate, his share goes to his heirs at law. A conveyance by one tenant in common of his share causes his grantee to become a tenant in common with his former tenants in common. In sum, a tenancy in common may be created by grant, purchase, device, or the operation of law.

Tenancy in common may be terminated by a partition giving each co-owner a specific portion or by merger (when one person acquires all the interests of the other co-owners). The partition may be voluntary, where each co-owner releases to the others that portion he is to relinquish. Where agreement is not possible or where minors who cannot participate in a voluntary partition are involved, one of the co-owners may bring an action at law for compulsory partition. The court may decree a partition if an equitable division can be made of specific portions of the property so that each co-owner will become the sole owner of that portion set aside for him. If there is disagreement over the manner of apportioning specific interests, the court may order the property sold and the proceeds of the sale divided among the parties according to their respective interests.

TENANCY BY THE ENTIRETIES

At common law, the wife lost much of her individuality as a legal person upon her marriage. Her legal status merged with that of her husband, who was considered the legal representative of the unit. As a result of this concept of the legal unity of spouses, there developed a kind of co-ownership between the husband and the wife, tenancy by the entirety. A conveyance or devise to a husband and wife during the continuation of the marriage caused the entire estate to vest in them as one person.

Tenancy by the entirety may be created by grant, purchase, gift, or devise. It is not an estate of inheritance. In most respects, it resembles the joint tenancy in that the four unities are essential. However, it differs in that neither spouse can disturb the right of survivorship by conveying his interest to another party, as may be done in a joint tenancy. Each spouse is considered to be the owner of the entire property; therefore, any action affecting title must be done in the name of both. Legally, joint tenants are said to be seized of a share of the whole, whereas tenants by the entirety are seized of the whole and not of a share. A grant "to John Jones and Mary Jones, husband and wife, as tenants by the entirety with right of survivorship" creates a tenancy by the entirety. Land held in this manner is free from the creditors of one spouse alone until the nondebtor spouse dies.

As a rule, the tenancy by the entirety may be terminated by death, divorce, annulment, or a joint conveyance of the property. Generally, estates held in tenancy by the entirety are not subject to partition during the continuance of the marriage. If divorce or annulment occurs, the former spouses become tenants in common. Upon the death of one of the co-owners, the survivor possesses the entire estate in severalty; the heirs take nothing.

COMMUNITY PROPERTY

The adoption in some states of the form of ownership known as community property is largely the result of the influence of Spanish civil law. In the Spanish legal system, the wife was considered an individual in her own right, just as the husband was in his. Although state statutes are not uniform, community property is generally defined as that property owned in common by husband and wife during the continuation of the marriage. Property acquired during marriage by the individual or joint effort of the parties to the marriage is considered as belonging to the marital unit, with each spouse owning an undivided one-half interest. The husband and wife share equally in property acquired during their marriage, even though one spouse may have earned or gained more than the other or though one may have earned or gained nothing.

Ownership of community property does not depend on who happens to hold legal title, as long as the property was acquired during the marriage and not purchased with separate funds. Whichever spouse acquires the property, title to half the acquisition passes automatically by operation of law to the other party. Likewise, a gift to both spouses is community property. However, property owned prior to the marriage or acquired by one spouse during the marriage by gift, inheritance, devise, or bequest remains the separate property of, and is controlled by the spouse owning it.

Community property laws usually give the husband the right of management and the power to sell the personal, but not real, property. As administrator of the property, the husband is subject to all the fiduciary obligations of an administrator. If he wastes the property or attempts to use it for his own benefit, his spouse may maintain an action against him or against any person who knowingly participated in such fraudulent use of the property. His right of management does not extend to the wife's separate property unless she expressly wishes to include it.

Termination of the tenancy of community property may be accomplished in a number of ways. Community property cannot be partitioned, but divorce terminates the tenancy and partition then is possible. Upon the death of either spouse, the community property is used to pay the debts; the remainder is divided equally between the surviving spouse and the heirs of the deceased. Neither party may make a will disposing of the community property in excess of his or her half interest, but each may dispose of his or her separate property and his or her share of the community property. The statutes and court decisions of the various states may, of course, vary the methods of termination. Arizona, California, Idaho, Louisiana, Nevada, New Mexico, Texas and Washington are community property states.

LEGAL PRINCIPLES

The common forms of co-ownership of land are joint tenancy, tenancy in common, tenancy by the entirety, community property, and tenancy in partnership.

Joint tenancy has unities of time, title, interest, and possession. It is also distinguished by the right of survivorship.

A conveyance to two or more persons without special designation will be regarded as a tenancy in common, with the only unity required being that of possession.

A suit for partition will divide co-interests in real property.

In tenancy by the entirety, neither party may convey his interest in the property to a third person without the consent of the other.

In states where the theory of community property is recognized, property acquired during marriage by the individual or joint effort of the spouses belongs to the marital unit.

CASE FOR REVIEW

ZAMISKA v. ZAMISKA

296 A.2d 722 (Pa. 1972)

Mike Zamiska and George Zamiska were father and son. On December 26, 1957, Mike Zamiska executed a deed conveying the title in certain land to Mike Zamiska and George Zamiska "as joint tenants and as in common with the right of survivorship." Upon his father's death (intestate) on July 18, 1970, George claimed complete title in the land. Other children and grandchildren of Mike Zamiska, claiming the 1957 deed created only a tenancy in common in the grantees, instituted an action in equity asking the court to declare that George's ownership was limited to an undivided one-half interest.

At common law joint tenancies were favored, and the doctrine of survivorship was a recognized incident to a joint estate. But the courts of the United States have generally been opposed to the creation of such estates, the presumption being that all tenants, who are not husband and wife, hold jointly as tenants in common, unless a clear intention to the contrary is shown.

Since the issue was decided on the pleadings below, our inquiry is limited to whether the deed involved expressed the intent to create a joint tenancy with the right of survivorship with sufficient clarity to overcome the statutory presumption to the contrary.

The pertinent phrase in the deed is: "Mike Zamiska and George Zamiska as Joint tenants and as in common with the right of survivorship."

While the term "entireties" is not an element instantly, [it] is clear we cannot disregard the words "with the right of survivorship" in the instant deed as meaningless. It is true that if we were to look merely to the words in the deed "as Joint tenants and as in common," we would have an ambiguity since joint tenancy implies the term "survivorship" and "in common" implies the opposite. However, the use of the words "Joint tenants" in connection with the operative words "with the right of survivorship" removes the ambiguity and makes it clear that the intention of the parties was to create a joint tenancy, with the passage of the title to the survivor upon the death of the other.

Appellants next contend the phrase "with the right of survivorship" is not a magic phrase and this Court recently saw fit to disregard it in Michael's Estate, 421 Pa. 207, . . . (1966).

In the present case, however, it is abundantly clear that the designation "with the right of survivorship" applies to Mike and George Zamiska, father and son.

Lastly, appellants argue that in the deed, there are other expressions affirmatively indicating that a tenancy in common was intended to be created. They point in particular to the use of the words "their heirs, and assigns" rather than "his heirs, and assigns." This Court answered this identical contention in Maxwell v. Saylor, . . . 359 Pa. at page 97. . . .

It is contended by plaintiffs that the phrase in the deed "their heirs and assigns" as in conflict with, and serves to negative [sic] any presumed intention to create a right of survivorship; this argument fails, however, in view of the fact that 'their heirs and assigns' are not words of purchase but of limitation, such being their time-honored use for the purpose of conveying a fee simple title.

CASE PROBLEMS

1. This is an action by Calvin Keith for the possession of certain property. The pertinent facts are as follows: In 1949, Ed Nunn and wife, Katie L. Nunn, executed and recorded a warranty deed conveying the real property which is the subject of this suit to themselves and to their grandson, Calvin C. Keith, as joint tenants, with right of survivorship. Katie L. Nunn died intestate in 1962 and later that year Ed Nunn married the appellant, Estella Nunn. In 1965, Ed Nunn and wife, Estella, executed and recorded a warranty deed conveying an undivided one-half interest in subject property to themselves for their joint lives with remainder to the survivor in fee simple. Ed Nunn died in 1967 and his widow claimed the property. Decide the claims to the property.

2. Roy Martin and his wife, Alice, their son, Hiram, and Hiram's wife, Myrna, acquired title to a two hundred and forty-acre farm. The deed ran to Roy Martin and Alice Martin, as joint tenants with the right of survivorship, and to Hiram Martin and Myrna Martin, also as joint tenants with the right of survivorship. Alice Martin died in 1960; three years later Roy remarried. By his will he left his entire estate to his second wife when he died in 1965, but upon his death Hiram and Myrna assumed complete control of the farm. Were they entitled to the property?

3. Fields willed his real property to his two sons, William and Thomas, "share and share alike." Plaintiffs, heirs of William, bring an action against defendants, heirs of Thomas, for partition, claiming that the grant of the testator created a tenancy-in-common in the sons. Defendants argue that the words created a joint tenancy in the sons and that, as William died before Thomas, the estate went to defendants by survivorship. Decide.

4. A clause in a will provided: "I give, bequeath, and devise my old homestead to my son, James, and my sister, Mary, as joint tenants. It is my desire that my son and sister shall have the right and privilege to occupy the premises during their lifetime and that, upon the death of one, the title is to vest in the survivor." The son brought an action for partition, raising the question of whether a joint tenancy or a joint life estate with contingent remainder to the survivor had been created. Decide.

5. Hubert and his wife, Wilma, were owners in joint tenancy of a tract of land that they had contracted to sell to Stone. When Hubert died, Wilma continued to collect the payments under the terms of the real estate contract, but refused to turn over any part of the proceeds to Barnes, the executor of Hubert's estate. Barnes brought an action against Wilma to collect one-half of the proceeds arising out of the contract. Decide.

6. By a deed dated April 11, 1974, John and Mary Yoder conveyed a tract of land consisting of approximately eighty acres in Kent County to Willard Short, a single man, and Emma Short, a single woman, "their heirs and assigns," The habendum clause stated that the lands and premises sold to the Shorts and "their heirs and assigns" were for their use "jointly and not as common tenants, forever." What form of ownership was conveyed?

7. The deed by which Dale Richardson acquired title to certain land contained the following words of conveyance in its granting clause: "Convey and warrant to Ray Richardson, Dale Richardson, Yvonne Richardson, and Len Richardson, in

equal proportions. In case of the death of any one or more of the grantees, his or her interest in said land shall go in equal proportions to the other surviving grantees then living." What form of ownership was conveyed?

8. This is an action by an air force officer against his wife for divorce. The Domestic Relations Court, Dallas County, entered a decree, which awarded to the wife a proportionate part of the officer's future military retirement pay benefits which would not become payable to him for eleven more years. The officer appealed from the portion of the decree awarding the wife a share of the retirement benefits alleging that these benefits are not part of the "community property." Decide.

WILLS AND INTESTATE SUCCESSION

WILLS AND INTESTATE SUCCESSION   51

The will is one of the oldest legal instruments known to modern man. It is primarily an expression of the desires of an individual, in a form permitted by law, in regard to the disposition of his property after his death. A will may also cover such items as the manner in which the deceased's funeral is to be conducted, the appointment of a guardian for his children and the appointment of an executor for his estate. However, we are concerned with wills here only insofar as they operate as transfers of title to property after the death of the testators. If a disposition of property is to take effect prior to death, the document directing the disposition is not a will, even though it may be designated as such. If an instrument calls for the transfer of a title to property after death, it may be a will, even though designated a contract, deed, or the like.

In our system of property, a man has a right to exercise some control over the transfer of his property at his death. If his will fulfills the various statutory requirements prescribed by state law, a property owner may dispose of his property in any manner he chooses. The power to devise usually includes all forms of property that could have been transferred by the owner in his lifetime. Furthermore, the testator may revoke, destroy, or cancel his will at any time, since it does not take effect until his death; there is no such thing as an irrevocable will. However, upon his death it takes immediate effect as a disposition of property.

TERMINOLOGY

Before going on to a discussion of the law of wills, it is necessary to understand a few technical terms. When a person dies having made out a will he is said to have died *testate*. The person making the will, if male, is designated the *testator;* a female is a *testatrix*. The person to whom real property is willed is called a *devisee,* and the disposition itself is a *devise*. A money gift under a will is referred to as a *legacy,* and the recipient is a *legatee*. A *bequest* includes any form of personal property passing under a will, and is a more general term than legacy.

ESSENTIALS OF A WILL

The formal requirements for the valid execution of wills are governed by statute. Although laws may vary somewhat in different states, the requirements described below are fairly standard in all jurisdictions. There is some

463

disagreement over whether the statutes in force at the time of execution of the will or those in force at the time of the testator's death govern its construction. The trend of court decisions seems to be toward upholding the validity of wills that fulfill the statutory requirements at the time of execution. The reasoning behind this is that a statute should not impair a will already made, nor should it aid a will that was defectively executed. (See Figure 51-1)

TESTATOR'S AGE

The original English *Statute of Wills* (1540) included no age requirement for testators. This rule was adopted in the United States at the time of the separation from England and, until recently, was still followed in a few states. At the present time, however, every state fixes by statute a minimum age for making a will. In general, any person of legal age and sound mind may make a will. While twenty-one years is usually specified, some states merely provide that the of lawful age. In some states, also, the age requirement differs for personal and real property. Usually a greater age is required for the devise of real property. Any age requirement must be met at the time of execution of the will.

Apart from a specific statutory provision making a criminal sentenced to life inprisonment civilly dead, conviction for a crime does not affect capacity to make a will. The disability formerly attached to an alien's capacity has now been abolished by statute.

TESTAMENTARY INTENT

A will generally must be evidenced by a writing that gives credence to the testator's intention that the document take effect only upon his death. The intent that certain persons shall become owners of certain property upon the death of the testator is called *testamentary intent*. Although evidence of testamentary intent is usually in writing, any device that results in a permanent record may be used.

FORM

Although the permanent record required for a valid will need take no particular form, if it is written on more than one sheet of paper it should be clear that the sheets are part of the same document. Form is not a basic requirement of a will; it is the evidence of its execution and its proper publication to witnesses of its character that is essential. Therefore, the only requirement regarding form is that the intention of the testator be formally expressed. The testator need not use any particular words as long as his language indicates an intention to make a gift of property. Attestation by two or more witnesses is almost universal, as is the requirement that the testator sign the document.

LAST WILL AND TESTAMENT

I, Patrick Michaels, of Wausaukee, Marinette County, Wisconsin, of sound mind and disposing memory, and more than twenty-one (21) years of age, do hereby make, publish and declare this as and for my last will and testament, and I do hereby revoke any and all former wills and codicils thereto by me at any time made.

First. I hereby direct that all debts, funeral expenses, and any taxes incurred by reason of my death shall by paid by my Executor out of the principal of my residuary estate.

Second. I have four (4) children, namely Marie, Susan, John, and David; and, having them in mind, I intend to make provision for them.

Third. I give Five Thousand Dollars ($5,000.00) to my daughter Marie, if living; if not then to my residuary estate.

I give Five Thousand Dollars ($5,000.00) to my daughter Susan, if living; if not then to my residuary estate.

I give Five Thousand Dollars ($5,000.00) to my son John, if living; if not then to my residuary estate.

I give Five Hundred Dollars ($500.00) to St. Augustine Church, Wausaukee, Marinette County, Wisconsin, to use in any manner they deem necessary.

The remainder of my property, both real and personal, I give to my son David.

Fourth. I hereby name, nominate and appoint my son David as executor of this my last will and testament to serve without the necessity of furnishing bond.

In witness whereof, I do hereunto subscribe my name to this my last will and testament on this 22nd day of November, 1977.

_____

The foregoing instrument, consisting of one typewritten page, including the page on which this attestation clause appears, was at the date thereof signed, published, and declared by the said Patrick Michaels to be his last will and testament, in the presence of each of us, who at his request and in his presence and in the presence of each other, have subscribed our names as witnesses thereto; and we hereby certify that the above-named testator was of sound and disposing mind and memory at the time of the execution thereof and over twenty-one (21) years of age.

_____

_____

Figure 51-1

PUBLICATION

It is a statutory requirement that wills be publicized. To accomplish this the person making the will must inform the attesting witnesses that the document he is signing before them is intended to be his last will and testament. The testator must then sign the will, or, if he is unable to write, must either place his mark upon the document or procure some person to sign on his behalf in his presence and under his direction. The signature need not be written; even using a rubber stamp will be sufficient if that is the complete act by which the testator intends to authenticate the instrument. Whatever means is employed, the law usually requires that the signer's mark be placed at the end of the will to prevent fraudulent additions to the document. If the will consists of several pages, it is wise for the testator to initial the pages, other than the last, which he signs.

ATTESTATION

Attestation is the act of witnessing the execution or formal signing of a will. It is the signing of the document by the required number of witnesses after a clause stating that the witness observed the execution of the will or that the testator acknowledged the document as his will. Although most states require two witnesses, some require three. Three is advisable in all cases, since one or more of the witnesses may be difficult to locate at a later date or the will may be probated in a state requiring three witnesses. The usual statutory requirement is that witnesses must be competent and credible and not have any beneficial interest in the will. However, any witness who is also a beneficiary may, if he chooses, renounce his legacy and thus remove this disqualification.

TESTAMENTARY CAPACITY

A person who intends to make a will must give evidence of testamentary capacity when he executes it. This is not to imply that he must be absolutely sound in every respect, but the proponents of the will must establish that the testator had sufficient mental capacity at the time he executed his will to know the natural objects of his bounty, to understand the kind and the extent of his property, to understand what he was doing in making a will, and to dispose of the property according to a plan formulated by him. An individual might be quite eccentric and still be of sound mind for the purposes of making a will. He may also be elderly and in poor health, yet be capable of disposing of his property. These factors do not necessarily disqualify a testator but they may be cited along with other evidence, to show that the proper testamentary capacity was lacking.

REVOCATION

Since a will has no legal effect prior to the death of the testator, it may be revoked in whole or in part at any time prior to this event. Revocation may be by an act of the testator or by the operation of law. However, it is necessary that the intention to revoke be apparent; hence, the same degree of mental capacity is required for revocation of a will as for its execution.

BY ACT OF THE TESTATOR

To be effective, a will must be published as the testator's last will and testament. If a person makes two wills, the first document is revoked by the second so far as the latter is inconsistent with the first or specifically revokes it. To avoid undue litigation, most states have enacted statutes setting forth the conditions that must be met for revocation to be effective. In these states revocation is merely a matter of complying with the statute.

Any deliberate destruction, cancellation, or mutilation of his will by the testator operates as a revocation. Accidental action will not cause revocation if the validity of the will can be proved by the introduction of proper and sufficient evidence. The physical acts necessary to revoke a will may be performed by the testator himself or by someone acting at his request and in his presence.

BY OPERATION OF LAW

Statutes usually provide that a change in the family relations of the testator may have the effect of a revocation. As a rule, if a testator marries after making a will and then dies, the will is revoked in the absence of an agreement to the contrary. The subsequent birth or adoption of a child for whom no provision is made in a will works as a revocation in that the child inherits the same property as he would have had if the testator died intestate. In the absence of a statute to the contrary, divorce alone does not revoke a will.

PROBATE

To probate a will is to institute proceedings in a proper court to establish its authenticity as a testamentary document. Probate is necessary to give legal status to the will. Proceedings are generally instituted by a petition entered at the request of a person designated in the will or by someone involved in an action concerning the testator's estate. Usually the request is made by the executor of the estate. For a will to be admitted to probate, it must conform to the statutory requirements for a genuine will.

WILL CONTESTS

The purpose of a will contest is to determine whether the document in its entirety is valid or invalid. A will contest may be had upon the following grounds:

1. lack of testamentary capacity of the testator;
2. failure to meet statutory requirements;
3. fraud, duress, or undue influence in inducing the making of the will, or
4. revocation.

PROBLEMS OF CONSTRUCTION

Interested parties, beneficiaries or heirs under the statutes of descent and distribution, may request the court to construe the meaning of ambiguous or doubtful clauses in a will. Ambiguity may arise from contradictory clauses in the instrument itself, or because there may be two persons answering to the name and description of a beneficiary. In each instance the court must make a judgment concerning the actual meaning of the language employed in the will.

The problem of construction is primarily one of giving effect to the true intention of the testator, insofar as his intention can be determined from the contents of the will and the circumstances of the case. (An exception arises where the testator attempted to make a disposition which the law regards as illegal.) The court cannot, in the absence of an illegal disposition, give a different intent to the words of the testator, even where the will does not provide for what the court deems a just disposition. The following rules will usually be considered by the courts:

1. The actual intent of the testator must be ascertained.
2. The entire will must be read, not merely parts of the document.
3. The court will presume the legality of the instrument.
4. Partial intestacy will be avoided if possible since it is presumed that the testator intended to dispose of his entire estate by the will.

CODICILS

A testator may change or modify his will by adding to it one or more new paragraphs, called codicils. A codicil, to be effective, must be executed with the same formalities as the will itself. It is a testamentary disposition subsequent to a will by which the will is altered, added to, or subtracted from, but in no instance totally revoked.

The testator may not modify his will merely by crossing out parts of it or inserting names or clauses, even if witnesses attest to such alterations. The entire will would have to be republished to make the changes effective.

SPECIAL WILLS

A *holographic will* is one entirely handwritten by the testator and signed by him. It is usually valid without an attestation. Where it is executed before witnesses in accordance with statutory requirements, its validity will be recognized in all states. Unless there is a controlling statute, no part of a holographic will may be printed. Thus it cannot be written on stationery that has a letterhead or on a sheet of paper that contains a printed date.

A *nuncupative will* is an oral will made and declared by the testator, in the presence of disinterested witnesses, to be his last will. No particular language is required, but the testator's statement must clearly and unequivocally show that this was his intention. Generally, a will of this type can be made only during the last illness of the testator and is effective only in regard to personal property. Jurisdictions that recognize nuncupative wills usually limit the amount that can be claimed; the maximum allowed ranges from $200 to $1000. Usually, also, the will must be reduced to writing and probated within a certain period.

Most state statutes allow soldiers' and sailors' wills to dispose of personal property without complying with the formalities required of other wills.

INTESTATE SUCCESSION

Intestate succession is one of the oldest privileges accorded the institution of property rights. According to our system of landholding, when a property owner dies, the title to his lands must pass to someone else. In the absence of a will title to real property of a decedent passes, by inheritance, to his heirs— those persons who by law are entitled to his property. The privilege of inheriting, or succeeding to, the ownership of the decedent's property is called the *right of succession.* It is usually confined to the blood line of the decedent; relatives by marriage, other than the surviving spouse, are thus excluded. Those persons entitled to inherit an intestate's real property are commonly called his "heirs," while those taking personalty are called "next of kin."

Intestate succession has its origin in English feudal law. Under this system, complete ownership as we know it today was not possible, nor was it possible to freely transfer title to real property. The king possessed the supreme right over the land. Blackstone comments, "The king is esteemed in the eyes of the law as the original proprietor of all the lands in the Kingdom." It was, therefore, at the will of the sovereign that land was transferred or, on the other hand, forfeited to the Crown upon the death of the holder. In return for grants of land, the Crown was assured of military services from its subjects whenever an armed force was needed. Any alienation of title from the family of the transferee was forbidden, lest the land fall into the hands of an enemy of the Crown. Since it was essential for the king to keep parcels of land intact in order to maintain a standing army, it became the rule that the eldest son alone should be the heir entitled to the property. This was called the *law of primogeniture.* A decedent could not violate this rule by attempting to make a devise of his property in his will. It was not until near the end of the thirteenth century, when military service was no longer of primary importance, that females were allowed to inherit under the laws of intestate succession.

INTESTACY

A person has the right but not the duty to make a will. If for some reason a man dies without having made a will, or if a will exists that does not effectively dispose of his property, he is said to have died intestate. The disposition of his property will be carried out in accordance with the statutes of descent and distribution of the state where the real property is located. These statutes may or may not make a disposition similar to what the decedent would have provided had he made a will. Since inheritance is a privilege granted by the state, it may be regulated and, hence, changed at any time by the state. For example, the state may change the class of designated heirs, or it may provide that intestate property should revert to the state. The statutes of descent and distribution set forth a rigid formula for determining who will receive the property of the decedent. The law makes no exceptions among the heirs based on need; for this reason alone it is better for the heirs when the decedent has made a plan for the effective disposition of his estate.

INHERITANCE STATUTES

Inheritance statutes seek to ensure an orderly transfer of title to property and to accomplish what the decedent ought to have provided for in an orderly plan to take effect upon his death. In effect, they attempt (1) to distribute the decedent's property through a practical and workable system with regard for the public interest and (2) to distribute it in a manner that would approximate the decedent's desires had he made a formal expression of his intent. The usual state laws not only decide who will inherit but also the order in which they will do so and the extent of their share.

INTESTATE PROPERTY

An intestate's property consists of his assets which survive him at the time of his death. Any present interest in property will descend to his heir or heirs. The distribution of real property will be made in accordance with the law of the jurisdiction where the property is located, whereas the distribution of the personal property will be controlled by the law of the jurisdiction where the decedent resided at the time of his death.

ORDER OF SUCCESSION

The persons entitled to a share of the intestate property are determined as of the date of death of the intestate. If any of this group should die, their rights do not lapse but become part of their estate.

The statutory formula generally provides that the first distribution shall be to the decedent's surviving spouse and surviving descendants. The surviving spouse is entitled to a one-third or one-half interest in the estate. This share varies if there are children of the decedent. If there are no children, the surviving spouse will take an enlarged part and in some states will take the entire estate. A divorced spouse, of course, is completely excluded. The expression "surviving descendants" includes children, grandchildren, great grandchildren, and other lineal or blood descendants. This class of heirs also includes a child of the intestate born after his death. In many jurisdictions, an adopted child inherits in the same manner as the surviving children. Also, many states provide that an illegitimate child can inherit from his mother.

If there are no descendants, the statutes usually provide that the ascendants of the deceased shall inherit. Ascendants include persons to whom one is related in the ascending line, such as parents, grandparents, and great grandparents.

Next in line of succession are the collateral heirs, who are not descendants of the decedent but are related to him through a common ancestor. Collateral heirs belong to the same ancestral stock but are not in the direct line of descent; they include brothers and sisters, nieces and nephews, uncles and aunts, and cousins, in that order. The relationship of these persons is usually not questioned but must be proved in the event of a dispute. In-laws do not share in the property. Yet interestingly enough, in the absence of a statutory provision to the contrary, a person who murders the decedent cannot be deprived of sharing in the estate if he is legally entitled to do so. Finally, if all the classes of possible heirs are exhausted and there is no one to inherit the estate, it will escheat to the state after a specified period. (See Figure 51-2)

PER CAPITA OR PER STIRPES DISTRIBUTION

If all the heirs stand in the same degree of relationship to the decedent, they share equally in his estate. For example, where there are three children, each child takes one-third share. This is referred to as a per capita distribution. If there are also grandchildren, they inherit nothing because the first group, or class, of heirs is intact and has procedence over them. If, however, one of the decedent's three children was deceased and left two children, the distribution would be somewhat different. The two living children would still take a one-third share, and the grandchildren whose parent had died would each take a one-sixth share. The grandchildren would merely divide the share of their deceased parent. This is called a per stirpes distribution. Some states permit grandchildren to inherit on a per capita basis.

ADMINISTRATION OF ESTATES

The purpose of the administration of any estate is to provide an efficient and impartial method to protect the interests of the creditors of the decedent and to distribute the assets of the estate to those persons who are entitled to share in the estate. The methods for accomplishing this are to be found in the state *probate code.*

The person charged with the administration of the decedent's estate is his *personal representative.* If a person designates a representative in his will, this person will be his executor, if male; executrix, if female. Where there is no designation, or where the person designated is unable or unwilling to serve, the court will appoint an administrator, if male; an administratrix, if female. A person must be competent to make a will in order to act as a personal representative. The duties of the *personal representative* are to discover and collect the assets of the decedent, pay the lawful claims against the estate, and distribute the balance to the persons entitled thereto, subject to the approval of the court.

472

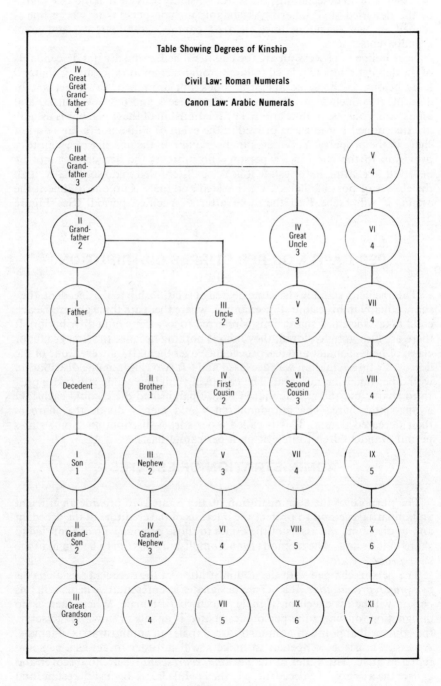

Figure 51-2

LEGAL PRINCIPLES

A will is the expression of an individual's wishes with regard to the final disposition of his property.

Since a will has no effect until the death of the testator, he may revoke it at any time.

A person, when making his will, must be of legal age to do so.

The individual drawing up his will is the testator. He must be legally competent at the time the will is executed.

A will need take no particular form, as long as the intent of the testator is made clear.

Wills must be published and attested to as a final disposition of property.

Testamentary capacity means that the person making a will knew what he was doing with regard to his property and the natural objects of his bounty.

Probate gives effect to a will.

A codicil is a formal addition to a will.

A holographic will is one entirely handwritten by the testator.

A nuncupative will is an oral will.

Inheritance is the method by which title to real property passes in the absence of a will.

A person dies intestate when he dies without making a will.

Inheritance statutes attempt to accomplish what the decedent ought to have accomplished by a will.

The persons entitled to inherit are determined by statute as of the date of death of the intestate.

Depending on the circumstances, a per capita or a per stirpes distribution may be made.

The personal representative will dispose of the decedent's estate, subject to the approval of the court.

CASE FOR REVIEW

ALLEN ET. AL. v. BROMBERG ET. AL.

147 Ala. 317 (1906)

A bill . . . was filed to enjoin the probate of a will in the probate court of Mobile county, upon the allegation that its execution was in violation of a contract, made between the textatrix and her husband, to execute similar wills, with the same executors, each in favor of the other for life, with remainder to certain public charities. . . .

It cannot be doubted that a person may make a valid agreement to dispose of his property by will in a particular way, and that a court of equity will require its performance. . . .

It is not claimed, of course, that any court has the power to compel a person to execute a last will and testament carrying out his agreement to bequeath a legacy; for this can be done only in the lifetime of the testator, and no breach of the agreement can be assumed as long as he lives, and after death he is no longer capable of doing the thing agreed by him. But the theory on which the courts proceed is to construe such agreeement, unless void under the statute of frauds or for some other reason, to bind the property of the testator or intestate so far as to fasten a trust on it in favor of the promisees, and to enforce such trust against the heirs and personal representatives of the deceased or others holding under them charged with notice of the trust. The courts do not set aside the will in such cases, but the executor, heir, or devisee is made a trustee to perform the contract. [*Bolman* v. *Overall,* 80 Ala. 451, 2 South. 624, 60 Am.Rep. 107.]

As a contract for the execution of a will with particular provisions can be specifically enforced only by fastening a trust on the property of the testator in favor of the promisee and enforcing such trust against the personal representatives and others claiming under the will violating the terms of the contract, it is necessary that the will be first probated, "for it cannot be recognized in any forum until admitted to probate." *Describes* v. *Wilmer,* 69 Ala. 25, 44 Am.Rep. 501. Nor does the fact that the agreement embraced the appointment of the same executors in both wills give equity to the bill. As stated, no breach of the agreement in any of its parts can be assumed as long as the testator lives, and after his death he is no longer capable of doing the thing agreed upon. Such agreement could be specifically enforced only by setting aside the latter will and probating the former. This could not be done. A will is in its very nature ambulatory, subject to revocation during the life of him who signed it, and is revoked by the execution of another will. . . . After such revocation it can be revived only by the expressed intention of the testator himself. . . .

For the reasons above given, a decree will be here rendered dissolving the injunction and dismissing the bill for want of equity.

CASE PROBLEMS

1. An Illinois statute required that a person's will "shall be attested and subscribed in the presence of the testator by two or more competent witnesses, who saw him subscribe or heard him acknowledge the same." Freeman executed a will and had two witnesses sign it after informing them that he had executed it, but they did not see him sign the will. After his death the will was offered for probate. Was it entitled to be probated?

2. Ford executed a will, then executed a second will that contained a clause expressly revoking all previous wills. He did not, however, destroy the first will. Neither the first nor the second will contained any provision for his only son, who had left home some years before. Ford and his son were later reconciled. Just before his death he said before witnesses that he wanted his son to have everything, and mutilated the second will. Was the second will properly revoked?

3. By his will Heath bequeathed one-third of his estate to Morse. When the will was probated, it was found that the bequest to Morse had been crossed out; at the bottom of the will was the typewritten statement, "Under no condition do I wish Morse to be included in this will." Both the will and the final addition were signed by Heath. The will was witnessed and acknowledged, but the addition was not. There was no evidence to indicate when or under what circumstances the changes

had been made, or where the will had been kept. Trust Company brought an action against Morse to obtain a declaratory judgment to determine his interest under the will. Decide.

4. In 1947 the deceased made a will, and in 1957 he executed another declaring it to be his last will. By the first he gave all property to his mother; in the second he gave her a life estate and added a group of legacies. The second will contained no express reference to the first. At the time of his death the first will was not disclosed. Six years later his heirs learned of its existence and petitioned for its probate, seeking to set aside the earlier proceedings. Decide.

5. Plaintiff took an action to contest the probating of the deceased's will, a single sheet of paper. On the face of the sheet appeared two additions: between the attestation and the date, the words, "Not any good—December 11, 1967"; and between the date and the signature, "Changed my mind." On the back of the sheet, not signed, is the phrase, "This is no good; will try to make another December 10, 1966." None of these markings strike across the original words, Decide.

6. Noxon, a resident of Connecticut, died intestate on November 28, 1971. Mrs. Noxon petitioned for administration, claiming that she was the widow and that the only heir-at-law and next of kin of the deceased was his sister, Mary. Administration being granted, the court of probate distributed the estate between the widow and Elizabeth Potter, who as an infant had been adopted by Mr. and Mrs. Noxon in Wisconsin. The sister brought an action to appeal the orders of distribution. Decide.

7. Ada Wardell, a resident of the city and county of San Francisco, died leaving as survivors her husband, two sons and a daughter. Before her death, she had made her last will and testament, whereby she disposed of all her real and personal estate to her husband for life, and the remainder to her two sons. No provision was made in the will for the daughter. Her name was not mentioned in it, and it does not appear by anything in the will itself that the omission was intentional. The daughter was born out of lawful wedlock. She had never been legitimated by the subsequent intermarriage of her parents, or by acknowledgement or adoption by her father. Having been omitted from the will, she resisted the disposition of the property made by it, claiming that, as overlooked heir of her mother, she was entitled to a distributive share in the estate. Decide.

8. Smyth's cousins filed a petition against his aunt-administratrix for the right to appeal from a probate judge's decree of distribution granting the balance of his estate to the aunt as decedent's only heir-at-law. The court denied the petition, holding that the decree of distribution was in conformity with the principle that the aunt of a man who dies intestate takes to the exclusion of decedent's cousins and that the cousins had no right to appeal from the decree. Is this a sound decision?

TRUSTS 52

A *trust* is a fiduciary relationship in which one person holds a property interest, subject to an equitable obligation to keep or use that interest for the benefit of another. The *trust property* is the interest in property which the trustee holds, subject to the rights of the beneficiary. The *settlor* is the person who transfers the trust property to the trustee and thereby causes the trust to come into existence. He may also be called the trustor, donor, or creator of the trust.

The *trustee* is the individual or corporation which holds the trust property for the benefit of the beneficiary, according to the instructions of the settlor. The *beneficiary* is the person for whose benefit the trust property is held by the trustee. The same person may be both the settlor and the beneficiary of a particular trust.

There can be no private trust without a beneficiary either (a) specifically named or (b) so described that he is ascertainable from facts existing when the trust is created. If part of a trust is invalid, the valid portion will hold if it can be separated from the invalid portion.

The *trust instrument* is the document in which the settlor expresses an intent to create a trust and sets forth rights and duties of the beneficiaries and powers of the trustee.

ELEMENTS OF A TRUST

There are five basic elements of a trust, namely: (1) a person competent to create the trust; (2) indication of trust intent; (3) designation of the trust res (property); (4) designation of the parties; and, (5) valid trust purpose.

The settlor should manifest by some definite expression his final and specific intention that a trust should arise with respect to some particular property. No particular words are required, as long as some "external expression" is shown. It must be a direct command to the trustee to manage the trust property. Anything less, such as a mere expression of a "hope," "wish," recommendation or suggestion that the property be so used, are precatory words which merely create unenforceable moral obligations. However, where such precatory words are coupled with other factors, the courts may find sufficient trust intent.

Generally, the intent to create a trust must be expressed at a time when the settlor owns the property in which he intends to create the trust. Also, the settlor must have intended the trust to take effect immediately, and not at a future time.

In certain situations, the law implies or infers a trust intention. In a situation where the owner of property acquired it in such a manner as to be under equitable duty to convey it to another because his acquisition was by fraud, duress, mistake, etc., and he would be unjustly enriched if he were permitted to retain the property, the law will impose a constructive trust on that property. In a case where it appears that the settlor, in conveying the property, did not make an effective disposition of the beneficial interest and did not intend that the person taking or holding title should have the beneficial interest, the law will declare a resulting trust. There are three types of resulting trusts, namely: (1), invalid trusts where an effective transfer is made, but for some reason the trust cannot be enforced; (2) situations where the amount of property transferred to the trust proves excessive for the purposes of the trust; and, (3) purchase money resulting trusts, where one party pays to a second party the consideration for a transfer of property, but has title taken in the name of a third party. In these situations there is a presumption that the first party intended the third party to hold as trustee for the first party.

There are three requirements for a trust res. It must be (1) an existing interest in property, (2) capable of ownership and alienation, and (3) sufficiently identifiable or identified. These are the only essential elements in every kind of trust.

The final element of a trust is trust purpose. Ordinarily, a trust may be created for any purpose that is not contrary to public policy. Occasionally, however, a trust or some provision therein may be held completely invalid if it appears that the settlor was attempting to accomplish an objective which is either illegal or requires the commission of a criminal or tortious act by the trustee or for some other reason would be contrary to public policy.

TYPES OF TRUSTS

LIVING TRUSTS

A living trust is a personal trust created by an individual during his lifetime for the benefit of himself or some other person or object. The settlor may declare himself trustee for some other person's benefit or he may be one of the trustees for his own benefit. He can create a trust with another person as trustee for the benefit of himself and another person. However, he cannot create a trust with himself as sole trustee and sole beneficiary.

A settlor can put into a living trust any kind of property that he as testator could leave in a trust under a will. He has the advantage of selecting the property which he and his trustee think will be well adapted to trust administration. A testator, however, leaves in trust whatever property he owns at the time of his death.

INSURANCE TRUSTS

An insurance trust is any living trust which consists wholly or partly of life insurance contracts made during the lifetime of the insured and of the insurance proceeds after the death of the insured. Insurance trusts may be either personal insurance trusts or business insurance trusts. Personal insurance trusts are those created by individuals for individuals, institutions, or other groups capable of being beneficiaries but in which no provision regarding a business or business interest is involved. Business insurance trusts are created by the business or by individuals for the liquidation of a business or business interest.

CHARITABLE TRUSTS

A charitable trust is one created for a charitable purpose. A charitable trust must be (1) for the benefit of an indefinite number of persons, as distinct from specified individuals; (2) for a charitable object; and (3) for an unlimited duration. A charitable trust has tax advantages over other kinds of trusts.

Since a charitable trust can be created to last indefinitely it occasionally happens that a trust may outlive the particular charitable purpose for which it was created. The "Cy Pres" doctrine may then be invoked by the court to apply the trust in a manner as nearly like the settlor's intention as possible. The doctrine may be invoked whenever it appears that either the particular charitable purpose designated by the settlor has been fully accomplished without exhausting the trust estate; or that the particular purpose designated has become impossible, illegal, or at least impracticable.

SPENDTHRIFT TRUSTS

Trust provisions restraining the beneficiary from wasting the income from the trust property during his lifetime create spendthrift trusts. Such income or the right thereto cannot be disposed of by the beneficiary or reached by his creditors so long as they are in the hands of the trustee nor can the creditors of the beneficiary reach the corpus of the trust. Such income after it has been received by the beneficiary is subject to the claims of the beneficiary's creditors and to disposition voluntarily by the beneficiary.

CREATION OF A TRUST

The principal methods of creating a trust are: (1) declaration by the owner of property that he holds it in trust for another; (2) transfer of property by the owner to another as trustee for the transferor or third persons; (3) a promise enforceable under the law of contracts; or (4) the exercise of a power or appointment.

If the transfer of property by the owner to another is made by the owner during his lifetime, it is done so in an inter vivos trust. The creation of a trust of this kind requires an effective, present transfer of the trust res. There must be a legally adequate delivery of the trust res to the trustee. There must be a physical transfer of possession of personal property to the trustee; and there must have been an effective conveyance of total to real property.

If an effective transfer has been made, a valid trust exists even if the trustee has not been made aware of it. Neither notice to, nor acceptance by, the trustee is esstential to the creation of a trust. Nor is notice to the beneficiary that the settlor intends to create a trust, or has created one, necessary for the validity or completion of the trust.

The Statute of Frauds requires that trusts concerning land must be evidenced by some writing signed by the party empowered to impress the trust upon the property. It is the original status of the trust res which is determinative of its status as "real" or "personal" at the time of transfer.

A testamentary trust is one created in a decedent's will, or by other testamentary act. (See Figure 53-1) It is the operative effect of the trust, which determines whether it is "testamentary"; not simply whether it is created inter vivos or by last will and testament. An inter vivos trust will be held "testamentary" in effect whenever the beneficiaries can be ascertained only by some future testamentary act by the trustor, such as by reference to beneficiaries who are "to be designated in my will."

Another element which is important in the creation of a testamentary trust is the use of "pour-over" provisions in the decedent's will. A "pour-over" provision is an attempted sift by the decedent to a pre-existing trust, whereby other assets of his estate are added to this trust and are administered and distributed as part of that trust. There is little problem in sustaining the "pour-over" provision where the inter vivos trust was (1) in existence at the time that the decedent executed his will; and (2) was by its terms non-modifiable.

TRUST ADMINISTRATION

A trustee has the authority and powers that are conferred upon him (1) by the express provisions in the trust instrument, (2) by virtue of being "necessary or appropriate" to carry out the trust purposes, and (3) by statute or court decree. Powers implied by law include the power of sale, the power to lease, and the power to incur reasonable expenses. The power to mortgage or pledge the trust estate, and the power to borrow money on the security of the trust estate must be expressed in the trust instrument. Most trust powers are discretionary; however, the trustee may be required to act in a particular way. In this situation, the power is imperative and he must exercise the power as it is conferred. If the power is discretionary, the scope of judicial review is ordinarily limited to the question of whether the trustee has abused his power. Unless otherwise specified, the powers granted to the trustees attach to the office and not the person. The trustee may employ agents and servants to perform various acts and to exercise various powers if the delegation is consistent with the trustee's general duty of care owed to beneficiaries.

Upon acceptance of the trust, the trustee is under a duty to the beneficiaries to administer the trust in accordance with its terms. He must exercise that degree of care and skill which a reasonably prudent businessman would exercise in dealing with his own property, even if he is not paid for his services. If he possesses or held himself out to possess special skills or knowledge, he is duty-bound to exercise such skills or ability.

The trustee is under a duty of absolute loyalty to the beneficiaries and must administer the trust solely for their benefit. It is a violation of this duty of loyalty for the trustee to engage personally in any financial transaction involving the trust property. The trustee may, however, recover reasonable compensation for services rendered to the trust beyond those ordinarily required of him as trustee.

TRUST PROVISION

In the event my said wife shall not survive me for at least thirty (30) days, or in the event that we die as a result of a common accident or catastrophe or under such circumstances as to make it difficult to determine which died first, I direct that the provisions for my wife as set forth in ITEM III above (of Last Will and Testament) shall not pass to her, but, in lieu thereof, I give, devise and bequeath all the property as described in ITEM III to my children, share and share alike, or to their heirs, per stirpes, subject to the following conditions:

If any of my said children are minors at the time of my death, I direct that all of said estate be held by my wife's brother, Robert John, in trust, for the use and benefit of said minor child or children until said child or children become self-supporting. I give my trustee absolute discretion in determining the amount of assistance necessary, even if it requires the use of a substantial part or all of the corpus of said trust, with the further right to invest said trust funds as an ordinary prudent person would do, and the right to terminate the assistance to any one or more of said children when at his absolute discretion he believes said child or children to no longer need such assistance. It is my desire that my trustee shall have sufficient power to assist those of my children who, because of tender years, may not be able to properly support themselves and thus may require more assistance than those who are more mature. I further direct that when my youngest child reaches the age of 18 years, the trust shall terminate and the corpus remaining, if any, shall be equally divided among my children, or their heirs, per stirpes.

I direct that no bond be required of the said Robert John, in the event he acts as trustee as hereinabove set forth.

Figure 52-1

The trustee is under a duty to the beneficiary to take and keep control of the trust property in accordance with the terms of the trust. He is under an affirmative duty to take possession of the tangible assets of the trust and of the documents representative of any intangible assets as soon as is reasonably possible after he becomes trustee. Furthermore, the trustee is under a duty to safeguard and preserve the trust estate. He is also under a duty to enforce all rights or claims belonging to the trust and to defend any action against the trust, unless it would be unreasonable to make such defense.

The trustee must keep trust assets separate from his individual assets or the assets of any other trust which he is administering. He must earmark it so as to evidence its ownership by the trust in whatever way is practical. The trustee is under a duty to the beneficiary to make the trust property productive. He must use reasonable care and skill to develop an income from the assets of the trust estate and to rid the estate of assets which are non-productive. Whether there is a duty to invest depends upon the terms of the trust. A trustee who fails to make the trust property productive is liable to the beneficiaries for the amount of income which normally would accrue from proper investment. He is held to a standard of good faith, sound discretion, and care in making the trust investment.

Where the trustee has breached any of these duties, the beneficiary may seek equitable relief and/or damages. When damages are sought, the trustee is personally liable to the beneficiaries for any loss or depreciation in value of the trust estate resulting from his breach of trust. The trustee is also personally liable to the beneficiaries for any profit made by him through the breach of trust, or for any profit which would have accrued to the trust estate if there had been no breach. The trustee is also chargeable with interest at prevailing rates on the total sums owing to the beneficiaries from the time of the estate. Where the trustee has utilized trust funds or assets to acquire other property, the beneficiaries can either enforce a constructive trust or an equitable lien on the property acquired to secure their claim for damages and interest.

The trust instrument may contain a provision to the effect that "my trustee shall not be liable for errors of judgment or carelessness, nor for any breach of trust unless willfull."Such provisions are called "exculpatory clauses." They are not effective or valid insofar as they attempt to relieve the trustee from liability for bad faith, intentional breach of trust, or gross negligence. Nor do they effect the trustee's liability to creditors of the trust.

The trustee is personally liable to all parties with whom he deals in the course of the trust administration, unless he has specifically disclaimed personal liability, or as otherwise provided by statute. The disclaimer must be explicit to qualify as a sufficient disclaimer. If there is a valid disclaimer, and if the trustee had acted properly in making the contract, the trustee cannot be held personally liable. Wherever a trustee is personally liable on a contract in the course of his administration, and the contract is a proper and prudent one, he is entitled to indemnification from the trust estate.

The trustee is personally liable for torts committed by him or any agent in the course of administering the trust. A trustee can never indemnify himself out of the trust property for tort liability incurred where he was personally at fault. However, where the trustee was not personally at fault, he is allowed to indemnify himself from the trust estate to the extent of his liability.

TERMINATION OF TRUSTS

The trustee has only such power to terminate the trust as is conferred upon him by the trust instrument. Where he exercises a discretionary power to terminate, he may be subject to judicial action for abuse of discretion.

Beneficiaries may force a modification or termination of the trust in situations where: (a) all of the beneficiaries agree to modify or terminate the trust; and (b) each of the beneficiaries is legally competent; and (c) such modification or termination will not defeat the "trust purpose" of the settlor in creating the trust.

A trust terminates by operation of law when (1) there is an expiration of the trust term, (2) the trust purpose is fulfilled or impossible, (3) there has been a merger of the legal and beneficial interests, or (4) there is a destruction or consumption of the trust estate.

LEGAL PRINCIPLES

A trust is as a fiduciary relationship in which one person (the trustee) holds a property interest (the trust res of property) subject to an equitable obligation to keep or use that interest for the benefit of another (the beneficiary).

The settlor of a trust is a person who causes the trust to come into existence.

The trust instrument is the document in which the settlor expresses an intent to form a trust and sets forth the trust terms.

Trusts are classified with respect to the manner of their origin and their method of creation.

It is essential to the creation of an express trust that the settlor should manifest by some external expression his definite intention that a trust should arise with respect to some particular property in which he has an interest.

Constructive trusts arise whenever the owner of property has acquired it in such a way as to be under equitable duty to convey it to another, and when he would be unjustly enriched if he were permitted to retain the property.

A living trust is a personal trust created by an individual during his lifetime for the benefit of himself or of some other person or object.

The Statute of Frauds requiring trusts to be proved by a writing relates only to interests in land.

A charitable trust must be for the public benefit or for the benefit of some particular class of the public, indefinite in number.

When a charitable trust outlives its particular purpose, the court may apply the Cy Pres Doctrine and administer the trust in a manner "as nearly like" the settlor's plan as nearly as possible.

In administering the terms of the trust, the trustee must exercise that degree of care and skill which a reasonably prudent businessman would exercise in dealing with his own property.

Where the trustee breaches any of his duties, the beneficiary may seek equitable relief or damages.

The trustee is liable to all parties with whom he contracts in the course of the trust administration, unless he has specifically disclaimed against personal liability.

The trustee is personally liable for torts committed by him in the course of administering the trust.

The settlor has no power to modify or revoke an inter vivos trust unless he retains that power when creating the trust.

The beneficiaries can compel a modification or termination of the trust only when all of the beneficiaries agree to modify or terminate the trust, and the modification or termination will not defeat the purpose of the settlor in creating the trust.

A trust terminates by operation of law when any of the following occur: the trust term expires; the trust purpose is fulfilled or becomes impossible; the trust estate is merged with another or the trust estate is destroyed or consumed.

CASE FOR REVIEW

SHAW v. JOHNSON

59 P.2d 876 (Cal. 1936)

This action was brought to declare a trust in the proceeds of a life insurance policy written by the Pacific Mutual Life Insurance Company upon the life of Frances Tyler Shaw, deceased.... When the cause went to trial, the only controversy remaining was one between the defendant, as executor of the last will of the deceased, and plaintiffs, who claimed as beneficiaries of an alleged trust created by the deceased. The insurance company had paid into court the proceeds of the policy subject to the determination of the rights of the rival claimants. The trial court entered its judgment declaring the trust in favor of plaintiffs, appointing the Crocker First National Bank of San Francisco as trustee in the place of the San Francisco Bank, which had been named as trustee in the trust agreement executed by the deceased but had declined to act as such trustee, and awarding plaintiffs attorneys' fees and costs to be paid out of the trust funds.

In urging the invalidity of the trust, appellant seems to contend most seriously that the instrument creating the trust was incomplete and that "there was no delivery." ... It is true that the trust instrument was drawn in form to be signed by the San Francisco Bank as trustee and that amount of the compensation to be paid to the trustee was left in blank. But the fact that the trustee had not executed the instrument and thereafter refused to act cannot affect the validity of the trust.... Even the omission to name a trustee is not fatal for a trust will not be allowed to fail for want of a trustee even though none be named. "It is sufficient if the subject matter of the trust, the purpose thereof, and the persons beneficially interested are indicated with reasonable certainty." Estate of. McCray, 204, Cal. 399.... It follows that the mere omission to fix the compensation of the trustee by the trust instrument does not invalidate the trust. Under some circumstances, as in a case where it appears from the evidence that the trustor unquestionably intends that the consent of the trustee shall be a condition precedent to the creation of the trust, the trust might be held not to come into existence until such consent is obtained, but the trial court was justified in finding and concluding that such was not the case here. The trust instrument read: "Witnesseth: The trustor has conveyed or intends to convey, assign, and transfer, *and by these presents does convey, assign, and transfer,*" the policy to the trustee named. The policy, the notice of change of beneficiary to the San Francisco Bank duly executed by the trustor, and the trust instrument duly executed by the trustor were all delivered to the trustor's attorney with directions to "go ahead with the matter and close it up." The documents were forwarded by said attorney to the insurance company with directions to "make the necessary endorsements on the policy to effect this change." The trustor had thereby done everything within her power to create a valid trust with respect to the proceeds of the policy, and we find no merit in appellant's claims relating to either the alleged incompleteness of the trust instrument or the alleged lack of delivery.

Appellant seems to claim the change of beneficiary was not accomplished as the policy provided: "Such change shall take effect on the endorsement of the same on this policy by the company and not before." It is well settled, however, that such a provision in a policy is for the protection of the insurer; that the failure of the insurer to make the endorsement on the policy cannot defeat the rights of the new beneficiary when the insured has made a substantial compliance with the requirements for effecting a change; and the rule should be applied with great liberality when the insurer has paid the money into court and has no further interest in the litigation.

CASE PROBLEMS

1. H. Moulton created an inter vivos trust, under the terms of which the income from the corpus was to be paid in equal shares to three beneficiaries: his daughter Katherine, and her two children Henry and Catherine, in equal shares, for life. Upon the death of any beneficiary, his or her share was to go to the survivor or survivors, and upon the death of the last survivor, the corpus was to be paid to the issue of Henry and Catherine. Katherine, Henry, and Catherine attempted to evade the trust provisions by assigning their life interests to the children of Henry and Catherine. The trustee objected to the assignments. Decide.
2. Charles Fable died in 1964, leaving a will in which he bequeathed that the residue of his property "be distributed by said trustee to such charitable and educational purposes as it may deem wise and prudent." The question presented was whether this gift constituted a valid charitable trust. Decide.
3. Elizabeth Gift died in 1965, leaving a duly executed will which read in part, as follows:

   Third: All the rest, residue and remainder of my property, real, personal, and mixed and wherever situated, I give, devise and bequeath to Katherine Clauson, as Turstee, for the purpose of converting it into cash and making distribution thereof in accordance with a memorandum of instructions prepared by me and delivered to her.

   After her death a memorandum making a number of specific bequests was found in an envelope with her will in her safe deposit box. The envelope was addressed to Miss Clauson. The memorandum and the will had been placed in the safe deposit box by Miss Clauson at Mrs. Gift's request some time after the execution of the will. Miss Clauson did not, at that time, know the contents of either document. The heirs claimed valid trust was never created. Decide.
4. In 1963, and again in 1970, W. Mussey conveyed certain parcels of land to his wife Caroline without consideration, and she, in order to confirm the nature of the transaction, signed a statement as follows:

   "145 Warren Avenue, Boston, Mass., December 6, 1970. December 3, 1970, Mussey transferred a mortgage to me, also the store in Cornhill he deeded to me, both to be held in trust for him by me just the same as I hold this house we are now living in, to be held for him in trust by me. He can sell it or do just the same with it as before, as it is his just the same."

   The question was whether the property which was conveyed to Caroline was held by her upon a valid trust for her husband. Decide.
5. John Shain was one of the founders of the Shaker Society. He and the cofounders, as well as persons becoming members, turned all their property over to

creditors and the like. The original "covenant" of 1814 was confirmed and enlarged by a new "covenant" in 1844 purporting to "release and quit claim to the acting trustees of the church, all our private, personal right, title, interest, claim, and demand of, in, and to the estate, interest, property, and appurtenances so consecrated, devoted, and given up". The grantors declared that they would "never hereafter, neither directly nor indirectly, under any circumstances whatever . . . make or require any account of any interest, property, labor, or service, nor any division thereof. . . ." The Society was dissolved in 1910, owning a large amount of property. This action, by persons claiming to be his heirs, sought to impose a resulting trust on such portion of the property of the Society as represents the share transferred to it by John Shain. Decide.

6. The will of Edmund Read provided in part that:

> "I further direct and empower the said Trust Company, if at any time it shall become necessary owing to bad health or accident to my said son, to use so much of the said principal as they may deem necessary for his medical care and comfort during said sickness and convalescence."

His son John applied for an advance of $1500 out of principal so that he might spend some time in Florida on advice of his physican. The remaindermen objected claiming the trustee should sell some real estate to obtain the money. Decide.

7. The plaintiff entered into a written agreement with the defendant trust company, under which she delivered certain securities and other property to it. An express trust of personal property was thereby created, a so-called living trust. The agreement grants broad powers to the trustee to deal with the fund, in the trustee's discretion and contains a provision stating that the trust is irrevocable and unalterable.

In January, 1960, the plaintiff served a written notice on the defendant purporting to revoke the trust. The complaint, among other things, alleged that at the date of the service of the notice of revocation the plaintiff was the owner of the trust corpus and entitled to its immediate possession. Decide.

8. Action by trustee requested the construction of the last will and testament of I. W. Harper, which read in part as follows:

> "I give my said home farm to The Illinois Society of Retired College Professors, Inc., whose address is now 216 W. Main Street, Springfield, Illinois, for use as a home. This farm is not to be sold or leased but shall be used, operated and farmed by the said Society."

Decide.

DEEDS

Real property today is usually acquired by purchase, the first step being an agreement in the form of a contract to purchase. Thus, people who own real estate acquire their property by buying and paying for it, with the transfer of ownership evidenced by a deed of grant. A deed is a written instrument in which the grantor expresses an intention to pass an interest in real property to the grantee. In the case of a gift of real estate, ownership is also transferred by deed. It is the appropriate form under modern law for the conveyance of any interest in land.

To be effective as a conveyance, the grant must be signed by the grantor and there must be actual physical delivery of the deed, accompanied by words or conduct signifying the grantor's intention to be bound by its provisions. In other words, a deed is an instrument formally executed by the grantor to the grantee, which upon delivery to the grantee makes him the owner of the grantor's rights in the property. It is the final step in a real estate transaction.

Deeds differ in the kind of interest they convey: (1) a *quit claim* deed conveys the interest of the grantor, if any, without specify the interest, and makes no warranties; (2) a *bargain and sale* deed conveys title but does not contain any convenants or warranties; (3) a *general warranty* deed transfers a specified interest and obligates the grantor on certain warranties (See Figure 53-1)(4) a *special warranty* deed contains some special warranty by the grantor that may be an addition to or a limitation on the general warranties. The only requirements as to form for the drafting of a deed are those specified by statute in various states. However, several items must be included in every deed to effectively transfer title to real estate.

COMPETENT PARTIES

In general, anyone who has the legal capacity to contract is qualified to execute a deed. The disabilities of married women have been removed in most states, although many states do not permit either a husband or wife to deed away property without the consent of the other spouse.

Care should be taken in the drafting of the deed to clearly identify the grantor. If possible, he should be described exactly as he was described in the instrument creating his estate. A valid deed must also name the grantee. Legal capacity is not a requisite (minors may therefore be grantees), but the grantee must be a legal person.

WORDS OF GRANT

Since the object of a deed is to convey property, its essence is found in the words of grant. These words must define effectively the extent of the interest

488

Know all Men by these Presents

That,

                             the Grantor   , who claim   title by or through
instrument recorded in Volume   , Page   ,
County Recorder's Office, for the consideration of
                                        received to   full satisfaction of

                     the Grantee   , whose TAX MAILING ADDRESS will be

Give, Grant, Bargain, Sell and Convey *unto the said Grantee ,   , do*
           heirs and assigns, the following described premises, situated in the
of   , County of   and State of Ohio:

be the same more or less, but subject to all legal highways.

Figure 53-1

To Have and to Hold *the above granted and bargained premises, with the appurtenances thereof, unto the said Grantee   heirs and assigns forever.*

And   ,

the said Grantor   , do for   and   heirs, executors and administrators, covenant with the said Grantee   ,   heirs and assigns, that at and until the ensealing of these presents,

well seized of the above described premises, as a good and indefeasible estate in FEE SIMPLE, and have good right to bargain and sell the same in manner and form as above written, and that the same are **free from all incumbrances whatsoever**

and that   will **Warrant and Defend** *said premises, with the appurtenances thereunto belonging, to the said Grantee   ,   heirs and assigns, against all lawful claims and demands whatsoever*

And for valuable consideration

*   do   hereby remise, release and forever quit-claim unto the said Grantee   ,*

heirs and assigns, all   right and expectancy of **Dower** *in the above described premises.*

In Witness Whereof,   *have hereunto set   hand , the*

*   day of   , in the year of our Lord one thousand nine hundred and*

Signed and acknowledged in presence of

_____   _____

_____   _____

_____   _____

State of Ohio, } *ss.   Before me, a*

*   County,* }   *in and for said County and State, personally appeared the above named*

who acknowledged that   did sign the foregoing instrument and that the same is   free act and deed.

In Testimony Whereof *I have hereunto set my hand and official seal, at*

this   day of   A. D. 19

_____

_____

This instrument prepared by _____

Warranty Deed

TO

19

Transferred

COUNTY AUDITOR

Mr. Robert J. Shedlarz
Attorney at Law
Stef Navarre Rd. S. W.
Canton, Ohio 44706

Figure 53-1

taken by the purchaser. Thus, while there is no prescribed language, it is necessary to use words that show the intent to sell, convey, or grant the estate to the named grantee in some form in the instrument. If the grantor wishes to limit subsequent use of the land, he must express this intention in the granting clause. The granting clause determines the extent of the grantee's estate. It is sometimes referred to as the *habendum clause.*

DESCRIPTION

The description employed by the instrument must be such that the exact property conveyed can be located with reasonable certainty. The description should accord with the description in the contract of sale, but if that descriptionis only a general description in terms of street address, it is desirable to have a detailed description in the deed.

WARRANTIES

A general warranty deed ordinarily grants the following warranties: (1) a covenant of seisen; (2) a covenant of the right to convey; (3) a covenant against encumbrances; (4) a covenant for quiet enjoyment; and (5) a covenant for further assurances.

A *covenant of seisen* is a guaranty that the grantor owns the exact estate that he intends to convey to the grantee. It is a covenant to the effect that the grantor has and conveys the title described in the conveyance. In a quit claim deed, the grantor purports to convey his interest, if any, to the grantee and, in the absence of fraud, if the grantor had nothing, the grantee gets nothing.

A *covenant of right to convey* is a guaranty that the grantor has the right to make the conveyance.

A *convenant against encumbrances* is an undertaking by the grantor that no lien or burden not described in the conveyance is outstanding against the property. In other words, he warrants that the property is free from any encumbrances such as mortgages, tax liens, mechanic's liens, or judgment liens, except those, if any, detailed in the deed.

A *covenant for quiet enjoyment* is a general warranty that the grantee will not be dusturbed by possessory or title claims not already disclosed, and, if such are established and are settled by the grantee, that the grantor will reinburse him for the sums expended. Actually, the grantor agrees to defend the title to the property against all who claim to have a superior title.

A *covenant for further assurance* is a promise by the grantor that he will execute any additional document that may be required to perfect the title of the grantee.

EXECUTION

The deed must be completed by the signature of the the grantor. Before affixing his signature, the grantor should make certain that everything is in order—that the spelling and form of the names is correct, that the description of the property is accurate, and that anything else necessary to effect a proper legal conveyance has been done. Witnesses were not required at common law; however, some jurisdictions now require a *testimonium clause* in deeds, in which a witness attests to the grantor's signing of the deed.

ACKNOWLEDGMENT

An acknowledgment is a statement of the grantor, under oath, that the act of conveyance is free and voluntary on his part. Many states require an acknowledgment as a condition for receiving the deed in the public records. In some jurisdictions statutory enactments make it an essential to the execution of a valid deed.

DELIVERY AND ACCEPTANCE

Delivery is essential to the completion of a conveyance. Even though a deed has been properly executed in every detail, title does not pass to the grantee until there is a proper delivery of the deed, which places the instrument beyond the authority and control of the grantor. That is, the grantor must deliver the deed with the intent that it is to take effect as a deed and convey an interest in the property and that title shall pass irrevocably, even where possession and enjoyment are indefinitely postponed. Manual delivery of the deed to the grantee or someone authorized to accept delivery for him is the safest method, since it leaves no doubt as to whether proper delivery has been made.

Part of the requirement of delivery is the acceptance of the deed by the grantee. This, like delivery, is a matter of intention. Acceptance may be verbal or may be evidenced by such acts as conveying or mortgaging the land or asserting rights with respect to it (for example, cultivating it) that are incidents of ownership and not consistent with nonownership.

LEGAL PRINCIPLES

Transfer of ownership to property is evidenced by a deed. Deeds may be classified according to the interest conveyed or the number of parties executing the instrument.

There are no legal specifications regarding the form of a deed.

Any competent person may execute a deed.

The words of grant describe the extent of the interest conveyed.

An exact description of property conveyed is necessary to ensure that it can be located with reasonable certainty.

Warranties are promises made in the deed.

Execution is the completion of the deed.

An acknowledgment is a statement by the grantor that he is making a voluntary conveyance of his property.

Delivery is essential to the completion of a conveyance.

CASE FOR REVIEW

GRANT v. FOURTH NATIONAL BANK OF COLUMBUS

194 S.E.2d 913 (Ga. 1972)

On July 6, 1962, Mrs. Grant entered into an agreement with Mr. Anthony to lend him ten thousand dollars, to be evidenced by a promissory note of even date and a security deed on certain land therein referred to. They agreed that if Mrs. Grant would make such loan and if it was not paid at the time of his death then Mrs. Grant, if still living, might have the land for the amount or the security deed. A copy of the agreement was annexed to the complaint. . . .

Pursuant to the agreement, Mrs. Grant made the loan of ten thousand dollars and took in return Mr. Anthony's note for ten thousand dollars, dated July 6, 1962, which was secured by the security deed of the same date, a copy of the plat referred to therein being attached to the complaint. She did all things required of her by the terms of the agreement.

At the time of Mr. Anthony's death nothing had been repaid on the loan. In accordance with the agreement the property thereby vested in Mrs. Grant immediately upon Mr. Anthony's death and she is entitled to have the property conveyed to her. . . .

Mrs. Grant, on or about January 25, 1971, duly presented to the administrator a demand that it execute a deed conveying to her the property and at the same time advised it that she was prepared to tender the security deed; but the administrator refused to accept the tender and refused to give its assent to the conveyance and to execute the required documents of conveyance.

She then tendered to the court the note and security deed, marking the note "paid in full", declaring the security deed to be satisfied and authorizing the court to cancel it of record.

She alleged that title to the property should be decreed in her in accordance with the agreement, and that the administrator should be required to specifically perform the agreement, and execute and deliver to her a proper deed.

Upon the trial, at the close of its evidence, the administrator moved to dismiss . . . upon . . . grounds . . . that specific performance could not be decreed because the security deed contained a description of the land which was vague and void for indefiniteness. . . .

We now proceed with Mrs. Grant's first enumeration, that the trial court erred in granting the administrator's motion to dismiss the counterclaim on the basis that the description of the security deed in question is void for lack of definiteness.

The description is as follows:

All that lot, tract and parcel of land situate, lying and being in Land Lots 29, 36 and 37 of the Ninth District of Muscogee County, Georgia, said property containing approximately 109.1 acres, more or less, and being more particularly described as follows: Beginning at the point where Land Lots 28, 29, 36 and 37, said District, intersect and from said beginning point, thence westerly along the line dividing Land Lots 28 and 29 a distance of 250 feet, more or less, to a point; thence, in a northerly direction a distance of 1,365 feet, more or less, to a point on the right of way line of the Southern Railway property; thence along said railroad right of way in a northwesterly direction a distance of 280 feet, more or less, to a point; thence, easterly a distance of 3020 feet, more or less, to a point on the northern side of the Columbus-Manchester Expressway; thence, south 42 degrees, 35 minutes west along the said expressway, a distance of 2106.2 feet to a point where the northern side of the expressway intersects the line dividing Land Lots 36 and 37, said District; thence west along the line dividing Land Lots 36 and 37, said District, a distance of 700 feet, more or less, to a fence; thence southerly a distance of 650 feet, more or less, along said fence, to a point on the northern side of said expressway; thence, southwesterly along the northern side of said expressway a distance of 1342.2 feet to a point where the northern line of the expressway intersects the line dividing Land Lots 28 and 37, said District; thence north along the line dividing Land Lots 28 and 37 a distance of 1595 feet, more or less, to the point of beginning. . . .

The description then recites that the property is that shown on a plat attached thereto.

The administrator's attacks upon this description are basically as follows: that the distances of the boundary lines are indefinite because most are qualified by the words "more or less" without otherwise showing terminal points; and that the directional bearings are indefinite, since they almost entirely recite "easterly", "northerly", "westerly" or "southerly" and the signals are not otherwise fixed.

However, the plat has two keys which, in our opinion, do render the description sufficient.

First, a scale of one inch to 400 feet is shown on the face of the plat. This can be employed to locate precisely every call in the description, terminal points and configurations, thus making certain the references "more or less".

Second, a designation for north also appears on the face of the plat. With this it is possible to identify the exact bearings stated in the description. . . .

With these two aids the lines on the plat can be measured and the footage computed in accordance with the scale. Thus the tract of land intended to be included in the security deed should become apparent.

It should be noted that the word "*northwesterly*" in the call, "thence along said railroad right of way in a northwesterly direction a distance of 280 feet, more or less, to a point . . .", is a typographical error and should recite "northeasterly". (Emphasis supplied.) However, such an inaccuracy does not necessarily invalidate the description. . . .

For the foregoing reasons we conclude that the trial court erred in striking Mrs. Grant's counterclaim for specific performance of the agreement upon this particular ground.

CASE PROBLEMS

1. This was an action to quiet title of land. It appeared from the record that the land belonged to John W. Caldwell, and the plaintiff, as his administrator, was entitled to recover it, unless Caldwell had conveyed it to the defendant. The paper relied upon as a conveyance of the property is as follows:

   State of Georgia, Floyd County: This indenture made this 16th day of August, 1904, between J. W. Caldwell of the one part, and Mrs. Nannie E.

Caldwell, his wife, of the other part, for the consideration of love and con [af]fection does will all the tract or parcel of land as follows, twenty acres of land in the South west corner of lot #55 in 22nd and third district of Georgia. I will that Mrs. Nannie E. Caldwell hold the pond and ginnery on said lot of land. . . .

Decide.

2. Wood delivered to his daughter, Eleanor, a deed to real estate that reserved a life estate to the grantor. At the time he handed her the deed, he said, "This is for you. Don't record it until my death, but upon my death, you get the deed on record. Furthermore, you are going to have to take care of it." The daughter, who was living with her father, kept the deed in a trunk that was accessible to him. When a brother-in-law threatened to destroy it, she had the deed recorded. On learning of the recording, Wood said, "Just let it be, just like it is." After his death, his other heirs sued to have the deed to the daughter set aside on the ground that it had never been delivered to her. Decide.

3. An action is brought by a daughter to partition lands owned by her father and brother, the defendant. When his daughter left home to go to another state, the father, desiring his son to have the old family farm and home, deeded it to him, stating that the deed was contingent on the sister's not coming back; otherwise she was to have all the property. The daughter later returned home. Decide.

4. Defendant conveyed premises to plaintiff by a deed that read in part, "hereby covenants and agrees that it is seized of an indefeasible estate in fee simple and that the same are free from all encumbrances." Plaintiff, showing that defendant had given a railroad contractual rights to lay track and forever operate trains along the avenue on which the premises abut, sought an action to cancel the deed alleging that he was not conveyed a fee simple. Decide.

5. The facts established by the evidence were that the defendant MacAdam, an attorney-at-law, acted as attorney for plaintiff's husband and, after the death of plaintiff's husband, acted as attorney for plaintiff. After Mr. Green's death, MacAdam advised Mrs. Green that it would be to her best interests to permit him to completely manage the miscellaneous property left by her husband. He thereafter made some attempts to find purchasers. In April 1954, MacAdam requested the plaintiff to sign several blank deeds stating in substance that they were for use in effectuating a sale. Accordingly, plaintiff attached her signature to several blank forms of quitclaim deed which she left with MacAdam. The plaintiff objected to a sale made by MacAdam. Decide.

6. Plaintiff brought an action seeking to eject defendants from property that he claimed under a deed purporting to grant the property "the lawful heirs of C. Hickel." Five years after the execution of the first, another deed was made to defendants' grantor, who had been in continuous possession. Defendants claim that the original deed was void because of uncertainty. Decide.

7. Plaintiff brought an action to eject defendants, who produced as their claim to title a deed to "a tract of land containing 5000 acres lying in our middle district, on the west fork of Cane Creek, the waters of the Elk River, beginning at a hickory and running north 1000 poles to a write oak." Plaintiff contended that this description was not sufficient in law to locate the grant and that, therefore, the deed was void. Decide.

8. Plaintiff brought an action charging alteration of a deed by the erasure of the name, "Hamilton Pry," and of a "W" in plaintiff's name. Declaring that the deed was filed on behalf of defendant, who claimed to be a purchaser for value, plaintiff alleged that the alteration canceled the deed and that defendant had no title thereby. Decide.

PERSONAL PROPERTY   54

Property rights are classified in law according to the nature of the object claimed. Immovable property—land and those things permanently attached to it—is considered real property, whereas movable items, or *chattels,* are designated as personal property. Automobiles, shares of stock, and jewelry, for example, are personal property. Since it can be easily moved about, personal property is of a more temporary character than real property. Land can be possessed and controlled; personal property may not only be possessed and controlled, it may also be handled, manually transferred, altered, and destroyed with relative ease.

OWNERSHIP AND POSSESSION

The terms "ownership" and "possession" are not synonymous. They refer to two separate rights to property—rights that need not be held by the same person. The owner *has title* to the things he owns; he has a series of rights in the property, which are protected by law. Possession, on the other hand, is simply the right to control a physical object. It may be a right of ownership or may be had temporarily by one who is not the owner. For example, if A rents his house to B, A retains ownership but B takes possession.

Possession may be *actual* or *constructive.* Actual possession indicates physical control over an object. Constructive possession indicates that while possessor's legal rights o the article still exist, the article is not under his physical control. For example, a man has actual possession of anything he carries on his person, such as a watch or a wallet; he would have only constructive possession of these same items had he left them at home.

CLASSES OF PERSONAL PROPERTY

Personal property is classified as *chattels real* and *chattels personal.* Chattels real are temporary interests in land; a prime example is a lease for a specified period. At one's death, these interests do not pass directly to one's heirs, but to an executor for administration.

Chattels personal may be tangible or intangible. Tangible chattels personal include all movable property, even large items such as animals, cars, and standing trees that have been sold and are to be removed from the land. Intangible chattels personal include things to which one has a right of possession but for which legal, not physical, action must be taken before they may be enjoyed. Negotiable instruments held, bank accounts, insurance policies, and stock certificates represent intangible personal property.

Tangible chattels personal are sometimes called *choses (things) in posses-sion.* Intangible chattels personal are often referred to as *choses in action.* In addition to the examples given above, any legal action based on breach of contract is a chose in action.

ACQUISITION OF TITLE

OCCUPATION

There are certain things of which no person is the immediate owner. Property in its natural state over which no one has ever taken full and com-plete control belongs to the first person taking possession of it. Taking and holding possession of ownerless property is called occupation. For example, in the absence of restrictions imposed by game laws, anyone who acquired dominion or control over a wild animal becomes its owner. If, after capture, the animal escapes and returns to its former wild state, it reverts to its ownerless status. However, if a domesticated animal escapes, the owner retains title.

PATENT AND COPYRIGHT

If the absence of a legitimate agreement to the contrary, a product belongs to its creator. This rule extends to the works of artists and inventors. At common law the creator of a literary or an artistic work had an absolute property right in his production as long as it remained unpublished. This right to intellectual production exists in respect to expressed ideas whether or not they are entirely original, as long as they are the result of mental labor.

Under federal statutory provisions a *copyright* is available to authors to allow them the exclusive right to possess, make, publish, and sell copies of their intellectual productions or to authorize others to do so for a period of twenty-eight years, with the privilege of renewal for an additional term of twenty-eight years. A copyright may be secured for books, musical com-positions, motion pictures, and similar productions, provided the work is an original expression of an idea and not contrary to public policy or statutes. The work must be published in order to qualify for federal copyright pro-tection.

A *patent* is available to one who has given concrete expression to an idea. It gives the creator an exclusive right to make, use, market, and authorize others to make, use, and market the invention for a period of seventeen years, and is not renewable. After the expiration of the seventeen-year period, the patent expires and the public is free to manufacture and market the article. For a patent to be granted, an invention must be a new and useful contribution in the area of art, machinery, manufacturing, or the composition of matter, or a new and useful improvement thereof. The specific elements of patentability are (1) novelty, (2) utility, and (3) non-obviousness.

ACCESSION

A literal definition of the term "accession" is "something added." Property may be acquired by accession by an addition to, or an increase of, a thing already owned. Property that is permanently attached to other property becomes a part of the larger unit.

As a rule, repairs become a part of the article repaired. Also, when materials are furnished to another for manufacture of a product, title to the finished product belongs to the owner of the materials. For example, if the owner of a quantity of cloth employs a tailor to make a suit for him, title to the suit belongs to the owner of the principal goods, in this case, the cloth. This rule accords with both reason and the intent of the parties.

Some difficulty arises when changes in property are made against the wishes or without the consent of the owner. Where such an act is done intentionally and willfully, it constitutes trespass; a trespasser cannot acquire title by accession, regardless of the degree of change. In fact, the conscious wrong-doer will usually lose all the benefit of his labor and skill. If the act was unintentional, the innocent trespasser may in some cases acquire title to the property. For example, when he has greatly increased the value of the goods, the courts may allow him to acquire title, but the increase in value must be substantial in relation to the original value. In other instances, whether title passes by accession depends on whether the labor and materials of the unintentional trespasser have changed the property into a different specie. For example, a man taking possession of an amount of lumber, unaware that the lumber belongs to another, and building a boat with it would acquire title by accession.

The rules of accession relate to the right of the original owner to obtain the return of property taken from him. Under other rules of property and tort law, the person taking the owner's property from him, however innocently, is liable for money damages representing the value of the property at the time and place of conversion. Even if it is decided that the owner cannot recover his actual property, he may recover its money value.

GIFTS

A gift is a voluntary transfer of property from one person to another without compensation. Because the donor receives no compensation, or consideration, a gift must be actually delivered to the donee to be effective. Delivery signifies that the donor gives up all ownership of his property and that he intends to part with dominion over it.

Although delivery is essential to a valid gift, the item need not always be manually transferred to the donee. Delivery can be irrevocable if the property is turned over to a third party with instructions to give it to the donee. Frequently an item, because of its size and location, is incapable of immediate transfer. In such instances, an irrevocable gift may be made by delivery of something that symbolizes dominion over the property, such as a key to an antique desk, a deed to a plot of land, or a passbook to a savings-account. A voluntary, uncompensated delivery with intent to give the recipient title, dominion, and control immediately constitutes a gift.

Most gifts are *inter vivos* gifts; that is, they are made during the lifetime of the donor and take effect immediately and irrevocably upon delivery of the property. A gift *causa mortis* is made when the donor, in contemplation of his death, delivers personal property to the donee with the intent that the donee shall own it if he (the donor) dies. This is a conditional gift and can be revoked by the donor. Where apprehension of death is not a factor, a gift is considered absolute.

CONFUSION

Confusion involves an intermingling of the goods of different owners where the goods of each owner retain their original form and characteristics but because of the intermingling can no longer be identified or separated. Confusion occurs most often in connection with so-called *fungible goods,* such as grain, hay, and similar property, which are of such a nature that one unit cannot be distinguished from another. Fungible goods are usually sold by weight or measure. When the fungible property of a number of owners is mixed (assuming no misconduct), the result is an undivided ownership of the total mass by the various owners. If the goods are all of the same kind and quality and the amounts contributed by each are known, each owns a proportionate share in the total mass. Should there be a loss, it too will be divided proportionately.

Confusion may exist when any goods belonging to different owners are so intermingled that they cannot be identified, separated, and returned to their respective owners. Such items as cattle, timber, or fowl are sometimes intermixed so as to constitute confusion of property.

Confusion of goods resulting from the misconduct of one of the parties causes title to the entire mass to pass temporarily to the innocent party or parties. If the wrongdoer is unable to show that his proportion of the total is of the same quality as the entire mass, he loses all interest. If it is of the same quality, the wrongdoer may claim his portion of the mass by presenting evidence of the amount added by him. These rules do not apply when the goods are (1) mixed by consent of the various owners, (2) mixed by accident, (3) able to be identified, or (4) of equal kind and quality.

ABANDONMENT OR LOSS

Property is said to be abandoned whenever possession is given up by the true owner who indicates by words or conduct that he has no intention of ever reclaiming it. Ownership of abandoned property may be assumed by the first person taking possession and control of it. The original owner cannot sue for conversion because it was his intention to give up all claims to the property. Since abandonment is a matter of intent, it must be determined by the jury upon consideration of all the circumstances.

Questions of abandonment are harder to resolve than questions of casual loss. Title to lost property remains with the true owner. However, until the true owner is found, the finder may keep the lost item, and his title is good against everyone except the true owner. To qualify as a finder, a person must have discovered the whereabouts of the goods in question and must have taken them into his possession. Conflicts sometimes arise when lost goods are discovered on property owned by someone other than the finder. Such disputes are usually resolved in favor of the finder because what was lost was possession, and the finder assumed possession. He does not assume the title, which was not lost. In the absence of a statutory requirement, the finder is not entitled to a reward.

Unclaimed property is said to be mislaid or misplaced when it was intentionally placed by the owner at a certain spot and his manner indicated that he intended to return for it. The owner of the premises upon which the property is left is entitled to hold it until the true owner is located. When property is left in a public place, the finder is entitled to possession.

SALE

Purchase is the most common way of acquiring ownership. In most cases, the sale and purchase of goods is regulated by the Uniform Commercial Code. Generally, the purchaser acquires no better title than that the seller had. Therefore, neither a person who innocently purchases stolen property from a thief nor any subsequent purchaser acquires any title because the thief had none. A purchaser of stolen goods acquires only possession of the property. (See Chapters on Sales 39-42).

WILLS AND INHERITANCE

A person may leave a will wherein he leaves his personal property to certain parties as bequests or legacies. When a person dies intestate, his personal property is passed on, or distributed, to the person or persons who are his next of kin by the operation of law. Property thus acquired is said to have been inherited. (See Chapter 51, Wills and Intestate Succession).

OPERATION OF LAW

Personal property may be sold pursuant to a court order—for example, at a tax sale or sale by a trustee in bankruptcy for the benefit of creditors. In this situation a judgment is had against the individual and his property is sold to pay the judgment. A judgment entered against personal property ordinarily has no effect upon the title unless the action was to determine title to the property.

LEGAL PRINCIPLES

The term "property" is used to designate both an object owned and rights or interests in the object.

Possession is the right to control a physical object. It may be actual or constructive.

Personal property is classified as chattels real and chattels personal.

Occupation is the taking and holding possession of ownerless property.

Copyrights and patents are designed to protect the original works of artists and authors.

Accession, in order to transfer title, must represent a significant increase in value.

A gift is an absolute transfer of property from one person to another without payment of compensation.

Confusion results when goods of different owners are so mixed that they cannot be identified and separated.

Property is abandoned when possession and title have been voluntarily relinquished by the true owner.

Property is mislaid when its whereabouts are forgotten by an owner who temporarily set it aside with the intention of reclaiming possession.

Generally, a purchaser acquires the same title to property as the seller held.

Title to property may be acquired as a bequest or by the operation of law.

CASE FOR REVIEW

IN RE ESTATE OF McDOWELL

345 N.Y.S.2d 828 (1973)

A hearing was held on April 11, 1973, in connection with the claim by the estate that a rocking chair, described as having principally sentimental value, was in the possession of Arthur C. McDowell. The executrix, who is the sister and co-beneficiary in the estate with Arthur C. McDowell, claimed that a rocking chair was removed from her father's living quarters and is presently in the possession of her brother and that it, in fact, belongs to the estate. It was conceded by Arthur C. McDowell that he did, in fact, have the chair. He claimed gift and admitted that he had removed the chair from the premises of the deceased on July 21, 1972, the day before his death. In support of this claim a son of claimant, presently in the United States Navy, stated that some years ago and prior to May of 1968 the deceased had told his father that he would give the chair to him and keep it in the family and that later, apparently in 1970 when he was on leave, that the decedent, the witness's grandfather, told Arthur McDowell, "You can have the chair." However, it remained in the apartment of the deceased until the day before his death.

The claimant's daughter testified that back in 1968 the decedent had told her father that he could have the chair and that on the second occasion, some six or seven months before the death of the decedent, he told her father, "Take it upstairs." Her father said that he did not have enough room and that he would leave it in the premises owned by the deceased. That is the only proof that was offered concerning the title to the rocking chair.

The burden of proving that a gift was made is upon the one asserting it, and such proof must be established by clear, convincing and satisfactory evidence. . . . Assuming this Court accepts the testimony of the claimant's daughter we would have, at best, an offer to remove the chair from the premises which was declined and the curious result that the chair was, in fact, moved almost immediately before the death of the decedent. The elements of gift are intent, delivery and acceptance. The element of delivery is the apparent stumbling block to a finding of gift in the case at bar, "To consummate a gift whether inter vivos or causa mortis, the property must be actually delivered and the donor must surrender the possession and dominion thereof to the donee." . . . Effective delivery must put the subject of the gift out of the Testator's possession and control.

Under all the circumstances claimant failed to prove an effective delivery, actual or constructive. It is to be noted that the subject of this controversy is a chair which is clearly identifiable but without any apparent value other than of a sentimental nature.

It is accordingly the decision of this Court that the claimant, Arthur C. McDowell, has failed to establish ownership to the rocking chair by reason of his alleged claim of gift and that title thereto belongs to the estate.

In view of the nature of the claim herein and in view of the circumstances developed upon the hearing herein the Court, as a part of this decision, . . . Directs that Mildred M. Hoover remain as executrix for an indefinite period of time and she is. . .Directed not to attempt to sell the chair to a third party and, since the property cannot reasonably be divided and/or sold that the use of the rocking chair be shared equally. Although it may sound strange, substantial justice would prevail if the respondent, Arthur C. McDowell, were to have the use of the chair up to and including July 1, 1973, on which date he is then directed to make the rocking chair available to the executrix, who will take possession of it until the end of December 1973. The executrix is then . . . Directed to return the chair to her brother for a six month period. This arrangement to continue unless terminated voluntarily between parties or until one or the other is deceased.

Since the chair has only nominal and/or sentimental value, it again would appear that substantial justice would prevail if on the death of either the brother or sister the chair becomes the sole property of the survivor thereof and such direction shall accordingly be contained in the order embracing this decision.

CASE PROBLEMS

1. The defendant was operating a subway railway. The plaintiff, while a passenger on the railway, saw a package on a seat opposite him left by a passenger who had alighted. He picked up the package, examined it and found no name or mark upon it. He had no idea who owned it. He disembarked at the first subsequent station stop, taking the package with him. He was about ten feet from the car when a railway guard touched him on the shoulder and said, "What are you going to do with that package?" He replied, "I am going to keep this and advertise for the owner." Forthwith the general trainmaster of the defendant, Mr. Blewitt, asked the same question, to which the passenger replied, "What authority have you?" and Blewitt stated, "I am the superintendent of this line." The plaintiff then said, "I guess that is immaterial. I am going to keep this package and advertise for the owner. I will give you my name and address." Blewitt said, "No, I don't want anything like that; either turn the package over to the railroad company or I will have you arrested." The plaintiff replied, "If you have made up your mind to do that, I will go with you to an officer." The plaintiff claimed the property was lost. Decide.

2. Sophia, a servant at Ham's hotel, found three $20 bills in the lobby. She told Ham, who said he thought that the money belonged to a salesman, a transient guest of the hotel. Sophia gave it to the proprietor to return to the salesman. It was afterward ascertained that the salesman had not lost the money, nor had anyone else claimed it. Sophia demanded the money be returned to her and, when Ham refused, brought an action to compel him to return it. Decide.

3. This was an action by Dolitsky against Savings Bank to recover $100 allegedly found by Dolitsky. Dolitsky rented a safe deposit box from the Savings Bank. The safe-deposit vault of the bank is in the basement and the vault area is walled off. Only box renters and officers and employees of the bank are admitted to this area. On November 7, 1971, Dolitsky requested access to her box and while she was in the booth and looking through an advertising folder which had been placed there by the bank she found a $100 bill. She turned the bill over to the attendant. Dolitsky waited one year. During that time no one made a claim for it. Dolitsky demanded that the bank surrender the bill to her alleging that she was entitled to the bill as finder. The bank claimed the bill was mislaid property and that it owed a duty to keep the bill for the rightful owner. Decide.

4. Richard Bunt and his wife, Rachel, had a joint checking account. Rachel claims to have deposited in the account more than $3500 of her separate funds. On October 28, 1965, Mr. Bunt, without his wife's knowledge, withdrew $8000 for the purchase of National Securities stock. The stock certificate was issued to "Richard H. Bunt & Marlys Fairbanks as Jt Wr of Surv & not as Tenants in Common." Until his death, Mr. Bunt received and retained the dividends therefrom. Marlys claimed the stock as donee by right of survivorship. Rachel brought this action to have herself declared the owner of the stock. Decide.

5. Hardy bought ten tickets from the YMCA for a lottery on a Buick. On one of the ticket stubs he wrote the name of his niece, Dixie Williams, a minor, then returned the stub to the center. Later he phoned the niece's mother to tell her that he had bought a chance for Dixie. The chance with Dixie's name won, and Hardy sued the YMCA, claiming that the Buick belonged to him. Decide.

6. When Burns' automobile, which was insured by Farm Bureau Insurance Company, was stolen, the insurance company paid him under the policy. The car was later found in the possession of Mosel, who had purchased it from a car dealer. The identity of the thief was never established, but both Mosel and the car dealer had acted in good faith. The thief had apparently installed a new engine; Mosel had also made additions to the car. The insurance company sued Mosel to recover the automobile. Decide.

7. Plaintiffs and defendant owned adjoining tracts of timberlands. In the winter of 1963 plaintiffs, mistaken as to the boundary of their land, cut from Mining Company's lands a quantity of wood, which they hauled to and piled on the bank of Portage Lake. Next spring Mining Company took possession of the wood, disposing of it for its own purposes. Plaintiffs brought suit for the value of their labor. It was not clearly shown in court whether Mining Company had knowledge of plaintiffs' activities at the time of the cutting and hauling. Decide.

8. Eaton brings an action of replevin to recover a fishing-boat foresail, which was made from a length of canvas that he had given to Hall. The canvas cost $40.63; it was shown that in making the sail Hall incurred additional expenses of about $10 for labor and from $5 to $8 for materials. Both had agreed at the outset that the sail was to be Eaton's property until Hall paid for the canvas. Hall never paid, and later sold the sail to Chase, who sold it to defendant. What are the rights in the foresail?

A contract whereby possession of personal property is surrendered by the owner for a particular purpose with provisions for its return upon completion of that purpose forms a bailment. Three conditions are essential to a bailment contract: (1) the bailor must retain title and ownership; (2) the bailee must have temporary possession and control of the property; and (3) the ultimate possession of the property must revert to the bailor, unless he orders it transferred to a third party.

A bailment relationship generally arises in one of two ways; first, when the owner surrenders articles of personal property to another for the purpose of having some service performed upon them; and second, when a person borrows or rents personal property from the owner in order to use it for his own purposes. Thus, leaving clothes with a dry cleaner, a car for a tune-up, or a television with a repairman create bailment relationships. The person receiving the surrendered property in these cases is assumed to be skilled and experienced in his profession and is expected to return the property upon completion of his service. A bailment relationship also exists when a man borrows his neighbor's lawn mower or rents a car for a business trip; the bailee is expected to take care of the property while it is in his possession. In either form of bailment contract, it is the voluntary delivery of the personal property by the owner to the second party that creates the bailment relationship.

BAILMENT DISTINGUISHED FROM A SALE

In both a bailment and a sale there is a transfer of possession of personal property according to an agreement. The difference between the two transactions lies in the fact that a sale implies a transfer of title, while in a bailment title to the goods remains with the bailor. If A transfers 1000 chickens to B on the condition that B is to give him 1000 chickens of like kind in three years, the transaction is a sale and not a bailment. Although the transaction appears similar to a bailment, it cannot be one because the goods originally transferred are not the same goods that will be transferred in three years. B can return any chickens of like kind and still fulfill the contract.

TYPES OF BAILMENTS

Bailments may be (1) for the sole benefit of the bailor, (2) for the sole benefit of the bailee, or (3) for the mutual benefit of bailor and bailee.

In a bailment for the sole benefit of the bailor, the bailee receives no compensation for the service he promises to render to the bailor's property.

He merely performs the service as a courtesy. (For example, a man may care for a neighbor's pet while the neighbor is on vacation.) However, his acceptance of possession of the property constitutes a form of contract; thus he is required to carry out his promise in a suitable manner. He is liable for any gross negligence or for any failure to exercise prudence in handling the property when he could have done so with little or no sacrifice on his part.

In a bailment for the sole benefit of the bailee, the bailor delivers his property to be used and returned by the bailee without expectation of compensation. (An example would be borrowing a neighbor's dog for a hunting trip.) The obligations of the bailee are greater in this case; he is required to exercise great care and is responsible for any loss incurred as a result of negligence. Included in the bailee's exercise of care is his obligation to ensure the proper return of the property as determined by the bailment agreement.

A mutual benefit bailment is an agreement by which one of the parties is given possession of the other's property for a specific purpose, to their mutual advantage. The bailor benefits from some service, while the bailee benefits from the compensation agreed upon, or vice versa. The bailee is responsible for any loss resulting from his neglect to exercise ordinary care, but not for losses that result in spite of such care, which are considered beyond his control. On the other hand if the property causes the bailee injury or loss while he is using it, the bailor is responsible. The law requires that the property be reasonably fit for service when it is presented to the bailee; if it is not, the bailor must notify the bailee of all known defects. Even where the bailor did not know of the defects, but through normal diligence should have been aware of them, he is responsible for any resultant injury. For example, a man who rents an automobile has a right to assume that it is free from defects and is usable as a means of transportation. (See Figure 55-1)

CONTRACTS RELIEVING LIABILITY

It is often desirable for bailees to make provisions in the bailment contract to protect themselves from any loss resulting from their negligence or the negligence of their employees. An ordinary private bailee (one whose services are not offered to the public at large but to certain persons only) may put any provision he wishes into the contract as long as the bailor is willing to accept the terms. If the provisions are not agreeable to him, the bailor is free to bargain or to contract with someone else whose terms are more satisfactory to him. However, where the provision relieving the bailee of liability would defeat the real purpose of the contract, it is unenforceable.

As a rule, a bailee who provides services to the general public may not contract to exempt himself from liability arising out of his own negligence. For example, the operator of a checkroom, a common carrier, or a parking lot operator may not relieve itself of liability arising from the negligence of any of its employees. A bailee may limit its liability for a loss or for damage to bailed goods that arises from specified causes or causes over which it has no control, but for such limitations to be effective, the bailor and bailee must mutually agree to them. Thus, the operator of a checkroom cannot limit his liability merely by printing limitations on the back of the tickets used in the checking

Figure 55-1

operation. It must be shown that the bailor was made aware of the limitations and had actual knowledge of them. (See Chapter 10 The Agreement). A parking lot, for example, may limit its liability to the auto itself, refusing responsibility for packages left in the car by posting notice of this fact in a prominent place within the lot. (See Figure 55-2)

DENIAL OF TITLE

Unless he has yielded possession to someone having a superior title, by accepting the bailed property, the bailee is estopped from denying the bailor's

Figure 55-2

title to it. He cannot retain possession of the property merely because he can prove the bailor does not hold title. Ownership is not a requirement of a bailment, merely possession. To keep the property from the bailor's possession, therefore, the bailee must show that he has turned it over to someone who has a better title or who is acting for the true owner. In fact, should a thief enter into a bailment relationship, the bailee must return the goods to the thief upon completion of the bailment. For example, if a thief takes a stolen coat to the cleaners, upon completion of the cleaning the coat must be returned to him in the absence of an asserted claim by the owner.

DUTIES OF THE BAILEE

The duties of the bailee are to exercise due care with respect to the article while it is in his possession and to surrender it to the bailor at the termination of the bailment. As long as he exercises the proper degree of care, he is not responsible for the loss of the article. If a tailor's shop is burned through no fault of the tailor and A's suit is destroyed, the tailor is not responsible to A for its value.

The value of the object and its nature also determine, to a certain extent, the degree of care that must be exercised by the bailee. Obviously, a work of art should be more carefully watched and protected than a commonplace item that has less intrinsic value and is easier to replace. Also, it matters little where an item is kept unless it is perishable, in which case it should be kept in proper storage.

The bailor and bailee can, in the contract, agree on specific terms regarding care and storage of the bailed goods and can thereby increase or decrease the responsibility of the bailee. If the contract is silent or if the bailee is a firm who deals with the general public, the previously mentioned requirements apply.

BREACH OF THE BAILMENT CONTRACT

A bailment is granted under specific conditions and for a certain purpose, as set forth in the bailment agreement. The bailee is bound to operate within the limitations of the agreement. If he exceeds or abuses the authority vested in him by the bailor in any way, he is absolutely liable for any damage, whether or not the damage resulted from his own actual negligence. When the bailee treats the property in other than the prescribed manner or uses it for other than the purpose specified in the contract, he is similarly liable for any resulting loss or damage.

RIGHTS OF THE BAILEE

One of the most important rights of the commercial bailee is a lien upon the property. He may retain possession until the bailor has performed his end of the contract. However, this right entitles the bailee only to the possession of the thing bailed; he can neither use it nor sell it unless the contract so provides.

Not all bailees can assert liens. The most common type of bailee who possesses a lien is an artisan, one who does some work on the object and thus increases its value. For example, a television repairman or a tailor possesses a lien on the property bailed. Persons who store articles for compensation such as warehousemen or garage owners, also have a lien on the property. A carrier who transports goods has a lien to enforce payment of freight charges. Statutes commonly give carriers, warehousemen, and other classes of public bailees the power to sell the object in order to enforce their lien.

RIGHTS OF THE BAILOR

The bailor can demand the surrender of the object held by the bailee upon the fulfillment of his obligations under the bailment contract. For example, if A, having stored an object with B, tenders to B the proper storage charges and B refuses to give up the article for some reason, A can assert that B has converted (assumed illegal possession of) the article and can sue him for its reasonable value.

TERMINATION

A bailment may be terminated in several ways. The conclusion of the bailment may be predetermined in the contract; it may be stipulated for a particular time or may be automatic upon fulfillment of a given condition. The contract may give the bailor the right to end the contract at any time by demanding the goods or by paying the bailee the amount due for his services.

A bailment is terminated by the operation of law if the property is lost or destroyed through no fault of the bailee. Death, insanity, or bankruptcy will end the relationship if it is thereby impossible for the bailee to perform his duties.

Finally, if either party violates the agreement, the injured party has the option of rescinding the bailment agreement and bringing suit for whatever damages resulted from the breach.

SPECIAL BAILMENTS

SAFE-DEPOSIT BOXES

In the rental of a safe-deposit box, the box and the property in the box remain in possession of the bank. This situation is somewhat complicated because neither party can gain access to the box without the other party's key. Also, although in possession of the bank, the bank has no knowledge or control over the contents of the box. Courts do not agree on the exact nature of the relationship, however, there is considerable opinion that it is a bailment situation.

COMMON CARRIER

A common carrier holds himself out to transport for a fee, the property of anyone who desires to employ him. The carrier, as bailee, is the insurer of the property he carries for others. This liability begins when goods are delivered to and accepted by the carrier. The only exception is if the damage is caused by an act beyond his control, such as by an act of God, a public enemy, or if the damage is caused by the nature of the goods. Liability terminates after the carrier has fulfilled his contract of carriage. U.C.C. Section 7-307 gives the carrier a possessory lien on the goods in his possession.

INNKEEPERS

The owner of a hotel or motel holds himself out to provide food and lodging to travelers. Although the guest does not give up possession of his property, the owner is the insurer of that property. Acts over which he has no control, as in the case of the common carrier, limit this liability. Several states have enacted legislation which also limits the strict liability standard.

WAREHOUSEMAN

A warehouseman holds himself out to the general public to store, for a fee, goods for parties desiring to negotiate with him. U.C.C. Section 7-204 provides that the warehouseman is under a duty to exercise that degree of care "a reasonably careful man would exercise under like circumstances." Liability is determined by the agreed valuation clauses in the warehouse receipt. The Code also provides that increased rates may be charged based on increased valuation and that the bailor has the right to demand an increase in the agreed valuation. The warehouseman is not an insurer of the goods. However, U.C.C. Section 7-203 imposes a duty on the warehouseman to deliver goods which are in conformity with the description in the warehouse receipt or to answer in damages. Where the contents of the packages are unknown, the warehouseman must note this fact in a conspicuous manner on the warehouse receipt. The obligation of the warehouseman begins when he assumes control of the goods and ceases when he delivers the goods to the proper person. The warehouseman may terminate storage under Section 7-206, which cannot take effect less than thirty days after he notifies the bailor. He may sell the goods if they are not removed upon proper termination of the storage under Section 7-210.

LEGAL PRINCIPLES

A bailment is a contract whereby possession of personal property is surrendered by the owner with provision for its return upon the completion of the purpose of the agreement.

The difference between a sale and a bailment is that a sale involves transfer of both title and possession, whereas a bailment is a transfer of possession only.

Bailments may be (1) for the sole benefit of the bailor, (2) for the sole benefit of the bailee, or (3) for mutual benefit.

A private bailee may contract away the results of its negligence, whereas a public bailee may merely limit its liability.

What constitutes due care is determined by the nature of the bailment and the value of the object bailed.

The mutual benefit bailment gives the bailee a lien on the property bailed.

The bailor can demand the surrender of the goods held by the bailee upon fulfillment of his contract.

CASE FOR REVIEW

SAMPLES v. GEARY

292 S.W. 1066 (1927)

This is an action in damages for the loss of a fur piece alleged to have been owned by the plaintiff. . . . The record shows defendant, Geary, was operating dancing school at 3032 Prospect Avenue in Kansas City, Mo., and on the evening of March 29, 1924, plaintiff, with two young women companions, attended. Upon arrival each paid the sum of 50 cents, of which 40 cents was for the wraps. Plaintiff testified at the trial in the circuit court that she was the owner of a certain fur piece, which was worn that night by Elsie Miller, one of her companions; that each of the young women was given a cardboard check for presentation at the checking window with the articles they desired to check. These checks were taken up by the young man in charge of the checking room and claim checks given therefor. The articles so received were then placed in wooden boxes or shelves, arranged along the inner walls of the checking room, each box having a number corresponding to the number of the claim check issued.

Plaintiff testified that Miss Miller placed the fur piece in her coat, folded the coat with the fur inside, put her hat on the bundle, surrendered her checking slip to the check boy, and received a claim check. In these statements plaintiff was corroborated by Elsie Miller and Esther McCullough, her companions on the occasion in question and who testified in her behalf. When they were ready to leave the hall, Miss Miller presented her claim check to the boy and received in return her coat and hat, but the fur piece was missing.

Payment for the fur was demanded of defendant but was refused, and this suit followed. The defense was that defendant did not receive the fur piece, but if it was received it was concealed from the view of the check boy and was not actually delivered and checked as a loose article and a separate check issued therefor, after the custom of defendant's dancing school; that no additional charge was made for such separate check. . . .

The term "bailment" has been variously defined. . . . The term signifies a contract resulting from the delivery of goods by bailor to bailee on condition that they be restored to the bailor, according to his directions, so soon as the purposes for which they were bailed are answered. . . .

"The law is well settled that in order to constitute such bailment, the parties must have intended that there should be a return or delivery of the identical thing bailed." [*Coleman* v. *Lipscombe*, 18 Mo.App. 447.]

Defendant argues that the only articles bailed were the hat and coat; that the fur piece was not delivered for the reason that it was concealed and completely hidden in the coat, according to plaintiff's testimony, and could not have been seen or detected.

Under this showing, we think the position of defendant that there was no legal delivery and acceptance of the fur piece is correct.

. . . "The party who is sought to be charged as bailee must accept the property, because the relation is founded upon contract, and the duty and liability springing therefrom cannot be thrust upon one without his knowledge or consent." [*Bertig Bros.* v. *Norman*, 101 Ark. 75, 81]

Since the relation of bailee and bailor is founded upon contract, there must be a meeting of minds to make the contract valid. In this case, the fur piece being concealed, the bailee did not know it was there, the minds of the parties did not meet, and there was no acceptance by defendant of the article in question.

CASE PROBLEMS

1. Weinberg was a holder of a "Parkcard" issued by Wayco for which he paid $10.50 per month and which entitled him to park his automobile at Wayco's garage. Entrance to the garage was gained by inserting the "Parkcard" into a slot causing the entrance gate to open. After securing admission to the garage with the Parkcard, Weinberg parked his own car, locked it, and took the keys with him. When he returned to his automobile in the evening of September 27, he found it had been broken into and certain personal property stolen. The automobile had not been moved. He alleged responsibility on the part of the garage. Decide.

2. Plaintiff took her auto for repairs to Fox Sales, located in the industrial section of the city and bounded on two sides by railroad yards. The rear of Fox's shop was out of the sight and hearing of passers-by. The two rear doors were secured nightly by padlocks. Because vandals had been breaking windows and stealing equipment, Fox also employed a night watchman, but he often failed to report for duty. On one of the nights when the watchman was absent, a thief broke the locks on the two rear doors and stole plaintiff's car. It was later found in a damaged condition, and plaintiff sued Fox for the damages. Decide.
3. The plaintiff was a guest at a luncheon held at the defendant's hotel. She hung her mink jacket in an unattended cloakroom on the main floor across from the lobby desk. After the luncheon and ensuing party, the plaintiff went to the cloakroom to retrieve her jacket and discovered it was gone. She brought an action against the hotel for the cost of a new coat. Decide.
4. Plaintiff placed $10,000 in a safe-deposit box that she had rented from defendant company. In consequence of the company's negligence, the money was stolen. Plaintiff asked for a judgment for the $10,000 loss, with interest and costs. Decide.
5. Plaintiff stored certain household furniture with defendant, who later, without the knowledge or consent of plaintiff, moved his storage business to a new location nearby. At the new location the goods were destroyed by fire, no question of negligence being involved. Plaintiff brought an action to recover the value of the furniture. Decide.
6. Allen checked his traveling bag at the parcel checking room of the Pacific Company in the Union Station at Portland, Oregon. When he presented his claim check for its return, it could not be found. At the time the bag was checked Pacific gave Allen a claim check which had printed on one side the following:

> Notice—Liability for loss of, damage or delay to any parcel limited to not to exceed $25.00 unless at time of deposit value is declared and paid for at the rate of 10 cents for each $25.00 or fraction thereof for thirty days or less. No parcel valued in excess of $250.00 will be accepted.

On the reverse side was printed:

> Date and time of delivery.
> For Excess Liability See Notice on Opposite Side.

There was also posted a sign at this parcel room to the same effect as the printing on the check. Allen claimed that since his attention was not called to the limitations, he was not bound by them. Decide.
7. Welge owned a sofa and chair that Baena agreed to reupholster. The work was not done according to the agreement, and Welge refused to accept the finished furniture on the ground that it no longer had any value to him. Baena sued for the contract price; Welge filed a counterclaim for the value of the furniture. Decide.
8. Fishermen's clothing and provisions, stored in a locked compartment, were allegedly stolen from a fishing vessel left by plaintiff in defendant's shipyard for repairs. An action was brought to recover the value of the items stolen. Decide.

PART IX
FINANCIAL TRANSACTIONS

A secured transaction usually involves the lending of money and the placing of some form of collateral with the lender to ensure that the money is repaid on the due date. Pre-code devices to effect secured transactions varied and were fashioned primarily on the idea of legal title or possession of the collateral by the lender. Court decisions were based largely on the form of the instrument used. The recording statutes designed to give the public notice of the security arrangement varied from state to state. Prior to the adoption of the U.C.C., secured creditors were subject to many risks due to legal technicalities as well as to differences in the law. The U.C.C. replaced the pledge, chattel mortgage, conditional sale, factor's lien, and other devices intended as security with a single device known as a *security interest.*

A security interest results from the execution by the parties of a document called a *security agreement,* which *vests in the creditor security rights in the personal property and fixtures of the debtor* covered therein (U.C.C. 9-102) (Goods, documents, negotiable instruments, general intangibles, chattel rights, and chattel paper are frequently listed items.) The parties to the agreement are the debtor who is giving the security interest and the secured party in whose favor the interest is. The debtor's property, as listed in the security agreement, is the collateral for the arrangement, and the creditor may collect his debt out of such property in the event of nonpayment. For example, if Albert borrows $1500 from the Last National Bank and uses his automobile as security for the loan, Albert (the debtor) has entered into a security agreement with the Last National Bank (the secured party); the automobile is the collateral that can be claimed by the bank if the debt is not paid when it becomes due.

The Code applies to any transaction, regardless of its form, that is intended to create a security interest. Its approach is largely functional. The primary test is the intention of the parties to create a security arrangement and the purpose served by the security interest in the transaction.

THE SECURITY AGREEMENT

The security agreement must be in writing, unless the security arrangement is a possessory one and the secured party is in possession of the collateral. The formal requirements are minimal; tthe agreement must be signed by the debtor and must contain a description of the collateral. In addition, when the security interest covers crops, or when it covers oil, gas, or minerals to be extracted or timber to be cut, a description of the land concerned must be included. Aside from these basic features, the agreement may include any provision that the parties deem necessary to the transaction. (U.C.C. 9-203) The standard form of pre-code security arrangements (the chattel mortgage or conditional sales contract) is considered sufficient to satisfy the requirements of the Code for a valid security agreement, which is really nothing more than a basic loan or sale agreement between the secured party and the debtor. (See Figure 56-1)

● ● ● ● ● ● ● ● ● ● ● ● ● ● ● ● ● ● ●

FIRST NATIONAL BANK OF AKRON   ORIGINAL

SECURITY AGREEMENT

Date_____, 19____

Debtor_____ Secured Party_____
      (Purchaser)   (Seller)

Address of Debtor_____
      (Street and City)   (County)   (State)

Secured Party does hereby sell and convey to Debtor the following described property, hereinafter referred to as "Chattel(s)", to wit:

Manufacturer	Description of Article Sold	New or Used	Model No.	Serial No.	Cash Price

After thorough examination, I hereby buy and accept delivery of the fore-going chattels to be kept and/or installed at the above address and I will pay you therefor the total of payments provided herein.

For valuable consideration, and as security for the total of payments, evidenced by my (our) note, I hereby give a security interest in the above described chattels to you, irrespective of any retaking or re-delivery thereof or the granting of any renewals or extension of said note.

Except as hereinafter provided Debtor shall remain in quiet and peaceable possession of Chattel(s).

Debtor does hereby covenant and agree that any and all equipment, accessories and parts now or hereafter attached or added to Chattel(s) shall at once by accession become a part thereof and of this grant; that Secured Party may correct patent errors herein; that any notice to Debtor shall be sufficiently given if mailed to Debtor's said address; that Chattel(s) shall remain personal property and shall not become a part of the realty no matter how annexed thereto; that said note and this Security Agreement contain the entire agreement and no oral agreement shall be binding. In the event of any default in the payment of any installment when due on said note, or if Debtor misuses, abuses, sells, or attempts to sell, secretes or attempts to secrete, encumber or attempts to encumber, removes or attempts to remove Chattel(s) from said County; or if Secured Party shall for any reason deem said indebtedness insecure then the Secured Party may at its option and without notice, elect to treat the balance unpaid on said note immediately due and payable, whereupon Debtor agrees, upon demand, to deliver Chattel(s) to Secured Party and Secured Party may without notice or demand, with or without the aid of legal process, make use of such force as may be necessary to enter upon, with or without breaking into any premises where the Chattel(s) may be found, and take possession thereof and sell and dispose of the same together with Debtor's equity or redemption at such place or places and at such time or times as Secured Party may deem advisable, at public auction or private sale, at the option of the Secured Party without demand or notice or advertisement, the same being hereby expressly waived, at which sale, if public, Secured Party may purchase Chattel(s) and such sale, whether public or private, shall be conclusively deemed a proper sale, and apply the proceeds after deducting all expenses in connection therewith to the payment of said note, returning the overplus, if any, to Debtor. Debtor waives all claims, damages, and demands upon Secured Party arising out of the repossession, retention, reparation and sale of the aforesaid. Any purchaser hereof and of said note will take same free from any defenses thereto and or claims, demands and setoffs of Debtor against Secured Party.

If Debtor shall well and truly pay the said note according to its tenor and shall keep and perform the covenants and agreements contained herein according to the true intent and meaning thereof, then this Security Agreement shall be terminated, otherwise the same shall be and remain in full force and virtue in law.

If the Debtor wishes to satisfy in full this contract before final maturity, he shall receive a partial refund of the finance charge, based on the rule of 78's, after deduction of a $10.00 acquisition charge. When the amount of the refund is less than $1.00 no refund will be made.

A "late charge" (five (5) cents per $1.00, maximum $3.00) will be assessed on any payment more than ten (10) days past due.

This Security Agreement shall be binding upon the Debtor, his heirs, executors, administrators, successors and assigns and shall inure to the benefit of the Secured Party, its heirs, executors, administrators, successors and assigns.

Debtor acknowledges receipt of a true copy of this Security Agreement.

1. Cash Price	$_____
2. Less: Cash Down Payment ....$_____	
3. Trade-in ....$_____	
4. Total Down Payment...........	$_____
Description of Trade-in	
5. Unpaid Balance of Cash Price	$_____
6. Other charges	
	$_____
7. Amount Financed	$_____
8. **FINANCE CHARGE**	$_____
9. Total of Payments	$_____
10. Deferred Payment Price (1+6+8)	$_____
11. **ANNUAL PERCENTAGE RATE**	_____%

Total of payments is:

Payable in_____consecutive monthly installments of ...... $_____
each, except the last installment shall be .... $_____
First Installment Due _____, 19____

Purchaser(s)

Witness_____

Witness_____   _____
RETAIL APPLIANCE SECURITY AGREEMENT

THIS INSTRUMENT WAS PREPARED BY _____

BUYER'S RIGHT TO CANCEL

YOU MAY CANCEL THIS AGREEMENT OR PURCHASE BY MAILING A WRITTEN NOTICE TO THE SELLER POSTMARKED NOT LATER THAN MIDNIGHT OF THE THIRD BUSINESS DAY AFTER THE DATE THIS AGREEMENT WAS SIGNED. YOU MAY USE THIS PAGE AS THAT NOTICE BY WRITING "I HEREBY CANCEL" AT THE BOTTOM AND ADDING YOUR NAME AND ADDRESS. THIS NOTICE MUST BE MAILED TO:

Form 955

Figure 56-1

COLLATERAL

Collateral may be classified as tangible personal property, intangible personal property, or property representative of a legal obligation. Due to the myriad legal problems that crop up where intangible and representative property is involved, of concern primarily to the practicing attorney, our discussion will center on tangible property.

The Code established four categories of tangible property; consumer goods, equipment, farm products, and inventory. (U.C.C. 9-109).

Consumer goods are those used or bought primarily for personal, family, or household use.

Equipment consists of tangible personal property that is used or bought for use primarily in a business, in farming, in a profession, in a nonprofit organization, or in a governmental agency. (Into this classification also fall all goods not included in the categories of inventory, farm products, or consumer goods.)

Farm products include crops or livestock used or produced in farming operations and the products of crops or livestock in their unmanufactured state, if they are in the possession of a debtor who is engaged in farming operations. Neither equipment nor inventory may be included in this category.

Inventory consists of tangible personal property that is held by a person for sale or lease or to be furnished under a contract of service, whether the goods be raw materials, work in process, or materials used or consumed in a business. The inventory of a debtor cannot be classified as equipment.

An item of tangible personal property is properly classified on the basis of its nature and intended use by the debtor. For example, a refrigerator in a dealer's store is inventory; when used in a home, it is a consumer good; when used by a doctor to store medicine, it is equipment. Sheep raised by a farmer are considered farm products, whereas the wool in the hands of a manufacturer is considered inventory. For a proper classification it is necessary for the secured party to know the intended use of the goods and to make certain that the actual use coincides with the intended use.

ATTACHMENT

Attachment is the process whereby the lender acquires an interest in the property of the debtor and qualifies as a secured party. It is necessary to the creation of a security interest; a purported interest does not exist unless it attaches to specific collateral. The secured party may create a security interest, yet he may not acquire rights in the debtor's property. The Code, Sec. 9-204, gives the following prerequisites for attachment of a security interest: (1) an agreement that it attach must be executed; (2) the secured party must have given value to the debtor; and (3) the debtor must have acquired legal or equitable rights in the collateral. It is not necessary that these events occur in any special order.

According to the Code, Sec. 1-201(44), a person gives "value" for rights if he acquires them

    (a) in return for a binding commitment to extend credit or for the extension of immediately available credit. . .;
    (b) as security for or in total or partial satisfaction of a pre-existing claim; or
    (c) by accepting delivery pursuant to a per-existing contract for purchase; or
    (d) generally, in return for any consideration sufficient to support a simple contract.

In other words, giving value means that the lender either gives up something or legally commits himself to do so.

A debtor acquires rights in collateral when the collateral has potential existence or is the specific property of the debtor. For example, he has no rights in fish until they are caught, crops until they are planted, or timber until it is cut. Therefore, the secured party's interest will not attach until there exists actual property for the debtor to have acquired rights in as either the legal or the equitable owner.

FUTURE ADVANCES

The Code provides that a security agreement may be drafted to include a provision covering future advances of funds. In fact, the financing statement may include any past, present, or future indebtedness that is to be incurred by the debtor. The security interest will attach when value is given by the secured party. (U.C.C. 9-204)

AFTER-ACQUIRED PROPERTY

A security agreement may provide that collateral, whenever acquired, shall secure all obligations covered by the agreement. Where such a claim is made part of the agreement, a security interest attaches in favor of the secured party as soon as the debtor acquires legal or equitable rights in additional property. For example, on July 1, a financial institution may lend $5000 to a retail store owner and take a security interest not only on the debtor's inventory as of July 1 but on all subsequent inventory. The security interest protects the loan of $5000, because the inventory in the store at any one time stands as security for whatever is due at that time. This allows the debtor to continue to carry on business without impairing the security interest of the lender. The Code, Sec. 9-204, limits the use of the after-acquired property clause by not allowing a security interest to attach to crops that become such more than one year after the execution of the security agreement or to consumer goods that are given as additional security unless the debtor acquires rights in them within ten days after the secured party gives value. In this latter situation, if the security agreement covers an electric range and all other goods bought by the debtor after the execution of the agreement, the security interest will attach only to such additional goods as the debtor acquires within ten days after the secured party gives the original value. Likewise, a security interest in after-acquired property may be defeated if the debtor acquires property subject to a purchase money security agreement.

"FLOATING LIENS"

There are certain situations in which it is necessary for the debtor to have absolute control over the collateral. For example, there are numerous sales in which no actual security is given: the sales are merely entered as accounts receivable. The debtor also has control over the collateral where inventory is the subject of a secured transaction. In other words, it may be necessary that the debtor have the right to use, sell, or otherwise dispose of the collateral without disturbing the lien of the secured party. This "floating lien" concept is made possible by the after-acquired property clause and a statement in the Code allowing the debtor to use, commingle, or dispose of all or part of the collateral in these circumstances. Therefore, the amount of the debt and the actual collateral are constantly changing where the security agreement contains an after-acquired property clause and a provision for future advances of money. (By revised U.C.C. 9-203 (3) proceeds are automatically covered unless specifically excluded).

There are, of course, risks inherent in inventory financing under the floating-lien concept. The good-faith purchaser in the regular course of a business transaction will purchase property free from the secured party's interest in the collateral. Likewise, a purchase money security interest has priority over the secured party's interest in inventory.

LEGAL PRINCIPLES

The U.C.C. replaces all previous security devices with the concept of the "security interest."

Whether an arrangement creates a security interest is determined by the intention of the parties.

The security agreement must be signed by the debtor and must contain a description of the collateral.

Tangible goods are classified as consumer goods, equipment, farm products, or inventory. A proper classification is determined on the basis of the nature of the goods and their intended use by the debtor.

Attachment is the process whereby the lender acquires an interest in the property of the debtor and qualifies as a secured party.

Attachment relates to the creation of the security interest and its attachment to the collateral. For the lender to acquire an interest in the property of the debtor, there must be an agreement, the secured party must give value to the debtor, and the debtor must have a legal or equitable interest in the property covered by the security interest.

Future advances of funds and "after-acquired" property may be included in the security agreement.

The "floating lien" concept is useful in financing inventory, since it allows the debtor to use the property without disturbing the lien of the secured party.

CASE FOR REVIEW

IN RE UNITED THRIFT STORES, INC.

242 F. Supp. 714 (1965)

Redisco is a subsidiary of American Motors Corporation, and is engaged in the business of financing Kelvinator electric home appliances sold to distributors by the American Motors Sales Corporation. United Thrift was engaged in the business of buying Kelvinator and other brand appliances, and selling them to retail dealers.

On March 12, 1963, a financing statement, pursuant to the Uniform Commercial Code N.J.S.A. 12A:1—101 et seq., was filed with the Secretary of State of New Jersey. This statement covered "[i]nventory of Kelvinator appliances and products including Kelvinator refrigerators, washers, dryers, freezers, and other Kelvinator gas and electrical applicances."United Thrift was named as debtor, and Redisco as the secured party. Proceeds of collateral were also noted as being covered. There is no indication of termination of financing on the statement before the Court.

On March 22, 1963, the Secretary of State certified that he had searched his files under the Uniform Commercial Code, and found four previously recorded, secured parties for United Thrift as debtor. Redisco thereupon duly sent notices, informing the other secured party that it "has or expects to acquire a purchase money security interest in inventory of Kelvinator electrical and gas appliances . . . which [it] . . . will from time to time deliver or cause to be delivered to United Thrift. . . ."

Four separate agreements were thereafter entered into between the Kelvinator Division of the American Motors Sales Corporation, United Thrift, and Redisco. These agreements, on identical printed forms prepared by Redisco, are entitled "Redisco Wholesale Floor Plan." Each agreement contains three sections, as follows: (1) a bill of sale from the Kelvinator Division to Redisco for the articles listed by model and serial numbers; (2) a trust receipt from United Thrift to Redisco, covering the same articles and setting forth a release amount opposite each item; and (3) a signed, but incompleted, promissory note from United Thrift to Redisco, which bears the same identification number as the trust receipt.

In the section labeled "trust receipt", United Thrift acknowledges the receipt of the listed appliances, acknowledges that they are the property of Redisco and will be returned to Redisco on demand, and agrees "not to sell, loan, deliver, pledge, mortgage, or otherwise dispose of said articles to any other person until after payment of amounts shown in Release Amount column below." The trust receipts do not indicate thereon that any payments have been made, or any appliances released, pursuant thereto.

The trust receipts also provide that the total release amounts are the "Amount of Promissory Note," A portion of the trust receipts further provides for terms of payment in either 90 days or one-third in 30, 60 and 90 days.

. . . This Court will address itself only to the question of whether Redisco has a valid security interest. . . .

The term "security agreement", which is defined in N.J.S.A. § 12A:9—105(1) (h)as "an agreement which creates or provides for a security interest", is used in the Code in place of such terms as "trust receipt." A "security interest" is defined under N.J.S.A. § 12A:1—201(37) as an interest in personal property which secures payment of an obligation. Finally, N.J.S.A. § 12A:9—201 provides that "a security agreement is effective according to its terms between the parties . . . and against creditors."

The four trust receipts in this case meet the requirements of N.J.S.A. § 12A:9—203(1)(b) for a valid security agreement since they are written agreements signed by United Thrift, grant security interest in collateral, and contain a description of said collateral. The financing statement between Redisco and United Thrift also meets the filing requirements in N.J.S.A. § 12A:9—401 et seq. Pursuant to N.J.S.A. § 12A:9—201 (1), the security interest herein attached when the agreements were made, value was given, and United Thrift received possession of the collateral. Under N.J.S.A. § 12A:9—302 and N.J.S.A. § 12A:9—303 (1), said security interests were perfected when they attached.

The financing statement in this case between Redisco and United Thrift was executed and filed prior to the making of the security agreements. . . . N.J.S.A. § 12A:9—402(1) provides that "[a] financing statement may be filed before a security agreement is made or a security interest otherwise attaches." Under N.J.S.A. § 12A:9—303(1), where the financing statement is filed before the security interest attaches, the security interest is perfected when it does so attach. Thus, the Code clearly contemplates that the financing statement may be filed prior to the making of the security agreement, and that a security interest need not be in existence at the the financing statement is filed. . . .

However, the Code contains no requirements with regard to method of payment affecting the validity of a security interest. . . . In fact, N.J.S.A. § 12A:9—205 provides that a "security interest is not invalid . . . by reason of the failure of the secured party to require the debtor to account for proceeds or replace collateral." Thus, under the Code, payment is not relevant to the question of validity of a security interest, and there is no requirement of "policing" of collateral by the secured party.

Moreover, this Court does not agree that payment of release amounts and payment on 30-60-90 day terms are contradictory methods of payment. The only testimony in this case regarding payment was given by James K. Marlowe, the authorized, agent of Redisco in this matter, who was the sole witness at the hearing. He testified that each term payment was applied to reduce the total indebtedness of the particular trust receipt, and not to release particular appliances. Thus, the release amount of each appliance was reduced proportionately by the term payments that were received, but no single appliance was released because none of the trust receipts was fully paid. Redisco's security interest in the collateral was thereby protected while any part of the total indebtedness on each agreement remained unpaid.

Since Redisco's security interests are valid under the Code, and since United Thrift is in default by reason of its failure to make payments as provided in the security agreements, Redisco is entitled to take possession of the collateral, or to obtain the proceeds thereof.

CASE PROBLEMS

1. Burroughs had leased to Electric a standard machine for a term of two years. In the lease a list price of the machine was established and a monthly rental was set. The lease contained a purchase option provision granting Electric the right to purchase the machine at the list price during the term of the lease. During that time Electric went bankrupt. Trustee claimed this was a secured transaction. Decide.

2. The defendant purchased a Chevrolet pickup truck from the plaintiff who retained a purchase money security interest in the collateral. The defendant indicated that he intended to use the truck in his business. In point of fact, he had never used it in business, but only for his own purposes. The trustee in bankruptcy claimed the collateral was improperly classified as business equipment. Decide.

3. In the description on a security agreement, the collateral was described as "One (1) 1967 Dodge, 6 cyl. D-100 pickup, serial #1161-702080." Everything was correct except the last digit, which should have been eight and not zero. Defendant claimed the security agreement was fatally defective. Decide.

4. Anderson Cadillac, Inc., a dealer, purchased new automobiles from the manufacturer and gave the bank a security interest. Were the automobiles consumer goods? If Anderson operated a car-rental service, would the cars be classified as consumer goods?

5. Minneapolis-Moline Company gave Shepler a dealer's franchise to sell its farm equipment. If the equipment were the subject of a later security agreement, how would the collateral be classified?

6. U.G.I. sold a "one-household laundry dryer" to Henry by a sales agreement in the form of a lease, under which title was retained by U.G.I. until all installments were paid. Henry later sold the dryer to McFalls, a dealer in used appliances, for resale. If the dryer subsequently becomes the subject of security interest, how should the collateral be classified?

7. Trust Company filed a financing statement that contained the following provision: "The financing statement covers the following types of property. All present and future accounts receivable submitted." The debtor subsequently went bankrupt. Trustee contended that provision does not cover after-acquired property. Decide.

8. Girard Bank financed the purchase of new cars by Lepley Ford, Inc., an automobile dealer. A security agreement was executed between the bank and the dealer covering "all cars purchased by Lepley," and proper filing made. The dealer later sold the cars purchased as the result of this transaction, buying other cars with the proceeds. When Lepley became insolvent, Girard claimed it was entitled to a security interest in the subsequently-purchased cars that were in the hands of Lepley's receiver. The receiver contended that the right of the bank did not go beyond the cash proceeds and was lost once the proceeds were spent in any way. Decide.

The rights and liabilities of the paries in relation to collateral are established by the security interest that attaches to the collateral. This, however, does not afford any protection to the secured party in relation to other creditors of the debtor, subsequent security interests, or possible claims in bankruptcy. To protect himself from the claims of subsequent parties, the secured party must "perfect" his interest; that is, he must make his interest immune to attacks by lien creditors who are without knowledge of it and also make it enforceable against subsequent purchasers of the property.

A security interest in personal property or fixtures may be perfected when (1) a financing statement has been filed, (2) the secured party has assumed possession of the collateral, or (3) there is attachment of the security interest. (U.C.C. 9-303(1)) The concept of perfection is based on the assumption that if the proper steps are taken, proper notice has been given to anyone who may be transacting business with the debtor that the secured party has a security interest in the collateral.

FILING

The usual method of perfecting a security interest is by filing a financing statement in the proper place, ordinarily a central location within the state or county. (U.C.C. 9-401) A financing statement is a document signed by both the debtor and the secured party that contains an address of the secured party from which information concerning the security interest may be obtained, a mailing address of the debtor, and a statement indicating the types of collateral or describing the items included. Its function is to alert the public to the possible existence of a security interest in the collateral. When the financing statement covers crops growing or to be grown or goods that are or will become fixtures by being attached to real property, the statement must also contain a description of the real estate concerned. A copy of the security agreement is sufficient as a financing statement if it contains the necessary information, is signed by both parties, and contains the addresses of both parties.

Generally, a financing statement will not include a maturity date. Where a date is included, however, perfection continues for sixty days after maturity. The Code, Sec. 9—403, states that in the absence of a maturity date, the filing of a financing statement for the purpose of perfecting a security interest is effective for five years from the date of filing and may be renewed for another five years by the filing of a continuation statement signed by the secured party. (A proposed 1972 amendment would make financing statements effective for

5 years unless renewed before it lapses.) Therefore, perfection may continue indefinitely by a proper filing of continuation statements. However, the Code provides for the filing of a termination statement whenever there is no outstanding secured obligation and no commitment to make advances. Where the secured party fails to send in a termination statement within ten days after the debtor demands it, the secured party is liable to the debtor for one hundred dollars, plus any losses caused to the debtor as a result of such failure. (See Figure 57-1)

89070 • COLUMBUS BANK NOTE CO., DUBLIN, OHIO 43017

UNIFORM COMMERCIAL CODE — FINANCING STATEMENT — FORM UCC-2

INSTRUCTIONS
1. This form is designed to avoid double typing when filing with more than one office. Place this form over Form UCC-1.
2. PLEASE TYPE this form. Fold only along perforation for mailing.
3. Send all 3 copies with interleaved carbon paper to the filing officer. Enclose filing fee.
4. If the space provided for any item(s) on the form is inadequate the item(s) should be continued on additional sheets, preferably 5" x 8" or 8" x 10". Only one copy of such additional sheets need be presented to the filing officer with a set of three copies of the financing statement. Long schedules of collateral, indentures, etc., may be on any size paper that is convenient for the secured party.
5. If collateral is crops or goods which are or are to become fixtures, describe generally the real estate and give name of record owner.
6. When a copy of the security agreement is used as a financing statement it is requested that it be accompanied by a completed but unsigned set of these forms, without extra fee.
7. At the time of original filing, filing officer will return third copy as an acknowledgement. At a later date, secured party may date and sign the termination legend and use third copy as a Termination Statement.

This FINANCING STATEMENT is presented to a filing officer for filing pursuant to the Uniform Commercial Code   3 Maturity date (if any):

1 Debtor(s) (Last Name First) and address(es)	2 Secured Party(ies) and address(es)	For Filing Officer (Date, Time, Number, and Filing Office)
	FIRST NATIONAL BANK OF AKRON 106 SOUTH MAIN STREET AKRON, OHIO 44308	

4 This financing statement covers the following types (or items) of property:

Check ☒ if covered: ☐ Proceeds of Collateral are also covered ☐ Products of Collateral are also covered No. of additonal sheets presented:

Filed with:

FIRST NATIONAL BANK OF AKRON — AKRON, OHIO

By: .... Signature(s) of Debtor(s)   By: .... Signature(s) of Secured Party(ies)

Filing Officer Copy - Alphabetical   *This form of financing statement is approved by the Secretary of State.*
STANDARD FORM — UNIFORM COMMERCIAL CODE — FORM UCC-2   COLUMBUS BANK NOTE CO., DUBLIN, OHIO

Figure 57-1

Filing is required in the case of all tangible property. The Code, Sec. 9—401, allows three methods of filing: a central filing system in the office of a named state official, usually the secretary of state; a local filing system in the county where the goods are located; or a combination of these systems. Better business practice would dictate filing both locally and centrally whenever practical.

The place of filing is dictated by the nature of the goods and their intended use by the debtor. For example, a security interest in fixtures would be filed at the same place as a mortgage on the real estate concerned would be filed or recorded.[1] When the business is statewide, a security interest should be filed in the county where the principal place of business is located and in the office of the secretary of state. A filing that is made in the proper place continues effective even though the debtor's residence or place of business or the location of the collateral or its use, whichever of these controlled the original filing, is thereafter changed. A filing which is made in good faith in the wrong place or in only one place when dual filing is required will be effective with regard to that collateral as against any person who has knowledge of the contents of the financing statement (U.C.C. 9-401(2))

POSSESSION

A security interest in letters of credit, goods, instruments, negotiable documents, or chattel paper may be perfected by the secured party's taking possession of the collateral. With the secured party in possession of the collateral, no filing is required to give public notice of his security interest. (U.C.C. 9-302(1))

A security interest is perfected by possession from the time possession is taken; it continues so long as possession is retained. Actually, the secured party is given a twenty-one day period, from the time the security interest attaches, during which his interest is perfected even though he does not take possession. This grace period is applicable (1) where the secured party gave new value (not for an antecedent debt) to the debtor and there is written security agreement and (2) in transactions involving negotiable documents pledged as security for a present loan of money. The twenty-one day period also applies where the secured party makes the goods available to the debtor for the purpose of ultimate sale or exchange or for loading, unloading, storing, shipping, transshipping, manufacturing, processing, or otherwise dealing with them in a manner preliminary to their exchange or sale. (U.C.C. 9-304)

A NON-FILING PERFECTION

In certain situations perfection can occur or attach as soon as an agreement is made to extend credit on collateral in which the debtor has an interest.

Attachment as a method of non-filing perfection is limited to transactions involving installment sales to consumers and sales of farm equipment with a purchase price not exceeding $2500. For example, the owner of an appliance store who sells a stereo on a conditional sales contract to a customer does not have to file a financing statement. The security interest is considered as being perfected by virtue of its attachment to the stereo. Attachment does not apply if the collateral is either a fixture or a motor vehicle required to be licensed. A security interest in a motor vehicle is perfected by a notation on the title or, in nontitle states, by filing a financing statement. Attachment provides protection for the secured party against those parties who have knowledge of the transaction. Filing is the best protection available to the second party. (U.C.C. 9-302)

PURCHASE MONEY SECURITY INTERESTS

A security interest is a "purchase money security interest" to the extent that it is taken or retained by the seller of the collateral (especially goods) to secure all or part of the purchase price. (U.C.C. 9-312 (3)) This type of security interest is made available to anyone financing a transaction to enable the debtor to acquire or obtain the use of collateral. A 10-day grace period following the date upon which the secured party gives value is allowed by the code, during which a purchase money security interest is perfected without filing in cases where filing is required for protection. A purchase money security interest has priority over a prior perfected interest in the same collateral.

PRIORITIES

Since it frequently happens that more than one party has, or claims to have, an interest in the same collateral, the Code provides rules to resolve these controversies. (U.C.C. 9-312, 9-313) The nature of the collateral, its intended use, and the relationship of the parties will affect the application of these rules. Since many of the technical regulations regarding handling and recording of instruments are of value only to the practicing attorney, we will emphasize here the priorities involved in claims concerning personal property and fixtures.

The common law lien of goods left for repair, improvement, storage, or transportation is superior to a perfected security interest if the claimant retains possession of the goods, even though this lien is second in point of time. For example, a garage has a lien on an automobile it repairs; a watchmaker has a lien on a watch he repairs. In both cases the goods may be retained until the debtor pays for the services.

A security interest that attaches to goods before they become fixtures takes priority over the claims of persons having an interest in the real estate. The type of personal property pertinent here would be such items as lighting fixture, built-in appliances, or installed elevators.

If a security interest in goods is perfected and the goods afterwards become part of a finished product, the security interest continues in the product if the goods are so processed that their identity is lost. For example, a security interest on nuts and bolts would continue if they were used as components of a machine. Where goods are affixed to other goods, a security interest perfected before they become accessions has priority over a security interest in the whole and over subsequent purchasers of the whole. Examples of this type of personal property would be the motor of an automobile or a television picture tube.

The priorities of a purchase money security interest depend on whether the goods are inventory. The holder of a purchase money security interest in inventory has priority over a security interest obtained under an after-acquired arrangement, provided (1) he perfects his interest prior to giving possession to the debtor and (2) he notifies the holder of the prior claims. Where the collateral is other than inventory, the purchase money interest is superior if it is perfected prior to giving possession to the debtor or within ten days thereafter.

LEGAL PRINCIPLES

In order to protect himself from the claims of parties resulting from events subsequent to his own arrangement with the debtor, the secured party must perfect his security interest by giving notice of his claim.

Perfection is accomplished by (1) filing a financing statement, (2) taking possession of the collateral, or (3) attachment.

Filing must be done in the proper time, in the proper form, and at the proper place, as prescribed by the U.C.C.

A "purchase money security interest" is obtained at the time of purchase of goods and involves the furnishing of financing by the seller or a financing agency to enable a buyer to purchase or to use goods.

Priorities of conflicting claims are affected by the nature of the collateral, its intended use, and the relationship of the parties.

CASE FOR REVIEW

NATIONAL CASH REGISTER CO. v. FIRESTONE & CO.

191 N.E.2d 471 (Mass 1963)

On June 15, 1960, the plaintiff, a manufacturer of cash registers, and one Edmund Carroll, doing business in Canton as Kozy Kitchen, entered into a conditional sale contract for a cash register. On November 18, 1960, the defendant, which was in the financing business, made a loan to Carroll, who conveyed certain personal property to the defendant as collateral under a security agreement. The defendant filed a financing statement with the Town Clerk of Canton on November 18, 1960, and with the Secretary of State on November 22, 1960. Between November 19 and November 25 the plaintiff delivered a cash register to Carroll in Canton. On November 25, the contract of June 15 was canceled and superseded by a new contract for the same cash register but providing for different terms of payment. The plaintiff filed a financing statement with respect to this contract with the Town Clerk of Canton on December 20 and with the Secretary of State on December 21. Carroll subsequently became in default both on the contract with the plaintiff and on the security agreement with the defendant. In December the defendant took possession of the cash register, and although notified on January 17, 1961, of the plaintiff's asserted right sold it at auction on the following day.

The defendant's security agreement recites that Carroll in consideration of $1911 paid by it does

> hereby grant, sell, assign, transfer and deliver to Grantee the following goods, chattels, and automobiles, namely: The business located at and numbered 574 Washington Street, Canton, Mass. together with all its goodwill, fixtures, equipment and merchandise. The fixtures specifically consist of the following: All contents of luncheonette including equipment such as: booths and tables; stand and counter; tables; chairs; booths; steam tables; salad unit, potato

peeler; U.S. Slicer; range; case; fryer; compressor; bobtail; milk dispenser; silex; 100 Class air conditioner; signs; pastry case; mixer; dishes; silverware; tables; hot fudge; Haven Ex.; 2 door stationwagon 1957 Ford A57R107215 together with all property and articles now, and which may hereafter be, used or mixed with, added or attached to, and/or substituted for, any of the foregoing described property.

In the defendant's financing statement the detailed description of the "types (or items) of property" is the same as the words in supplied italics in the security agreement. There is no specific reference to a cash register in either document, and no mention in the defendant's financing statement of property to be acquired thereafter.

. . . the principal issue is whether the defendant's earlier security interest effectively covers the cash register.

. . . we are of opinion that the security agreement is broad enough to include the cash register, which concededly did not have to be specifically described. The agreement covers "All contents of luncheonette including equipment such as," which we think covers all those contents and does not mean "equipment, to wit." There is a reference to "all property and articles now, and which may hereafter be, used . . . with, [or] added . . . to . . . any of the foregoing described property." We infer that the cash register was used with some of the other equipment even though the case stated does not expressly state that the luncheonette was operated.

The plaintiff's next argument is that the financing statement is insufficient because it incorrectly describes the debtor as "Carroll, Edmund d/b/a Cozy Kitchen 574 Wash. St. Canton, Mass." The specific objection is that "Cozy" should be "Kozy." This word, however, is merely part of the name and style under which the debtor, an individual, did business. The Uniform Commercial Code, § 9-402(5), reads: "A financing statement substantially complying with the requirements of this section is effective even though it contains minor errors which are not seriously misleading. "The name of the debtor, Carroll, is correctly given. It should have been and, for aught that appears, was correctly indexed under "C." With the name of the debtor accurately stated, the spelling of "Cozy" is, at most, a minor error which is not "seriously misleading."

We now come to the question whether the defendant's financing statement should have mentioned property to be acquired thereafter before a security interest in the cash register could attach. The Code, G.L. c. 106, § 9—402(1), reads in part:

A financing statement is sufficient if it is signed by the debtor and the secured party, gives an address of the secured party from which information concerning the security interest may be obtained, gives a mailing address of the debtor and contains a statement indicating the types, or describing the items, of collateral.

. . . In view of the broad purposes of the act we do not give a restrictive construction to the provision which sets forth what constitutes a "sufficient" financing statement. The defendant's financing statement is signed by the debtor and the secured party and gives both the address of the latter from which information is to be obtained and the mailing address of the debtor. . . . We observe nothing to exclude the cash register, or any "equipment" for that matter, from the system of "notice filing," the adoption of which the comment discloses to be the intent of the section for all purposes and not just for some. That "the alternative procedure of filing" a copy of the security agreement may be the simple solution for some types of collateral does not bar notice filing. Filing a copy of the security agreement is not exclusive but is an alternative procedure.

The words, "All contents of luncheonette," including, as we have held, all equipment, were enough to put the plaintiff on notice to ascertain what those contents were. This is not a harsh result as to the plaintiff, to which, as we have indicated . . . made available a simple and sure procedure for completely protecting its purchase money security interest.

CASE PROBLEMS

1. The state statute requires that a filing be made in the county where the debtor has his "principal place of business." The secured party filed in the county that the debtor corporation lists as its place of business. The defendant claimed that this was an improper filing because this is not the place where it really operates. Decide.
2. The creditor originally listed the debtor as residing at 108 South Main, and a few years later he moved on to 229 East Third. At the last address he went bankrupt. The trustee wanted to void the earlier financing because of the change of address. Decide.
3. Brown and his wife bought an automobile in New York from plaintiff under an installment sales contract. Plaintiff immediately perfected his security interest in New York; he therefore, under the U.C.C., had a perfected security interest in the automobile in Pennsylvania when Brown drove the car to Pittsburgh the next day and sold it to defendant. Was defendant a buyer in the ordinary course of business who took the car free of plaintiff's perfected security interest?
4. Nutrodynamics, Inc., delivered to Ivers-Lee a quantity of pills for placement in foil packages and then in shipping containers suitable for delivery to Nutrodynamics customers. The packaged pills were in the possession of Ivers-Lee when Beck instituted an action against Nutrodynamics to attach the pills. Approximately 193 cartons of the packaged pills were levied upon and taken into possession by the sheriff, Ivers-Lee intervened, claiming to have, at common law, by virtue of materials, labor, and services rendered, an artisan's lien to the goods that had priority over Beck's attachment. Decide.
5. A financing statement described the collateral as 800 head of cattle, plus "any increase thereof by birth or purchase." The security agreement, mentioned only 800 head of cattle. A dispute later arose regarding cattle purchased by the debtor after the closing of the deal. Decide.
6. Alfred Carl and his wife Sheila were operating a small business under the name Carriage Card and Record Shop. They borrowed money from the local bank and put the store's inventory up as collateral for the loan. The bank named the debtor as the Carriage Card and Record Shop and filed in the proper place. The couple later went bankrupt. The Trustee claimed the use of the trade name was not sufficient. Decide.
7. A Kansas bank secured a loan with a security agreement describing the cattle, the DeLaval milking equipment, and the feed. However, in the financing statement the creditor simply filled in the description with the words "All the personal property." The farmer went bankrupt and the bank claimed a perfected security interest in the cattle, feed, and machinery. Decide.

8. A credit company originally made a loan to a homeowner, secured by his household furniture. A financing statement was properly filed. The loan was subsequently paid off, but the filed financing statement was never taken off the books. Later, the creditor made another loan to the homeowner, secured by the same furniture and relied on the old financing statement to perfect the new loan. Decide.

ENDNOTE

1. Under the 1972 Code Amendments, it is not sufficient that a fixture filing is made in the office where real estate priorities are recorded. It must be added to the real estate records where it can be found by a standard title search. Arizona, Arkansas, Connecticut, Illinois, Iowa, Kansas, Nevada, North Carolina, North Dakota, Oregon, Texas, Virginia, West Virginia, and Wisconsin have adopted this admendment.

RIGHTS AND REMEDIES 58

The rights and duties of the parties to a secured transaction are determined by reference to the security agreement and to the Uniform Commercial Code. The debtor and the secured party generally reach an understanding with respect to the nature of the secured transaction, possession of the collateral, the terms of repayment, and the conditions that will amount to default by the debtor. Article 9 of the Code, which deals with secured transactions, does not define what constitutes default by the debtor, but it does establish rules governing the rights and duties of the parties in absence of an agreement regarding default. The remedies found in the security agreement and in the Code, Sec. 9—501, include repossession, sale, acceptance of the collateral in satisfaction of the debt, judgment on the debt, judicial sale, and other judicial procedures.

The rights and obligations of the parties with respect to certain procedures cannot be varied by the security agreement. These rights and duties relate to (1) the surplus on the disposition of collateral, (2) the procedure to be followed in disposing of collateral, (3) acceptance of the collateral in full satisfaction of the debt. (4) the right of the debtor to redeem the collateral, and (5) the liability of the secured party if he fails to comply with the proper procedure after the debtor's default. In general, the rules governing the rights and duties of the parties vary prior to default, after default, and according to whether the goods are in the possession of the debtor or the secured party.

RIGHTS OF SECURED PARTIES

A secured party must use reasonable care in the custody and preservation of the collateral in his possession. Unless otherwise agreed, the following rules apply when the collateral is in the possession of the secured party:

1. Reasonable expenses incurred in the custody, preservation, use, or operation of the collateral are chargeable to the debtor and are secured by the collateral.
2. The risk of accidental loss or damage is with the debtor.
3. The secured party may hold, as additional security, any increase or profits (except money) received from the collateral; money, unless given to the debtor, shall be applied to reduce the debt.
4. The secured party must keep the collateral identifiable, but fungible property may be commingled.
5. The secured party may repledge the collateral upon terms that do not impair the debtor's right to redeem it.

The Code, Sec. 9—207(3), provides that "a secured party is liable for any loss caused by his failure to meet any obligation imposed but does not lose his security interest."

The agreement may allow the secured party the right to use or operate the collateral—for example, when the collateral is a going business, it may be operated in such a manner as to preserve its value. If this is the case, the risk of loss and duty to insure will be with the secured party.

RIGHTS OF THE DEBTOR

The provisions of the security agreement govern the duties of the debtor with respect to collateral in his possession and cover such items as taxes, insurance, and use and maintenance. The only provision in the Code concerning the duties of the debtor is in Sec. 9—205, which states: "A security interest is not invalid or fraudulent against creditors by reason of liberty in the debtor to use, commingle or dispose of all or part of the collateral."

The debtor has the right to compel the secured party to state what balance is owed and also to specify in what collateral there is a security interest. To accomplish this, the debtor may send to the secured party a written statement from time to time specifying what he (the debtor) believes to be the amount of the debt as of a stated date and the collateral held by the secured party. He has the right to request that the secured party indicate whether the statements are correct. If the secured party has assigned the contract and the security interest to a third person, he must furnish the debtor with the name and address of his successor in the interest. If the secured party fails to disclose the name and address of any party to whom he has assigned any of his rights against the debtor he is liable to the debtor for any loss caused thereby. The debtor is entitled to a statement once every six months without charge to him.

DEFAULT BY THE DEBTOR

The Code Secs. U.C.C. 9—502, 9—503 gives the secured party the right to take peaceable possession of the collateral, if it is not already in his possession, upon default of the debtor. The secured party also has the right to avail himself of any legal process to enforce the debt against the debtor, as well as to foreclose his interest in the property. Although the appropriate judicial procedure will vary from state to state, generally it amounts to *obtaining a judgment against the debtor, levying on the specific property used as collateral,* and the *sale under execution* of the collateral.

The secured party may sell, lease, or otherwise dispose of any or all of the collateral in its current condition or following any commercially reasonable preparation or processing. (U.C.C. 9—504) *A sale may be private or public, at any time and place, and on any terms, as long as the secured party acts in a commercially reasonable manner.* The secured party must give the debtor reasonable advance notice of a resale unless the goods are perishable, threaten to decline speedily in value, or are of a type customarily sold on a recognized market. When the collateral is disposed of after default, it destroys all the debtor's interest and discharges any security interest or lien that was attached to the property. The secured party must apply the proceeds of the disposition first to the expenses of retaking and resale, then to the debt. *He must account to the debtor for any surplus; unless otherwise agreed, the debtor is liable for any deficiency.* Where the debtor has paid 60 percent or more of the purchase price of the goods, the secured party must resell them within ninety days after repossession unless the debtor has signed a written waiver of his right to require the resale. If the secured party fails to resell the goods within the specified time, the debtor may sue him for conversion of the collateral.

In the case of any other default, the secured party may give written notice that he intends to retain the collateral in satisfaction of his claim. (U.C.C. 9—505) If the debtor does not object to this proposal within thirty days from the receipt of notification, the secured party may do so and the secured claim is discharged. Where written objection is made within the prescribed time, the seller must proceed to dispose of the collateral by resale or in any other reasonable manner. *If the objection to retention is not made both in writing and within the thirty-day period, the secured party may ignore it.*

At any time before the secured party has disposed of the collateral or entered into a contract for its disposition, or before the obligation has been discharged by the secured party's acceptance of the collateral, the debtor may redeem the collateral unless the parties have otherwise agreed in writing after default. (U.C.C. 9—506) Before redemption can be accomplished, the debtor must tender to the secured party the amount owed to him, as well as the expenses reasonably incurred by the latter in retaking, holding, and preparing the collateral for disposition and in arranging for the sale, attorney's fees, and legal expenses.

DEFAULT BY THE SECURED PARTY

Where it can be established that the secured party is not complying with the code provisions with respect to the disposition of collateral, disposition may be ordered or restrained upon appropriate terms and conditions. When the sale has taken place, the secured party is liable for any loss and loses his right to recover any deficiency if the loss is greater than the debt.

Sec. 9—507(1) of the Code authorizes injunctive relief where resale has not yet been made or when a binding contract for resale has not yet been entered into.

LEGAL PRINCIPLES

The rights and remedies of the secured party and the debtor are determined by reference to the security agreement and the Uniform Commercial Code.

A secured party must be reasonable in his care of secured property left in his possession. Any expenses of care are borne by the debtor.

When the secured party is allowed use of the collateral, interested parties should consult the security agreement for conditions of use.

The debtor may use the secured property.

The debtor may compel the secured party to furnish him information concerning the collateral and the debt.

In the event of default by the debtor, the secured party may sell, be forced to sell, or may retain the collateral in satisfaction of the debt.

In the event of default by the secured party, the debtor is authorized to employ injunctive relief or bring suit for money damages.

CASE FOR REVIEW

FUENTES v. SHEVIN

407 U.S. 67 (1972)

Margarita Fuentes is a resident of Florida. She purchased a gas stove and service policy from the Firestone Tire and Rubber Company (Firestone) under a conditional sales contract calling for monthly payments over a period of time. A few months later, she purchased a stereophonic phonograph from the same company under the same sort of contract.

For more than a year, Mrs. Fuentes made her installment payments. But then, with only about $200 remaining to be paid, a dispute developed between her and Firestone over the servicing of the stove. Firestone instituted an action in a small claims court for repossession of both the stove and the stereo, claiming that Mrs. Fuentes had refused to make her remaining payments. Simultaneously with the filing of that action and before Mrs. Fuentes had ... received a summons to answer its complaint, Firestone obtained a writ of replevin ordering a sheriff to seize the disputed goods at once.

In conformance with Florida procedure, Firestone had only to fill in the blanks on the appropriate form documents and submit them to the clerk of the small claims court. The clerk signed and stamped the documents and issued a writ of replevin. Later the same day, a local deputy sheriff and an agent of Firestone went to Mrs. Fuentes' home and seized the stove and stereo.

Shortly thereafter, Mrs. Fuentes instituted the present action in a federal district court, challenging the constitutionality of the Florida prejudgment replevin procedures under the Due Process Clause of the Fourteenth Amendment . . .

The primary question in the present case is whether these state statutes are constitutionally defective in failing to provide for hearings "at a meaningful time." The Florida replevin process guarantees an opportunity for a hearing after the seizure of goods, and the Pennsylvania process allows a postseizure hearing if the aggrieved party shoulders the burden of initiating one. But neither the Florida nor Pennsylvania statute provides for notice or an opportunity to be heard *before* the seizure. The issue is whether procedural due process in the context of these cases requires an opportunity for a hearing *before* the State authorizes its agents to seize property in the possession of a person upon the application of another.

. . . If the right to notice and a hearing is to serve its full purpose, . . . it is clear that it must be granted at a time when the deprivation can still be prevented.

At a later hearing, an individual's possessions can be returned to him if it was unfairly or mistakenly taken in the first place. Damages may even by awarded to him for the wrongful deprivation. But no later hearing and no damage award can undo the fact that the arbitrary taking that was subject to the right of procedural due process has already occurred.

> That the hearing required by due process is subject to waiver, and is not fixed in form does not affect its root requirement that an individual be given an opportunity for a hearing *before* he is deprived of any significant property interest, except for extraordinary situations where some valid governmental interest is at stake that justifies postponing the hearing until after the event.

There are "extraordinary situations" that justify postponing notice and opportunity for a hearing. Thus, the Court has allowed summary seizure of property to collect the internal revenue of the United States, to meet the needs of a national war effort, to protect against the economic disaster of a bank failure, and to protect the public from misbranded drugs and contaminated food.

The Florida and Pennsylvania prejudgment replevin statutes serve no such important governmental or general public interest. They allow summary seizure of a person's possessions when no more than private gain is directly at stake. The replevin of chattels, as in the present cases, may satisfy a debt or settle a score. But state intervention in a private dispute hardly compares to state action furthering a war effort or protecting the public health.

Nor do the broadly drawn Florida and Pennsylvania statutes limit the summary seizure of goods to special situations demanding prompt action. There may be cases in which a creditor could make a showing of immediate danger that a debtor will destroy or conceal disputed goods. But the statutes before us are not "narrowly drawn to meet such unusual condition." Sniadach v. Family Finance Corp., . . . 23 L Ed 2d 339, 352. And no such unusual situation is presented by the facts of these cases.

The statutes, moreover, abdicate effective state control over state power. Private parties, serving their own private advantage, may unilaterally invoke state power to replevy goods from another. No state official participates in the decision to seek a writ; no state official reviews the basis for the claim to repossession; and no state official evaluates the need for immediate seizure. There is not even a requirement that the plaintiff provide any information to the court on these matters. The State acts largely in the dark. . . . We hold that the Florida and Pennsylvania prejudgment replevin provisions work a deprivation of property without due process of law insofar as they deny the right to a prior opportunity to be heard before chattels are taken from their possessor. Our holding, however, is a narrow one. We do not question the power of a State to seize goods before a final judgment in order to protect the security interests of creditors so long as those creditors have tested their claim to the goods through the process of a fair prior hearing. The nature and form of such prior hearings, moreover, are legitimately open to many potential variations and are a subject, at this point, for legislation—not adjudication. Since the essential reason for the requirement of a prior hearing is to prevent unfair and mistaken deprivations of property, however, it is axiomatic that the hearing must provide a real test. . . .

CASE PROBLEMS

1. Shaw purchased an automobile from Country Motors. The seller financed the purchase, with Shaw executing a contract and a judgment note. Country sold the contract and note to Alliance Corporation, which, when the installments were not paid on the purchase price, entered judgment on the note, repossessed the car, and sold it at a private sale for a nominal amount. No notice was given to Shaw of any of the proceedings. He later petitioned the court to open the judgment to permit him to show the true value of the automobile, so that the balance owed on the purchase price could be reduced by the fair value of the car. Decide.

2. The seller repossessed a truck from a debtor who was in default. Before reselling the truck by private sale seller gave the debtor more than a week's notice, by certified mail, of the proposed resale. Debtor, who was living on a rural route, presumably received a notice from the post office that this piece of mail was being held for him, but he did not pick it up until two weeks after the sale. Debtor claims that he had no notice of the proposed resale. Decide.

3. The seller of an aircraft retook the craft when the debtor defaulted on his payments, and resold the plane to the person who had been using it under a lease arrangement with the debtor. The sale was worked out with the lessee for $22,500, after the seller had contracted five or six other operators in the trade and one aircraft broker. The plane was not advertised for sale. The sale price option in the security agreement with the original debtor at the time of the retaking was $75,000. Was the sale "commercially reasonable?" Decide.

4. Associates held a perfected interest in an automobile owned by McCurry, Inc., which sold the car to Taylor, Inc. When installment payments due Associates were not made, it repossessed the automobile. Taylor brought suit to recover. Associates showed that McCurry and Taylor were both under the management of Fred McCurry, that the two corporations had common officers, shareholders, and employees, and that Fred McCurry had applied for the state certificate of title in the name of Taylor. Who is entitled to the automobile?

5. Adrian Chemical Company owed more than $7000 rent to Kirk. To protect him, Adrian gave Kirk a judgment note for the amount of the overdue rent and entered into an agreement giving Kirk a security interest in Adrian's office, laboratory, and plant equipment. Kirk entered judgment on the note and, about six months later, issued execution. The sheriff served the execution process and advertised the date of the sale of Adrian's property. Before the sale could take place, Adrian went into bankruptcy, and Kirk filed a petition claiming the property covered by the security agreement. The referee in bankruptcy and the district court refused to recognize Kirk's claim, holding that he was merely a general creditor. Was the decision correct?

6. The plaintiff addressed a letter to Carriage Barn, Inc., Route 202, Oakland, New Jersey, purporting to give notice to Carriage Barn that the plaintiff intended to sell at private sale the collateral which had previously been repossessed. The letter was delivered to the president of Carriage Barn at 1184 Ridgewood Avenue, Ridgewood, New Jersey. The defendant claims that notice was never received. Decide.

7. Smith borrowed $14,710 from plaintiff and executed a security agreement and financing statement covering a corn crop and other personal property. Subsequently, the defendant purchased all this corn from Smith, credited his account for $10,403.26 and paid him a balance of $2425. Plaintiff brought this action to recover the proceeds of the corn. Decide.

8. A security agreement covering a truck contained a clause allowing the seller upon default to take "immediate possession of the property . . . without notice or

demand." To do this the vendor was authorized to enter upon any premises the property may be." Buyer was in default and seller removed the truck from the lot of another by towing it away. Buyer brought an action claiming that repossession was improper. Decide.

BANKRUPTCY   59

The individual, the partnership, or the corporation may sometimes be faced with situations in which there is no cash available to meet liabilities. Whenever a liquidity crisis arises, the debtor may look to society for relief from his debts so he can resume business operations.

Bankruptcy laws represent a practical manner of dealing with debtors who have made impractical business decisions. They are designed to reduce the possible waste of resources when business mistakes have to be corrected. The law, in effect, allows a fair distribution of the debtor's assets among his creditors and discharges him from the burden of his debts. This serves the interest of society and it enables the debtor to again become a productive member of society.

UNITED STATES BANKRUPTCY LEGISLATION

The Constitution of the United States (Article 1, Section 8, Clause 4) provides that "the Congress shall have power . . . to establish . . . uniform laws on the subject of bankruptcies throughout the United States." The present Bankruptcy Act, passed in 1898, was due in large measure to the financial depression which lasted from 1892 until 1896 and produced a very large number of business failures. Although it has been amended from time to time, the most complete revision being the Chandler Act of 1938, the present bankruptcy law is basically that of the 1898 act.

TYPES OF BANKRUPTCY

There are two types of bankruptcy—voluntary and involuntary. Proceedings which seek the liquidation of a bankrupt's assets and their distribution to his creditors are initiated by the filing of a voluntary petition by the debtor. It is not necessary that the petitioner be insolvent. The debtor's object is to obtain a discharge from his debts. The amount of his liabilities is immaterial, so long as he owes money. The debtor will be entitled to a discharge in bankruptcy as long as he has committed no fraudulent acts. Any person, partnership or corporation may become bankrupt in a voluntary proceeding, except a "municipal, railroad, insurance, or banking corporation or a building and loan association." The insolvencies of the excepted classes are handled under other laws.

An involuntary petition in bankruptcy is an action taken to have a debtor who has committed an act of bankruptcy adjudicated a bankrupt and his assets taken into custody for distribution to his creditors. Involuntary petitions may be filed against any natural person, partnership or moneyed business or commercial corporation having debts of $1000 or more, except wage earners, farmers, and specific classes of corporations exempt from voluntary proceedings. A wage earner is a person who works for hire, receiving compensation of $1500 or less per year. The determination of the status of wage earner is made as of the time of the commission of the act of bankruptcy. A farmer is one who personally engages in farming, and receives the principal part of his income from farming.

The object of an involuntary petition is to prevent an insolvent debtor from disposing of his assets or from paying some creditors to the exclusion of others. The alleged bankrupt is given an opportunity to appear, answer, and contest the claim asserted against him. If a debtor has twelve or more creditors, at least three are required to join together in filing an involuntary petition. When the debtor has fewer than twelve creditors, it is only necessary for one creditor to file the involuntary petition. Creditors may file an involuntary petition only if: (1) the debtor owes $1000 or more; (2) the debtor has committed an act of bankruptcy within four months of the filing of the involuntary petition against him; (3) the petitioning creditors have provable claims which total at least $500.

When an involuntary petition is filed, the clerk of the court issues a subpoena addressed to the alleged bankrupt. A copy of the petition along with the subpoena is given to the United States marshal for service upon the alleged bankrupt. The defendant has five days after the service is made to answer the petition. If he denies insolvency or the commission of an act of bankruptcy, he is entitled as a matter of right to a jury trial; other issues raised by the answer will be determined by a trial without jury. In most cases no contest is made but the petitioning creditor(s) should be prepared to prove all the allegations made in the petition.

With both voluntary and involuntary petitions an indemnity deposit is required to cover costs, consel fees, and the expense of sending out notices and of taking testimony. The party making the deposit may claim reimbursement as a cost of administration.

ACTS OF BANKRUPTCY

Six acts of bankruptcy are defined by the federal statute:

1. to convey, transfer, conceal, or remove, or to permit to be concealed or removed, any part of his property within four months preceding the filing of the bankruptcy petition and with intent to hinder, delay, or defraud his creditors or any of them;
2. to transfer while insolvent, and within the same four months period, any portion of his property to one or more of his creditors, resulting in a preference to such creditors over other creditors;
3. to permit, while insolvent, a creditor to obtain a lien through legal proceedings, and to fail to have such lien vacated or discharged at least five days before a sale or final disposition of any property thereby affected;

4. to permit while insolvent any creditor to obtain through legal proceedings any levy, attachment, judgment, or other lien, and to fail to have it vacated or discharged within thirty days;

5. to make a general assignment for the benefit of his creditors, or while insolvent to have a receiver or trustee appointed or put in charge of his property;

6. to have admitted in writing his inability to pay his debts and his willingness to be adjudged a bankrupt on that ground.

Although most involuntary petitions are uncontested, caution should be exercised in alleging the commission of an act of bankruptcy because the court may require proofs if the objection should be contested by the debtor. As a general rule, the above described first act of bankruptcy is not easy to ascertain or prove. Fraudulent transfers are almost always concealed, and even if there is no actual intent to defraud, the transfer would not be publicized by the transferor.

The second act of bankruptcy (the giving of a preference), is frequently not difficult to prove. The businessman in financial difficulty usually cannot put off all creditors. Some will threaten suit and usually receive payment. The payment of any creditor to the exclusion of others of the same class constitutes a preference. Financial records in the business normally supply such proof.

On the other hand, if the debtor refuses to pay and the creditor obtains an attachment, levy, judgment, or other lien or judicial preference which is not vacated or discharged within the period provided, the debtor may commit the third or fourth act of bankruptcy. These acts of bankruptcy are easily proved. The judgments are matters of record and are either published or easily disvered.

The purpose of the fifth act of bankruptcy is to protect one creditor from other creditors who have designed an unfair composition of creditors. The frustrated creditor may file a petition in bankruptcy based on such an assignment or receivership as an act of bankruptcy, to gain a court administered distribution of the debtor's assets. (See contracts: Chapter 11, Consideration)

Any debtor who is guilty of the sixth act of bankruptcy should be amenable to the bankruptcy law because it amounts to an invitation to his creditors to file a petition against him. The debtor does not wish to undertake the proceeding himself.

INSOLVENCY

The definition of insolvency should be noted at this point because of its importance in determining whether or not the debtor has committed an act of bankruptcy. The act declares a person to be insolvent "whenever the aggregate of his property exclusive of any property which he may have conveyed, transferred, concealed, removed or permitted to be concealed or removed with intent to defraud, hinder or delay his creditors, shall not at a fair valuation be sufficient in amount to pay his debts." A fair valuation of property does not mean what could be realized on a forced sale, nor does it mean what could be realized after waiting an indefinite time. It means rather what the debtor could realize if he were permitted to continue in business and was given a reasonable time to dispose of his property at market value.

PARTIES IN BANKRUPTCY

The *bankrupt* is the person seeking a discharge from his liabilities. The act authorizes the court to appoint *receivers* to take charge of the property of bankrupts and to protect the interests of creditors after the filing of the petition. The court will not appoint the receiver unless the court is satisfied that the appointment is necessary "to preserve the estate or to prevent loss thereto." The receiver is a temporary appointee whose principal function is to care for and protect the assets of the estate until a trustee is elected and qualified. The receiver, upon his appointment, will proceed immediately to take possession of the assets and business holdings of the bankrupt.

At the first creditor's meeting, one or three *trustees* are selected by the creditors. The court makes the appointment if no selection is made. The trustee is to collect the bankrupt's property and to account for all monies collected and disbursed. Such disbursements must be made by check. Ownership of the bankrupt's property, except that which is exempt (wearing apparel, wages, jewelry, tools of trade), passes by operation of law to the trustee upon appointment and qualification. In addition, the trustee possesses the following power:

1. to void certain preferences;
2. to recover certain preferentially transferred property;
3. to collect and reduce to money the property of the estate;
4. to assume or reject claims;
5. to set apart the bankrupt's exemptions;
6. to pay dividends (proportion of the assets available for distribution must be distributed at uniform rate) to creditors within ten days after they are declared by the referee; and,
7. to make a final report of his activities to the court.

To relieve the court of the burden of handling the details of bankruptcy administration, the judicial office of "referee in bankruptcy" was created by the Bankruptcy Act. *Referees* in bankruptcy are appointed by the district judges and generally serve for a term of six years. They can be reappointed for another term. For practical purposes, the referee is the judge in a bankruptcy proceeding. They are vested with all the powers of bankruptcy courts except those specifically reserved by the act for the judges. Wherever the term "court," as distinguished from the word "judge," appears in the act, it includes, by definition, the referee to whom the proceeding has been referred. The orders of a referee have the same force and effect as decisions rendered by the district court, subject, however, to review by the judge within the period for review prescribed by the act. The referee has most of the powers of a judge, including the power to administer oaths, examine witnesses, require production of documents, conduct examinations, and generally to hear controversies relating to property in the possession of the bankrupt.

THE COURTS OF BANKRUPTCY

The courts of bankruptcy are the district courts of the United States and of its territories and possessions and the District Court of the United States for the District of Columbia. Bankruptcy proceedings may be held in that district in which the debtor had his or its principal place of business, residence or domicile for the greatest portion of the preceding six months.

LEGAL PRINCIPLES

The Bankruptcy Act allows a fair distribution of the debtor's assets among his creditors and discharges him from his debts.
Congress has the power to establish uniform laws on bankruptcy.
There are two types of bankruptcy—voluntary and involuntary.
Six acts of bankruptcy are defined by the act.
Insolvency is the inability of the debtor to meet his debts as they occur.
The trustee administers the estate of the bankrupt.
The referee is the judge in a bankruptcy proceeding.
The district courts are the courts of bankruptcy.

CASES FOR REVIEW

WINKLEMAN v. OGAMI

123 F.2d 78 (1941)

This appeal is from an order adjudging appellant a bankrupt. The . . . appellant's sole contention [is] that a creditor who has received a voidable preference is not qualified and may not be counted as a petitioning creditor in an involuntary proceeding unless the first surrenders or offers to surrender the preference.

The bankrupt has more than twelve creditors. Three of them joined in the bankruptcy petition. One of the three is concededly qualified. As to the other two, the bankrupt offered evidence tending to prove that they had received voidable preferences and had made no offer to return them.

> . . . Three or more creditors who have provable claims fixed as to liability and liquidated as to amount against any person which amount in the aggregate in excess of the value of securities held by them, if any, to $500 or over; or if all of the creditors of such persons are less than twelve in number, then one of such creditors whose claim equals such amount may file a petition to have him adjudged a bankrupt.

Presumably the three creditors who joined in the petition be have provable claims fixed as to liability and liquidated as to amount. There is nothing in the agreed statement to indicate the contrary, nor does appellant contend otherwise. He concedes the right of the two creditors in question to join in the petition but attacks their "qualification to be counted as one of the required number of petitioning creditors under the statute".

On its face the statute is plain. A creditor who has received a voidable preference may nevertheless prove his claim, although it may not be allowed unless the preference is surrendered or except upon condition that it be surrendered. . . . Notwithstanding he has receive a preference, he has a "provable claim". . . . In re Hornstein, D.C., 122 F. 266, 272-275, and the statute in terms requires no higher qualification than that on the part of a petitioning creditor.

Subdivision e of the statute, on which appellant leans, has a purpose quite distinct from that of subdivision b. It proceeds upon the theory that creditors in certain categories, such as employees, relatives, or stockholders of the debtor, as well as those who have received preferences, will, in the nature of things, be averse to joining in a petition to have their debtor adjudged an involuntary bankrupt; hence they are not to be counted in computing the number of creditors for the purpose of determining whether one petitioning creditor is sufficient or whether three must join. If, as is here contended, the subdivision means that the creditors enumerated in it shall not be "counted either for or against the petition", it necessarily follows that employees and relatives of the debtor, although having provable claims, are on the mere score of relationship debarred from initiating an involuntary adjudication. Congress manifestly did not intend that, nor does the statute admit of such interpretation. The subdivision, however, makes no distinction between such creditors and those holding preferences.

We see no persuasive reason for engrafting extra-statutory limitations on those provisions of the Chandler Act which prescribe the qualifications of petitioning creditors, since terms having elsewhere in the law a well defined meaning were deliberately used. A creditor who has received a voidable preference gains no advantage over his fellows by helping put his debtor in bankruptcy; rather, he places himself in a position where he impliedly offers to relinquish any preference he may be held to have received and in any event subjects himself to the necessity of so doing. Nor does the agreed statement before us disclose any circumstance that could properly be thought, on considerations of a general nature, to estop appellees from seeking an adjudication.

HARRIS v. CAPEHART-FARNSWORTH CORP.

207 F.2d 512 (1953)

. . . So far as . . . pertinent, the amended petition alleges:

. . . That . . . Albert F. Harris, Edward J. Harris and Emmeline Harris, both as copartners doing business as Southwest Distributing Company, and as individuals, owe debts to the amount of $1,000.00 and over;

That your petitioners are creditors of . . . Albert F. Harris, Edward J. Harris and Emmeline Harris, . . . having provable claims against the copartnership and against them as individuals fixed as to liability and liquidated as to amount, in excess of the value of securities held by them, if any, of over $500.00. . . .

That . . . Albert F. Harris, Edward J. Harris and Emmeline Harris, the alleged bankrupts, are insolvent in that the aggregates of their property are not sufficient at a fair valuation to pay their debts, and that within the four months preceding the filing of this petition and while insolvent, as aforesaid, they committed acts of bankruptcy: . . .

In the amended petition the alleged bankrupt is charged in substantially the words of the statute with having suffered or permitted while insolvent a creditor to obtain a lien upon its property through legal proceedings or distraint, and not having vacated or discharged such lien within thirty days from the date thereof, or at least five days before the date set for any sale or other disposition of such property. In addition to the general allegation following the words of the statute the petition sets forth the name of the creditor in whose favor a judgment had been permitted to be entered, states the date and amount of the judgment, alleges that the judgment has become final and that said judgment had not been vacated and discharged within thirty days from the date said judgment was rendered or within thirty days from the date upon which it became final and a lien. It is argued that the mere entry of the judgment was not sufficient to create a lien upon the bankruptcy property. However, the petition alleged that it became a lien and the motion must be taken as admitting as true this allegation. The manner in which it became a lien is not material as the ultimate fact that it became a lien was admitted by the motion. We think the allegation set out the facts with reference to the alleged act of bankruptcy with sufficient particularity.

In view of our conclusion as to the sufficiency of the allegation charging the alleged bankrupt with permitting a judgment to be rendered against it which became a lien and which had not been vacated, we deem it unnecessary to consider with particularity the other three charges as to acts of bankruptcy committed by the alleged bankrupt.

CASE PROBLEMS

1. The defendant, Tyler, set up his exempt status from involuntary proceedings as a farmer whose principal business was tilling the soil. It was alleged that some years earlier the defendant had left his farm and moved to a nearby community. However, he made an agreement with his son to farm the 400 acres and expressly agreed that he would assist in the operations. The defendant further alleged that the farm animals and crops were owned in equal shares. Decide.

2. Brown claimed to be exempt from bankruptcy as a farmer or one engaged in tilling the soil. It is shown that Brown had acquired more than 4000 acres of farmland, which he operated on a "cooperative" arrangement in which the tenant furnished tools and labor, and Brown furnished the land and half the harvesting expenses. It was shown that Brown spent some time with his tenants. However, although the crops were sold and shared in halves there was no real partnership. In addition, Brown found a grain-buying firm in which he was a substantial stockholder and vice-president. Decide.

3. Plaintiff alleged that the defendant, Shingle, while insolvent, caused and suffered a creditor, Meyer, to obtain a judgment against him in Jefferson County, Missouri. It was claimed that in the action the defendant filed a voluntary

appearance and confession of judgment, and that execution followed against the accounts due the defendant, and that this was done with intent to prefer a creditor. Decide.

4. Plaintiff, trustee in bankruptcy of Mrs. Lee, brought this action to set aside a quitclaim deed which the bankrupt had given her mother, while insolvent, for property. It appeared that Mrs. Lee's mother owned the property in question but in 1954 conveyed it to herself and daughter as joint tenants, apparently to avoid the probate in the event of the mother's death. The daughter had given no consideration for the transfer and exercised no control over the property. The deed was given by the daughter to her mother immediately proceding the bankruptcy action. Decide.

5. Ace Building Company leased a building to Fitch, and loaned him $10,000, payable in installments, to enable Fitch to purchase fixtures and inventory. Fitch defaulted on notes as they became due and owed several months rent. Ace was aware that Fitch intended to quit his business because he had returned the keys to Ace, leaving all the fixtures on the premises. Ace secured a judgment against Fitch and had his assets sold on execution sale. On that day, Fitch was insolvent and was adjudged a bankrupt less than four months from the date of the sale. Trustee claimed the sale was a preferential transfer. Decide.

6. Loser filed a voluntary petition in bankruptcy on July 1, 1973 and was adjudicated a bankrupt on the same date. Winner, a creditor, filed a timely objection to discharge. It was alleged that Loser, within twelve months immediately preceding the filing of the petition, withdrew $2000 from his checking account with which he made payments to several of his creditors. Loser admitted he withdrew the money, knowing he was going bankrupt. Decide.

7. Eagan endorsed Brady's note to People's Merchants Trust Company. Brady paid the bank while insolvent. Eagan knew of the payment and had "reasonable cause to believe" that Brady was insolvent at the time. Less than four months later Brady became bankrupt. The trustee alleged the amount of payment to Eagan was a preferential transfer. Decide.

8. Creditors attempted to place a company in bankruptcy by virtue of a statement in writing by the company admitting its inability to pay its debts and expressing a willingness to be adjudged bankrupt. The owner alleged the firm was solvent and offers proof of this claim. Decide.

BANKRUPTCY PROCEEDINGS   60

A decree of adjudication in bankruptcy is merely a statement by the court that a person is declared a bankrupt. It is the first order entered in the bankruptcy proceedings and gives the court jurisdiction over the assets and business affairs of the bankrupt. After the adjudication, the referee takes charge of the bankrupt's estate for the purposes of an orderly administration.

MEETINGS OF CREDITORS

The first step in the bankruptcy proceeding in which the creditors participate is a meeting of creditors. The referee is required to call this meeting not less than ten nor more than thirty days after the adjudication. The first order of business is the allowance of claims, which have either been previously filed or which are filed at the meeting. Only the holders of claims which have been allowed are entitled to vote concerning the selection of the trustee. Holders of secured or priority claims may vote only to the extent that the amount of their claim exceeds the value of their security or the amount of priority to the extent that they are unsecured creditors. The referee may allow such claims, either provisionally or permanently, at the first meeting.

The duty of giving notice to the creditors is imposed upon the referee. Notices are given by mail. Ten days notice is mandatory for all meetings of creditors, for all proposed sales of property with certain limited exceptions, for the audit of all accounts and for the hearing of all applications for compensation. Except for exempt property the trustee is authorized to sell the estate of the bankrupt. It is the duty of the trustee to determine what property is exempt and report the items and the estimated value to the court as soon as practical.

A qualified and disinterested appraiser appointed by the referee appraises the property of the bankrupt. This appraisal provides a measure for the trustee, the referee, and the creditor as to the adequacy or inadequacy of any bids made for the purchase of the property of the bankrupt. Ordinarily the sales are made at auction. The trustee may never sell for less than 75 percent of the appraised value unless the lower price was been approved by the referee. Ten days notice by mail of all proposed sales must be given to the creditors. This protects against collusive sales for the benefit of the bankrupt or some creditor favored by the trustee. The court can order a sale without notice under certain conditions, such as where perishable property is involved.

DUTIES OF BANKRUPT

In general, the duties of the bankrupt are his required attendance at meetings, the filing of schedules and submission to an examination under oath. He is required to obey all lawful orders of the court, including a direction to attend any special meetings. If he is requested by the trustee or referee, he must corroborate or deny claims which have been filed. The sole ground for refusing to answer questions during an examination is the privilege against self-incrimination. Failure on the part of the bankrupt to perform his duties may result in the denial of his discharge from his debts and perhaps in an imprisonment for contempt.

PROVABLE CLAIMS

Provable claims are entitled to share on a pro rata (proportionate) basis in the dividends and, with few exceptions, such sharing in the distribution will discharge the debt of the bankrupt. Section 63a of the Bankruptcy Act lists the claims which are provable and, therefore, allowable by the referee. They are the following:

1. fixed liabilities owing at the time of the petition, whether then payable or not;
2. taxable costs where bankrupt was plaintiff or defendant;
3. debts based upon an open account or a contract, express or implied; (This would include the bulk of claims).
4. debts reduced to judgment after petition has been filed;
5. an award by a workmen's compensation board where the injury occured prior to adjudication;
6. a damage claim based upon negligence if an action was instituted prior to filing of the petition in bankruptcy and if it is pending at such time:
7. since 1938, contingent claims—claims against bankrupt sureties, guarantors, endorsers and other accomodation parties; and
8. claims for anticipatory breach of excutory contracts. Bankruptcy itself constitutes an anticipatory breach.

PREFERRED CREDITORS

The transfer of any property of a debtor to or for the benefit of a creditor made or suffered by such debtor while insolvent and within four months before the filing by or against him of the petition is considered a preference. The effect of the transfer could enable such creditor to obtain a greater percentage of his claim than some of the other creditors of the same class. This is deemed a voidable transfer. Some transfers during insolvency cannot be avoided. Otherwise, no business firm could pay any of its debts during a period of financial crisis without committing an act of bankruptcy. Preferences may be avoided by the trustee if the creditor receiving it or his agent had reasonable cause to believe the debtor insolvent when the transfer was made. Mere suspicion is not enough.

The following are exceptions to the recoverable preference rule:

1. payment of a fully secured claim;
2. transfer of property for a present consideration;

3. a mortgage to secure a loan although the mortgagee took the security with the knowledge of the debtor's insolvency;
4. any debtor of a bankrupt may set off against the amount he owes the bankrupt estate any sum which the estate owes him.

PRIORITY OF CLAIMS

Because there may be some estates with very few assets, the order of priority of payment is important. The Act sets up five classes of priority claimants. Every claim of each preceding class must be paid in full before the next class may receive any distribution. Within a particular class, each claimant shares pro rata if the estate is insufficient to satisfy all such claims.

The first group in order of priority would be those cases involving the cost of administration. The more important are the costs of preserving the estate; filing fees for the referees' salary and expense fund; cost of creditors in recovering fraudulently transferred or concealed assets; expenses of witnesses; fees of attorneys representing the petitioning creditors, the receiver and trustee, and the bankrupt; receiver's and trustee's commissions; and the actual expenses of administering the estate and conducting hearings.

The second group includes wages and commissions, not to exceed $600 to each claimant, which have been earned from and owed by the debtor within three months before the beginning of preceedings, and are due to workmen, servants, or salesmen on salary or commission basis.

The third priority is for the costs and expenses incurred by creditors (as distinguished from the trustee) in successfully opposing, revoking or setting aside a confirmation of an arrangement or a discharge in bankruptcy, or in securing evidence resulting in a conviction for an offense under the Act.

Taxes legally due and owing by the bankrupt to the United States or any state or any subdivision thereof is next in priority. This section relates to taxes which bacame due prior to bankruptcy.

The last group would include debts holding priority by federal law (federal government and its sureties), and rents entitled to priority under state law, not to exceed amounts accruing during the three months prior to the date of bankruptcy.

After priority claims have been paid in full, general creditors will share the remaining fund pro rata.

DENIAL OF DISCHARGE

The trustee or any creditor may object to the discharge of debts being granted to the bankrupt on any one or more of the following grounds:

1. that the bankrupt has committed an offense punishable by imprisonment under the Bankruptcy Act;
2. that the bankrupt, with intent to conceal his financial condition, destroyed, mutilated, falsified, concealed, or failed to keep books of account or records from which his financial condition and business transactions could be ascertained;

3. that the bankrupt, while engaged in business or as an executive of a corporation, obtained for such business money or property on credit by a materially false statement in writing made for the purpose of obtaining credit;

4. that the bankrupt, at any time during the twelve months preceding the filing of the bankruptcy petition, removed, destroyed, or concealed any of his property or permitted any of his property to be removed, destroyed, or concealed with the intent to hinder, delay, or defraud any of his creditors;

5. that the bankrupt in the course of the proceedings refused to obey any lawful order of the court, or to answer any material question approved by the court;

6. that within six years the bankrupt obtained a discharge in a voluntary bankruptcy proceeding; or

7. that the bankrupt has failed to explain satisfactorily any losses of assets or deficiency of assets to meet his liabilities.

The objecting party is required to file written specifications of the grounds for his objections. The objections to discharge are heard by the referee in a trial-type hearing. The objecting parties have the initial burden of proof. However, if it is shown to the satisfaction of the court that there are reasonable grounds for believing that the bankrupt has committed any act sufficient to bar his discharge, the burden of disproving shifts to the bankrupt. A bankrupt who is refused a discharge remains liable on all his obligations. The creditors retain their claims in full.

NONDISCHARGEABLE DEBTS

The principal purpose of the Bankruptcy Act is to grant a discharge to the debts of a bankrupt. The general rule is that debts which are provable are dischargeable. However, there are certain types of liability that cannot be discharged. The discharge will not apply to a debt or a liability that is not scheduled, unless the particular creditor proves his claim then scheduled, or knows of the bankruptcy proceeding. A bankrupt will not be discharged of any debts or liabilities that become due after the filing of the petition. Other debts not dischargeable are:

1. alimony or maintenance for the bankrupt's wife or children—past as well as future alimony;

2. taxes due the United States government or any state government or any subordinate governmental authority;

3. liabilities for obtaining property by false pretenses or false representations;

4. liability for willful and malicious injuries to the person or property of another, except liability due to negligence;

5. wages which have been earned within three months before the date of commencement of the proceedings in bankruptcy due to workmen, servants, clerks, or traveling or city salesmen, on salary or commission basis, whole or part time, whether or not he was selling exclusively for the bankrupt;

6. claims due for money of an employee received or retained by the employer as security for the faithful performance of the contract of employment.

The death or insanity of a bankrupt does not abate the proceedings. They are continued as if he had not died or become insane. However, bankruptcy proceedings cannot be instituted against the estate of a deceased person.

There is always the risk that the estate will be exhausted before all claims are filed, as the act does not restrict the court's power to declare a final dividend before the six-month period for filing claims has expired, except that a final dividend cannot be declared until three months have elapsed after the first dividend. Although it is unlikely that the court would permit the estate to be exhausted through a distribution to general creditors before the period for filing claims has expired, the importance of filing proofs of debt promptly cannot be overemphasized.

DEBTOR RELIEF

The Chandler Act of 1938 also makes a provision for other types of debtor relief:

1. *Composition and Extension Arrangements.* An arrangement is defined XI of the Bankruptcy Act as "any plan of a debtor for the settlement, satisfaction, or extension of the time of payment of his unsecured debts upon any terms." This phase of debtor relief is initiated by the filing of a petition for debt relief in the federal district court by the debtor himself. His petition contains a declaration either of his inability to meet his debts as they mature or his insolvency; it also details his proposal to his creditors for an extension or a composition as the case may be. In order for the creditors to pass judgment on a proposed plan the debtor must be prepared with schedules of his assets and liabilities, a statement of affairs and a listing of his binding contracts. Dissenting creditors have a right to object to these proposed plans. The objections will be given a hearing by the referee. If a plan is agreed upon and confirmed it is effective. Once effective, it binds both the assenting and dissenting creditors. Composition and extension arrangements are applicable only to unsecured debts and only to those not specifically excluded from the Bankruptcy Act.

2. *Wage Earners' Arrangements.* This arrangement is restricted to unsecured debts and to those wage earners with a limited income. A wage earner is an individual whose principal income is derived from wages, salary or commissions. Again proceedings are initiated by the debtor who must be prepared to file the same documents as he would for composition or extension arrangements. This plan allows for greater flexibility in repayment in recognition of the changing circumstances of the debtor. Repayment amounts may be increased or decreased: the length of time may be lengthened or shortened dependent upon the immediate circumstances of the debtor. All other provisions are the same as above.

3. *Real Property Arrangements.* Initiation and schedules here again follow the pattern described above. In real property arrangements secured creditors are involved. The purpose of this particular arrangement is to grant the debtor time in which to work out a plan of rehabilitation and prevent foreclosures which result in forced sales and substantial loss of equity. In this arrangement the creditors as well as the debtor may initiate a plan. According to the Bankruptcy Act: "Real property arrangements, a special type, available only to a limited but very common class of debtors who have debts that are secured by mortgages or real estate liens. They are restricted to individuals."

4. *Corporate Reorganization.* In corporate reorganization the bankruptcy proceedings may be either voluntary or involuntary. The directors have the authority to file a voluntary petition but this is seldom done without the approval of the stockholders. This provision applies to all corporations that are not in the excepted class which includes municipals, banks, insurance companies, and railroads. According to the capital structure, the indebtedness, and other circumstances of the specific corporation involved, the plans under the corporate reorganization provisions may vary widely. It may call for a complete financial renovation and the formation of a new corporation out of the old corporation and any of its subsidiaries. Also, under this provision the submitted plan may alter the rights of secured as well as unsecured creditors.

A corporation seeking a change in the corporate capital structure with or without a change in its debt structure may apply to a federal court for such reorganization under Chapter X of the Bankruptcy Act. If relief is sought simply with respect to debt, such relief must be applied for under the "arrangements" section of the act. A petition for reorganization may be submitted by either stockholders or creditors. The petition may be filed during the course of bankruptcy proceedings.

The plan for reorganization must be approved by two-thirds of the creditors and a majority of the stockholders affected. After such approval, the court will confirm the plan if it is satisfied that the plan is feasible and is in the best interests of the creditors. The reorganization is then binding upon the corporations, its stockholders, and its creditors. In the event of a failure to effect a corporate reorganization, any bankruptcy proceeding that may have been suspended by the petition for reorganization is reopened.

LEGAL PRINCIPLES

An adjudication in bankruptcy is decree by a court stating that a person is declared a bankrupt.

The first order of business at the meeting of creditors is the allowance of claims.

Holders of secured claims may vote only to the extent that the amount of their claim exceeds the amount of their security.

Ten days notice must be given for the meetings.

Bankruptcy sales are ordinarily made at auction.

The bankrupt must obey all lawful orders of the court.

The effect of a preferential transfer is to give one creditor an advantage over other creditors.

Because there may be some estates with limited assets, the order of priority of payment is important.

The bankrupt may be denied a discharge of his debts.

There are certain debts which cannot be discharged.

Death or insanity of the bankrupt does not abate the proceedings; bankruptcy proceedings may not, however, be initiated against the estate of a deceased person.

The Chandler Act of 1938 makes a provision for other types of debtor relief.

CASES FOR REVIEW

RICCIO v. GENERAL MOTORS ACCEPTANCE CORPORATION

203 A.2d 92 (Conn. 1963)

The plaintiff, as trustee of the bankrupt estate of Jamarc Sewing Machine Company, Inc., hereinafter referred to as Jamarc, which had on February 7, 1961, filed a petition in bankruptcy and was adjudicated a bankrupt, brings this action under . . . the Bankruptcy Act . . . to recover because of an alleged preferential transfer suffered or made by the bankrupt on February 3, 1961, within four months before the filing of the petition and when the bankrupt was insolvent, the effect of which was to enable the defendant to obtain a greater percentage of its debt than other creditors of the same class. It is further alleged that at the date of the transfer the defendant had reasonable cause to believe that the enforcement of the transfer would work a preference within the meaning of the act. In paragraph 5 of the complaint, the plaintiff alleged that "on [February 3, 1961] Jamarc . . . was insolvent and . . . indebted to defendant and divers other creditors of the same class upon unsecured indebtedness provable in bankruptcy."

However, . . . a preference is voidable by the trustee in bankruptcy only upon proof . . . that the creditor receiving or to be benefited by the preference had reasonable cause to believe that the debtor was insolvent. If any one of the elements of a preference . . . is wanting, there is no necessity of considering an avoidance of the transfer . . . since a preference . . . itself has not been established. Just as the trustee in his suit to recover property preferentially transferred must include allegations, in his statement of claim, of all the elements of the alleged voidable preference, so also must the trustee introduce evidence at the trial to sustain all such averments that have not been admitted. The law places upon the trustee (or receiver) the unmistakable burden of proving by a fair preponderance of all the evidence every essential, controverted element resulting in the composite voidable preference.

In order to prove that a preference be effected under . . . the Act, a transfer of property must be made or suffered by the debtor "while insolvent." 3 Collier, op. cit. § 60.30, p. 889. As in the other elements of a preference, the burden of proof is on the trustee to show insolvency at the time of the transfer.

Id. § 60.30, p. 893. The transfer may be voluntary or involuntary. The term "suffered," as used in the act, does not require any conscious participation by the debtor. .... The insolvency must be in the bankruptcy sense, as defined by § 1(19) of the Bankruptcy Act.

> ... A person shall be deemed insolvent within the provisions of the title whenever the aggregate of his property, exclusive of any property which he may have conveyed, transferred, concealed, removed, or permitted to be concealed or removed, with intent to defraud, hinder, or delay his creditors, shall not at a fair valuation be sufficient in amount to pay his debts. [A]n adjudication in bankruptcy, standing alone, creates no presumption and warrants no inference that the debtor was insolvent for any period before the petition in bankruptcy was filed, regardless whether the same was voluntary or involuntary. ...

Applying the foregoing principles to the controverted issue of insolvency at the time of the transfer in the present case, we point out that it was incumbent on the trustee to introduce into evidence a statement of the assets and liabilities of the bankrupt. There is nothing in the record before us showing the financial condition of the bankrupt, such as inventories, bankruptcy appraisals, trustee's reports, orders confirming bankruptcy sales, or even the bankrupt's own schedules. ... It was the duty of the trustee not only to plead but to prove, and for the court to make a finding, that on February 3, 1961— the date of the alleged transfer—the bankrupt's debts exceeded the aggregate fair value of its assets. A failure to prove and find this indispensable and essential element must result in a finding that the preference, if any, is not voidable.

CHARLES EDWARD & ASSOCIATES v. ENGLAND

301 F.2d 572 (1962)

The Referee fixed November 10, 1958, as the time for filing objections to the discharges of the individual partners as well as the partnership itself. Prior to that date, the Trustee petitioned the Referee for an order extending the time within which to file objections. By inadvertence, the . . . petition requested time within which to object to the discharges of the individual partners but no such request was made for the partnership. The order granting the extension was likewise limited to the individuals.

Within the extended time, the Trustee filed objections to the discharges of both the partnership and the individual partners. The . . . pertinent specifications charged:

1. The individual partners failed to keep partnership records;

2. The partnership transferred property to the individual partners with intent to defraud partnership creditors within one year from the filing of the bankruptcy petition. . . .

The failure to keep or preserve books of account or records from which a bankrupt's financial condition and business transactions might be obtained is a ground for the denial of a discharge in bankruptcy under the Bankruptcy Act (Act), 11 U.S.C.A. § 32, sub. c(2).

Specification 1 charges:

. . . That said Bankrupt copartnership and each of the bankrupt individual members thereof failed to keep books or records from which the financial condition of said bankrupt copartnership might be ascertained in that they, and each of them, wholly failed and neglected at all times during the existence of said copartnership to maintain books or records relating to the accounts payable of said copartnership.

Appellants contend that this specification charges misconduct against the partnership and not against the individual partners, and they claim that any other construction would disregard the entity theory of partnership.

Although the Bankruptcy Act of 1938 adopted the entity theory for some purposes and the aggregate theory for other purposes, the entity theory is specifically rejected in § 5, sub. j of the Act, 11 U.S.C.A. § 23, sub. j, which provides that the discharge of a partnership does not discharge the individual partners from partnership debts.

Under either theory, a partner who has engaged in conduct proscribed by the Act, either on behalf of the partnership or on his own behalf, is not entitled to a discharge.

The transfer of property with intent to hinder, delay or defraud creditors, within twelve months of the filing of a petition in bankruptcy, is also a ground for the denial of a discharge in bankruptcy. 11 U.S.C.A. § 32, sub. c(4).

Specification 2 charges:

. . . That at times subsequent to the first day of the twelve months immediately preceding the filing of the individual partners' petitions in bankruptcy, and also at items [sic] subsequent to the first day of the twelve months immediately preceding the filing of the petition in bankruptcy against the said bankrupt copartnership, the said partnership, while continually insolvent, the individual members thereof having full knowledge of such partnership insolvency and with intent to defraud the partnership creditors, transferred to the individual members thereof, property of said partnership, to wit, cash in the sum of $22,819.07 or thereabouts.

CASE PROBLEMS

1. In bankruptcy proceedings, a number of creditors sought a review of orders of the referee. It appears that the referee concluded that one Ratchford had the votes of a majority of claims, therefore, he confirmed his appointment as trustee. The same day, the referee, after deciding that a certain claim should be withdrawn, called Ratchford to inform him that with the claim and vote withdrawn he was not properly elected and that the referee would appoint a successor. The plaintiffs challenged these actions. Decide.
2. In an involuntary proceeding in bankruptcy the defendant claimed to be a workman. It was alleged that the defendant gave music lessons and had additional income from rental properties. Decide.
3. Petitioner claimed a priority on a contract for services as an actress in a motion picture, in which she was to be paid a weekly sum over a five-week period. Petitioner claimed this service entitled her to the priority granted for workmen. Decide.
4. Smith was involved in an automobile accident. Jones, the driver of the other vehicle, was injured. Jones brought suit against Smith in a state court and was

awarded damages. Smith petitioned for a discharge in bankruptcy. The Jones judgment was listed in the bankruptcy proceedings, and Smith was discharged by the bankruptcy court from all debts. Jones claimed the unsatisfied judgment should not be discharged. Decide.

5. Robinson intentionally drove his car across the newly sodded lawn of Early, causing a considerable amount of damage to the property. Suit was brought by Early for these damages. Judgment was entered against Robinson, who thereafter went into and was discharged in bankruptcy. Early brought an action to collect the debt claiming it was not discharged. Decide.

6. The defendant made loans to the plaintiff in 1939 and 1946 totaling about $200,000. The monies were invested in real estate and loans and not until 1950 was a settlement made of the account when the plaintiff gave the defendant a promissory note. The note was not paid and in 1956 the plaintiff filed a bankruptcy action. The plaintiff had, since 1950, lost or destroyed all original records of his business transactions, keeping only limited memos. Plaintiff appealed an order denying him a discharge in bankruptcy. Decide.

7. Plaintiff received an assignment of wages not yet earned but to be due from the employer, defendant, as security for an existing debt. Shortly thereafter the debtor filed a petition in bankruptcy and listed the debt of the plaintiff. The debtor was discharged in January, 1970. On March 3, 1970, the plaintiff notified defendant of the assignment. Defendant contended the claim was discharged. Decide.

8. Debtor obtained a discharge in bankruptcy which covered his debt to Creditor. Subsequently Debtor promised to pay the debt, and Creditor obtained a judgment in a state court based on that subsequent promise. More than six years after the first discharge, Debtor again became bankrupt. Creditor sought to have his debt excepted from Debtor's second discharge. Decide.

GLOSSARY

Abandoned property. Property the title to which has been surrendered by the owner.

Abate. To reduce or put a stop to a nuisance; to reduce or decrease a legacy because the estate is insufficient.

Ab initio. From the beginning. An agreement is said to be "void ab initio" if it at no time had any legal validity.

Abrogate. To annul, repeal.

Abstract. A history of the title to land, consisting of a summary of all transactions that may in any manner affect the land, or any estate or interest therein, together with a statement of all liens or liabilities to which the title may be subject.

Acceleration clause. A provision in a contract or another legal instrument that upon the occurence of a stated event, the time for performance shall be advanced.

Acceptance. The act by which a person obligates himself, or the inference that a person intends to obligate himself, to the terms of a contract offered him. Also, the act by which the person on whom a draft is drawn assents to the request of the drawer to pay it or makes himself liable to pay it when it falls due.

Accession. The acquisition of title to all property produced by, or united to, one's original property.

Accessory after the fact. One who, after a felony has been committed, knowingly assists the felon.

Accessory before the fact. One who was not present at the commission of a crime but who nevertheless had some part in its commission.

Accommodation paper. A negotiable instrument to which the acceptor, drawer, or endorser has put his name, without consideration, for the purpose of benefiting or accommodating some other party who desires to raise money on it and who is to pay the instrument when it becomes due.

Accord and satisfaction. The substitution of a second agreement between contracting parties in satisfaction of a former one, and the execution of the latter agreement. Accord is the agreement to substitute; satisfaction is the performance of the accord.

Accretion. The acquisition of title to additional land when land already owned is built up by gradual deposits made by natural causes.

Acknowledgment. The act by which a party who has executed an instrument goes before a competent officer or court and affirms that its execution was a genuine and voluntary act on his part; certification by an authorized person on the face of an instrument that it has been acknowledged.

Action. A suit brought to enforce a right.

Act of God. Any injury or damage that happens by the direct and exclusive operation of natural forces, without human intervention, and that could not have been prevented or escaped from by any reasonable degree of care or diligence.

Adjudication. The giving or pronouncing of a judgment in a case; also, the judgment given.

Ad litem. While an action is pending.

Administrator. A person appointed by the court to administer the estate of a deceased person.

Advisory opinion. An opinion rendered by the court when there is no actual controversy before it upon a matter submitted to obtain the court's opinion.

Affidavit. A written declaration made voluntarily and confirmed by the oath of the party making it, taken before a person having authority to administer such an oath.

Affiant. One who makes or attests to an affidavit.

A fortiori. By a stronger reason.

Agency. A relationship created by an express or implied contract or by law whereby one party (the principal) delegates the transaction of some business to another person (the agent), who undertakes a commercial transaction for him.

Agent. One who represents and acts for another under an agency relationship.

Aleatory contract. A contract under which all risks without exception are assumed by the parties.

Alienability. Transferability.

Alienation. The transfer of property from one person to another.

Allegation. The statement of a party to an action, made in a pleading, setting forth the charges he expects to prove.

Allege. To state or charge, to make an allegation.

Allonge. A paper attached to a commercial paper that provides additional space for endorsements.

Alluvion. An addition made to land by accretion.

Alteration. Any material change of the terms of a written instrument.

Ambulatory. Not effective.

Amicus curiae. A friend of the court, a person appointed by the court to assist in litigation by offering his opinion on some important matter of law.

Amortize. To provide for the paying of a debt in installments.

Ancillary. Auxiliary.

Annexation. The attachment of personalty to real property in such a manner as to make it part of the realty.

Answer. In a pleading, the written statement made by the defendant setting forth his defense.

Antenuptial contract. A contract made prior to marriage between a prospective wife and her prospective husband.

Appeal. The removal of an adjudicated case from a trial court to a court of appellate jurisdiciton for the purpose of obtaining a review or retrial.

Appearance. A coming into court as plaintiff or as defendant.

Appellant. A party who takes an appeal from one court to another.

Appellate jurisdiction. The power of a court to hear cases on appeal from another court or an administrative agency.

Appellee. The party in a legal action against whom an appeal is taken.

Appurtenance. An incidental adjunct to some thing that is considered the principal thing.

Arbitration. An agreement to submit a matter in dispute to selected persons and to accept their decision or award as a substitute for the decision of a court.

Arrest of judgment. The act of staying a judgment or refusing to render judgment in an action at law after the verdict has been given, for some matter appearing on the face of the record that would render the judgment, if given, reversible.

Assault. A threat of an "offensive or injurious touch" to a person, made by another person who is able to carry out the threat.

Assumpsit. A form of action brought to recover damages for the nonperformance of a contract.

Assurance. A conveyance whereby an estate being transferred is assured to the transferee with all controversies, doubts, and difficulties affecting his quiet enjoyment of the property either prevented or removed.

Attachment. Seizure of the property of a debtor by the service of process upon a third person who is in possession of the property.

Attest. To act as a witness to.

Attestation clause. A clause at the end of an instrument stating that the document has been properly executed.

"Attractive nuisance." The courts hold a landowner liable for injuries sustained by small children while they were playing on his land if they were reasonably attracted there by something on the property.

Averment. A positive statement of fact.

Avulsion. A sudden addition to land by the action of water.

Bad faith. The intent to mislead, deceive, or take unfair advantage of another.

Bailment. The giving up of the possession of personal property to another for some purpose, upon the accomplishment of which the goods are to be redelivered to the owner.

Battery. An unlawful beating, wrongful physical violence, or "offensive touch" inflicted on another without his consent.

Bearer. The holder of a commercial paper.

Beneficiary. A person for whose benefit property is held by a trustee, administrator, or executor.

Bequeath. To give personal property to another by a will.

Bequest. A gift of personal property by will.

Bill. A formal, written declaration, complaint, or statement of fact.

Bill in equity. The complaint in an action in equity.

Bill of particulars. A written statement giving the details of the demand for which an action is brought, or of a defendant's counterclaim against such a demand, furnished by one of the parties to the other, either voluntarily or in compliance with a court order.

Bill of sale. Written evidence of the completion of a sale.

Blank endorsement. The signing of one's name to a commercial paper.

Blue Sky laws. Laws regulating the sale of stocks and bonds to the general public.

Bona fide. In good faith.

Brief. A written statement of a party's case.

Burden of proof. The necessity of proving the facts at issue in court.

Case. A dispute to be resolved in a court of law or equity.

Case law. Legal principles evolved from case decisions.

Cause of action. The right to bring a legal action.

Caveat emptor. Let the buyer beware.

Caveat venditor. Let the seller beware.

Certificate of deposit. A writing that acknowledges that the person named has deposited in the issuing bank a specified sum of money and that the bank will repay the money to the named individual, or to his order, or to some other person named in the instrument as payee.

Cestui que trust. A person who is the beneficial owner, or beneficiary, of property held in trust.

Charter. A grant of authority to exist as a corporation, issued by a state.

Chattel. An article of personal property.

Chattel mortgage. An instrument of sale of personalty that conveys the title of the property to the mortgagee and specifies the terms of defeasance.

Check. A draft drawn upon a deposit of funds in a bank directing the unconditional payment on demand of a sum certain in money to the person named on the instrument, or to his order, or to bearer.

Chose in action. A right to personal property that is not in the owner's possession, but to which he has a right of action for its possession.

Chose in possession. Personal property that is in the owner's possession and to which he has a right of possession.

Circumstantial evidence. Evidence relating to the circumstances of a case from which the jury may deduce what actually happened.

Civil rights. Private rights, protected by law, of members of society.

Close. An area of land bounded by a visible enclosure.

Cloud on title. Evidence that a third person has a claim to property.

Class action. A legal action brought by a limited number of persons on behalf of a larger number of persons similarly situated.

Codicil. An addition to a will, executed in the same manner as the will itself.

Cognovit. Admission by the defendant of the legitimacy of the plaintiff's claim.

Collateral heirs. Persons descended from a common ancestor but in different lines; cousins, for example.

Collusion. An agreement between two or more persons to defraud, or a conspiracy for some other illegal purpose.

Color of title. Apparent title; the misleading appearance that someone owns something, when in fact legitimate title may lie elsewhere.

Commodatum. A loan of property to be returned in kind and without payment.

Common law. A body of unwritten law based on the customs, habits, and usages of society.

Complainant. The plaintiff in a legal or an equitable pleading.

Complaint. The first pleading on the part of the plaintiff in a civil action (corresponding to a declaration in common law). Also, a charge, preferred before a court in order to begin prosecution, that the person named (or a certain person whose name is unknown) has committed a certain offense, together with an offer to prove the facts alleged.

Composition. An agreement between an insolvent debtor and his creditors whereby the latter agree to accept an amount less than the whole of their claims, to be distributed pro rata, in discharge and satisfaction of the entire debt.

Compos mentis. Of sound mind.

Compounding a felony. The offense committed by a person who, after having been directly injured by a felony, makes an agreement with the felon that he will not prosecute him, on the condition that the latter will make reparation or will tender him a bribe.

Concealment. The failure to volunteer relevant facts not apparent to the other party.

Conditional sale. A sale under the terms of which the passage of title depends on the performance of a stated act.

Confession of judgment. The act by which a debtor permits a judgment to be entered against him by his creditor without any legal proceedings having taken place.

Confusion. The mixing of goods of a similar nature belonging to different owners under such circumstances that the owner of one portion may become the owner of the entirety.

Connivance. Secret or indirect consent to, or permission for, the commission of an unlawful act.

Consanguinity. Blood relationship; the relationship that exists between persons descended from a common ancestor.

Conservator. The court-appointed guardian of an insane person's estate.

Consideration. The inducement to a contract; the thing of value which induces a contracting party to enter into a contract.

Consignee. One to whom a consignment is made; the person to whom goods are shipped for sale.

Consignor.   One who sends or makes a consignment; a shipper of goods.

Conspiracy.   An agreement between two or more persons to work together to commit a criminal act.

Constructive.   Inferred, legally interpreted to be so; construed by the courts to have a particular character or meaning other than or beyond what is actually expressed.

Contempt.   Conduct that is disruptive of a legislative or judicial proceeding or disobedience of a lawful order of a legislative or judicial body.

Contract.   An agreement enforceable in a court of law.

Contribution.   The sharing of a loss or a payment among several individuals; also reimbursement of a surety who has paid the entire debt by his co-sureties.

Contributory negligence.   Negligence on the part of the plaintiff that contributes to his injury. At common law a person guilty of such negligence cannot recover damages.

Conversion.   The unauthorized assumption of ownership of goods belonging to another.

Copyright.   A grant to an author or publisher of an exclusive right to publish and sell a literary work for a period of twenty-eight years, renewable for a second twenty-eight years.

Corporation.   An artificial legal person, created by the state, which for some purposes may act as a natural person and be treated as such.

Corporeal property.   Property that is discernible by the senses and may be seen and handled (as opposed to incorporeal property, which cannot be seen or handled and exists only in contemplation).

Corpus delicti.   Evidence that a crime has been committed.

Costs.   An allowance made to a successful party for his court costs in prosecuting or defending a suit. Costs rarely include attorney's fees.

Counterclaim.   A claim made by the defendant against the plaintiff; a cross-complaint.

"Court above"—"Court below."   The "court above" is the court to which a case is removed for review; the "court below" is the court from which the case is removed.

Court of record.   A court in which a permanent record is kept of proceedings.

Covenant.   An agreement or promise of two or more parties, given in a written, signed, and delivered deed, by which one party promises the other that something either is done or shall be done, or by which one party stipulates the truth of certain facts. Also, a promise contained in such an agreement.

Covenants of title.   Covenants made by the grantor of real property that guarantee such matters as his right to make the conveyance, his ownership of the property, and the freedom of the property from encumbrances.

Covert.   Covered, protected, sheltered.

Coverture.   The condition or state of a married woman; her legal status.

Crime.   A violation of the law punishable as an offense against the state.

Cross-complaint.   A conterclaim made by the defendant against the plaintiff.

Cross examination.   The examination of a party's witness by the attorney for the other party.

Culpable.   Evil or criminal.

Curtesy.   The common law right of a husband in the real property of his deceased wife, when there are surviving children who would also be capable of inheriting.

Cypres Doctrine.   As nearly as possible. When a trust cannot be carried out literally, an effort will be made to approximation the intent of the settler.

Damage.   Loss or injury to one's person or property caused by the negligence or intentional actions of another.

Damages.   Compensation claimed or awarded in a suit for damage suffered.

Deceit. A fraudulent misrepresentation made by one or more persons to another who is ignorant of the true facts, to his injury.

Declaration. The initial pleading filed by the plaintiff upon beginning his action, also called the complaint or petition.

Deed. An instrument purporting to convey an interest in real property, delivered by the party who is to be bound thereby and accepted by the party to whom the contract is given.

Defalcation. Embezzlement.

Default. Failure to perform.

Defeasance clause. A term of a mortgage that enables the mortgagor to defeat a foreclosure claim of the mortagee by paying off the amount of his obligation.

Defendant. The against person against whom a declaration or complaint is filed and who is named therein.

Deficiency judgment. A judgment against a debtor for the amount that still remains due after a mortgage foreclosure that did not discharge the full amount of the debt.

De jure. Of right; legitimate, lawful.

Delictum. A tort.

Delivery. The physical or constructive transfer of an instrument or of goods from one person to another.

Demise. (1) A conveyance of an estate to another for life, for a term of years, or at will; a lease. (2) Death or decease.

Demonstrative evidence. Evidence that consists of physical objects.

Demurrer. A plea by the defendant that concedes the truth of the facts in the case but alleges that the plaintiff does not have a cause of action.

De novo. Anew, over again.

Deponent. One who takes an oath in writing that certain facts are true.

Deposition. The testimony of a witness in response to questioning, not given in court, but taken for use in court.

Derivative action. Action brought by shareholders to enforce a corporate cause of action.

Descent. Hereditary succession.

Devise. A testamentary disposition of real property by the donor's will.

Dictum. A statement of law by a judge in an opinion that is not essential to the determination of that controversy.

Directed verdict. An instruction by the trial judge to the jury to return a verdict in favor of one of the parties to an action. The party requests the instruction.

Disparagement of goods. The making of false and derogatory statements about the economic goods of another.

Domestic corporation. A corporation chartered by the state in which it is doing business.

Domicile. The home of a person; the state in which a corporation was incorporated.

Dominant tenement. The tract of land benefited by an easement to which another tract, the servient tenement, is subject.

Dower. An estate for life, to which a widow is entitled, in that portion of her husband's estate to which she has not given up her right during the marriage.

Drawee. The person to whom a draft is addressed and who is requested to pay the sum of money therein named.

Drawer. The person drawing a draft and addressing it to the drawee.

Due care. The degree of care that a reasonable man can be expected to exercise in order to prevent harm that, under given circumstances, is reasonably foreseeable should such care not be taken.

Duress. A use of force or threat of force that deprives the victim of free will.

Earnest. A payment of a part of the price of goods sold, or a delivery of part of such goods, in order to make a contract binding.

Easement A right that inheres in the owner of one parcel of land, by reason of his ownership, to use the land of another for a special purpose.

Ejectment. An action to determine the title to certain land.

Emancipation. The act by which all rights and obligations in regard to a child are given up by his parents.

Embezzlement. The fraudulent appropriation to one's own use of benefit of property or money entrusted to the appropriator by another.

Eminent domain. The right of the government to take private property for public use in the name of the people.

Encumbrance. A claim or lien that affects title to real property.

Endorsee. The person to whom draft, promissory note, or other commercial paper is assigned by endorsement and who therefore has cause of action if payment is not made.

Endorsement. The signature of a payee, a drawee, or accomodation endorser, or a holder of a negotiable instrument, written on the back of the instrument, in order to transfer it to another.

Endorser. One who makes an endorsement.

Entirety. The whole (as opposed to a part). When land is conveyed to a husband and wife jointly, both own the entirety.

Equitable. Just, fair, or right; existing in equity.

Equity. A field of jurisdiction different in its origin, theory, and methodology from the common law.

Equity of redemption. The right of the mortgagor of an estate to redeem it, after the estate has been forfeited by a breach of a condition of the mortgage, by paying the amount of the debt, the interest, and other costs of foreclosure.

Error. A mistaken judgment or incorrect belief of a trial court as the existence or effect of matters of fact, or a false of mistaken conception or application of the law. (1) *Assignment of errors.* A statement of the errors upon which an appellant will rely, submitted to assist an appellate court in its examination of the transcript of a case under appeal. (2) *Harmless error.* An error committed during the progress of a trial that was not prejudicial to the rights of the party assigning it and for which, therefore, an appellate court will not reverse a judgment. (3) *Reversible error.* An error in original proceedings for which an appellate court will reverse the judgment under review.

Escheat. The reversion of the property of a decedent to the government when there is no legal heir.

Escrow. A deed that is held by a third person until a specified condition is fulfilled.

Estate. An interest in land or in any other subject of property.

Estoppel. A rule of law designed to prevent a person from denying a fact that his conduct influenced others to believe was true.

Et ux. And his wife.

Eviction. The act of depriving a person of the possession of lands held by him, pursuant to a court order.

Evidence. Any type of proof legally presented at a trial through witnesses, records, documents, or physical objects, for the purpose of inducing belief in the mind of the court or the jury as to the truth or falsity of the facts at issue.

Exception. A formal objection to the action of the court raised during a trial, implying that the objecting party does not agree with the decision of the court and that he will seek a reversal of the judgment handed down.

Ex contractu. From or out of a contract. The term is usually used to refer to a cause of action arising from a contract.

Ex delicto. From a tort or crime.

Executed. Completed; fully carried into effect.

Executor. A person appointed by a testator to carry out the directions and requests in his will and to dispose of his property according to the testamentary provisions of the will.

Executory. Something that is yet to be executed or performed; that which is incomplete or dependent upon a future performance or event.

Exemplary damages. Damages in excess of the amount needed to compensate the plaintiff for his injury, awarded to punish the defendant for malicious or willful conduct.

Exemption. A privilege allowed by law to a debtor by which he may hold a certain amount of property or certain classes of property free from all liability—free from seizure and sale by court order or from attachment by his creditors.

Ex parte. On one side only; by one party; done for, or on behalf of, one party only.

Express. Set forth in direct and appropriate language (as opposed to that which is implied from conduct).

Fee simple. The most complete form of ownership of real property.

Fee tail. A common law form of inheritance under which property descends only to a certain class of heirs.

Felony. An offense punishable by confinement in prison or by death, or an offense expressly deemed a felony by statute.

Fiction. An assumption of the law.

Fixture. Personal property attached to real property in such a manner that it is considered part of the realty.

F.O.B. Free on board. A shipping term designating a seller's intention to deliver goods on board a car or ship at a designated place without charge to the buyer.

Forcible detainer. The offense of keeping possession of lands by force and without legal authority.

Forcible entry. An offense or a private wrong committed by taking possession of lands by force and without legal authority.

Foreclosure. A proceeding by which the rights of the mortgagee of real property are enforced against the mortgagor.

Forgery. The fraudulent making of an instrument that, if genuine, would appear to create contractual liability in another.

Franchise. Any special privilege conferred by a governmental body upon an individual or a corporation.

Fraud. An intentional misinterpretation of a material fact made in order to deprive another of his rights or to induce him to enter into a contract.

Fungible goods. Goods of a class in which any unit is the equivalent of any other unit.

Future estate. An estate that will not take effect until the termination of the present estate.

Garnishment. See Attachment.

General creditor. A creditor who has an unsecured claim against a debtor.

General issue. A plea that denies every material allegation in the plaintiff's complaint.

General verdict. The ordinary form of verdict, either for the plaintiff or for the defendant.

Gift causa mortis. A gift made by the donor in contemplation of his supposedly imminent death.

Good faith. Honest intentions.

Grant. To convey real property.

Gratuitous bailment. A bailment for the benefit of the bailor.

Gravamen. The material part or gist of a charge.

Guaranty. A promise to be responsible for the performance of another.

Habeus corpus. A writ obtained to test whether a prisoner is being lawfully held.

Habendum clause. The clause in a deed describing the estate granted.

Hearsay. Evidence attested by a witness that is derived not from his personal knowledge but from what others have told him.

Heirs. Persons entitled to receive an estate or a portion of an estate that a decedent has not effectively disposed of by will.

Hereditaments. Things capable of being inherited.

Holder. The person in possession of a negotiable instrument.

Holographic will. A will entirely handwritten by the testator.

Homestead. Real estate occupied as a home. It is exempt within certain limitations from attachment by creditors.

Hung jury. A jury that are unable to agree upon a verdict.

Illusory. Appears to be, but is not.

Immunity. Freedom from legal duties and obligations.

Impanel. To make a list of those who have been selected for a jury.

Implied. Found from the circumstances of the case.

Inchoate. Not perfect or perfected.

Indicia. A sign or indication.

Indictment. The formal written accusation of a crime, presented by a grand jury.

Infant. A person under the age of twenty-one years; a minor.

Information. In criminal law, an accusation by a public officer (as distinguished from a finding by a grand jury) that is made the basis of a prosecution for a crime.

Injunction. An order issued by a court of equity directing a person or a group to do, or to refrain from doing, a specified act.

Injury. Any wrong or damage to the person, rights, reputation, or property of another.

In pari delicto. In equal fault; equally guilty.

In personam. Against a specific person (as opposed to *In rem*).

In re. In the matter.

In rem. Against a thing; directed at specific property or at a specific right or status.

Insolvency. A state in which debts and liabilities exceed assets.

Interpleader. A form of action by which a third person who holds property or monies to which he has no claim and against whom conflicting claims are made may bring the complaining parties into court to settle their claims.

Inter se. Between or among themselves.

Inter vivos. Any transaction that takes place among living persons.

Intestate. Without a will.

Intestate succession. A distribution, directed by statute, of property owned by a decedent and not effectively disposed of by will.

Ipso facto. By the fact itself.

Jeopardy. Danger, peril. A person is said to be in jeopardy when he is officially charged with a crime before a court of law.

Jointly. Acting together. When persons are jointly liable, they all must be sued or none can be sued.

Jointly and severally. Acting together and separately. Anyone so liable can sue (or be sued) with or without the others joining (or being joined) in the action.

Joint tenancy. An estate in entirety held by two or more persons with the right of survivorship.

Judgment. The final order of a court, entered upon the completion of an action.

Judgment note. A note authorizing a judgment to be entered against a debtor if the note is not paid when it falls due.

Judgment on the pleadings. A judgment entered upon the request of either party to an action after the pleadings have been filed, when it is apparent from the content of the pleadings that one party is entitled to a decision in his favor without proceeding further.

Judicial sale. A sale made under a court order by an officer appointed to make the sale.

Jurisdiction. The power and authority conferred upon a court, either constitutionally or by statute.

Laches. An equitable principle that discourages delay in the enforcement of legal rights.

"Last clear chance." In accident cases, the courts hold that if the defendant had the last clear chance to avoid an accident, he is liable even though the plaintiff may have been guilty of contributory negligence.

Leading question. A question during a cross-examination that suggests to the witness what his response should be.

Lease. A conveyance of lands or tenements to a person for life, for a term of years, or at will, in consideration of a return of rent or some other form of compensation.

Leasehold. An estate held under a lease; an estate for a fixed term of years.

Legacy. A bequest of personal property by will.

Legal tender. A medium of exchange that the law compels a creditor to accept in payment of a debt when it is legally offered to him by the debtor.

Lessee. One to whom a lease is made.

Lessor. One who grants a lease.

Let. To demise, to lease.

Letters of administration. The formal instrument that appoints an administrator, issued by the court having jurisdiction over an estate. They empower him to enter upon the discharge of his administratorial duties.

Letters testamentary. The formal instrument that appoints an executor, issued by the court having jurisdiction over a decedent's property. They empower him to enter upon the discharge of his duties as executor.

Levy. To exact, collect, gather, seize.

Lex loci. The law of the place where an accident occurred.

Lex loci contractus. The law of the place where a contract was made.

Lex loci fori. The law of the place where an action was brought.

License. A personal privilege.

Lien. A claim against, or a right to, property.

Life estate. An estate the duration of which is limited to the life of the person named in the grant; a freehold estate that cannot be passed on to one's heirs.

Life tenant. One who holds an estate in lands for the period of his own life or that of another person named.

Limitation. Anything that defines or limits, either by words or by implication, the time during which an estate granted may be enjoyed.

Lineal heirs. Those directly descended from an ancestor; children or grandchildren, for example.

Liquidated. Determined, clarified, fixed.

Liquidated damages. Damages that must be paid, in the amount stipulated by a contract, in the event of a breach of the contract.

Lis pendens. A suit pending; the filing of legal notice that there is a dispute about the title to property.

Maker. One who executes a legal instrument.

Malfeasance. The performance of an unlawful act.

Malum in se.   An act that is wrong in itself.

Malum prohibitum.   An act that is prohibited by law.

Mandamus.   A court order compelling an individual to fulfill an official duty.

Marshalling assets.   The distributing of a partner's assets upon termination of a partnership so as to obtain the greatest benefit for his creditors.

Maturity.   The due date of an instrument.

Mechanic's lien.   A claim created by statute for the benefit of persons supplying materials for the construction of a building, giving them a lien on the building.

Mens rea.   The state of mind of the actor.

Merchantable.   Of good quality; salable in the regular course of business.

Merger.   A joining of two corporations whereby one company retains its original identity.

Mesne.   Intermediate, intervening.

Minor.   A person who is under the age of legal competence specified by statute; usually, a person under twenty-one years of age.

Misdemeanor.   A crime that is neither a felony nor treason.

Misfeasance.   The performing of a lawful act in an improper manner.

Misrepresentation.   An intentionally false statement of fact.

Mitigation of damages.   The duty of the plaintiff to avoid increasing his damages and to limit them where possible.

Moiety.   One-half.

Moot case.   A hypothetical or nonexisting controversy.

Moratorium.   A temporary suspension of the enforcement of debts.

Mutuality.   Reciprocation of understanding. Both parties to a contract must have a clear understanding of the legal obligations of their agreement.

Necessaries.   That which is reasonably needed to maintain one's accustomed standard of living.

Negative covenant.   An agreement in a deed to refrain from doing something.

Negligence.   The failure to do something that a reasonable man would do, or the commission of an act that a reasonable man would not commit, that results, in an ordinary and natural sequence, in damage to another.

Negotiable instrument.   An instrument containing an obligation for the payment of a sum certain in money, the legal title to which may be transferred from one person to another by endorsement and delivery by the holder or by delivery only.

Nil debit.   A plea that the defendant owes nothing.

Nisi prius.   A trial court (as distinguished from an appellate court).

Nolo contendere.   A plea which has the effect of a guilty plea in a criminal action.

Nominal damages.   A token sum awarded to the plaintiff when he has suffered no actual damage.

Non compos mentis.   Not sound of mind; insane.

Nuncupative will.   An oral will.

Non est factum.   A plea that a note sued on was never made or executed.

Nonfeasance.   The neglect or failure to do something that one ought to do.

Non obstante veredicto.   A judgment given that is contrary to the verdict of the jury.

Nonsuit.   An abandonment of suit by the plaintiff.

Novation.   Release by agreement from a contractual obligation by substitution of a third party for the original obligor.

Nudum pactum.   An agreement or promise made without consideration and thus not legally enforceable under normal circumstances.

Nuisance.   Improper personal conduct, or the unreasonable use by a person of his own property, that obstructs the rights of others or of the public and produces material inconvenience or hardship.

Obliteration. An erasure or crossing out that makes all or portions of a will impossible to read. Sections so altered are considered to be revoked when the changes were made by the testator for the purpose of revocation.

Occupation. Taking possession of property; a method of acquiring title to personal property that is in an ownerless state.

Operation of law. The automatic attaching of certain legal consequences to certain facts.

Opinion evidence. The conclusions that a witness draws from what he has observed (as opposed to the observation itself).

Option. A contract to hold an offer open for a fixed period of time.

Ordinance. A statutory enactment of the legislative branch of a municipal government.

Ostensible agency. An implied agency that exists when a supposed principal by his conduct induces another to believe that a third person is his agent, although the principal never actually employed him.

Ostensible partner. A partner whose name is publicly made known (as opposed to a silent partner).

Parol. Oral, spoken.

Parol evidence rule. The construction that additional evidence is not considered by the courts to alter a contract that is complete on its face.

Partition. A division of real property between co-owners.

Patent. The giving of a privilege or property by a government to one or more individuals. (1) The conveyance by which a government grants lands in the public domain to an individual.(2) The privilege given to an inventor allowing him the exclusive right to make and sell his invention for a definite period of time.

Pawn. A bailment of goods to a creditor as security for a debt; a pledge.

Payee. One to whom a negotiable instrument is made payable.

Payer, payor. One who pays a negotiable instrument.

Per curiam opinion. An opinion written with the concurrence of all the members of the court.

Perform. To do any action, other than making payment, in discharge of a contract.

Performance. The fulfillment of a contractual obligation according to the terms of the agreement.

Perpetual succession. The right of a corporation to carry on its corporate existence for an unlimited period of time.

Per se. By itself; standing alone; not related to other matters.

Per stirpes. The distribution of a decedent's estate according to degree of relationship.

Petition. The first pleading by the plaintiff in a civil case, also called the complaint.

Petty jury, petit jury. The twelve-man jury in a trial court.

Plaintiff. One who brings an aciton.

Plaintiff in error. A party who bases his appeal on an error in a judgment rendered by a trial court.

Plead. To make, deliver, or file a pleading.

Pleadings. The papers filed by the parties in an action.

Pledge. A bailment of goods as security for a debt.

Pledgee. One to whom the goods are pledged.

Pledgor. The party delivering the goods in a pledge.

Police power. The power of the state to enact laws for the protection of the public health, safety, welfare, and morals.

Polling the jury. Asking each member of the jury in open court how he voted on the verdict.

Possessory lien. The right to retain property as security for a debt.

Postdate. To record a date later than the date of execution on an instrument.

Precatory. Indicating a desire or wish.

Preference. The payment of money or the transfer of property to one creditor in priority to other creditors.

Prescription. The acquisition of title to incorporeal hereditaments by virtue of having used or enjoyed them for a long period of time.

Presentment. The exhibition of a draft to the drawee for his acceptance or to the drawer or acceptor for payment; also, the exhibition of a promissory note to the party liable, with a demand for payment.

Presumption. An inference of the truth or falsehood of a proposition or a fact, in the absence of actual certainty as to its truth or falsehood, by a process of probable reasoning.

Prima facie. At first sight; on first appearance; presumably.

Privileged communication. A communication concerning which a witness may refuse to testify in open court because of his relationship with the person from whom he received the information; a communication between a lawyer and his client, for example.

Privity. An immediate relationship. A party to a contract is said to have "privity" with regard to the making of a contract.

Probate. The act or process of proving the validity of a will.

Process. A court order informing the defendant that he is required to appear in court.

Promissory note. A promise in writing to pay a specified sum within a certain time, on demand, or at sight, to a named person, to his order, or to bearer.

Promoters. The organizers of a corporation.

Prosecute. To bring suit and carry on an action against a person in court.

Pro tanto. For so much; as far as it goes.

Protest. A formal, written statement, made by a notary at the request of the holder of a commercial paper, that the draft or note was presented for payment (or acceptance) and that payment (or acceptance) was refused. The protest also states the reasons if any, given, for the dishonor.

Proximate cause. That act which is the effective cause of an injury; an act from which the injury could reasonably be expected to result.

Proximate damage. Damage that is a reasonably foreseeable result of an action.

Punitive damages. Damages over and above the amount necessary to compensate an injured party. They are imposed to punish a wrongdoer.

Qualified acceptance. A conditional or modified acceptance of a draft that in some way changes the terms of the instrument.

Qualified endorsement. An endorsement containing the words "without recourse," or words of similar import, evidencing the endorser's intent not to be bound should the primary party fail to pay.

Quantum meruit. As much as he deserved.

Quasi. As it if were; having the characteristics of.

Quasi contract. A contract implied in law.

Quid pro quo. Something for something.

Quiet title. An action brought to settle claims against the title to a piece of property.

Quit claim deed. A deed purporting to transfer whatever interest, if any, the grantor has in the property concerned.

Quorum. The minimum number of persons that must be present before business can be transacted.

Quo warranto. An action compelling someone (usually a corporation) to show by whose authority he is transacting business.

Ratification. The acceptance of responsibility for, and the undertaking of the obligations incurred by, a previous act committed either by oneself or by one's agent.

Real property. A general term for land and everything attached to it.

Receipt. Acceptance of something delivered.

Receiver. A person appointed by the court to collect the rents and profits of land, or the growth of personal estates, or to transact other business that the court thinks not reasonable that either party should transact or that a party is incompetent to transact.

Recognizance. An obligation entered into before a court or magistrate to do a particular act—for example, to appear in court or to pay a debt.

Recoupment. The right of the defendant to obtain a reduction in the amount of the plaintiff's damages because the plaintiff, too, has failed to comply with certain obligations or conditions of the contract.

Recovery. The collection of a debt through an action at law. (See also *Right of Recovery.*)

Redemption. A buying back of property. A mortgage conveys the title to property to the mortgagee, subject to a right of redemption of the mortgagor: The mortgagor has a right to defeat the conveyance of the title by paying the amount of the debt secured by the mortgage.

Reimbursement. A surety's right to be repaid by his principal for debts paid on the principal's behalf.

Release. The giving up of a right or privilege by the person in whom it existed to the person against whom it might have been demanded or enforced.

Remainder. An estate that takes effect and may be enjoyed only after another estate is determined.

Remand. To send a case back to a trial court for a new trial in accordance with the decision of an appellate court.

Remedial. Pertaining to a legal remedy, or to the form or procedural details of such a remedy, that is to be taken after a legal or an equitable wrong has been committed.

Remedy. The means by which the violation of a right is prevented or compensated for.

Replevin. A personal action brought to recover possession of goods taken from one unlawfully.

Rescission. Cancellation of a contract by one or both parties.

Residuary. Constituting the residue; entitled to the residue.

Residuary devisee. The person named in a will to take all the real property that remains after the specified devises have been granted.

Residuary estate. The part of a testator's estate and effects that remains after all particular devises and bequests have been made.

Residuary legatee. The person to whom a testator bequeaths the residue of his personal estate, after the payment of all other legacies are specifically mentioned in the will.

Respondeat superior. A legal maxim that a master is liable in certain cases for the wrongful acts of his servant, and a principal for those of his agent.

Respondent. One who makes an answer to or argues against an appeal.

Reversal. The decision of an appellate court to annul or vacate a judgment or decree of a trial court.

Revocation. The recall of some power, authority, or thing granted; also, the destruction or voiding of a legal document.

Right of entry. The right of taking or resuming possession of land by entering peaceably on it.

Right of recovery. A right of action deriving from a legal wrong committed in a given case.

Right to redeem. The right of a debtor whose property has been mortgaged, then sold to another to pay a debt, to repurchase the property.

Riparian. Relating to the bank of a river.

"Run with the land." Certain covenants in a deed to land are deemed to "run" or pass with the land in order that whoever owns the land is bound by or entitled to the benefit of the covenants, even though the agreements are not in the public record.

Sale or return. A sale in which, although title passes to the buyer at the time of the agreement, he has the option of returning title to the seller.

Satisfaction. The act of discharging an obligation owed to a party by paying what is due him or what is awarded to him by the judgment of a court.

Scienter. Knowingly.

Scintilla. A spark, a remaining particle; hence, the least evidence.

Scire facias. A judicial writ, founded upon some record, requiring the person against whom it is brought to show cause why the party bringing it should not be able to enforce or annul that record.

Seal. An impression on wax or some other substance used at common law to authenticate legal documents.

Seisin. Possession with the intention to claim a freehold interest.

Set-off. A counterclaim, a cross-demand.

Severable contract. A contract one part of which may be separated from the other parts and performed or enforced alone.

Severalty. The sole ownership of real property.

Severance. The separating of anything from the land.

Silent partner. A partner whose name or connection with a firm is not known to the public (as opposed to an ostensible or acknowledged partner).

Slander. Oral defamation of character.

Slander per se. Words slanderous in themselves whether or not damage can be proven to result from them. To have a case, it is necessary merely to allege that they have been published.

Simple contract. A contract based on consideration, not on any special formal document.

Special agent. An agent authorized to conduct a specific transaction.

Special appearance. A person's appearance in court for a specific purpose, without his submitting to the jurisdiction of the court.

Special damages. Damages that are the actual and natural, although not the necessary, result of the proximate cause of an injury. They must be proven according to the special circumstances of a particular case.

Specific performance. An equitable remedy by which a contracting party is compelled to perform his obligations under the terms of the contract.

Stare decisis. To stand by that which has been decided. A case decision serves as a legal precedent in the deciding of subsequent similar cases.

Statute of frauds. A statute that requires certain contracts to be in writing before they will be accepted as valid, enforceable contracts. It is designed to prevent contracts based upon perjured testimony.

Statute of limitations. A statute that limits the period of time in which an enforceable cause of action may be brought.

Stipulation. An agreement between opposing counsel that they will accept certain things in evidence without the necessity of proof.

Stoppage in transitu. The right of an unpaid seller to stop goods before they arrive at the buyer's destination.

Subrogation. The substitution of one thing for another, or of one person in place of another, with respect to rights, claims, or securities.

Subscribe. To write one's name at the bottom or end of a writing.

Substantive law. That part of the law that creates, defines, and regulates rights (as opposed to procedural law, which prescribes methods of enforcing rights or obtaining remedies for this invasion).

Sui generis. Of its own kind or class.

Sui juris. Of his own right; having legal capacity to manage his own affairs.

Summary. Immediate; rendered without a jury.

Summary judgment. A judgment entered by a court when no substantial dispute of fact exists and one party can be shown to have no true cause of action.

Summary proceeding. A brief proceeding, usually conducted with less formality than a normal court proceeding.

Summons. A writ served upon a defendant to secure his appearance in court.

Surety. A person who makes himself liable for the obligations of another.

Survivorship. The right of a surviving tenant (or tenants) to take the share (or shares) of a tenant who dies.

Tangible. Having physical qualities.

Tenancy at sufferance. An illegal staying on by a tenant after a lease has expired.

Tenancy at will. The possession of land for an indefinite period of time that may be terminated at any time by either party without notice being given.

Tenancy for years. A tenancy for any fixed period of time. (The period may be less than year.)

Tenancy from year to year. A tenancy that continues indefinitely from year to year (or any other period of time) until terminated.

Tenancy in common. The ownership of property by two or more persons.

Tenancy in partnership. The form of ownership of partnership property that was created by the Uniform Partnership Act.

Tender. An unconditional offer by a party who is able to complete an obligation.

Tenor. The true meaning or effect of an instrument.

Terminable fee. An estate that may be terminated upon the occurrence of some event.

Testamentary capacity. The capacity to make a will.

Testate. Having left a will.

Testate succession. The distribution of a testator's estate according to the terms of his will.

Testator, testatrix. One who makes a will.

Third party beneficiary. A third person who is directly benefited by the making of a contract to which he is not a party.

Toll the statute. To stop the operation of the time period specified by the statute of limitations.

Tort. A wrong committed upon the person or property of another; an invasion of a private right.

Tort feasor. One who commits a tort.

Tortious. Wrongful.

Transcript. A copy of a writing; a court record.

Transitory action. An action brought against a defendant in any county where service or process may be obtained.

Trespass. (1) An injury to the person, property, or rights of another. (2) A common law action for money damages for injury to one's person, property, or rights.

Trier of fact. Usually, a jury.

Trover. An action against a person who has wrongfully converted another's goods to his own use. The action is for damages, not for the return of the goods.

Trust. An equitable right to land or other property, held for a beneficiary by another person, in whom the legal title rests.

Trust deed. An instrument that is substituted for and serves as a mortgage, by which the legal title to real property is placed in one or more trustees, to secure the repayment of a sum of money or the performance of other conditions.

Trustee. One appointed to execute a trust; a person in whom an estate, interest, or power is vested under an agreement that he shall administer or exercise if for the benefit or use of another.

Ultra vires. Beyond the powers conferred upon a corporation by its charter.

Undisclosed principal. A principal whose existence and identity are unknown to third parties.

Undue influence. Dominance of one person in a fiduciary relationship over another, sufficient to inhibit or destroy the weaker party's free will.

Unilateral contract. A contract consisting of a promise made by one party in return for an act to be done by the other.

Unincorporated association. A combination of two or more persons to achieve a common end.

Universal agent. An agent authorized to commit any act that the principal himself might lawfully perform.

Usury. The charging of an illegally high interest rate.

Vacation of judgment. The setting aside of a judgment by a court.

Valid. Legally sufficient.

Vendee. A purchaser, a buyer.

Vendor. A seller.

Venire. To appear in court. A writ of venire is used to summon a jury.

Veracity. Truthfulness.

Verdict. The decision of a jury.

Vested. Accrued, settled, absolute; not contingent upon anything; having an immediate right to the enjoyment of property.

Void. Having no legal effect; not binding.

Voidable. Subject to being declared ineffectual. A contract is voidable when one party has grounds for refusing to perform his obligations.

Voidable preference. A preference given by a bankrupt person or firm to one creditor over others. It may be set aside by the trustee in bankruptcy.

Voir dire examination. An examination to determine the qualifications of a juror or witness.

Volenti non fit injuria. He who consents cannot be injured.

Voluntary nonsuit. A means available to the plaintiff for stopping a trial in a civil suit.

Waiver. The giving up of a legal right.

Ward. A person under the care of court.

Warrant. A guaranty that certain facts are true as represented.

Warranty of authority. An implied warranty that an agent possesses the authority that he represents himself as possessing.

Waste. A reduction in value to property caused by the person in possession.

Watered stock. Stock recorded in the books of a corporation as being fully paid when in fact it is not.

Will. The legal expression of a person's wishes regarding the disposition of his property after his death.

Witness. An individual who testifies under oath in a legal action.

Writ of certiorari. An order from an appellate court to a lower court requesting the record of a case that is to be reviewed by the appellate court.

Writ of entry. An action to recover the possession of real property.

Writ of error. The order of an appellate court authorizing a lower court to remit to it the official record of the proceedings in a case where an error sufficient to invalidate the verdict is claimed.

APPENDIX
UNIFORM COMMERCIAL CODE
Selected Sections
[1972 Amendments]

ARTICLE ONE—GENERAL PROVISIONS

PART 1

Short Title, Construction, Application and Subject Matter of the Act

§ 1-101. **Short Title.**—This Act shall be known and may be cited as Uniform Commercial Code.

§ 1-102 **Purposes; Rules of Construction; Variation by Agreement.**—
(1) This Act shall be liberally construed and applied to promote its underlying purposes and policies.
(2) Underlying purposes and policies of this Act are
  (a) to simplify, clarify and modernize the law governing commercial transactions;
  (b) to permit the continued expansion of commercial practices through custom, usage and agreement of the parties;
  (c) to make uniform the law among the various jurisdictions.
(3) The effect of provisions of this Act may be varied by agreement, except as otherwise provided in this Act and except that the obligations of good faith, diligence, reasonableness and care prescribed by this Act may not be disclaimed by agreement but the parties may by agreement determine the standards by which the performance of such obligations is to be measured if such standards are not manifestly unreasonable.
(4) The presence in certain provisions of this Act of the words "unless otherwise agreed" or words of similar import does not imply that the effect of other provisions may not be varied by agreement under subsection (3).
(5) In this Act unless the context otherwise requires
  (a) words in the singular number include the plural, and in the plural include the singular.
  (b) words of the masculine gender include the feminine and the neuter, and when the sense so indicates words of the neuter gender may refer to any gender.

§ 1-103. **Supplementary General Principles of Law Applicable.**—Unless displaced by the particular provisions of this Act, the principles of law and equity, including the law merchant and the law relative to capacity to contract, principal and agent, estoppel, fraud, misrepresentation, duress, coercion, mistake, bankruptcy, or other validating or invalidating cause shall supplement its provisions.

§ 1-104. **Construction Against Implicit Repeal.**—This Act being a general act intended as a unified coverage of its subject matter, no part of it shall be deemed to be impliedly repealed by subsequent legislation if such construction can reasonably be avoided.

§ 1-105. **Territorial Application of the Act; Parties' Power to Choose Applicable Law.**—
(1) Except as provided hereafter in this section, when a transaction bears a reasonable relation to this state and also to another state or nation the parties may agree

that the law either of this state or of such other state or nation shall govern their rights and duties. Failing such agreement this Act applies to transactions bearing an appropriate relation to this state.

(2) Where one of the following provisions of this Act specifies the applicable law, that provision governs and a contrary agreement is effective only to the extent permitted by the law (including the conflict of laws rules) so specified:

Rights of creditors against sold goods. Section 2-402.

Applicability of the Article on Bank Deposits and Collections. Section 4-102.

Bulk transfers subject to the Article on Bulk Transfers. Section 6-102.

Applicability of the Article on Investment Securities. Section 8-106.

Perfection provisions of the Article on Secured Tansactions. Section 9-103.

§ **1-106. Remedies to Be Liberally Administered.—**
(1) The remedies provided by this Act shall be liberally administered to the end that the aggrieved party may be put in as good a position as if the other party had fully performed but neither consequential or special nor penal damages may be had except as specifically provided in this Act or by other rule of law.

(2) Any right or obligation declared by this Act is enforceable by action unless the provision declaring it specifies a different and limited effect.

§ **1-107. Waiver or Renunciation of Claim or Right After Breach.—**Any claim or right arising out of an alleged breach can be discharged in whole or in part without consideration by a written waiver or renunciation signed and delivered by the aggrieved party.

§ **1-108. Severability.—**If any provision or clause of this Act or application thereof to any person or circumstances is held invalid, such invalidity shall not affect other provisions or applications of the Act which can be given effect without the invalid provision or application, and to this end the provisions of this Act are declared to be severable.

§ **1-109. Section Captions.—**Section captions are parts of this Act.

PART 2

General Definitions and Principles of Interpretation

§ **1-201. General Definitions.—**Subject to additional definitions contained in the subsequent Articles of this Act which are applicable to specific Articles or Parts thereof, and unless the context otherwise requires, in this Act:

(1) "Action" in the sense of a judicial proceeding includes recoupment, counterclaim, set-off, suit in equity and any other proceedings in which rights are determined.

(2) "Aggrieved party" means a party entitled to resort to a remedy.

(3) "Agreement" means the bargain of the parties in fact as found in their language or by implication from other circumstances including course of dealing or usage of trade or course of performance as provided in this Act (Sections 1-205 and 2-208). Whether an agreement has legal consequences is determined by the provisions of this Act, if applicable; otherwise by the law of contracts (Section 1-103). (Compare "Contract".)

(4) "Bank" means any person engaged in the business of banking.

(5) "Bearer" means the person in possession of an instrument, document of title, or security payable to bearer or indorsed in blank.

(6) "Bill of lading" means a document evidencing the receipt of goods for shipment issued by a person engaged in the business of transporting or forwarding goods, and includes an airbill. "Airbill" means a document serving for air transportation as a bill

of lading does for marine or rail transportation, and includes an air consignment note or air waybill.

(7) "Branch" includes a separately incorporated foreign branch of a bank.

(8) "Burden of establishing" a fact means the burden of persuading the triers of fact that the existence of the fact is more probable than its non-existence.

(9) "Buyer in ordinary course of business" means a person who in good faith and without knowledge that the sale to him is in violation of the ownership rights or security interest of a third party in the goods buys in ordinary course from a person in the business of selling goods of that kind but does not include a pawnbroker. [All persons who sell minerals or the like (including oil and gas) at wellhead or minehead shall be deemed to be persons in the business of selling goods of that kind.] "Buying" may be for cash or by exchange of other property or on secured or unsecured credit and includes receiving goods or documents of title under a pre-existing contract for sale but does not include a transfer in bulk or as security for or in total or partial satisfaction of a money debt.

(10) "Conspicuous": A term or clause is conspicuous when it is so written that a reasonable person against whom it is to operate ought to have noticed it. A printed heading in capitals (as: NON-NEGOTIABLE BILL OF LADING) is conspicuous. Language in the body of a form is "conspicuous" if it is in larger or other contrasting type or color. But in a telegram any stated term is "conspicuous". Whether a term or clause is "conspicuous" or not is for decision by the court.

(11) "Contract" means the total legal obligation which results from the parties' agreement as affected by this Act and any other applicable rules or law. (Compare "Agreement".)

(12) "Creditor" includes a general creditor, a secured creditor, a lien creditor and any representative of creditors, including an assignee for the benefit of creditors, a trustee in bankruptcy, a receiver in equity and an executor or administrator of an insolvent debtor's or assignor's estate.

(13) "Defendant" includes a person in the position of defendant in a cross-action or counterclaim.

(14) "Delivery" with respect to instruments, documents of title, chattel paper or securities means voluntary transfer of possession.

(15) "Document of title" includes a bill of lading, dock warrant, dock receipt, warehouse receipt or order for the delivery of goods, and also any other document which in the regular course of business or financing is treated as adequately evidencing that the person in possession of it is entitled to receive, hold and dispose of the document and the goods it covers. To be a document of title a document must purport to be issued by or addressed to a bailee and purport to cover goods in the bailee's possession which are either identified or are fungible portions of an identified mass.

(16) "Fault" means wrongful act, omission or breach.

(17) "Fungible" with respect to goods or securities means goods or securities of which any unit is, by nature or usage of trade, the equivalent of any other like unit. Goods which are not fungible shall be deemed fungible for the purposes of this Act to the extent that under a particular agreement or document unlike units are treated as equivalents.

(18) "Genuine" means free of forgery or counterfeiting.

(19) "Good faith" means honesty in fact in the conduct or transaction concerned.

(20) "Holder" means a person who is in possession of a document of title or an instrument or an investment security drawn, issued or indorsed to him or to his order or to bearer or in blank.

(21) To "honor" is to pay or to accept and pay, or where a credit so engages to purchase or discount a draft complying with the terms of the credit.

(22) "Insolvency proceedings" includes any assignment for the benefit of creditors or other proceedings intended to liquidate or rehabilitate the estate of the person involved.

(23) A person is "insolvent" who either has ceased to pay his debts in the ordinary course of business or cannot pay his debts as they become due or is insolvent within the meaning of the federal bankruptcy law.

(24) "Money" means a medium of exchange authorized or adopted by a domestic or foreign government as a part of its currency.

(25) A person has "notice" of a fact when

(a) he has actual knowledge of it; or

(b) he has received a notice or notification of it; or

(c) from all the facts and circumstances known to him at the time in question he has reason to know that it exists.

A person "knows" or has "knowledge" of a fact when he has actual knowledge of it. "Discover" or "learn" or a word or phrase of similar import refers to knowledge rather than to reason to know. The time and circumstances under which a notice or notification may cease to be effective are not determined by this Act.

(26) A person "notifies" or "gives" a notice or notification to another by taking such steps as may be reasonably required to inform the other in ordinary course whether or not such other actually comes to know of it. A person "receives" a notice or notification when

(a) it comes to his attention; of

(b) it is duly delivered at the place of business through which the contract was made or at any other place held out by him as the place for receipt of such communications.

(27) Notice, knowledge or a notice or notification received by an organization is effective for a particular transaction from the time when it is brought to the attention of the individual conducting that transaction, and in any event from the time when it would have been brought to his attention if the organization had exercised due diligence.

(28) "Organization" includes a corporation, government or governmental subdivision or agency, business trust, estate, trust, partnership or association, two or more persons having a joint or common interest, or any other legal or commercial entity.

(29) "Party", as distinct from "third party", means a person who has engaged in a transaction or made an agreement within this Act.

(30) "Person" includes an individual or an organization (See Section 1-102).

(31) "Presumption" or "presumed" means that the trier of fact must find the existence of the fact presumed unless and until evidence is introduced which would support a finding of its nonexistence.

(32) "Purchase" includes taking by sale, discount, negotiation, mortgage, pledge, lien, issue or re-issue, gift or any other voluntary transaction creating an interest in property.

(33) "Purchaser" means a person who takes by purchase.

(34) "Remedy" means any remedial right to which an aggrieved party is entitled with or without resort to a tribunal.

(35) "Representative" includes an agent an officer of a corporation or association, and a trustee, executor or administrator of an estate, or any other person empowered to act for another.

(36) "Rights" includes remedies.

(37) "Security interest" means an interest in personal property or fixtures which secures payment or performance of an obligation. The retention or reservation of title by a seller of goods nonwithstanding shipment or delivery to the buyer (Section 2-401) is limited in effect to a reservation of a "security interest". The term also includes any interest of a buyer of accounts [or] chattel paper which is subject to Article 9. The special property interest of a buyer of goods on identification of such goods to a contract for sale under Section 2-401 is not a "security interest", but a buyer may also acquire a "security interest" by complying with Article 9. Unless a lease or consignment is intended as security, reservation of title thereunder is not a "security interest" but a

consignment is in any event subject to the provisions on consignment sales (Section 2-326). Whether a lease is intended as security is to be determined by the facts of each case; however,

(a) the inclusion of an option to purchase does not of itself make the lease one intended for security, and

(b) an agreement that upon compliance with the terms of the lease the lessee shall become or has the option to become the owner of the property for no additional consideration or for a nominal consideration does make the lease one intended for security.

(38) "Send" in connection with any writing or notice means to deposit in the mail or deliver for transmission by any other usual means of communication with postage or cost of transmission provided for and properly addressed and in the case of an instrument to an address specified thereon or otherwise agreed, or if there be none to any address specified thereon or otherwise agreed, or if there be none to any address reasonable under the circumstances. The receipt of any writing or notice within the time at which it would have arrived if properly sent has the effect of a proper sending.

(39) "Signed" includes any symbol executed or adopted by a party with present intention to authenticate a writing.

(40) "Surety" includes guarantor.

(41) "Telegram" includes a message transmitted by radio, teletype, cable, any mechanical method of transmission, or the like.

(42) "Term" means that portion of an agreement which relates to a particular matter.

(43) "Unauthorized" signature or indorsement means one made without actual, implied or apparent authority and includes a forgery.

(44) "Value". Except as otherwise provided with respect to negotiable instruments and bank collections (Sections 3-303, 4-208 and 4-209) a person gives "value" for rights if he acquires them

(a) in return for a binding commitment to extend credit or for the extension of immediately available credit whether or not drawn upon and whether or not a charge-back is provided for in the event of difficulties in collection; or

(b) as security for or in total or partial satisfaction of a pre-existing claim; or

(c) by accepting delivery pursuant to a pre-existing contract for purchase; or

(d) generally, in return for any consideration sufficient to support a simple contract.

(45) "Warehouse receipt" means a receipt issued by a person engaged in the business of storing goods for hire.

(46) "Written" or "writing" includes printing, typewriting or any other intentional reduction to tangible form.

§ 1-202. **Prima Facie Evidence by Third Party Documents.**—A document in due form purporting to be a bill of lading, policy or certificate of insurance, official weigher's or inspector's certificate, consular invoice, or any other document authorized or required by the contract to be issued by a third party shall be prima facie evidence of its own authenticity and genuineness and of the facts stated in the document by the third party.

§ 1-203. **Obligation of Good Faith**—Every contract or duty within this Act imposes an obligation of good faith in its performance or enforcement.

§ 1-204. **Time; Reasonable Time; "Seasonably".**—

(1) Whenever this Act requires any action to be taken within a reasonable time, any time which is not manifestly unreasonable may be fixed by agreement.

(2) What is a reasonable time for taking any action depends on the nature, purpose and circumstances of such action.

(3) An action is taken "seasonably" when it is taken at or within the time agreed or if no time is agreed at or within a reasonable time.

§ 1-205. Course of Dealing and Usage of Trade—

(1) A course of dealing is a sequence of previous conduct between the parties to a particular transaction which is fairly to be regarded as establishing a common basis of understanding for interpreting their expressions and other conduct.

(2) A usage of trade is any practice or method of dealing having such regularity of observance in a place, vocation or trade as to justify an expectation that it will be observed with respect to the transaction in question. If it is established that such usage is embodied in a written trade code or similar writing the interpretation of the writing is for the court.

(3) A course of dealing between parties and any usage of trade in the vocation or trade in which they are engaged or of which they are or should be aware give particular meaning to and supplement or qualify terms of an agreement.

(4) The express terms of an agreement and an applicable course of dealing or usage of trade shall be construed wherever reasonable as consistent with each other; but when such construction is unreasonable express terms control both course of dealing and usage of trade and course of dealing controls usage of trade.

(5) An applicable usage of trade in the place where any part of performance is to occur shall be used in interpreting the agreement as to that part of the performance.

(6) Evidence of a relevant usage of trade offered by one party is not admissible unless and until he has given the other party such notice as the court finds sufficient to prevent unfair surprise to the latter.

§1-206. Statute of Frauds for Kinds of Personal Property Not Otherwise Covered.—

(1) Except in the cases described in subsection (2) of this section a contract for the sale of personal property is not enforceable by way of action or defense beyond five thousand dollars in amount or value of remedy unless there is some writing which indicates that a contract for sale has been made between the parties at a defined or stated price, reasonably identifies the subject matter, and is signed by the party against whom enforcement is sought or by his authorized agent.

(2) Subsection (1) of this section does not apply to contracts for the sale of goods (Section 2-201) nor of securities (Section 8-319) nor to security agreements (Section 9-203).

§ 1-207. Performance or Acceptance Under Reservation of Rights.—A party who with explicit reservation of rights performs or promises performance or assents to performance in a manner demanded or offered by the other party does not thereby prejudice the rights reserved. Such words as "without prejudice", "under protest" or the like are sufficient.

§ 1-208. Option to Accelerate at Will.—A term providing that one party or his successor in interest may accelerate payment or performance or require collateral or additional collateral "at will" or "when he deems himself insecure" or in words of similar import shall be construed to mean that he shall have power to do so only if he in good faith believes that the prospect of payment or performance is impaired. The burden of establishing lack of good faith is on the party against whom the power has been exercised.

ARTICLE TWO—SALES

PART 1

Short Title, General Construction and Subject Matter

§ 2-101. **Short Title.**—This Article shall be known and may be cited as Uniform Commercial Code—Sales.

§ 2-102. **Scope; Certain Security and Other Transactions Excluded From This Article.**—Unless the context otherwise requires, this Article applies to transactions in goods; it does not apply to any transaction which although in the form of an unconditional contract to sell or present sale is intended to operate only as a security transaction nor does this Article impair or repeal any statute regulating sales to consumers, farmers or other specified classes of buyers.

§ 2-103. **Definitions and Index of Definitions.**—

(1) In this Article unless the context otherwise requires

(a) "Buyer" means a person who buys or contracts to buy goods.

(b) "Good faith" in the case of a merchant means honesty in fact and the observance of reasonable commercial standards of fair dealing in the trade.

(c) "Receipt" of goods means taking physical possession of them.

(d) "Seller" means a person who sells or contracts to sell goods. . . .

§ 2-104. **Definitions: "Merchant"; "Between Merchants"; "Financing Agency."**—

(1) "Merchant" means a person who deals in goods of the kind or otherwise by his occupation holds himself out as having knowledge or skill peculiar to the practices or goods involved in the transaction or to whom such knowledge or skill may be attributed by his employment of an agent or broker or other intermediary who by his occupation holds himself out as having such knowledge or skill.

(2) "Financing agency" means a bank, finance company or other person who in the ordinary course of business makes advances against goods or documents of title or who by arrangement with either the seller or the buyer intervenes in ordinary course to make or collect payment due or claimed under the contract for sale, as by purchasing or paying the seller's draft or making advances against it or by merely taking it for collection whether or not documents of title accompany the draft. "Financing agency" includes also a bank or other person who similarly intervenes between persons who are in the position oo seller and buyer in respect to the goods (Section 2-707).

(3) "Between merchants" means in any transaction with respect to which both parties are chargeable with the knowledge or skill of merchants.

§ 2-105. **Definitions: Transferability; "Goods"; "Future" Goods; "Lot"; "Commercial Unit."**—

(1) "Goods" means all things (including specially manufactured goods) which are movable at the time of identification to the contract for sale other than the money in which the price is to be paid, investment securities (Article 8) and things in action. "Goods" also includes the unborn young of animals and growing crops and other identified things attached to realty as described in the section on goods to be severed from realty (Section 2-107).

(2) Goods must be both existing and identified before any interest in them can pass. Goods which are not both existing and identified are "future" goods. A purported present sale of future goods or of any interest therein operates as a contract to sell.

(3) There may be a sale of a part interest in existing identified goods.

(4) An undivided share in an identified bulk of fungible goods is sufficiently identified to be sold although the quantity of the bulk is not determined. Any agreed proportion of such a bulk or any quantity thereof agreed upon by number, weight or other measure may to the extent of the seller's interest in the bulk be sold to the buyer who then becomes an owner in common.

(5) "Lot" means a parcel or a single article which is the subject matter of a separate sale or delivery, whether or not it is sufficient to perform the contract.

(6) "Commercial unit" means such a unit of goods as by commercial usage is a single whole for purposes of sale and division of which materially impairs its character or

value on the market or in use. A commercial unit may be a single article (as a machine) or a set of articles (as a suite of furniture or an assortment of sizes) or a quantity (as a bale, gross, or carload) or any other unit treated in use or in the relevant market as a single whole.

§ 2-106 Definitions: "Contract"; "Agreement"; Contract for sale"; "Sale"; "Present Sale"; "Conforming" to Contract; "Termination"; "Cancellation."—

(1) In This Article unless the context otherwise requires "contract" and "agreement" are limited to those relating to the present or future sale of goods. "Contract for sale" includes both a present sale of goods and a contract to sell goods at a future time. A "sale" consists in the passing of title from the seller to the buyer for a price (Section 2-401). A "present sale" means a sale which is accomplished by the marking of the contract.

(2) Goods or conduct including any part of a performance are "conforming" or conform to the contract when they are in accordance with the obligations under the contract.

(3) "Termination" occurs when either party pursuant to a power created by agreement or law puts an end to the contract otherwise than for its breach. On "termination" all obligations which are still executory on both sides are discharged but any right based on prior breach or performance survives.

(4) "Cancellation" occurs when either party puts an end to the contract for breach by the other and its effect is the same as that of "termination" except that the cancelling party also retains any remedy for breach of the whole contract or any unperformed balance.

§ 2-107. Goods to Be Severed From Realty: Recording.—

(1) A contract for the sale of minerals or the like [(including oil and gas)] or a structure or its materials to be removed from realty is a contract for the sale of goods within this Article if they are to be severed by the seller but until severance a purported present sale thereof which is not effective as a transfer of an interest in land is effective only as a contract to sell.

(2) A contract for the sale apart from the land of growing crops or other things attached to realty and capable of severance without material harm thereto but not described in subsection (1) [or of timber to be cut] is a contract for the sale of goods within this Article whether the subject matter is to be severed by the buyer or by the seller even though it forms part of the realty at the time of contracting, and the parties can be identification effect a present sale before severance.

(3) The provisions of this section are subject to any third party rights provided by the law relating to realty records, and the contract for sale may be executed and recorded as a document transferring an interest in land and shall then constitute notice to third parties of the buyer's rights under the contract for sale.

PART 2

Form, Formation and Readjustment of Contract

§ 2-201. Formal Requirements; Statute of Frauds.—

(1) Except as otherwise provided in this section a contract for the sale of goods for the price of $500 or more is not enforceable by way of action or defense unless there is some writing sufficient to indicate that a contract for sale has been made between the parties and signed by the party against whom enforcement is sought or by his authorized agent or broker. A writing is not insufficient because it omits or incorrectly states a term agreed upon but the contract is not enforceable under this paragraph beyond the quantity of goods shown in such writing.

(2) Between merchants if within a reasonable time a writing in confirmation of the contract and sufficient against the sender is received and the party receiving it has reason to know its contents, it satisfies the requirements of subsection (1) against such party unless written notice of objection to its contents is given within ten days after it is received.

(3) A contract which does not satisfy the requirements of subsection (1) but which is valid in other respects is enforceable

(a) if the goods are to be specially manufactured for the buyer and are not suitable for sale to others in the ordinary course of the seller's business and the seller, before notice of repudiation is received and under circumstances which reasonably indicate that the goods are for the buyer, has made either a substantial beginning of their manufacture or commitments for their procurement; or

(b) if the party against whom enforcement is sought admits in his pleading, testimony or otherwise in court that a contract for sale was made, but the contract is not enforceable under this provision beyond the quantity of goods admitted; or

(c) with respect to goods for which payment has been made and accepted or which have been received and accepted (Sec. 2-606).

§ 2-202.   **Final Written Expression: Parol or Extrinsic Evidence**—Terms with respect to which the confirmatory memoranda of the parties agree or which are otherwise set forth in a writing intended by the parties as a final expression of their agreement with respect to such terms as are included therein may not be contradicted by evidence of any prior agreement or of a contemporaneous oral agreement but may be explained or supplemented

(a) by course of dealing or usage of trade (Section 1-205) or by course of performance (Section 2-208); and

(b) by evidence of consistent additional terms unless the court finds the writing to have been intended also as a complete and exclusive statement of the terms of the agreement.

§ 2-203.   **Seals Inoperative.**—The affixing of a seal to a writing evidencing a contract for sale or an offer to buy or sell goods does not constitute the writing a sealed instrument and the law with respect to sealed instruments does not apply to such a contract or offer.

§ 2-204.   **Formation in General.**—

(1) A contract for sale of goods may be made in any manner sufficient to show agreement, including conduct by both parties which recognizes the existence of such a contract.

(2) An agreement sufficient to constitute a contract for sale may be found even though the moment of its making is undetermined.

(3) Even though one or more terms are left open a contract for sale does not fail for indefiniteness if the parties have intended to make a contract and there is a reasonably certain basis for giving an appropriate remedy.

§ 2-205.   **Firm Offers.**—An offer by a merchant to buy or sell goods in a signed writing which by its terms gives assurance that it will be held open is not revocable, for lack of consideration, during the time stated or if no time is stated for a reasonable time, but in no event may such period of irrevocability exceed three months; but any such term of assurance on a form supplied by the offeree must be separately signed by the offeror.

§ 2-206.   **Offer and Acceptance in Formation of Contract.**—

(1) Unless otherwise unambiguously indicated by the language or circumstances

(a) an offer to make a contract shall be construed as inviting acceptance in any manner and by any medium reasonable in the circumstances.

(b) an order or other offer to buy goods for prompt or current shipment shall be construed as inviting acceptance either by a prompt promise to ship or by the prompt or current shipment of conforming or non-conforming goods, but such a shipment of non-conforming goods does not constitute an acceptance if the seller seasonably notifies the buyer that the shipment is offered only as an accommodation to the buyer.

(2) Where the beginning of a requested performance is a reasonable mode of acceptance an offeror who is not notified of acceptance within a reasonable time may treat the offer as having lapsed before acceptance.

§ 2-207. Additional Terms in Acceptance or Confirmation.—

(1) A definite and seasonable expression of acceptance or a written confirmation which is sent within a reasonable time operates as an acceptance even though it states terms additional to or different from those offered or agreed upon, unless acceptance is expressly made conditional on assent to the additional or different terms.

(2) The additional terms are to be construed as proposals for addition to the contract. Between merchants such terms become part of the contract unless:

(a) the offer expressly limits acceptance to the terms of the offer;

(b) they materially alter it; or

(c) notification of objection to them has already been given or is given within a reasonable time after notice of them is received.

(3) Conduct by both parties which recognizes the existence of a contract is sufficient to establish a contract for sale although the writings of the parties do not otherwise establish a contract. In such case the terms of the particular contract consist of those terms on which the writings of the parties agree, together with any supplementary terms incorporated under any other provisions of this Act.

§ 2-208. Course of Performance or Practical Construction.—

(1) Where the contract for sale involves repeated occasions for performance by either party with knowledge of the nature of the performance and opportunity for objection to it by the other, any course of performance accepted or acquiesced in without objection shall be relevant to determine the meaning of the agreement.

(2) The express terms of the agreement and any such course of performance, as well as any course of dealing and usage of trade, shall be construed whenever reasonable as consistent with each other; but when such construction is unreasonable, express terms shall control course of performance and course of performance shall control both course of dealing and usage of trade (Section 1-205).

(3) Subject to the provisions of the next section on modification and waiver, such course of performance shall be relevant to show a waiver or modification of any term inconsistent with such course of performance.

§ 2-209. Modification, Rescission and Waiver.—

(1) An agreement modifying a contract within this Article needs no consideration to be binding.

(2) A signed agreement which excludes modification or rescission except by a signed writing cannot be otherwise modified or rescinded, but except as between merchants such a requirement on a form supplied by the merchant must be separately signed by the other party.

(3) The requirements of the statute of frauds section of this Article (Section 2-201) must be satisfied if the contract as modified is within its provisions.

(4) Although an attempt at modification or rescission does not satisfy the requirements of subsection (2) or (3) it can operate as a waiver.

(5) A party who has made a waiver affecting an executory portion of the contract may retract the waiver by reasonable notification received by the other party that strict performance will be required of any term waived, unless the retraction would be unjust in view of a material change of position in reliance on the waiver.

§ 2-210. Delegation of Performance; Assignment of Rights.—

(1) A party may perform his duty through a delegate unless otherwise agreed or unless the other party has a substantial interest in having his original promisor perform or control the acts required by the contract. No delegation of performance relieves the party delegating of any duty to perform or any liability for breach.

(2) Unless otherwise agree' all rights of either seller or buyer can be assigned except where the assignment would materially change the duty of the other party, or increase materially the burden or risk imposed on him by his contract, or impair materially his chance of obtaining return performance. A right to damages for breach of the whole contract or a right arising out of the assignor's due performance of his entire obligation can be assigned despite agreement otherwise.

(3) Unless the circumstances indicate the contrary a prohibition of assignment of "the contract" is to be construed as barring only the delegation to the assignee of the assignor's performance.

(4) An assignment of "the contract" or of "all my rights under the contract" or an assignment in similar general terms is an assignment of rights and unless the language or the circumstances (as in an assignment for security) indicate the contrary, it is a delegation of performance of the duties of the assignor and its acceptance by the assignee constitutes a promise by him to perform those duties. This promise is enforceable by either the assignor or the other party to the original contract.

(5) The other party may treat any assignment which delegates performance as creating reasonable grounds for insecurity and may without prejudice to his rights against the assignor demand assurances from the assignee (Section 2-609).

PART 3

General Obligation and Construction of Contract

§ 2-301. General Obligations of Parties.—The obligation of the seller is to transfer and deliver and that of the buyer is to accept and pay in accordance with the contract.

§ 2-302. Unconscionable Contract or Clause.—

(1) If the court as a matter of law finds the contract or any clause of the contract to have been unconscionable at the time it was made the court may refuse to enforce the contract, or it may enforce the remainder of the contract without the unconscionable clause, or it may so limit the application of any unconscionable clause as to avoid any unconscionable result.

(2) When it is claimed or appears to the court that the contract or any clause thereof may be unconscionable the parties shall be afforded a reasonable opportunity to present evidence as to its commercial setting, purpose and effect to aid the court in making the determination.

§ 2-303. Allocation or Division of Risks.—Where this Article allocates a risk or a burden as between the parties "unless otherwise agreed," the agreement may not only shift the allocation but may also divide the risk or burden.

§ 2-304. Price Payable in Money, Goods, Realty, or Otherwise.—

(1) The price can be made payable in money or otherwise. If it is payable in whole or in part in goods each party is a seller of the goods which he is to transfer.

(2) Even though all or part of the price is payable in an interest in realty the transfer of the goods and the seller's obligations with reference to them are subject to this Article, but not the transfer of the interest in realty or the transferor's obligations in connection therewith.

§2-305. Open Price Term.—

(1) The parties if they so intend can conclude a contract for sale even though the price is not settled. In such a case the price is a reasonable price at the time for delivery

if:

    (a) nothing is said as to price; or

    (b) the price is left to be agreed by the parties and they fail to agree; or

    (c) the price is to be fixed in terms of some agreed market or other standard as set or recorded by a third person or agency and it is not so set or recorded.

(2) A price to be fixed by the seller or by the buyer means a price for him to fix in good faith.

(3) When a price left to be fixed otherwise than by agreement of the parties fails to be fixed through fault of one party the other may at his option treat the contract as cancelled or himself fix a reasonable price.

(4) Where, however, the parties intend not to be bound unless the price be fixed or agreed and it is not fixed or agreed there is no contract. In such a case the buyer must return any goods already received or if unable so to do much pay their reasonable value at the time of delivery and the seller must return any portion of the price paid on account.

§ 2-306. Output, Requirements and Exclusive Dealings.—

(1) A term which measures the quantity by the output of the seller or the requirements of the buyer means such actual output or requirements as may occur in good faith, except that no quantity unreasonably disproportionate to any stated estimate or in the absence of a stated estimate to any normal or otherwise comparable prior output or requirements may be tendered or demanded.

(2) A lawful agreement by either the seller or the buyer for exclusive dealing in the kind of goods concerned imposes unless otherwise agreed an obligation by the seller to use best efforts to supply the goods and by the buyer to use best efforts to promote their sale.

§ 2-307. Delivery in Single Lot or Several Lots.—Unless otherwise agreed all goods called for by a contract for sale must be tendered in a single delivery and payment is due only on such tender but where the circumstances give either party the right to make or demand delivery in lots the price if it can be apportioned may be demanded for each lot.

§ 2-308. Absence of Specified Place for Delivery.—Unless otherwise agreed.

    (a) the place for delivery of goods is the seller's place of business or if he has none his residence; but

    (b) in a contract for sale of identified goods which to the knowledge of the parties at the time of contracting are in some other place, that place is the place for their delivery; and

    (c) documents of title may be delivered through customary banking channels.

§ 2-309. Absence of Specific Time Provisions; Notice of Termination.—

(1) The time for shipment or delivery of any other action under a contract if not provided in this Article or agreed upon shall be a reasonable time.

(2) Where the contract provides for successive performances but is indefinite in duration it is valid for a reasonable time but unless otherwise agreed may be terminated at any time by either party.

(3) Termination of a contract by one party except on the happening of an agreed event requires that reasonable notification be received by the other party and an agreement dispensing with notification is invalid if its operation would be unconscionable.

§ 2-310. Open Time for Payment or Running of Credit; Authority to Ship Under Reservation.—Unless otherwise agreed.

    (a) payment is due at the time and place at which the buyer is to receive the goods even though the place of shipment is the place of delivery; and

    (b) if the seller is authorized to send the goods he may ship them under reservation, and pay tender the documents of title, but the buyer may inspect the goods after their arrival before payment is due unless such inspection is inconsistent with the terms of the contract (Section 2-513); and

(c) if delivery is authorized and made by way of documents of title otherwise than by subsection (b) then payment is due at the time and place at which the buyer is to receive the documents regardless of where the goods are to be received; and

(d) where the seller is required or authorized to ship the goods on credit the credit period runs from the time of shipment but post-dating the invoice or delaying its dispatch will correspondingly delay the starting of the credit period.

§ 2-311. Options and Cooperation Respecting Performance.—

(1) An agreement for sale which is otherwise sufficiently definite (subsection (3) of Section 2-204) to be a contract is not made invalid by the fact that it leaves particulars of performance to be specified by one of the parties. Any such specification must be made in good faith and within limits set by commercial reasonableness.

(2) Unless otherwise agreed specifications relating to assortment of the goods are at the buyer's option and except as otherwise provided in subsections (1) (c) and (3) of Section 2-319 specifications or arrangements relating to shipment are at the seller's option.

(3) Where such specification would materially affect the other party's performance but is not seasonably made or where one party's cooperation is necessary to the agreed performance of the other but is not seasonably forthcoming, the other party in addition to all other remedies

(a) is excused for any resulting delay in his own performance; and

(b) may also either proceed to perform in any reasonable manner or after the time for a material part of his own performance treat the failure to specify or to co-operate as a breach by failure to deliver or accept the goods.

§ 2-312. Warranty of Title and Against Infringement; Buyer's Obligation Against Infringement.—

(1) Subject to subsection (2) there is in a contract for sale a warranty by the seller that

(a) the title conveyed shall be good, and its transfer rightful; and

(b) the goods shall be delivered free from any security interest or other lien or encumbrance of which the buyer at the time of contracting has no knowledge.

(2) A warranty under subsection (1) will be excluded or modified only by specific language or by circumstances which give the buyer reason to know that the person selling does not claim title in himself or that he is purporting to sell only such right or title as he or a third person may have.

(3) Unless otherwise agreed a seller who is a merchant regularly dealing in goods of the kind warrants that the goods shall be delivered free of the rightful claim of any third person by way of infringement or the like but a buyer who furnishes specifications to the seller must hold the seller harmless against any such claim which arises out of compliance with the specifications.

§ 2-313. Express Warranties by Affirmation, Promise, Description, Sample.—

(1) Express warranties by the seller are created as follows:

(a) Any affirmation of fact or promise made by the seller to the buyer which relates to the goods and becomes part of the basis of the bargain creates an express warranty that the goods shall conform to the affirmation or promise.

(b) Any description of the goods which is made part of the basis of the bargain creates an express warranty that the goods shall conform to the description.

(c) Any sample or model which is made part of the basis of the bargain creates an express warranty that the whole of the goods shall conform to the sample or model.

(2) It is not necessary to the creation of an express warranty that the seller use formal words such as "warrant" or "guarantee" or that he have a specific intention to

make a warranty, but an affirmation merely of the value of the goods or a statement purporting to be merely the seller's opinion or commendation of the goods does not create a warranty.

§ 2-314. Implied Warranty: Merchantability; Usage of Trade.—

(1) Unless excluded or modified (Section 2-316), a warranty that the goods shall be merchantable is implied in a contract for their sale if the seller is a merchant with respect to goods of that kind. Under this section the serving for value of food or drink to be consumed either on the premises or elsewhere is a sale.

(2) Goods to be merchantable must be at least such as

(a) pass without objection in the trade under the contract description; and

(b) in the case of fungible goods, are of fair average quality within the description; and

(c) are fit for the ordinary purposes for which such goods are used; and

(d) run, within the variations permitted by the agreement, of even kind, quality and quantity within each unit and among all units involved; and

(e) are adequately contained, packaged, and labeled as the agreement may require; and

(f) conform to the promises or affirmations of fact made on the container or label if any

(3) Unless excluded or modified (Section 2-316) other implied warranties may arise from course of dealing or usage of trade.

§ 2-315. Implied Warranty: Fitness for Particular Purpose.—

Where the seller at the time of contracting has reason to know any particular purpose for which the goods are required and that the buyer is relying on the seller's skill or judgment to select or furnish suitable goods, there is unless excluded or modified under the next section an implied warranty that the goods shall be fit for such purpose.

§ 2-316. Exclusion or Modification of Warranties.—

(1) Words or conduct relevant to the creation of an express warranty and words or conduct tending to negate or limit warranty shall be construed wherever reasonably as consistent with each other; but subject to the provisions of this Article on parol or extrinsic evidence (Section 2-202) negation or limitation is inoperative to the extent that such construction is unreasonable.

(2) Subject to subsection (3), to exclude or modify the implied warranty of merchantability or any part of it the language must mention merchantability and in case of a writing must be conspicuous, and to exclude or modify any implied warranty of fitness the exclusion must be by a writing and conspicuous. Language to exclude all implied warranties of fitness is sufficient if it states, for example, that "There are no warranties which extend beyond the description on the face hereof."

(3) Notwithstanding subsection (2)

(a) unless the circumstances indicate otherwise, all implied warranties are excluded by expressions like "as is," "with all faults" or other language which in common understanding calls the buyer's attention to the exclusion of warranties and makes plain that there is no implied warranty; and

(b) when the buyer before entering into the contract has examined the goods or the sample or model as fully as he desired or has refused to examine the goods there is no implied warranty with regard to defects which an examination ought in the circumstances to have revealed to him; and

(c) an implied warranty can also be excluded or modified by course of dealing or course of performance or usage of trade.

(4) Remedies for breach of warranty can be limited in accordance with the provisions of this Article on liquidation or limitation of damages and on contractual modification of remedy (Sections 2-718 and 2-719).

§ 2-317. Cumulation and Conflict of Warranties Express or Implied.—Warranties whether express or implied whall be construed as consistent with each other and as cumulative, but if such construction is unreasonable the intention of the parties shall determine which warranty is dominant. In ascertaining that intention the following rules apply:

(a) Exact or technical specifications displace an inconsistent sample or model or general language of description.

(b) A sample from an existing bulk displaces inconsistent general language of description.

(c) Express warranties displace inconsistent implied warranties other than an implied warranty of fitness for a particular purpose.

§ 2-318. Third Party Beneficiaries of Warranties Express or Implied.—A seller's warranty whether express or implied extends to any natural person who is in the family or household of his buyer or who is a guest in his home if it is reasonable to expect that such person may use, consume or be affected by the goods and who is injured in person by breach of the warranty. A seller may not exclude or limit the operation of this section.

§ 2-319. F.O.B. and F.A.S. Terms.—

(1) Unless otherwise agreed the term F.O.B. (which means "free on board") at a named place, even though used only in connection with the stated price, is a delivery term under which

(a) when the term is F.O.B. the place of shipment, the seller must at that place ship the goods in the manner provided in this Article (Section 2-504) and bear the expense and risk of putting them into the possession of the carrier; or

(b) when the term is F.O.B. the place of destination, the seller must at his own expense and risk transport the goods to that place and there tender delivery of them in the manner provided in this Article (Section 2-503);

(c) when under either (a) or (b) the term is also, F.O.B. vessel, car or other vehicle, the seller must in addition at his own expense and risk load the goods on board. If the term is F.O.B. vessel the buyer must name the vessel and in an appropriate case the seller must comply with the provisions of this Article on the form of bill of lading (Section 2-323).

(2) Unless otherwise agreed the term F.A.S. vessel (which means "free alongside") at a named port, even though used only in connection with the stated price, is a delivery term under which the seller must

(a) at his own expense and risk deliver the goods alongside the vessel in the manner usual in that port or on a dock designated and provided by the buyer; and

(b) obtain and tender a receipt for the goods in exchange for which the carrier is under a duty to issue a bill of lading.

(3) Unless otherwise agreed in any case falling within subsection (1) (a) or (c) or subsection (2) the buyer must seasonably give any needed instructions for making delivery, including when the term is F.A.S. or F.O.B. the loading berth of the vessel and in an appropriate case its name and sailing date. The seller may treat the failure of needed instructions as a failure of cooperation under this Article (Section 2-311). He may also at his option move the goods in any reasonable manner preparatory to delivery or shipment.

(4) Under the term F.O.B. vessel or F.A.S. unless otherwise agreed the buyer must make payment against tender of the required documents and the seller may not tender nor the buyer demand delivery, of the goods in substitution for the documents.

§ 2-320. C.I.F. and C. & F. Terms.—

(1) The term C.I.F. means that the price includes in a lump sum the cost of the goods and the insurance and freight to the named destination. The term C. & F. or C.F. means that the price so includes cost and freight to the named destination.

(2) Unless otherwise agreed and even though used only in connection with the stated price and destination, the term C.I.F. destination or its equivalent requires the seller at his own expense and risk to

(a) put the goods into the possession of a carrier at the port for shipment and obtain a negotiable bill or bills of lading covering the entire transportation to the named destination; and

(b) load the goods and obtain a receipt from the carrier (which may be contained in the bill of lading) showing that the freight has been paid or provided for; and

(c) obtain a policy or certificate of insurance, including any war risk insurance, of a kind and on terms then current at the port of shipment in the usual amount, in the currency of the contract, shown to cover the same goods covered by the bill of lading and providing for payment of loss to the order of the buyer or for the account of whom it may concern; but the seller may add to the price the amount of the premium for any such war risk insurance; and

(d) prepare an invoice of the goods and procure any other documents required to effect shipment or to comply with the contract; and

(e) forward and tender with commercial promptness all the documents in due form and with any indorsement necessary to perfect the buyer's rights.

(3) Unless otherwise agreed the term C. & F. or its equivalent has the same effect and imposes upon the seller the same obligations and risks as a C.I.F. term except the obligation as to insurance.

(4) Under the term C.I.F. or C. & F. unless otherwise agreed the buyer must make payment against tender of the required documents and the seller may not tender nor the buyer demand delivery of the goods in substitution for the documents.

§ 2-321. C.I.F. or C. & F.: "Net Landed Weights"; "Payment on Arrival"; Warranty of Condition on Arrival.—Under a contract containing a term C.I.F. or C. & F.

(1) Where the price is based on or is to be adjusted according to "net landed weights," "delivered weights," "out turn" quantity or quality or the like, unless otherwise agreed the seller must reasonably estimate the price. The payment due on tender of the documents called for by the contract is the amount so estimated but after final adjustment of the price a settlement must be made with commercial promptness.

(2) An agreement described in subsection (1) or any warranty of quality or condition of the goods on arrival places upon the seller the risk of ordinary deterioration, shrinkage and the like in transportation but has no effect on the place or time of identification to the contract for sale or delivery or on the passing of the risk of loss.

(3) Unless otherwise agreed where the contract provides for payment on or after arrival of the goods the seller must before payment allow such preliminary inspection as is feasible; but if the goods are lost delivery of the documents and payment are due when the goods should have arrived.

§ 2-322. Delivery "Ex-Ship". —

(1) Unless otherwise agreed a term for delivery of goods "ex-ship" (which means from the carrying vessel) or in equivalent language is not restricted to a particular ship and requires delivery from a ship which has reached a place at the named port of destination where goods of the kind are usually discharged.

(2) Under such a term unless otherwise agreed

(a) the seller must discharge all liens arising out of the carriage and furnish the buyer with a direction which puts the carrier under a duty to deliver the goods; and

(b) the risk of loss does not pass to the buyer until the goods leave the ship's tackle or are otherwise properly unloaded.

§ 2-323.   Form of Bill of Lading Required in Overseas Shipments: "Overseas."—

(1) Where the contract contemplates overseas shipment and contains a term C.I.F. or C. & F. or F.O.B. vessel, the seller unless otherwise agreed must obtain a negotiable bill of lading stating that the goods have been loaded on board or, in the case of a term C.I.F. or C. & F., received for shipment.

(2) Where in a case within subsection (1) a bill of lading has been issued in a set of parts, unless otherwise agreed if the documents are not to be sent from abroad the buyer may demand tender of the full set; otherwise only one part of the bill of lading need be tendered. Even if the agreement expressly requires a full set.

(a) due tender of a single part is acceptable within the provisions of this Article on cure of improper delivery (subsection (1) of Section 2-508); and

(b) even though the full set is demanded, if the documents are sent from abroad the person tendering an incomplete set may nevertheless require payment upon furnishing an indemnity which the buyer in good faith deems adequate.

(3) A shipment by water or by air or a contract contemplating such shipment is "overseas" insofar as by usage of trade or agreement it is subject to the commercial, financing or shipping practices characteristic of international deep water commerce.

§ 2-324.   "No Arrival, No Sale" Term.—Under a term "no arrival, no sale" or

terms of the like meaning, unless otherwise agreed,

(a) the seller must properly ship conforming goods and if they arrive by any means he must tender them on arrival but he assures no obligation that the goods will arrive unless he has caused the non-arrival; and

(b) where without fault of the seller the goods are in part lost or have so deteriorated as no longer to conform to the contract or arrive after the contract time, the buyer may proceed as if there had been casualty to identified goods (Section 2-613).

§ 2-325.   "Letter of Credit" Term; "Confirmed Credit."—

(1) Failure of the buyer seasonably to furnish an agreed letter of credit is a breach of the contract for sale.

(2) The delivery to seller of a proper letter of credit suspends the buyer's obligation to pay. If the letter of credit is dishonored, the seller may on seasonable notification to the buyer require payment directly from him.

(3) Unless otherwise agreed the term "letter of credit" or "banker's credit" in a contract for sale means an irrevocable credit issued by a financing agency of good repute and, where the shipment is overseas, of good international repute. The term "confirmed credit" means that the credit must also carry the direct obligation of such an agency which does business in the seller's financial market.

§ 2-326.   Sale on Approval and Sale or Return; Consignment Sales and Rights of Creditors.—

(1) Unless otherwise agreed, if delivered goods may be returned by the buyer even though they conform to the contract, the transaction is

(a) a "sale on approval" if the goods are delivered primarily for use, and

(b) a "sale or return" if the goods are delivered primarily for resale.

(2) Except as provided in subsection (3), goods held on approval are not subject to the claims of the buyer's creditors until acceptance; goods held on sale or return are subject to such claims while in the buyer's possession.

(3) Where goods are delivered to a person for sale and such person maintains a place of business at which he deals in goods of the kind involved, under a name other than the name of the person making delivery, then with respect to claims of creditors of the

person conducting the business the goods are deemed to be on sale or return. The provisions of this subsection are applicable even though an agreement purports to reserve title to the person making delivery until payment or resale or uses such words as "on consignment" or "on memorandum." However, this subsection is not applicable if the person making delivery

(a) complies with an applicable law providing for a consignor's interest or the like to be evidenced by a sign, or

(b) establishes that the person conducting the business is generally known by his creditors to be substantially engaged in selling the goods of others, or

(c) complies with the filing provisions of the Article on Secured Transactions (Article 9).

(4) Any "or return" term of a contract for sale is to be treated as a separate contract for sale within the statute of frauds section of this Article (Section 2-201) and as contradicting the sale aspect of the contract within the provisions of this Article on parol or extrinsic evidence (Section 2-202).

§ 2-327. Special Incidents of Sale on Approval and Sale or Return.—

(1) Under a sale on approval unless otherwise agreed.

(a) although the goods are identified to the contract the risk of loss and the title do not pass to the buyer until acceptance; and

(b) use of goods consistent with the purpose of trial is not acceptance but failure seasonably to notify the seller of election to return the goods is acceptance, and if the goods conform to the contract acceptance of any part is acceptance of the whole; and

(c) after due notification of election to return, is at the seller's risk and expense but a merchant buyer must follow any reasonable instructions.

(2) Under a sale or return unless otherwise agreed

(a) the option to return extends to the whole or any commercial unit of the goods while in substantially their original condition, but must be exercised seasonably; and

(b) the return is at the buyer's risk and expense.

§ 2-328. Sale by Auction.—

(1) In a sale by auction if goods are put up in lots each lot is the subject of a separate sale.

(2) A sale by auction is complete when the auctioneer so announces by the fall of the hammer or in other customary manner. Where a bid is made while the hammer is falling in acceptance of a prior bid the auctioneer may in his discretion reopen the bidding or declare the goods sold under the bid on which the hammer was falling.

(3) Such a sale is with reserve unless the goods are in explicit terms put up without reserve. In an auction with reserve the auctioneer may withdraw the goods at any time until he announces completion of the sale. In an auction without reserve, after the auctioneer calls for bids on an article or lot, that article or lot cannot be withdrawn unless no bid is made within a reasonable time. In either case a bidder may retract his bid until the auctioneer's announcement of completion of the sale, but a bidder's retraction does not revive any previous bid.

(4) If the auctioneer knowingly receives a bid on the seller's behalf or the seller makes or procures such a bid, and notice has not been given that liberty for such bidding is reserved, the buyer may at his option avoid the sale or take the goods at the price of the last good faith bid prior to the completion of the sale. This subsection shall not apply to any bid at a forced sale.

PART 4

Title, Creditors and Good Faith Purchasers

§ 2-401. Passing of Title; Reservation for Security; Limited Application of This Section.—Each provision of this Article with regard to the rights, obligations and remedies of the seller, the buyer, purchasers or other third parties applies irrespective of title to the goods except where the provision refers to such title. Insofar as situations are not covered by the other provisions of this Article and matters concerning title become material the following rules apply:

(1) Title to goods cannot pass under a contract for sale prior to their identification to the contract (Section 2-501), and unless otherwise explicitly agreed the buyer acquires by their identification a special property as limited by this Act. Any retention or reservation by the seller of the title (property) in goods shipped or delivered to the buyer is limited in effect to a reservation of a security interest. Subject to these provisions and to the provisions of the Article on Secured Transactions (Article 9), title to goods passes from the seller to the buyer in any manner and on any conditions explicitly agreed on by the parties.

(2) Unless otherwise explicitly agreed title passes to the buyer at the time and place at which the seller completes his performance with reference to the physical delivery of the goods, despite any reservation of a security interest and even though a document of title is to be delivered at a different time or place; and in particular and despite any reservation of a security interest by the bill of lading.

    (a) if the contract requires or authorizes the seller to send the goods to the buyer but does not require him to deliver them at destination, title passes to the buyer at the time and place of shipment; but

    (b) if the contract requires delivery at destination, title passes on tender there.

(3) Unless otherwise explicitly agreed where delivery is to be made without moving the goods,

    (a) if the seller is to deliver a document of title, title passes at the time when and the place where he delivers such documents; or

    (b) if the goods are at the time of contracting already identified and no documents are to be delivered, title passes at the time and place of contracting.

(4) A rejection or other refusal by the buyer to receive or retain the goods, whether or not justified, or a justified revocation of acceptance revests title to the goods in the seller. Such revesting occurs by operation of law and is not a "sale."

§ 2-402. Rights of Seller's Creditors Against Sold Goods.—

(1) Except as provided in subsections (2) and (3), rights of unsecured creditors of the seller with respect to goods which have been identified to a contract for sale are subject to the buyer's rights to recover the goods under this Article (Sections 2-502 and 2-716).

(2) A creditor of the seller may treat a sale or an identification of goods to a contract for sale as void if as against him a retention of possession by the seller is fraudulent under any rule of law of the state where the goods are situated, except that retention of possession in good faith and current course of trade by a merchant-seller for a commercially reasonable time after a sale or identification is not fraudulent.

(3) Nothing in this Article shall be deemed to impair the rights of creditors of the seller

    (a) under the provisions of the Article on Secured Transactions (Article 9); or

    (b) where identification to the contract or delivery is made not in current course of trade but in satisfaction of or as security for a preexisting claim for money, security or the like and is made under circumstances which under any rule of law of the state where the goods are situated would apart from this Article constitute the transaction a fraudulent transfer or voidable preference.

§ 2-403. Power to Transfer; Good Faith Purchase of Goods; "Entrusting."—

(1) A purchaser of goods acquires all title which his transferor had or had power to transfer except that a purchaser of a limited interest acquires rights only to the extent of the interest purchased. A person with voidable title has power to transfer a good title to

a good faith purchaser for value. When goods have been delivered under a transaction of purchase the purchaser has such power even though

(a) the transferor was deceived as to the identity of the purchaser, or

(b) the delivery was in exchange for a check which is later dishonored, or

(c) it was agreed that the transaction was to be a "cash sale," or

(d) the delivery was procured through fraud punishable as larcenous under the criminal law.

(2) Any entrusting of possession of goods to a merchant who deals in goods of that kind gives him power to transfer all rights of the entruster to a buyer in ordinary course of business.

(3) "Entrusting" includes any delivery and any acquiescence in retention of possession regardless of any condition expressed between the parties to the delivery or acquiescence and regardless of whether the procurement of the entrusting or the possessor's disposition of the goods have been such as to be larcenous under the criminal law.

(4) The rights of other purchasers of goods and of lien creditors are governed by the Articles on Secured Transactions (Article 9), Bulk Transfers (Article 6) and Documents of Title (Article 7).

PART 5

Performance

§ 2-501.   Insurable Interest in Goods; Manner of Identification of Goods.—

(1) The buyer obtains a special property and an insurable interest in goods by identification of existing goods as goods to which the contract refers even though the goods so identified are non-conforming and he has an option to return or reject them. Such identification can be made at any time and in any manner explicitly agreed to by the parties. In the absence of explicit agreement identification occurs.

(a) when the contract is made if it is for the sale of goods already existing and identified;

(b) if the contract is for the sale of future goods other than those described in paragraph (c), when goods are shipped, marked or otherwise designated by the seller as goods to which the contract refers:

(c) when the crops are planted or otherwise become growing crops or the young are conceived if the contract is for the sale of unborn young to be born within twelve months after contracting or for the sale of crops to be harvested within twelve months or the next normal harvest season after contracting whichever is longer.

(2) The seller retains an insurable interest in goods so long as title to or any security interest in the goods remains in him and where the identification is by the seller alone he may until default or insolvency or notification to the buyer that the identification is final substitute other goods for those identified.

(3) Nothing in this section impairs any insurable interest recognized under any other statute or rule of law.

§ 2-502.   Buyer's Right to Goods on Seller's Insolvency.—

(1) Subject to subsection (2) and even though the goods have not been shipped a buyer who has paid a part or all of the price of goods in which he has a special property under the provisions of the immediately preceding section may on making and keeping good a tender of any unpaid portion of their price recover them from the seller if the seller becomes insolvent within ten days after receipt of the first installment on their price.

(2) If the identification creating his special property has been made by the buyer he acquires the right to recover the goods only if they conform to the contract for sale.

§ 2-503. Manner of Seller's Tender of Delivery.—

(1) Tender of delivery requires that the seller put and hold conforming goods at the buyer's disposition and give the buyer any notification reasonably necessary to enable him to take delivery. The manner, time and place for tender are determined by the agreement and this Article, and in particular

    (a) tender must be at a reasonable hour, and if it is of goods they must be kept available for the period reasonably necessary to enable the buyer to take possession; but

    (b) unless otherwise agreed the buyer must furnish facilities reasonably suited to the receipt of the goods.

(2) Where the case is within the next section respecting shipment tender requires that the seller comply with its provisions.

(3) Where the seller is required to deliver at a particular destination tender requires that he comply with subsection (1) and also in any appropriate case tender documents as described in subsections (4) and (5) of this section.

(4) Where goods are in the possession of a bailee and are to be delivered without being moved

    (a) tender requires that the seller either tender a negotiable document of title covering such goods or procure acknowledgment by the bailee of the buyer's right to possession of the goods; but

    (b) tender to the buyer of a nonnegotiable document of title or of a written direction to the bailee to deliver is sufficient tender unless the buyer seasonbly objects, and receipt by the bailee of notification of the buyer's rights fixes those rights as against the bailee to honor the non-negotiable document of title or to obey the direction remains on the seller until the buyer has had a reasonable time to present the document or direction, and a refusal by the bailee to honor the document or to obey the direction defeats the tender.
direction defeats the tender.

(5) Where the contract requires the seller to deliver documents

    (a) he must tender all such documents in correct form, except as provided in this Article with respect to bills of lading in a set (subsection (2) of Section 2-323); and

    (b) tender through customary banking channels is sufficient and dishonor of a draft accompanying the documents constitutes non-acceptance or rejection.

§ 2-504. Shipment by Seller.—

Where the seller is required or authorized to send the goods to the buyer and the contract does not require him to deliver them at a particular destination, then unless otherwise agreed he must

    (a) put the goods in the possession of such a carrier and make such a contract for their transportation as may be reasonable having regard to the nature of the goods and other circumstances of the case; and

    (b) obtain and promptly deliver or tender in due form any document necessary to enable the buyer to obtain possession of the goods or otherwise required by the agreement or by usage of trade; and

    (c) promptly notify the buyer of the shipment.
Failure to notify the buyer under paragraph (c) or to make a proper contract under paragraph (a) is a ground for rejection only if material delay or loss ensues.

§ 2-505. Seller's Shipment Under Reservation.—

(1) Where the seller has identified goods to the contract by or before shipment;

    (a) his procurement of a negotiable bill of lading to his own order or otherwise reserves in him a security interest in the goods. His procurement of the bill to the order of a financing agency or of the buyer indicates in addition only the seller's expectation of transferring that interest to the person named.

    (b) a non-negotiable bill of lading to himself or his nominee reserves possession of the goods as security but except in a case of conditional delivery (subsection (2) of

Section 2-507) a non-negotiable bill of lading naming the buyer as consignee reserves no security interest even though the seller retains possession of the bill of lading.

(2) When shipment by the seller with reservation of a security interest is in violation of the contract for sale it constitutes an improper contract for transportation within the preceding section but impairs neither the rights given to the buyer by shipment and identification of the goods to the contract nor the seller's powers as a holder of a negotiable document.

§ 2-506. Rights of Financing Agency.—

(1) A financing agency by paying or purchasing for value a draft which relates to a shipment of goods acquires to the extent of the payment or purchase and in addition to its own rights under the draft and any document of title securing it any rights of the shipper in the goods including the right to stop delivery and the shipper's right to have the draft honored by the buyer.

(2) The right to reimbursement of a financing agency which has in good faith honored or purchased the draft under commitment to or authority from the buyer is not impaired by subsequent discovery of defects with reference to any relevant document which was apparently regular on its face.

§ 2-507. Effect of Seller's Tender; Delivery on Condition.—

(1) Tender of delivery is a condition to the buyer's duty to accept the goods and, unless otherwise agreed, to his duty to pay for them. Tender entitles the seller to acceptance of the goods and to payment according to the contract.

(2) Where payment is due and demanded on the delivery to the buyer of goods or documents of title, his right as against the seller to retain or dispose of them is conditional upon his making the payment due.

§ 2-508. Cure by Seller of Improper Tender or Delivery; Replacement.—

(1) Where any tender or delivery by the seller is rejected because non-conforming and the time for performance has not yet expired, the seller may seasonably notify the buyer of his intention to cure and may then within the contract time make a conforming delivery.

(2) Where the buyer rejects a non-conforming tender which the seller had reasonable grounds to believe would be acceptable with or without money allowance the seller may if he seasonably notifies the buyer have a further reasonable time to substitute a conforming tender.

§ 2-509. Risk of Loss in the Absence of Breach.—

(1) Where the contract requires or authorizes the seller to ship the goods by carrier

  (a) if it does not require him to deliver them at a particular destination, the risk of loss passes to the buyer when the goods are duly delivered to the carrier even though the shipment is under reservation (Section 2-505); but

  (b) if it does require him to deliver them at a particular destination and the goods are there duly tendered while in the possession of the carrier, the risk of loss passes to the buyer when the goods are there duly so tendered as to enable the buyer to take delivery.

(2) Where the goods are held by a bailee to be delivered without being moved, the risk of loss passes to the buyer

  (a) on his receipt of a negotiable document of title covering the goods; or

  (b) on acknowledgment by the bailee of the buyer's right to possession of the goods; or

  (c) after his receipt of a non-negotiable document of title or other written direction to deliver, as provided in subsection (4) (b) of Section 2-503.

(3) In any case not within subsection (1) or (2), the risk of loss passes to the buyer on his receipt of the goods if the seller is a merchant; otherwise the risk passes to the buyer on tender of delivery.

(4) The provisions of this section are subject to contrary agreement of the parties and to the provisions of this Article on sale on approval (Section 2-327) and on effect of breach on risk of loss (Section 2-510).

§ 2-510. Effect of Breach on Risk of Loss.—

(1) Where a tender or delivery of goods so fails to conform to the contract as to give a right of rejection the risk of their loss remains on the seller until cure or acceptance.

(2) Where the buyer rightfully revokes acceptance he may to the extent of any deficiency in his effective insurance coverage treat the risk of loss as having rested on the seller from the beginning.

(3) Where the buyer as to conforming goods already identified to the contract for sale repudiates or is otherwise in breach before risk of their loss has passed to him, the seller may to the extent of any deficiency in his effective insurance coverage treat the risk of loss as resting on the buyer for a commercially reasonable time.

§ 2-511. Tender of Payment by Buyer; Payment by Check.—

(1) Unless otherwise agreed tender of payment is a condition to the seller's duty to tender and complete any delivery.

(2) Tender of payment is sufficient when made by any means or in any manner current in the ordinary course of business unless the seller demands payment in legal tender and gives any extension of time reasonably necessary to procure it.

(3) Subject to the provisions of this Act on the effect of an instrument on an obligation (Section 3-802), payment by check is conditional and is defeated as between the parties by dishonor of the check on due presentment.

§ 2-512. Payment by Buyer Before Inspection.—

(1) Where the contract requires payment before inspection non-conformity of the goods does not excuse the buyer from so making payment unless

(a) the non-conformity appears without inspection; or

(b) despite tender of the required documents the circumstances would justify injunction against honor under the provisions of this Act (Section 5-114).

(2) Payment pursuant to subsection (1) does not constitute an acceptance of goods or impair the buyer's right to inspect or any of his remedies.

§ 2-513. Buyer's Right to Inspection of Goods.—

(1) Unless otherwise agreed and subject to subsection (3), where goods are tendered or delivered or identified to the contract for sale, the buyer has a right before payment or acceptance to inspect them at any reasonable place and time and in any reasonable manner. When the seller is required or authorized to send the goods to the buyer, the inspection may be after their arrival.

(2) Expenses of inspection must be borne by the buyer but may be recovered from the seller if the goods do not conform and are rejected.

(3) Unless otherwise agreed and subject to the provisions of this Article on C.I.F. contracts (subsection (3) of Section 2-321), the buyer is not entitled to inspect the goods before payment of the price when the contract provides

(a) for delivery "C.O.D." or on other like terms; or

(b) for payment against documents of title, except where such payment is due only after the goods are to become available for inspection.

(4) A place or method of inspection fixed by the parties is presumed to be exclusive but unless otherwise expressly agreed it does not postpone identification or shift the place for delivery or for passing the risk of loss. If compliance becomes impossible, inspection shall be as provided in this section unless the place or method fixed was clearly intended as an indispensable condition failure of which avoids the contract.

§ 2-514. When Documents Deliverable on Acceptance; When on Payment.—

Unless otherwise agreed documents against which a draft is drawn are to be delivered to the drawee on acceptance of the draft if it is payable more than three days after presentment; otherwise, only on payment.

§ **2-515. Preserving Evidence of Goods in Dispute.**—In furtherance of the adjustment of any claim or dispute

(a) either party on reasonable notification to the other and for the purpose of ascertaining the facts and preserving evidence has the right to inspect, test and sample the goods including such of them as may be in the possession or control of the other; and

(b) the parties may agree to a third party inspection or survey to determine the conformity or condition of the goods and may agree that the findings shall be binding upon them in any subsequent litigation or adjustment.

PART 6

Breach, Repudiation and Excuse

§ **2-601. Buyer's Rights on Improper Delivery.**—Subject to the provisions of this Article on breach in installment contracts (Section 2-612) and unless otherwise agreed under the sections on contractual limitations of remedy (Sections 2-718 and 2-719), if the goods or the tender of delivery fail in any respect to conform to the contract, the buyer may

(a) reject the whole; or

(b) accept the whole; or

(c) accept any commercial unit or units and reject the rest.

§ **2-602. Manner and Effect of Rightful Rejection.**—

(1) Rejection of goods must be within a reasonable time after their delivery or tender. It is ineffective unless the buyer seasonably notifies the seller.

(2) Subject to the provisions of the two following sections on rejected goods (Sections 2-603 and 2-604).

(a) after rejection any exercise of ownership by the buyer with respect to any commercial unit is wrongful as against the seller; and

(b) if the buyer has before rejection taken physical possession of goods in which he does not have a security interest under the provisions of this Article (subsection (3) of Section 2-711), he is under a duty after rejection to hold them with reasonable care at the seller's disposition for a time sufficient to permit the seller to remove them; but

(c) the buyer has no further obligations with regard to goods rightfully rejected.

(3) The seller's rights with respect to goods wrongfully rejected are governed by the provisions of this Article on Seller's remedies in general (Section 2-703).

§ **2-603. Merchant Buyer's Duties as to Rightfully Rejected Goods.**—

(1) Subject to any security interest in the buyer (subsection (3) of Section 2-711), when the seller has no agent or place of business at the market of rejection a merchant buyer is under a duty after rejection of goods in his possession or control to follow any reasonable instructions received from the seller with respect to the goods and in the absence of such instructions to make reasonable efforts to sell them for the seller's account if they are perishable or threaten to decline in value speedily. Instructions are not reasonable if on demand indemnity for expenses is not forthcoming.

(2) When the buyer sells goods under subsection (1), he is entitled to reimbursement from the seller or out of the proceeds for reasonable expenses of caring for and selling them, and if the expenses include no selling commission then to such commission as is usual in the trade or if there is none to a reasonable sum not exceeding ten per cent on the gross proceeds.

(3) In complying with this section the buyer is held only to good faith and good faith conduct hereunder is neither acceptance nor conversion nor the basis of an action for damages.

§ 2-604. **Buyer's Options as to Salvage of Rightfully Rejected Goods.**—Subject to the provisions of the immediately preceding section on perishables if the seller gives no instructions within a reasonable time after notification of rejection the buyer may store the rejected goods for the seller's account or reship them to him or resell them for the seller's account with reimbursement as provided in the preceding section. Such action is not acceptance or conversion.

§ 2-605. **Waiver of Buyer's Objections by Failure to Particularize.**—
(1) The buyer's failure to state in connection with rejection a particular defect which is ascertainable by reasonable inspection precludes him from relying on the unstated defect to justify rejection or to establish breach

(a) where the seller could have cured it if stated seasonably; or

(b) between merchants when the seller has after rejection made a request in writing for a full and final written statement of all defects on which the buyer proposes to rely.

(2) Payment against documents made without reservation of rights precludes recovery of the payment for defects apparent on the face of the documents.

§ 2-606. **What Constitutes Acceptance of Goods.**—
(1) Acceptance of goods occurs when the buyer

(a) after a reasonable opportunity to inspect the goods signifies to the seller that the goods are conforming or that he will take or retain them in spite of their non-conformity; or

(b) fails to make an effective rejection (subsection (1) of Section 2-602), but such acceptance does not occur until the buyer has had a reasonable opportunity to inspect them; or

(c) does any act inconsistent with the seller's ownership; but if such act is wrongful as against the seller it is an acceptance only if ratified by him.

(2) Acceptance of a part of any commercial unit is acceptance of that entire unit.

§ 2-607. **Effect of Acceptance; Notice of Breach; Burden of Establishing Breach After Acceptance; Notice of Claim or Litigation to Person Answerable Over.**—
(1) The buyer must pay at the contract rate for any goods accepted.

(2) Acceptance of goods by the buyer precludes rejection of the goods accepted and if made with knowledge of a nonconformity cannot be revoked because of it unless the acceptance was on the reasonable assumption that the non-conformity would be seasonably cured but acceptance does not of itself impair any other remedy provided by this Article for non-conformity.

(3) Where a tender has been accepted

(a) the buyer must within a reasonable time after he discovers or should have discovered any breach notify the seller of breach or be barred from any remedy; and

(b) if the claim is one for infringement or the like (subsection (3) of Section 2-312) and the buyer is sued as a result of such a breach he must so notify the seller within a reasonable time after he receives notice of the litigation or be barred from any remedy over for liability established by the litigation.

(4) The burden is on the buyer to establish any breach with respect to the goods accepted.

(5) Where the buyer is sued for breach of a warranty or other obligation for which his seller is answerable over

(a) he may give his seller written notice of the litigation. If the notice states that the seller may come in and defend and that if the seller does not do so he will be bound in any action against him by his buyer by any determination of fact common to the two litigations, then unless the seller after seasonable receipt of the notice does come in and defend he is so bound.

(b) if the claim is one for infringement or the like (subsection (3) of Section 2-312) the original seller may demand in writing that his buyer turn over to him control of the litigation including settlement or else be barred from any remedy over and if he also agrees to bear all expense and to satisfy any adverse judgment, then unless the buyer after seasonable receipt of the demand does turn over control the buyer is so barred.

(6) The provisions of subsections (3), (4) and (5) apply to any obligation of a buyer to hold the seller harmless against infringement or the like (subsection (3) of Section 2-312).

§ 2-608. Revocation of Acceptance in Whole or in Part.—

(1) The buyer may revoke his acceptance of a lot or commercial unit whose non-conformity substantially impairs its value to him if he has accepted it

(a) on the reasonable assumption that its non-conformity would be cured and it has not been seasonably cured; or

(b) without discovery of such nonconformity if his acceptance was reasonably induced either by the difficulty of discovery before acceptance or by the seller's assurances.

(2) Revocation of acceptance must occur within a reasonable time after the buyer discovers or should have discovered the ground for it and before any substantial change in condition of the goods which is not caused by their own defects. It is not effective until the buyer notifies the seller of it.

(3) A buyer who so revokes has the same rights and duties with regard to the goods involved as if he had rejected them.

§ 2-609. Right to Adequate Assurance of Performance.—

(1) A contract for sale imposes an obligation on each party that the other's expectation of receiving due performance will not be impaired. When reasonable grounds for insecurity arise with respect to the performance of either party the other may in writing demand adequate assurance of due performance and until he receives such assurance may if commercially reasonable suspend any performance for which he has not already received the agreed return.

(2) Between merchants the reasonableness of grounds for insecurity and the adequacy of any assurance offered shall be determined according to commercial standards.

(3) Acceptance of any improper delivery or payment does not prejudice the aggrieved party's right to demand adequate assurance of future performance.

(4) After receipt of a justified demand failure to provide within a reasonable time not exceeding thirty days such assurance of due performance as is adequate under the circumstances of the particular case is a repudiation of the contract.

§ 2-610. Anticipatory Repudiation.—When either party repudiates the contract with respect to a performance not yet due the loss of which will substantially impair the value of the contract to the other, the aggrieved party may

(a) for a commercially reasonable time await performance by the repudiating party; or

(b) resort to any remedy for breach (Section 2-703 or Section 2-711), even though he has notified the repudiating party that he would await the latter's performance and has urged retraction; and

(c) in either case suspend his own performance or proceed in accordance with the provisions of this Article on the seller's right to identify goods to the contract notwithstanding breach or to salvage unfinished goods (Section 2-704).

§ 2-611.   Retraction of Anticipatory Repudiation.—

(1) Until the repudiating party's next performance is due he can retract his repudiation unless the aggrieved party has since the repudiation cancelled or materially changed his position or otherwise indicated that he considers the repudiation final.

(2) Retraction may be by any method which clearly indicates to the aggrieved party that the repudiating party intends to perform, but must include any assurance justifiably demanded under the provisions of this Article (Section 2-609).

(3) Retraction reinstates the repudiating party's rights under the contract with due excuse and allowance to the aggrieved party for any delay occasioned by the repudiation.

§ 2-612.   "Installment Contract"; Breach.—

(1) An "installment contract" is one which requires or authorizes the delivery of goods in separate lots to be separately accepted, even though the contract contains a clause "each delivery is a separate contract" or its equivalent.

(2) The buyer may reject any installment which is non-conforming if the nonconformity substantially impairs the value of that installment and cannot be cured or if the non-conformity is a defect in the required documents; but if the non-conformity does not fall within subsection (3) and the seller gives adequate assurance of its cure the buyer must accept that installment.

(3) Whenever non-conformity or default with respect to one or more installments substantially impairs the value of the whole contract there is a breach of the whole. But the aggrieved party reinstates the contract if he accepts a non-conforming installment without seasonably notifying of cancellation or if he brings an action with respect only to past installments or demands performance as to future installments.

§ 2-613.   Casualty to Identified Goods.—

Where the contract requires for its performance goods identified when the contract is made, and the goods suffer casualty without fault of either party before the risk of loss passes to the buyer, or in a proper case under a "no arrival, no sale" term (Section 2-324) then

(a) if the loss is total the contract is avoided; and

(b) if the loss is partial or the goods have so deteriorated as no longer to conform to the contract the buyer may nevertheless demand inspection and at his option either treat the contract as avoided or accept the goods with due allowance from the contract price for the deterioration or the deficiency in quantity but without further right against the seller.

§ 2-614.   Substituted Performance.—

(1) Where without fault of either party the agreed berthing, loading, or unloading facilities fail or an agreed type of carrier becomes unavailable or the agreed manner of delivery otherwise becomes commercially impracticable but a commercially reasonable substitute is available, such substitute performance must be tendered and accepted.

(2) If the agreed means or manner of payment fails because of domestic or foreign governmental regulation, the seller may withhold or stop delivery unless the buyer provides a means or manner of payment which is commercially a substantial equivalent. If delivery has already been taken, payment by the means or in the manner provided by the regulation discharges the buyer's obligation unless the regulation is discriminatory, oppressive or predatory.

§ 2-615.   Excuse by Failure of Presupposed Conditions.—

Except so far as a seller may have assumed a greater obligation and subject to the preceding section on substituted performance:

(a) Delay in delivery or non-delivery in whole or in part by a seller who complies with paragraphs (b) and (c) is not a breach of his duty under a contract for sale if performance as agreed has been made impracticable by the occurrence of a contingency the non-occurrence of which was a basic assumption on which the contract was made or by compliance in good faith with any applicable foreign or domestic governmental regulation or order whether or not it later proves to be invalid.

(b) Where the causes mentioned in paragraph (a) affect only a part of the seller's capacity to perform, he must allocate production and deliveries among his customers but may at his option include regular customers not then under contract as well as his own requirements for further manufacture. He may so allocate in any manner which is fair and reasonable.

(c) The seller must notify the buyer seasonably that there will be delay or non-delivery and, when allocation is required under paragraph (b), of the estimated quota thus made available for the buyer.

§ 2-616. Procedure on Notice Claiming Excuse.—

(1) Where the buyer receives notification of a material or indefinite delay or an allocation justified under the preceding section he may by written notification to the seller as to any delivery concerned, and where the propective deficiency substantially impairs the value of the whole contract under the provisions of this Article relating to breach of installment contracts (Section 2-612), then also as to the whole,

(a) terminate and thereby discharge any unexecuted portion of the contract; or

(b) modify the contract by agreeing to take his available quota in substitution.

(2) If after receipt of such notification from the seller the buyer fails so to modify the contract within a reasonable time not exceeding thirty days the contract lapses with respect to any deliveries affected.

(3) The provisions of this section may not be negated by agreement except in so far as the seller has assumed a greater obligation under the preceding section.

PART 7

Remedies

§ 2-701. Remedies for Breach of Collateral Contracts Not Impaired.—Remedies for breach of any obligation or promise collateral or ancillary to a contract for sale are not impaired by the provisions of this Article.

§ 2-702. Seller's Remedies on Discovery of Buyer's Insolvency.—

(1) Where the seller discovers the buyer to be insolvent he may refuse delivery except for cash including payment for all goods theretofore delivered under the contract, and stop delivery under this Article (Section 2-705).

(2) Where the seller discovers that the buyer has received goods on credit while insolvent he may reclaim the goods upon demand made within ten days after the receipt, but if misrepresentation of solvency has been made to the particular seller in writing within three months before delivery the ten day limitation does not apply. Except as provided in this subsection the seller may not base a right to reclaim goods on the buyer's fraudulent or innocent misrepresentation of solvency or of intent to pay.

(3) The seller's right to reclaim under subsection (2) is subject to the rights of a buyer in ordinary course or other good faith purchaser or lien creditor under this Article (Section 2-403). Successful reclamation of goods excludes all other remedies with respect to them.

§ 2-703. Seller's Remedies in General.—Where the buyer wrongfully rejects or revokes acceptance of goods or fails to make a payment due on or before delivery or repudiates with respect to a part or the whole, then with respect to any goods directly affected and, if the breach is of the whole contract (Section 2-612), then also with respect to the whole undelivered balance, the aggrieved seller may

(a) withhold delivery of such goods;

(b) stop delivery by any bailee as hereafter provided (Section 2-705);

(c) proceed under the next section respecting goods still unidentified to the contract;

(d) resell and recover damages as hereafter provided (Section 2-706);

(e) recover damages for non-acceptance (Section 2-708) or in a proper case the price (Section 2-709);

(f) cancel.

§ 2-704. Seller's Right to Identify Goods to the Contract Notwithstanding Breach or to Salvage Unfinished Goods.—

(1) An aggrieved seller under the preceding section may

(a) identify to the contract conforming goods not already identified if at the time he learned of the breach they are in his possession or control;

(b) treat as the subject of resale goods which have demonstrably been intended for the particular contract even though those goods are unfinished.

(2) Where the goods are unfinished an aggrieved seller may in the exercise of reasonable commercial judgment for the purposes of avoiding loss and of effective realization either complete the manufacture and wholly identify the goods to the contract or cease manufacture and resell for scrap or salvage value or proceed in any other reasonable manner.

§ 2-705. Seller's Stoppage of Delivery in Transit or Otherwise.—

(1) The seller may stop delivery of goods in the possession of a carrier or other bailee when he discovers the buyer to be insolvent (Section 2-702) and may stop delivery of carload, truckload, planeload or larger shipments of express or freight when the buyer repudiates or fails to make a payment due before delivery or if for any other reason the seller has a right to withhold or reclaim the goods.

(2) As against such buyer the seller may stop delivery until

(a) receipt of the goods by the buyer; or

(b) acknowledgment to the buyer by any bailee of the goods except a carrier that the bailee holds the goods for the buyer; or

(c) such acknowledgment to the buyer by a carrier by reshipment or as warehouseman; or

(d) negotiation to the buyer of any negotiable document of title covering the goods.

(3) (a) To stop delivery the seller must so notify as to enable the bailee by reasonable diligence to prevent delivery of the goods.

(b) After such notification the bailee must hold and deliver the goods according to the directions of the seller but the seller is liable to the bailee for any ensuing charges or damages.

(c) If a negotiable document of title has been issued for goods the bailee is not obliged to obey a notification to stop until surrender of the document.

(d) A carrier who has issued a non-negotiable bill of lading is not obliged to obey a notification to stop received from a person other then the consignor.

§ 2-706. Seller's Resale Including Contract for Resale.—

(1) Under the conditions stated in Section 2-703 on seller's remedies, the seller may resell the goods concerned or the undelivered balance thereof. Where the resale is made in good faith and in a commercially reasonable manner the seller may recover the difference between the resale price and the contract price together with any incidental damages allowed under the provisions of this Article (Section 2-710), but less expenses saved in consequence of the buyer's breach.

(2) Except as otherwise provided in subsection (3) or unless otherwise agreed resale may be at public or private sale including sale by way of one or more contracts to sell or of identification to an existing contract of the seller. Sale may be as a unit or in parcels and at any time and place and on any terms but every aspect of the sale including the method, manner, time, place and terms must be commercially reasonable. The resale

must be reasonably identified as referring to the broken contract, but it is not necessary that the goods be in existence or that any or all of them have been identified to the contract before the breach.

(3) Where the resale is at private sale the seller must give the buyer reasonable notification of his intention to resell.

(4) Where the resale is at public sale

    (a) only identified goods can be sold except where there is a recognized market for a public sale of futures in goods of the kind; and

    (b) it must be made at a usual place or market for public sale if one is reasonably available and except in the case of goods which are perishable or threaten to decline in value speedily the seller must give the buyer reasonable notice of the time and place of the resale; and

    (c) if the goods are not to be within the view of those attending the sale the notification of sale must state the place where the goods are located and provide for their reasonable inspection by prospective bidders; and

    (d) the seller may buy.

(5) A purchaser who buys in good faith at a resale takes the goods free of any rights of the original buyer even though the seller fails to comply with one or more of the requirements of this section.

(6) The seller is not accountable to the buyer for any profit made on any resale. A person in the position of a seller (Section 2-707) or a buyer who has rightfully rejected or justifiably revoked acceptance must account for any excess over the amount of his security interest, as hereinafter defined (subsection (3) of Section 2-711).

§ 2-707. "Person in the Position of a Seller."—

(1) A "person in the position of a seller" includes as against a principal an agent who has paid or become responsible for the price of goods on behalf of his principal or anyone who otherwise holds a security interest or other right in goods similar to that of a seller.

(2) A person in the position of a seller may as provided in this Article withold or stop delivery (Section 2-705) and resell (Section 2-706) and recover incidental damages (Section 2-710).

§ 2-708. Seller's Damages for Nonacceptance or Repudiation.—

(1) Subject to subsection (2) and to the provisions of this Article with respect to proof of market price (Section 2-723), the measure of damages for non-acceptance or repudiation by the buyer is the difference between the market price at the time and place for tender and the unpaid contract price together with any incidental damages provided in this Article (Section 2-710), but less expenses saved in consequence of the buyer's breach.

(2) If the measure of damages provided in subsection (1) is inadequate to put the seller in as good a position as performance would have done then the measure of damages is the profit (including reasonable overhead) which the seller would have made from full performance by the buyer, together with any incidental damages provided in this Article (Section 2-710), due allowance for costs reasonably incurred and due credit for payments or proceeds of resale.

§ 2-709. Action for the Price.—

(1) When the buyer fails to pay the price as it becomes due the seller may recover, together with any incidental damages under the next section, the price

    (a) of goods accepted or of conforming goods lost or damaged within a commercially reasonable time after risk of their loss has passed to the buyer; and

    (b) of goods identified to the contract if the seller is unable after reasonable effort to resell them at a reasonable price or the circumstances reasonably indicate that such effort will be unavailing.

(2) Where the seller sues for the price he must hold for the buyer any goods which have been identified to the contract and are still in his control except that if resale becomes possible he may resell them at any time prior to the collection of the judgment. The net proceeds of any such resale must be credited to the buyer and payment of the judgment entitles him to any goods not resold.

(3) After the buyer has wrongfully rejected or revoked acceptance of the goods or has failed to make a payment due or has repudiated (Section 2-610), a seller who is held not entitled to the price under this section shall nevertheless be awarded damages for non-acceptance under the preceding section.

§ 2-710.   **Seller's Incidental Damages.**—Incidental damages to an aggrieved seller include any commercially reasonable charges, expenses or commissions incurred in stopping delivery, in the transportation, care and custody of goods after the buyer's breach, in connection with return or resale of the goods or otherwise resulting from the breach.

§ 2-711.   **Buyer's Remedies in General, Buyer's Security Interest in Rejected Goods.**—

(1) Where the seller fails to make delivery or repudiates or the buyer rightfully rejects or justifiably revokes acceptance then with respect to any goods involved, and with respect to the whole if the breach goes to the whole contract (Section 2-612), the buyer may cancel and whether or not he has done so may in addition to recovering so much of the price as has been paid

(a) "cover" and have damages under the next section as to all the goods affected whether or not they have been identified to the contract; or

(b) recover damages for non-delivery as provided in this Article (Section 2-713).

(2)   Where the seller fails to deliver or repudiates the buyer may also

(a)   if the goods have been identified recover them as provided in this Article (Section 2-502); or

(b)   in a proper case obtain specific performance or replevy the goods as provided in this article (Section 2-716).

(3)   On rightful rejection or justifiable revocation of acceptance a buyer has a security interest in goods in his possession or control for any payments made on their price and any expenses reasonably incurred in their inspection, receipt, transportation, care and custody and may hold such goods and resell them in like manner as an aggrieved seller (Section 2-706).

§ 2-712.   **"Cover"; Buyer's Procurement of Substitute Goods.**—

(1) After a breach within the preceding section the buyer may "cover" by making in good faith and without unreasonable delay any reasonable purchase of or contract to purchase goods in substitution for those due from the seller.

(2) The buyer may recoved from the seller as damages the difference between the cost of cover and the contract price together with any incidental or consequential damages as hereinafter defined (Section 2-715), but less expenses saved in consequence of the seller's breach.

(3) Failure of the buyer to effect cover within this section does not bar him from any other remedy.

§ 2-713.   **Buyer's Damages for Non-Delivery or Repudiation.**—

(1) Subject to the provisions of this Article with respect to proof of market price (Section 2-723), the measure of damages for non-delivery or repudiation by the seller is the difference between the market price at the time when the buyer learned of the breach and the contract price together with any incidental and consequential damages provided in this Article (Section 2-715), but less expenses saved in consequence of the seller's breach.

(2) Market price is to be determined as of the place for tender or, in cases of rejection after arrival or revocation of acceptance, as of the place of arrival.

§ 2-714. Buyer's Damages for Breach in Regard to Accepted Goods.—

(1) Where the buyer has accepted goods and given notification (subsection (3) of Section 2-607) he may recover as damages for any non-conformity of tender the loss resulting in the ordinary course of events from the seller's breach as determined in any manner which is reasonable.

(2) The measure of damages for breach of warranty is the difference at the time and place of acceptance between the value of the goods accepted and the value they would have had if they had been as warranted, unless special circumstances show proximate damages of a different amount.

(3) In a proper case any incidental and consequential damages under the next section may also be recovered.

§ 2-715. Buyer's Incidental and Consequential Damages.—

(1) Incidental damages resulting from the seller's breach include expenses reasonably incurred in inspection, receipt, transportation and care and custody of goods rightfully rejected, and any commercially reasonable charges, expenses or commissions in connection with effecting cover and any other reasonable expense incident to the delay or other breach.

(2) Consequential damages resulting from the seller's breach include.

(a) any loss resulting from general or particular requirements and needs of which the seller at the time of contracting had reason to know and which could not reasonably be prevented by cover or otherwise; and

(b) injury to person or property proximately resulting from any breach of warranty.

§ 2-716. Buyer's Right to Specific Performance of Replevin.—

(1) Specific performance may be decreed where the goods are unique or in other proper circumstances.

(2) The decree for specific performance may include such terms and conditions as to payment of the price, damages, or other relief as the court may deem just.

§ 2-717. Deduction of Damages From the Price.—The buyer on notifying the seller of his intention to do so may deduct all or any part of the damages resulting from any breach of the contract from any part of the price still due under the same contract.

§ 2-718. Liquidation or Limitation of Damages; Deposits.—

(1) Damages for breach by either party may be liquidated in the agreement but only at an amount which is reasonable in the light of the anticipated or actual harm caused by the breach, the difficulties of proof of loss, and the inconvenience or nonfeasibility of otherwise obtaining an adequate remedy. A term fixing unreasonably large liquidated damages is void as a penalty.

(2) Where the seller justifiably withholds delivery of goods because of the buyer's breach, the buyer is entitled to restitution of any amount by which the sum of his payments exceeds

(a) The amount to which the seller is entitled by virtue of terms liquidating the seller's damages in accordance with subsection (1), or

(b) in the absence of such terms, twenty per cent of the value of the total performance for which the buyer is obligated under the contract or $500, whichever is smaller.

(3) The buyer's right to restitution under subsection (2) is subject to offset to the extent that the seller establishes.

(a) a right to recover damages under the provisions of this Article other than subsection (1), and

(b) the amount or value of any benefits received by the buyer directly or indirectly by reason of the contract.

(4) Where a seller has received payment in goods their reasonable value or the proceeds of their resale shall be treated as payments for the purposes of subsection (2); but if the seller has notice of the buyer's breach before reselling goods received in part performance, his resale is subject to the conditions laid down in this Article on resale by an aggrieved seller (Section 2-706).

§ 2-719. Contractual Modification or Limitation of Remedy.—

(1) Subject to the provisions of subsections (2) and (3) of this section and of the preceding section on liquidation and limitation of damages.

(a) the agreement may provide for remedies in addition to or in substitution for those provided in this Article and may limit or alter the measure of damages recoverable under this Article, as by limiting the buyer's remedies to return of the goods and repayment of the price or to repair and replacement of non-conforming goods or parts; and

(b) resort to a remedy as provided is optional unless the remedy is expressly agreed to be exclusive, in which case it is the sole remedy.

(2) Where circumstances cause an exclusive or limited remedy to fail of its essential purpose, remedy may be had as provided in this Act.

(3) Consequential damages may be limited or excluded unless the limitation or exclusion is unconscionable. Limitation of consequential damages for injury to the person in the case of consumer goods is prima facie unconscionable but limitation of damages where the loss is commercial is not.

§ 2-720. Effect of "Cancellation" or "Rescission" on Claims for Antecedent Breach.—Unless the contrary intention clearly appears, expressions of "cancellation" or "rescission" of the contract or the like shall not be construed as a renunciation or discharge of any claim in damages for an antecedent breach.

§ 2-721. Remedies for Fraud.—Remedies for material misrepresentation or fraud include all remedies available under this Article for non-fraudulent breach. Neither rescission or a claim for rescission of the contract for sale nor rejection or return of the goods shall bar or be deemed inconsistent with a claim for damages or other remedy.

§ 2-722. Who Can Sue Third Parties for Injury to Goods.—Where a third party so deals with goods which have been identified to a contract for sale as to cause actionable injury to a party to that contract

(a) a right of action against the third party is in either party to the contract for sale who has title to or a security interest or a special property or an insurable interest in the goods; and if the goods have been destroyed or converted a right of action is also in the party who either bore the risk of loss under the contract for sale or has since the injury assumed that risk as against the other;

(b) if at the time of the injury the party plaintiff did not bear the risk of loss as against the other party to the contract for sale and there is no arrangement between them for disposition of the recovery, his suit or settlement is, subject to his own interest, as a fiduciary for the other party to the contract;

(c) either party may with the consent of the other sue for the benefit of whom it may concern.

§ 2-723. Proof of Market Price: Time and Place.—

(1) If an action based on anticipatory repudiation comes to trial before the time for performance with respect to some or all of the goods, any damages based on market price (Section 2-708 or Section 2-713) shall be determined according to the price of such goods prevailing at the time when the aggrieved party learned of the repudiation.

(2) If evidence of a price prevailing at the times or places described in this Article is not readily available the price prevailing within any reasonable time before or after the

time described or at any other place which in commercial judgment or under usage of trade would serve as a reasonable substitute for the one described may be used, making any proper allowance for the cost of transporting the goods to or from such other place.

(3) Evidence of a relevant price prevailing at a time or place other than the one described in this Article offered by one party is not admissible unless and until he has given the other party such notice as the court finds sufficient to prevent unfair surprise.

§ 2-724. **Admissibility of Market Quotations.**—Whenever the prevailing price or value of any goods regularly bought and sold in any established commodity market is in issue, reports in official publications or trade journals or in newspapers or periodicals of general circulation published as the reports of such market shall be admissible in evidence. The circumstances of the preparation of such a report may be shown to affect its weight but not its admissibility.

§ 2-725. **Statute of Limitations in Contracts for Sale.**—
(1) An action for breach of any contract for sale must be commenced within four years after the cause of action has accrued. By the original agreement the parties may reduce the period of limitation to not less than one year but may not extend it.

(2) A cause of action accrues when the breach occurs, regardless of the aggrieved party's lack of knowledge of the breach. A breach of warranty occurs when tender of delivery is made, except that where a warranty explicitly extends to future performance of the goods and discovery of the breach must await the time of such performance the cause of action accrues when the breach is or should have been discovered.

(3) Where an action commenced within the time limited by subsection (1) is so terminated as to leave available a remedy by another action for the same breach such other action may be commenced after the expiration of the time limited and within six months after the termination of the first action unless the termination resulted from voluntary discontinuance or from dismissal for failure or neglect to prosecute.

(4) This section does not alter the law on tolling of the statute of limitations nor does it apply to causes of action which have accrued before this Act becomes effective.

ARTICLE THREE—COMMERCIAL PAPER

PART 1

Short Title, Form and Interpretation

§ 3-101. **Short Title.**—This Article shall be known and may be cited as Uniform Commercial Code—Commercial Paper.

§ 3-102. **Definitions and Index of Definitions.**—
(1) In this Article unless the context otherwise requires
(a) "Issue" means the first delivery of an instrument to a holder or a remitter.
(b) An "order" is a direction to pay and must be more than an authorization or request. It must identify the person to pay with reasonable certainty. It may be addressed to one or more such persons jointly or in the alternative but not in succession.
(c) A "promise" is an undertaking to pay and must be more than an acknowledgment of an obligation.
· (d) "Secondary party" means a drawer or endorser.
(e) "Instrument" means a negotiable instrument. . . .

§ 3-103. Limitations on Scope of Article.—

(1) This Article does not apply to money, documents of title or investment securities.

(2) The provisions of this Article are subject to the provisions of the Article on Bank Deposits and Collections (Article 4) and Secured Transactions (Article 9).

§ 3-104. Form of Negotiable Instruments; "Draft"; "Check"; "Certificate of Deposit"; "Note."—

(1) Any writing to be a negotiable instrument within this Article must
    (a) be signed by the maker or drawer; and
    (b) contain an unconditional promise or order to pay a sum certain in money and no other promise, order, obligation or power given by the maker or drawer except as authorized by this Article; and
    (c) be payable on demand or at a definite time; and
    (d) be payable to order or to bearer.

(2) A writing which complies with the requirements of this section is
    (a) a "draft" ("bill of exchange") if it is an order;
    (b) a "check" if it is a draft drawn on a bank and payable on demand;
    (c) a "certificate of deposit" if it is an acknowledgment by a bank of receipt of money with an engagement to repay it;
    (d) a "note" if it is a promise other than a certificate of deposit.

(3) As used in other Articles of this Act, and as the context may require, the terms "draft", "check", "certificate of deposit" and "note" may refer to instruments which are not negotiable within this Article as well as to instruments which are so negotiable.

§ 3-105. When Promise or Order Unconditional.—

(1) A promise or order otherwise unconditional is not made conditional by the fact that the instrument
    (a) is subject to implied or constructive conditions; or
    (b) states it consideration, whether performed or promised, or the transaction which gave rise to the instrument, or that the promise or order is made or the instrument matures in accordance with or "as per" such transaction; or
    (c) refers to or states that it arises out of a separate agreement; or
    (d) states that it is drawn under a letter of credit; or
    (e) states that it is secured, whether by mortgage, reservation of title or otherwise; or
    (f) indicates a particular account to be debited or any other fund or source from which reimbursement is expected; or
    (g) is limited to payment out of a particular fund or the proceeds of a particular source, if the instrument is issued by a government or governmental agency or unit; or
    (h) is limited to payment out of the entire assets of a partnership, unincorporated association, trust or estate by or on behalf of which the instrument is issued.

(2) A promise or order is not unconditional if the instrument
    (a) states that it is subject to or governed by any other agreement; or
    (b) states that it is to be paid only out of a particular fund or source except as provided in this Section.

§ 3-106. Sum Certain.—

(1) The sum payable is a sum certain even though it is to be paid
    (a) with stated interest or by stated installments; or
    (b) with stated different rates of interest before and after default or a specified date; or
    (c) with a stated discount or addition if paid before or after the date fixed for payment; or

(d) with exchange or less exchange, whether at a fixed rate or at the current rate; or

(e) with costs of collection or an attorney's fee or both upon default.

(2) Nothing in this Section shall validate any term which is otherwise illegal.

§ 3-107. Money.—

(1) An instrument is payable in money if the medium of exchange in which it is payable is money at the time the instrument is made. An instrument payable in "currency" or "current funds" is payable in money.

(2) A promise or order to pay a sum stated in a foreign currency is for a sum certain in money and, unless a different medium of payment is specified in the instrument, may be satisfied by payment of that number of dollars which the stated foreign currency will purchase at the buying sight rate for that currency on the day on which the instrument is payable or, if payable on demand, on the date of demand. If such an instrument specifies a foreign currency as the medium of payment the instrument is payable in that currency.

§ 3-108. Payable on Demand.—Instruments payable on demand include those payable at sight or on presentation and those in which no time for payment is stated.

§ 3-109. Definite Time.—

(1) An instrument is payable at a definite time if by its terms it is payable

(a) on or before a stated date or at a fixed period after a stated date; or

(b) at a fixed period after sight; or

(c) at a definite time subject to any acceleration; or

(d) at a definite time subject to extension at the option of the holder, or to extension to a further definite time at the option of the maker or acceptor or automatically upon or after a specified act or event.

(2) An instrument which by its terms is otherwise payable only upon an act or event uncertain as to time of occurrence is not payable at a definite time even though the act or event has occurred.

§ 3-110. Payable to Order.—

(1) An instrument is payable to order when by its terms it is payable to the order or assigns of any person therein specified with reasonable certainty, or to him or his order, or when it is conspicuously designated on its face as "exchange" or the like and names a payee. It may be payable to the order of

(a) the maker or drawer; or

(b) the drawee; or

(c) A payee who is not maker, drawer or drawee; or

(d) two or more payees together or in the alternative; or

(e) an estate, trust or fund, in which case it is payable to the order of the representative of such estate, trust or fund or his successors; or

(f) an office, or an officer by his title as such in which case it is payable to the principal but the incumbent of the office or his successors may act as if he or they were the holder; or

(g) a partnership or unincorporated association, in which case it is payable to the partnership or association and may be indorsed or transferred by any person thereto authorized.

(2) An instrument not payable to order is not made so payable by such words as "payable upon return of this instrument properly indorsed."

(3) An instrument made payable both to order and to bearer is payable to order unless the bearer words are handwritten or typewritten.

§ 3-111. Payable to Bearer.—An instrument is payable to bearer when by its terms it is payable to

(a) bearer or the order of bearer; or

(b) a specified person or bearer; or

(c) "cash" or the order of "cash", or any other indication which does not purport to designate a specific payee.

§ 3-112.   Terms and Omissions Not Affecting Negotiability.—

(1) The negotiability of an instrument is not affected by

(a) the omission of a statement of any consideration or of the place where the instrument is drawn or payable; or

(b) a statement that collateral has been given for the instrument or in case of default on the instrument the collateral may be sold; or

(c) a promise or power to maintain or protect collateral or to give additional collateral; or

(d) a term authorizing a confession of judgment on the instrument if it is not paid when due; or

(e) a term purporting to waive the benefit of any law intended for the advantage or protection of any obligor; or

(f) a term in a draft providing that the payee by indorsing or cashing it acknowledges full satisfaction of an obligation of the drawer; or

(g) A statement in a draft drawn in a set of parts (Section 3-801) to the effect that the order is effective only if no other part has been honored.

(2) Nothing in this Section shall validate any term which is othewise illegal.

§ 3-113.   Seal.—An instrument otherwise negotiable is within this Article even though it is under a seal.

§ 3-114.   Date, Antedating, Postdating.—

(1) The negotiability of an instrument is not affected by the fact that it is undated, antedated or postdated.

(2) Where an instrument is antedated or postdated the time when it is payable is determined by the stated date if the instrument is payable on demand or at a fixed period after date.

(3) Where the instrument or any signature thereon is dated, the date is presumed to be correct.

§ 3-115.   Incomplete Instruments.—

(1) When a paper whose contents at the time of signing show that it is intended to become an instrument is signed while still incomplete in any necessary respect it cannot be enforced until completed, but when it is completed in accordance with authority given it is effective as completed.

(2) If the completion is unauthorized the rules as to material alteration apply (Section 3-407), even though the paper was not delivered by the maker or drawer; but the burden of establishing that any completion is unauthorized is on the party so asserting.

§ 3-116.   Instruments Payable to Two or More Persons.—An instrument payable to the order of two or more persons

(a) if in the alternative is payable to any one of them and may be negotiated, discharged or enforced by any of them who has possession of it;

(b) if not in the alternative is payable to all of them and may be negotiated, discharged or enforced only by all of them.

§ 3-117.   Instruments Payable With Words of Description.—An instrument made payable to a named person with the addition of words describing him

(a) as agent or officer of a specified person is payable to his principal but the agent or officer may act as if he were the holder;

(b) as any other fiduciary for a specified person or purpose is payable to the payee and may be negotiated, discharged or enforced by him;

(c) in any other manner is payable to the payee unconditionally and the additional words are without effect on subsequent parties.

§ 3-118. Ambiguous Terms and Rules of Construction.—The following rules apply to every instrument:

(a) Where there is doubt whether the instrument is a draft or a note the holder may treat it as either. A draft drawn on the drawer is effective as a note.

(b) Handwritten terms control typewritten and printed terms, and typewritten control printed.

(c) Words control figures except that if the words are ambiguous figures control.

(d) Unless otherwise specified a provision for interest means interest at the judgment rate at the place of payment from the date of the instrument, or if it is undated from the date of issue.

(e) Unless the instrument otherwise specifies two or more persons who sign as maker, acceptor or drawer or indorser and as a part of the same transaction are jointly and severally liable even though the instrument contains such words as "I promise to pay."

(f) Unless otherwise specified consent to extension authorizes a single extension for not longer than the original period. A consent to extension, expressed in the instrument, is binding on secondary parties and accommodation makers. A holder may not exercise his option to extend an instrument over the objection of a maker or acceptor or other party who in accordance with Section 3-604 tenders full payment when the instrument is due.

§ 3-119. Other Writings Affecting Instrument.—

(1) As between the obligor and his immediate obligee or any transferee the terms of an instrument may be modified or affected by any other written agreement executed as a part of the same transaction, except that a holder in due course is not affected by any limitation of his rights arising out of the separate written agreement if he had no notice of the limitation when he took the instrument.

(2) A separate agreement does not affect the negotiability of an instrument.

§ 3-120. Instruments "Payable Through" Bank.—An instrument which states that it is "payable through" a bank or the like designates that bank as a collecting bank to make presentment but does not of itself authorize the bank to pay the instrument.

§ 3-121. Instruments Payable at Bank.—A note or acceptance which states that it is payable at a bank is not of itself an order or authorization to the bank to pay it.

§ 3-122. Accrual of Cause of Action.—

(1) A cause of action against a maker or an acceptor accures

(a) in the case of a time instrument on the day after maturity;

(b) in the case of a demand instrument upon its date or, if no date is stated, on the date of issue.

(2) A cause of action against the obligor of a demand or time certificate of deposit accrues upon demand, but demand on a time certificate may not be made until on or after the date of maturity.

(3) A cause of action against a drawer of a draft or an indorser of any instrument accrues upon demand following dishonor of the instrument. Notice of dishonor is a demand.

(4) Unless an instrument provides otherwise, interest runs at the rate provided by law for a judgment

(a) in the case of a maker acceptor or other primary obligor of a demand instrument, from the date of demand;

(b) in all other cases from the date of accrual of the cause of action.

PART 2

Transfer and Negotiation

§ 3-201.   Transfer: Right to Indorsement.—

(1) Transfer of an instrument vests in the transferee such rights as the transferor has therein, except that a transferee who has himself been a party to any fraud or illegality affecting the instrument or who as a prior holder had notice of a defense or claim against it cannot improve his position by taking from a later holder in due course.

(2) A transfer of a security interest in an instrument vests the foregoing rights in the the transferee to the extent of the interest transferred.

(3) Unless otherwise agreed any transfer for value of an instrument not then payable to bearer gives the transferee the specifically enforceable right to have the unqualified indorsement of the transferor. Negotiation takes effect only when the indorsement is made and until that time there is no presumption that the transferee is the owner.

§ 3-202.   Negotiation.—

(1) Negotiation is the transfer of an instrument in such form that the transferee becomes a holder. If the instrument is payable to order it is negotiated by delivery with any necessary indorsement; if payable to bearer it is negotiated by delivery.

(2) An indorsement must be written by or on behalf of the holder and on the instrument or on a paper so firmly affixed thereto as to become a part thereof.

(3) An indorsement is effective for negotiation only when it conveys the entire instrument or any unpaid residue. If it purports to be of less it operates only as a partial assignment.

(4) Words of assignment, condition, waiver, guaranty, limitation or disclaimer of liability and the like accompanying an indorsement do not affect its character as an indorsement.

§ 3-203.   Wrong or Misspelled Name.—Where an instrument is made payable to a person under a misspelled name or one other than his own he may indorse in that name or his own or both; but signature in both names may be required by a person paying or giving value for the instrument.

§ 3-204.   Special Indorsement; Blank Indorsement.—

(1) A special indorsement specifies the person to whom or to whose order it makes the instrument payable. Any instrument specially indorsed becomes payable to the order of the special indorsee and may be further negotiated only by his indorsement.

(2) An indorsement in blank specifies no particular indorsee and may consist of a mere signature. An instrument payable to order and indorsed in blank becomes payable to bearer and may be negotiated by delivery alone until specially indorsed.

(3) The holder may convert a blank indorsement into a special indorsement by writing over the signature of the indorser in blank any contract consistent with the character of the indorsement.

§ 3-205.   Restrictive Indorsements.—An indorsement is restrictive which either

(a) is conditional; or

(b) purports to prohibit further transfer of the instrument; or

(c) includes the words "for collection", "for deposit", "pay any bank", or like terms signifying a purpose of deposit or collection; or

(d) otherwise states that it is for the benefit or use of the indorser or of another person.

§ 3-206. Effect of Restrictive Indorsement.—

(1) No restrictive indorsement prevents further transfer or negotiation of the instrument.

(2) An intermediary bank, or a payor bank which is not the depositary bank, is neither given notice nor otherwise affected by a restrictive indorsement of any person except the bank's immediate transferor or the person presenting for payment.

(3) Except for an intermediary bank, any transferee under an indorsement which is conditional or includes the words "for collection", "for deposit", "pay any bank", or like terms (subparagraphs (a) and (c) of Section 3-205) must pay or apply any value given by him for or on the security of the instrument consistently with the indorsement and to the extent that he does so he becomes a holder for value. In addition such transferee is a holder in due course if he otherwise complies with the requirements of Section 3-302 on what constitutes a holder in due course.

(4) The first taker under an indorsement for the benefit of the indorser or another person (subparagraph (d) of Section 3-205) must pay or apply any value given by him for or on the security of the instrument consistently with the indorsement and to the extent that he does so he becomes a holder for value. In addition such taker is a holder in due course if he otherwise complies with the requirements of Section 3-302 on what constitutes a holder in due course. A later holder for value is neither given notice nor otherwise affected by such restrictive indorsement unless he has knowledge that a fiduciary or other person has negotiated the instrument in any transaction for his own benefit or otherwise in breach of duty (subsection (2) of Section 3-304).

§ 3-207. Negotiation Effective Although It May Be Rescinded.—

(1) Negotiation is effective to transfer the instrument although the negotiation is
   (a) made by an infant, a corporation exceeding its powers, or any other person without capacity; or
   (b) obtained by fraud, duress or mistake of any kind; or
   (c) part of an illegal transaction; or
   (d) made in breach of duty.

(2) Except as against a subsequent holder in due course such negotiation is in an appropriate case subject to rescission, the declaration of a constructive trust or any other remedy permitted by law.

§ 3-208. Reacquisition.—Where an instrument is returned to or required by a prior party he may cancel any indorsement which is not necessary to his title and reissue or further negotiate the instrument, but any intervening party is discharged as against the reacquiring party and subsequent holders not in due course and if his indorsement has been cancelled is discharged as against subsequent holders in due course as well.

PART 3

Rights of a Holder

§ 3-301. Rights of a Holder.—The holder of an instrument whether or not he is the owner may transfer or negotiate it and, except as otherwise provided in Section 3-603 on payment or satisfaction, discharge it or enforce payment in his own name.

§ 3-302. Holder in Due Course.—

(1) A holder in due course is a holder who takes the instrument
   (a) for value; and
   (b) in good faith; and
   (c) without notice that it is overdue or has been dishonored or of any defense against or claim to it on the part of any person.

(2) A payee may be a holder in due course.

(3) A holder does not become a holder in due course of an instrument:

(a) by purchase of it at judicial sale or by taking it under legal process; or

(b) by acquiring it in taking over an estate; or

(c) by purchasing it as part of a bulk transaction not in regular course of business of the transferor.

(4) A purchaser of a limited interest can be a holder in due course only to the extent of the interest purchased.

§ 3-303. Taking for Value.—A holder takes the instrument for value

(a) to the extent that the agreed consideration has been performed or that he acquires a security interest in or a lien on the instrument otherwise than by legal process; or

(b) when he takes the instrument in payment of or as security for an antecedent claim against any person whether or not the claim is due; or

(c) when he gives a negotiable instrument for it or makes an irrevocable commitment to a third person.

§ 3-304. Notice to Purchaser.—

(1) The purchaser has notice of a claim or defense if

(a) the instrument is so incomplete, bears such visible evidence of forgery or alteration, or is otherwise so irregular as to call into question its validity, terms or ownership or to create an ambiguity as to the party to pay; or

(b) the purchaser has notice that the obligation of any party is voidable in whole or in part, or that all parties have been discharged.

(2) The purchaser has notice of a claim against the instrument when he has knowledge that a fiduciary has negotiated the instrument in payment of or as security for his own debt or in any transaction for his own benefit or otherwise in breach of duty.

(3) The purchaser has notice that an instrument is overdue if he has reason to know

(a) that any part of the principal amount is overdue or that there is an uncured default in payment of another instrument of the same series; or

(b) that acceleration of the instrument has been made; or

(c) that he is taking a demand instrument after demand has been made or more than a reasonable length of time after its issue. A reasonable time for a check drawn and payable within the states and territories of the United States and the District of Columbia is presumed to be thirty days.

(4) Knowledge of the following facts does not of itself give the purchaser notice of a defense or claim

(a) That the instrument is antedated or postdated;

(b) that it was issued or negotiated in return for an executory promise or accompanied by a separate agreement, unless the purchaser has notice that a defense or claim has arisen from the terms thereof;

(c) that any party has signed for accommodation;

(d) that an incomplete instrument has been completed, unless the purchaser has notice of any improper completion;

(e) that any person negotiating the instrument is or was a fiduciary;

(f) that there has been default in payment of interest on the instrument or in payment of any other instrument, except one of the same series.

(5) The filing or recording of a document does not of itself constitute notice within the provisions of this Article to a person who would otherwise be a holder in due course.

(6) To be effective notice must be received at such time and in such manner as to give a reasonable opportunity to act on it.

§ 3-305.   Rights of Holder in Due Course.—To the extent that a holder is a holder in due course he takes the instrument free from

(1) all claims to it on the part of any person; and

(2) all defenses of any party to the instrument with whom the holder has not dealt except

(a) infancy, to the extent that it is a defense to a simple contract; and

(b) such other incapacity, or duress, or illegality of the transaction, as renders the obligation of the party a nullity; and

(c) such misrepresentation as has induced the party to sign the instrument with neither knowledge nor reasonable opportunity to obtain knowledge of its character or its essential terms; and

(d) discharge in insolvency proceedings; and

(e) any other discharge of which the holder has notice when he takes the instrument.

§ 3-306.   Rights of One Not Holder in Due Course.—Unless he has the rights of a holder in due course any person takes the instrument subject to

(a) all valid claims to it on the part of any person; and

(b) all defenses of any party which would be available in an action on a simple contract; and

(c) the defenses of want or failure of consideration, non-performance of any condition precedent, non-delivery, or delivery for a special purpose (Section 3-408); and

(d) the defense that he or a person through whom he holds the instrument acquired it by theft, of that payment or satisfaction to such holder would be inconsistent with the terms of a restrictive indorsement. The claim of any third person to the instrument is not otherwise available as a defense to any party liable thereon unless the third person himself defends the action for such party.

§ 3-307.   Burden of Establishing Signatures, Defenses and Due Course.—

(1) Unless specifically denied in the pleadings each signature on an instrument is admitted. When the effectiveness of a signature is put in issue

(a) the burden of establishing it is on the party claiming under the signature; and

(b) the signature is presumed to be genuine or authorized except where the action is to enforce the obligation of a purported signer who has died or become incompetent before proof is required.

(2) When signatures are admitted or established, production of the instrument entitles a holder to recover on it unless the defendant establishes a defense.

(3) After it is shown that a defense exists a person claiming the rights of a holder in due course has the burden of establishing that he or some person under whom he claims is in all respects a holder in due course.

PART 4

Liability of Parties

§ 3-401.   Signature.—

(1) No person is liable on an instrument unless his signature appears thereon.

(2) A signature is made by use of any name, including any trade or assumed name, upon an instrument, or by any word or mark used in lieu of a written signature.

§ 3-402.   Signature in Ambiguous Capacity.—Unless the instrument clearly indicates that a signature is made in some other capacity it is an indorsement.

§ 3-403. Signature by Authorized Representative.—

(1) A signature may be made by an agent or other representative, and his authority to make it may be established as in other cases of representation. No particular form of appointment is necessary to establish such authority.

(2) An authorized representative who signs his own name to an instrument

(a) is personally obligated if the instrument neither names the person represented nor shows that the representative signed in a representative capacity;

(b) except as otherwise established between the immediate parties, is personally obligated if instrument names the person represented but does not show that the representative signed in a representative capacity, or if the instrument does not name the person represented but does show that the representative signed in a representative capacity.

(3) Except as otherwise established the name of an organization preceded or followed by the name and office of an authorized individual is a signature made in a representative capacity.

§ 3-404. Unauthorized Signatures.—

(1) Any unauthorized signature is wholly inoperative as that of the person whose name is signed unless he ratifies it or is precluded from denying it; but it operates as the signature of the unauthorized signer in favor of any person who in good faith pays the instrument or takes it for value.

(2) Any unauthorized signature may be ratified for all purposes of this Article. Such ratification does not of itself affect any rights of the person ratifying against the actual signer.

§ 3-405. Imposters; Signature in Name of Payee.—

(1) An indorsement by any person in the name of a named payee is effective if

(a) an imposter by use of the mails or otherwise has induced the maker or drawer to issue the instrument to him or his confederate in the name of the payee; or

(b) a person signing as or on behalf of a maker or drawer intends the payee to have no interest in the instrument; or

(c) an agent or employee of the maker or drawer has supplied him with the name of the payee intending the latter to have no such interest.

(2) Nothing in this Section shall affect the criminal or civil liability of the person so indorsing.

§ 3-406. Negligence Contributing to Alteration or Unauthorized Signature.—

Any person who by his negligence substantially contributes to a material alteration of the instrument or to the making of an unauthorized signature is precluded from asserting the alteration or lack of authority against a holder in due course or against a drawee or other payor who pays the instrument in good faith and in accordance with the reasonable commercial standards of the drawee's or payor's business.

§ 3-407. Alteration.—

(1) Any alteration of an instrument is material which changes the contract of any party thereto in any respect, including any such change in

(a) the number or relations of the parties; or

(b) an incomplete instrument, by completing it otherwise than as authorized; or

(c) the writing as signed, by adding to it or by removing any part of it.

(2) As against any person other than a subsequent holder in due course

(a) alteration by the holder which is both fraudulent and material discharges any party whose contract is thereby changed unless that party assents or is precluded from asserting the defense;

(b) no other alteration discharges any party and the instrument may be enforced according to its original tenor, or as to incomplete instruments according to the authority given.

(3) A subsequent holder in due course may in all cases enforce the instrument according to its original tenor, and when an incomplete instrument has been completed, he may enforce it as completed.

§ 3-408. Consideration.—Want or failure of consideration is a defense as against any person not having the rights of a holder in due course (Section 3-305), except that no consideration is necessary for an instrument or obligation thereon given in payment of or as security for an antecedent obligation of any kind. Nothing in this Section shall be taken to displace any statute outside this Act under which a promise is enforceable notwithstanding lack or failure of consideration. Partial failure of consideration is a defense pro tanto whether or not the failure is in an ascertained or liquidated amount.

§ 3-409. Draft Not an Assignment.—

(1) A check or other draft does not of itself operate as an assignment of any funds in the hands of the drawee available for its payment, and the drawee is not liable on the instrument until he accepts it.

(2) Nothing in this Section shall affect any liability in contract, tort or otherwise arising from any letter of credit or other obligation or representation which is not an acceptance.

§ 3-410. Definition and Operation of Acceptance.—

(1) Acceptance is the drawee's signed engagement to honor the draft as presented. It must be written on the draft, and may consist of his signature alone. It becomes operative when completed by delivery or notification.

(2) A draft may be accepted although it has not been signed by the drawer or is otherwise incomplete or is overdue or has been dishonored.

(3) Where the draft is payable at a fixed period after sight and the acceptor fails to date his acceptance the holder may complete it by supplying a date in good faith.

§ 3-411. Certification of a Check.—

(1) Certification of a check is acceptance. Where a holder procures certification the drawer and all prior indorsers are discharged.

(2) Unless otherwise agreed a bank has no obligation to certify a check.

(3) A bank may certify a check before returning it for lack of proper indorsement. If it does so the drawer is discharged.

§ 3-412. Acceptance Varying Draft.—

(1) Where the drawee's proffered acceptance in any manner varies the draft as presented the holder may refuse the acceptance and treat the draft as dishonored in which case the drawee is entitled to have his acceptance cancelled.

(2) The terms of the draft are not varied by an acceptance to pay at any particular bank or place in the continental United States, unless the acceptance states that the draft is to be paid only at such bank or place.

(3) Where the holder assents to an acceptance varying the terms of the draft each drawer and indorser who does not affirmatively assent is discharged.

§ 3-413. Contract of Maker, Drawer and Acceptor.—

(1) The maker or acceptor engages that he will pay the instrument according to its tenor at the time of his engagement or as completed pursuant to Section 3-115 on incomplete instruments.

(2) The drawer engages that upon dishonor of the draft and any necessary notice of dishonor or protest he will pay the amount of the draft to the holder or to any indorser who takes it up. The drawer may disclaim this liability by drawing without recourse.

(3) By making, drawing or accepting the party admits as against all subsequent parties including the drawee the existence of the payee and his then capacity to indorse.

§ 3-414. Contract of Indorser; Order of Liability.—

(1) Unless the indorsement otherwise specifies (as by such words as "without recourse") every indorser engages that upon dishonor and any necessary notice of

dishonor and protest he will pay the instrument according to its tenor at the time of his indorsement to the holder or to any subsequent indorser who takes it up, even though the indorser who takes it up was not obligated to do so.

(2) Unless they otherwise agree indorsers are liable to one another in the order in which they indorse, which is presumed to be the order in which their signatures appear on the instrument.

§ 3-415. Contract of Accommodation Party.—

(1) An accommodation party is one who signs the instrument in any capacity for the purpose of lending his name to another party to it.

(2) When the instrument has been taken for value before it is due the accommodation party is liable in the capacity in which he has signed even though the taker knows of the accommodation.

(3) As against a holder in due course and without notice of the accommodation oral proof of the accommodation is not admissible to give the accommodation party the benefit of discharges dependent on his character as such. In other cases the accommodation character may be shown by oral proof.

(4) An indorsement which shows that it is not in the chain of title is notice of its accommodation character.

(5) An accommodation party is not liable to the party accommodated, and if he pays the instrument has a right of recourse on the instrument against such party.

§ 3-416. Contract of Guarantor.—

(1) "Payment guaranteed" or equivalent words added to a signature mean that the signer engages that if the instrument is not paid when due he will pay it according to its tenor without resort by the holder to any other party.

(2) "Collection guaranteed" or equivalent words added to a signature mean that the signer engages that if the instrument is not paid when due he will pay it according to its tenor, but only after the holder has reduced his claim against the maker or acceptor to judgment and execution has been returned unsatisfied, or after the maker or acceptor has become insolvent or it is otherwise apparent that it is useless to proceed against him.

(3) Words of guaranty which do not otherwise specify guarantee payment.

(4) No words of guaranty added to the signature of a sole maker or acceptor affect his liability on the instrument. Such words added to the signature of one of two or more makers or acceptors create a presumption that the signature is for the accommodation of the others.

(5) When words of guaranty are used presentment, notice of dishonor and protest are not necessary to charge the user.

(6) Any guaranty written on the instrument is enforcible notwithstanding any statute of frauds.

§ 3-417. Warranties on Presentment and Transfer.—

(1) Any person who obtains payment or acceptance and any prior transferor warrants to a person who in good faith pays or accepts that

(a) he has a good title to the instrument or is authorized to obtain payment of acceptance on behalf of one who has a good title; and

(b) he has no knowledge that the signature of the maker or drawer is unauthorized, except that this warranty is not given by a holder in due course acting in good faith

(i) To a maker with respect to the maker's own signature; or

(ii) To a drawer with respect to the drawer's own signature, whether or not the drawer is also the drawee; or

(iii) to an acceptor of a draft if the holder in due course took the draft after the acceptance or obtained the acceptance without knowledge that the drawer's signature was unauthorized; and

(c) the instrument has not been materially altered, except that this warranty is not given by a holder in due course acting in good faith

(i) to the maker of a note; or

(ii) To the drawer of a draft whether or not the drawer is also the drawee; or

(iii) to the acceptor of a draft with respect to an alteration made prior to the acceptance if the holder in due course took the draft after the acceptance, even though the acceptance provided "payable as originally drawn" or equivalent terms; or

(iv) to the acceptor of a draft with respect to an alteration made after the acceptance.

(2) Any person who transfers an instrument and receives consideration warrants to his transferee and if the transfer is by indorsement to any subsequent holder who takes the instrument in good faith that

(a) he has a good title to the instrument or is authorized to obtain payment or acceptance on behalf of one who has a good title and the transfer is otherwise rightful; and

(b) all signatures are genuine or authorized; and

(c) the instrument has not been materially altered; and

(d) no defense of any party is good against him; and

(e) he has no knowledge of any insolvency proceeding instituted with respect to the maker or acceptor or the drawer of an unaccepted instrument.

(3) By transferring "without recourse" the transferor limits the obligation stated in subsection (2) (d) to a warranty that he has no knowledge of such a defense.

(4) A selling agent or broker who does not disclose the fact that he is acting only as such gives the warranties provided in this Section, but if he makes such disclosure warrants only his good faith and authority.

§ 3-418. **Finality of Payment or Acceptance.**—Except for recovery of bank payments as provided in the Article on Bank Deposits and Collections (Article 4) and except for liability for breach of warranty on presentment under the preceding section, payment or acceptance of any instrument is final in favor of a holder in due course, or a person who has in good faith changed his position in reliance on the payment.

§ 3-419. **Conversion of Instrument; Innocent Representative.**—

(1) An instrument is converted when

(a) a drawee to whom it is delivered for acceptance refuses to return it on demand; or

(b) any person to whom it is delivered for payment refuses on demand either to pay or to return it; or

(c) it is paid on a forged indorsement.

(2) In an action against a drawee under subsection (1) the measure of the drawee's liability is the face amount of the instrument. In any other action under subsection (1) the measure of liability is presumed to be the face amount of the instrument.

(3) Subject to the provisions of this Act concerning restrictive indorsements a representative, including a depositary or collecting bank, who has in good faith and in accordance with the reasonable commercial standards applicable to the business of such representative dealt with an instrument or its proceeds on behalf of one who was not the true owner is not liable in conversion or otherwise to the true owner beyond the amount of any proceeds remaining in his hands.

(4) An intermediary bank or payor bank which is not a depositary bank is not liable in conversion solely by reason of the fact that proceeds of an item indorsed restrictively (Sections 3-205 and 3-206) are not paid or applied consistently with the restrictive indorsement of an indorser other than its immediate transferor.

PART 5

Presentment, Notice of Dishonor and Protest

§ 3-501. **When Presentment, Notice of Dishonor, and Protest Necessary or Permissible.** —

(1) Unless excused (Section 3-511) presentment is necessary to charge secondary parties as follows:

(a) presentment for acceptance is necessary to charge the drawer and indorsers of a draft where the draft so provides, or is payable elsewhere than at the residence or place of business of the drawee, or its date of payment depends upon such presentment. The holder may at his option present for acceptance any other draft payable at a stated date;

(b) presentment for payment is necessary to charge any indorser;

(c) in the case of any drawer, the acceptor of a draft payable at a bank or the maker of a note payable at a bank, presentment for payment is necessary, but failure to make presentment discharges such drawer, acceptor or maker only as stated in Section 3-502(1) (b).

(2) Unless excused (Section 3-511)

(a) notice of any dishonor is necessary to charge any indorser;

(b) in the case of any drawer, the acceptor of a draft payable at a bank or the maker of a note payable at a bank notice of any dishonor is necessary, but failure to give such notice discharges such drawer, acceptor or maker only as stated in Section 3-502(1) (b).

(3) Unless excused (Section 3-511) protest of any dishonor is necessary to charge the drawer and indorsers of any draft which on its face appears to be drawn or payable outside of the states and territories of the United States and the District of Columbia. The holder may at his option make protest of any dishonor of any other instrument and in the case of a foreign draft may on insolvency of the acceptor before maturity make protest for better security.

(4) Notwithstanding any provision of this Section, neither presentment nor notice of dishonor nor protest is necessary to charge an indorser who has indorsed an instrument after maturity.

§ 3-502. **Unexcused Delay; Discharge.** —

(1) Where without excuse any necessary presentment or notice of dishonor is delayed beyond the time when it is due

(a) Any indorser is discharged; and

(b) any drawer or the acceptor of a draft payable at a bank or the maker of a note payable at a bank who because the drawee or payor bank becomes insolvent during the delay is deprived of funds maintained with the drawee or payor bank to cover the instrument may discharge his liability by written assignment to the holder of his rights against the drawee or payor bank in respect of such funds, but such drawer, acceptor or maker is not otherwise discharged.

(2) Where without excuse a necessary protest is delayed beyond the time when it is due any drawer or indorser is discharged.

§ 3-503. **Time of Presentment.** —

(1) Unless a different time is expressed in the instrument the time for any presentment is determined as follows:

(a) where an instrument is payable at or a fixed period after a stated date any presentment for acceptance must be made on or before the date it is payable:

(b) where an instrument is payable after sight it must either be presented for acceptance or negotiated within a reasonable time after date or issue whichever is later;

(c) where an instrument shows the date on which it is payable presentment for payment is due on that date;

(d) where an instrument is accelerated presentment for payment is due within a reasonable time after the acceleration;

(e) with respect to the liability of any secondary party presentment for acceptance or payment of any other instrument is due within a reasonable time after such party becomes liable thereon.

(2) A reasonable time for presentment is determined by the nature of the instrument, any usage of banking or trade and the facts of the particular case. In the case of an uncertified check which is drawn and payable within the United States and which is not a draft drawn by a bank the following are presumed to be reasonable periods within which to present for payment or to initiate bank collection:

(a) with respect to the liability of the drawer, thirty days after date or issue whichever is later; and

(b) with respect to the liability of an endorser, seven days after his indorsement.

(3) Where any presentment is due on a day which is not a full business day for either the person making presentment or the party to pay or accept, presentment is due on the next following day which is a full business day for both parties.

(4) Presentment to be sufficient must be made at a reasonable hour, and if at a bank during its banking day.

§ 3-504.   How Presentment Made.—

(1) Presentment is a demand for acceptance or payment made upon the maker, acceptor, drawee or other payor by or on behalf of the holder.

(2) Presentment may be made

(a) by mail, in which event the time of presentment is determined by the time of receipt of the mail; or

(b) through a clearing house; or

(c) at the place of acceptance or payment specified in the instrument or if there be none at the place of business or residence of the party to accept or pay. If neither the party to accept or pay nor anyone authorized to act for him is present or accessible at such place presentment is excused.

(3) It may be made

(a) to any one of two or more makers, acceptors, drawees or other payors; or

(b) to any person who has authority to make or refuse the acceptance or payment.

(4) A draft accepted or a note made payable at a bank in the continental United States must be presented at such bank.

(5) In the cases described in Section 4-210 presentment may be made in the manner and with the result stated in that section.

§ 3-505.   Rights of Party to Whom Presentment is Made.—

(1) The party to whom presentment is made may without dishonor require

(a) exhibition of the instrument; and

(b) reasonable identification of the person making presentment and evidence of his authority to make it if made for another; and

(c) that the instrument be produced for acceptance or payment at a place specified in it, or if there be none at any place reasonable in the circumstances; and

(d) a signed receipt on the instrument for any partial or full payment and its surrender upon full payment.

(2) Failure to comply with any such requirements invalidates the presentment but the person presenting has a reasonable time in which to comply and the time for acceptance or payment runs from the time of compliance.

§ 3-506.   Time Allowed for Acceptance or Payment.—

(1) Acceptance may be deferred without dishonor until the close of the next business day following presentment. The holder may also in a good faith effort to obtain

acceptance and without either dishonor of the instrument or discharge of secondary parties allow postponement of acceptance for an additional business day.

(2) Except as a longer time is allowed in the case of documentary drafts drawn under a letter of credit, and unless an earlier time is agreed to by the party to pay, payment of an instrument may be deferred without dishonor pending reasonable examination to determine whether it is properly payable, but payment must be made in any event before the close of business on the day of presentment.

§ 3-507.   Dishonor; Holder's Right of Recourse; Term Allowing Re-Present-ment.—

(1) An instrument is dishonored when

(a) a necessary or optional presentment is duly made and due acceptance or payment is refused or cannot be obtained within the prescribed time or in case of bank collections the instrument is seasonably returned by the midnight deadline (Section 4-301); or

(b) presentment is excused and the instrument is not duly accepted or paid.

(2) Subject to any necessary notice of dishonor and protest, the holder has upon dishonor an immediate right of recourse against the drawers and indorsers.

(3) Return of an instrument for lack of proper indorsement is not dishonor.

(4) A term in a draft or an indorsement thereof allowing a stated time for re-presentment in the event of any dishonor of the draft by nonacceptance if a time draft or by nonpayment if a sight draft gives the holder as against any secondary party bound by the term an option to waive the dishonor without affecting the liability of the secondary party and he may present again up to the end of the stated time.

§ 3-508.   Notice of Dishonor.—

(1) Notice of dishonor may be given to any person who may be liable on the instrument by or on behalf of the holder or any party who has himself received notice, or any other party who can be compelled to pay the instrument. In addition an agent or bank in whose hands the instrument is dishonored may give notice to his principal or customer or to another agent or bank from which the instrument was received.

(2) Any necessary notice must be given by a bank before its midnight deadline and by any other person before midnight of the third business day after dishonor or receipt of notice of dishonor.

(3) Notice may be given in any reasonable manner. It may be oral or written and in any terms which identify the instrument and state that it has been dishonored. A mis-description which does not mislead the party notified does not vitiate the notice. Sending the instrument bearing a stamp, ticket or writing stating that acceptance or payment has been refused or sending a notice of debit with respect to the instrument is sufficient.

(4) Written notice is given when sent although it is not received.

(5) Notice to one partner is notice to each although the firm has been dissolved.

(6) When any party is in insolvency proceedings instituted after the issue of the instrument notice may be given either to the party or to the representative of his estate.

(7) When any party is dead or incompetent notice may be sent to his last known address or given to his personal representative.

(8) Notice operates for the benefit of all parties who have rights on the instrument against the party notified.

§ 3-509.   Protest; Noting for Protest.—

(1) A protest is a certificate of dishonor made under the hand and seal of a United States consul or vice consul or a notary public or other person authorized to certify dishonor by the law of the place where dishonor occurs. It may be made upon infor-mation satisfactory to such person.

(2) The protest must identify the instrument and certify either that due presentment has been made or the reason why it is excused and that the instrument has been dishonored by non-acceptance or nonpayment.

(3) The protest may also certify that notice of dishonor has been given to all parties or to specified parties.

(4) Subject to subsection (5) any necessary protest is due by the time that notice of dishonor is due.

(5) If, before protest is due, an instrument has been noted for protest by the officer to make protest, the protest may be made at any time thereafter as of the date of the noting.

§ 3-510.   **Evidence of Dishonor and Notice of Dishonor.**—The following are admissible as evidence and create a presumption of dishonor and of any notice of dishonor therein shown:

(a) a document regular in form as provided in the preceding section which purports to be a protest;

(b) the purported stamp or writing of the drawee, payor bank or presenting bank on the instrument or accompanying it stating that acceptance or payment has been refused for reasons consistent with dishonor;

(c) any book or record of the drawee, payor bank, or any collecting bank kept in the usual course of business which shows dishonor, even though there is no evidence of who made the entry.

§ 3-511.   **Waived or Excused Presentment, Protest or Notice of Dishonor or Delay Therein.**—

(1) Delay in presentment, protest or notice of dishonor is excused when the party is without notice that it is due or when the delay is caused by circumstances beyond his control and he exercises reasonable diligence after the cause of the delay ceases to operate.

(2) Presentment or notice or protest as the case may be is entirely excused when

(a) the party to be charged has waived it expressly or by implication either before or after it is due; or

(b) such party has himself dishonored the instrument or has countermanded payment or otherwise has no reason to expect or right to require that the instrument be accepted or paid; or

(c) by reasonable diligence the presentment or protest cannot be made or the notice given.

(3) Presentment is also entirely excused when

(a) the maker, acceptor or drawee of any instrument except a documentary draft is dead or in insolvency proceedings instituted after the issue of the instrument; or

(b) acceptance or payment is refused but not for want of proper presentment

(4) Where a draft has been dishonored by nonacceptance a later presentment for payment and any notice of dishonor and protest for nonpayment are excused unless in the meantime the instrument has been accepted.

(5) A waiver of protest is also a waiver of presentment and of notice of dishonor even though protest is not required.

(6) Where a waiver of presentment or notice of protest is embodied in the instrument itself it is binding upon all parties; but where it is written above the signature of an indorser it binds him only.

PART 6

Discharge

§ 3-601.   **Discharge of Parties.**—

(1) The extent of the discharge of any party from liability on an instrument is governed by the sections on

(a) payment or satisfaction (Section 3-603); or

(b) tender of payment (Section 3-604); or

(c) cancellation or renunciation (Section 3-605); or

(d) impairment of right or recourse or of collateral (Section 3-606); or

(e) reacquisition of the instrument by a prior party (Section 3-208); or

(f) fraudulent and material alteration (Section 3-407); or

(g) certification of a check (Section 3-411); or

(h) acceptance varying a draft (Section 3-412); or

(i) unexcused delay in presentment or notice of dishonor or protest (Section 3-502).

(2) Any party is also discharged from his liability on an instrument to another party by any other act or agreement with such party which would discharge his simple contract for the payment of money.

(3) The liability of all parties is discharged when any party who has himself no right of action or recourse on the instrument

(a) reacquires the instrument in his own right; or

(b) is discharged under any provisions of this Article, except as otherwise provided with respect to discharge for impairment of recourse or of collateral (Section 3-606).

§ 3-602. Effects of Discharge Against Holder in Due Course.—No discharge of any party provided by this Article is effective against a subsequent holder in due course unless he has notice thereof when he takes the instrument.

§ 3-603. Payment or Satisfaction.—

(1) The liability of any party is discharged to the extent of his payment or satisfaction to the holder even though it is made with knowledge of a claim of another person to the instrument unless prior to such payment or satisfaction the person making the claim either supplies indemnity deemed adequate by the party seeking the discharge or enjoins payment or satisfaction by order of a court of competent jurisdiction in an action in which the adverse claimant and the holder are parties. This subsection does not, however, result in the discharge of the liability

(a) of a party who in bad faith pays or satisfies a holder who acquired the instrument by theft or who (unless having the rights of a holder in due course) holds through one who so acquired it; or

(b) of a party (other than an intermediary bank or a payor bank which is not a depositary bank) who pays or satisfies the holder of an instrument which has been restrictively indorsed in a manner not consistent with the terms of such restrictive indorsement.

(2) Payment of satisfaction may be made with the consent of the holder by any person including a stranger to the instrument. Surrender of the instrument to such a person gives him the rights of a transferee (Section 3-201).

§ 3-604. Tender of Payment.—

(1) Any party making tender of full payment to a holder when or after it is due is discharged to the extent of all subsequent liability for interest, costs and attorney's fees.

(2) The holder's refusal of such tender wholly discharges any party who has a right of recourse against the party making the tender.

(3) Where the maker or acceptor of an instrument payable otherwise than on demand is able and ready to pay at every place of payment specified in the instrument when it is due, it is equivalent to tender.

§ 3-605. Cancellation and Renunciation.—

(1) The holder of an instrument may even without consideration discharge any party

(a) in any manner apparent on the face of the instrument or the indorsement, as by intentionally cancelling the instrument or the party's signature by destruction or mutilation, or by striking out the party's signature; or

(b) by renouncing his rights by a writing signed and delivered or by surrender of the instrument to the party to be discharged.

(2) Neither cancellation nor renunciation without surrender of the instrument affects the title thereto.

§ 3-606. Impairment of Recourse or of Collateral.—

(1) The holder discharges any party to the instrument to the extent that without such party's consent the holder

(a) without express reservation of rights releases or agrees not to sue any person against whom the party has to the knowledge of the holder a right of recourse or agrees to suspend the right to enforce against such person the instrument or collateral or otherwise discharges such person, except that failure or delay in effecting any required presentment, protest or notice of dishonor with respect to any such person does not discharge any party as to whom presentment, protest or notice of dishonor is effective or unnecessary; or

(b) unjustifiably impairs any collateral for the instrument given by or on behalf of the party or any person against whom he has a right of recourse.

(2) By express reservation of rights against a party with a right of recourse the holder preserves

(a) all his rights against such party as of the time when the instrument was originally due; and

(b) the right of the party to pay the instrument as of that time; and

(c) all rights of such party to recourse against others.

PART 7

Advice of International Sight Draft
(omitted)

PART 8

Miscellaneous

§ 3-801. omitted.

§ 3-802. Effect of Instrument on Obligation for Which It Is Given.—

(1) Unless otherwise agreed where an instrument is taken for an underlying obligation

(a) the obligation is pro tanto discharged if a bank is drawer, maker or acceptor of an instrument and there is no recourse on the instrument against the underlying obligor; and

(b) in any other case the obligation is suspended pro tanto until the instrument is due or if it is payable on demand until its presentment. If the instrument is dishonored action may be maintained on either the instrument or the obligation; discharge of the underlying obligor on the instrument also discharges him on the obligation.

(2) The taking in good faith of a check which is not postdated does not of itself so extend the time on the original obligation as to discharge a surety.

§ 3-803. Notice to Third Party.—Where a defendant is sued for breach of an obligation for which a third person is answerable over under this Article he may give the third person written notice of the litigation, and the person notified may then give similar notice to any other person who is answerable over to him under this Article. If

the notice states that the person notified may come in and defend and that if the person notified does not do so he will in any action against him by the person giving the notice be bound by any determination of fact common to the two litigations, then unless after seasonable receipt of the notice the person notified does come in and defend he is so bound.

§ 3-804. **Lost, Destroyed or Stolen Instruments.**—The owner of an instrument which is lost, whether by destruction, theft or otherwise, may maintain an action in his own name and recover from any party liable thereon upon due proof of his ownership, the facts which prevent his production of the instrument and its terms. The court may require security indemnifying the defendant against loss by reason of further claims on the instrument.

§ 3-805. **Instruments Not Payable to Order or to Bearer.**—This Article applies to any instrument whose terms do not preclude transfer and which is otherwise negotiable within this Article but which is not payable to order or to bearer, except that there can be no holder in due course of such an instrument.

ARTICLE FOUR—BANK DEPOSITS AND COLLECTIONS

PART 1

General Provisions and Definitions

§ 4-101. **Short Title.**—This Article shall be known and may be cited as Uniform Commercial Code—Bank Deposits and Collections.

§ 4-102. **Applicability.**—
(1) To the extent that items within this Article are also within the scope of Articles 3 and 8, they are subject to the provisions of those Articles. In the event of conflict the provisions of this Article govern those of Article 3 but the provisions of Article 8 govern those of this Article.
(2) The liability of a bank for action or non-action with respect to any item handled by it for purposes of presentment, payment or collection is governed by the law of the place where the bank is located. In the case of action or non-action by or at a branch or separate office of a bank, its liability is governed by the law of the place where the branch or separate office is located.

§ 4-103. **Variation by Agreement; Measure of Damages; Certain Action Constituting Ordinary Care.**—
(1) the effect of the provisions of this Article may be varied by agreement except that no agreement can disclaim a bank's responsibility for its own lack of good faith or failure to exercise ordinary care or can limit the measure of damages for such lack or failure; but the parties may by agreement determine the standards by which such responsibility is to be measured if such standards are not manifestly unreasonable.
(2) Federal reserve regulations and operating letters, clearing house rules, and the like, have the effect of agreements under subsection (1), whether or not specifically assented to by all parties interested in items handled.
(3) Action or non-action approved by this Article or pursuant to Federal Reserve regulations or operating letters constitutes the exercise of ordinary care and, in the absence of special instructions, action or non-action consistent with clearing house rules and the like or with a general banking usage not disapproved by this Article, prima facie constitutes the exercise of ordinary care.
(4) The specification or approval of certain procedures by this Article does not constitute disapproval of other procedures which may be reasonable under the circumstances.

(5) The measure of damages for failure to exercise ordinary care in handling an item is the amount of the item reduced by an amount which could not have been realized by the use of ordinary care, and where there is bad faith it includes other damages, if any, suffered by the party as a proximate consequence.

§ 4-104. Definitions and Index of Definitions.—

(1) In this Article unless the context otherwise requires

(a) "Account" means any account with a bank and includes a checking, time, interest or savings account;

(b) "Afternoon" means the period of a day between noon and midnight;

(c) "Banking day" means that part of any day on which a bank is open to the public for carrying on substantially all of its banking functions;

(d) "Clearing house" means any association of banks or other payors regularly clearing items;

(e) "Customer" means any person having an account with a bank or for whom a bank has agreed to collect items and includes a bank carrying an account with another bank;

(f) "Documentary draft" means any negotiable or non-negotiable draft with accompanying documents, securities or other papers to be delivered against honor of the draft;

(g) "Item" means any instrument for the payment of money even though it is not negotiable but does not include money;

(h) "Midnight deadline" with respect to a bank is midnight on its next banking day following the banking day on which it receives the relevant item or notice or from which the time for taking action commences to run, whichever is later;

(i) "Properly payable" includes the availability of funds for payment at the time of decision to pay or dishonor;

(j) "Settle" means to pay in cash, by clearing house settlement, in a charge or credit or by remittance, or otherwise as instructed. A settlement may be either provisional or final;

(k) "Suspends payments" with respect to bank means that it has been closed by order of the supervisory authorities, that a public officer has been appointed to take it over or that it ceases or refuses to make payments in the ordinary course of business.

(2) Other definitions applying to this Article and the sections in which they appear are:

"Collecting bank"	Section 4-105.
"Depositary bank"	Section 4-105.
"Intermediary bank"	Section 4-105.
"Payor bank"	Section 4-105.
"Presenting bank"	Section 4-105.
"Remitting bank"	Section 4-105.

(3) The following definitions in other Articles apply to this Article:

"Acceptance"	Section 3-410.
"Certificate of deposit"	Section 3-104.
"Certification"	Section 3-411.
"Check"	Section 3-104.
"Draft"	Section 3-104.
"Holder in due course"	Section 3-302.
"Notice of dishonor"	Section 3-508.
"Presentment"	Section 3-504.
"Protest"	Section 3-509.
"Secondary party"	Section 3-102.

(4) In addition Article 1 contains general definitions and principles of construction and interpretation applicable throughout this Article.

§ **4-105.** **"Depositary Bank"; "Intermediary Bank"; "Collecting Bank"; "Payor Bank"; "Presenting Bank"; "Remitting Bank"**—In this Article unless the context otherwise requires:

(a) "Depositary bank" means the first bank to which an item is transferred for collection even though it is also the payor bank.

(b) "Payor bank" means a bank by which an item is payable as drawn or accepted;

(c) "Intermediary bank" means any bank to which an item is transferred in course of collection except the depositary or payor bank;

(d) "Collecting bank" means any bank handling the item for collection except the payor bank;

(e) "Presenting bank" means any bank presenting an item except a payor bank;

(f) "Remitting bank" means any payor or intermediary bank remitting for an item.

§ **4-106.** **Separate Office of a Bank.**—A branch or separate office of a bank [maintaining its own deposit ledgers] is a separate bank for the purpose of computing the time within which and the place at or to which action may be taken or notices or orders shall be given under this Article.

Note: The brackets are to make it optional with the several states whether to require a branch to maintain its own deposit ledgers in order to be considered to be a separate bank for certain purposes under Article 4. In some states "maintaining its own deposit ledgers" is a satisfactory test. In others branch banking practices are such that this test would not be suitable.

§ **4-107.** **Time of Receipt of Items.**—

(1) For the purpose of allowing time to process items, prove balances and make the necessary entries on its books to determine its position for the day, a bank may fix an afternoon hour of two P.M. or later as a cut-off hour for the handling of money and items and the making of entries on its books.

(2) Any item or deposit of money received on any day after a cut-off hour so fixed or after the close of the banking day may be treated as being received at the opening of the next banking day.

§ **4-108.** **Delays.**—

(1) Unless otherwise instructed, a collecting bank in a good faith effort to secure payment may, in the case of specific items and with or without the approval of any person involved, waive, modify or extend time limits imposed or permitted by this Act for a period not in excess of an additional banking day without discharge of secondary parties and without liability to its transferor or any prior party.

(2) Delay by a collecting bank or payor bank beyond time limits prescribed or permitted by this Act or by instructions is excused if caused by interruption of communication facilities, suspension of payments by another bank, war, emergency conditions or other circumstances beyond the control of the bank provided it exercises such diligence as the circumstances require.

PART 2

Collection of Items: Depositary and Collecting Banks

§ **4-201.** **Presumption and Duration of Agency Status of Collecting Banks and Provisional Status of Credits; Applicability of Article; Item Indorsed "Pay Any Bank".**—

(1) Unless a contrary intent clearly appears and prior to the time that a settlement given by a collecting bank for an item is or becomes final (subsection (3) of Section

630

4-211 and Section 4-212 and 4-213) the bank is an agent or sub-agent of the owner of the item and any settlement given for the item is provisional. This provision applies regardless of the form of indorsement or lack of indorsement and even though credit given for the item is subject to immediate withdrawal as of right or is in fact withdrawn; but the continuance of ownership of an item by its owner and any rights of the owner to proceeds of the item are subject to rights of a collecting bank such as those resulting from outstanding advances on the item and valid rights of setoff. When an item is handled by banks for purposes of presentment, payment and collection, the relevant provisions of this Article apply even though action of parties clearly establishes that a particular bank has purchased the item and is the owner of it.

(2) After an item has been indorsed with the words "pay any bank" or the like, only a bank may acquire the rights of a holder

    (a) until the item has been returned to the customer initiating collection; or

    (b) until the item has been specially endorsed by a bank to a person who is not a bank.

§ 4-202. Responsibility for Collection; When Action Seasonable.—

(1) A collecting bank must use ordinary care in

    (a) presenting an item or sending it for presentment; and

    (b) sending notice of dishonor or non-payment or returning an item other than a documentary draft to the bank's transferor [or directly to the depositary bank under subsection (2) of Section 4-212] (*see note to Section 4-212*) after learning that the item has not been paid or accepted, as the case may be; and

    (c) settling for an item when the bank receives final settlement; and

    (d) making or providing for any necessary protest; and

    (e) notifying its transferor of any loss or delay in transit within a reasonable time after discovery thereof.

(2) A collecting bank taking proper action before its midnight deadline following receipt of an item, notice or payment acts seasonably; taking proper action within a reasonably longer time may be seasonable but the bank has the burden of so establishing.

(3) Subject to subsection (1) (a), a bank is not liable for the insolvency, neglect, misconduct, mistake or default of another bank or person or for loss or destruction of an item in transit or in the possession of others.

§ 4-203. Effect of Instructions.—Subject to the provisions of Article 3 concerning conversion of instruments (Section 3-419) and the provisions of both Article 3 and this Article concerning restrictive indorsements only a collecting bank's transferor can give instructions which affect the bank or constitute notice to it and a collecting bank is not liable to prior parties for any action taken pursuant to such instructions or in accordance with any agreement with its transferor.

§ 4-204. Methods of Sending and Presenting; Sending Direct to Payor Bank.—

(1) A collecting bank must send items by reasonably prompt method taking into consideration any relevant instructions, the nature of the item, the number of such items on hand, and the cost of collection involved and the method generally used by it or others to present such items.

(2) A collecting bank may send

    (a) any item direct to the payor bank;

    (b) any item to any non-bank payor if authorized by its transferor; and

    (c) any item other than documentary drafts to any non-bank payor, if authorized by Federal Reserve regulation or operating letter, clearing house rule or the like.

§ 4-205. Supplying Missing Indorsement; No Notice From Prior Indorsement.—

(1) A depositary bank which has taken an item for collection may supply any indorsement of the customer which is necessary to title unless the item contains the words

"payee's indorsement required" or the like. In the absence of such a requirement a statement placed on the item by the depositary bank to the effect that the item was deposited by a customer or credited to his account is effective as the customer's indorsement.

(2) An intermediary bank, or payor bank which is not a depositary bank, is neither given notice nor otherwise affected by a restrictive indorsement of any person except the bank's immediate transferor.

§ 4-206. **Transfer Between Banks**—Any agreed method which identifies the transferor bank is sufficient for the item's further transfer to another bank.

§ 4-207. **Warranties of Customer and Collecting Bank on Transfer or Presentment of Items; Time for Claims.**—

(1) Each customer or collecting bank who obtains payment or acceptance of an item and each prior customer and collecting bank warrants to the payor bank or other payor who in good faith pays or accepts the item that

    (a) he has a good title to the item or is authorized to obtain payment or acceptance on behalf of one who has a good title; and

    (b) he has no knowledge that the signature of the maker or drawer is unauthorized,except that this warranty is not given by any customer or collecting bank that is a holder in due course and acts in good faith

        (i) to a maker with respect to the maker's own signature; or

        (ii) to a drawer with respect to the drawer's own signature, whether or not the drawer is also the drawee; or

        (iii) to an acceptor of an item if the holder in due course took the item after the acceptance or obtained the acceptance without knowledge that the drawer's signature was unauthorized; and

    (c) the item has not been materially altered, except that this warranty is not given by any customer or collecting bank that is a holder in due course and acts in good faith

        (i) to the maker of a note; or

        (ii) to the drawer of a draft whether or not the drawer is also the drawee; or

        (iii) to the acceptor of an item with respect to an alteration made prior to the acceptance if the holder in due course took the item after the acceptance, even though the acceptance provided "payable as originally drawn" equivalent terms; or

        (iv) to the acceptor of an item with respect to an alteration made after the acceptance.

(2) Each customer and collecting bank who transfers an item and receives a settlement or other consideration for it warrants to his transferee and to any subsequent collecting bank who takes the item in good faith that

    (a) he has a good title to the item or is authorized to obtain payment or acceptance on behalf of one who has a good title and the transfer is otherwise rightful; and

    (b) all signatures are genuine or authorized; and

    (c) the item has not been materially altered; and

    (d) no defense of any party is good against him; and

    (e) he has no knowledge of any insolvency proceeding instituted with respect to the maker or acceptor or the drawer of an unaccepted item.

In addition each customer and collecting bank so transferring an item and receiving a settlement or other consideration engages that upon dishonor and any necessary notice of dishonor and protest he will take up the item.

(3) The warranties and the engagement to honor set forth in the two preceding subsections arise notwithstanding the absence of endorsement or words of guaranty or warranty in the transfer or presentment and a collecting bank remains liable for their breach despite remittance to its transferor. Damages for breach of such warranties or engagement to honor shall not exceed the consideration received by the customer or

collecting bank responsible plus finance changes and expenses related to the item, if any.

(4) Unless a claim for breach of warranty under this section is made within a reasonable time after the person claiming learns of the breach, the person liable is discharged to the extent of any loss caused by the delay in making claim.

§ 4-208. Security Interest of Collecting Bank in Items, Accompanying Documents and Proceeds.—

(1) A bank has a security interest in an item and any accompanying documents or the proceeds of either

(a) in case of an item deposited in an account to the extent to which credit given for the item has been withdrawn or applied;

(b) in case of an item for which it has given credit available for withdrawal as of right, to the extent of the credit given whether or not the credit is drawn upon and whether or not there is a right of charge-back; or

(c) if it makes an advance on or against the item.

(2) When credit which has been given for several items received at one time or pursuant to a single agreement is withdrawn or applied in part the security interest remains upon all the items, any accompanying documents or the proceeds of either. For the purpose of this section, credits first given are first withdrawn.

(3) Receipt by a collecting bank of a final settlement for an item is a realization on its security interest in the item, accompanying documents and proceeds. To the extent and so long as the bank does not receive final settlement for the item or give up possession of the item or accompanying documents for purposes other than collection, the security interest continues and is subject to the provisions of Article 9 except that

(a) no security agreement is necessary to make the security interest enforceable (subsection (1)(b) of Section 9-203); and

(b) no filing is required to perfect the security interest; and

(c) the security interest has priority over conflicting perfected security interests in the item, accompanying documents or proceeds.

§ 4-209. When Bank Gives Value for Purposes of Holder in Due Course.—

For purposes of determining its status as a holder in due course, the bank has given value to the extent that it has a security interest in an item provided that the bank otherwise complies with the requirements of Section 3-302 on what constitutes a holder in due course.

§ 4-210. Presentment by Notice of Item Not Payable by, Through or at a Bank; Liability of Secondary Parties.—

(1) Unless otherwise instructed, a collecting bank may present an item not payable by, through or at a bank by sending to the party to accept or pay a written notice that the bank holds the item for acceptance or payment. The notice must be sent in time to be received on or before the day when presentment is due and the bank must meet any requirement of the party to accept or pay under Section 3-505 by the close of the bank's next banking day after it knows of the requirement.

(2) Where presentment is made by notice and neither honor nor request for compliance with a requirement under Section 3-505 is received by the close of business on the day after maturity or in the case of demand items by the close of business on the third banking day after notice was sent, the presenting bank may treat the item as dishonored and charge any secondary party by sending him notice of the facts.

§ 4-211. Media of Remittance; Provisional and Final Settlement in Remittance Cases.—

(1) A collecting bank may take in settlement of an item

(a) a check of the remitting bank or of another bank on any bank except the remitting bank; or

(b) a cashier's check or similar primary obligation of a remitting bank which is a member of or clears through a member of the same clearing house or group as the collecting bank; or

(c) appropriate authority to charge an account of the remitting bank or of another bank with the collecting bank; or

(d) if the item is drawn upon or payable by a person other than a bank, a cashier's check, certified check or other bank check or obligation.

(2) If before its midnight deadline the collecting bank properly dishonors a remittance check or authorization to charge on itself or presents or forwards for collection a remittance instrument of or on another bank which is of a kind approved by subsection (1) or has not been authorized by it, the collecting bank is not liable to prior parties in the event of the dishonor of such check, instrument or authorization.

(3) A settlement for an item by means of a remittance instrument or authorization to charge is or becomes a final settlement as to both the person making and the person receiving the settlement

(a) if the remittance instrument or authorization to charge is of a kind approved by subsection (1) or has not been authorized by the person receiving the settlement and in either case the person receiving the settlement acts seasonably before its midnight deadline in presenting, forwarding for collection or paying the instrument or authorization, —at the time the remittance instrument or authorization is finally paid by the payor by which it is payable;

(b) if the person receiving the settlement has authorized remittance by a non-bank check or obligation or by a cashier's check or similar primary obligation of or a check upon the payor or other remitting bank which is not of a kind approved by subsection (1)(b),—at the time of the receipt of such remittance check or obligation; or

(c) if in a case not covered by subparagraphs (a) or (b) the person receiving the settlement fails to seasonably present, forward for collection, pay or return a remittance instrument or authorization to it to charge before its midnight deadline,—at such midnight deadline.

§ 4-212. Right of Charge-Back or Refund.—

(1) If a collecting bank has made provisional settlement with its customer for an item and itself fails by reason of dishonor, suspension of payments by a bank or otherwise to receive a settlement for the item which is or becomes final, the bank may revoke the settlement given by it, charge back the amount of any credit given for the item to its customer's account or obtain refund from its customer whether or not it is able to return the items if by its midnight deadline or within a longer reasonable time after it learns the facts it returns the item or sends notification of the facts. These rights to revoke, chargeback and obtain refund terminate if and when a settlement for the item received by the bank is or becomes final (subsection (3) of Section 4-211 and subsections (2) and (3) of Section 4-213).

[(2) Within the time and manner prescribed by this section and Section 4-301, an intermediary or payor bank, as the case may be, may return an unpaid item directly to the depositary bank and may send for collection a draft on the depositary bank and obtain reimbursement. In such case, if the depositary bank has received provisional settlement for the item, it must reimburse the bank drawing the draft and any provisional credits for the item between banks shall become and remain final.]

> **Note:** *Direct returns is recognized as an innovation that is not yet established bank practice, and therefore, Paragraph 2 has been bracketed. Some lawyers have doubts whether it should be included in legislation or left to development by agreement.*

(3) A depositary bank which is also the payor may charge-back the amount of an item to its customer's account or obtain refund in accordance with the section governing return of an item received by a payor bank for credit on its books (Section 4-301).

(4) The right to charge-back is not affected by

(a) prior use of the credit given for the item; or

(b) failure by any bank to exercise ordinary care with respect to the item but any bank so failing remains liable.

(5) A failure to charge-back or claim refund does not affect other rights of the bank against the customer or any other party.

(6) If credit is given in dollars as the equivalent of the value of an item payable in a foreign currency the dollar amount of any charge-back or refund shall be calculated on the basis of the buying sight rate for the foreign currency prevailing on the day when the person entitled to the charge-back or refund learns that it will not receive payment in ordinary course.

§ 4-213. Final Payment of Item by Payor Bank; When Provisional Debits and Credits Become Final; When Certain Credits Become Available for Withdrawal.—

(1) An item is finally paid by a payor bank when the bank has done an of the following, whichever happens first:

(a) paid the item in cash; or

(b) settled for the item without reserving a right to revoke the settlement and without having such right under statute, clearing house rule or agreement; or

(c) completed the process of posting the item to the indicated account of the drawer, maker or other person to be charged therewith; or

(d) made a provisional settlement for the item and failed to revoke the settlement in the time and manner permitted by statute, clearing house rule or agreement.

Upon a final payment under subparagraphs (b), (c) or (d) the payor bank shall be accountable for the amount of the item.

(2) If provisional settlement for an item between the presenting and payor banks is made through a clearing house or by debits or credits in an account between them, then to the extent that provisional debits or credits for the item are entered in accounts between the presenting and payor banks or between the presenting and successive prior collecting banks seriatim, they become final upon final payment of the item by the payor bank.

(3) If a collecting bank receives a settlement for an item which is or becomes final (subsection (3) of Section 4-211, subsection (2) of Section 4-213) the bank is accountable to its customer for the amount of the item and any provisional credit given for the item in an account with its customer becomes final.

(4) Subject to any right of the bank to apply the credit to an obligation of the customer, credit given by a bank for an item in an account with its customer becomes available for withdrawal as of right

(a) in any case where the bank has received a provisional settlement for the item,—when such settlement becomes final and the bank has had a reasonable time to learn that the settlement is final;

(b) in any case where the bank is both a depositary bank and a payor bank and the item is finally paid,—at the opening of the bank's second banking day following receipt of the item.

(5) A deposit of money in a bank is final when made but, subject to any right of the bank to apply the deposit to an obligation of the customer, the deposit becomes available for withdrawal as of right at the opening of the bank's next banking day following receipt of the deposit.

§ 4-214. Insolvency and Preference.—

(1) Any item in or coming into the possession of a payor or collecting bank which suspends payment and which item is not finally paid shall be returned by the receiver, trustee or agent in charge of the closed bank to the presenting bank or the closed bank's customer.

(2) If a payor bank finally pays an item and suspends payments without making a settlement for the item with its customer or the presenting bank which settlement is or becomes final, the owner of the item has a preferred claim against the payor bank.

(3) If a payor bank gives or a collecting bank gives or receives a provisional settlement for an item and thereafter suspends payments, the suspension does not prevent or interfere with the settlement becoming final if such finality occurs automatically upon the lapse of certain time or the happening of certain events (subsection (3) of Section 4-211, subsections (1) (d), (2) and (3) of Section 4-213).

(4) If a collecting bank receives from subsequent parties settlement for an item which settlement is or becomes final and suspends payments without making a settlement for the item with its customer which is or becomes final, the owner of the item has a preferred claim against such collecting bank.

PART 3

Collection of Items: Payor Banks

§ 4-301. Deferred Posting; Recovery of Payment by Return of Items; Time of Dishonor.—

(1) Where an authorized settlement for a demand item (other than a documentary draft) received by a payor bank otherwise than for immediate payment over the counter has been made before midnight of the banking day of receipt the payor bank may revoke the settlement and recover any payment if before it has made final payment (subsection (1) of Section 4-213) and before its midnight deadline it

(a) returns the item; or

(b) sends written notice of dishonor or nonpayment if the item is held for protest or is otherwise unavailable for return.

(2) If a demand item is received by a payor bank for credit on its books it may return such item or send notice of dishonor and may revoke any credit given or recover the amount thereof withdrawn by its customer, if it acts within the time limit and in the manner specified in the preceding subsection.

(3) Unless previous notice of dishonor has been sent an item is dishonored at the time when for purposes of dishonor it is returned or notice sent in accordance with this section.

(4) An item is returned:

(a) as to an item received through a clearing house, when it is delivered to the presenting or last collecting bank or to the clearing house or is sent or delivered in accordance with its rules; or

(b) in all other cases, when it is sent or delivered to the bank's customer or transferor or pursuant to his instructions.

§ 4-302. Payor Bank's Responsibility for Late Return of Item.—In the absence of a valid defense such as breach of a presentment warranty (subsection (1) of Section 4-207), settlement effected or the like, if an item is presented on and received by a payor bank the bank is accountable for the amount of

(a) a demand item other than a documentary draft whether properly payable or not if the bank, in any case where it is not also the depositary bank, retains the item beyond midnight of the banking day of receipt without settling for it or, regardless of whether it is also the depositary bank, does not pay or return the item or send notice of dishonor until after its midnight deadline; or

(b) any other properly payable item unless within the time allowed for acceptance or payment of that item the bank either accepts or pays the item or returns it and accompanying documents.

§ 4-303. When Items Subject to Notice, Stop-Order, Legal Process or Setoff; Order in Which Items May Be Charged or Certified.—

(1) Any knowledge, notice or stop-order received by, legal process served upon or setoff exercised by a payor bank, whether or not effective under other rules of law to terminate, suspend or modify the bank's right or duty to pay an item or to charge its customer's account for the item, comes too late to so terminate, suspend or modify such right or duty if the knowledge, notice, stop-order or legal process is received or served and a reasonable time for the bank to act thereon expires or the setoff is exercised after the bank has done any of the following;

(a) accepted or certified the item;

(b) paid the item in cash;

(c) settled for the item without reserving a right to revoke the settlement and without having such right under statute, clearing house rule or agreement;

(d) completed the process of posting the item to the indicated account of the drawer, maker or other person to be charged therewith or otherwise has evidenced by examination of such indicated account and by action its decision to pay the item; or

(e) become accountable for the amount of the item under subsection (1) (d) of Section 4-213 and Section 4-302 dealing with the payor bank's responsibility for late return of items.

(2) Subject to the provisions of subsection (1) items may be accepted, paid, certified or charged to the indicated account of its customer in any order convenient to the bank.

PART 4

Relationship Between Payor Bank and Its Customer

§ 4-401. When Bank May Charge Customer's Account.—

(1) As against its customer, a bank may charge against his account any item which is otherwise properly payable from that account even though the charge creates an overdraft.

(2) A bank which in good faith makes payment to a holder may charge the indicated account of its customer according to

(a) the original tenor of his altered item; or

(b) the tenor of his completed item, even though the bank knows the item has been completed unless the bank has notice that the completion was improper.

§ 4-402. Bank's Liability to Customer for Wrongful Dishonor.—A payor bank is liable to its customer for damages proximately caused by the wrongful dishonor of an item. When the dishonor occurs through mistake liability is limited to actual damages proved. If so proximately caused and proved damages may include damages for an arrest or prosecution of the customer or other consequential damages. Whether any consequential damages are proximately caused by the wrongful dishonor is a question of fact to be determined in each case.

§ 4-403. Customer's Right to Stop Payment; Burden of Proof of Loss.—

(1) A customer may by order to his bank stop payment of any item payable for his account but the order must be received at such time and in such manner as to afford the bank a reasonable opportunity to act on it prior to any action by the bank with respect to the item described in Section 4-303.

(2) An oral order is binding upon the bank only for fourteen calendar days unless confirmed in writing within that period. A written order is effective for only six months unless renewed in writing.

(3) The burden of establishing the fact and amount of loss resulting from the payment of an item contrary to a binding stop payment order is on the customer.

§ **4-404.   Bank Not Obligated to Pay Check More Than Six Months Old.**—A bank is under no obligation to a customer having a checking account to pay a check, other than a certified check, which is presented more than six months after its date, but it may charge its customer's account for a payment made thereafter in good faith.

§ **4-405.   Death or Incompetence of Customer.**—

(1) A payor or collecting bank's authority to accept, pay or collect an item or to account for proceeds of its collection of otherwise effective by incompetence of a customer of either bank existing at the time the item is issued or its collection undertaken if the bank does not know of an adjudication of incompetence. Neither death nor incompetence of a customer revokes such authority to accept, pay, collect or account until the bank knows of the fact of death or of an adjudication of incompetence and has reasonable opportunity to act on it.

(2) Even with knowledge a bank may for ten days after the date of death pay or certify checks drawn on or prior to that date unless ordered to stop payment by a person claiming an interest in the account.

§ **4-406.   Customer's Duty to Discover and Report Unauthorized Signature or Alteration.**—

(1) When a bank sends to its customer a statement of account accompanied by items paid in good faith in support of the debit entries or holds the statement and items pursuant to a request or instructions of its customer or otherwise in a reasonable manner makes the statement and items available to the customer, the customer must exercise reasonable care and promptness to examine the statement and items to discover his unauthorized signature or any alteration on an item and must notify the bank promptly after discovery thereof.

(2) If the bank establishes that the customer failed with respect to an item to comply with the duties imposed on the customer by subsection (1) the customer is precluded from asserting against the bank

   (a) his unauthorized signature or any alteration on the item if the bank also establishes that it suffered a loss by reason of such failure; and

   (b) an unauthorized signature or alteration by the same wrongdoer on any other item paid in good faith by the bank after the first item and statement was available to the customer for a reasonable period not exceeding fourteen calendar days and before the bank receives notification from the customer of any such unauthorized signature or alteration.

(3) The preclusion under subsection (2) does not apply if the customer establishes lack of ordinary care on the part of the bank in paying the item(s).

(4) Without regard to care or lack of care of either the customer or the bank a customer who does not within one year from the time the statement and items are made available to the customer (subsection (1)) discover and report his unauthorized signature or any alteration on the face or back of the item or does not within three years from that time discover and report any unauthorized indorsement is precluded from asserting against the bank such unauthorized signature or endorsement or such alteration.

(5) If under this section a payor bank has a valid defense against a claim of a customer upon or resulting from payment of an item and waives or fails upon request to assert the defense the bank may not assert against any collecting bank or other prior party presenting or transferring the item a claim based upon the unauthorized signature or alteration giving rise to the customer's claim.

§ 4-407. Payor Bank's Right to Subrogation on Improper Payment.—If a payor bank has paid an item over the stop payment order of the drawer or maker or otherwise under circumstances giving a basis for objection by the drawer or maker, to prevent unjust enrichment and only to the extent necessary to prevent loss to the bank by reason of its payment of the item, the payor bank shall be subrogated to the rights

    (a) of any holder in due course on the item against the drawer or maker; and

    (b) of the payee or any other holder of the item against the drawer or maker either on the item or under the transaction out of which the item arose; and

    (c) of the drawer or maker against the payee or any other holder of the item with respect to the transaction out of which the item arose.

PART 5

Collection of Documentary Drafts

§ 4-501. Handling of Documentary Drafts; Duty to Send for Presentment and to Notify Customer of Dishonor.—A bank which takes a documentary draft for collection must present or send the draft and accompanying documents for presentment and upon learning that the draft has not been paid or accepted in due course must seasonably notify its customer of such fact even though it may have discounted or bought the draft or extended credit available for withdrawal as of right.

§ 4-502. Presentment of "On Arrival" Drafts.—When a draft or the relevant instructions require presentment "on arrival", "when goods arrive" or the like, the collecting bank need not present until in its judgment a reasonable time for arrival of the goods has expired. Refusal to pay or accept because the goods have not arrived is not dishonor; the bank must notify its transferor of such refusal but need not present the draft again until it is instructed to do so or learns of the arrival of the goods.

§ 4-503. Responsibility of Presenting Bank for Documents and Goods; Report of Reasons for Dishonor; Referee in Case of Need.—Unless otherwise instructed and except as provided in Article 5 a bank presenting a documentary draft

    (a) must deliver the documents to the drawee on acceptance of the draft if it is payable more than three days after presentment; otherwise, only on payment; and

    (b) upon dishonor, either in the case of presentment for acceptance or presentment for payment, may seek and follow instructions from any referee in case of need designated in the draft or if the presenting bank does not choose to utilize his services it must use diligence and good faith to ascertain the reason for dishonor, must notify its transferor of the dishonor and of the results of its effort to ascertain the reasons therefor and must request instructions.

But the presenting bank is under no obligation with respect to goods represented by the documents except to follow any reasonable instructions seasonably received; it has a right to reimbursement for any expense incurred in following instructions and to prepayment of or indemnity for such expenses.

§ 4-504. Privilege of Presenting Bank to Deal With Goods; Security Interest for Expenses.—

    (1) A presenting bank which, following the dishonor of a documentary draft, has seasonably requested instructions but does not receive them within a reasonable time may store, sell, or otherwise deal with the goods in any reasonable manner.

    (2) For its reasonable expenses incurred by action under subsection (1) the presenting bank has a lien upon the goods or their proceeds, which may be forclosed in the same manner as an unpaid seller's lien.

ARTICLE FIVE—LETTERS OF CREDIT

§ **5-101. Short Title.**—This Article shall be known and may be cited as Uniform Commercial Code—Letters of Credit.

§ **5-102. Scope.**—

(1) This Article applies

(a) to a credit issued by a bank if the credit requires a documentary draft or a documentary demand for payment; and

(b) to a credit issued by a person other than a bank if the credit requires that the draft or demand for payment be accompanied by a document of title: and

(c) to a credit issued by a bank or other person if the credit is not within subparagraphs (a) or (b) but conspicuously states that it is a letter of credit or is conspicuously so entitled.

... [The remaining portion of this article omitted as it contains material not usually covered in Business Law.]

ARTICLE SIX—BULK TRANSFERS

§ **6-101. Short Title.**—This Article shall be known and may be cited as Uniform Commercial Code—Bulk Transfers.

§ **6-102. "Bulk Transfer"; Transfers of Equipment; Enterprises Subject to This Article; Bulk Transfers Subject to This Article.**—

(1) A "bulk transfer" is any transfer in bulk and not in the ordinary course of the transferor's business of a major part of the materials, supplies, merchandise or other inventory (Section 9-109) of an enterprise subject to this Article.

(2) A transfer of a substantial part of the equipment (Section 9-109) of such an enterprise is a bulk transfer if it is made in connection with a bulk transfer of inventory, but not otherwise.

(3) The enterprises subject to this Article are all those whose principal business is the sale of merchandise from stock, including those who manufacture what they sell.

(4) Except as limited by the following section all bulk transfers of goods located within this State are subject to this Article.

§ **6-103. Transfers Excepted From This Article.**—The following transfers are not subject to this Article:

(1) Those made to give security for the performance of an obligation;

(2) General assignments for the benefit of all the creditors of the transferor, and subsequent transfers by the assignee thereunder;

(3) Transfers in settlement or realization of a lien or other security interests;

(4) Sales by executors, administrators, receivers, trustees in bankruptcy, or any public offer under judicial process;

(5) Sales made in the course of judicial or administrative proceedings for the dissolution or reorganization of a corporation and of which notice is sent to the creditors of the corporation pursuant to order of the court or administrative agency;

(6) Transfers to a person maintaining a known place of business in this State who becomes bound to pay the debts of the transferor in full and gives public notice of that fact, and who is solvent after becoming so bound;

(7) A transfer to a new business enterprise organized to take over and continue the business, if public notice of the transaction is given and the new enterprise assumes the debts of the transferor and he receives nothing from the transaction except an interest in the new enterprise junior to the claims of creditors;

(8) Transfers of property which is exempt from execution.

§ 6-104. Schedule of Property, List of Creditors.—

(1) Except as provided with respect to auction sales (Section 6-108), a bulk transfer subject to this Article is ineffective against any creditor of the transferor unless:

    (a) The transferee requires the transferor to furnish a list of his existing creditors prepared as stated in this section; and

    (b) The parties prepare a schedule of the property transferred sufficient to identify it; and

    (c) The transferee preserves the list and schedule for six months next following the transfer and permits inspection of either or both and copying therefrom at all reasonable hours by any creditor of the transferor, or files the list and schedule in (*a public office to be here identified*).

(2) The list of creditors must be signed and sworn to or affirmed by the transferor or his agent. It must contain the names and business addresses of all creditors of the transferor, with the amounts when known, and also the names of all persons who are known to the transferor to assert claims against him even though such claims are disputed.

(3) Responsibility for the completeness and accuracy of the list of creditors rests on the transferor, and the transfer is not rendered ineffective by errors or omissions therein unless the transferee is shown to have had knowledge.

§ 6-105. Notice to Creditors.—

In addition to the requirements of the preceding section, any bulk transfer subject to this Article except one made by auction sale (Section 6-108) is ineffective against any creditor of the transferor unless at least ten days before he takes possession of the goods or pays for them, whichever happens first, the transferee gives notice of the transfer in the manner and to the persons hereafter provided (Section 6-107).

[§ 6-106. Application of the Proceeds.—

In addition to the requirements of the two preceding sections:

(1) Upon every bulk transfer subject to this Article for which new consideration becomes payable except those made by sale at auction it is the duty of the transferee to assure that such consideration is applied so far as necessary to pay those debts of the transferor which are either shown on the list furnished by the transferor (Section 6-104) or filed in writing in the place stated in the notice (Section 6-107) within thirty days after the mailing of such notice. This duty of the transferee runs to all the holders of such debts, and may be enforced by any of them for the benefit of all.

(2) If any of said debts are in dispute the necessary sum may be withheld from distribution until the dispute is settled or adjudicated.

(3) If the consideration payable is not enough to pay all of the said debts in full distribution shall be made pro rata.]

    Note: *This section is bracketed to indicate division of opinion as to whether or not it is a wise provision, and to suggest that this is a point on which State enactments may differ without serious damage to the principle of uniformity.*

    In any State where this section is omitted, the following parts of sections, also bracketed in the text, should also be omitted, namely:

        Section 6-107(2)(e).

            6-108(3)(c).

            6-109(2).

    In any State where this section is enacted, these other provisions should be also.

§ 6-107. The Notice.—

(1) The notice to creditors (Section 6-105) shall state:

    (a) that a bulk transfer is about to be made; and

(b) the names and business addresses of the transferor and transferee, and all other business names and addresses used by the transferor within three years last past so far as known to the transferee; and

(c) whether or not all the debts of the transferor are to be paid in full as they fall due as a result of the transaction, and if so, the address to which creditors should send their bills.

(2) If the debts of the transferor are not to be paid in full as they fall due or if the transferee is in doubt on that point then the notice shall state further:

(a) the location and general description of the property to be transferred and the estimated total of the transferor's debts;

(b) the address where the schedule of property and list of creditors (Section 6-104) may be inspected;

(c) whether the transfer is to pay existing debts and if so the amount of such debts and to whom owing;

(d) whether the transfer is for new consideration and if so the amount of such consideration and the time and place of payment; and

[(e) if for new consideration the time and place where creditors of the transferor are to file their claims.]

(3) The notice in any case shall be delivered personally or sent by registered mail to all the persons shown on the list of creditors furnished by the transferor (Section 6-104) and to all other persons who are known to the transferee to hold or assert claims against the transferor.

§ 6-108. Auction Sales; "Auctioneer".—

(1) A bulk transfer is subject to this Article even though it is by sale at auction, but only in the manner and with the results stated in this section.

(2) The transferor shall furnish a list of his creditors and assist in the preparation of a schedule of the property to be sold, both prepared as before stated (Section 6-104).

(3) The person or persons other than the transferor who direct, control or are responsible for the auction are collectively called the "auctioneer". The auctioneer shall:

(a) receive and retain the list of creditors and prepare and retain the schedule of property for the period stated in this Article (Section 6-104);

(b) give notice of the auction personally or by registered mail at least ten days before it occurs to all persons shown on the list of creditors and to all other persons who are known to him to hold or assert claims against the transferor; [and]

[(c) assure that the net proceeds of the auction are applied as provided in this Article (Section 6-106).]

(4) Failure of the auctioneer to perform any of these duties does not affect the validity of the sale or the title of the purchasers, but if the auctioneer knows that the auction constitutes a bulk transfer such failure renders the auctioneer liable to the creditors of the transferor as a class for the sums owing to them from the transferor up to but not exceeding the net proceeds of the auction. If the auctioneer consists of several persons their liability is joint and several.

§ 6-109. What Creditors Protected.—

(1) The creditors of the transferor mentioned in this Article are those holding claims based on transactions occurring before the bulk transfer, but creditors who become such after notice to creditors is given (Sections 6-105 and 6-107) are not entitled to notice.

[(2) Against the aggregate obligation imposed by the provisions of this Article concerning the application of the proceeds (Section 6-106 and subsection (3)(c) of 6-108) the transferee or auctioneer is entitled to credit for sums paid to particular creditors of the transferor, not exceeding the sums believed in good faith at the time of the payment to be properly payable to such creditors.]

§ 6-110. Subsequent Transfers.—When the title of a transferee to property is subject to a defect by reason of his noncompliance with the requirements of this Article, then:

(1) a purchaser of any such property from such transferee who pays no value or who takes with notice of such noncompliance takes subject to such defect, but

(2) a purchaser for value in good faith and without such notice takes free of such defect.

§ 6-111. Limitation of Actions and Levies.—No action under this Article shall be brought nor levy made more than six months after the date on which the transferee took possession of the goods unless the transfer has been concealed. If the transfer has been concealed, actions may be brought or levies made within six months after its discovery.

> **Note to Article 6:** *Section 6-106 is bracketed to indicate division of opinion as to whether or not it is a wise provision, and to suggest that this is a point on which State enactments may differ without serious damage to the principal of uniformity.*
>
> *In any State where Section 6-106 is not enacted, the following parts of sections, also bracketed in the text, should also be omitted, namely;*
> *Sec. 6-107(2)(e)*
> *6-108(3)(c)*
> *6-109(2).*

In any State where Section 6-106 is enacted, these other provisions should be also.

ARTICLE SEVEN—WAREHOUSE RECEIPTS, BILLS OF LADING AND OTHER DOCUMENTS OF TITLE

Part 1

General

§ 7-101. Short Title.—This Article shall be known and may be cited as Uniform Commercial Code—Documents of Title

. . . [The remaining portion of this article ommitted as it contains material not usually covered in Business Law.]

ARTICLE EIGHT—INVESTMENT SECURITIES

PART 1

Short Title and General Matters

§ 8-101. Short Title.— This Article shall be known and may be cited as Uniform Commercial Code—Investment Securities.

§ 8-102. Definitions and Index of Definitions.—

(1) In this Article unless the context otherwise requires

(a) A "security" is an instrument which

(i) is issued in bearer or registered form; and

(ii) is of a type commonly dealt in upon securities exchanges or markets or commonly recognized in any area in which it is issued or dealt in as a medium for investment; and

(iii) is either one of a class or series or by its terms is divisible into a class or series of instruments; and

(iv) evidences a share, participation or other interest in property or in an enterprise or evidences an obligation of the issuer.

(b) A writing which is a security is governed by this Article and not by Uniform Commercial Code—Commercial Paper even though it also meets the requirements of that Article. This Article does not apply to money.

(c) A security is in "registered form" when it specifies a person entitled to the security or the rights it evidences and when its transfer may be registered upon books maintained for that purpose by or on behalf of an issuer or the security so states.

(d) A security is in "bearer form" when it runs to bearer according to its terms and not by reason of any indorsement.

(2) "Proper form" means regular on its face with regard to all formal matters.

(3) A "subsequent purchaser" is a person who takes other than by original issue.

(4) Other definitions applying to this Article or to specified Parts thereof and the sections in which they appear are:

"Adverse claim"   Section 8-301.
"Bona fide purchaser"   Section 8-302.
"Broker"   Section 8-303.
"Guarantee of signature"   Section 8-402.
"Intermediary Bank"   Section 4-105.
"Issuer"   Section 8-201.
"Overissue"   Section 8-104.

(5) In addition Article 1 contains general definitions and principles of construction and interpretation applicable throughout this Article.

§ 8-103.   Issuer's Lien.—A lien upon a security in favor of an issuer thereof is valid against a purchaser only if the right of the issuer to such lien is noted conspicuously on the security.

§ 8-104.   Effect of Overissue; "Overissue."—The provisions of this Article which validate a security or compel its issue or reissue do not apply to the extent that validation, issue or reissue would result in overissue; but

(a) if an identical security which does not constitute an overissue is reasonably available for purchase, the person entitled to issue or validation may compel the issuer to purchase and deliver such a security to him against surrender of the security, if any, which he holds; or

(b) if a security is not so available for purchase, the person entitled to issue or validation may recover from the issuer the price he or the last purchaser for value paid for it with interest from the date of his demand.

(2) "Overissue" means the issue of securities in excess of the amount which the issuer has corporate power to issue.

§ 8-105.   Securities Negotiable; Presumptions.—

(1) Securities governed by this Article are negotiable instruments.

(2) In any action on a security

(a) unless specifically denied in the pleadings, each signature on the security or in a necessary indorsement is admitted;

(b) when the effectiveness of a signature is put in issue the burden of establishing it is on the party claiming under the signature but the signature is presumed to be genuine or authorized;

(c) when signatures are admitted or established production of the instrument entitles a holder to recover on it unless the defendant establishes a defense or a defect going to the validity of the security; and

(d) after it is shown that a defense or defect exists the plaintiff has the burden of establishing that he or some person under whom he claims is a person against whom the defense or defect is ineffective (Section 8-202).

§ **8-106. Applicability.**—The validity of a security and the rights and duties of the issuer with respect to registration of transfer are governed by the law (including the conflict of laws rules) of the jurisdiction of organization of the issuer.

PART 2

Issue—Issuer

§ **8-201. "Issuer."**—

(1) With respect to obligations on or defenses to a security "issuer" includes a person who

(a) places or authorizes the placing of his name on a security (otherwise than as authenticating trustee, registrar, transfer agent or the like) to evidence that it represents a share, participation or other interest in his property or in an enterprise or to evidence his duty to perform an obligation evidenced by the security; or

(b) directly or indirectly creates fractional interests in his rights or property which fractional interests are evidenced by securities; or

(c) becomes responsible for or in place of any other person described as an issuer in this section.

(2) With respect to obligations on or defenses to a security a guarantor is an issuer to the extent of his guaranty whether or not his obligation is noted on the security.

(3) With respect to registration of transfer (Part 4 of this Article) "issuer" means a person on whose behalf transfer books are maintained.

§ **8-202. Issuer's Responsibility and Defenses; Notice of Defect or Defense.**—

(1) Even against a purchaser for value and without notice, the terms of a security include those stated on the security and those made part of the security by reference to another instrument, indenture or document or to a constitution, statute, ordinance, rule, regulation, order or the like to the extent that the terms so referred to do not conflict with the stated terms. Such a reference does not of itself charge a purchaser for value with notice of a defect going to the validity of the security even though the security expressly states that a person accepting it admits such notice.

(2) (a) A security other than one issued by a government or governmental agency or unit even though issued with a defect going to its validity is valid in the hands of a purchaser for value and without notice of the particular defect unless the defect involves a violation of constitutional provisions in which case the security is valid in the hands of a subsequent purchaser for value and without notice of the defect.

(b) The rule of subparagraph (a) applies to an issuer which is a government or governmental agency or unit only if either there has been substantial compliance with the legal requirements governing the issue or the issuer has received a substantial consideration for the issue as a whole or for the particular security and a stated purpose of the issue is one for which the issuer has power to borrow money or issue the security.

(3) Except as otherwise provided in the case of certain unauthorized signatures on issue (Section 8-205), lack of genuineness of a security is a complete defense even against a purchaser for value and without notice.

(4) All other defenses of the issuer including nondelivery and conditional delivery of the security are ineffective against a purchaser for value who has taken without notice of the particular defense.

(5) Nothing in this section shall be construed to affect the right of a party to a "when, as and if issued" or a "when distributed" contract to cancel the contract in the event of a material change in the character of the security which is the subject of the contract or in the plan or arrangement pursuant to which such security is to be issued or distributed.

§ 8-203. Staleness as Notice of Defects or Defenses.—

(1) After an act or event which creates a right to immediate performance of the principal obligation evidenced by the security or which sets a date on or after which the security is to be presented or surrendered for redemption or exchange, a purchaser is charged with notice of any defect in its issue or defense of the issuer

(a) if the act or event is one requiring the payment of money or the delivery of securities or both on presentation or surrender of the security and such funds or securities are available on the date set for payment or exchange and he takes the security more than one year after that date; and

(b) if the act or event is not covered by paragraph (a) and he takes the security more than two years after the date set for surrender or presentation or the date on which such performance became due.

(2) A call which has been revoked is not within subsection (1).

§ 8-204. Effect of Issuer's Restrictions on Transfer.—Unless noted conspicuously on the security a restriction on transfer imposed by the issuer even though otherwise lawful is ineffective except against a person with actual knowledge of it.

§ 8-205. Effect of Unauthorized Signature on Issue.—An unauthorized signature placed on a security prior to or in the course of issue is ineffective except that the signature is effective in favor of a purchaser for value and without notice of the lack of authority if the signing has been done by

(a) an authenticating trustee, registrar, transfer agent or other person entrusted by the issuer with the signing of the security or of similar securities or their immediate preparation for signing; or

(b) an employee of the issuer or of any of the foregoing entrusted with responsible handling of the security.

§ 8-206. Completion or Alteration of Instrument.—

(1) Where a security contains the signatures necessary to its issue or transfer but is incomplete in any other respect

(a) any person may complete it by filling in the blanks as authorized; and

(b) even though the blanks are incorrectly filled in, the security as completed is enforceable by a purchaser who took it for value and without notice of such incorrectness.

(2) A complete security which has been improperly altered even though fraudulently remains enforceable but only according to its original terms.

§ 8-207. Rights of Issuer With Respect to Registered Owners.—

(1) Prior to due presentment for registration of transfer of a security in registered form the issuer or indenture trustee may treat the registered owner as the person exclusively entitled to vote, to receive notifications and otherwise to exercise all the rights and powers of an owner.

(2) Nothing in this Article shall be construed to affect the liability of the registered owner of a security for calls, assessments or the like.

§ 8-208. Effect of Signature of Authenticating Trustee, Registrar or Transfer Agent.—

(1) A person placing his signature upon a security as authenticating trustee, registrar, transfer agent or the like warrants to a purchaser for value without notice of the particular defect that

(a) the security is genuine and in proper form; and

(b) his own participation in the issue of the security is within his capacity and within the scope of the authorization received by him from the issuer; and

(c) he has reasonable grounds to believe that the security is within the amount the issuer is authorized to issue.

(2) Unless otherwise agreed, a person by so placing his signature does not assume responsibility for the validity of the security in other respects.

PART 3

Purchase

§ 8-301. Rights Acquired by Purchaser; "Adverse Claim"; Title Acquired by Bona Fide Purchaser.—

(1) Upon delivery of a security the purchaser acquires the rights in the security which his transferor had or had actual authority to convey except that a purchaser who has himself been a party to any fraud or illegality affecting the security or who as a prior holder had notice of an adverse claim cannot improve his position by taking from a later bona fide purchaser. "Adverse claim" includes a claim that a transfer was or would be wrongful or that a particular person is the owner of or has an interest in the security.

(2) A bona fide purchaser in addition to acquiring the rights of a purchaser also acquires the security free of any adverse claim.

(3) A purchaser of a limited interest acquires rights only to the extent of the interest purchased.

§ 8-302. "Bona Fide Purchaser."—A "bona fide purchaser" is a purchaser for value in good faith and without notice of any adverse claim who takes delivery of a security in bearer form or of one in registered form issued to him or indorsed to him or in blank.

§ 8-303. "Broker."—"Broker" means a person engaged for all or part of his time in the business of buying and selling securities, who in the transaction concerned acts for, or buys a security from or sells a security to a customer. Nothing in this Article determines the capacity in which a person acts for purposes of any other statute or rule to which such person is subject.

§ 8-304. Notice to Purchaser of Adverse Claims.—

(1) A purchaser (including a broker for the seller or buyer but excluding an intermediary bank) of a security is charged with notice of adverse claims if

(a) the security whether in bearer or registered form has been indorsed "for collection" or "for surrender" or for some other purpose not involving transfer; or

(b) the security is in bearer form and has on it an unambiguous statement that it is the property of a person other than the transferor. The mere writing of a name on a security is not such a statement.

(2) The fact that the purchaser (including a broker for the seller or buyer) has notice that the security is held for a third person or is registered in the name of or indorsed by a fiduciary does not create a duty of inquiry into the rightfulness of the transfer or constitute notice of adverse claims. If, however, the purchaser (excluding an intermediary bank) has reason to know that the proceeds are being used or that the transaction is for the individual benefit of the fiduciary, the purchaser is charged with notice of adverse claims.

§ 8-305. Staleness as Notice of Adverse Claims.—An act or event which creates a right to immediate performance of the principal obligation evidenced by the security or which sets a date on or after which the security is to be presented or surrendered for redemption or exchange does not of itself constitute any notice of adverse claims except in the case of a purchase.

(a) after one year from any date set for such presentment or surrender for redemption or exchange; or

(b) after six months from any date set for payment of money against presentation or surrender of the security if funds are available for payment on that date.

§ 8-306. Warranties on Presentment and Transfer—

(1) A person who presents a security for registration of transfer or for payment or exchange warrants to the issuer that he is entitled to the registration, payment or exchange. But a purchaser for value without notice of adverse claims who receives a new, reissued or re-registered security on registration of transfer warrants only that he has no knowledge of any unauthorized signature (Section 8-311) ia necessary indorsement.

(2) A person by transferring a security to a purchaser for value warrants only that
   (a) his transfer is effective and rightful; and
   (b) the security is genuine and has not been materially altered; and
   (c) he knows no fact which might impair the validity of the security.

(3) Where a security is delivered by an intermediary known to be entrusted with delivery of the security on behalf of another or with collection of a draft or other claim against such delivery, the intermediary by such deliver warrants only his own good faith and authority even though he has purchased or made advances against the claim to be collected against the delivery. A broker is not an intermediary within the meaning of this subsection.

(4) A pledgee or other holder for security who redelivers the security received, or after payment and on order of the debtor delivers that security to a third person makes only the warranties of an intermediary under subsection (3).

(5) A broker gives to his customer and to the issuer and a purchaser the warranties provided in this section and has the rights and privileges of a purchaser under this section. The warranties of and in favor of the broker acting as an agent are in addition to applicable warranties given by and in favor of his customer.

§ 8-307. Effect of Delivery Without Indorsement; Right to Compel Indorsement.—Where a security in registered form has been delivered to a purchaser without a necessary indorsement he may become a bona fide purchaser only as of the time the indorsement is supplied, but against the transferor the transfer is complete upon delivery and the purchaser has a specifically enforceable right to have any necessary indorsement supplied.

§ 8-308. Indorsement, How Made; Special Indorsement; Indorser Not a Guarantor; Partial Assignment.—

(1) An indorsement of a security in registered form is made when an appropriate person signs on it or on a separate document an assignment or transfer of the security or a power to assign or transfer it or when the signature of such person is written without more upon the back of the security.

(2) An indorsement may be in blank or special. An indorsement in blank includes an indorsement to bearer. A special indorsement specifies the person to whom the security is to be transferred, or who has power to transfer it. A holder may convert a blank indorsement into a special indorsement.

(3) "An appropriate person" in subsection (1) means
   (a) the person specified by the security or by special indorsement to be entitled to the security; or
   (b) where the person so specified is described as a fiduciary but is no longer serving in the described capacity,—his successor; or
   (c) where the security or indorsement so specifies more than one person as fiduciaries and one or more are no longer serving in the described capacity,—the remaining fiduciary or fiduciaries, whether or not a successor has been appointed or qualified; or

(d) where the person so specified is an individual and is without capacity to act by virtue of death, incompetence, infancy or otherwise.— his executor, administrator, guardian or like fiduciary; or

(e) where the security or indorsement so specifies more than one person as tenants by the entirety or with right of survivorship and by reason of death all cannot sign,— the survivor or survivors; or

(f) a person having power to sign under applicable law or controlling instrument; or

(g) to the extent that any of the foregoing persons may act through an agent,—his authorized agent.

(4) Unless otherwise agreed the indorser by his indorsement assumes no obligation that the security will be honored by the issuer.

(5) An indorsement purporting to be only of part of a security representing units intended by the issuer to be separately transferable is effective to the extent of the indorsement.

(6) Whether the person signing is appropriate is determined as of the date of signing and an indorsement by such a person does not become unauthorized for the purposes of this Article by virtue of any subsequent change of circumstances.

(7) Failure of a fiduciary to comply with a controlling instrument or with the law of the state having jurisdiction of the fiduciary relationship, including any law requiring the fiduciary to obtain court approval of the transfer, does not render his indorsement unauthorized for the purposes of this Article.

§ 8-309.　**Effect of Indorsement Without Delivery.**—An indorsement of a security whether special or in blank does not constitute a transfer until delivery of the security on which it appears or if the indorsement is on a separate document until delivery of both the document and the security.

§ 8-310.　**Indorsement of Security in Bearer Form.**—An indorsement of a security in bearer form may give notice of adverse claims (Section 8-304) but does not otherwise affect any right to registration the holder may possess.

§ 8-311.　**Effect of Unauthorized Indorsement.**—Unless the owner has ratified an unauthorized indorsement or is otherwise precluded from asserting its effectiveness

(a) he may assert its ineffectiveness against the issuer or any purchaser other than a purchaser for value and without notice of adverse claims who has in good faith received a new, reissued or reregistered security on registration of transfer; and

(b) an issuer who registers the transfer of a security upon the unauthorized indorsement is subject to liability for improper registration (Section 8-404).

§ 8-312.　**Effect of Guaranteeing Signature or Indorsement.**—

(1) Any person guaranteeing a signature of an indorser of a security warrants that at the time of signing

(a) the signature was genuine; and

(b) the signer was an appropriate person to indorse (Section 8-308); and

(c) the signer had legal capacity to sign.

But the guarantor does not otherwise warrant the rightfulness of the particular transfer.

(2) Any person may guarantee an indorsement of a security and by so doing warrants not only the signature (subsection 1) but also the rightfulness of the particular transfer in all respects. But no issuer may require a guarantee of indorsement as a condition to registration of transfer.

(3) The foregoing warranties are made to any person taking or dealing with the security in reliance on the guarantee and the guarantor is liable to such person for any loss resulting from breach of the warranties.

§ 8-313. When Delivery to the Purchaser Occurs; Purchaser's Broker as Holder.—

(1) Delivery to a purchaser occurs when

(a) he or a person designated by him acquires possession of a security; or

(b) his broker acquires possession of a security specially indorsed to or issued in the name of the purchaser; or

(c) his broker sends him confirmation of the purchase and also by book entry or otherwise identifies a specific security in the broker's possession as belonging to the purchaser; or

(d) with respect to an identified security to be delivered while still in the possession of a third person when that person acknowledges that he holds for the purchaser.

(2) Except as specified in subparagraphs (b) and (c) of subsection (1) the purchaser is not the holder of securities held for him by his broker despite a confirmation of purchase and a book entry and other indication that the security is part of a fungible bulk held for customers and despite the customer's acquisition of a proportionate property interest in the fungible bulk.

§ 8-314. Duty to Deliver, When Completed.—

(1) Unless otherwise agreed where a sale of a security is made on an exchange or otherwise through brokers

(a) the selling customer fulfills his duty to deliver when he places such a security in the possession of the selling broker or of a person designated by the broker or if requested causes an acknowledgment to be made to the selling broker that it is held for him; and

(b) the selling broker including a correspondent broker acting for a selling customer fulfills his duty to deliver by placing the security or a like security in the possession of the buying broker or a person designated by him or by effecting clearance of the sale in accordance with the rules of the exchange on which the transaction took place.

(2) Except as otherwise provided in this section and unless otherwise agreed, a transferor's duty to deliver a security under a contract of purchase is not fulfilled until he places the security in form to be negotiated by the purchaser in the possession of the purchaser or of a person designated by him or at the purchaser's request causes an acknowledgment to be made to the purchaser that it is held for him. Unless made on an exchange a sale to a broker purchasing for his own account is within this subsection and not within subsection (1).

§ 8-315. Action Against Purchaser Based Upon Wrongful Transfer.—

(1) Any person against whom the transfer of a security is wrongful for any reason, including his incapacity, may against anyone except a bona fide purchaser reclaim possession of the security or obtain possession of any new security evidencing all or part of the same rights or have damages.

(2) If the transfer is wrongful because of an unauthorized indorsement, the owner may also reclaim or obtain possession of the security or new security even from a bona fide purchaser if the ineffectiveness of the purported indorsement can be asserted against him under the provisions of this Article on unauthorized indorsements (Section 8-311).

(3) The right to obtain or reclaim possession of a security may be specifically enforced and its transfer enjoined and the security impounded pending the litigation.

§ 8-316. Purchaser's Right to Requisites for Registration of Transfer on Books.—

Unless otherwise agreed the transferor must on due demand supply his purchaser with any proof of his authority to transfer or with any other requisite which may be necessary to obtain registration of the transfer of the security but if the transfer is not for value a transferor need not do so unless the purchaser furnishes the necessary expenses. Failure to comply with a demand made within a reasonable time gives the purchaser the right to reject or rescind the transfer.

§ 8-317 Attachment or Levy Upon Security.—
(1) No attachment or levy upon a security or any share or other interest evidenced thereby which is outstanding shall be valid until the security is actually seized by the officer making the attachment or levy but a security which has been surrendered to the issuer may be attached or levied upon at the source.

(2) A creditor whose debtor is the owner of a security shall be entitled to such aid from courts of appropriate jurisdiction, by injunction or otherwise, in reaching such security or in satisfying the claim by means thereof as is allowed at law or in equity in regard to property which cannot readily be attached or levied upon by ordinary legal process.

§ 8-318. No Conversion by Good Faith Delivery.—An agent or bailee who in good faith (including observance of reasonable commercial standards if he is in the business of buying, selling or otherwise dealing with securities) has received securities and sold, pledged or delivered them according to the instructions of his principal is not liable for conversion although the principal had no right to dispose of them.

§ 8-319. Statute of Frauds—A contract for the sale of securities is not enforceable by way of action or defense unless
(a) there is some writing signed by the party against whom enforcement is sought or by his authorized agent or broker sufficient to indicate that a contract has been made for sale of a stated quantity of described securities at a defined or stated price; or

(b) delivery of the security has been accepted or payment has been made but the contract is enforceable under this provision only to the extent of such delivery or payment; or

(c) within a reasonable time a writing in confirmation of the sale or purchase and sufficient against the sender under paragraph (a) has been received by the party against whom enforcement is sought and he has failed to send written objection to its contents within ten days after its receipt; or

(d) the party against whom enforcement is sought admits in his pleading, testimony or otherwise in court that a contract was made for sale of a stated quantity of described securities at a defined or stated price.

PART 4

Registration

§ 8-401. Duty of Issuer to Register Transfer.—
(1) Where a security in registered form is presented to the issuer with a request to register transfer, the issuer is under a duty to register the transfer as requested if
(a) the security is indorsed by the appropriate person or persons (Section 8-308); and

(b) reasonable assurance is given that those endorsements are genuine and effective (Section 8-402); and

(c) the issuer has no duty to inquire into adverse claims or has discharged any such duty (Section 8-403); and

(d) any applicable law relating to the collection of taxes has been complied with; and

(e) the transfer is in fact rightful or is to a bona fide purchaser.

(2) Where an issuer is under a duty to register a transfer of a security the issuer is also liable to the person presenting it for registration or his principal for loss resulting from any unreasonable delay in registration or from failure or refusal to register the transfer.

§ 8-402. Assurance That Indorsements Are Effective.—

(1) The issuer may require the following assurance that each necessary indorsement is genuine and effective.

(a) in all cases, a guarantee of the signature (subsection (1) of Section 8-312) of the person indorsing; and

(b) where the indorsement is by an agent, appropriate assurance of authority to sign;

(c) where the indorsement is by a fiduciary, an appropriate certificate of appointment or incumbency dated within sixty days before the date of presentation for transfer;

(d) where there is more than one fiduciary, reasonable assurance that all who are required to sign have done so;

(e) where the indorsement is by a person not covered by any of the foregoing, assurance appropriate to the case corresponding as nearly as may be to the foregoing.

(2) A "guarantee of the signature" in subsection (1) means a guarantee signed by or on behalf of a person reasonably believed by the issuer to be responsible. The issuer may adopt standards with respect to responsibility provided such standards are not manifestly unreasonable.

(3) "An appropriate certificate of appointment or incumbency" in subsection (1) means

(a) in the case of a fiduciary appointed or qualified by a court, a certificatd issued by or under the direction or supervision of that court; and

(b) otherwise, a certificate issued by or on behalf of a person reasonably believed by the issuer to be qualified so to certify. The issuer may adopt standards with respect to qualification provided such standards are not manifestly unreasonable.

(4) If the issuer has notice that the transfer may be wrongful, it may require reasonable assurance beyond that specified in this section. But if an issuer elects to investigate the requested transfer and both requires and obtains a copy of a will, trust, indenture, articles of co-partnership, bylaws or other controlling instrument it is put on notice of all matters contained therein affecting the transfer.

§ 8-403. Limited Duty of Inquiry.—

(1) An issuer to whom a security is presented for registration is under a duty to inquire into adverse claims if

(a) a notification of an adverse claim is received at a time and in a manner which affords the issuer a reasonable opportunity to act on it prior to the issuance of a new, reissued or re-registered security; or

(b) the issuer has notice of an adverse claim by electing to require a controlling instrument as provided in the last subsection of the preceding section.

(2) The issuer may discharge any duty of inquiry by any reasonable means, including notifying an adverse claimant by registered or certified mail at the address furnished by him or if there be no such address at his residence or regular place of business that the security has been presented for registration of transfer by a named person, and that the transfer will be registered unless within thirty days from the date of mailing the notification, either

(a) an appropriate restraining order, injunction or other process issues from a court of competent jurisdiction; or

(b) an indemnity bond sufficient in the issuer's judgment to protect the issuer and any transfer agent, registrar or other agent of the issuer involved, from any loss which it or they may suffer by complying with the adverse claim is filed with the issuer.

(3) Except to the extent that an issuer has notice by electing to require a controlling instrument as provided in the last subsection of the preceding section or receives notification of an adverse claim under subsection (1) of this section, where a security presented for registration is indorsed by the appropriate person or persons the issuer is under no duty to inquire into adverse claims. In particular

(a) an issuer registering a security in the name of a fiduciary is not bound to inquire into the existence, extent, or correct description of the fiduciary relationship;

(b) an issuer registering transfer on an indorsement by a fiduciary is not bound to inquire whether the transfer is made in compliance with a controlling instrument or with the law of the state having jurisdiction of the fiduciary relationship, including any law requiring the fiduciary to obtain court approval of the transfer; and

(c) the issuer is not charged with notice of the contents of any court record or file or other recorded or unrecorded document even though the document is in its possession and even though the transfer is made on the indorsement of a fiduciary to the fiduciary himself or to his nominee.

§ 8-404. Liability and Non-Liability for Registration.—

(1) Except as otherwise provided in any law relating to the collection of taxes, the issuer is not liable to the owner or any other person suffering loss as a result of the registration of a transfer of a security if

(a) there were on or with the security the necessary indorsements (Section 8-308); and

(b) the issuer had no duty to inquire into adverse claims or has discharged any such duty (Section 8-403).

(2) Where an issuer has registered a transfer of a security to a person not entitled to it the issuer on demand must deliver a like security to the true owner unless

(a) the registration was pursuant to subsection (1); or

(b) the owner is precluded from asserting any claim for registering the transfer under subsection (1) of the following section; or

(c) such delivery would result in overissue, in which case the issuer's liability is governed by Section 8-104.

§ 8-405. Lost, Destroyed and Stolen Securities.—

(1) Where a security has been lost, apparently destroyed or wrongfully taken and the owner fails to notify the issuer of that fact within a reasonable time after he has notice of it and the issuer registers a transfer of the security before receiving such a notification, the owner is precluded from asserting against the issuer any claim for registering the transfer under the preceding section or any claim to a new security under this section.

(2) Where the owner of a security claims that the security has been lost, destroyed or wrongfully taken, the issuer must issue a new security in place of the original security if the owner

(a) so requests before the issuer has notice that the security has been acquired by a bona fide purchaser; and

(b) files with the issuer a sufficient indemnity bond; and

(c) satisfies any other reasonable requirements imposed by the issuer.

(3) If, after the issue of the new security, a bona fide purchaser of the original security presents it for registration of transfer, the issuer must register the transfer unless registration would result in overissue, in which event the issuer's liability is governed by Section 8-104. In addition to any rights on the indemnity bond, the issuer may recover the new security from the person to whom it was issued or any person taking under him except a bona fide purchaser.

§8-406.   Duty of Authenticating Trustee, Transfer Agent or Registrar.—

(1)   Where a person acts as authenticating trustee, transfer agent, registrar, or other agent for an issuer in the registration of transfers of its securities or in the issue of new securities or in the cancellation of surrendered securities

(a) he is under a duty to the issuer to exercise good faith and due diligence in performing his functions; and

(b) he has with regard to the particular functions he performs the same obligation to the holder or owner of the security and has the same rights and privileges as the issuer has in regard to those functions.

(2)   Notice to an authenticating trustee, transfer agent, registrar or other such agent is notice to the issuer with respect to the functions performed by the agent.

ARTICLE NINE—SECURED TRANSACTIONS

PART 1

Short Title, Applicability and Definitions

§ 9-101.   Short Title.—This Article shall be known and may be cited as Uniform Commercial Code—Secured Transactions.

§ 9-102.   Policy and [Subject Matter] of Article.—

(1)   Except as otherwise provided in Section 9-103 on multiple state transactions and in Section 9-104 on excluded transactions, this Article applies so far as concerns any personal property and fixtures within the jurisdiction of this State

(a) to any transaction (regardless of its form) which is intended to create a security interest in personal property or fixtures including goods, documents, instruments, general intangibles, chattel paper of accounts and also

(b) to any sale [or] accounts or chattel paper.

(2)   This Article applies to security interests created by contract including pledge, assignment, chattel mortgage, chattel trust, trust deed, factor's lien, equipment trust, conditional sale, trust receipt, other lien or title retention contract and lease or consignment intended as security. This Article does not apply to statutory liens except as provided in Section 9-310.

(3)   The application of this Article to a security interest in a secured obligation is not affected by the fact that the obligation is itself secured by a transaction or interest to which this Article does not apply.

§ 9-103* [Perfection of Security Interests in Multiple State Transactions—

(1) Documents, instruments and ordinary goods.

(a) This subsection applies to documents and instruments and to goods other than those covered by a certificate of title described in subsection (2), mobile goods described in subsection (3), and minerals described in subsection (5).

(b) Except as otherwise provided in this subsection, perfection and the effect of perfection or non-perfection of a security interest in collateral are governed by the law of the jurisdiction where the collateral is when the last event occurs on which is based the assertion that the security interest is perfected or unperfected.

(c) If the parties to a transaction creating a purchase money security interest in goods in one jurisdiction understand at the time that the security interest attaches that the goods will be kept in another jurisdiction, then the law of the other jurisdiction governs the perfection and the effect of perfection or non-perfection of the security interest from the time it attaches until thirty days after the debtor receives possession of the goods and thereafter if the goods are taken to the other jurisdiction before the end of the thirty-day period.

(d) When collateral is brought into and kept in this state while subject to a security interest perfected under the law of the jurisdiction from which the collateral was removed, the security interest remains perfected, but if action is required by Part 3 of this Article to perfect the security interest,

(i) if the action is not taken before the expiration of the period of perfection in the other jurisdiction or the end of four months after the collateral is brought into this state, whichever period first expires, the security interest becomes unperfected at the end of that period and is thereafter deemed to have been unperfected as against a person who became a purchaser after removal;

(ii) if the action is taken before the expiration of the period specified in subparagraph (i), the security interest continues perfected thereafter;

(iii) for the purpose of priority over a buyer of consumer goods (subsection (2) of Section 9-307), the period of the effectiveness of a filing in the jurisdiction from which the collateral is removed is governed by the rules with respect to perfection in subparagraphs (i) and (ii).

(2) Certificate of title.

(a) This subsection applies to goods covered by a certificate of title issued under a statute of this state or of another jurisdiction under the law of which indication of a security interest on the certificate is required as a condition of perfection.

(b) Except as otherwise provided in this subsection, perfection and the effect of perfection or non-perfection of the security interest are governed by the law (including the conflict of laws rules) of the jurisdiction issuing the certificate until four months after the goods are removed from that jurisdiction and thereafter until the goods are registered in another jurisdiction, but in any event not beyond surrender of the certificate. After the expiration of that period, the goods are not covered by the certificate of title within the meaning of this section.

(c) Except with respect to the rights of a buyer described in the next paragraph, a security interest, perfected in another jurisdiction otherwise than by notation on a certificate of title, in goods brought into this state and thereafter covered by a certificate of title issued by this state is subject to the rules stated in paragraph (d) of subsection (1).

(d) If goods are brought into this state while a security interest therein is perfected in any manner under the law of the jurisdiction from which the goods are removed and a certificate of title is issued by this state and the certificate does not show that the goods are subject to the security interest or that they may be subject to security interests not shown on the certificate, the security interest is subordinate to the rights of a buyer of the goods who is not in the business of selling goods of that kind to the extent that he gives value and receives delivery of the goods after issuance of the certificate and without knowledge of the security interest.

(3) Accounts, general intangibles and mobile goods.

(a) This subsection applies to accounts (other than an account described in subsection (5) on minerals) and general intangibles and to goods which are mobile and which are of a type normally used in more than one jurisdiction, such as motor vehicles, trailers, rolling stock, airplanes, shipping containers, road building and construction machinery and commercial harvesting machinery and the like, if the goods are equipment or are inventory leased or held for lease by the debtor to others, and are not covered by a certificate of title described in subsection (2).

(b) The law (including the conflict of laws rules) of the jurisdiction in which the debtor is located governs the perfection and the effect of perfection or non-perfection of the security interest.

(c) If, however, the debtor is located in a jurisdiction which is not a part of the United States, and which does not provide for perfection of the security interest by filing or recording in that jurisdiction, the law of the jurisdiction in the United States in which the debtor has its major executive office in the United States governs the perfection and the effect of perfection or non-perfection of the security interest through filing. In the alternative, if the debtor is located in a jurisdiction which is not a part of the United States or Canada and the collateral is accounts or general intangibles for money due or to become due, the security interest may be perfected by notification to the account debtor. As used in this paragraph, "United States" includes its territories and possessions and the Commonwealth of Puerto Rico.

(d) A debtor shall be deemed located at his place of business if he has one, at his chief executive office if he has more than one place of business, otherwise at his residence. If, however, the debtor is a foreign air carrier under the Federal Aviation Act of 1958, as amended, it shall be deemed located at the designated office of the agent upon whom service of process may be made on behalf of the foreign air carrier.

(e) A security interest perfected under the law of the jurisdiction of the location of the debtor is perfected until the expiration of four months after a change of the debtor's location to another jurisdiction, or until perfection would have ceased by the law of the first jurisdiction, whichever period first expires. Unless perfected in the new jurisdiction before the end of that period, it becomes unperfected thereafter and is deemed to have been unperfected as against a person who became a purchaser after the change.

(4) Chattel paper. The rules stated for goods in subsection (1) apply to a possessory security interest in chattel paper. The rules stated for accounts in subsection (3) apply to a non-possessory security interest in chattel paper, but the security interest may not be perfected by notification to the account debtor.

(5) Minerals. Perfection and the effect of perfection or non-perfection of a security interest which is created by a debtor who has an interest in minerals or the like (including oil and gas) before extraction and which attaches thereto as extracted, or which attaches to an account resulting from the sale thereof at the wellhead or minehead are governed by the law (including the conflict of laws rules) of the jurisdiction where in the well head or minehead is located.]

*[This section 9-103 has been completely rewritten]

§ 9-104.   Transactions Excluded From Article.—This Article does not apply

(a) to a security interest subject to any statute of the United States such as the Ship Mortgage Act, 1920, to the extent that such statute governs the rights of parties to and third parties affected by transactions in particular types of property; or

(b) to a landlord's lien; or

(c) to a lien given by statute or other rule of law for services or materials except as provided in Section 9-310 on priority of such liens; or

(d) to a transfer of a claim for wages, salary or other compensation of an employee, or

(e) to a transfer by a government or governmental subdivision or agency; or

(f) to a sale of accounts or chattel paper as part of a sale of the business out of which they arose, or an assignment of accounts or chattel paper which is for the purpose of a collection only, or a transfer of a right to payment under a contract to an assignee who is also to do the performance under the contract or a transfer of a single account to an assignee in whole or partial satisfaction of a preexisting indebtedness; or

(g) to a transfer of an interest or claim in or under any policy of insurance, except as provided with respect to proceeds (Section 9-306) and priorities in proceeds (Section 9-312); or

(h) to a right represented by a judgment; (other than a judgment taken on a right to payment which was collateral); or

(i) to any right of set-off; or

(j) except to the extent that provision is made for fixtures in Section 9-313, to the creation or transfer of an interest in or lien on real estate, including a lease or rents thereunder; or

(k) to a transfer in whole or in part of any claim arising out of tort; or

(l) to a transfer of an interest in any deposit account (Subsection (1) of Section 9-105), except as provided with respect to proceeds (Section 9-106) and priorities in proceeds (Section 9-312).

§ 9-105. Definitions and Index of Definitions.—

(1) In this Article unless the context otherwise requires:

(a) "Account debtor" means the person who is obligated on an account, chattel paper, contract right or general intangible;

(b) "Chattel paper" means a writing or writings which evidence both a monetary obligation and a security interest in or a lease of specific goods. When a transaction is evidenced both by such a security agreement or a lease and by an instrument or a series of instruments, the group of writings taken together constitutes chattel paper;

(c) "Collateral" means the property subject to a security interest, and includes accounts, contract rights and chattel paper which have been sold;

(d) "Debtor" means the person who owes payment or other performance of the obligation secured, whether or not he owns or has rights in the collateral, and includes the seller of accounts, contract rights or chattel paper. Where the debtor and the owner of the collateral are not the same person, the term "debtor" means the owner of the collateral in any provision of the Article dealing with the collateral, the obligor in any provision dealing with the obligation, and may include both where the context so requires;

[(e) "Deposit account" means a demand, time, savings, passbook or like account maintained with a bank, savings and loan association, credit union or like organization, other than an account evidenced by a certificate of deposit;]

[(f)] "Document" means document of title as defined in the general definitions of Article 1 (Section 1-201), [and a receipt of the kind described in subsection (2) of Section 7-201;]

[(g) "Encumbrance" includes real estate mortgages and other liens on real estate and all other rights in real estate that are not ownership interests.]

[(h)] "Goods" includes all things which are movable at the time the security interest attaches or which are fixtures (Section 9-313), but does not include money, documents, instruments, accounts, chattel paper, general intangibles, or minerals or the like (including oil and gas) before extraction. "Goods" also includes standing timber which is to be cut and removed under a conveyance or contract for sale, the unborn young of animals, and growing crops.

[(i)] "Instrument" means a negotiable instrument (defined in Section 3-104), or a security (defined in Section 8-102) or any other writing which evidences a right to the payment of money and is not itself a security agreement or lease and is of a type which is in ordinary course of business transferred by delivery with any necessary indorsement or assignment;

[(j) "Mortgage" means a consensual interest created by a real estate mortgage, a trust deed on real estate, or the like;]

[(k) An advance is made "pursuant to commitment"if the secured party has bound himself to make it, whether or not a subsequent event of default or other event not within his control has relieved or may relieve him from his obligation.]

[(l)] ["Security agreement" means an agreement which] creates or provides for a security interest;

[(m)] "Secured party" means a lender, seller or other person in whose favor there is a security interest, including a person to whom accounts, (contract rights) or chattel paper have been sold. When the holders of obligations issued under an indenture of trust, equipment trust agreement or the like are represented by a trustee or other person, the representative is the secured party;

[(n) "Transmitting utility" means any person primarily engaged in the railroad, street railway or trolley bus business, the electric or electronics communications transmission business, the transmission of goods by pipeline, or the transmission or the production and transmission of electricity, steam, gas or water, or the provision of sewer service.]

(2) Other definitions applying to this Article and the sections in which they appear are: . . .

§ **9-106. Definitions: "Account"; "Contract Right"; "General Intangibles."—** "Account" means any right to payment for goods sold or leased or for services rendered [which is not evidenced by an instrument or chattel paper whether or not it has been earned by performance] "General intangibles" means any personal property (including things in action) other than goods, accounts, chattel paper, documents, instruments [and money] . . .

§ **9-107. Definitions: "Purchase Money Security Interest."**—A security interest is a "purchase money security interest" to the extent that it is

(a) taken or retained by the seller of the collateral to secure all or part of its price; or

(b) taken by a person who by making advances or incurring an obligation gives value to enable the debtor to acquire rights in or the use of collateral if such value is in fact so used.

§ **9-108. When After-Acquired Collateral Not Security for Antecedent Debt.—** Where a secured party makes an advance, incurs an obligation, releases a perfected security interest, or otherwise gives new value which is to be secured in whole or in part by after-acquired property his security interest in the after-acquired collateral shall be deemed to be taken for new value and not as security for an antecedent debt if the debtor acquires his rights in such collateral either in the ordinary course of his business or under a contract of purchase made pursuant to the security agreement within a reasonable time after new value is given.

§ **9-109. Classification of Goods; "Consumer Goods"; "Equipment"; "Farm Products"; "Inventory."**—Goods are

(1) "consumer goods" if they are used or brought for use primarily for personal, family or household purposes;

(2) "equipment" if they are used or bought for use primarily in business (including farming or a profession) or by a debtor who is a non-profit organization or a governmental subdivision or agency or if the goods are not included in the definitions of inventory, farm products or consumer goods;

(3) "farm products" if they are crops or livestock or supplies used or produced in farming operations or if they are products of crops or livestock in their unmanufactured states (such as ginned cotton, woolclip, maple syrup, milk and eggs), and if they are in the possession of a debtor engaged in raising, fattening, grazing or other farming operations. If goods are farm products they are neither equipment nor inventory;

(4) "inventory" if they are held by a person who holds them for sale or lease or to be furnished under contracts of service or if he has so furnished them, or if they are raw materials, work in process or materials used or consumed in a business. Inventory of a person is not to be classified as his equipment.

§ **9-110. Sufficiency of Description.**—For the purposes of this Article any description of personal property or real estate is sufficient whether or not it is specific if it reasonably identifies what is described.

§ **9-111. Applicability of Bulk Transfer Laws.**—The creation of a security interest is not a bulk transfer under Article 6 (see Section 6-103).

§ **9-112. Where Collateral Is Not Owned by Debtor.**—Unless otherwise agreed, when a secured party knows that collateral is owned by a person who is not the debtor, the owner of the collateral is entitled to receive from the secured party any surplus under Section 9-502(2) or under Section 9-504(1), and is not liable for the debt or for any deficiency after resale, and he has the same right as the debtor

    (a) to receive statements under Section 9-208;

    (b) to receive notice of and to object to a secured party's proposal to retain the collateral in satisfaction of the indebtedness under Section 9-505;

    (c) to redeem the collateral under Section 9-506;

    (d) to obtain injunctive or other relief under Section 9-507(1) and

    (e) to recover losses caused to him under Section 9-208(2).

§ **9-113. Security Interests Arising Under Article on Sales.**—A security interest arising solely under the Article on Sales (Article 2) is subject to the provisions of this Article except that to the extent that and so long as the debtor does not have or does not lawfully obtain possession of the goods

    (a) no security agreement is necessary to make the security interest enforceable; and

    (b) no filing is required to perfect the security interest; and

    (c) the rights of the secured party on default by the debtor are governed by the Article on Sales (Article 2).

§ **9-114. Consignment—**

(1) A person who delivers goods under a consignment which is not a security interest and who would be required to file under this Article by paragraph (3) (c) of Section 2-326 has priority over a secured party who is or becomes a creditor of the consignee and who would have a perfected security interest in the goods if they were the property of the consignee, and also has priority with respect to identifiable cash proceeds received on or before delivery of the goods to a buyer, if

    (a) the consignor complies with the filing provision of the Article on Sales with respect to consignments (paragraph (3) (c) of Section 2-326) before the consignee receives possession of the goods; and

    (b) the consignor gives notification in writing to the holder of the security interest if the holder has filed a financing statement covering the same types of goods before the date of the filing made by the consignor; and

    (c) the holder of the security interest receives the notification within five years before the consignee receives possession of the goods; and

    (d) the notification states that the the consignor expects to deliver goods on consignment to the consignee, describing the goods by item or type.

(2) In the case of a consignment which is not a security interest and in which the requirements of the preceding subsection have not been met, a person who delivers goods to another is subordinate to a person who would have a perfected security interest in the goods if they were the property of the debtor.]*

*This section new in 1972.

PART 2

Validity of Security Agreement and Rights of Parties Thereto

§ **9-201. General Validity of Security Agreement.**—Except as otherwise provided by this Act a security agreement is effective according to its terms between the parties, against purchasers of the collateral and against creditors. Nothing in this Article validates any charge or practice illegal under any statute or regulation thereunder governing usury, small loans, retail installment sales, or the like or extends the application of any such statute or regulation to any transaction not otherwise subject thereto.

§ 9-202. **Title to Collateral Immaterial.**— Each provision of this Article with regard to rights, obligations and remedies applies whether title to collateral is in the secured party or in the debtor.

§ 9-203. **[Attachment and] Enforceability of Security Interest; Proceeds, Formal Requisites.**—

[(1) Subject to the provisions of Section 4-208 on the security interest of a collecting bank and Section 9-113 on a security interest arising under the Article on Sales, a security interest is not enforceable against the debtor or third parties with respect to the collateral and does not attach unless

(a) the collateral is in the possession of the secured party pursuant to agreement, or the debtor has signed a security agreement which contains a description of the collateral and in addition, when the security interest covers crops growing or to be grown or timber to be cut, a description of the land concerned; and

(b) value has been given; and

(c) the debtor has rights in the collateral.

(2) A security interest attaches when it becomes enforceable against the debtor with respect to the collateral. Attachment occurs as soon as all of the events specified in subsection (1) have taken place unless explicit agreement postpones the time of attaching.

(3) Unless otherwise agreed a security agreement gives the secured party the rights to proceeds provided by Section 9-306]

[(4)] A transaction, although subject to this Article, is also subject to the "Consumer Finance Act" . . . "The Retail Installment Sales Act" . . .and in the case of conflict between the provisions of this Article and any such statute, the provisions of such statute control. Failure to comply with any applicable statute has only the effect which is specified therein.

§ 9-204. **When Security Interest Attaches; After-Acquired Property; Future Advances.**—

[(1) Except as provided in subsection (2), a security agreement may provide that any or all obligations covered by the security agreement are to be secured by after-acquired collateral.

(2) No security interest attaches under an after-acquired property clause to consumer goods other than accessions (Section 9-314) when given as additional security unless the debtor acquires rights in them within ten days after the secured party gives value.]

[(3)] Obligations covered by a security agreement may include future advances or other value whether or not the advances or value are given pursuant to commitment [(Subsection (1) of Section (1) of Section 9-105)]

§ 9-205. **Use or Disposition of Collateral Without Accounting Permissible.**—A security interest is not invalid or fraudulent against creditors by reason of liberty in the debtor to use, commingle or dispose of all or part of the collateral (including returned or repossessed goods) or to collect or compromise accounts, contract rights or chattel paper, or to accept the return of goods or make repossessions, or to use, commingle or dispose of proceeds, or by reason of the failure of the secured party to require the debtor to account for proceeds or replace collateral. This Section does not relax the requirements of possession where perfection of a security interest depends upon possession of the collateral by the secured party or by a bailee.

§ 9-206. Agreement Not to Assert Defenses Against Assignee; Modification of Sales Warranties Where Security Agreement Exists.—

(1) Subject to any statute or decision which establishes a different rule for buyers of consumer goods, an agreement by a buyer that he will not assert against an assignee any claim or defense which he may have against the seller is enforceable by an assignee who takes his assignment for value, in good faith and without notice of a claim or defense, except as to defenses of a type which may be asserted against a holder in due course of a negotiable instrument under the Article on Commercial Paper (Article 3). A buyer who as part of one transaction signs both a negotiable instrument and a security agreement makes such an agreement.

(2) When a seller retains a purchase money security interest in goods the Article on Sales (Article 2) governs the sale and any disclaimer, limitation or modification of the seller's warranties.

§ 9-207. Rights and Duties When Collateral Is in Secured Party's Possession.—

(1) A secured party must use reasonable care in the custody and preservation of collateral in his possession. In the case of an instrument or chattel paper reasonable care includes taking necessary steps to preserve rights against prior parties unless otherwise agreed.

(2) Unless otherwise agreed, when collateral is in the secured party's possession

    (a) reasonable expenses (including the cost of any insurance and payment of taxes or other charges) incurred in the custody, preservation, use or operation of the collateral are chargeable to the debtor and are secured by the collateral;

    (b) the risk of accidental loss or damage is on the debtor to the extent of any deficiency in any effective insurance coverage;

    (c) the secured party may hold as additional security any increase or profits (except money) received from the collateral, but money so received, unless remitted to the debtor, shall be applied in reduction of the secured obligation;

    (d) the secured party must keep the collateral identifiable but fungible collateral may be commingled;

    (e) the secured party may repledge the collateral upon terms which do not impair the debtor's right to redeem it.

(3) A secured party is liable for any loss caused by his failure to meet any obligation imposed by the preceding subsections but does not lose his security interest.

(4) A secured party may use or operate the collateral for the purpose of preserving the collateral or its value or pursuant to the order of a court of appropriate jurisdiction or, except in the case of consumer goods, in the manner and to the extent provided in the security agreement.

§ 9-208. Request for Statement of Account or List of Collateral.—

(1) A debtor may sign a statement indicating what he believes to be the aggregate amount of unpaid indebtedness as of a specified date and may send it to the secured party with a request that the statement be approved or corrected and returned to the debtor. When the security agreement or any other record kept by the secured party identifies the collateral a debtor may similarly request the secured party to approve or correct a list of the collateral.

(2) The secured party must comply with such a request within two weeks after receipt by sending a written correction or approval. If the secured party claims a security interest in all of a particular type of collateral owned by the debtor he may indicate that fact in his reply and need not approve or correct an itemized list of such collateral. If the secured party without reasonable excuse fails to comply he is liable for any loss caused to the debtor thereby; and if the debtor has properly included in his request a good faith statement of the obligation or a list of the collateral or both, the secured party may claim a security interest only as shown in the statement against persons misled by his failure to comply. If he no longer has an interest in the obligation or collateral at the

time the request is received he must disclose the name and address of any successor in interest known to him and he is liable for any loss caused to the debtor as a result or failure to disclose. A successor in interest is not subject to this Section until a request is received by him.

(3) A debtor is entitled to such a statement once every 6 months without charge. The secured party may require payment of a charge not exceeding $10 for each additional statement furnished.

PART 3

Rights of Third Parties; Perfected and Unperfected

Security Interests: Rules of Priority

§ 9-301. Persons Who Take Priority Over Unperfected Security Interests: [Right of] "Lien Creditor."—

(1) Except as otherwise provided in subsection (2), an unperfected security interest is subordinate to the rights of

(a) persons entitled to priority under Section 9-312;

(b) a person who becomes a lien creditor and before [the security interest] is perfected;

(c) in the case of goods, instruments, documents, and chattel paper, a person who is not a secured party and who is a transferee in bulk or other buyer not in ordinary course of business, [or is a buyer of farm products in the ordinary course of business] to the extent that he gives value and receives delivery of the collateral without knowledge of the security interest and before it is perfected;

(d) in the case of accounts, contract rights, and general intangibles, a person who is not a secured party and who is a transferee to the extent that he gives value without knowledge of the security interest and before it is perfected.

(2) If the secured party files with respect to a purchase money security interest before or within ten days after the [debtor takes possession] collateral comes into possession of the debtor, he takes priority over the rights of a transferee in bulk or of a lien creditor which arise between the time the security interest attaches and the time of filing.

(3) A "lien creditor" means a creditor who has acquired a lien on the property involved by attachment, levy or the like and includes as assignee for benefit of creditors from the time of assignment, and a trustee in bankruptcy from the date of the filing of the petition or a receiver in equity from the time of appointment. Unless all the creditors represented had knowledge of the security interests such a representative of creditors is a lien creditor without knowledge even though he personally has knowledge of the security interest.

[(4) A person who becomes a lien creditor while a security interest is perfected takes subject to the security interest only to the extent that it secures advances made before he becomes a lien creditor or within 45 days thereafter or made without knowledge of the lien or pursuant to a commitment entered into without knowledge of the lien.]

§ 9-302. When Filing is Required to Perfect Security Interest; Security Interests to Which Filing Provisions of This Article Do Not Apply.—

(1) A financing statement must be filed to perfect all security interests except the following:

(a) a security interest in collateral in possession of the secured party under Section 9-305;

(b) a security interest temporarily perfected in instruments or documents without delivery under Section 9-304 or in proceeds for a 10 day period under Section 9-306;

[(c) a security interest created by an assignment of a beneficial interest in a trust of a decedent's estate;]

(d) a purchase money security interest in consumer goods; but filing is required [for a motor vehicle required to be registered; and fixture filing is required for priority over conflicting interests in fixtures to the extent provided in Section 9-313;]

(e) an assignment of accounts or contract rights which does not alone or in conjunction with other assignments to the same assignee transfer a significant part of the outstanding accounts or contract rights of the assignor;

(f) a security interest of a collecting bank (Section 4-208) or arising under the Article on Sales (see Section 9-113) or covered in subsection (3) of this section.

[(g) an assignment for the benefit of all the creditors of the transferor, and subsequent transfers by the assignee thereunder.]

(2) If a secured party assigns a perfected security interest, no filing under this Article is required in order to continue the perfected status of the security interest against creditors of and transferees from the original debtor.

[(3) The filing of a financing statement otherwise required by this Article is not necessary or effective to perfect a security interest in property subject to

(a) a statute or treaty of the United States which provides for a national or international registration or a national or international certificate of title or which specifies a place of filing different from that specified in this Article for filing of the security interest; or

(b) the following statutes of this state; [[list any certificate of title statute covering automobiles, trailers, mobile homes, boats, farm tractors, or the like, and any central filing statue*.]]; but during any period in which collateral is inventory held for sale by a person who is in the business of selling goods of that kind, the filing provisions of this Article (Part 4) apply to a security interest in that collateral created by him as debtor; or

(c) a certificate of title statute of another jurisdiction under the law of which indication of a security interest on the certificate is required as a condition of perfection (subsection (2) of Section 9-103).

(4) Compliance with a statute or treaty described in subsection (3) is equivalent to the filing of a financing statement under this Article, and a security interest in property subject to the statute or treaty can be perfected only by compliance therewith except as provided in Section 9-103 on multiple state transactions. Duration and renewal of perfection of a security interest perfected by compliance with the statute or treaty are governed by the provisions of the statute or treaty; in other respects the security interest is subject to this Article.

*Note: *It is recommended that the provisions of certificate of title acts for perfection of security interests by notation on the certificates should be amended to exclude coverage of inventory held for sale.*]

§ 9-303. When Security Interest is Perfected; Continuity of Perfection.—

(1) A security interest is perfected when it has attached and when all of the applicable steps required for perfection have been taken. Such steps are specified in Sections 9-302, 9-304, 9-306. If such steps are taken before the security interest attaches, it is perfected at the time when it attaches.

(2) If a security interest is originally perfected in any way permitted under this Article and is subsequently perfected in some other way under this article, without an intermediate period when it was unperfected, the security interest shall be deemed to be perfected continuously for the purposes of this Article.

§ 9-304. Perfection of Security Interest in Instruments, Documents and Goods Covered by Documents; Perfection by Permissive Filing; Temporary Perfection Without Filing or Transfer of Possession.—

(1) A security interest in chattel paper or negotiable documents may be perfected by filing. A security interest in [money or] instruments (other than instruments which constitute part of chattel paper) can be perfected only by the secured party's taking possession, except as provided in subsections (4) and (5) [of this section and subsections (2) and (3) of Section 9-306 on Proceeds.]

(2) During the period that goods are in the possession of the issuer of a negotiable document therefor, a security interest in the goods is perfected by perfecting a security interest in the document, and any security interest in the goods otherwise perfected during such period is subject thereto.

(3) A security interest in goods in the possession of a bailee other than one who has issued a negotiable document therefor is perfected by issuance of a document in the name of the secured party or by the bailee's receipt of notification of the secured party's interest or by filing as to the goods.

(4) A security interest in instruments or negotiable documents is perfected without filing or the taking of possession for a period of 21 days from the time it attaches to the extent that it arises for new value given under a written security agreement.

(5) A security interest remains perfected for a period of 21 days without filing where a secured party having a perfected security interest is an instrument, a negotiable document or goods in possession of a bailee other than one who has issued a negotiable document therefor

(a) makes available to the debtor the goods or documents representing the goods for the purpose of ultimate sale or exchange or for the purpose of loading, unloading, storing, shipping, trans-shipping, manufacturing, processing or otherwise dealing with them in a manner preliminary to their sale or exchange; [but priority between conflicting security interests in goods is subject to subsection (3) of Section 9-312; or]

(b) delivers the instrument to the debtor for the purpose of ultimate sale or exchange or of presentation, collection, renewal or registration of transfer.

(6) After the 21 day period in subsections (4) and (5) perfection depends upon compliance with applicable provisions of this Article.

§ 9-305.   When Possession by Secured Party Perfects Security Interest Without Filing.— A security interest in letters of credit and advices of credit (subsection (2) (a) of Section 5-116), goods, instruments, [money] negotiable documents or chattel paper may be perfected by the secured party's taking possession of the collateral. If such collateral other than goods covered by a negotiable document is held by a bailee, the secured party is deemed to have possession from the time the bailee receives notification of the secured party's interest. A security interest is perfected by possession from the time possession is taken without relation back and continues only so long as possession is retained, unless otherwise specified in this Article. The security interest may be otherwise perfected as provided in this Article before or after the period of possession by the secured party.

§ 9-306.   "Proceeds"; Secured Party's Rights on Disposition of Collateral

(1) ["Proceeds" includes whatever is received upon the sale, exchange, collection or other disposition of collateral or proceeds. Insurance payable by reason of loss or damage to the collateral is proceeds, except to the extent that it is payable to a person other than a party to the security agreement.] Money, checks, [deposit accounts,] and the like are "cash proceeds". All other proceeds are "non-cash proceeds".

(2) Except where this Article otherwise provides, a security interest continues in collateral notwithstanding sale, exchange or other disposition thereof unless [the disposition was] authorized by the secured party in the security agreement or otherwise, and also continues in any identifiable proceeds including collections received by the debtor.

(3) The security interest in proceeds is a continuously perfected security interest if the interest in the original collateral was perfected but it ceases to be a perfected

security interest and becomes unperfected ten days after receipt of the proceeds by the debtor unless

[(a) a filed financing statement covers the original collateral and the proceeds are collateral in which a security interest may be perfected by filing in the office or offices where the financing statement has been filed and, if the proceeds are acquired with cash proceeds, the description of collateral in the financing statement indicates the types of property constituting the proceeds; or]

[(b) a filed financing statement covers the original collateral and the proceeds are identifiable cash proceeds; or]

[(c)] the security interest in the proceeds is perfected before the expiration of the ten day period.

[Except as provided in this section, a security interest in proceeds can be perfected only by the methods or under the circumstances permitted in this Article for original collateral of the same type.]

(4) In the event of insolvency proceeding instituted by or against a debtor, a secured party with a perfected security interest in proceeds has a perfected security interest [only in the following proceeds:]

(a) in identifiable non-cash proceeds[,] [and in separate deposit accounts containing only proceeds;]

(b) in identifiable cash proceeds in the form of money which is [neither] commingled with other money [nor] deposited in a [deposit] account prior to the insolvency proceedings;

(c) in identifiable cash proceeds in the form of checks and the like which are not deposited in a [deposit] account prior to the insolvency proceedings; and

(d) in all cash and [deposit] accounts of the debtor [in which] proceeds have been commingled [with other funds,] but the perfected security interest under this paragraph (d) is

(i) subject to any right of set-off; and

(ii) limited to an amount not greater than the amount of any cash proceeds received by the debtor within ten days before the institution of the insolvency proceedings [less the sum of (I) the payments to the secured party on account of cash proceeds received by the debtor during such period and (II) the cash proceeds received by the debtor during such period to which the secured party is entitled under paragraphs (a) through (c) of this subsection (4).]

(5) If a sale of goods results in an account or chattel paper which is transferred by the seller to a secured party, and if the goods are returned to or are repossessed by the seller or the secured party, the following rules determine priorities:

(a) If the goods were collateral at the time of sale for an indebtedness of the seller which is still unpaid, the original security interest attaches again to the goods and continues as a perfected security interest if it was perfected at the time when the goods were sold. If the security interest was originally perfected by a filing which is still effective, nothing further is required to continue the perfected status; in any other case, the secured party must take possession of the returned or repossessed goods or must file.

(b) An unpaid transferee of the chattel paper has a security interest in the goods against the transferor. Such security interest is prior to a security interest asserted under paragraph (a) to the extent that the transferee of the chattel paper was entitled to priority under Section 9-308.

(c) An unpaid transferee of the account has a security interest in the goods against the transferor. Such security interest is subordinate to a security interest asserted under paragraph (a).

(d) A security interest of an unpaid transferee asserted under paragraph (b) or (c) must be perfected for protection against creditors of the transferor and purchasers of the returned or repossessed goods.

§ 9-306.01. Debtor Disposing of Collateral and Failing to Pay Secured Party Amount Due under Security Agreement; Penalties for Violation.—

(1) It is unlawful for a debtor under the terms of a security agreement (a) who has no right of sale or other disposition of the collateral or (b) who has a right of sale or other disposition of the collateral and is to account to the secured party for the proceeds of any sale or other disposition of the collateral, to sell or otherwise dispose of the collateral and willfully and wrongfully to fail to pay the secured party the amount of said proceeds due under the security agreement.

(2) An individual convicted of a violation of this Section shall be punished by imprisonment in the penitentiary for not less than one year nor more than ten years.

(3) A corporation convicted of a violation of this Section shall be punished by a fine of not less than two thousand dollars nor more than ten thousand dollars.

(4) In the event the debtor under the terms of a security agreement is a corporation or a partnership, any officer, director, manager, or managerial agent of the debtor who violates this Section or causes the debtor to violate this Section shall, upon conviction thereof, be punished by imprisonment in the penitentiary for not less than one year nor more than ten years.

§ 9-307. Protection of Buyers of Goods.—

(1) A buyer in ordinary course of business (subsection (9) of Section 1-201) other than a person buying farm products from a person engaged in farming operations takes free of a security interest created by his seller even though the security interest is perfected and even though the buyer knows of its existence.

(2) In the case of consumer goods, a buyer takes free of a security interest even though perfected if he buys without knowledge of the security interest, for value and for his own personal, family or household purposes or his own farming operations unless prior to the purchase the secured party has filed a financing statement covering such goods.

[(3) A buyer other than a buyer in ordinary course of business (subsection (1) of this section) takes free of a security interest to the extent that it secures future advances made after the secured party acquires knowledge of the purchase, or more than 45 days after the purchase, whichever first occurs, unless made pursuant to a commitment entered into without knowledge of the purchase and before the expiration of the 45 day period.]

§ 9-308.* Purchase of Chattel Paper and Instruments—[A purchaser of chattel paper or an instrument who gives new value and takes possession of it in the ordinary course of his business has priority over a security interest in the chattel paper or instrument

(a) which is perfected under Section 9-304 (permissive filing and temporary perfection) or under Section 9-306 (perfection as to proceeds) if he acts without knowledge that the specific paper or instrument is subject to a security interest; or

(b) which is claimed merely as proceeds of inventory subject to a security interest (Section 9-306) even though he knows that the specific paper or instrument is subject to the security interest.]

*This section was redrafted in 1972.

§ 9-309. Protection of Purchasers of Instruments and Documents.—Nothing in this Article limits the rights of a holder in due course of a negotiable instrument (Section 3-302) or a holder to whom a negotiable document of title has been duly negotiated (Section 7-501) or a bona fide purchaser of a security (Section 8-301) and such holders or purchasers take priority over an earlier security interest even though perfected. Filing under this Article does not constitute notice of the security interest to such holders or purchasers.

§ 9-310. Priority of Certain Liens Arising by Operation of Law.—When a person in the ordinary course of his business furnishes services or materials with respect to goods subject to a security interest, a lien upon goods in the possession of such person given by statute or rule of law for such materials or services takes priority over a perfected security interest unless the lien is statutory and the statute expressly provides otherwise.

§ 9-311. Alienability of Debtor's Rights: Judicial Process.—The debtor's rights in collateral may be voluntarily or involuntarily transferred (by way of sale, creation of a security interest, attachment, levy, garnishment or other judicial process) notwithstanding a provision in the security agreement prohibiting any transfer or making the transfer constitute a default.

§ 9-312. Priorities Among Conflicting Security Interests in the Same Collateral.—

[(1) The rules of priority stated in other sections of this Part and in the following sections shall govern when applicable: Section 4-208 with respect to the security interests of collecting banks in items being collected, accompanying documents and proceeds; Section 9-103 on security interests related to other jurisdictions; Section 9-114 on consignments.]

(2) A perfected security interest in crops for new value given to enable the debtor to produce the crops during the production season and given not more than three months before the crops become growing crops by planting or otherwise takes priority over an earlier perfected security interest to the extent that such earlier interest secures obligations due more than six months before the crops become growing crops by planting or otherwise, even though the person giving new value had knowledge of the earlier security interest.

[(3) A perfected purchase money security interest in inventory has priority over a conflicting security interest in the same inventory and also has priority in identifiable cash proceeds received on or before the delivery of the inventory to a buyer if

(a) the purchase money security interest is perfected at the time the debtor receives possession of the inventory; and

(b) the purchase money secured party gives notification in writing to the holder of the conflicting security interest if the holder had filed a financing statement covering the same types of inventory (i) before the date of the filing made by the purchase money secured party, or (ii) before the beginning of the 21 day period where the purchase money security interest is temporarily perfected without filing or possession (subsection (5) of Section 9-304); and

(c) the holder of the conflicting security interest receives the notification within five years before the debtor receives possession of the inventory; and

(d) the notification states that the person giving the notice has or expects to acquire a purchase money security interest in inventory of the debtor, describing such inventory by item or type.]

(4) A purchase money security interest in collateral other than inventory has priority over a conflicting security interest in the same collateral [or its proceeds] if the purchase money security interest is perfected at the time the debtor receives possession of the collateral or within 10 days thereafter.

(5) In all cases not governed by other rules stated in this section (including cases of purchase money security interests which do not qualify for the special priorities set forth in subsections (3) and (4) of this section), priority between conflicting security interests in the same collateral shall be determined] according to the following rules:

(a) Conflicting security interests rank according to priority in time of filing or perfection. Priority dates from the time a filing is first made covering the collateral or the time the security interest is first perfected, whichever is earlier, provided that there is no period thereafter when there is neither filing nor perfection.

(b) So long as conflicting security interests are unperfected, the first to attach has priority.]

[(6) For the purposes of subsection (5) a date of filing or perfection as to collateral is also a date of filing or perfection as to proceeds.

(7) If future advances are made while a security interest is perfected by filing or the taking of possession, the security interest has the same priority for the purposes of subsection (5) with respect to the future advances as it does with respect to the first advance. If a commitment is made before or while the security interest is so perfected, the security interest has the same priority with respect to advances made pursuant thereto. In other cases a perfected security interest has priority from the date the advance is made.]

§ 9-313.   Priority of Security Interests in Fixtures.—

[(1) In this section and in the provisions of Part 4 of this Article referring to fixture filing, unless the context otherwise requires

(a) goods are "fixtures" when they become so related to particular real estate that an interest in them arises under real estate law

(b) a "fixture filing" is the filing in the office where a mortgage on the real estate would be filed or recorded of a financing statement covering goods which are or are to become fixtures and conforming to the requirements of subsection (5) of Section 9-402

(c) a mortgage is a "construction mortgage" to the extent that it secures an obligation incurred for the construction of an improvement on land including the acquisition cost of the land, if the recorded writing so indicates.

(2) A security interest under this Article may be created in goods which are fixtures or may continue in goods which become fixtures, but no security interest exists under this Article in ordinary building materials incorporated into an improvement on land.

(3) This Article does not prevent creation of an encumbrance upon fixtures pursuant to real estate law.

(4) A perfected security interest in fixtures has priority over the conflicting interest of an encumbrancer or owner of the real estate where

(a) the security interest is a purchase money security interest, the interest of the encumbrancer or owner arises before the goods become fixtures, the security interest is perfected by a fixture filing before the goods become fixtures or within ten days thereafter, and the debtor has an interest of record in the real estate or is in possession of the real estate; or

(b) the security interest is perfected by a fixture filing before the interest of the encumbrancer or owner is of record, the security interest has priority over any conflicting interest of a predecessor in title of the encumbrancer or owner, and the debtor has an interest of record in the real estate or is in possession of the real estate; or

(c) the fixtures are readily removable factory or office machines or readily removable replacements of domestic appliances which are consumer goods, and before the goods become fixtures the security interest is perfected by any method permitted by this Article; or

(d) the conflicting interest is a lien on the real estate obtained by legal or equitable proceedings after the security interest was perfected by any method permitted by this Article.

(5) A security interest in fixtures, whether or not perfected, has priority over the conflicting interest of an encumbrancer or owner of the real estate where

(a) the encumbrancer or owner has consented in writing to the security interest or has disclaimed an interest in the goods as fixtures; or

(b) the debtor has a right to remove the goods as against the encumbrancer or owner. If the debtor's right terminates, the priority of the security interest continues for a reasonable time.

(6) Notwithstanding paragraph (a) of subsection (4) but otherwise subject to subsections (4) and (5), a security interest in fixtures is subordinate to a construction mortgage recorded before the goods become fixtures if the goods become fixtures before the completion of the construction. To the extent that it is given to refinance a construction mortgage, a mortgage has this priority to the same extent as the construction mortgage.

(7) In cases not within the preceding subsections, a security interest in fixtures is subordinate to the conflicting interest of an encumbrancer or owner of the related real estate who is not the debtor.]

[(8)] When [all owners and encumbrancers] the real estate, he may, on default, subject to the provisions of Part 5, remove his collateral from the real estate but he must reimburse any encumbrancer or owner of the real estate who is not the debtor and who has not otherwise agreed for the cost of repair of any physical injury, but not for any diminution in value of the real estate caused by the absence of the goods removed or by any necessity for replacing them. A person entitled to reimbursement may refuse permission to remove until the secured party gives adequate security for the performance of this obligation.

§ 9-314. Accessions.—

(1) A security interest in goods which attaches before they are installed in or affixed to other goods takes priority as to the goods installed or affixed (called in this section "accessions") over the claims of all persons to the whole except as stated in subsection (3) and subject to Section 9-315(1).

(2) A security interest which attaches to goods after they become part of a whole is valid against all persons subsequently acquiring interests in the whole except as stated in subsection (3) but is invalid against any person with an interest in the whole at the time the security interest attaches to the goods who has not in writing consented to the security interest or disclaimed an interest in the goods as part of the whole.

(3) The security interests described in subsections (1) and (2) do not take priority over

(a) a subsequent purchaser for value of any interest in the whole; or

(b) a creditor with a lien on the whole subsequently obtained by judicial proceedings; or

(c) a creditor with a prior perfected security interest in the whole to the extent that he makes subsequent advances

if the subsequent purchase is made, the lien by judicial proceedings obtained or the subsequent advance under the prior perfected security interest is made or contracted for without knowledge of the security interest and before it is perfected. A purchaser of the whole at a foreclosure sale other than the holder of a perfected security interest purchasing at his own foreclosure sale is a subsequent purchaser within this Section.

(4) When under subsections (1) or (2) and (3) a secured party has an interest in accessions which has priority over the claims of all persons who have interests in the whole, he may on default subject to the provisions of Part 5 remove his collateral from the whole but he must reimburse any encumbrancer or owner of the whole who is not the debtor and who has not otherwise agreed for the cost of repair of any physical injury but not for any diminution in value of the whole caused by the absence of the goods removed or by any necessity for replacing them. A person entitled to reimbursement may refuse permission to remove until the secured party gives adequate security for the performance of this obligation.

§ 9-315. Priority When Goods Are Commingled or Processed.—

(1) If a security interest in goods was perfected and subsequently the goods or a part thereof have become part of a product or mass, the security interest continues in the product or mass if

(a) the goods are so manufactured, processed, assembled or commingled that their identity is lost in the product or mass; or

(b) a financing statement covering the original goods also covers the product into which the goods have been manufactured, processed or assembled.

In a case to which paragraph (b) applies, no separate security interest in that part of the original goods which has been manufactured, processed or assembled into the product may be claimed under Section 9-314.

(2) When under subsection (1) more than one security interest attaches to the product or mass, they rank equally according to the ratio that the cost of the goods to which each interest originally attached bears to the cost of the total product or mass.

§ 9-316. Priority Subject to Subordination.—Nothing in this Article prevents subordination by agreement by any person entitled to priority.

§ 9-317. Secured Party Not Obligated on Contract of Debtor.—The mere existence of a security interest or authority given to the debtor to dispose of or use collateral does not impose contract or tort liability upon the secured party for the debtor's acts or omissions.

§ 9-318. Defenses Against Assignee; Modification of Contract After Notification of Assignment; Term Prohibiting Assignment Ineffective; Identification and Proof of Assignment.—

(1) Unless an account debtor has made an enforceable agreement not to assert defenses or claims arising out of a sale as provided in Section 9-206 the rights of an assignee are subject to

(a) all the terms of the contract between the account debtor and assignor and any defense or claim arising therefrom; and

(b) any other defense or claim of the account debtor against the assignor which accrues before the account debtor receives notification of the assignment.

(2) So far as the right to payment [or a part thereof] under an assigned contract [has not been fully earned by performance,] and notwithstanding notification of the assignment, any modification of or substitution for the contract made in good faith and in accordance with reasonable commercial standards is effective against an assignee unless the account debtor has otherwise agreed but the assignee acquires corresponding rights under the modified or substituted contract. The assignment may provide that such modification or substitution is a breach by the assignor.

(3) The account debtor is authorized to pay the assignor until the account debtor receives notification that the [amount due or to become due] has been assigned and that payment is to be made to the assignee. A notification which does not reasonably identify the rights assigned is ineffective. If requested by the account debtor, the assignee must seasonably furnish reasonable proof that the assignment has been made and unless he does so the account debtor may pay the assignor.

(4) A term in any contract between an account debtor and an assignor [is ineffective if it] prohibits assignment of an account [or prohibits creation of a security interest in a general intangible for money due or to become due or requires the account debtor's consent to such assignment or security interest.]

PART 4

FILING

§ 9-401. Place of Filing; Erroneous Filing; Removal of Collateral

First Alternative Subsection (1)

(1) The proper place to file in order to perfect a security interest is as follows:

[(a) when the collateral is timber to be cut or is minerals or the like (including oil and gas) or accounts subject to subsection (5) of Section 9-103, or when the financing statement is filed as a fixture filing (Section 9-313) and] the collateral is goods which are or are to become fixtures, then in the office where a mortgage on the real estate would be filed or recorded;

(b) in all other cases, in the office of the Secretary of State.

Second Alternative Subsection (1)

(1) The proper place to file in order to perfect a security interest is as follows:

(a) when the collateral is equipment used in farming operations, or farm products, or accounts, [contract rights] or general intangibles arising from or relating to the sale of farm products by a farmer, or consumer goods, then in the office of the . . . . in the county of the debtor's residence or if the debtor is not a resident of this state then in the office of the . . . . in the county where the goods are kept, and in addition when the collateral is crops [growing or to be grown] in the office of the . . . . in the county where the land [on which the crops are growing or to be grown] is located;

(b) when the collateral is [timber to be cut or is minerals or the like (including oil and gas) or accounts subject to subsection (5) of Section 9-103, or when the financing statement is filed as a fixture filing (Section 9-313) and the collateral is goods which are or are to become fixtures,] then in the office where a mortgage on the real estate would be filed or recorded;

(c) in all other cases, in the office of the Secretary of State.

Third Alternative Subsection (1)

(1) The proper place to file in order to perfect a security interest is as follows:

(a) when the collateral is equipment used in farming operations, or farm products, or accounts, [contract rights] or general intangibles arising from or relating to the sale of farm products by a farmer, or consumer goods, then in the office of the . . . . in the county of the debtor's residence or if the debtor is not a resident of this state then in the office of the . . . . in the county where the goods are kept, and in addition when the collateral is crops growing or to be grown in the office of the . . . . in the county where the land [on which the crops are growing or to be grown] is located;

(b) when the collateral is [goods which at the time the security interest attaches are or are to become fixtures] timber to be cut or is minerals or the like (including oil and gas) or accounts subject to subsection (5) of Section 9-103, or when the financing statement is filed as a fixture filing (Section 9-313) and the collateral is goods which are or are to become fixtures, then in the office where a mortgage on the real estate [concerned] would be filed or recorded;

(c) in all other cases, in the office of the Secretary of State and in addition, if the debtor has a place of business in only one county of this state, also in the office of . . . . of such county, or, if the debtor has no place of business in this state, but resides in the state, also in the office of . . . . of the county in which he resides.

Note: *One of the three alternatives should be selected as subsection (1).*

(2) A filing which is made in good faith in an improper place or not in all of the places required by this section is nevertheless effective with regard to any collateral as to which the filing complied with the requirements of this Article and is also effective

with regard to collateral covered by the financing statement against any person who has knowledge of the contents of such financing statement.

(3) A filing which is made in the proper place in this State continues effective even though the debtor's residence or place of business or the location of the collateral or its use, whichever controlled the original filing, is thereafter changed.

(4) [The] rules stated in Section 9-103 determine whether filing is necessary in this State.

[(5) Notwithstanding the preceding subsections, and subject to subsection (3) of Section 9-302, the proper place to file in order to perfect a security interest in collateral, including fixtures, of a transmitting utility is the office of the Secretary of State. This filing constitutes a fixture filing (Section 9-313) as to the collateral described therein which is or is to become fixtures.

(6) For the purposes of this section, the residence of an organization is its place of business if it has one or its chief executive office if it has more than one place of business.]

> **Note:** *Subsection (6) should be used only if the state chooses the Second or Third Alternative Subsection (1).*

§ 9-402. Formal Requisites of Financing Statement; Amendments; Mortgage as Financing Statement—

(1) A financing statement is sufficient if it [gives the names of the debtor and the secured party,] is signed by the debtor, gives an address of the secured party from which information concerning the security interest may be obtained, gives a mailing address of the debtor and contains a statement indicating the types, or describing the items, of collateral. A financing statement may be filed before a security agreement is made or a security interest otherwise attaches. When the financing statement covers crops growing or to be grown [or goods which are or are to become fixtures,] the statement must also contain a description of the real estate concerned. [When the financing statement covers timber to be cut or covers minerals or the like (including oil and gas) or accounts subject to subsection (5) of Section 9-103, or when the financing statement is filed as a fixture filing (Section 9-313) and the collateral is goods which are or are to become fixtures, the statement must also comply with subsection (5).] A copy of the security agreement is sufficient as a financing statement if it contains the above information and is signed by [the debtor. A carbon, photographic or other reproduction of a security agreement or a financing statement is sufficient as a financing statement if the security agreement so provides or if the original has been filed in this state.]

(2) A financing statement which otherwise complies with subsection (1) is sufficient [when] it is signed by the secured party [instead of the debtor] if it is filed to perfect a security interest in

(a) collateral already subject to a security interest in another jurisdiction when it is brought into this state, [or when the debtor's location is changed to this state.] Such a financing statement must state that the collateral was brought into this state [or that the debtor's location was changed to this state] under such circumstances; [or]

(b) proceeds under Section 9-306 if the security interest in the original collateral was perfected. Such a financing statement must describe the original collateral; [or

(c) collateral as to which the filing has lapsed; or

(d) collateral acquired after a change of name, identity or corporate structure of the debtor (subsection (7).]

(3) A form substantially as follows is sufficient to comply with subsection (1):

Name of debtor (or assignor) ....

Address..

Name of secured party or assignee)......................................

Address..

1. This financing statement covers the following types (or items) of property:
(Describe)..
2. (If collateral is crops) The above described crops are growing or are to be grown on:
(Describe Real Estate) ....
[3. (If applicable) The above goods are to become fixtures on*]

*Where appropriate substitute either "The above timber is standing on. . . ." or "The above minerals or the like (including oil and gas) or accounts will be financed at the wellhead or minehead of the well or mine located on. . . ."

[(Describe Real Estate) ....
and this financing statement is to be filed [for record] in the real estate records. (If the debtor does not have an interest of record) The name of a record owner is]
....
4. (If [proceeds or] products of collateral are claimed) Products of the collateral are also covered.

(use
whichever
is
applicable)
{
....
Signature of Debtor (or Assignor)
....
Signature of Secured Party (or Assignee)

(4) A financing statement may be amended by filing a writing signed by both the debtor and the secured party. An amendment does not extend the period of effectiveness of a financing statement.] [If] any amendment adds collateral, it is effective as to the added collateral only from the filing date of the amendment. [In this Article, unless the context otherwise requires, the term "financing statement" means the original financing statement and any amendments.

(5) A financing statement covering timber to be cut or covering minerals or the like (including oil and gas) or accounts subject to subsection (5) of Section 9-103, or a financing statement filed as a fixture filing (Section 9-313) where the debtor is not a transmitting utility, must show that it covers this type of collateral, must recite that it is to be filed [for record] in the real estate records, and the financing statement must contain a description of the real estate [sufficient if it were contained in a mortgage of the real estate to give constructive notice of the mortgage under the law of this state.] If the debtor does not have an interest of record in the real estate, the financing statement must show the name of a record owner.

(6) A mortgage is effective as a financing statement filed as a fixture filing from the date of its recording if (a) the goods are described in the mortgage by item or type, (b) the goods are or are to become fixtures related to the real estate described in the mortgage, (c) the mortgage complies with the requirements for a financing statement in this section other than a recital that it is to be filed in the real estate records, and (d) the mortgage is duly recorded. No fee with reference to the financing statement is required other than the regular recording and satisfaction fees with respect to the mortgage.

(7) A financing statement sufficiently shows the name of the debtor if it gives the individual, partnership or corporate name of the debtor, whether or not it adds other trade names or the names of partners. Where the debtor so changes his name or in the case of an organization its name, identity or corporate structure that a filed financing statement becomes seriously misleading, the filing is not effective to perfect a security interest in collateral acquired by the debtor more than four months after the change, unless a new appropriate financing statement is filed before the expiration of that time. A filed financing statement remains effective with respect to collateral transferred by the debtor even though the secured party knows of or consents to the transfer.]

[(8)] A financing statement substantially complying with the requirements of this section is effective even though it contains minor errors which are not seriously misleading.

§ 9-403. What Constitutes Filing; Duration of Filing; Effect of Lapsed Filing; Duties of Filing Officer.—

(1) Presentation for filing of a financing statement and tender of the filing fee or acceptance of the statement by the filing officer constitutes filing under this Article.

[(2) Except as provided in Subsection (6)] a filed financing statement is effective for a period of five years from the date of filing. The effectiveness of a filed financing statement lapses on the expiration of [the five] year period unless a continuation statement is filed prior to the lapse. [If a security interest perfected by filing exists at the time insolvency proceedings are commenced by or against the debtor, the security interest remains perfected until termination of the insolvency proceedings and thereafter for a period of sixty days or until expiration of the five year period, whichever occurs later.] Upon lapse the security interest becomes unperfected, [unless it is perfected without filing. If the security interest becomes unperfected upon lapse, it is deemed to have been unperfected as against a person who became a purchaser or lien creditor before lapse.]

(3) A continuation statement may be filed by the secured party [(i) within six months before and sixty days after a stated maturity date of five years or less, and (ii) otherwise] within six months prior to the expiration of the five year period specified in subsection (2). Any such continuation statement must be signed by the secured party, identify the original statement by file number and state that the original statement is still effective. [A continuation statement signed by a person other than the secured party of record must be accompanied by a separate written statement of assignment signed by the secured party of record and complying with subsection (2) of Section 9-405, including payment of the required fee.] Upon timely filing of the continuation statement, the effectiveness of the original statement is continued for five years after the last date to which the filing was effective whereupon it lapses in the same manner as provided in subsection (2) unless another continuation statement is filed prior to such lapse. Succeeding continuation statements may be filed in the same manner to continue the effectiveness of the original statement. Unless a statute on disposition of public records provides otherwise, the filing officer may remove a lapsed statement from the files and destroy it [immediately if he has retained a microfilm or other photographic record, or in other cases after one year after the lapse. The filing officer shall so arrange matters by physical annexation of financing statements to continuation statements or other related filings, or by other means, that if he physically destroys the financing statements of a period more than five years past, those which have been continued by a continuation statement or which are still effective under subsection (6) shall be retained.]

[(4) Except as provided in subsection (7) a] filing officer shall mark each statement with a [consecutive] file number and with the date and hour of filing and shall hold the statement [or a microfilm or other photographic copy thereof] for public inspection. In addition the filing officer shall index the statements according to the name of the debtor and shall note in the index the file number and the address of the debtor given in the statement.

[(5) The uniform fee for filing and indexing and for stamping a copy furnished by the secured party to show the date and place of filing for an original financing statement or for a continuation statement shall be $ . . . . if the statement is in the standard form prescribed by the [Secretary of State] and otherwise shall be $ . . . ., plus in each case, if the financing statement is subject to subsection (5) of Section 9-402, $ . . . . The uniform fee for each name more than one required to be indexed shall be $ . . . . The secured party may at his option show a trade name for any person and an extra uniform indexing fee of $ . . . . shall be paid with respect thereto.

(6) If the debtor is a transmitting utility (subsection (5) of Section 9-401) and a filed financing statement so states, it is effective until a termination statement is filed. A real estate mortgage which is effective as a fixture filing under subsection (6) of Section 9-402 remains effective as a fixture filing until the mortgage is released or satisfied of record or its effectiveness otherwise terminates as to the real estate.

(7) When a financing statement covers timber to be cut or covers minerals or the like (including oil and gas) or accounts subject to subsection (5) of Section 9-103, or is filed as a fixture filing, [it shall be filed for record and] the filing officer shall index it under the names of the debtor and any owner of record shown on the financing statement in the same fashion as if they were the mortgagors in a mortgage of the real estate described, and, to the extent that the law of this state provides for indexing of mortgages under the name of the mortgagee, under the name of the secured party as if he were the mortgagee thereunder, or where indexing is by description in the same fashion as if the financing statement were a mortgage of the real estate described.]

§ 9-404. Termination Statement

[(1) If a financing statement covering consumer goods is filed on or after . . . ., then within one month or within ten days following written demand by the debtor after there is no outstanding secured obligation and no commitment to make advances, incur obligations or otherwise give value, the secured party must file with each filing officer with whom the financing statement was filed, a termination statement to the effect that he no longer claims a security interest under the financing statement, which shall be identified by file number. In other cases whenever there is no outstanding] secured obligation and no commitment to make advances, incur obligations or otherwise give value, the secured party must on written demand by the debtor send the debtor, [for each filing officer with whom the financing statement was filed,] a [termination] statement [to the effect] that he no longer claims a security interest under the financing statement, which shall be identified by file number. A termination statement signed by a person other than the secured party of record must be accompanied by a [separate written] statement [of assignment signed] by the secured party of record [complying with subsection (2) of Section 9-405, including payment of the required fee.] If the affected secured party fails to [file such a termination statement as required by this subsection, or to] send such a termination statement within ten days after proper demand therefor he shall be liable to the debtor for one hundred dollars, and in addition for any loss caused to the debtor by such failure.

(2) On presentation to the filing officer of such a termination statement he must note it in the index. [If he has received the termination statement in duplicate, he shall return one copy of the termination statement to the secured party stamped to show the time of receipt thereof. If the filing officer has a microfilm or other photographic record of the financing statement, and of any related continuation statement, statement of assignment and statement of release, he may remove the originals from the files at any time after receipt of the termination statement, or if he has no such record, he may remove them from the files at any time after one year after receipt of the termination statement.]

[(3) If the termination statement is in the standard form prescribed by the Secretary of State,] the uniform fee for filing and indexing [the] termination statement shall be $ . . . ., [and otherwise shall be $ . . . ., plus in each case an additional fee of $ . . . . for each name more than one against which the termination statement is required to be indexed.]

Note: *The date to be inserted should be the effective date of the revised Article 9.*

§ 9-405. Assignment of Security Interest; Duties of Filing Officer; Fees.—

(1) A financing statement may disclose an assignment of a security interest in the collateral described in the [financing] statement by indication in the [financing]

statement of the name and address of the assignee or by an assignment itself or a copy thereof on the face or back of the statement. On presentation to the filing officer of such a financing statement the filing officer shall mark the same as provided in Section 9-403(4). The uniform fee for filing, indexing and furnishing filing data for a financing statement so indicating an assignment shall be $ . . . . [if the statement is in the standard form prescribed by the Secretary of State and otherwise shall be $ . . . ., plus an additional fee of $ . . . . for each name more than one against which the financing statement is required to be indexed.]

(2) A secured party may assign of record all or a part of his rights under a financing statement by the filing [in the place where the original financing statement was filed] of a separate written statement of assignment signed by the secured party of record and setting forth the name of the secured party of record and the debtor, the file number and the date of filing of the financing statement and the name and address of the assignee and containing a description of the collateral assigned. A copy of the assignment is sufficient as a separate statement if it complies with the preceding sentence. On presentation to the filing officer of such a separate statement, the filing officer shall mark such separate statement with the date and hour of the filing. He shall note the assignment on the index of the financing statement [or in the case of a fixture filing. or a filing covering timber to be cut, or covering minerals or the like (including oil and gas or accounts subject to subsection (5) of Section 9-103, he shall index the assignment under the name of the assignor as grantor and, to the extent that the law of this state provides for indexing the assignment of a mortgage under the name of the assignee, he shall index the assignment of the financing statement under the name of the assignee. The uniform fee for filing, indexing and furnishing filing data about such a separate statement of assignment shall be $ . . . . . . if the statement is in the standard form prescribed by the Secretary of State and otherwise shall be $ . . . ., plus in each case an additional fee of $ . . . . for each name more than one against which the statement of assignment is required to be indexed. Notwithstanding the provisions of this subsection, an assignment of record of a security interest in a fixture contained in a mortgage effective as a fixture filing (subsection (6) of Section 9-402) may be made only by an assignment of the mortgage in the manner provided by the law of this state other than this Act.]

(3) After the disclosure or filing of an assignment under this section, the assignee is the secured party of record.

§ **9-406. Release of Collateral; Duties of Filing Officer; Fees—**A secured party of record may by his signed statement release all or a part of a collateral described in a filed financing statement. The statement of release is sufficient if it contains a description of the collateral being released, the name and address of the debtor, the name and address of the secured party, and the file number of the financing statement. [A statement of release signed by a person other than the secured party of record must be accompanied by a separate written statement of assignment signed by the secured party of record and complying with subsection (2) of Section 9-405, including payment of the required fee.] Upon presentation of such a statement [of release] to the filing officer he shall mark the statement with the hour and date of filing and shall note the same upon the margin of the index of the filing of the financing statement. The uniform fee for filing and noting such a statement of release shall be $ . . . . [if the statement is in the standard form prescribed by the [Secretary of State] and otherwise shall be $ . . . ., plus in each case an additional fee of $ . . . . for each name more than one against which the statement of release is required to be indexed.

[§ **9-407. Information From Filing Officer]***

[(1) If the person filing any financing statement, termination statement, statement of assignment, or statement release, furnishes the filing officer a copy thereof, the filing officer shall upon request note upon the copy the file number and date and hour of the filing of the original and deliver or send the copy to such person.]

[(2) Upon request of any person, the filing officer shall issue his certificate showing whether there is on file on the date and hour stated therein, any presently effective financing statement naming a particular debtor and any statement of assignment thereof and if there is, giving the date and hour of filing of each such statement and the names and addresses of each secured party therin. The uniform fee for such or certicate shall be $ . . . . . .[plus $ . . . . . for each financing statement and for each statement of assignment reported therein.] if the request for the certificate is in the standard form prescribed by the [Secretary of State] and otherwise shall be $ . . . . [plus $ . . . . for each financing statement and for each statement of assignment reported therein.] Upon request the filing officer shall furnish a copy of any filed financing statement or statement of assignment for a uniform fee of $ . . . . per page.]

*This section optional.

§ **9-408. Financing Statements Covering Consigned or Leased Goods—***A consignor or lessor of goods may file a financing statement using the terms "consignor," "consignee," "lessor," "lessee" or the like instead of the terms specified in Section 9-402. The provisions of this Part shall apply as appropriate to such a financing statement but its filing shall not of itself be a factor in determining whether or not the consignment or lease is intended as security (Section 1-201(37). However, if it is determined for other reasons that the consignment or lease is so intended, a security interest of the consignor or lessor which attaches to the consigned or leased goods is perfected by such filing.

*This section new in 1972.

PART 5

Default

§ **9-501. Default; Procedure When Security Agreement Covers Both Real and Personal Property.—**
(1) When a debtor is in default under a security agreement, a secured party has the rights and remedies provided in this Part and except as limited by subsection (3) those provided in the security agreement. He may reduce his claim to judgment, foreclose or otherwise enforce the security interest by any available judicial procedure. If the collateral is documents the secured party may proceed either as to the documents or as to the goods covered thereby. A secured party in possession has the rights, remedies and duties provided in Section 9-207. The rights and remedies referred to in this subsection are cumulative.
(2) After default, the debtor has the rights and remedies provided in this Part, those provided in the security agreement and those provided in Section 9-207.
(3) To the extent that they give rights to the debtor and impose duties on the secured party, the rules stated in the subsections referred to below may not be waived or varied except as provided with respect to compulsory disposition of collateral [(subsection (3) of Section 9-504 and] Section 9-505) and with respect to redemption of collateral (Section 9-506) but the parties may by agreement determine the standards by which the fulfillment of these rights and duties is to be measured if such standards are not manifestly unreasonable:
    (a) subsection (2) of Section 9-502 and subsection (2) of Section 9-504 insofar as they require accounting for surplus proceeds of collateral;
    (b) subsection (3) of Section 9-504 and subsection (1) of Section 9-505 which deal with disposition of collateral;

(c) subsection (2) of Section 9-505 which deals with acceptance of collateral as discharge of obligation;

(d) Section 9-506 which deals with redemption of collateral; and

(e) subsection (1) of Section 9-507 which deals with the secured party's liability for failure to comply with this Part.

(4) If the security agreement covers both real and personal property, the secured party may proceed under this Part as to the personal property or he may proceed as to both the real and the personal property in accordance with his rights and remedies in respect to the real property in which case the provisions of this Part do not apply.

(5) When a secured party has reduced his claim to judgment the lien of any levy which may be made upon his collateral by virtue of any execution based upon the judgment shall relate back to the date of the perfection of the security interest in such collateral. A judicial sale, pursuant to such execution, is a foreclosure of the security interest by judicial procedure within the meaning of this Section, and the secured party may purchase at the sale and thereafter hold the collateral free of any other requirements of this Article.

§ 9-502. Collection Rights of Secured Party.—

(1) When so agreed and in any event on default the secured party is entitled to notify an account debtor or the obligor on an instrument to make payment to him whether or not the assignor was theretofore making collections on the collateral, and also to take control of any proceeds to which he is entitled under Section 9-306.

(2) A secured party who by agreement is entitled to charge back uncollected collateral or otherwise to full or limited recourse against the debtor and who undertakes to collect from the account debtors or obligors must proceed in a commercially reasonable manner and may deduct his reasonable expenses of realization from the collections. If the security agreement secures an indebtedness, the secured party must account to the debtor for any surplus, and unless otherwise agreed, the debtor is liable for any deficiency. But, if the underlying transaction was a sale of accounts or chattel paper, the debtor is entitled to any surplus or is liable for any deficiency only if the security agreement so provides.

§ 9-503. Secured Party's Right to Take Possession After Default.—Unless otherwise agreed a secured party has on default the right to take possession of the collateral. In taking possession a secured party may proceed without judicial process if this can be done without breach of the peace or may proceed by action.

If the security agreement so provides the secured party may require the debtor to assemble the collateral and make it available to the secured party at a place to be designated by the secured party which is reasonably convenient to both parties. Without removal a secured party may render equipment unusable, and may dispose of collateral on the debtor's premises under Section 9-504.

§ 9-504. Secured Party's Right to Dispose of Collateral After Default; Effect of Disposition.—

(1) A secured party after default may sell, lease or otherwise dispose of any or all of the collateral in its then condition or following any commercially reasonable preparation or processing. Any sale of goods is subject to the Article on Sales (Article 2). The proceeds of disposition shall be applied in the order following to

(a) the reasonable expenses of retaking, holding, preparing for sale [or lease,] selling, [leasing] and the like and, to the extent provided for in the agreement and not prohibited by law, the reasonable attorneys' fees and legal expenses incurred by the secured party;

(b) the satisfaction of indebtedness secured by the security interest under which the disposition is made;

(c) the satisfaction of indebtedness secured by any subordinate security interest in the collateral if written notification of demand therefor is received before distribution of the proceeds is completed. If requested by the secured party, the holder of a subordinate security interest must seasonably furnish reasonable proof of his interest, and unless he does so, the secured party need not comply with his demand.

(2) If the security interest secures an indebtedness, the secured party must account to the debtor for any surplus, and, unless otherwise agreed, the debtor is liable for any deficiency. But if the underlying transaction was a sale of accounts or chattel paper, the debtor is entitled to any surplus or is liable for any deficiency only if the security agreement so provides.

(3) Disposition of the collateral may be by public or private proceedings and may be made by way of one or more contracts. Sale or other disposition may be as a unit or in parcels and at any time and place and on any terms but every aspect of the disposition including the method, manner, time, place and terms must be commercially reasonable. Unless collateral is perishable or threatens to decline speedily in value or is of a type customarily sold on a recognized market, reasonable notification of the time and place of any public sale or reasonable notification of the time after which any private sale or other intended disposition is to be made shall be sent by the secured party to the debtor, if he has not signed after default a statement renouncing or modifying his right to notification of sale. In the case of consumer goods no other notification need be sent. In other cases notification shall be sent to any other secured party from whom the secured party has received (before sending his notification to the debtor or before the debtor's renunciation of his rights) written notice of a claim of an interest in the collateral. The secured party may buy at any public sale and if the collateral is of a type customarily sold in a recognized market or is of a type which is the subject of widely distributed standard price quotations he may buy at private sale.

(4) When collateral is disposed of by a secured party after default, the disposition transfers to a purchaser for value all of the debtor's rights therein, discharges the security interest under which it is made and any security interest or lien subordinate thereto. The purchaser takes free of all such rights and interests even though the secured party fails to comply with the requirements of this Part or of any judicial proceedings

    (a) in the case of a public sale, if the purchaser has no knowledge of any defects in the sale and if he does not buy in collusion with the secured party, other bidders or the person conducting the sale; or

    (b) in any other case, if the purchaser acts in good faith.

(5) A person who is liable to a secured party under a guaranty, indorsement, repurchase agreement or the like and who receives a transfer of collateral from the secured party or is subrogated to his rights has thereafter the rights and duties of the secured party. Such a transfer of collateral is not a sale or disposition of the collateral under this Article.

§ 9-505. Compulsory Disposition of Collateral; Acceptance of the Collateral as Discharge of Obligation.—

(1) If the debtor has paid 60 percent of the cash price in the case of a purchase money security interest in consumer goods or 60 percent of the loan in the case of another security interest in consumer goods, and has not signed after default a statement renouncing or modifying his rights under this Part a secured party who has taken possession of collateral must dispose of it under Section 9-504 and if he fails to do so within ninety days after he takes possession the debtor at his option may recover in conversion or under Section 9-507(1) on secured party's liability.

(2) In any other case involving consumer goods or any other collateral a secured party in possession may, after default, propose to retain the collateral in satisfaction of the obligation. Written notice of such proposal shall be sent to the debtor [if he has not signed after default a statement renouncing or modifying his rights under this subsec-

tion. In the case of consumer goods no other notice need be given. In other cases notice shall be sent to any other secured party from whom the secured party has received (before sending his notice to the debtor or before the debtor's renunciation of his rights) written notice of a claim of an interest in the collateral. If the secured party receives objection in writing from a person entitled to receive notification within twenty-one days after the notice was sent, the secured party must dispose of the collateral under Section 9-504.] In the absence of such written objection the secured party may retain the collateral in satisfaction of the debtor's obligation.

§ **9-506. Debtor's Right to Redeem Collateral.**—At any time before the secured party has disposed of collateral or entered into a contract for its disposition under Section 9-504 or before the obligation has been discharged under Section 9-505(2) the debtor or any other secured party may unless otherwise agreed in writing after default redeem the collateral by tendering fulfillment of all obligations secured by the collateral as well as the expenses reasonably incurred by the secured party in retaking, holding, and preparing the collateral for disposition, in arranging for the sale, and to the extent provided in the agreement and not prohibited by law, his reasonable attorneys' fees and legal expenses.

§ **9-507. Secured Party's Liability for Failure to Comply With This Part.**—

(1) If it is established that the secured party is not proceeding in accordance with the provisions of this Part disposition may be ordered or restrained on appropriate terms and conditions. If the disposition has occurred the debtor or any person entitled to notification or whose security interest has been made known to the secured party prior to the disposition has a right to recover from the secured party any loss caused by a failure to comply with the provisions of this Part. If the collateral is consumer goods, the debtor has a right to recover in any event an amount not less than the credit service charge plus 10 percent of the principal amount of the debt or the time price differential plus 10 percent of the cash price.

(2) The fact that a better price could have been obtained by a sale at a different time or in a different method from that selected by the secured party is not of itself sufficient to establish that the sale was not made in a commercially reasonable manner. If the secured party either sells the collateral in the usual manner in any recognized market therefor or if he sells at the price current in such market at the time of his sale or if he has otherwise sold in conformity with reasonable commercial practices among dealers in the type of property sold he has sold in a commercially reasonable manner. The principles stated in the two preceding sentences with respect to sales also apply as may be appropriate to other types of disposition. A disposition which has been approved in any judicial proceeding or by any bona fide creditors' committee or representative of creditors shall conclusively be deemed to be commercially reasonable, but this sentence does not indicate that any such approval must be obtained in any case nor does it indicate that any disposition not so approved is not commercially reasonable.

INDEX